The A to Z of Food

LIVE TO EAT OR EAT TO LIVE?

Dear Wendy Mair,
Thank you for your interest!
All the best,
Federico

Navigating food and dietary choices in a complex world.

FEDERICO FILIPPI

To my Mother,

for her love, wisdom

and encouragement

Contents

SECTION THREE
Navigating Food and Dietary Choices

Preface

There has never been a time in our cultural history when there has been a greater proliferation of books and opinions about food, cookery, diets, and "lifestyle". This is the era of celebrity chefs, superfoods, veganism, gluten-free diets, intermittent fasting, molecular gastronomy and endless series of television cookery programmes and hordes of Instagram and YouTube "influencers".[1] On the other hand, daily time spent cooking by the average Briton has been diminishing year on year for decades. Fast food, or rather junk food, is the norm rather than the exception. Similar trends, albeit less extreme, can be observed everywhere else in continental Europe. In Italy, in the 1980s, my kitchen-dwelling mother was already becoming a rare breed. Fast food, ready meals, flavoured crisps, and microwaves are now everywhere. We find ourselves in a paradoxical situation: the less we cook, the more we watch other people cooking on television and buy recipe books, never to be used. This odd alienation suggests that for many cooking and cuisine is a "hobby" or perhaps an aspiration or a lifestyle. This, as I will lay out, is a huge misunderstanding: surely cookery is not a hobby, nor a fashion, but rather an essential life skill, a harbinger of civilisation, an act of care for oneself and for others, as well as a connection to the land, the seas, and the seasons.

It may be legitimate to ask why, in the midst of such an abundance of books and ideas, my own contribution would be required or welcome. My long background in traditional Italian cookery and agriculture has kept me far from faddish and fashionable trends and more interested in preserving great cuisine and growing the best possible crops in the best possible soil, which should be the first duty of any culture. Whilst admitting to a weakness for MasterChef and, most regrettably, for the odd Coca-Cola (the corporation got me when I was an infant... that's my excuse), I have been on the periphery of this cultural trend, as an observer rather than as a participant.

At the same time, obesity is fast increasing, as are eating disorders. Some awareness of the disastrous impacts of industrial agriculture on the environment and of the horrors of factory farming is slowly seeping into public consciousness. Concern about diets, dieting and the healthiness of foods has also increased, with a mushrooming of diets, trends, and fads that

[1] I have had to join this category, with some regret, or you may never have had the opportunity to come across this book! See Instagram: @cook.farmer.fred

all seem to share similar characteristics: superficiality (Eliminate gluten! Eliminate all sugar!), mutual exclusivity (Fats are good! Fats are bad!) and fanaticism, as vegan and raw food trends amply demonstrate.

The human trigger behind this book was my former colleague and dear friend Alexander. Like others in our open plan office off Cannon Street, he had observed my enthusiastic consumption of less-than-ordinary foods and put up with my brief but regular musings about, say, the need for pigs to be happy and the horror that is Monster Munch. Being on the somewhat corpulent side, and forever looking for THE diet that would finally fix him, and fed up with the aforementioned musings, he asked: "Why don't YOU tell me what and how I should eat? Why don't you write me a diet?" The following weekend, in a three-hour splurge of creativity and amusement (I did enjoy telling him what NOT to do, as much as what to do…), I typed up a six-page document outlining my philosophy, strong recommendations and suggested diet. The document made its way round several colleagues and, apparently, it was read out loud in the HR Practice. Alex, and a couple of others, said: "You should write a book!" A seed was planted, pun intended, and this book is the end result.

For the record, one can lead a horse (or indeed an ox, as I can personally attest) to water but cannot make it drink. Alex did take up a few ideas and habits from the original document but did not quite embrace them as he could and should have. I remain hopeful.

Introduction

I am not an old man but even in my relatively short time I have witnessed a coming and going of countless diets, nutritional theories, and a degree of flipping and flopping that is rare to find in other subject matters. In the 1950s and 1960s, red meat and whole milk were actively promoted as the sort of foods good parents should actively feed their children. Growing up in the 1980s, the main demon was saturated animal fat. By then, oversized chicken breasts and "lean meat", as well as skimmed, homogenised milk and "low fat" ultra-processed foods, made their meteoric rise into the average diets and red meat and full-fat products, whilst never losing popularity, became items that raised suspicion and guilt. Today, sugar is the primary evil, to the point that, if you were to follow NHS dietary guidelines verbatim, "Coke Zero" could somehow manage to be perceived as a relatively healthier product than organic fruit juice. Hundreds of mutually exclusive diet plans and programmes have been devised and promoted over the years. Detox and cleansing plans continue to hold sway, and the supplements and "protein" sectors continue to grow.

The speed and inconsistency with which both nutritional advice and diets come and go is perhaps a reflection of the short-termism inherent in a mature consumer society, where products, superficial ideas and fashions must perennially be superseded, upgraded, and repackaged. A toxic mixture of public ignorance, marketing, advertising and pseudoscience has led to an ever-changing proliferation of bad ideas, fads and fashions. As ever, it is not as simple as that: there are multiple causes and conditions which explain this extraordinary state of affairs, which cannot simply be reduced to the ills of 21st century consumerism.

Looking further into the past, we could point to the historically unprecedented rate of urbanisation and abandonment of the land which began in the late 19th century and early 20th century and accelerated in the post-war period. In Europe, we have gone from over half the population living off the land, in some capacity or other, to less than 5% in the space of a couple of generations. Whatever the merits and demerits of mass urbanisation it has to be recognised for what it is: a revolutionary and relatively sudden seismic change in our social, economic and ecological relations. Such a drastic change had to have an impact on our worldview, our psyche and on our relationships with the natural world, with domestic plants and animals and, consequently, with what we eat and how we eat it.

There have undoubtedly been vast improvements over the last century. Postwar Europeans have been living lives of unprecedented comfort, and the same is true in many other parts of the world. Hunger, famines and stunted growth have, by and large, been confined to a past that is no longer in living memory. Food items that used to be very occasional luxuries, even for the affluent, are now widely available. At the click of a button, a phone call away or just a stroll down the high street, a cornucopia of foods and ingredients from all over the world is available: if one knows what to buy and when to buy it, all sorts of boons and bounties are there for the taking.

The downsides, which have become more pronounced as the decades have rolled on, are equally stark and historically abnormal. We may no longer have to worry about a lack of food (at least for now, in spite of the fact that we are not self-sufficient in Britain), but we also have an unprecedented problem with dysfunctional and unhealthy eating. We can witness, on a daily basis, a broad range of paradoxes and abnormalities. A clear example is the widespread and unprecedented problem of obesity, which cannot be underestimated. Obesity is accompanied by the relatively novel problem of eating disorders, which emerged from the peculiar conditions of contemporary culture, and for which there is almost no pre-War record. We live in a society where there are people who will eat themselves, or indeed starve themselves, to an early grave. This is abnormal.

At the same time, a fear of fat as a food source remains, in spite of the recent demonisation of sugar. This fat phobia, which as I will argue in this book is based on simple misunderstandings, somehow coexists with the "body positivity" movement and "fat is beautiful" activism. So, perversely, animal fat (say, in whole milk or lard) is bad, but human fat on an obese person can potentially be celebrated. I have news: being fat is not beautiful and there is nothing inherently wrong with butter, whole milk, or pork belly. Indeed, in the past, good farmers knew that fat, especially animal fat, was, if anything, the most precious and nutritious gift of the land and would have been rightly horrified by intentionally impoverished foods like skimmed milk. It is no coincidence that the English language still has expressions that celebrate the value of fat: "the cream of the crop", "saving the bacon" and "the fat of the land".

Another historically abnormal phenomenon is the unprecedented level of meat consumption. We have gone from meat scarcity to meat excess, especially of certain types and cuts of meat. I never tire of giving a simple example of the dramatic changes that have taken place in a few decades. My mother, who grew up in affluence and comfort in residential Rome, recalls how, in the late 1950s, there was one girl in her class who aroused the envy of all her classmates. Why? Because she had the audacity of bringing in the occasional chicken sandwich for her school lunch. Her father had made a fortune in post-war real estate developments and chicken was a luxury that only a very tiny minority could afford to consume as an everyday food. Fast forward to the present day and the poorer one is in the UK, or indeed in the United States, the more likely one is to consume vast quantities of chicken, more so than the wealthy. Think Chicken Cottage, KFC, and the £3-4 whole chicken available at many supermarkets. At the same time, in the midst of such meat abundance, there are those who have embraced the wholesale rejection of all animal products: vegans. I am fairly confident that in the days when poultry was an occasional luxury, there were almost no vegans at all. Could one extreme be correlated to the other?

The abundance of food, especially animal products, has led to an increase in height and to the disappearance of diseases of scarcity and malnutrition like pellagra, scurvy, and rickets. However, we now have a whole set of what might be called "diseases of abundance". With the industrialisation of food production, the increase in quantity has gradually been accompanied by a decrease in quality. Whilst great products are still available, generally speaking, the precious chicken of old has been replaced by the £3-4 factory-farmed, abused, pale and sick animal sold in supermarkets. Similarly, the agrochemical arsenal used to produce the hybrid wheat in most of our bread has turned the average loaf into an unhealthy product, as opposed to the stuff of life. It is no coincidence that the diseases of abundance, from all types of cancer to heart disease and diabetes, can all be directly linked to the diets and habits of urban life.

Other dramatic changes have been forgotten or are largely unknown: the changes to our landscapes, to land use and to agricultural practice. Even though most people are aware, on an abstract level, of the mass extinction of several animal species, these are usually perceived as exotic and removed. The plight of the rhino or koala, or indeed the deforestation of the Amazon, is more likely to be associated with the devastation of the natural world than anything more domestic. However, the changes around the corner from us have been significant and equally problematic. Here in England, over the last century, we have lost most of our meadows, ripped up thousands of miles of hedgerows and several animal and plant species have either disappeared or declined. Whilst most large species of animal, such as the wolf, disappeared well before the Industrial Age, the decline in insect and bird life, not to mention the decline of fish such as cod, is recent and devastating. As the late Jim Lovelock used to recall, the scale and beauty of the countryside just outside of London as recently as the 1920s and 1930s is something that very few people have experienced or can even imagine. Whilst there are still several pockets and areas of natural wealth and beauty left in this country, ours is in an impoverished environment.

All this is connected to food. The main reason for the depletion of our ecosystems is industrial agriculture and mass urbanisation. In turn, this has led to a fundamental lack of ecological knowledge and connection. Many a contemporary Briton lacks direct experience of very basic activities: he or she has never tried milking a cow, has never caught a fish, butchered an animal, climbed a tree or grown a vegetable from seed. Or indeed cooked many meals. The same holds true on the Continent or indeed in any nation and culture that has undergone similar patterns of transformation.

The fervent move to the cities and the near-universal adoption of the automobile have been accompanied by changes in ideology and custom. To many contemporary minds, some of these will either be taken for granted or seen as indisputable goods. One such change has been the gradual abandonment of traditional religion and the rise of science and "scientism". I will not be the first to argue that we are inherently ideological beings and that the end of one ideology is generally followed by the adoption of another. This is undoubtably the era of science, materialism, reductionism and determinism. How does this relate to food? At the farm level, it has resulted in the conversion of living systems driven by biology and the Sun to factory systems driven by the input-output logic of all industrial units. The dance and rhythm of the seasons, of prey and predator, of bug and bird, of fields and muck has been replaced by chemistry, genetics and machinery. It is no wonder that the farm animal has been reduced to an object in such a system. Sadly, Pascal's vision of the soulless, mechanical animal has been applied to the modern farm. I have had the displeasure of hearing farmers and food industry representatives refer to themselves as being in "the protein business" and to animals as mere "protein". This is an example of Reductionism 101 and has deep implications for how we think about living creatures and about the food we eat.

Michael Pollan, in his worthy critiques, talked about "nutritionism": the belief that a food item is best understood as the combination of its fundamental nutrients (e.g., chicken breast: 165 calories, 31 grams of protein and 3.6 grams of fat) and that this is all one needs to know about such food item. Such reductive thinking, as I will argue throughout this book, is what leads to the world of Coke Zero, protein powders, molecular gastronomy and other such developments. This worldview has also led to a general faith in the advice of those wearing a white coat. I would find it odd to presume that the best-placed advisor on how to raise an animal or how to feed a child is necessarily a scientist. That is not to say that science has not done much to inform us about many things that we did not previously know, but it is not, and should not be, the only route to knowledge, especially on matters which are not reducible to simple categories and equations. I must briefly clarify the difference between nutritional advice and dieting, as I will be dealing with both extensively. The former is the output of nutritional science, the latter is the practical application of such advice. For example, a nutritionist may argue that carbohydrates or sugar are the problem; a diet, such as the Atkins or Ketogenic diet, will prescribe how to act on such advice. Be that as it may, it is science and scientists that people look up to when thinking about what to eat, how and when.

Lastly, and I may lose some of my more progressive audience here, I must point to another obvious radical change that has swept over our culture over the last couple of generations: the decline of the traditional family and of what I would call "matriarchal cookery". Whatever one's opinions about the family and the traditional divisions of labour, it is easy to see how such a dramatic change has led to a revolution in eating habits. Growing up in the 1980s in Rome, my very traditional kitchen-dwelling mother was already a species on the way to extinction. Her mother and grandmother had not encouraged her to cook, nor had they encouraged her to be a housewife, in fact, quite the opposite. My mother taught herself how to cook once she had children and by the early 80s, it was already normal for many mothers not to cook, especially in middle-class, bourgeois urban Italy. It was already becoming normal for children not to know the names of many vegetables, presuming they were even eating them. I remember the first ever McDonald's to open in Italy, in Piazza Di Spagna. I also remember the contrast between my disgust and my classmates' enthusiasm for it. There are now over 500 McDonald's restaurants in Italy, which I see as a national and cultural failing and capitulation.

As my dear old boss David used to say about many things: "we are where we are". The question is: could there be a compromise between the best of the past and the best of modernity? Can we have our chicken and eat it? As I will argue, there is a path towards "normality", in the best sense of the word, and towards a sane, rational, serene approach towards food. What follows does not need to be taken on faith. All that is required is an open mind and a willingness to experiment and change. The first part of the book will be historical and theoretical and is the philosophical foundation for the claims and recommendations you will find in the rest of the book. Section two is a collection of polemical essays on popular trends in the world of food. If you don't want to run the risk of boredom and want to skip ahead and go straight to the diets, "food rules" and recommendations in the third section... feel free to do so... and refer back to the first sections as and when required. Happy reading!

SECTION 1

A Very Brief History of Food and Nutrition

Chapter 1

LIVE TO EAT OR EAT TO LIVE?

Many years ago, my old colleague Vince (another victim slash beneficiary of my musings) came to the belief that I was too obsessed with food. He snapped: "I eat to live; I don't live to eat!" Nothing new in this old saying of course, but it got me thinking. Am I too much of a "foodie"? Is it wrong, when visiting a new city somewhere in the world, to be as interested in finding the best restaurant as in finding the best art gallery or cathedral? When I visited Florence, I was certainly as excited by the prospect of trying its great beef dishes[2] as I was by visiting the Cathedral of Santa Maria del Fiore. In Seville, it was crucial for me to find the best tapas, as it was to visit the Plaza de Toros. Is too much of my income going towards the finest food items?

One could argue that the £5.95 jar of tuna in organic olive oil currently sitting in my pantry, or indeed the odd bag of fine Marron glacé,[3] are extravagances I could do without. Indeed, I could do without them, but then again, I probably spend less of my disposable income on other things people deem more desirable. Should one spend more time thinking about what one will wear to work or on a date than one does thinking about what to make with those partridges in the freezer? The short answer to the preceding questions, at least for Yours Truly, is a resounding "No". Clearly, we should not live to eat but we should also not eat to

[2] Tuscany is home to a unique beef breed, the Chianina, a white giant of a bovine, possibly the tallest in the world, standing at 6 ft at the shoulder. In Florence there are a host of wonderful beef dishes, from the enormous and unparalleled Fiorentina T-Bone steak to several slow cooked beef dishes, all the way to tripe.

[3] In spite of its French name and reputation, this is as much a Piemontese delicacy as it is a Lyonnaise one: it originates from what was then the Savoyard State, comprising both North-West Italy and South-East France. In France they are often referred to as Marron de Turin, given that the chestnuts from Valle di Susa in the Province of Turin are traditionally used to manufacture this delicacy. Overall, both the French and the Italians can claim the candied chestnut as part of their shared culture.

live. In between these extremes, there in undoubtedly an acceptable spectrum of subjective experience that can and will vary from person to person.

Apart from the fact that "foodie" is an expression that makes me cringe, I have never felt that my commitment to food and cookery is excessive or misplaced, or indeed needed a label. This goes back to my introductory remarks: it is neither a hobby, nor a fad, and as such needs no nomenclature. But let us briefly consider the definition of the cringeworthy expression, which is defined, according to the Cambridge Dictionary, as "a person who loves food and is very interested in different types of food".[4] This seems uncontroversial and fairly common, and nothing to be apologetic about. Gluttony is a sin, we are told, but this is not a definition of gluttony. It is perhaps the "love", or at least an excess of it, that the Vinces of this world find an unpalatable step too far and lead to the accusation of "living to eat", which I guess is indeed a fair definition of gluttony. But, then again, if one "eats to live", love is redundant or at the very least optional. If one eats to live, food has to be perceived through a purely utilitarian lens: it is a means to an end, never an end in itself. The aesthetic, hedonistic, communal and ritual dimensions, arguably so important to any food culture, are always bound to be secondary or optional for the utilitarian.

So, what is the utility of food? At its most basic level, it is indeed a bare physical necessity. We need to eat in order to live, in spite of what breatharians might claim.[5] Without wanting to dwell on primary school-level biology, it is clear that just like other living creatures on this planet, we need energy and nutrients in order to survive, reproduce and so on. Food is living fuel for living creatures. Whilst food scarcity and hunger are problems that the readers of this book are highly unlikely to have ever experienced, it is a reoccurring and timeless historical problem. As I look through my comfortably bursting freezer, which in itself is an extraordinary recent invention and luxury, it is easy to forget that food is first and foremost what we need in order to survive and live. Having said that, as we shall see, it would be a mistake to associate a less utilitarian approach to food and the "foodie" approach with bourgeois whims and aspirations. Whilst an interest in overrated Michelin-star restaurants may well reflect such whims and aspirations, most traditional food cultures do not simply "eat to live". Other considerations are always at play. All we need to do is think about the peasant culinary traditions of Europe: intertwined with poverty and scarcity, one finds celebration, pleasure, ritual, decoration and great skill in the kitchen.

This truism brings me back to the word fuel, which is often associated with food in contemporary language. Food is not just fuel, in spite of what Huel manufactures may like to

[4] https://dictionary.cambridge.org/dictionary/english/foodie

[5] Breatharians claim to be able to live through breath alone or with a very reduced food intake, with breath providing sufficient energy...

suggest.[6] Food is many things, such as pleasure, health, community, conversation, tradition, festivity, family, acts of love, the seasons, nature, landscape and memory. As with any other aspect of life, we should remember what makes us distinctly human and attempt to aim for the best possible version of ourselves. Indeed, as good old Aristotle would have argued, and as I will elucidate later, the nutritive and appetitive is something we share with other animals. It would be demeaning and unwise for us to simply satisfy these urges without any recourse to those facets of our nature that are uniquely human; namely reason and virtue.[7] It is only by appreciating the truth of human exceptionalism that we can appreciate why we may go to great lengths to source a rare ingredient lacking in any real substance or nutrition, why we decorate cakes, why we eat with elaborate cutlery and table paraphernalia, why we forbid one food and consecrate another and why we feed the poor.

We must not eat to live if we are to fulfil our human potential. Imagine we used the same rationale to make sense of two other basic necessities of life: clothing and shelter. If we only wore clothes to keep warm, or only built shelter to keep out of the elements, we would have a very impoverished culture. In fact, we would hardly have any culture at all: a purely utilitarian approach to the necessities of life kills off all sophistication, charm and complexity. The ascetic or monk will be exempted from this precept, but not the rest of us. It is no coincidence that great civilisations, unlike primitive cultures, have produced varied, rich, complex cuisines, manufactured beautiful textiles and ornaments, and have also built palaces, castles, temples, and manicured gardens. We want more than the prevention of public nudity and exposure to the elements when we manufacture, purchase and wear clothes. We recognise the need for embellishment, for aesthetic pleasure and attractiveness, both in our own eyes and those of others, and the need for identity, role-playing and ritual. Similarly, the beauty of a home, of a neighbourhood or of a city is not determined by the presence of double glazing or efficient plumbing, as important as these may be. One of the many reasons why the quasi-Soviet style tower blocks built in many parts of Britain in the post-war period were such a bad idea was that they were not built with people in mind, whose aesthetic needs are as important for the soul as warmth is for the body.

If food were just fuel, it would, in extremis, make sense to forego all the valuable things that enrich our experience of food and just quietly refill, three or four times a day, on our own, in the bathroom, with tasteless powders, said to be nutritionally sound by its manufacturers and teams of boffins in white coats. It is not alarmist to say that in contemporary culture we have taken some steps towards this food dystopia. Apart from the popularity of the aforementioned Huel, which, in my opinion, is a miserable and unnecessary replacement for

[6] The name is a contraction of Human Fuel: https://uk.huel.com/pages/about-us

[7] This is a rough version of one of Aristotle's main ideas in the *Nicomachean Ethics*.

an actual meal, the very idea of replacing food with scientifically sound artificial replacements is on the rise. For a start, this idea is promoted by diets that advocate so-called total diet replacement (TDR) or the partial substitution of food for highly processed shakes, powders, and tasteless bars.

There are two main problems with this approach. The first is that, apart from the fact that a reduction in calorie intake cannot be an end in itself, calorie intake reduction via the substitution of food with replacements is simply not necessary nor desirable: real food can provide better and healthier solutions. The second problem is that it lacks any educational and reformative element. In fact, it actively promotes a less educated and very misguided reductionist approach to food and diet. I distinctly recall two former colleagues[8] who had decided to embark on a course promoting a total diet replacement plan, where all meals were substituted with the aforementioned powders and bars. They claimed that the aim of the diet, apart from drastic calorie reduction, was to inculcate the view that food was primarily fuel and nutrition, rather than pleasure, and that a period of complete abandonment of actual food and cooked meals would cement that idea in their minds.

Apart from the fact that, even if calorie reduction and weight loss were to be the main goal of diet, there are far better and healthier ways to achieve this, it is obvious that the "patient", having shed the desired pounds through the meal replacement plan, is then left with the prospect of having to learn how and what to eat all over again. Let's face it: he or she only ended up on such a dietary regime as a result of poor eating habits and a lack of basic knowledge about what to buy, cook and eat in the first place. Surely, any diet must involve a long-term educational plan. The severity and short-termism of these artificial diets also have another negative effect: it confirms the idea, in the mind of the patient, that only through a punishing regime of unpleasant, lab-formulated nutrition can health and body shape be restored. This is a great falsehood. Even obese patients can, and should, be taught how to enjoy food and derive pleasure and comfort from the very foods and meals which will make them well.

The other threat to real food comes from elements within the environmental movement and scientific community. An eminent exponent of this trend was the aforementioned Jim Lovelock, the man behind the fascinating and intriguing Gaia Theory. Lovelock argued that, in order to preserve the biosphere and avoid the destruction of life as we know it, we must leave as much of the Earth's surface as possible entirely unfettered by human activity, especially agriculture, and allow natural processes to take over and regenerate those self-regulating mechanisms required for the maintenance of life on Earth. The ideal food

[8] I've had many colleagues over the years. I am not picking on them; my comments also apply to acquaintances and friends outside of the office!

production of the future would have to come from factories, capable of manufacturing proteins, carbohydrates, and other fundament nutrients out of thin air.[9] Lovelock hoped for, and in part prophesied, a future where food could be obtained through synthetic manufacture, by combining basic elements (carbon, nitrogen, hydrogen) from the air, with water and trace elements, all powered by clean energy. The resulting sugars and proteins could then serve as feedstock for meat and plant cultures and any other edible junk food[10] that could be manufactured thereof. "Real food", such as vegetables grown in soil and meat and fish from animals would be rare luxuries likely consumed by the very rich,[11] in the way that the rich may now consume Beluga caviar and the most expensive champagne.

Most recently the environmentalist George Monbiot promoted a very similar idea to Lovelock's: the gradual abandonment of farming and other traditional forms of food production.[12] There has indeed been a lot of progress made in what we could call futuristic food production. Monbiot has toured cultured meat production facilities and, most impressively in his mind, a factory in Finland, belonging to the tech firm Solar Foods,[13] producing synthetic proteins in a manner very reminiscent of what Lovelock envisaged for the future. The company's product is designed to be appropriate for future space travel and the potential colonisation of Mars... *"Take your protein pills and put your helmet on"*[14]... comes to mind.

Jesting aside, if we presume, as Monbiot must, that there is simply no way to produce food without destroying the prospect of a viable civilisation, then one would have to resign oneself to the prospect of cultured meat burgers, synthetic chicken, and futuristic pancakes like the one Monbiot declared he would be happy to eat every morning. In this brave new world, we would need to eat to live, foregoing any other consideration. As I will argue throughout this book, this is neither a necessity nor an unavoidable destiny. In other words, we can have our cake and eat it, quite literally. We need to reform and improve food production and our cultural norms, often in radical ways, but any attempt to bypass the fundamental laws of nature will lead us further away from where we need to be. We need to embrace the fact that we share this planet with plants and animals, most of which are domesticated, and that our attitude to food must satisfy both our mammalian urges and our uniquely human desire for beauty, culture, and consolation.

[9] J. Lovelock, 2006, The Revenge of Gaia, pages 169-170.

[10] His words, not mine!

[11] Ibidem, page 171.

[12] G. Monbiot, 2023, Regenesis: Feeding the World Without Devouring the Planet. See also Monbiot's Channel 4 Documentary: *Apocalypse Cow: How Meat Killed The Planet, 2020*

[13] https://solarfoods.fi

[14] David Bowie, Space Oddity, 1969.

IN A NUTSHELL

- Don't live to eat and don't eat to live.
- Food is not just fuel.
- Express your full human potential in all affairs, including food. Don't feed like an animal.
- Beware of futuristic dystopias: they are neither necessary nor desirable.

Apocalypse Cow? Cows grazing on pasture near my old field. Credit: @escapetheofficejob

Chapter 2

INGREDIENTS AND PRODUCE

One day my friend Ronnie asked me to teach him some classic Italian dishes. In spite of never having been to Italy, he has eaten many a *Spaghetti al Pomodoro* (spaghetti with tomato sauce) over the years, which has become a rather popular dish in the UK and around the world. There are many horrific home and restaurant versions of it, not to mention ready-made, microwaveable versions. I guess the same is true of good old "Spag Bol" and *Lasagne*. Following a brief raid of my larder for a few ingredients, I made my way to Ronnie's Battersea flat, where I cooked the dish for him, with enthusiastic commentary to go alongside it. Having devoured a hefty dish, and after much praise and gratitude, Ronnie asked me to write down the recipe for him, so that he could match the memories of the demo with some clear instructions. Normally, recipes are given as a list of ingredients, followed by instructions. Not so with my recipes. My email to Ronnie began as follows:

"Preliminary Thoughts:

- Ronnie, I cannot emphasise this enough: the outcome of the recipe will only be as good as the ingredients you use. Technique and recipe are important, of course, but without quality ingredients, it's a non-starter.
- Please ask me for advice if you struggle getting some of the ingredients."

I then went on to list the ingredients, with details of how to source them, literally *how to buy them*. This may seem incredibly patronising, not that Ronnie found it so,[15] and some home cooks may feel that recipe instructions should not extend to shopping instructions. However, as I explained to Ronnie, we can take any dish, from scrambled eggs to chicken curry and *Spaghetti al Pomodoro* and perform a simple experiment. We buy the same items on the

[15] Ronnie is my best culinary disciple! Not that there is much competition.

ingredients list, but from radically different sources. We then follow the recipe word for word and use exactly the same tools and technique. We will, at the end of this experiment, have very different dishes, both in terms of their flavour, texture, and impact on our health. The quality and texture of the pasta, not to mention the quality and provenance of the tomatoes and of every other ingredient, will be absolutely crucial to the outcome.

I had to break the news to Ronnie that this was the case even for the least obvious ingredient in a *Spaghetti al Pomodoro*: the small amount of olive oil used for frying. Olive oil, unfortunately, generally cannot cost less than £15-20 a litre if it is going to be any good. Things to look for: cold pressed, single estate or single olive variety, region of provenance, some indication of growing methods, and more.[16] The average bottle of Napolina or Filippo Berio olive oil, in my opinion, is simply not a good product. The good news is that the olive oil requirement in *Spaghetti al Pomodoro* is low, and olive oil can in any case be used with parsimony and thrift.[17] It is better to buy half a litre of good oil and use less of it than to buy a litre of cheap oil and use it in great quantities. If you can afford to pay more for olive oil and can also afford to use it liberally, so much the better. However, quality must always come above quantity. Unfortunately, there are no short cuts available and no way of getting around this inescapable truth.

Not All Chickens are Created Equal: The Experiment

If any reader is sceptical about this, they must perform a simple experiment. Instead of a dish that requires several steps and processes, as well as multiple ingredients, I recommend much simpler dishes with one or two dominant ingredients and very simple processes.

For example:

- Roast chicken
- Poached eggs on toast
- Strawberries and cream

The roast chicken, a simple and popular dish dominated by one common ingredient, is the most obvious example. The reader does not need to take my word for it. Here is a simple experiment:

[16] More on this in Chapter 11.

[17] I am very often guilty of using it quite liberally myself, but it is not necessary.

1. Buy a Red Tractor certified chicken from one of the main supermarkets.
2. Buy a chicken that comes from a good farm. For the purpose of the experiment, I will refer to Abbey Home Organic Farm.[18] This is a farm I personally visited in 2016 and 2024 and which I will use as an example for that very reason. There are many other farms that provide similar standards.[19]

Some field notes on our chickens:

Red Tractor Chicken

- The Red Tractor label is a minimum guarantee of welfare widely used across the UK. It generally reflects standard industry practice across the country and goes marginally beyond the minimum legal welfare standards, with slightly reduced stocking density for meat chickens, for example. There are farms both in the UK and overseas that have even lower standards than the Red Tractor Assurance standards. The Red Tractor scheme at least does not permit caged broilers[20] and hens.
- The animals are not fed, as they are in many poultry farms, prophylactic antibiotics or hormonal growth promoters and their feed does not contain meat and bone meal, poultry by-products[21] or tallow. They are however fed with the standard low-quality feed usually made up of processed GM soya, wheat, maize, and a host of additives. The overbred birds live short and miserable lives and never develop proper bone and muscle structure.
- Unfortunately, the Red Tractor standards permit 100% indoor production and allow a shocking stocking rate of 38kg/m2.[22] For the layman, presuming an average weight of 1.5kg per bird, that's up to 20 broilers per square meter (10.76 square feet). 20!
- These animals never see the light of day, live in overcrowded barns where the noise and the smell of faeces and ammonia will be overwhelming to the unaccustomed, and unpleasant to those working there, who need to wear some sort of protection. The birds often suffer "hock burns". These are skin burns caused by continuous exposure to faeces: a fancy way of saying that they live, 24/7, on top of their own poo.
- After around 6 weeks of fast growth, they are cramped inside cages on a truck, which will take them on a long journey to an industrial slaughterhouse, where their comfort and welfare will always come second to speed and efficiency.

[18] http://www.theorganicfarmshop.co.uk

[19] See Chapter 11 for details on how to identify and purchase quality poultry.

[20] A broiler is a chicken raised for meat rather than eggs.

[21] Believe it or not, poultry remains (a rendered down mix of chicken manure, dead chickens, feathers, and spilled feed) are fed to livestock in some countries, including the United States. This is now illegal in the UK.

[22] https://redtractorassurance.org.uk/wp-content/uploads/2022/08/Chicken-V5.1-Standards-FINAL.pdf

- This chicken can cost less than £3 per kg at major supermarkets.

Abbey Home Farm Organic Chicken

Laying hens at Abbey Home Farm. They had just been moved to fresh grassland and were having a good time amongst the feeders. It was full of flowering chicory, which had clearly been sown for the benefit of the soil and birds.

- Abbey Home Farm, on the other hand, is a 1,625-acre Gloucestershire farm I had the pleasure of visiting on an academic field trip in 2016 and, more recently, on a personal visit during the summer of 2024. It is a textbook English mixed organic farm, producing cereals, vegetables, fruits, herbs and flowers. There are dairy cows, beef cattle, sheep, pigs, laying hens and broilers. The farm has a lovely farm shop and café for the community and provides many other goods and services, including timber and woodland produce.
- Its laying hens and broilers, unlike those in the Red Tractor-approved sheds, live in open chicken houses with large openings, with plenty of space, with outdoor access to rich grassland all year round (unless they wish to remain inside when it is too hot or cold or when they sleep at night) and can do what chickens both need and like to do: scratching, nesting, running around, establishing a pecking order, feeding on whatever herbs and insects come their way.

- Inside the little houses, fresh wood shavings are spread out on a regular basis, to keep things clean and, as I can testify, the birds had plenty of space and comfort. The inevitable ammonia-like smell of chicken poo was minimal, and the birds were relaxed and free of the various conditions of confinement, including hock burns.

The broilers coming and going between feeding sessions. It was a very hot summer's day, and the birds mostly stayed in the shade to keep cool.

- The chicken houses and movable fencing are rotated around the grassland, which gives the birds regular access to fresh vegetation and replenishes the soil.
- Their compound feed will be based on organic cereals and legumes grown without pesticides, herbicides, and fungicides, and will also not contain the types of additives found in conventional feeds. Ideally, a farm the size of Abbey Home Farm could grow and manufacture its own feed. It would be more sustainable and economically viable in the long run, I believe.
- The birds are slaughtered after 12-14 weeks on site. One of the chicken houses is literally used for small-scale, humane slaughter.[23]
- The chicken costs £11.50 per kg.

[23] Daylesford Organic Farm, the grand farm belonging to Lady Bamford, not many miles away from Abbey Home Farm, also has its own slaughterhouse and not just for the broilers, but for all the livestock. This is just one of many examples that demonstrates the superiority of organic farming. Conventional farms, including chicken factory farms, never slaughter their own animals.

- To all intents and purposes, this is the kind of chicken any reasonable person will immediately want to eat.

To continue our experiment:

3. Prepare both chickens using exactly the same tools, methods, cooking times, temperature, and additional ingredients (such as olive oil/butter, salt, black pepper, and rosemary). Keep it simple.

What this simple experiment will inevitably reveal is that:

- The colour, texture and density of the chickens will be completely different.
- The body shape and bone structure (try to break the leg bones on both) will also be very different.
- The taste and intensity of flavour of the chickens will be remarkably different.

You may well (albeit the results of blind tests have usually been one-sided in favour of the organic chickens) feel that the flavour of the Red Tractor chicken is more to your liking. That would be a great shame, and I would recommend you persevere with the happy chickens for health and ethical reasons. However, what is clearly not subjective, but a matter of fact, is the following:

- Not all chickens are born equal. Nor do they die equal. Nor do they taste equal.
- The outcome of any chicken dish will be dependent on the kind of chicken the cook sources and uses.
- Therefore: the first step towards a successful recipe, from the simplest to the most complex, is the selection of its ingredients.

The same experiment with the two other simple dishes listed above, poached eggs on toast and strawberries and cream, will reveal exactly the same truth. The quality of the two basic ingredients in each of these dishes will determine the quality of the dishes. The dreadful loaves that pass for bread in many supermarkets and eggs from Red Tractor egg farms will produce something altogether different from the same dish made with real bread and eggs from happy hens living in conditions comparable to those living at Abbey Home Farm. Similarly, out-of-season, heavily sprayed strawberries flown in from California or the Netherlands, coupled with cream from stationary Holsteins eating tonnes of dry feed in a smelly barn, will not produce the classic British dessert that could be produced by using British organic strawberries in June with cream from happy Jersey cows eating grass.

So, what are the most basic criteria by which to select our ingredients and produce?

Ingredients and Produce: Basic Criteria

Edibility

The first basic criteria that determine whether an ingredient is good or not is its edibility and digestibility. Most of this will be pretty obvious, but it is important to remind ourselves of this simple truth when the suitability of many contemporary ingredients and mutually exclusive diets is considered:

- We are able to eat, digest and gain nutrition from all manner of foods, of different origins and levels of quality.
- Edibility and digestibility are not very selective for us humans and are not indicative of quality.
- Therefore, edibility is a good indicator of what we *cannot* eat, rather than what we *should* eat.
- We cannot eat any grasses and barks, as we are not herbivores and cannot digest cellulose.
- We cannot eat several species of plants and mushrooms, which are toxic or indigestible to us.
- Some animals can also be toxic to us. There are at times intricate ways around this: the pufferfish, eaten in Japan, is an extreme example of getting a meal from something that is potentially lethal.
- Many ingredients require cooking in order to be digestible. Most of our grain staples (e.g., rice, wheat, corn) need cooking in order to be eaten and digested properly. Other staples (e.g., potatoes, beans) are toxic and completely inedible unless they are cooked.
- Some toxins we can ingest and process due to other benefits conferred by the foods that contain them (e.g., caffeine, alcohol), but an excess of these will lead to poisoning.
- Not all humans can digest certain foods. Milk is a good example, as some ethnic groups are lactose intolerant. Your ancestry may limit some of the foods you can and cannot digest.

Flora, Fauna, and Fungi: Our Omnivorous Dominion

The flip side of the above is that edibility is also a good indicator of what we *can* eat. As will be discussed at length in my challenge to veganism, it is quite clear that, if a Martian David Attenborough studied our species with the spirit of an impartial naturalist, he would have to conclude that we are omnivorous creatures. Good ingredients *can* come, but do not *necessarily* come, as other criteria come into play, from the following categories:

- Wild mammals, birds, fish, crustaceans, reptiles, amphibians, and several invertebrates.
- Wild plants, fruits, nuts, honey, and fungi.
- Domesticated/farmed animals and their several raw products (meat, blood, milk, eggs, honey).
- Cultivated grains and pulses.
- Cultivated vegetables, tubers, herbs, fruits, and nuts.
- Spices, flavourings, and mild intoxicants (e.g., saffron, vanilla, coffee, tea, black pepper)
- Miscellaneous other (e.g., sea salt, algae, cacti)
- This is truly a cornucopia of potential ingredients, and we clearly are lords and masters here on Earth, whether we like it or not.[24]

Even the least theologically minded reader cannot deny the validity of the fundamental truth contained in our ancient myths: unlike other animals, we have the ability to choose what we eat and have unique power over other creatures and the land that sustains us.

As Nature Intended

At the risk of getting carried away and upsetting secular sensibilities, I would like to suggest that the chief moral implication of dominion is stewardship and responsibility: our power and ability to make choices have given us the potential to do things very well or very badly, very responsibly or very irresponsibly. I will therefore suggest and explain throughout this book, a very simple idea that I have already anticipated with our chicken experiment: that there are objectively good and bad ways of procuring the innumerable potential ingredients listed above. In and of themselves, all these ingredients provide us with good food and nutrition, and we are ideally suited to live off them. This is always the case, provided that these ingredients are inherently healthy, wholesome, and *natural*. I can already hear roars of disapproval from some of my readers, who can now picture me as a sandal-wearing hippy pontificating from a crop circle. I will therefore pre-empt some of the potential objections and counter arguments.

[24] As I listed the many boons that nature provides, I could not help but be reminded of these familiar passages:

"Let them have dominion over the fish of the sea, and over the birds of the air, and over all the wild animals of the earth, and over every creeping thing that creeps upon the earth." (Genesis 1:26)

"Every plant bearing seed, which is upon the face of all the earth, and every tree with seed in its fruit; you shall have them for food." (Genesis 1:29)

> "Everything is part of nature, by definition: both chickens in our experiment are 'natural'."

If we wish to define everything that exists as natural, whether we are talking about an iceberg or a nuclear power station, we are simply limiting our use of language, avoiding the issue, and engaging in a pointless exercise in sophistry. In the realm of ingredients and produce, the distinction between natural and unnatural is quite clear: an ingredient is "natural" if it arises through the timeless processes of nature, an ingredient is unnatural if it does not. What do I mean by "the timeless processes of nature"? I mean the fundamental relationships between Sun, atmosphere, water, soil, flora, fauna, and fungi that have always sustained life on Earth: what we humans call biology or ecology. Nature has her laws and rhythms and what we can observe and come to know, in our imperfect and limited ways, is that all plants and animals live, decay, and die according to their specific and innate roles in the grand, interconnected cycle of life. It follows that any given species of animal will have its innate needs, propensities, and reciprocal relationships with other living creatures.

Herbivores, for example, are perfectly designed for living in a mutually beneficial relationship with grassland, which they feed from and maintain. Herbivores tend to keep large-scale tree cover and forests away, fertilise the grasses, spread their seeds and soften the soil with their hooves, helping germination. They are prey animals that need to live in herds and need to be on the move. Therefore, a herbivore that lives more or less in this manner lives as its nature intended. On the other hand, a herbivore living away from grassland, away from the sun and the rain, locked inside a barren feedlot or barn, on concrete floors, living in its own faeces,[25] feeding on grains,[26] additives and hormones is not living as its nature intended. This, in a nutshell, is where a clear distinction between natural and unnatural can be drawn and why our Abbey Home Farm chicken, able to satisfy its fundamental needs and instincts, provides a healthy, natural ingredient, unlike its unfortunate Red Tractor counterpart living in its own poo. As I will argue in far more detail later, there is wisdom and prudence in allowing natural processes to be the foundation of our nutrition and health and there is a heavy price to pay for disregarding them. Humans can be part of the web of life, if they choose to, and their participation in the intricate soil-plant-animal cycles of the Earth is natural by definition.

> "Apart from wild plants and animals, everything else that we domesticate cannot be considered to be natural, given that it has been modified by human activity and does not exist in the wild."

[25] One of the reasons why herbivores are animals that are regularly on the move is that, like all animals, they do not want to live in their own poo.

[26] For which their ruminant stomachs are not designed.

This was an argument used by Richard Dawkins to justify the use of genetically modified crops[27] in response to Prince (now King) Charles' worthy campaigns against them. Dawkins argues that domestication has always involved human modification of plants, which are, therefore, not natural: *"agriculture has always been unnatural"*.[28] We are told that humans have been manipulating the genes of crops for millennia by selectively breeding plants with desirable traits and that therefore genetically modified crops are simply a continuation and improvement of the same process. There are two significant problems with this line of argument. The first problem is the mistaken assumption that domesticated plants and animals (potatoes, pigs, apples etc..) are *not natural* in virtue of the fact that their characteristics have been shaped by human desires and activities. This is simply not the case. Humans have historically only domesticated those plants and animals that were inherently suitable for domestication, and which thrived by living in mutual dependence with humans. Unless we believe that all human interaction with the natural world is inherently *unnatural*, domestication is simply one of many natural processes, no less natural than gathering, hunting, and fishing. Even ants domesticate other insects and cultivate mushrooms, after all, as the relationship is mutually beneficial for both ants and their domesticates.

Secondly, Professor Dawkins, as a biologist, ought to be able to understand the dramatic difference between the gradual changes that domesticated crops undergo through a farmer's seed selections and cultivation methods, and the changes that crops undergo through the targeted alteration of the crop's genetics. GM technology produces crops that could NEVER, under any circumstance, occur through the process of domestication. The genes inserted in a transgenic maize or soy crop could never possibly end up there through natural selection, because no plant can absorb the genetic material of completely different species. On the other hand, when a farmer selects the seeds of a crop that produced a particularly high yield or exhibited particularly high resistance to fungal disease, he is simply *favouring* the natural development of desirable traits in the plant for the next generation. The changes to a domesticated maize plant over time are neither random nor limitless in their potential: it will always be a maize plant, with maize genetics, with no genes from other plant and animal species. Farmers do not literally select crop characteristics: we tip the odds in our favour by selecting desirable plants and Mother Nature does the rest, if she allows it... I will let Virginia farmer and educator Joel Salatin highlight the essential difference between domesticated crops and transgenic crops, with his trademark humour and common sense:

[27] See: https://www.theguardian.com/science/2000/may/21/gm.food1

Similar arguments have been made by other proponents of genetic modification, such as Matt Ridley and Sean Rickard.

[28] https://www.theguardian.com/science/2000/may/21/gm.food1

> *"In all historic selective breeding programs, the penetrating male and the hollow female sex organs had to fit, to embrace, to connect. That a human was outside the breeding chamber selecting which pairs to mate did not override this compatible plumbing requirement. You could spend a lifetime putting a corn plant and a moth in the same room, but they just won't get it together. You could play soft music, light some candles, add some incense, deliver pizza, wash dishes, give diamond rings, go to Vegas – whatever. You could do that all day, every day, for a million years, and I guarantee you that the corn and moth would not get it on. It just wouldn't happen."*[29 30]

The difference between traditional domestication and genetic modification is one of *kind*, not of *degree*.

That traditional domestication is a natural process is highlighted by the fact that the historical dominance of crops like wheat and barley in agriculture is not accidental, it is the result of ecological and botanical constraints and opportunities which were not of our choosing. Indeed, there are very few wild animals and plants which possess the characteristics that make them suitable for domestication. The vast majority of large-seeded grass species are concentrated in Eurasia, with very few in the Americas, Sub-Saharan Africa, and Australia. The best candidates for domestication, due to seed size and cultivability, wild emmer wheat and wild barley, were only found in Eurasia. In other words, natural processes have determined both where and how agriculture could arise in the first place. The farmer can improve, adapt, and gradually transform the crop on a continuous, seasonal basis, by selecting the seeds of those plants with the most desirable qualities and replanting them. Over time, the crop changes and barely resembles its ancestor: that does not in any sense imply that the crop has become *unnatural*, nor that there is anything random or unexplainable about how the crop is transformed over time.

This argument equally applies to herbivorous livestock: it is no coincidence that agriculturalists have domesticated large herbivores like cattle, horses, donkeys, camels, sheep, and goats mostly in Eurasia, where there were plenty of wild herbivores suitable for domestication. The lack of any large mammals appropriately meeting the necessary criteria for domestication goes some way towards explaining why no domestication ever took place

[29] J. Salatin, 2011, Folks, This Ain't Normal: A Farmer's Advice for Happier Hens, Healthier People, and a Better World, page 280.

[30] NB: GM Bt corn contains genes from the bacterium Bacillus thuringiensis, rather than moth genes, but Salatin's hypothetical example is equally valid. Monsanto's Roundup Ready corn, on the other hand, has been designed to withstand spraying with Monsanto's Roundup herbicide: glyphosate. Any reasonable person should be suspicious of a crop so altered that it cannot die when sprayed with a toxic herbicide that kills all other plants around it... glyphosate is also often used at harvest time to dry up crop seeds uniformly before combining: a toxic kiss of death. This practice is commonly carried out on our oilseed rape crops in the UK.

in certain parts of the world, such as Australia. The large herbivores that we did manage to domesticate exhibit numerous fundamental natural features, including:

- The very fact that they are herbivores: these are animals that primarily feed on the one abundant plant source that humans cannot digest, namely grasses.
- Their tame, docile nature and herd behaviour: herbivorous herding animals, as well as being natural prey, are ideally suited to being led, manoeuvred, and protected in large numbers.
- Just like wheat and barley, which provide particularly desirable and useful sources of food, big herbivores provide a myriad of resources (meat, fat, milk, blood, skins, muscle power etc...) that no other animals can provide and make their domestication worthwhile.

Therefore, TO SUM UP:

1. Our crops and livestock are no less natural than wild plants and animals.
2. Domestication is a natural process.

"'Natural' is the most vague and misused word in food marketing: what does it even mean anymore?"

This objection is certainly valid, but this does not prevent the correct use of the word. Sadly, the food manufacturing and retail sectors, and their marketing and advertising efforts, aided by complicit governments and regulatory bodies, have done everything possible to mislead the public, through very effective misinformation campaigns and cheap psychological trickery.

The word "natural" is indeed now mostly meaningless in food packaging and advertising.

"Natural things, like cyanide (present in many plants), are not necessarily good for us: they might in fact kill you. Natural can be as dangerous as synthetic."

This oft-repeated argument is obviously true but irrelevant: some natural ingredients are toxic for us, others are not.[31] We can imagine and speculate that some of our earliest ancestors must have experimented with plants, fungi and the like and were met with mixed success. With some intoxicants, in spite of the fact that they offered no nutritional value, they persevered as they provided other potential benefits. Think of hallucinogens, tobacco,

[31] The journalist Steven Poole, in his misguided critique of organic farming, quipped: "Great white sharks, death cap mushrooms, and the venom of the black widow spider are also of natural origin, but you wouldn't necessarily want them sprinkled on your food" (S. Poole, 2012, You Aren't What You Eat, page 109).

opium poppies and coca plants. With others, that probably killed those first hypothetical human eaters, our ancestors quickly learnt to desist. As a seasoned forager of wild mushrooms, I know which mushrooms are edible and which ones would literally kill me, like the death cap or the destroying angel, members of the *Amanita* family. This wisdom has been passed onto me through countless generations of accumulated traditional knowledge. Interestingly, a mushroom that is toxic for humans may well be perfectly edible for an animal. The fly agaric mushroom, highly toxic and hallucinogenic, can be very dangerous if ingested in vast quantities. Reindeer, on the other hand, can eat it in vast quantities. It has been claimed that in some of the Northern shamanic traditions, such as those of the Saami people of Lapland, shamans were in the habit of drinking the urine of reindeer who had eaten the fly agaric mushroom,[32] as a sort of filtered hallucinogen. Be that as it may, the conclusion is clear: a plant or a fungus that is toxic to one animal may well be food for another animal and vice versa. All that we need here is caution and access to traditional knowledge: there should be no difficulty in avoiding nature's poisons. The other important point to make is that none of Nature's toxins in plants, fungi and animals have a negative effect on the environment as a whole. In fact, quite the opposite: they are part of the nutrient cycles, of prey-predator relationships and of plant defence mechanisms.

Pictures taken by the author in the New Forest, Hampshire, in 2022.

[32] There is speculation and uncertainty around this. The previously sceptical author of *Shroom: The Cultural History of the Magic Mushroom* (2006) later conceded that it was highly likely to be true: http://andy-letcher.blogspot.com/2011/09/taking-piss-reindeers-and-fly-agaric.html

On the other hand, humans have developed and synthesised a whole host of toxic substances, for various purposes, that are not only harmful to individual creatures but will destroy the very foundations for any sort of living systems to exist and reproduce. This has been repeatedly the case wherever and whenever these substances seep into the local air, soil, and water. The world is full of examples of disaster zones, both on land and at sea, where the effects of chemical factories, mining, nuclear technology, agrochemical pollution and toxic waste disposal, as well as accidental spills, have killed off or negatively affected the local ecology, often beyond repair, at least in the foreseeable future. It is also worth remembering that the arsenal of chemicals now routinely used in agriculture and food production is based on the same technologies used by chemical weapon manufacturers and indeed often manufactured by the very same companies. The infamous Agent Orange dropped on the land and people of Vietnam, Cambodia, and Laos over a ten-year period, was manufactured by Monsanto.[33] Other defoliants used during the same horrific war were manufactured by Dow Chemical, a major producer of the full destructive arsenal of industrial agriculture: pesticides, herbicides, GM seeds and so on.

If "natural" ingredients are the only way to go, should we only use "natural" medicines? Why can we use pharmaceuticals made in a factory but not synthetic ingredients?

There is plenty to be gained from using herbal medicine and similar practices when used properly and wisely. If I have a cold or sore throat, gargling fresh organic lemon juice, eating honey and drinking hot mint tea may be sufficient in arresting it without resorting to pharmaceuticals. However, none of this is particularly relevant as we are talking about completely different things. Food is a daily necessity and the foundation of health. Medicine, all things being equal, is an occasional need *in extremis* that we avoid unless absolutely necessary. Even the most useful, tried, and tested pharmaceuticals should be taken with caution and will have some negative side effects. Interestingly, one of the problems with industrial agriculture is precisely the fact that farm animals are routinely medicated, even pre-emptively, given the very fact that they are inherently unhealthy and need to be kept alive long enough to be useful. On farms where livestock are allowed to live as their nature intended, health is the norm and poor health and widespread disease the exception.

At the risk of repeating an old cliché, "let food be your medicine" (and your farm animals' medicine, I would add). In other words, eating well is the first prerequisite to good health and our best bet to avoid chronic disease, drugs, surgeries, and early graves.

[33] Monsanto is now part of Bayer, following the 2018 merger.

So... what sort of "natural food" should we seek?

Wild or Domesticated?

Once upon a time, all food came from the wild. If we take the last 50,000 years, usually referred to as the Upper Palaeolithic or Late Stone Age, about which we know a decent amount thanks to fairly consistent and well-preserved archaeological evidence, we know that agriculture took centre stage in the latter quarter of that period, during the last 10,000-12,000 years. We have, therefore, a very long past as hunters and gatherers: domestication and civilisation are relatively recent.

The vast majority of our food, apart from seafood, has come from domesticated plants and animals for thousands of years now and the recent debates around "Paleo diets" and the merits of wild foods versus domesticated foods are, in many ways, rather pointless. The vast majority of our food must come from agriculture if we are to even attempt to feed our growing populations sustainably. When selecting our ingredients, we should:

- Appreciate that wild foods (seafood, wild meat, fungi etc...) are potentially some of the best and most appropriate foods for us to eat, given our ancestry.
- Understand that we are nonetheless perfectly adapted to eating ingredients from domesticated plants and animals, which evolved in symbiosis with humans.
- Consider that whilst agriculture will always provide the bulk of our ingredients (with some marginal exceptions depending on geography and culture), it is desirable not to completely lose touch with our *wildness*, for both nutritional and cultural reasons.

Fresh or Preserved?

There is no question that there is much virtue in our produce being fresh. Fruits and vegetables, picked ripe and ready to eat, are unquestionably far better when they are very fresh, both nutritionally and in terms of the pleasure we get from them. Exposure to heat and travel, plus the passage of time, can turn something fresh, crunchy, and vibrant into a limp and tasteless product. These are living things which will eventually rot. Anybody who has had the opportunity to pick a tomato, a head of lettuce or an apple straight from a garden will know how the intensity of flavour and texture of a freshly picked crop differs from its supermarket counterpart. Similar experiences are available with seafood, which must be eaten as fresh as possible, for both sanitary and gastronomic reasons. Overall, an abundance of fresh produce is a great start to any diet. Historically, there has never been a better time in which to keep produce fresh for the longest possible time and to bring it to the cities at its prime, given the marvels of modern transportation, refrigeration, and storage. Provided we know how to select and buy the right produce, we have ample opportunities to eat produce fresh and at its best.

This should not lead us to conclude that food must always be fresh or that fresh is necessarily always better. Provided that high-quality ingredients and the right processes are used, we can and should buy products that are preserved, pickled, salted, frozen, smoked and fermented. In some cases, preserving brings out additional qualities to an ingredient: tomatoes, for example, when cooked and preserved as paste or sauce have more beneficial antioxidants bioavailable to humans, in the form of lycopene, than fresh tomatoes. Does that mean we should eat our tomatoes cooked and canned? No, it means that we should eat them both fresh and preserved. In the same way that all ingredients are inherently good for us, provided they are from the right sources, similarly, all traditional preservation methods are perfectly good, provided they are done with skill, prudence, and cleanliness, whether at home or in a manufacturing facility. In other words, just like all chickens are not born equal, not all dried pasta, canned tomatoes, biscuits, smoked herring, and jam are made in the same way. Wheat, tomatoes, herring, and fruit are inherently good ingredients. However, the way they are processed will greatly affect the final quality of the product. As will be explained in later chapters, reading labels and understanding processing methods are crucial when shopping for all sorts of products.

Processed or Unprocessed?

This brings us to an important point. There is unquestionably more discussion nowadays about the problems associated with "processed food", "processed meat" and industrial food processing in general. "Processed" has often become synonymous with "unhealthy" in alternative food circles. Much of this perception of processed food has emerged for all the right reasons, and it is mainly based on opposition to *ultra-processed foods* which, as clearly delineated by Brazilian epidemiologist Carlos Monteiro,[34] are in a class of their own and must be distinguished from "processed" food, which can be either good or bad. An increasing section of the public has come to realise that most food items in the supermarket, with their unpronounceable ingredients, additives, E numbers, emulsifiers and microwave instructions are fundamentally unhealthy. However, a blanket opposition to processed food and exultation of "fresh and natural" foods in alternative food circles has given food historian Rachel Laudan, a staunch defender of industrial agriculture, the opportunity to chastise the Slow Food movement and what she craftily refers to as "Culinary Luddism" in an impressive attack.[35] I will come back to her many criticisms, some of which are perfectly legitimate, some misguided straw man arguments, others outright wrong, throughout this book.

[34] Monteiro CA. Nutrition and health. The issue is not food, nor nutrients, so much as processing. Public Health Nutrition. 2009;12(5):729-731. doi:10.1017/S1368980009005291

[35] https://www.jacobinmag.com/2015/05/slow-food-artisanal-natural-preservatives/

For our immediate purposes here, we must clarify why processed food is not necessarily bad:

- Many of the raw materials of nature need cooking, processing, and transforming before they can be at their best or even edible.
- We don't need to do all this ourselves; we need to learn to find the right sources of processed foods and include them in our diet.
- Cooking and processing are one of our many distinguishing features as humans; we have been using fire and processing nature's raw materials since times immemorial. It's a good thing.
- It ought to be clear that, like growing food and raising animals, processing food can be done both very well and very badly.
- Industrial technology has made it possible to do both: it has allowed the cheap, mass production of excellent products and the cheap, mass production of very poor products.
- Sadly, the very poor products make up the majority of the market: for every can of organic tomato paste with no additives, there are dozens of flavoured crisp brands.
- Whilst the basis of our cookery should centre around the use of fresh, high-quality ingredients, processed foods have their place in a healthy diet and food culture.
- We need to learn how to clearly distinguish between processed foods and ultra-processed foods.

Cleanliness and Pollution

We live in an age of paradoxes. On the one hand, widespread sanitation and personal hygiene have been one of the great successes of the last century. Food poisoning, tainted food, rotten food and thoroughly unhygienic practices have massively declined in Europe and the type of food markets that can still be found in parts of Asia and Africa are thankfully not even conceivable for most of us. Similarly, water is relatively clean and waterborne illnesses like cholera are a thing of the past. On the other hand, industrial pollution, which poses a different type of threat, is now a mostly inescapable global problem. It has been proven that even the most seemingly pristine and remote environments, from the Arctic to great mountaintops, have been contaminated by plastics and other pollutants. We are very unlikely to get food poisoning from oysters and mussels or eat meat that has gone off, but we are highly likely to eat fish that contains mercury, pineapples that contain organophosphates and bread that contains glyphosate. We may no longer catch infectious diseases from food, but we are exposed to a host of pollutants that lead to all sorts of other ailments like cancer, infertility, and the many other diseases of modernity.

This means that, whilst our choices are necessarily constrained, the choices we can make really matter. We cannot avoid some mercury or microplastics in seafood, for example, and we cannot avoid the fact that the air and water that our crops live on will be relatively polluted, albeit to differing degrees depending on location. My current food growing project, Local Organic Growers CIC, is situated in Watford, Hertfordshire. One of the sites is very close to the M1, and the other is fairly close to the centre of town. Traffic noise can be heard at all times, and it would be a fair assumption to presume that, whilst this is not the most polluted part of England in which to grow crops, there is an inevitable amount of pollution in the air, water, and soil.

Of course, it could be much worse. Driving alongside the Mississippi in Louisiana during a family holiday one spring, we saw huge rice fields right next to oil refineries, petrochemical plants and miscellaneous factories. It was a vast industrial area, with a few desolate dwellings and very small towns scattered around. I remember the sadness of this spectacle and felt sorry for the farmers who lived and worked there and, inevitably, could not help but wonder about that rice! Apart from being grown with agrochemicals to begin with, the polluted water in which the rice is flooded and the heavy particles in the air must all result in a relatively toxic product.

Somewhere in Louisiana, by the Mississippi, 2019. Images taken by the Author.

Overall, we have to accept that some varying degrees of pollution and toxicity will be in all of our food. Whilst we can try to grow and source food from relatively less polluted parts of the land and seas, there is only so much we can do. What we can do, however, is at least select ingredients that were not *intentionally* polluted. The average conventional potato crop in the UK is sprayed repeatedly from the beginning to the end of its lifecycle with herbicides, fungicides, and pesticides. In fact, fields are usually sprayed with glyphosate to clear the field of any residual weeds before the potatoes are even planted and then sprayed again to dry out the crop just before harvest. This we can and should avoid and I will do my best to explain how to achieve that goal in further chapters.

Our potatoes in Watford.

IN A NUTSHELL

- Not all chickens are born equal. Or cows, or tomato plants for that matter.
- Animals do not like living in their own poo.
- Food is only ever as good as the quality of the ingredients from which it is made.
- There are no inherently bad ingredients.
- All edible plants, animals, fungi etc... whether wild or domesticated, are inherently good for us, provided they lived the life their nature intended.
- Appeals to nature in branding and advertising are almost meaningless.
- You can appreciate nature's wisdom with humility and gratitude without being a hippie.
- There can be no good food without good produce but there can be great food without any cooking or processing.
- Processed food is not inherently bad. Ultra-processed food is inherently bad.
- Large-scale manufacturing and industrial food processing is, in principle, a good thing, depending on what is being processed, how and why.
- Cleanliness and hygiene are non-negotiable.
- We can't do that much about global pollution and contaminated soils, air, and water.
- What we can do is avoid produce that has been subjected to a bombardment of agrochemicals and products from sick animals that live in their own poo.

Chapter 3

ORGANIC AND BEYOND ORGANIC

The fundamental importance of being able to draw qualitative distinctions between ingredients, as we did with our chickens, implies that the key to a good diet lies in developing the ability to make such qualitative judgments. This is far more important, as we shall see, than developing an understanding of nutrition science. Whilst of course, it is helpful to know that chicken is a source of protein, rather than a source of carbohydrates, this is of secondary importance when it comes to selecting what to eat and how. The emphasis on sound agricultural practice and on the wholesomeness of ingredients and produce should be the cornerstone of any reasonable approach to diet and cookery. In the previous chapter, an initial attempt was made to address the confusion around "natural" food and to make the case for its inclusion as a main criterion when assessing the quality of any food ingredient. Natural food is often, rightly, associated with the organic movement and with other alternative agricultural movements. What follows is a brief overview and defence of the principles behind this broad church, with a focus on Britain and America. Why aren't all chickens the same and why does it matter?

I first became aware of the organic movement in the 1980s, through my mother. Before there was even a language to define and describe organic food in Italy,[36] she had taken it upon herself to source produce that was seasonal, not sprayed with noxious chemicals and of clear origin. She made her own yoghurt and only bought eggs from hens that were "ruspanti", a word which roughly translates as "rustic", "traditional", "free-ranging" and "full of vitality". We ate quite moderate amounts of meat growing up but what meat we ate was exceptional, as

[36] No real distinction was made back then and the language of organic was simply not part of the culture, although there was certainly food grown according to organic principles, especially fruit and vegetables, as well as traditional dairy and pork products. Organic is now referred to as "biologico" in Italian, which is arguably more appropriate than "organic", as it defines a key distinction between conventional agriculture, which is based on chemistry, and organic agriculture, which is based on biology.

our butcher sourced it from the best farms raising animals in the traditional manner. I remember the smell and taste of the half lamb from the Roman countryside that used to be roasted every Christmas and Easter at our home. Fed on the grasses and shrubs of the Mediterranean, the sheep produced lambs that were completely different to those produced here in Britain. This, to be clear, was not a qualitative difference, as the best British lamb is as good as the best Roman lamb, but a difference of kind: a reflection of different soils, breeds, slaughter age, vegetation, and climate. This brings me to a key point: food should reflect healthy landscapes and soils and derive character from it. This was a major intuition of the founding fathers of the organic movement around the world: that there is an unbreakable and uncompromising connection between soil, vegetation, landscape and, ultimately, food and the people eating it.

This is a very different way to look at food from that which underpins the production and marketing of conventional food products like our unfortunate Red Tractor chickens. Much of the motivation behind the organic movement and other alternative agricultural movements has been the desire to move away from this relatively new, but now conventional, reductive view of food. Almost invariably, these alternative movements have tended to offer potential solutions to the short and long-term negative consequences of industrial agriculture.

The problems associated with industrial agriculture are manifold, interconnected and well-documented.[37]

They can be summarised as follows, in no particular order:

- Loss of organic matter and soil erosion.
- Water and air pollution.
- Loss of biodiversity and increased species extinction (both wild and domesticated plants and animals).
- Low food quality and variety.
- Dependence on fossil fuels, mined minerals and synthetic chemical inputs.
- Causes and exacerbates anthropogenic climate change.
- Lack of resilience, geographic diversity, and flexibility to cope with climatic extremes.
- Leads to desertification.
- Involves unskilled, dangerous, poorly compensated, precarious labour (e.g., industrial slaughterhouse work).
- Is inherently abusive and cruel to domesticated animals and ethically untenable.

[37] See, for example: S.R. Gliessman, 2006, Agroecology: The Ecology of Sustainable Food Systems, pages 8-17; N. Lampkin, 1990, Organic Farming, pages 6-8; P. Lymbery, 2014, Farmageddon: The True Cost of Cheap Meat.

- Carries great social costs (e.g., obesity and the "diseases of abundance": cancer, diabetes, heart disease etc..).
- Leads to the loss of cultural and culinary diversity and to the spread of homogenous "junk food" worldwide.
- Leads to rural depopulation and impoverishment and to the disappearance of traditional lifestyles.
- Leads to the loss of traditional landscapes and domesticated ecosystems (e.g., hedges, meadows, and orchards in England).

The impact of industrial agriculture on the planet as a whole is even recognised by some of industrial agriculture's staunchest proponents, such as Vaclav Smil. Smil, in spite of arguing that artificial nitrogen fertiliser has made it possible to feed the world's population and that we need *"substantial increases in the Haber-Bosch synthesis during the first half of the twenty-first century"*,[38] acknowledges that *"humans have transformed significant portions of all natural terrestrial biomes in destructive ways"*, *"have degraded, fragmented, and impoverished natural vegetation"* and, with *"their domesticated animals have become the dominant mammalian species on Earth"*.[39]

Organic and Alternative Agriculture: A Very Brief History

In 1909, as the process of industrialisation of agriculture was rapidly expanding, the American F.H. King (1848-1911) was reporting on the organic agricultural practices of the Far East, where the crucial importance of maintaining fertility for thousands of years for a very dense population had been remarkably successful. King contrasted this with the then already common practice of *"movement of feeding stuffs and mineral fertilisers to Western Europe and to the Eastern United States"* which *"began less than a century"* before the time of writing, and which King predicted could not *"be continued indefinitely in either Europe or America"*.[40] The following decade, Fritz Haber (1868-1934) claimed his Nobel Prize in 1918 for the synthesis of ammonia which, as we shall see later, was a major milestone in the development of industrial agriculture, as it became the standard method used to produce nitrogen fertiliser to this day.

Reacting to the spread of the new synthetic fertility model, Rudolf Steiner (1861-1925), the father of biodynamic agriculture, observed that *"fertility cannot be promoted entirely by*

[38] V. Smil, 2001, Enriching the Earth: Fritz Haber, Carl Bosch, and the transformation of world food production, page 206.

[39] V. Smil, 2013, Harvesting the biosphere: What we have taken from nature, page 235.

[40] F.H. King, 1911, Farmers of Forty Centuries, page 1.

artificial means; there must be knowledge of things that are directly connected with Nature herself."[41] Here in Britain, Lord Northbourne (1896-1982) later applied the theories of Rudolf Steiner to his family estate in Kent, and in 1939 travelled to Switzerland to visit the leading exponent of biodynamic agriculture, Dr Ehrenfried Pfeiffer (1899-1961). He went on to host the Betteshanger Summer School and Conference, the first biodynamic farming conference held in Britain. Subsequently, Lord Northbourne coined the term *"organic farming"* and the concept of *"the farm as organism"*, of *"organic versus chemical farming"*.[42] By comparing the farm to an organism, the term "organic", which is quite an odd term to describe a farming system, makes sense. The farm as "organism" is a living entity, whose vital elements and constituent parts are mutually interdependent, which is very different from the linear, input-output dynamic of industrial systems.

At around the same time, the great English botanist Sir Albert Howard (1873-1947), having spent many years in India, as well as other parts of the British Empire, published his *Agricultural Testament* (1940), which became one of the foundational texts for the organic movement, together with some of his earlier works, such as *The Waste Products of Agriculture* (1931). His work was motivated by what he saw as the deep flaws and grave consequences of the spread of industrial agriculture, with particular focus on Britain and her dominions. Domestic agricultural lands in Britain were increasingly reliant on artificial inputs and imported fertilisers, whilst colonial plantations were failing to maintain long-term soil fertility and crop health. His response was to apply scientific rigour and research methodology to the study of traditional farming methods, especially those of India, and to provide a modern alternative to industrial agriculture. He was one of the first to explicitly make the link between the health of soil, vegetation and animals and the health and vitality of human populations, which he believed would suffer from the gradual impoverishment of soils. Similar conclusions were drawn by the nutritionist Sir Robert McCarrison (1878-1960), who had spent seven years with the Hunza people of India (now Pakistan) and observed how the common chronic diseases that afflicted Europeans were notably absent from the local population. McCarrison attributed this anomaly to their diet, based upon whole foods from healthy plants, grown on carefully tended fields in which organic waste was dutifully returned. He compared this diet to the diet of the English working classes, already full of

[41] R. Steiner, Lecture X, 9 September 1924, Dornach, Switzerland.

[42] Lord Northbourne, 1940, Look to the Land, page 81. Northbourne's intuition has been entirely misunderstood by many of those who oppose organic farming. Steven Poole, in commenting on Northbourne's intuition, declares: "Of course an 'organic' farm is also stuffed to the brim with chemicals. Chemicals are all there is." (S. Poole, 2012, You Aren't What You Eat, page 108). This kind of nonsensical circular argument is used, as we will see, by all sorts of reductionists working across different disciplines related to food.

white bread and margarine, and concluded *that "the greatest single factor in the acquisition of good health is perfectly constituted food."*[43]

As recorded throughout Howard's work, by addressing soil health, plantations and crop fields would not only increase in productivity, but farmers would be able to reverse and prevent outbreaks of fungal disease and problems with insect pests and also be able to keep livestock healthy and disease free by feeding them with the healthy crops. In other words, the organic method is *inherently preventative*: it is about creating healthy soil conditions in the first place, so that plants and animals are strong, healthy, and self-reliant. Howard's innovative contributions to the study of humus and to the manufacture of composts were in stark contrast to the rising tide of agricultural chemistry and research emanating from such places as Rothamsted Experimental Station, founded by John Bennett Lawes (1814-1900), a pioneer in the manufacture of superphosphates, in 1843.

It may come as a shock to the readers, especially those who tend to a garden, to realise that whilst some forms of composting existed in all pre-Industrial agricultural societies, the systematic, large-scale, and "scientific" manufacture of compost is relatively recent. One can only wonder, with regret, how advanced in the large-scale manufacture and mass use of compost we would now be, as well as in the recycling of sewage and other biodegradable waste, had Howard, rather than Fritz Haber and the scientists at Rothamsted, been given the opportunity to lead agricultural progress. One also wonders how much better equipped we would be to deal with the many current crises in agriculture. A good example particularly relevant to Howard is the current threat to the world banana crop posed by fungal disease, which could potentially wipe out most of the world's banana plantations. At the root of the problem is the fact that most banana plantations are monocultures lacking in biodiversity, devoted to one banana variety, the Cavendish.

The Cavendish had replaced the previous dominant banana variety, the Gros Michel, that was grown as a monoculture throughout Central America until the 1950s, and which had been wiped out by fungal disease. The Cavendish may be facing the same demise: banana monocultures, lacking in all genetic diversity, are extremely susceptible to pests and disease. The depleted soils of banana monocultures do not tend to be nurtured with organic matter, are reliant on synthetic fertilisers, and the whole system is built upon heavy applications of toxic agrochemicals. As scientists will no doubt rush to create effective fungicides or genetically modified bananas resistant to the virus, which would only address the symptoms rather than the causes of the fungal threat, a very different approach could be taken to solve the problem: regenerating the soils with organic matter and green manures, creating

[43] P. Conford, 2001, The Origins of the Organic Movement, page 53.

polycultures by introducing other fruit crops to the plantations, growing a far more diverse mix of banana varieties, and other more enlightened measures.

On the other side of the Atlantic, in the United States, some of the concerns that motivated Howard were increasingly of interest to other likeminded scientists. Following the devastating impact of the Dust Bowl in the American Great Plains, Edward Faulkner (1886-1964) declared that US agriculture had used *"machinery towards bringing destruction to the soil in less time than any other people in the world's history"*.[44] The Dust Bowl had indeed been a disaster of agricultural origin. It is easy to forget, or simply not know in the first place, that a huge chunk of land running across the middle of the United States and Canada, stretching from Texas to Alberta, was natural grassland and prairie, populated by an enormous population of bison[45] and other herbivores, especially elk and antelope. In a relatively short period of time, this majestic ecosystem was greatly altered beyond recognition. For a start, the adoption and spread of horse culture amongst the Native American tribes greatly facilitated buffalo hunting and allowed several populations to permanently roam and hunt across the Plains.[46]

As Europeans and firearms gradually spread West, the buffalo came under unprecedented pressure. Following the profitable and short-lived buffalo skin and bone trade of the second half of the 19th century, and, most importantly, following the colonisation and permanent settlement of these lands by Europeans, the bison was almost completely exterminated and huge tracts of the Great Plains were indiscriminately ploughed up to grow annual crops such as wheat. The topsoil across the prairies was generally extremely deep and fertile, which encouraged settlers to grow crops intensely, without much rotation and without putting much organic matter back in the soil. Not many trees were planted, which could have at least offered wind break and water retention between ploughed-up fields. Consequently, soil erosion ensued, as did loss of moisture and drought. Combined with strong winds, it led to the literal blowing away of the topsoil and to the ruin of many farmers.

The American J. Russell Smith (1874-1966), similarly to Faulkner, was motivated by a concern over the soil erosion and infertility that he witnessed in a dusty, treeless landscape in China.[47] Smith's premise was that this was due to the inevitable consequences of deforestation followed by arable agriculture, which in turn would lead to desert, with only sheep and goats scavenging any remaining vegetation. The same conclusion had previously been reached

[44] E.H. Faulkner, 1945, Ploughman's Folly, page 11.

[45] For a fascinating account, see S. Rinella, 2009, American Buffalo: In Search of a Lost Icon.

[46] Such as the Comanches. For further reading, I recommend T. R. Fehrenbach, 2001, Comanches: The History of a People.

[47] J.R. Smith, 1953, Tree crops: A permanent agriculture.

by Richard St. Barbe Baker (1889-1982), an English biologist and botanist who dedicated his life to promoting and leading worldwide reforestation efforts. St Barbe Baker, having been posted to Kenya by the Colonial Office in 1920, had observed how the highlands had been denuded of tree cover, and stripped and kept bare by grazing goats.[48]

Like Faulkner, Smith believed that the United States, with its highly mechanised and reckless tillage, was undergoing this process of destruction at a greater speed than previous civilisations. This problem, which Smith argued was observable worldwide, was particularly prevalent on hilly ground where unless tree crops were maintained instead of tilled crops, destruction always followed. On flat lands, the problem was less prevalent, as soil erosion was less likely, or at least less rapid. Interestingly, Smith recalled the two-storey cropping system he observed on the island of Mallorca, where annual crops were grown between alleys of tree crops such as almonds and figs: agroforestry in other words, which he argued could work alongside reforested hillsides. The rest of Smith's work was dedicated to examining the tree crops with the most potential, as both food and fodder. Smith's insights undoubtedly informed some of the alternative agricultural movements that followed, especially those that wish to include far more tree cover and perennials in their system, such as agroforestry, permaculture[49] and forest gardening.[50]

In 2019, I had the pleasure of visiting Wakelyn Farm in Suffolk, belonging to the late Professor Martin Wolfe,[51] where he experimented with a form of agroforestry: an organic system combining the integration of arable crops (of staples such as wheat) with productive tree crops (like apples) in neat alley systems. Whilst the Professor's impressive and valuable work was incomplete, he demonstrated the practicality of growing crops through an agroforestry system on many acres of land, with a tractor. This is a system that could be significantly scaled up very efficiently, as it has been by a few farmers, such as Stephen Briggs in Cambridgeshire, who grows organic cereals, vegetables and apples on over 500 acres.[52] Over in the United States, with its swathes of flat arable land, agroforestry holds huge promise, as it combines biodiversity and resilience with high productivity and scalability.

[48] P. Conford, 2001, The Origins of the Organic Movement, pages 60-61.

[49] Broadly defined as "the conscious design and maintenance of agriculturally productive ecosystems which have the diversity, stability, and resilience of natural ecosystems." (Mollison, 1979). Permaculture places a particular emphasis on the central importance of perennial crops. For further reading, I recommend S. Holzer, 2004, Sepp Holzer's Permaculture and M. Shepard, 2013, Restoration Agriculture: Real-World Permaculture for Farmers.

[50] See M. Crawford, 2010, Creating a Forest Garden: Working with Nature to Grow Edible Crops.

[51] https://www.organicresearchcentre.com/news-events/news/professor-martin-wolfe/

[52] https://www.agricology.co.uk/resources/agroforestry-farming-future; https://www.woodlandtrust.org.uk/plant-trees/stephen-briggs/

Again, in the United States, J.I. Rodale (1898-1971), inspired by Howard and Steiner, founded a working organic farm for trials and experimentation in the 1940s, The Rodale Institute, which is still running today, and the Rodale Press, to teach and advocate organic methods to the wider public. Further work was done by Lady Eve Balfour (1898-1990) in England, who believed that mankind's health and future depended on how the soil was used, and that organic farming provided the solution. In 1943 Balfour published The Living Soil, based on the initial findings of the Haughley Experiment, the first experiment carried out to compare chemical and organic farming methods. This eventually led to the formation of a key international organic advocacy group, the Soil Association, which is the current organic certifying body in Britain. At around the same time, George Henderson advocated small-scale mixed farming systems, aimed at building up soil, and developed portable pastured livestock and poultry structures.[53] Inspired by Howard, Newman Turner (1913-1964) promoted a biological approach to fertility and a rejection of agrochemicals, with emphasis on the intensive use of pasture.[54]

There were several others on the pastoral side of the movement. Innovators such as the Frenchman Andre Voisin (1903-1964) introduced novel approaches to grass management and grazing,[55] developing a technique of rotational grazing which allowed, at a time in which the application of artificial fertilisers was increasingly perceived as the only method to increase grass production, to significantly increase dairy and meat productivity per hectare, without any inputs other than different management techniques. As Graham Harvey points out, this was an *"extraordinary finding"* which *"had it been acted upon by the government and farming establishment it might well have given Britain a healthy and sustainable food supply"*.[56] At present, in Britain, 41.1% of the land is covered in permanent grassland and rough grazing, rising to 45.8% if we include temporary grassland under 5 years old.[57] Much of our grassland could be managed far more efficiently and we are not alone. Indeed, in many parts of the pastoral world, overgrazing and undergrazing have been a historical and ongoing problem that has eroded soils, depleted fertility, led to the loss of biodiversity, to a loss of arboreal cover and to drier conditions.

In the United States, this pastoral counterculture has in some ways hankered back to the Jeffersonian ideal of the independent farmer and exultation of agrarian life. Through the 1960s and 1970s, with the growth of the environmental movement, influential farmers like

[53] G. Henderson, 1943, The Farming Ladder.

[54] N. Turner, 1951, Fertility Farming; 1955 Fertility Pastures.

[55] A. Voisin, 1959, Grass Productivity.

[56] G. Harvey, 2008, The Carbon Fields: How Our Countryside Can Save Britain, page 81.

[57] Agriculture in the United Kingdom 2022, page 25.

Wendell Berry argued for the agrarian ideal and against the environmental, cultural, and spiritual damage of the industrial takeover of agriculture and American society.[58] Charles Walters, founder of Acres U.S.A., Stan Parsons, founder of Ranching for Profit, Allan Savory, the Rhodesian founder of Holistic Management International and Allan Nation, founder of Stockman Grass Farmer, all contributed to this vision, with particular emphasis on pasture management and regenerative ranching, at a time when most livestock in the country had been increasingly housed in feedlots and fed grain-based diets. More recently, this approach has been popularised by the aforementioned Joel Salatin, who has presented his work as a call to sanity and return to normality, and by Will Harris, a sixth-generation Georgian farmer who converted his industrial system to a model in regenerative agriculture, which he defines as *"restarting the cycles of nature that the industrial, monocultural, input-heavy methods of modern land management broke"*.[59] Salatin, who promotes grass-based systems, has squarely placed his advocacy and practices as alternatives to the *"compartmentalized, reductionist, fragmented, linear thought process"*[60] of industrial agriculture. His productivity rates per acre are outstanding, by any measure, and all revolve around grass management and livestock. The potential of holistic, intensive, rotational grazing techniques arguably holds more promise for the 21st century than almost any other development in agriculture. The benefits are manifold and applicable to much of the Earth's landmass: from regenerating thin, eroded soils and reversing desertification to exponentially increasing meat and dairy productivity per acre.

Organic Principles Beyond Certification

I must clarify an important detail: from here onwards, for simplicity, I will refer to the word "organic" in a general sense, as a reference to organic principles, rather than to organic certification. All alternative agricultural movements share some basic principles which are consistent with the organic approach and method. The holistic grazing methods of Salatin, Harris and others, for example, are generally not certified by any organic body and yet are very consistent with organic principles. These farmers will not sell their products as "organic" and yet their products are often better than many products which are certified as organic. Indeed, organic certification, whilst a good guarantor of some *minimum* degree of quality, varies from country to country[61] and does not and cannot draw qualitative distinctions

[58] W. Berry, 1977, The Unsettling of America: Culture and Agriculture.

[59] W. Harris, 2023, A Bold Return to Giving a Damn. One Farm, Six Generations, and the Future of Food, page xiii.

[60] J. Salatin, 2007, Everything I Want To Do Is Illegal: War Stories From the Local Food Front, pages 3-4.

[61] US standards are looser than UK standards, for example.

between different certified organic products, nor can it include products that are not certified organic but are grown using organic methods. The latter are really important, as they make up a significant percentage of the current market. There are beef and lamb producers in the UK, for example, who raise their animals on healthy, clean pastures but do not, for all sorts of reasons, have organic certification. And yet, their productive methods are "organic". On the other hand, you may well find certified organic lamb from New Zealand in our supermarkets. Whilst no doubt a quality product, the local British uncertified equivalent may be a better option and far closer to the ethos of the organic movement.

The fact that there is wonderful organic produce that is not certified is something that I can vouch for through personal experience. The many crops I used to grow on my one-acre field in Hertfordshire ranged from potatoes and beans to cucumbers and beetroots. No fertilisers, pesticides, herbicides, or fungicides were ever used. The single major input into the field was manure from the cows and oxen, who grazed on pasture for much of the year. Vegetable waste, autumn leaf litter and other organic matter also found their way onto the field. A little seaweed was added to the soil in the polytunnel, and bags of seed compost were bought every season to start off the seeds before planting out onto the field. Crop rotation was practised, the field was never left fallow, it was grazed in between crops and ploughing was carried out once a year just before first planting in late March/early April. Some seeds/bulbs (tomatoes, chillies, and garlic) were saved and replanted year after year. The produce was as "organic" as it gets in England and, given the health and vitality of the soil, it was generally free from pest damage, blemishes, and fungal disease: it was mostly "picture perfect". And yet, legally, we could not sell our produce as "organic", as we did not have, nor did we need, certification, given the particular cultural and commercial dynamics at our farm and community.

Cows grazing in early spring on my old arable field in between crops. Credit: @escapetheofficejob

Basic Hallmarks of Organic Agriculture

The basic features of organic agriculture, certified or otherwise, can be summarised as follows:

Soil Health and the Preventative Principle

The fundamental premise of the organic method is that soil health is the key to plant, animal, and human health. An inherently fertile, rich, biologically active soil will provide plants what they need to be healthy throughout their life cycle, just as it does in the wild. Serious crop loss through pests and fungal disease is a *symptom* of a problem, rather than *the* problem.

Therefore, the good farmer addresses the problem, rather than the symptom. In 2019, when I was still at the farm, I suffered a relatively rare crop loss: my broad bean and pea crop completely succumbed to black aphids and slugs respectively and produced a very limited amount of beans and peas. Why? Because the area of the field in which these crops were planted was the most dried out, infertile, over-cultivated part of the field, where even weeds struggled to grow vigorously. A quick dig through hardened soil revealed a low worm population and a lack of water absorption. As a result, the plants grew stunted and weak, resulting in extreme susceptibility to the pests with which they usually coexist. Having grown both broad beans and peas very successfully in the past, I know that sowing the right varieties as early as possible in fertile soils leads to sturdy, strong plants, early flowering, and heavy crops. Any crop loss to black aphids and slugs is irrelevant, in the grand scheme of things: healthy crops have high yields, and a low percentage of crop loss or damage is not a problem.

The solution? Following the disappointing crop, I gradually mulched the soil with strawy manure and regularly mowed or grazed the weeds and grasses that were gradually coming through. The fertility boost and brief fallow period gradually addressed the problem, by returning that part of the field to what over the years I have experienced over and over again as the norm: healthy plants and heavy crops. Low yields and crop loss to disease and pests are the exception rather than the norm in organic agriculture.[62] When it does happen, it is generally the result of human mismanagement. The key to achieving results is to *prevent* problems by promoting soil health, rather than reacting to problems. This approach is the exact opposite of conventional agriculture. The conventional farmer systematically creates unhealthy conditions, in which plants, weak and exposed, cannot grow without continuous intervention. The farmer proceeds to routinely and pre-emptively treat the symptoms of ill health through the application of agrochemicals throughout the full life cycle of the plants. This secures a heavy crop, for sure, but at what cost?

Cyclical Fertility

The organic method is modelled on natural ecosystems. Nature is always dominated by cycles of birth, growth, death, and decay which underpin all living systems. Soil, plants, and animals are interdependent and inseparable, as a rule. Fertility is maintained by the continuous recycling of nutrients. There is no such thing as "waste" in nature and tomorrow's plants and animals are dependent on today's death, decay, and waste products: what Howard called the Law of Return. It is for this reason that the farmer looks upon manure and

[62] An exceptionally wet winter and spring, like in 2023/2024, can lead to an extraordinarily high slug population, which is problematic. But one can and must adapt to exceptional circumstances and the solutions do not lie in chemical sprays.

waste as fundamental resources, rather than as a nuisance. To put it in simple terms, it is impossible to underestimate the important of... pee and poo! As James Lovelock pointed out, the elimination of waste is not particularly efficient for animals: it involves the loss of a lot of nutrients, water, and heat energy.[63] If individual interest and survival were all that mattered, a more efficient way to eliminate waste would have evolved by now. Therefore, it seems as if animals have evolved features that are designed to benefit the survival of other species as much as their own survival.[64] In order for the soil to nourish the next generation of plants, it needs a large return from the animals who benefited from eating those plants or from eating other animals.

Perhaps the simplest and most accessible example of how fertility works through symbiosis and interdependence is provided by observing the relationship between soil, grass, herbivores, and predators. All four individual elements in this life cycle are entirely dependent on the other three. The soil takes nutrients from the waste of herbivores and their predators and gives nourishment to the grass. The grass takes its nutrition from the soil and gives nourishment to the herbivores. Herbivores take their nutrition from grass and give nourishment to the soil. Herbivores, through regular movement, grazing, herd behaviour and hoof action, maintain and protect the grass. Herbivores provide nutrition to the predators, who in turn give nourishment to the soil and encourage herd behaviour by the very threat of predation. The reality of this life cycle is of course more complex that this simple illustration. However, what is clear is that it is a self-contained life cycle which is sustainable, rich, and resilient by definition. The best organic farming systems are based on a replication and maintenance of the same kind of soil-plant-animal relationships.

For this reason, organic systems always require the integration of crops with livestock, of some kind or other. Nature is integrated, and cyclical, and a system based on biomimicry must obey this simple, yet profound, principle.

No Chemical Inputs

An uncompromising rejection of the agrochemical arsenal of conventional agriculture is at the heart of the organic method. The application of biocides is simply inconsistent with the creation of a complex, diverse web of life, which is ultimately what the organic farmer is trying to create. Starting from the soil, the application of nitrogenous compounds and mineral

[63] J. Lovelock, The Revenge of Gaia, 2006, pages 23-25.

[64] A similar example is the dissemination of plant species by the animals who benefit from them: many creatures, such as orangutans and tapirs, for example, literally seed the forest of their favourite fruit by pooping out seeds across the land. The poop also acts as a fertiliser and seed "starter" for the seeds to sprout.

fertilisers (especially in isolation, with no organic sources of fertility)[65] does not lead to a living soil: a soil rich in worms, microorganisms, fungi, and insect life. Organic agriculture has to centre around organic sources of fertility. With purely synthetic sources of fertility, soil becomes a largely sterile *medium* through which artificial nutrients are supplied to the roots of plants.

Herbicides will kill off any plants competing with the crops and poison soil and water in the process. Weeding, on the other hand, whilst laborious, allows for the biological recycling of unwanted plant matter. On my old one-acre field at the farm, as the wheel hoes passed through lines of beetroot (see images below) around 3-5 times over the course of 5-6 months, the weeds were automatically mulched and prevented from growing and seeding.[66] Ultimately, the extirpated weeds will go on to feed the next generation of crops.

[65] Should British agriculture ever convert to organic methods, the process of converting from synthetic to organic fertility would likely need to be gradual, given our enormous dependence on synthetic fertilisers. Synthetic fertiliser use will gradually need to decrease over time, with organic fertility becoming the basis of crop health. Mineral fertilisers could also be obtained from waste, as opposed to mining and the Haber Bosch process. As for herbicides and pesticides, we should just stop using these products, and never look back. These biocides are inherently toxic and completely incompatible with the organic method.

[66] Just to be clear, before I am accused of suggesting we should hand weed every field in England: on a large scale, weeding can be mechanised and far less labour intensive.

A massive crop of beetroot was grown with no input other than cow manure. Credit: @escapetheofficejob

Pesticides are also completely antithetic with the organic method. The indiscriminate elimination of insects through the application of pesticides will have a knock-on effect on all other life forms, especially birds,[67] given the crucial importance of insects in all temperate ecosystems. Our broad beans serve as an excellent example. The black aphids, believe it or not, are herded by ants, who protect and direct them in exchange for the sugary secretions the aphids produce from sucking the sap of the plant. In turn, ladybirds feed on the black aphids, which means that there is a constant war of attrition between the ants and the ladybirds; much like humans protecting sheep from wolves. Ladybirds themselves are eaten

[67] Not just birds of course, but the whole web of life. Pesticides are one of the reasons why hedgehogs have disappeared, for example.

by several animals, especially birds like swifts and swallows. Bees and bumblebees, of course, pollinate the broad beans: without their activity, no broad beans can ever form. All of this fascinating food chain is wiped out by pesticides, with the exception of bees, which are merely poisoned. The systematic use of pesticides on most of our agricultural land goes some way towards explaining the decline and depletion of so many life forms across our countryside. The organic farmer, on the other hand, accepts and maintains this kind of life cycle as part and parcel of farming. It undoubtedly takes more knowledge and skill to co-exist with the complexity of life on a farm and, at the same time, obtain heavy crops at harvest time. Seed variety, sowing time, weeding schedules, manuring, soil health, crop rotation etc... all play a crucial role in determining success or failure.

The rewards, however, make it all worthwhile. As I saw rare butterflies and birds descending on my field, as the bees buzzed from plant to plant, as I tasted, without fear of contamination, unwashed crops straight from the plant, I knew why it was worth renouncing the toxic chemical fixes of conventional farming. This brings me to a key point: a major reason for the rejection of agrochemicals is the simple fact that, in spite of what the industry and government agencies continuously claim, these substances are neither safe nor healthy. There is a reason why they must be applied with body protection resembling the space age uniforms worn by workers in nuclear power plants, why farmers do not step onto fields after spraying, why people who work in their manufacture or are regularly exposed to them contract terrible and often deadly illnesses. This is a common problem in many parts of the world, where both agricultural workers and communities living close to farmland pay a very heavy price for their exposure to agrochemicals. To differing and varying degrees, we are all affected by agrochemical toxicity.

A herbicide like glyphosate or pesticides like neonicotinoids and organophosphates are, and this must be made clear, toxic substances. Pesticides are substances that could be used, and indeed have been used, as poison for successfully committing suicide.[68] This is not to say that farmers commit suicide *because* of pesticides, but it does demonstrate that these are extremely poisonous, dangerous substances which anyone with suicidal intent can use successfully. The supposed "safety" of agrochemicals is based on a simple premise: in small quantities, they will not poison, nor kill you, at least not in the short term. This is generally the main measure of safety that regulatory agencies use to determine whether to approve a product or not.

[68] An estimated 140,000 people a year commit suicide with pesticides across the world each year, especially in low and middle-income countries like India, Sri Lanka, and China. See WHO 2024 report: https://www.who.int/publications/m/item/preventing-suicide-by-phasing-out-highly-hazardous-pesticides)

What is not considered, and cannot be considered, is the long-term effect of exposure to these chemicals, which are now found, albeit in diluted forms, across our conventional food chain and in our soils and waterways. At present, most of the arable land in the UK is sprayed with these toxic substances throughout the season, right up to harvest, depending on the crop. It is virtually impossible to test, in an experimental setting, whether the significant rise in cancer rates, degenerative diseases, neurological disorders, and reproductive dysfunctions that we have witnessed is directly correlated to the lifelong ingestion of "safe" amounts of pesticides and herbicides. No doubt other factors are at play, from air pollution and other environmental conditions to lifestyle choices and habits.

However, these "safe" chemicals are known, without a shadow of a doubt, to consistently cause these diseases when ingested in large quantities. A good example is organophosphates used in sheep dipping.[69] Sheep dipping is the norm in British sheep farming, with organic practice the exception, where it is forbidden. Organophosphates, banned as crop pesticides in the UK, are persistent, highly toxic, and potentially deadly chemicals. Their use has damaged the health of many sheep dippers in the post-war period and through to the 1990s,[70] especially following their compulsory use, which lasted until 1992. Organophosphate-based sheep dips continue to be legally sold and used in the UK, and whilst safety procedures and warnings do more to protect individual sheep dippers than they used to, these chemicals have entered our ecosystems and waterways and continue to do so unabated.

The alternative farmer cannot abide by these methods and their consequences. An objection often touted by the agribusiness lobby and their servile acolytes in academia and the media is that organic farmers do use pesticides, but older and outdated varieties of them. This is almost entirely false. Most certified and uncertified organic farmers, most alternative farmers à la Joel Salatin and Will Harris simply do not use any pesticides of any kind. There are some pesticides which are permitted by organic certifying bodies like the Soil Association.[71] However, these are mostly harmless plant extracts from garlic, neem, or tobacco, for example, and used on a small scale. There are some questionable old pesticides, such as copper compounds like the Bordeaux mixture, originally created in the 19th century to combat fungal disease in grapes, which some growers use sparingly when necessary. However, all this suggests is that there are a few grey areas and compromises, that organic standards can still improve and that not all farmers are equally faithful to organic principles.

[69] The practice of literally dipping sheep in an insecticide and fungicide bath.

[70] https://theecologist.org/2012/mar/28/ghosts-farming-britains-forgotten-sheep-farmers-poisoned-pesticides

[71] See https://www.soilassociation.org/media/25986/sa-gb-farming-growing.pdf pages 84-87.

The bottom line is that organic farming is based on a rejection of chemical inputs and looks to biological health as the basis for success.

Animal Welfare and Platonic Livestock

The industrialisation of agriculture has been a disaster for farm animals.[72] The segregation of crops and livestock, and the gradual emptying of the countryside as a result of mass urbanisation, has resulted in the majority of animals being confined to factory conditions, away from people. In Britain, thanks to our natural grasslands, more extensive than anywhere else across Europe, there are still many animals, mostly sheep and beef cattle, who have been spared this cruel fate. However, for many traditional farm animals, especially poultry, pigs and dairy cows, their integration into an industrial system has resulted in their complete objectification and commoditisation. As Harris insightfully points out: *"when you see a living creature as a product, when you produce meat instead of raise meat, and when your holy grail is efficiency, you can rationalise a lot of sins"*.[73]

The availability of abundant cheap cereal has permitted a massive expansion in the confined production of grain-eating livestock, especially chickens, and the feeding of grains to stationary bovines, who should not be eating grain as their main source of food in the first place. It is not the purpose of this section to document the many cruelties to which animals are inevitably subjected once integrated into the logic of industrial production. It is not difficult for the interested reader to find ample evidence and countless case studies, documentaries and video evidence of what is now the norm. The conditions in which our Red Tractor chickens are kept, which are not even the worst, are not a secret. There is no doubt that a close encounter with the miserable pigs living in indoor systems, or a quick whiff of the stink rising from the average poultry farm, would do a lot to awaken the conscience of the average consumer.

For our purposes what should be clear is the following: apart from serious health considerations, which are of course important, we cannot consider the fate of these animals as morally acceptable. The organic movement has done much to promote a very simple idea: that animals should be allowed to express their natural propensities, play their natural role around the farm, and satisfy their basic desires. All of this is denied in factory conditions. Our chickens, as we saw earlier, need access to the sun and to the shade, need to scratch, forage and moult, need to nest and, as per the Abbey Home Farm chickens, need to be able to keep clean and well groomed. They need to establish a pecking order and cannot be

[72] Cruelty towards animals is nothing new, of course, and animals have at times been mistreated since times immemorial, but the scale, methodology and philosophy of industrial agriculture is inherently cruel and abusive in a way that is radically different from anything that preceded it.

[73] W. Harris, 2023, A Bold Return to Giving a Damn. One Farm, Six Generations, and the Future of Food, page 115.

closely confined. When they are forcibly confined, they will lash out against one another with their beaks. The industrial egg industry's answer to the stress and aggression created by the very conditions that cause it in the first place is to trim the hens' beaks, rather than address the cause of the behaviour. Again, just as with crops, the industrial farmer always treats the symptoms, never the cause, of the self-inflicted problems. The same logic underpins tail docking in pigs: the only reasons pigs pick on each other's tails are the stress, boredom and aggression associated with forced close confinement. No happy outdoor pig needs to have its tail docked. The tail should only ever be removed when the slaughtered pig is on the butcher's table and can then become part of old-fashioned dishes that utilise these once valued off cuts.

Pigs roaming at Abbey Home Farm, 2024. The pigs have their tails!

On the organic farm, the nature of the animal is considered as the basis for any guideline on how to rear such an animal, prior to considering how to combine the need to respect the nature of the animal with our human needs. As nicely encapsulated by Salatin, we need to respect "the pigness of the pig".[74] We need to simply ask ourselves: what is it that a pig needs

[74] J. Salatin, 2010, The Sheer Ecstasy of Being a Lunatic Farmer, pages 118-132.

to do and likes to do in order to fulfil its "pigness"? Let us imagine a Platonic Pig, the ideal Form of the Pig, remembering that it is an intelligent, social, active, omnivorous mammal. This would be a creature that has abundant space and warm or cool shelter, depending on the season, and access to a combination of grass, woodland, and orchard, depending on the farm model and local ecology. It would have access to water and mud,[75] it would clean up and cultivate our harvested potato fields. It would forage some of its own food, especially in woods and forests covered by acorns, chestnuts, or hickory. It would pick fallen fruit in the orchard, root and dig around the hedges and be greedy for more food all the time. Being an omnivorous scavenger, it would get to eat, apart from some of our harvested crops like cereals, legumes and tubers, our kitchen and garden waste. The sow would make her own nest, the piglets would keep their tails. The breeding boar would copulate naturally and abundantly. When slaughter comes, it will be as painless and unexpected as possible, preferably on farm or very close to the farm.

Pigs doing what pigs do at Abbey Home Farm.

[75] Pigs do not have sweat glands, hence why they love mud baths, which keeps them nice and cool.

There is no real clash between our interests and those of the pig. Being a domesticated animal, its nature has also been shaped by our desires. It has also evolved to exist in the context of agriculture meaning that a lot of what it needs and likes to do is necessary for the ecological efficiency of the organic farm. An animal that eats all waste and turns it into valuable poop and meat is very important on a farm, as is an animal that puts on fat in time for winter. The natural functions of livestock, which are species-specific, are as important to an organic system as the direct outputs of these animals (e.g., milk, meat etc...). The fact that cows can feed on the waste of a wheat crop (namely straw) and on grass, which we cannot eat, and transform it into fertility is as important as the fact that they also produce milk. All of this is lost in the factory system, where only direct outputs matter and natural functions are routinely denied and eliminated or, in some cases, such as manure, are a hazardous nuisance to get rid of.

Seasonal and Local

It is common to see field upon field of dark, cultivated, lifeless soil in the grain baskets of England over winter. The reductionist approach of most arable farming, with only two or three crops and no animals, has simplified the seasons. There is a main growing season and a fairly tight harvest time over summer, with sowing to follow in fall or spring. That is about it. The organic farm, on the other hand, is a twelve-month-a-year operation that has to be rooted in what nature provides at each time of year and on the continuous cycles of growth, decay, and rebirth. My own personal motto has always been that at any given time, something should be sown, something should be growing, something should be harvested, even in the depths of winter. Being a mixed operation by definition, there should always be something that is harvestable or that can be slaughtered on the farm. The integration of main field crops, with field vegetables, fruit orchards, indoor cropping, and all sorts of livestock, will ensure that each month, each season will produce something specific and fresh. The organic farm is complex and varied, and each season has several dynamics, nuances, and rhythms. In Spring, for example, there will be fewer vegetables than at any other time of the year, but what is available is fantastic: mostly asparagus, spring greens, spinach, garden peas and broad beans. Birds are making eggs like there is no tomorrow,[76] so there is no better time to collect and sell eggs. Lambs are abundant and ready for slaughter. Cows are starting to make more milk. Grain crops and potatoes are still green and growing in the field. Fruit trees have flowered or are flowering. The shooting season is over, but the wood pigeons and

[76] As discussed in a later chapter, the fact that birds start making eggs again in spring explains why the egg is one of the symbols of Easter.

muntjacs are up for grabs.[77] There is a lot of firewood in store from winter. All of this is tied to the seasons in a way that the wheat-barley-oilseed rape model can never be.

A corollary of seasonality is locality; both at the farm level and further up the food chain. On the mixed farm, the choice of crops grown may reflect the local soil (e.g., carrots in the sandy soils of the East of England) and include the local crop varieties traditionally grown in the area,[78] the livestock may well be from the local breeds.[79] The preservation of domesticated plants and animals should be seen as a high priority, just as important as the preservation of their wild counterparts. A pig breed or apple variety is just as important to biodiversity as a hedgehog or wildflower species. On the organic farm, one would expect to see some local fruit varieties or sheep breeds and the availability of a broad range of ingredients needed to make local dishes. Even if the farm is mostly producing food for urban populations, especially cereals, we would nonetheless expect a reasonable percentage of the produce to be consumed locally. It is not normal for people in the countryside to shop at Tesco like someone living in East London. It is also not normal that in the cities, we are as likely to find produce from overseas as we are likely to find British produce. As I write this particular chapter, in May, with the asparagus season in full swing, supermarkets are still selling Peruvian and Mexican asparagus alongside our British crop. This makes no environmental, nutritional, or cultural sense. Localising production and shortening food chains has to be a crucial part of the organic vision.

Integration with Wilderness

Our landscapes, at least in Europe, are by and large domesticated landscapes, with pockets of wilderness in between and a few secluded wildlife areas. Industrial agriculture has done much to wipe out a lot of the species that could live within our domesticated landscapes, which make up 69% of the UK land mass. There is also no doubt that, across Britain, biodiversity is generally decreasing, as is ancient woodland and the rate of extinction of species, from bees and butterflies to birds and small mammals. Indeed, an estimated 97% of wildflower meadows were lost between the 1930s and 1984 and the area of crops treated with pesticides increased by 53% between 1990 and 2010.[80] The organic farm in based on a principle of compromise and co-existence. Compromise because we need most of our land

[77] Albeit, as my friend and mentor Ian in Devon taught me, we should spare the woodpigeons in spring, as they are having eggs and chicks, and wait until the summer before heading to the fields with our shotguns.

[78] Local crop varieties have almost entirely disappeared in England, far more so than in the rest of Europe. This is perhaps a legacy of being the first major industrial nation and of having less varieties to begin with, when compared to countries like France, Italy, and Spain.

[79] In Britain, we have done a far better job of preserving livestock breeds, albeit mainstream conventional production is built around a few breeds particularly suited to industrial practice: Holsteins for dairy and Large Whites for pork.

[80] https://nbn.org.uk/wp-content/uploads/2019/09/State-of-Nature-2019-UK-full-report.pdf

to live on and grow food, which means that there are limits to the degree to which land can be "rewilded".

Co-existence is however possible because the more self-sustaining, organic, and biodiverse an agricultural system is, the more likely it will include wild animals and high levels of biodiversity. A system driven by biology and living systems, rather than by agrochemicals and factories, will involve complex inevitable relationships with wild plants and animals, which thrive when chemicals and monocultures are abandoned. More life means more death too. A thriving, biodiverse farm will have more living, and dying, creatures, from insects to birds and mammals, as well as far more fish in the clear waters. This way of farming also requires a much greater willingness to manage pests[81] (from foxes threatening livestock to woodpigeons, rabbits, deer and squirrels eating crops) and to embrace the far greater opportunities to shoot, fish and hunt. This seems counterintuitive but, again, the organic system is one built on a virtuous compromise, on a best-case scenario that allows us to both feed ourselves and preserve ecosystems and biodiversity to the greatest degree possible.

British Organic Food

What would our diets look like if British agriculture were grass-based and organic? Whilst we are far away from that ideal, it is worthwhile running the hypothetical scenario,[82] as it reveals much about what our land does offer without agrochemical inputs and factory farms and can help us make better choices today. In a nutshell, there would be less of certain foods, more of others and greater diversity of outputs overall. There would be an inevitable decrease in cereal production, which is no bad thing as we eat too many grains in our diets and waste up to 44% of our bread.[83] The great success of industrial agriculture has been the ability to raise productivity per acre of grains, mostly wheat and barley in the UK, and almost eliminating crop rotations in the process. This has also allowed an increase in the production of grain-eating livestock, especially poultry, which is now the cheapest of meats, as well as turkey, pork, and dairy cows. The growing of traditional fodder crops, on the other hand, has almost disappeared, and legume (beans, peas etc...) and potato production is very low. As

[81] One issue Abbey Home Farm has is that crows regularly swoop in and eat the chicken feed, which would never happen on an industrial farm, and adds a lot of cost to the enterprise. I offered Hilary, the owner of the farm, my services as an all-round pest control man, but unfortunately, she is not keen on what she referred to as "blood sports"!

[82] A valuable attempt to investigate a potential scenario can be found in Feeding Britain from the Ground Up, 2022. The report can be downloaded online (https://sustainablefoodtrust.org/our-work/feeding-britain/).

Simon Fairlie also investigated this question (See. S. Fairlie, 2010, Meat. A Benign Extravagance, Chapter 9, Can Britain Feed Itself?)

[83] Estimates vary and exact figures cannot realistically be obtained, but even if we allow for a ± 10% margin of error, 34% or 54% are staggering numbers. Source: https://www.theguardian.com/food/2019/jan/29/campaign-launched-to-curb-the-waste-of-12bn-uk-bread-crusts

a country, we are reliant on imports of fruit and vegetables, which are not a major part of the national diet. We are also not in the habit of eating much of the carcass of livestock and there is a huge waste of eggs and milk.

A national organic agriculture would bring about significant changes, as outlined below:

Meat, Dairy and Eggs

Our grass-fed nation would rely on cattle and sheep as crucial food sources and as the basis for land management and fertility. We could not afford to feed that much cereal to cattle and would devote modest amounts for dairy cows. We would no longer be keeping demanding breeds like Holsteins, but rely on more hardy, undemanding breeds, like Dexters and Jerseys, that do extremely well on mostly grass. We would have to eat a lot more of the carcass and learn to honour different cuts of meat. We would start eating mutton again, which is currently only really eaten by the Islamic community or exported, and we would need to get over the misguided veal-eating taboo, with male calves no longer the unwanted offspring of dairy cows. We would no longer engage in the dubious practice of eating low-fat dairy and would milk more of our ewes. Goats should become a growing niche market, for both meat and milk. Goats are difficult to manage, given their notorious tendency to jump fences and break into the very places you don't want them, but they are an extremely low-input animal, that can be fed on all sorts of vegetation that no human or other livestock will eat.

On the other hand, poultry consumption would have to decrease dramatically, especially chicken. The pallid, soft, sickly chickens of our Red Tractor farm are the end result of cheap industrial grain and confinement, and no sustainable agricultural system can produce that much chicken. To a lesser degree, this is also true of eggs, which should cost more than they currently do, and their production should be lower in winter. We should be eating spent laying hens, cocks, and capons,[84] all of which have disappeared from our diets.[85] Geese would make a nationwide comeback, as they can be almost entirely grass-fed, and semi-wild ducks would also fit in well in organic farming systems, given their helpful slug-eating habits. We ought to start breeding lots of rabbits on farms too, as they can be fed on grass and vegetable waste: almost free food. A similar principle applies to domestic pigeon, eaten as squab, which used to be the norm on farms across Europe.

Pork would still be an important meat in Britain and sausages and bacon would still grace our tables, but with far more parsimony and higher costs. We would no longer feed them

[84] A castrated and fattened cockerel: it used to be a delicacy for special occasions. See "Vegan?" chapter.

[85] I have tried valiantly to find a farmer or butcher who would sell me an old hen, but to no avail. It would make the best possible broth and the meat, served with salsa verde or other condiments, would make a Sunday classic.

with imported maize and soya[86] in factory farms and would revert to our traditional breeds, like the Gloucestershire Old Spots, and rear them for much longer and much fatter than so-called "lean pork". Pigs are arguably the most environmentally sound livestock on Earth, given their ability to mop up waste everywhere on the farm, from cleaning fields to orchards, to the waste from dairy, grain, and brewery operations. We should reintroduce the feeding of swill and local food waste, which was foolishly banned in the UK, and every farm should either have pigs or send their waste along to farms that do. Finally, there would be more opportunities to eat wild meats, albeit it would always be a marginal part of the diet. The adoption of organic methods inevitably increases wild populations and creates niches for all sorts of animals, pests or otherwise. Regular culling would be more important than it is now, and we should expect certain species, like hares and woodcock, to become abundant again, and other already abundant species, like muntjac and rabbits, to increase in numbers.[87] I am personally excited by the return of the wild boar.

TO SUM UP:

- A lot of beef, veal, mutton, hogget, lamb, and some goat/kid - nose-to-tail eating.
- Plenty of milk and dairy (including ewe's and goat's milk and dairy products), albeit at higher cost - and all full fat (whole milk, butter, double cream, clotted cream, yoghurt, cheese).
- A lot less poultry overall, especially chicken and turkey.
- Less hen eggs, especially in winter. More duck and goose eggs.
- Less pork. Fatter pork.
- A lot more domestic geese, pigeons, rabbits.[88]
- More wild meats.

Oils and Fats

The general rule worldwide is that there is a reverse correlation in the availability of vegetable and animal fats, depending on how far North we are from the Equator. The further North we go, the more the land is likely to produce animal fats as opposed to vegetable fats. Fat is what allows animals to keep warm in the cold and what prevents plants from drying out in the heat. Plump fatty fruits like olives and nuts like walnuts, hazelnuts, and almonds grow

[86] In the UK our conventional pork and poultry production relies on countless "ghost acres" of land overseas, including the destructive soya monocultures of South America.

[87] See my own contribution on the subject: https://www.thelandmagazine.org.uk/articles/default-hunting

[88] We should also consider farming snails, which are a nutritious delicacy that require virtually no inputs to produce!

well in the Mediterranean[89] but not so well further North. In the tropics, there is an abundance of oily fruits, from avocados to cocoa and coconuts and scarcely any animal fats. In Northern regions, on the other hand, animals put on a lot more fat on their bodies and provide the bulk of dietary fats in the human diet. There are some vegetable oils that can be produced in Northern regions, especially oilseed rape, which is extensively grown in Canada and Britain, and sunflowers, grown across the continent but, overall, countries like Britain are on the Northern end of the spectrum. At present, much of our vegetable oil for the table is imported. There is nothing wrong, and here I must reveal my obvious bias, in importing olive oil or, say, sunflower oil. However, a lot of the vegetable oil imported into this country is of very low quality and, at the same time, we produce a vast amount of industrial oilseed rape, much of which is not consumed as oil. Currently, 8.9% of land planted with arable crops is growing oilseed rape,[90] which is the most important crop in UK agriculture after wheat and barley. Oilseed rape barely produces anything directly edible, with most of it ending up as animal feed or as feedstock for low-quality ultra-processed foods. With the animal fat phobia that has pervaded our culture for decades now, animal fats have decreased in popularity and usage. This is a great shame, as our best dairy farms produce butter that is second to none and should be used liberally as a staple food.

TO SUM UP:

- More butter, goose fat, lard, and tallow, replacing low-quality domestic oilseed rape and imports of other low-quality vegetable oils.
- We should consider introducing sunflowers and hemp into our cropping systems across Southern England.
- More high-quality vegetable oil imports.

Grains and Starchy Staples

There is no question that, on an acre-per-acre basis, wheat and barley production would drop, as would consumption, and a lower percentage of our fields would be planted with wheat and barley. Oat and rye yields, on the other hand, would be very similar. There would be far more legumes grown, which are necessary for fertility and highly nutritious. This may seem like a disaster to many, but the truth is that, apart from the enormous waste of wheat in our food chain (meaning that we could grow less grain, of higher quality, and not waste it), we eat too many grains-based foods anyway. Too many of our calories come from

[89] Being somewhere between the tropics and the cold North, the Mediterranean has the best of both worlds in many ways: plants that bear oily fruits and nuts and animals that produce fats. Sicily is a perfect example: the land produces olive oil, pistachios, walnuts, hazelnuts and almonds, but also sheep and cow's milk and a wonderful black skinned pig, the Suino Nero dei Nebrodi. See Chapter 8 for more details.

[90] Agriculture in the United Kingdom 2022, pages 25-26.

nutritionally denuded refined flour products, from bread to breakfast cereals and biscuits. This is a nation of beer, ale and stout drinkers and this industry relies on cheap grain. However, much of the cost to the consumer is through taxation: if barley was more scarce and more expensive, a drop in taxation would make up for the higher production costs.

On the other hand, the humble potato should be a key staple source of carbohydrates on these densely populated islands. To put this in context, we only plant potatoes on 2.9% of our cropped arable land.[91] Conventional yields oscillate between 40-45 tonnes per hectare,[92] organic yields reach 25 tonnes per hectare, but organic potatoes are denser and more nutritious. It is by far the most productive staple crop that can be grown in Britain, and we should extend its acreage very substantially.

TO SUM UP:

- Less bread but better bread.
- Less wheat flour-based foods.
- More oatmeal.
- A lot more potatoes.
- More legumes/pulses.
- Less beers/ales/stouts and spirits derived from grains (e.g., whisky, brandy).
- More cider, wine and spirits not derived from grains (e.g., vodka, gin).

Vegetables and Fruits

At present, national production and consumption of vegetables and fruits is woefully low. Even the much-touted 5 a day is quite low when portion sizes are taken into consideration.[93] In an organic regimen, farms would produce a far greater quantity of vegetables and polytunnels would be widely used, to provide more heat-loving crops. We would also massively increase the production of starchy, sugary field vegetables, like beetroot, carrot, sweetcorn, and squash, on arable land as part of our crop rotations, as well as more kale, cabbage, leeks, onions, and winter root vegetables. Mushrooms could be cultivated across organic farms without taking up additional acreage and limited resources. All these increases in production would provide a lot of additional, healthy calories which, alongside potatoes, would turn tubers and vegetables into major staples substituting a lot of the empty calories of today: crisps, white bread, crackers, biscuits and so on. The systematic planting of orchards around the country, in both urban and rural areas, and the spread of agroforestry

[91] Agriculture in the United Kingdom 2022, pages 25-26.

[92] https://www.gov.uk/government/statistics/agriculture-in-the-united-kingdom-2022/chapter-7-crops#potatoes

[93] See NHS Guidelines (https://www.nhs.uk/live-well/eat-well/5-a-day/portion-sizes/) according to which 7 cherry tomatoes or 7 strawberries count as one portion.

would increase fruit production and fruits like apples would be important daily foods. We should wish for the day in which, instead of bringing cheese and onion crisps, a Twix and a Coke as snacks, the average British child comes to school with an apple, a carrot and a 275ml bottle of beetroot juice.

TO SUM UP:

- A lot, lot more seasonal vegetables and herbs.
- A lot more seasonal fruit.
- A lot more preserved vegetables, jams, pickles.
- More cultivated mushrooms.

Sugars

Sugar forms an important part of the diet in Britain and, whilst it is certainly consumed in excess, it now suffers from an unjustified demonisation, much like red meat. The problem, as ever, is one of *quality* first and foremost, and of excessive consumption. Moderate daily amounts of high-quality sugar are not a problem, but an enrichment. The sugar beet industry on the East of England is the epitome of industrial monoculture production and no such thing as organic sugar beet production even exists in the UK. Most of the sugar beet is refined into white sugar and makes up a substantial percentage of the domestic market, with the rest imported from overseas. Given our limited land availability, we may be better off not producing sugar in the UK and focus on importing high-quality cane sugar instead. Most importantly, an organic and pasture-based system is hugely reliant on pollinators and provides exponentially more and better-quality feed for them. Bee numbers and honey production would increase once we give up agrochemicals, replacing some of our sugar consumption.

TO SUM UP:

- Lower sugar consumption.
- Lower white refined sugar consumption.
- If sugar is to be produced domestically, we must grow our sugar beets as part of an organic farming system.
- High-quality sugar cane imports.
- A lot more domestic honey.

Fish, Crustaceans and Molluscs

Our fisheries suffer from a double whammy: the consequences of water pollution, which are often directly linked to industrial agriculture, and the destructive practices of industrial fishing, with its bottom trawlers and other indiscriminate methods. Furthermore, fish farming suffers from many of the same environmental problems of other types of farming, with the added problem that farmed fish such as salmon, unlike chickens, are not even domesticated animals and are therefore inherently unsuitable for domestication. On some level, there is no such thing as "organic salmon" and sustainably farmed fish: more on this later.[94] That is not to say that all types of aquatic farming are unsustainable: mussels and oysters should be farmed far more extensively across the cleaner parts of the British Isles, as they require no feed and chemicals to produce.[95] The only way to replenish our fisheries is to tackle the causes of depletion. Britain, post her exit from the European Union, should take the opportunity to close her fisheries to all foreign fishing boats, ban the use of bottom trawling and other destructive methods for domestic fishermen and get rid of the absurd quota systems, which encourage enormous waste. Stricter fishing seasons should be imposed for some species, and a few areas should be kept as marine reserves. Over time, the seas would recover, and fish stocks increase.

Much of our river, stream and lake pollution is linked to run off from farms: a mixture of agrochemicals from fields and poorly managed manure from factory farms. The rest of freshwater pollution is down to poorly managed sewage works and industrial pollutants. Populations of trout and other once-abundant fish have plummeted. Again, the solution does not simply lie in trying to clean up rivers, but in cutting off the source of pollution in the first place. We should, again, expect an increase in freshwater fish over time.

TO SUM UP:

- Less domestic seafood for a few years; much more in the future.
- Far more use of abundant sea fish that currently has no commercial value or market, such as horse mackerel and pouting.
- More freshwater fish and farmed molluscs (mussels, oysters etc...).
- Sustainable fish imports (e.g., Icelandic cod, Alaskan salmon)

Imports and Exports

At present, Britain relies on imports for roughly 40% of its food.[96] Britain actually produces enough grains to be self-sufficient, even at the currently extravagant levels of consumption and waste, but we import a lot of other products, especially animal feed, pork, fruits, vegetables, and wine. Whilst it should be the goal of any agricultural system to supply as much of the domestic market as possible and have a certain degree of food security and self-sufficiency, the importing of products that cannot be produced domestically, and the export

[94] See chapters 10 & 11.

[95] We should also be cultivating a lot more seaweed: for food, animal feed and fertiliser.

[96] https://www.gov.uk/government/publications/uk-food-security-index-2024/uk-food-security-index-2024

of our own special and abundant products overseas, makes perfect economic and cultural[97] sense. It enriches our food culture to import Italian rice, French wine, or Spanish oranges and to return the favour by exporting Scotch whisky, English cheddar and Welsh lamb to the Continent. There are things we should not import, such as out-of-season crops that we can grow here perfectly well, and others that we should keep importing, provided we have criteria other than cost and aim for quality over quantity.

TO SUM UP:

- We should aim to base our diets on what we grow here in Britain, especially fresh food, and support local agriculture.
- We should import food wisely and selectively.
- Main food imports in no particular order: rice, pasta, chickpeas, lentils, vegetable oils, wine and other alcoholic drinks, cane sugar, maple syrup, honey, Continental cheeses and cold cuts, sustainable seafood, bananas, other exotic fruit, citrus fruits, olives, dates, nuts, spices, coffee, tea, cacao, sauces (e.g., soy sauce, mustard etc…)

We Are Not Luddites

One of the most common objections to organic agriculture is that it represents a modern-day Luddite approach. There is a widespread assumption that organic farming is a regression, a return to something archaic and gone by, motivated by sentimental and romantic notions of a pastoral idyll of the past. The critics of the organic movement and the staunch defenders of industrial agriculture pull no punches on this front, keen to highlight the reactionary impulses of their opponents:

> *"The Luddites may prevent innovation from raising food yields and drive us back to land-hungry organic farming."*[98]
>
> *"Those of us who grew up with a hoe in our hand have absolutely no nostalgia for days gone by"*[99].
>
> *"No amount of nostalgia for the pastoral foods of the distant past can wish away the fact that our ancestors lived mean, short lives, constantly afflicted with*

[97] In the sense that it is culturally enriching to have access to "exotics", as well as offering a nutritional advantage.

[98] Matt Ridley: http://www.rationaloptimist.com/blog/coping-with-only-six-billion/

[99] Blake Hurst: https://www.aei.org/articles/organic-illusions/

> *diseases, many of which can be directly attributed to what they did and did not eat"*[100].

The Hobbesian view of the past[101] has some merit, as does the claim that there have been elements of nostalgia for an imaginary past within the very broad alternative agricultural movement. I am not sure why anyone would expect otherwise: has there ever been a movement, in any walk of life, that is devoid of irrational ideas and ill-informed individuals? There have also been internal disagreements within the movement which, again, one would expect in any dynamic, diverse, loose movement about something as important as agriculture. I personally find, as did Albert Howard, that Rudolf Steiner's esoteric practices[102] are not necessary for successful farming and may, in opening the movement to charges of unscientific superstition, damage the movement as a whole. Having said that, the core practices of the biodynamic movement, esoteric practices excluded, are very sound and very consistent with Albert Howard's and biodynamic farms are often exemplary farms.

But let us come back to the general progressivist account of history that has dominated the worldview of an important faction of our intellectual culture and elite since the Enlightenment and the Industrial Revolution: that life has got infinitely better and that industrial agriculture has been a key reason for the progress achieved to date.[103] According to this narrative, Haber's synthesis of ammonia and, decades later, Norman Borlaug's Green Revolution, literally saved mankind from inevitable starvation and much of the unprecedented wealth and health around us can be traced back to these discoveries. The organic movement, by definition, not only denies the validity of these claims, but seeks to drag us back to pre-Industrial agriculture, with its lower productivity, enormous manual labour force and general drudgery. Taken at face value, this does not seem an unreasonable charge against the organic movement. However, to illustrate the deception, intentional or otherwise, of our opponents, I will briefly paint a picture of what agriculture might have looked like for the majority of peasants in Europe before the 20th century.

Imagine farming without any machinery, of any kind. Imagine no electricity, running water or sanitation. Imagine that you are either a sharecropper, having to give away a lot of your harvest to your landlord or, worse still, a landless peasant. Imagine the ownership of a pair of oxen or mules as a great luxury. Imagine no fuel, gas or central heating and having to collect or chop wood daily, with nothing more than an axe and saw. Imagine no

[100] Rachel Laudan; https://www.jacobinmag.com/2015/05/slow-food-artisanal-natural-preservatives/

[101] Hobbes famously argued that the natural condition of mankind is one in which life is *"solitary, poor, nasty, brutish, and short"* (L 186).

[102] Involving planting according to the movement of the moon and the planets, for example.

[103] Vaclav Smil, Matt Ridley, Sean Rickard, and Steven Pinker are typical exponents of this approach.

contraception, many children to feed and high mortality rates. Imagine no public health care, doctors, or vaccinations. Imagine being unable to source seeds and livestock from anywhere outside of your village or province. Imagine being unable to make compost with tools, boxes, forklifts, and tractors. Imagine having to spread dung by hand. Imagine ploughs and other metal tools being hard to replace, source and maintain. Imagine no greenhouses, polytunnels or protective nets and frames. Imagine no refrigeration, no plastic, no aluminium foil, no disinfectant, no toilet paper. Imagine all basic materials, from glass to cloth, being expensive and hard to get. Imagine that produce rots all the time and that storage is leaky and inadequate. Imagine being unable to keep mice and rats away from your food and home. Imagine no weather forecasts. Imagine no rescue or emergency services available when a flood, storm or other disaster strikes. Imagine no possibility of food aid when drought and crop failure strike. Imagine being illiterate and having little or no news of anything outside the farm and village.

I could go on, but a clear picture should have emerged in the reader's mind. There are parts of the world today where many aspects of this kind of life are not imaginary, but everyday reality, and an investigation of peasant life in parts of Africa, Latin America, India and South-East Asia will reveal stark similarities to the picture painted. What should also be clear is that this way of living and farming is subsistence farming, by definition, where the farmer produces a small surplus and just about feeds his family, on a good year. It is very hard to raise good crops and have any kind of efficiency and ability to make the most of the land in such hard circumstances: survival and subsistence are not consistent with productivity and flourishing. There is a name for all this: poverty. The reason why the subsistence farmers just depicted were so unproductive was not because they didn't have herbicides or because their cows ate grass and straw instead of maize and growth hormones, but because of everything else. The reason why Italian peasants in Veneto in the 19th century ate a diet almost exclusively composed of maize and suffered from pellagra as a result was that they had almost nothing and were extremely poor: it was not because they were waiting for synthetic ammonia and caged hens to come along.

Poverty and privation are not the result of poor agricultural practice, rather they are the result of a vicious cycle: poverty and privation prevent consistent, efficient, and productive agricultural practice, and poor agricultural outputs exacerbate poverty and privation. If farmers in many parts of Africa or India today are unproductive it is not because they don't have Roundup or GM maize seeds but because of *everything else* that they do not have. If the average African or Indian subsistence farmer had some electricity, clean running water, access to decent healthcare, a small tractor, some good tools, weather forecasts, modern storage facilities, some irrigation, modern composting pits, beehives, trees to plant etc... his productivity, using his traditional organic methods, would probably treble, at the very minimum. That is not to say his methods could not be improved, of course: overgrazing and poor maintenance of soil fertility is an old problem in parts of Africa, India and elsewhere around the world. But these can be addressed, as we just saw, with the kind of scientific and experimental approach to organic agriculture and grazing that the many pioneers of this broad movement have demonstrated.

No one in the organic movement is calling for a planned return to widespread poverty. The resources, comforts and many technologies that have transformed lives since the 19th century, are here to stay and have an enormous role to play in agriculture and its productivity and efficiency. The modern-day organic farmer has tools, facilities, social services, and public goods at his disposal that would have been unimaginable in the past. The potential crop productivity and ability to use every square inch of the land efficiently and to keep dense stocks of animals well-fed and healthy is unprecedented. The ability to use movable electric fencing to manage mob grazing, the ability to weed row crops or harvest potatoes with a tractor, the ability to store apples for up to 12 months and freeze tonnes of peas and cuts of lamb is also unprecedented. None of these technologies are inconsistent with the organic method and approach. Similarly, the industrial scaled-up manufacture of compost and bone meal, and the use of polytunnels and high-tech drip irrigation are also not inconsistent with the organic method and approach.

Old and new at the farm: traditional ploughs with electricity pylons in the background. Credit: @escapetheofficejob

TO SUM UP: the charge of Luddism is either disingenuous or a straw man argument, or both. The successful agriculture of the future will be one where appropriate technology and mechanisation are used to enhance natural processes and the productivity of agroecosystems. Organic agriculture looks back to the past in one crucial way: in an appreciation of the fact that the fundamental laws of nature, of fertility cycles, of soil-plant-animal integration are timeless and unbreakable. We disregard this reality at our peril and cost. The role of science is to help us understand the workings of this order and to allow us to tailor and improve our methods accordingly, with technology providing the tools required to implement these methods. What this means, however, is that there is an inherent precautionary principle embedded within the organic approach: a technology or novel method is only to be adopted if it complies with the laws of nature. Any innovation should be subjected to the following question: is it wise to adopt this innovation? Will it comply with the natural order? What are its long-term consequences? Just because *we can* do something, it does not mean *we should*.

The "Feed the World" Narrative and its Inadequacy

A corollary of the Luddism charge is the accusation that organic agriculture "cannot feed the world" and is not sufficiently productive. There are a number of problems with this line of argument, which I will briefly tackle below.

Comparing Productivity

Agricultural productivity is generally measured in terms of productivity per unit of labour: per agricultural worker, in other words. Under such terms, the average conventional arable farmer in East Anglia or Iowa is the most productive farmer, or indeed worker, in history. One man with a massive tractor and combine, and tonnes of fertiliser and agrochemicals, can cultivate literally thousands of acres of land and produce thousands of tonnes of wheat or maize or potatoes or whichever monoculture his field is devoted to. It is this sort of productivity that has allowed less than 1% of our population to work as farmers in North American and Western Europe. Under this metric, there is no question that the organic farmer, even the most technologically enhanced, will be far less productive. However, there are two problems with the hyper-productivity of the conventional farmer. The first is that he still relies on a great industrial ghost force: the miners, oil and gas drillers, factory workers and chemical plant operators who keep his inputs rolling in and build and supply his machines. It is a very energy and resource-intensive system, with the farmer standing somewhere in between the mine and the supermarket. The organic farm also relies on industrial inputs, especially fuel, but nowhere near to the same degree. With no synthetic fertilisers and agrochemicals, and with a grassland-based system with animals kept outdoors for much of the year, the ghost work force is much reduced. The second problem with the hyper-productivity of the conventional farmer is that it comes with huge costs and externalities.

The only way to farm thousands of acres solo is to grow a very narrow pattern of monocultures and unleash the full arsenal of agrochemicals available. Similarly, the only way for an individual farmer to raise thousands and thousands of chickens is to keep them in confinement in a massive, automated barn. This comes at a severe environmental cost, as it is simply impossible to look after the soil and be good stewards of the land by farming this way. It comes at the cost of quality, which is inevitably low, and it comes at a great social cost to rural communities. As clear from above, the modern organic farmer does not have to be a Luddite and even a nationwide adoption of organic methods would not necessitate a labour force anything like pre-War numbers. We would, however, need far more people working on the land. The only way to look after the land and be productive is to have people on the ground. The complexities of growing multiple field and tree crops, of keeping a mixture of pastured and movable livestock, of managing woodland and forestry, and of doing it all without chemicals and other short cuts, is labour intensive. To those who will inevitably claim that I am suggesting a back-to-the-land deportation of the urban masses, I will repeat: we need a greater agricultural labour force than the minuscule one we have now, but we do not need anything like the traditional agricultural labour force of old. Between 1% and 50% there are many numbers, such as 5 or 10%, for example. We would lose quite a few industrial, manufacturing and processing jobs too, which would be replaced by agricultural ones. Given the hazards and sheer bleakness of some of these jobs and given the current numbers of able-bodied unemployed in this country, the creation of land-based outdoor work should be seen as an additional benefit.

The other main way to measure productivity is productivity per unit of land: per acre or hectare. Under this metric, there is no doubt that for many crops, especially grains, industrial monoculture is far more productive. A monoculture of industrial wheat will yield more (approx. 6-9 tonnes per hectare in the UK) than an organic wheat monoculture (approx. 4-5 tonnes per hectare in the UK, usually at the lower end of that spectrum).[104] Organic wheat also needs to be grown in rotation[105] rather than in succession, which means that the fields will grow something else when not growing wheat. In England that is often temporary

[104] UK average is 4.2 tonnes, with exceptional yields reaching 7 tonnes https://www.fwi.co.uk/arable/crop-management/how-an-organic-pioneer-delivers-top-crop-yields. Ancient wheats, grown as landraces or as single varieties, will only yield 2-3 tonnes per hectare, but are very reliable, require very low fertility and can be grown with little rotation, and produce exceptional, nutritionally superior grains. Straw production is also very high with ancient grains, much higher than industrial grains, providing a lot of fodder.

[105] Apart from ancient varieties, as mentioned above. John Letts, an archaeobotanist and farmer in Oxfordshire, has been growing landraces of ancient wheats with no fertiliser nor rotations for years on end with steady yields of 2.5 tonnes per hectare.

grassland or clover, which is fed to livestock and provides fertility for the grain crops, but it could be legumes or other food and fodder crops instead. Be that as it may, overall, unquestionably, organic agriculture will produce lower grain yields. We should, however, keep in mind that there is a difference between calories and nutritional content. The mass of calories produced by conventional grain monocultures is not matched by nutritional content and quality. Furthermore, we should not simply fixate on comparing grain yields, as organic farms produce a greater diversity of outputs and can, at their best, potentially produce just as much, or even more, *food* per hectare, which could compensate for lower grain yields.

In any case, if we want to consider ways to compensate for lower grain yields, I would suggest the following strategies and ideas as a helpful starting point:

1) Far less grains should be fed to poultry, pigs, and dairy cattle to begin with. We are growing too much grain and using it wastefully on livestock. Growing a far lower percentage of the grain crop for animals leaves more grain available for human consumption, partly compensating for the lower yields. Animals should eat the waste of grain crops (straw, corn stalks etc...) and a low percentage of the grain harvest. At present, a very high percentage of the world's major crops (especially oilseed rape, barley, maize, and soya) are grown specifically to feed animals. For example, the herbicide-resistant GM soya crop, a major traded commodity which is extensively grown throughout North and South America,[106] is almost entirely dedicated to the production of low-quality feed for pigs, poultry and cattle.

2) Crop rotations in an organic system can include a higher percentage of high-yielding food crops, like potatoes, squash, large brassicas,[107] root crops, and sweetcorn, than conventional arable rotations that focus on just wheat, barley, and oilseed rape. As discussed earlier, in the UK we could make up for some of the grain shortfall by growing far more potatoes and sugary, starchy vegetables in our crop rotations, and including fruit trees within arable agroforestry systems. In the United States, the enormous swathes of land currently used for soya and corn in the Midwest should be used to implement mixed organic farming systems, with extensive grassland, tree crops and livestock spread across the land, intermixed with

[106] One of the primary causes for the progressive destruction of the Amazon, Cerrado and Gran Chaco is the expansion of industrial soya monoculture, which devastates wildlife, ecosystems and local communities wherever it spreads.

[107] There are huge, high yielding vegetable and fodder crop varieties that we should be growing extensively. Some giant kales, such as the Jersey Walking Stick, ought to be tested on a field scale. Why does Rothamsted and the other research centre show no interest whatsoever in this sort of crop, that can be grown organically on a field scale? Why so much interest in creating new hybrids and genetically modified crops when our endangered and rare domesticated heritage crops have so much great potential?

organic arable crops primarily grown for human consumption. [108] We would have less meat but possibly as much or more *food* on the table at the end of it, and without devastating the environment in the process. In tropical climates, diversification is even more applicable, as there are many very high-yielding crops that can be grown organically and in biodiverse agroforestry systems, such as bananas, plantains, coconuts, breadfruit, sweet potatoes, yams, sugar cane, cassava, taro, and peanuts. These crops may not be commodities tradable on the stock exchange, a cardinal sin in our system, but that is not a good reason not to grow more of them if feeding the world is the goal. Most of Borneo and Sumatra, for example, are in the process of being completely deforested in order to plant palm oil plantations in monocultures, entirely dependent on heavy applications of agrochemicals. Palm oil, another tradable commodity, is used as industrial feedstock for a lot of our processed junk food (from margarine to low-quality bread, biscuits and chocolate), for cosmetics and detergents, animal feed and so-called "biofuel".[109] If, hypothetically, two-thirds of the deforested land in Borneo and Sumatra currently used for palm oil could be used for agroforestry systems growing actual food crops, such as those listed above, mixed in with some cash crops,[110] these huge islands would grow far more food, with no chemicals, and be able to return the rest of the palm oil monocultures back to forest, or at the very least spare the remaining forest from being cut down. A very similar discourse applies to the maize and soya monocultures that have spread throughout the Amazon region. We could grow more and better food in biodiverse agroforestry systems and preserve what is left of the great forest.

3) Crop rotations in organic systems can allow for two crops per season, rather than just one. For example, stubble turnips or fodder rape can follow a wheat crop, or ryegrass and vetch can follow potatoes. These are high-yielding fodder crops that, again, can help to compensate for the lower yields of the main grain crop. Crops like turnips should definitely make a comeback. The cultivation of the turnip played a key role in the period often referred to as the British Agricultural Revolution which, unlike the Industrial Revolution, led to substantial increases in productivity without compromising the natural capital and long-term

[108] An even stronger argument is made by Mark Shepard, who argues that a monoculture of industrial corn produces less food and nutritional value per acre than a perennial polyculture producing a variety of fruits, nuts, and fodder (M. Shepard, 2013, Restoration Agriculture: Real-World Permaculture for Farmers, pages 153-183). I do not fully subscribe to Shepard's views, especially his overwhelmingly negative view of arable agriculture. Fruits, nuts, and fodder are not a direct and complete substitute for grains, of course, and we still need to devote a lot of our land to growing annual grain crops. But he is certainly correct in his criticism of industrial monoculture and in his promotion of perennial polycultures as an alternative. What is certainly the case is that a lot of the land currently devoted to industrial monocultures should be converted to systems dominated by perennial plants. It would certainly make sense for many of the boundless corn and soya fields of the Midwest to revert to grassland.

[109] There are few things more damaging to the environment than conventional biofuels made from industrial monocultures: oil and gas are relatively better.

[110] Including organic palm oil, which could certainly fit into a mixed tropical agroforestry system. The problem is not palm oil, but palm oil monoculture. Other cash crops like coffee and cacao would fit in very well too.

sustainability of the nation's agriculture. Charles Townshend (1674-1738), nicknamed "Turnip Townshend", did much to promote the cultivation of the turnip which gradually allowed for far greater stocking rates of cattle and sheep, particularly through winter, avoided the fallowing of arable land, encouraged the practice of folding and, consequently, of far heavier manuring and improvement of soils. The turnip was subsequently one of the four crops included in the Norfolk four-course rotation system introduced and promoted by Coke of Holkham (1752-1842) who Albert Howard considered to be one of the pioneers who led the restoration of British agriculture and who managed to *"achieve at long last an approach to Nature's Law of Return"*.[111]

Young Bhuri with the Author's stubble turnips at the farm, 2013.

Turnips aside, there are plenty of examples of two crop harvests per season that used to be practised around the world[112] which should be revisited and adapted to today's agriculture and its modern tools and efficiencies. In the North of Italy, in parts of Piemonte, it was common practice to grow fast-growing dwarf beans like the *Fagioli di Saluggia* straight after the barley harvest in late June/early July. Further South, the "stubble bean" or "second bean" (*Fagiolo Giallo della Stoppia di San Lorenzo*) was sown in the wheat stubble after harvest and

[111] A. Howard, 1947, The Soil and Health, page 52.

[112] Or still practiced in some cases. Traditional farmers in India often grow two crops per season. With the benefits of modern technology applied to organic farming, as previously explained, their production potential is very promising.

harvested at the end of summer. This kind of crop rotation secured a very substantial grain/legume combined harvest from each field in one season. Even with lower organic yields, it would compare very well with single conventional grain harvests.[113] In Japan, as recorded by Masanobu Fukuoka (1913-2008), the traditional Japanese rice-barley rotation guaranteed two harvests in one season. Again: a modern, mechanised organic version of this rotation would undoubtedly perform well when compared to an industrial monoculture of either barley or rice.

4) Mixed organic farming systems are far more resilient to climatic extremes and perform better in drought, flood, and extreme temperatures. This is because more trees and shrubs, more grassland and a living soil are better able to both absorb and retain moisture and are far less prone to runoff and soil erosion. Furthermore, growing a diverse mix of crops, better suited to local conditions, is a way of hedging bets, as some crops will always do better than others in any given season, whatever the conditions. Similarly, raising diverse, hardy, locally adapted breeds of livestock does make far more sense than raising a limited range of demanding breeds in intensive conditions. Monocultures and factory farms are inherently vulnerable, as all the eggs are literally in one basket. Therefore, especially as we head into an uncertain future, potentially characterised by more climatic extremes and unpredictability, organic agriculture will be better equipped to both adapt and maintain overall yields. I will not directly deal with the climate change debate throughout this book.[114] However, I will offer a brief take on the subject, from an agriculturalist's perspective. There is no doubt that human activities have always had an impact on the climate, even before the advent of the Industrial Revolution. This is because some of the regulating factors in the climate equation are soil, vegetation, and biological activity on Earth, both on land and in the oceans.[115] Whenever humans have cut down too many trees, have deforested, have overcultivated the land, have grazed irresponsibly and have mismanaged fresh water sources, drought, higher temperatures and desertification have tended to follow.

An obvious place to observe this effect is the Fertile Crescent, which was once a major cradle of agriculture, a relatively green and fertile land, and is now mostly an arid, dried-out landscape, unable to grow anywhere near enough food to feed its population. A similar process has taken place across North Africa and, in part, across the broader Mediterranean.

[113] A barley or wheat crop of 2.5/4 tonnes plus a bean crop of 2/2.5 tonnes would compare very well with the 6-8 tonnes of barley of wheat one would expect from a hectare of conventional arable land in the UK.

[114] As any rational person should be able to recognise, some of the factors regulating climate are clearly anthropogenic (our direct impact on the land, on vegetation and the seas, our vast range of industrial activities etc...) and other factors are clearly not (solar activity, volcanic activity, ocean currents etc...). I will indirectly deal with the issue of climate change when discussing meat consumption and veganism in chapter 6.

[115] This understanding of life on Earth is consistent with Lovelock's fascinating Gaia Theory. I disagree with many of Lovelock's environmental solutions, but his holistic understanding of life on Earth is most persuasive.

Similar effects have been recorded, and continue to be recorded, across huge areas of arid, increasingly unproductive land across the world (mostly in parts of Africa, Central Asia, China, Australia, the Western United States, and the Middle East) which have succumbed, or are gradually succumbing, to desertification. These lands have generally been over-cultivated, deforested, poorly grazed or water from finite sources of irrigation has run out. Once the vegetation dwindles, the land heats up, the rains decrease, drought increases and water runs out, which in turn kills off more vegetation and dries out more soil, in a positive feedback mechanism. The consequences of decimating rainforests are another poignant example of a positive feedback loop mechanism in action: when rainforests are cut down, precipitation inevitably plummets, temperatures rise, and the land dries out. As the aforementioned Fukuoka wisely observed, plants need rain, but rain also needs plants,[116] in a virtuous cycle of interdependence.

To sum up, a different approach to agriculture and land management would make a huge difference, arguably more than any of the various techno-fixes being promoted. A combination of water conservation, water management, soil regeneration, nutrient cycling, holistic grazing, and strategic sowing and planting, which has been proven to work,[117] could reverse desertification and gradually bring huge swathes of land into sustainable food production. None of this is possible with the current agricultural model, which can only make the problem worse and lead to more loss of agricultural land worldwide. Here in Britain, we would be far better prepared for increasing flood, drought, and other extremes that may come our way if we regenerated our landscape: protecting coastlines, replanting miles of hedges, practising agroforestry, regenerating soils and pastures, protecting woodland and reforesting as much as possible.[118] This is where our environmental efforts should be focused, instead of focusing on illusory "Net Zero" targets and on unrealistic energy transition strategies.

[116] See M. Fukuoka, 2012, Sowing Seeds in the Desert. In a nutshell: plants both absorb water from the atmosphere in the form of rainwater and release water into the atmosphere through evaporation. Humans have tended to only see one side of the equation: that plants need water. This is a mistake.

[117] There are plenty of relatively simple landscape management methods that have been proven to reverse desertification around the world. There are examples of successful small-scale projects in Africa, as part of the Great Green Wall initiatives, where degraded, desertified land has been regenerated and brought back to life simply by the mass digging of water harvesting structures, followed by the replanting of native species, both wild and domestic. Similar projects have succeeded in other parts of the world, usually on a small scale. When projects have failed, it was due to reductionist, unimaginative approaches: reforesting with monocultures of non-native species, for example. We could regreen so much of the planet with relatively simple methods: the limits are political and ideological, as opposed to technical.

[118] Even in cities and suburban environments the extensive planting of trees and all sorts of vegetation has a significant cooling effect, and aids water retention. We should also allow wildflowers to grow on public lands, the edges of motorways and other marginal terrains, and stop spraying and destroying square miles of perfectly good land for foolish reasons.

Share vs Spare

The preceding discussion brings us to an important point: well-tended soils, well-managed grazing and the maintenance of tree cover create agroecosystems. Unlike industrial monocultures and factory farms, which do not qualify as ecosystems, agroecosystems mimic many of the efficiencies and rhythms of wild ecosystems. The carbon, nutrient, mineral and water cycles of an agroecosystem, dominated by domesticated species, are similar to those of a wild ecosystem. They also allow some degree of co-existence with the wild. Given that much of the Earth's landmass is covered with agricultural activity, how we manage this land is arguably as important, if not more important, to the environment, climate patterns and biodiversity than how we manage wilderness. In spite of this obvious fact, it has now become popular to claim that, in fact, organic agriculture is even *worse* for the environment, as it takes up more land to produce the same amount of food as a conventional system. This idea is based on the erroneous presumption, which is correct if we are referring to conventional agriculture, that agricultural activity is inherently damaging and that the more land we can "leave for Nature" the better. This has also been referred to as the "share vs spare" debate. On the "spare" side of the debate, we find the whole juggernaut of conventional agribusiness interests and their investors and media outlets, with their "sustainable intensification" agenda. We also have environmentalists like Monbiot and Lovelock who, as we saw earlier, argue that the best-case scenario for the planet is one where we farm very intensely on agricultural land and spare the rest of the land for Mother Nature to do her business.

George Monbiot's account of the depleted uplands of Britain is not without some merit. British uplands do lack in tree and shrub cover, with British tree cover amongst the lowest in Europe. These terrains are often depleted in both fertility and biodiversity and the mixed hill and upland livestock farming that used to be common in Wales, for example, has been replaced by an overwhelming dominance of sheep. Conversely, the number of sheep farmers and shepherds has steadily fallen and the practice of unattended sheep, as depicted by James Rebanks,[119] has gradually increased since the 18th century. There are only a little more than 50,000 agricultural workers, not all sheep farmers, across Wales[120] for 1.765m hectares of agricultural land, most of which is devoted to pasture, to raise sheep and cattle, which amount to approximately 10.53m animals.[121] Consequently, there are certainly

[119] J. Rebanks, 2016, The Shepherd's Life.

[120] In Wales, 50,401 people were working in agriculture in 2021. 75% of these are farmers, business partners, directors and spouses. The remaining 25% are employees, incorporating regular employees, managers and casual workers.

See: https://research.senedd.wales/media/iuch3jz1/22-47-farming-sector-in-wales.pdf

[121] https://www.gov.wales/sites/default/files/statistics-and-research/2022-11/survey-agriculture-and-horticulture-june-2022-005.pdf

problems with overgrazing, undergrazing, low productivity and a lack of biodiversity in parts of the Welsh uplands, and in other parts of Britain. Overall, we could increase grass productivity, livestock productivity and biodiversity in this country if we focused on improving our grazing and land management practices.[122] Far from the vegan utopia, a diet rich in grass-fed dairy and red meat should be the goal of the sustainable agriculture of the future in Britain.

As everything said so far indicates, whilst we need to preserve as many wild ecosystems as possible, our best bet is to look after farmland and "share" it with Nature so that farmland too can play a role in maintaining the rhythms and cycles of the planet. The UK is a good example: the wholesale abandonment of industrial agriculture would have far more benefit to the country as a whole than any rewilding project would, given that most of our landmass is devoted to agriculture to begin with. Monbiot, in his argument for the rewilding of Britain, argues that sheep, as a *"woolly ruminant from Mesopotamia"*,[123] cannot be considered a native species. Our native vegetation has no natural defences against it, apparently, and therefore sheep should simply be removed from our uplands. I would argue that the distinction between native and invasive, following at least six thousand years of adaptation and breeding, becomes blurred and arbitrary. Over thousands of years, our grasses and pastures have developed, adapted, and co-evolved in symbiosis with our sheep, as have many of our shrubs: when does an animal and the vegetation it feeds on become native? How many thousands of years does it take? Would the displacement of sheep and the reintroduction of the forest bison and the moose, which Monbiot suggests as distinct possibilities,[124] represent a return to a more "native" fauna? Successful domestication, by definition, involves the gradual localisation and evolution of species and their environment. British sheep are "native", as are our grass and meadow flower species, in so far as the distinctive British sheep breeds are uniquely adapted to their specific regional terrains, climates and grasslands. The fact that it was forest, as opposed to grassland, that was the dominant vegetation of the British Isles in the Mesolithic does not logically entail that a substantial return to forest at the expense of grassland is necessarily desirable or ecologically sound.

Extensive rewilding entails a "spare" mentality: intensive industrial farming and dense populations in the lowlands and rewilding and abandoned communities in the uplands, with tourism the only viable economic option for those who remain. If we were to reform and

[122] By adopting methods such as silvopasture, which is closely related to agroforestry, and consists in the integration of tree and shrub cover with pasture and livestock. It would arguably be the best practice to integrate with rotational, holistic grazing.

[123] G. Monbiot, 2013, Feral, page 70.

[124] Ibidem, pages 124-126.

expand, rather than abandon, the farming of the uplands, more people, rather than less, would need to be employed and live in these remote places. Generous subsidies and resources would need to be given to landowners and tenants for planting trees, shrubs, and hedges, adopting far better grazing practices, steadily and mandatorily moving away from all chemicals, preserving livestock breeds and adopting a broad range of other beneficial measures. Between mismanaged grazing and denuded grassland on one hand and rewilding and the departure of sheep on the other, there is a sensible middle way, and plenty of reasonable policies available to facilitate the transition. None of this negates the possibility and indeed desirability of a few rewilded areas. Even in a densely populated country like Britain and even in a hypothetical future of post-industrial sustainable food production, there should be plenty of scope to restore a few of the most remote areas of the Highlands to forest with, perhaps, some carefully reintroduced species. The commendable work of Alan Watson Featherstone, discussed in detail by Monbiot, to restore parts of the Caledonian Forest, does not clash with our need to use most of our hills and uplands for farming, or indeed for stalking and shooting when appropriate. But, even in the best-case scenario, this will be the exception rather than the norm.

A woolly ruminant from Mesopotamia? Jacob sheep at Bagnell Farm, Somerset

The Unbearable Problem of Waste

Perhaps the chief problem with the "feed the world" narrative is that there is already plenty of food to feed the world's population, even if it keeps growing at predicted rates. Where there is still starvation, malnutrition and stunting around the world, it is not due to a scarce global food supply. Clearly, distribution is the main issue, rather than food availability. There are an estimated billion people who are obese and a similar number who do not have enough to eat: those who eat too much and those who eat too little. Many farmers and herders around the world do not have enough to eat, whilst people who have never grown a plant or raised an animal in their life and work in an office in a skyscraper are likely to consult dietary advice and feel the need to go to the gym to offset their excessive eating. This undeniable paradox indicates that we do not have a supply problem. There are many political, economic, social, and cultural reasons why distribution and inequality around the world are the way they are, and it is beyond the scope of this book to investigate them.

It is however worth examining another phenomenon which also puts a severe dent in the presumption, always used to justify industrial agriculture, genetic modification, factory farms etc..., that our main challenge in agriculture is to increase productivity so that we can "feed the world". That straightforward phenomenon is waste. At present, an estimated third of all food produced is wasted[125] and never ends up in a person's stomach. Let us assume, for sake of argument, and given the difficulty of obtaining accurate measurements, that it is actually just 20 or 25%. This would still be a staggering amount of food. In Britain, it is estimated that the following food items are wasted every day:[126]

- 2.9 million whole potatoes
- 1 million whole bananas
- 1.4 million whole tomatoes
- 360,000 whole oranges
- 33,000 whole apples
- 2.1 million whole carrots
- 170,000 whole onions
- 170,000 whole lettuces

[125] An estimated one fifth (19 per cent) of food available to consumers is wasted, at the retail, food service, and household level. That is in addition to the 13 per cent of the world's food lost in the supply chain, as estimated by FAO, from post-harvest up to and excluding retail. See the UN Environment Programme's Food Waste Index Report 2024: https://wedocs.unep.org/handle/20.500.11822/45230

[126] See the WRAP (Waste & Resources Action Programme) report on Food Surplus and Waste in the UK: https://www.wrap.ngo/resources/report/food-surplus-and-waste-uk-key-facts-updated-november-2023#download-file

- 2.7 million glasses' worth of milk
- 2.1 million slices' worth of ham
- The equivalent of 25 million slices of bread or 1,300,000 loaves

And this is just food wasted at home, we are discounting the waste in retail, manufacturing, restaurants, coffee shops, butcher shops, fishmongers etc... Let us pre-empt the scepticism of our industrial farming advocates: even if the figures were exaggerated, even if they were 50% above actual waste levels, it would still be an enormous amount of waste. We ought to see this as a national shame and regard it, as it used to be, as a sin. It is historically abnormal and unprecedented. In pre-war Italy, it would have been common for breadcrumbs to be collected off tables after meals and kept for cooking future meals. A lot of wonderful recipes, such as Pappa al Pomodoro, a bread and tomato soup from Tuscany, are made from stale, hard bread. Similar traditions would have been the norm in Britain and elsewhere.

That is not to say that waste is also not symptomatic of something positive: that we have unprecedented food abundance, that we do not need to collect breadcrumbs and can afford some degree of food waste. Comfort about food supplies, and not having to worry if the milk goes off or the bread goes mouldy, is a good thing. But between the understandable marginal waste that comes with comfort and prosperity and the absolute carelessness and wastefulness of today, there is an enormous gap. In poor countries, people cannot possibly waste food the way we do[127] and food waste is normally the result of poor storage, lack of refrigeration and inefficient transport logistics. As we saw earlier, a lot of the technologies we take for granted would make a huge difference to poor farming communities in Africa, India, and other countries around the world.

The other problem that we have is that there is a lot of systematic, planned waste in our food system. Under the dubious label of health and safety, huge amounts of perfectly good food are wasted and prevented from being eaten by man or beast. Just consider for a moment the amount of food that, having gone past its sell-by date, is systematically thrown away. Or the less than "perfect" food that doesn't even make the supermarket shelf to begin with. Or the absurd standards of size, weight and shape imposed on slaughterhouses, manufacturers, and distributors. Furthermore, not only is a lot of food prevented from being eaten, but it is also prevented from ending up in the only other two places where it should end up: as animal feed or compost. If the staff at Abbey Home Farm wanted to feed their leftover bread or milk

[127] In the Philippines, leftover food from restaurants (usually from fast food restaurants), referred to as *pagpag*, is scavenged from garbage sites and dumps and cooked. A small-scale cottage industry and trade revolves around *pagpag*. This is obviously a practice borne out of tragic degrees of poverty, and one that we should be grateful to be completely unfamiliar with. However, it is instructive to be aware of the lengths to which people around the world must go in order to feed themselves and should make us think twice before being so wasteful and careless with our own food.

to the pigs at the end of the business day at their farm shop, they would be breaking the law. If they have bags of vegetable peelings from their kitchens, these cannot legally be fed to pigs: it is unhealthy and unsafe, apparently. And yet, it is considered perfectly healthy and safe to keep pigs living in their own faeces inside a factory.[128] The aforementioned ban on swill[129] should not only be reversed, but food waste should, by law, either end up as swill or end up in composting sites. Homes should have compulsory food-only waste bins, to be collected by the council, and large municipal composting sites should be set up all around the country. High-energy, perfectly safe foods like old bread and fruit from retailers should be trucked to the nearest pig farms. Swill-making technology, which is institutional in Japan, hardly a nation known for its lack of cleanliness, should be the norm.

Before we worry about food running out or call for ever more productivity, let us take stock of how much food is currently wasted and take individual action. Even if no government policy does anything to address the problem, which is highly likely, individual citizens have no good reason to throw away food from their kitchens, nor to order too much food at a restaurant and leave half of it on the plate. The amount of waste and waistline expansion that we see all around us should also make us conclude that we should focus on quality, rather than quantity: buy less food overall, buy high-quality ingredients and do not waste them.

IN A NUTSHELL

- Organic agriculture is relatively recent and should not be confused with pre-industrial agriculture and visions of barefoot peasants leading oxen by the yoke.
- We are not Luddites.
- Sir Albert Howard was a great man, and we should have listened to him. It is not too late.
- There are other related "schools" of alternative agriculture that have arisen over the last century, which share the same ethos as the organic movement and are just as important.
- Healthy soil → healthy plants → healthy animals → healthy humans.
- Organic principles are more important than organic certification.

[128] The National Pig Association, an industry body representing commercial pig farmers, foolishly campaigns against feeding kitchen waste to pigs on disease prevention grounds but does not seem to mind the fact that most of the pigs in the UK, including those of their members, are usually kept in cruel, horrific, unsanitary conditions that seem perfectly designed to promote disease. See https://www.npa-uk.org.uk/Do_not_feed_food_waste_to_pigs-campaign_stepped_up.html

[129] Food waste that is cooked and fed to pigs.

- Holistic, regenerative grazing and allowing livestock to mimic wild herbivores could prevent desertification, restore soils and ecosystems, and bring a lot of the world's degraded land into food production.
- Agroforestry and silvopasture should be implemented worldwide: we need far more trees on both lowlands and uplands.
- We could feed the world without agrochemicals and factory farms.
- In Britain, we would eat a very different but much better diet if we got rid of agrochemicals and factory farms.
- Let's share land, not spare land.
- Poor distribution is one of the main reasons for both obesity and starvation around the world: not a lack of food.
- We already grow more than enough food to feed the world, but waste far too much of it.
- Food waste is an avoidable sin. Eat less, eat well and do not waste food.

Chapter 4

THE ROOTS OF INDUSTRIAL AGRICULTURE AND NUTRITION SCIENCE

The "organic vision" just laid out is at odds with the trends that have developed since the post-war period and have been accelerating over the last thirty years. Whilst there is undoubtedly a revival in the alternative agricultural movement, as well as many promising developments around the world, this is a niche vision with almost no backing (in fact direct opposition in most cases) from educational, academic, and governmental resources, not to mention from industry and financial institutions. It would be easy to simplify this problem by laying the blame on powerful vested interests. Whilst these are always crucial and undeniable, it would be disingenuous to ignore other fundamental reasons why we find ourselves firmly in the era of protein powders, Big Macs, obesity, pesticides, and factory farms. The first reason, often ignored by those in the organic and alternative food movement, is that both industrial agriculture and nutrition science did bring great benefits, especially at the beginning. Many of the negative outcomes were largely unpredictable and unintended. We cannot blame the first farmers to use herbicides for doing so, after generations of back-breaking labour. As I can personally testify, even by just looking after relatively small patches of land year after year without chemical inputs, weeding is a huge factor in all annual cultivations and a seemingly magical liquid that could make all weeds disappear must have been a temptation too great to resist for many.

We also cannot blame these farmers for ignoring the potential drawbacks of chemical fertilisers, which must have seemed absolutely miraculous when first used, as they simplified farming and increased yields of desirable crops very rapidly. We certainly cannot blame, and still cannot blame, our wholesale adoption of machinery and technologies that have freed us from astonishing levels of daily drudgery, from the farm all the way to the kitchen. Equally, we cannot blame those who tried to make King Henry IV's vision in 16th century France come true, when he apparently expressed the wish that every labourer in his realm should be able to put a chicken in the pot on Sundays.

The fact that now chicken is the most eaten meat on the planet and that, in fact, the poorer one is in Britain the more likely one is to be eating chicken, is an astounding, but unintended, outcome. The desire to create a system of production which would allow anyone the ability to be able to afford a hamburger on a regular basis and bring their family to a restaurant was unquestionably one of the initial motives of the nascent fast-food industry in post-War California and this, it must be said, was a benevolent motive. The many dreadful consequences of the fast-food industry were not cynically and systematically planned in the 1950s, it was only with the expansion and corporatisation of the industry that benevolent intentions gradually gave way to a harmful and predatory system.[130]

This does not mean that, even in the very early days of industrial agriculture, there weren't any wiser, dissenting voices. If only the Albert Howards of this world had been listened to... But this brings us to an important point: technological and scientific developments have been accompanied by developments in the world of ideas and by major cultural upheavals. We are ideological beings. How we view the world, the filters through which we choose to interpret it, is as important as any actual facts about the world. No age is devoid of great and small ideas, often competing with one another. In our culture, the Scientific Revolution, the Enlightenment, and the rise of industrial societies are generally perceived as part of what could be described as a "progress narrative", as a literal enlightenment and the dawn of a new and, in many ways, final era. Interestingly, in the 19th century, both the nascent industrial capitalist system and Marxism, committed to historical materialism, saw industrialisation as both a positive and inevitable step forward for mankind. One thing all totalitarian regimes in the 20th century had in common was a drive towards industrialisation,[131] with motorways and tractors symbols of undisputed progress. The rise of the natural sciences, industrialisation, mass urbanisation and the decline of rural life and traditional religion have changed and shaped our societies and our worldview in a relatively short time to a degree that is easy to ignore but impossible to overstate.

The reader might think that this is all a bit highfalutin (I thought we were talking about chickens, weren't we?!) and that there is no need to consider historical events from the 18th and 19th centuries to understand why we eat how we do. But, at the risk of needlessly repeating an old truism, understanding the past is the key to understanding the present and

[130] Harmful to children, who were and still are the primary marketing audience of fast-food companies, to their obese and unhealthy parents and relatives, to farmers reduced to producing cheap commodities on industrial farms, to workers in slaughterhouses and concentrated animal feeding operations, to farm animals, to wildlife and to the environment as a whole. It has also been harmful to superior food cultures that have been damaged and corrupted by the arrival of the fast-food industry as part of *Pax Americana*.

[131] The Khmer Rouge's short lived and small-scale experiment in Cambodia is a rare exception to this rule.

the future. Furthermore, the very fact that these dramatic and relatively rapid changes are largely taken for granted or barely acknowledged is in and of itself symptomatic of the fact that these have been ideological changes first and foremost. An ideology can be defined as a set of ideas through which we interpret and view the world. For our purposes, it is important to briefly consider how the scientific outlook, especially what has been aptly referred to as "scientism",[132] has shaped and continues to shape our relationship with food, the natural world and each other. In many ways, it makes the job of reform even harder, as minds are harder to change than mere policies.

None of what follows should be construed as an attack on science and the scientific method, nor as a primitivist attack on the value of industry and technology in agriculture and food production, as only a fool could deny their value. I will, however, argue that science is not only never fully divorced from ideology but that its increasing and ongoing encroachment into other sources of human knowledge is philosophically problematic and leads to many negative consequences. I will also argue that whilst science can and should inform our agricultural practices, dietary choices and eating habits, it should never do more than inform. There are many other reasons and motivations that should inform our agricultural practices, dietary choices and eating habits that do not and should not require scientific sanction.

Chemistry and the Origins of Nutrition Science

The discovery of macronutrients, like protein and carbohydrates, is relatively recent. Until the latter part of the 18th century, there had been a lot of speculation about the role of food in our bodies. However, it was only with what is often referred to as the Chemical Revolution, largely originating in France, that the identification of the main elements and the adoption of experimental procedures consistent with the scientific method that new understanding of the composition of food and its agency in the human body was gradually developed. Many of the initial breakthroughs are often attributed to Antoine Lavoisier, (1743-1794) considered a founding father of modern chemistry, who hypothesised the concept of metabolism, as in the combustion of food and oxygen into heat energy and water in the body. Through an experiment with guinea pigs, he had established that the heat emanating from the rodents' bodies came from the combustion of organic compounds within their internal tissues. Claude Berthollet (1748-1822), whose methods were an early example of the new quantitative approach, found that the gas emanating from decomposing animal matter was

[132] The belief that knowledge can **only** be derived through scientific enquiry and the belief that all questions are potentially answerable by science. Raymond Tallis defines scientism as *"the mistaken belief that the natural sciences (physics, chemistry, biology and their derivatives) can or will give a complete description and even explanation of everything, including human life."* (R. Tallis, 2016, Aping Mankind, page 15)

ammonia and that this gas was composed of a 3:1 hydrogen-nitrogen ratio. The presence of nitrogen in animal matter helped to distinguish it from sugars, starches, and fats.

By the early 1800s, the primary elements in food (carbon, nitrogen, hydrogen, and oxygen) had been identified and experiments continued to attempt to identify which elements played which role and how. François Magendie (1783-1855), in a series of cruel experiments, attempted to understand the role of nitrogen in food and to establish whether animals could absorb nitrogen from the atmosphere (in the manner of leguminous plants). He took single foods, like sugar, butter, and olive oil, that did not contain nitrogen and fed them as single foods to dogs. All dogs eventually got sick and died within a month or so. He concluded, therefore, that nitrogen uptake must come from food, from foods other than those that do not contain nitrogen and concluded that *"diversity and multiplicity of aliments is an important rule in hygiene"*.[133]

Similar efforts in plant nutrition were made by Jean Baptiste Boussingault (1801-1887), who demonstrated that leguminous crops (e.g., peas, beans, lentils) are able to absorb and utilise atmospheric nitrogen, unlike other staple crops. He then proceeded to experiment with livestock feed, measuring the nitrogen content in both feed and manure, and concluded that the animals, unlike the legumes, were obtaining their nitrogen from their feed instead of the atmosphere. These experiments, and similar other efforts throughout this period, led to the belief that nitrogen compounds were the key to the support of living things and that since plants alone were able to manufacture these, the animal kingdom depended on plant food to obtain the required nitrogen. Up until this point, nitrogenous compounds in animals had been referred to as albumin, casein, fibrin and so on and, in 1839, Dutch chemist Gerardus Johannes Mulder (1802-1880) came to refer to them as "protein" for the first time. By the mid-19th century, the three fundamental macronutrients, carbohydrates, fats, and proteins, had been identified.

This was aided by the gradual development of the periodic table, which had begun with Antoine Lavoisier, and of "atomic theory". Whilst schools of atomism were already present in Ancient Greece and India, the modern, scientific approach to atomic theory was still in its infancy. John Dalton (1766-1844) proposed that all matter was composed of atoms, which were the indivisible and indestructible building blocks of all things. He also postulated that all atoms within an element (say, oxygen) were identical, but that different elements had atoms of differing size and mass. The increasing understanding of both the elements and compounds led to the ability to identify molecular formulas. William Prout (1785-1850), for example, identified the molecular formula of urea, a very important compound present in urine that eventually became the main component of chemical fertiliser. The ability to identify the molecular composition of urea and

[133] F. Magendie, 1831, An Elementary Compendium of Physiology.

to recreate it through synthetic means, as Friedrich Wöhler (1800-1882) did in 1828, went on to have drastic consequences for both nutrition and agriculture: the ability to synthesise all sorts of molecules, without needing to obtain them from living things, would change nutrient cycles and ecosystems in unprecedented ways.

Justus von Liebig (1803-1873), the scientist who possibly had more influence on the future of agriculture than any other scientist (more on him later), also contributed to the nascent nutritional science of the 19th century. He had observed how pigs could be fattened on potatoes that were rich in starch and had almost no fat and therefore concluded, correctly, that animals had the internal ability to make complex molecules from more simple molecules, which explained how sugars and starches could be converted into fat. He was however proven wrong in his thesis that energy in the body, given the absence of sugars, starches and fats from muscles, must originate from proteins. The disproving of Liebig's theory came from the experiments into the conservation of energy by James Joule (1818-1889) and others. Johannes Wislicenus (1835-1902), Adolf Fick (1829-1901) and the latter's brother-in-law, Sir Edward Frankland (1825-1899), tested Liebig's theory in a series of experiments. By measuring the correlation between the ingestion of protein, energy expended through measurable activity and urea excreted, they concluded, beyond reasonable doubt, that protein alone could not have been responsible for the energy expended by the experimental subjects and that it must have also come from other sources, namely carbohydrates and/or fats.

The discovery of micronutrients had a similar timeline. A well-known early experiment on sailors was carried out by Dr James Lind (1716-1794), a physician in the British Navy. Scurvy had been a deadly problem for explorers, sailors (and pirates!) from the time of the discovery of the Americas. The benefits of citrus fruits as a cure for scurvy had already been sporadically attested by the Spanish, Portuguese, French and British explorers, but no formal experiment was performed until Dr Lind's trial. There was also an obvious technical difficulty: citrus were fresh products and could not be stored properly at sea. In his experiment, Lind gave seawater to some of the sailors, others vinegar, and the rest limes. Those given the limes were saved from scurvy, thanks to their vitamin C content. Lind and his contemporaries never identified the vitamin as the healing micronutrient, as vitamin C wasn't discovered until the 1930s. The acidic quality of citrus was usually believed to be the cure, which led to many errors, such as boiling down the citrus juice to make a concentrate, killing off the vitamin C in the process.

Christiaan Eijkman (1858-1930), a Dutchman working with indigenous people in Java, identified a local disease called beriberi, which caused heart problems and paralysis. He had observed that when chickens were fed the native diet of white rice, they developed the symptoms of beriberi but when the chickens were fed unprocessed brown rice they did not.

Eijkman went on to feed brown rice to human patients and they were cured. The outer rice bran contains vitamin B1, also known as thiamine, which was the deficiency causing the disease, as later discovered by Elmer Verner McCollum (1879-1967), a U.S. Department of Agriculture researcher at the University of Wisconsin. In 1912, McCollum began a series of nutrition experiments using rats. He discovered the first fat-soluble vitamin, vitamin A, and observed that rats were healthier when they were fed butter instead of lard, as butter contains more vitamin A. Other diseases were linked to vitamin deficiencies,[134] such as the already mentioned beriberi and rickets, brought on by a lack of vitamin D.

Dr Kazimierz Funk (1884-1967) was the first to coin the term "vitamins" in 1912 as vital factors in the diet. His work followed on from Eijkman's beriberi research and he succeeded in identifying the substance (later known as vitamin B1) and in identifying vitamins as those substances present in food which could prevent scurvy, beriberi, and pellagra (a disease caused by a deficiency of niacin, vitamin B3, usually associated with a diet almost exclusively made up of maize and its derivatives) and rickets. For the nascent science of nutrition, the discovery of micronutrients was in many ways a greater step forward than the discovery of macronutrients, at least in terms of raising its public profile and allowing it to gain tangible results, because it permitted immediate and successful cures of previously incurable diseases through the administration of single substances or dietary changes. From the 1920s onwards, nutrition science gradually became a branch of medicine, and vitamins and other supplements entered the consumer market.[135] It was not, however, until the post-war period that nutrition science, its language and shifting recommendations gradually became an omnipresent part of our culture.

Darwinism and Genetics

Other major 19th century developments in biological sciences which had long-term implications for agriculture and nutrition science were the beginning of the modern science of genetics and the theory of evolution by natural selection. Gregor Mendel (1822-1884), generally considered the father of modern genetics, carried out his famous experiments on pea plants over a period of eight years to investigate heredity. He established what came to be referred to as the laws of Mendelian inheritance, which were later accepted as negating and superseding the theory of blended inheritance, which was popular in the 19th century. As the name suggests, the theory held that progeny inherits a blend, or average, of the

[134] Some diseases were also linked to mineral deficiencies. Goitre, also known as "Derbyshire neck", was proven to be brought on by a lack of iodine by French Chemist Gaspard Adolphe Chatin (1813-1901).

[135] By 1960, the President of American Medical Association lamented that the public was afflicted by *"vitamania"*, and that *"ingenious advertising and misleading claims have helped cram Americans full of vitamins they don't need"* (H. Levenstein, 1993, Paradox of Plenty, page 167).

parents' characteristics. Charles Darwin (1809-1882), unaware of Mendel's work, also believed in a form of blended inheritance. Mendel deduced that genes come in pairs and are inherited as distinct units, one from each parent. Through his controlled experiments with peas, he tracked the segregation of parental genes and their appearance in the offspring as dominant or recessive traits and recognised the mathematical patterns of inheritance from one generation to the next.

Mendel's laws were not recognised until the beginning of the 20th century but went on to have a major impact on plant and animal breeding. Guided by the laws of heredity, breeders have been able to be more successful in selecting for traits, in being able to make predictions and accelerate the development of desired crop varieties, including hybrids. Unaware of Mendel's findings, Nazareno Strampelli (1862-1942) began working on the hybridisation of wheat in 1901, with similar approaches and methods to those used by Mendel. He eventually read Mendel's work in 1904 and went on to develop successful high-yielding hybrids that contributed to a substantial increase in Italian wheat production during the Battle of the Grain (1925-1943) and to the planting of these wheat varieties overseas, including in Latin America. These early breeding efforts led to the development of excellent wheat varieties such as Senatore Cappelli. Hybridization, in its early days, was overwhelmingly positive: it speeded up conventional breeding efforts and crop development. As we shall see later, this new knowledge and technical advancement eventually also led to many negative consequences and contributed to some of the worst aspects of industrial agriculture. As is often the case, technology is a double-edged sword, and we ignore its destructive potential at our peril.

The aforementioned Darwin, as well as Alfred Wallace (1823-1913) and others, on the other hand, had a more indirect but perhaps even more profound impact on food production and agriculture. They were influenced by Thomas Malthus (1766-1834), who argued that exponential population growth is at odds with limited natural resources and food supply: unchecked population growth outpaces food supply, leading to scarcity, starvation etc... and to an eventual natural rebalancing of population vis-à-vis food supply. The theory of evolution by natural selection aims to describe the process by which all living organisms, including humans, change over time as a result of changes in heritable traits. Organisms produce more offspring that are able to survive in their environment, given limited resources and competition for food supplies. The theory contends that those who are better equipped to survive grow to maturity, reproduce, and pass on their traits. Natural selection has often been referred to as *"survival of the fittest"*[136] because the "fittest" organisms, those most adapted to their environments, are the ones that

[136] The famous expression was coined by Herbert Spencer (1820-1903) in Principles of Biology (1864).

reproduce most successfully and are most likely to pass on their traits to the next generation. Traits later came to be understood as genes.

Whatever the scientific merits of the theory of evolution, it had a profound ideological impact which rippled across other disciplines. It challenged historical notions of human exceptionalism and provided an alternative to the traditional, Aristotelian teleological view of nature. By "freeing" mankind from the burden of stewardship and exceptional responsibility, and by portraying nature as lacking in any purpose, sanctity and intelligent design, evolutionary thinking gave the nascent industrial and scientific revolution added impetus and sense of authority.[137] Evolutionary thinking undoubtedly also fitted in very well with the rise of other ideas of the time and with the general ethos of the Victorian era. Karl Marx was onto something when he claimed that Darwin had projected the rules of Malthusian and Smithsonian economic liberalism onto the animal world: *"It is remarkable how Darwin rediscovers, among the beasts and plants, the society of England with its division of labour, competition, opening up of new markets, 'inventions' and Malthusian 'struggle for existence'."* [138]

One of the legacies of evolutionary thinking has been an excessive and arbitrary emphasis on what is perceived to be the competitive, ruthless, "survival of the fittest" aspects of nature. The Malthusian "zero-sum game" view of the natural world[139] inevitably invokes the primacy of struggle and, as Tennyson famously wrote in his poem, of *"nature red in tooth and claw"*.[140] A particularly relevant contemporary exponent of the worldview emerging from the 18-19th century scientific revolution is the aforementioned Richard Dawkins:

"The total amount of suffering per year in the natural world is beyond all decent contemplation. During the minute that it takes me to compose this sentence, thousands of animals are being eaten alive, many others are running for their lives, whimpering with fear, others are slowly being devoured from within by rasping parasites, thousands of all kinds are dying of starvation, thirst, and disease. It must be so. If there ever is a time of plenty, this very fact will automatically lead to an increase in the population until the natural state of starvation and misery is restored. In a universe of electrons and selfish genes, blind physical forces and genetic replication, some people are going to get hurt, other people are going to get lucky, and you won't find any rhyme or reason in it, nor any justice. The universe that we observe has precisely the properties we

[137] Enthusiasm for evolutionary thinking has always been, and continues to be, embedded within broader ideological concerns that have little do with science per se.

[138] Marx Engels Correspondence, 18 June 1862 (https://marxists.architexturez.net/archive/marx/index.htm).

[139] Competition and struggle in the natural world are no more prevalent and important than cooperation and symbiosis. Nature is far more complex and irreducible than any of our analyses of course, but the simplistic "survival of the fittest" paradigm that still dominates evolutionary thinking is particularly unhelpful.

[140] Lord A. Tennyson, In Memoriam A.H.H., Canto 56.

should expect if there is, at bottom, no design, no purpose, no evil, no good, nothing but pitiless indifference."[141]

The ideological shift that followed the scientific revolution led to an interesting and enduring paradox. On the one hand, it arbitrarily downgraded and demystified the status and value of humans. No longer endowed with a soul, we apparently became just another primate on an unremarkable planet. This way of thinking about ourselves, this *zeitgeist* which currently dominates both the sciences and the humanities has led to a reductionist, deterministic, and misanthropic understanding of ourselves. It has also led to a general confusion about the crucial distinctions between man and beast, and we have ended up animalising humans and humanising animals and misunderstanding both.[142]

For example, in one of the most popular books of our time, *"Sapiens. A Brief History of Mankind"*,[143] the author declares that, as time goes by, *"the less difference we find between us and other apes"* and that, at the level of the individual and small collective, *"on a one to one, even ten to ten basis"*, *"we are embarrassingly similar to chimpanzees"*.[144] Harari, who seems keen to highlight our lowly origins throughout his overrated tome, perhaps feels that his dubious assertions are supported by the fact that we humans share approximately 99% of our DNA with chimpanzees and bonobos and approximately 98% of our DNA with gorillas.[145] More strikingly still, humans, chimpanzees, and bonobos are apparently more closely related to one another than either is to gorillas or any other primate.[146] So, in other words, if DNA is the measure by which we understand living things, you and I are closer to chimpanzees than chimpanzees are to gorillas. And yet, it should be absolutely clear to any rational person who hasn't been bamboozled by Darwinian dogmatism that the differences between chimpanzees and gorillas are insignificant when compared to the differences between us and any of the great apes. No amount of DNA analysis and genomic sequencing should mislead us into demeaning self-delusion. We are not just another ape.

Back to our enduring paradox: having arbitrarily downgraded and demystified the status and value of humans, we have also freed ourselves from our exceptional place in the world and from the burden of responsibility. The scientific revolution gave us unparalleled licence and authority to ruthlessly pursue our goals and desires, with increasingly powerful technological

[141] R. Dawkins, 2008, River Out of Eden: A Darwinian View of Life, pages 131-132.

[142] As eloquently argued by Tallis: R. Tallis, 2016, Aping Mankind, "From Darwinism to Darwinitis", pages 147-182.

[143] Y.N. Harari, 2011, Sapiens. A Brief History of Mankind.

[144] Ibidem, page 42.

[145] https://www.scientificamerican.com/article/tiny-genetic-differences-between-humans-and-other-primates-pervade-the-genome/

[146] http://humanorigins.si.edu/evidence/genetics. Interestingly this article is entitled: *"What does it mean to be human?"* This is a good example of misguided scientism, as no comprehensive DNA analysis or genome sequencing could ever come close to address questions of meaning. It is simply the wrong question, in the wrong context.

tools. Lowly primates, but with self-administered authority to do as we wish. As will become clear, all of this has had a deep impact on agriculture, food production and our attitude towards ourselves and the natural world.

Industrial Agriculture: A Brief Overview

The developments in the natural sciences were accompanied by and closely related to the Industrial Revolution. The dawn of modern chemistry, the invention of the steam engine, the development of factory processes and mass production all contributed to the transformation of agriculture and food production. The main changes that occurred from the late 19th century onwards can briefly be summarised as follows:

From Biology to Chemistry

The aforementioned Justus von Liebig discovered that the three major plant macronutrients, now commonly referred to as NPK, are nitrogen, phosphorus, and potassium. His discovery, coupled with the gradual development of industrial processes and large-scale mining, gradually shifted the fertility of crops from biological to chemical processes. Phosphorus and potassium were gradually used as fertilisers during the 19th century, albeit on a much-reduced scale, and were obtained from bone ash, guano deposits and wood ash. From then on, and until the present day, phosphorus and potassium fertilisers have been mass-produced through mining phosphate and potash respectively.

The revolution in the nitrogen cycle was even more significant. Whilst making up most of the atmosphere, nitrogen fixation into useful nitrates is limited by the agency of bacterial activity in the soil. In agriculture, the maintenance of fertility required the careful cycling of nitrogen sources through sound management of manures and through the cultivation of plants that fix nitrogen[147] through symbiotic relationships with nitrogen-fixing bacteria. The Haber-Bosch process, discovered by the German chemists Fritz Haber (1868-1934) and Carl Bosch (1874-1940) on the eve of World War 1, enabled the artificial fixation of nitrogen directly from the atmosphere to make ammonia to be used for the manufacture of both explosives and fertilisers. Ammonia gradually became an unlimited source of artificial fertility that could be applied to soils.

Interestingly, Haber also developed chemical weapons to be used in the war effort and the insecticide Zyklon A. The technologies created for warfare became the technologies used

[147] Legumes: as discovered by Boussingault. However, the fertilising properties of legumes have been known since antiquity, well before the discovery of the nitrogen fixation process. In parts of Central Sicily, for example, the rotation of wheat and broad beans has been practiced since Roman colonisation.

for agriculture, with the same manufacturers often operating in both spheres. As we saw earlier, this trend continued well into the 60s and 70s, with Monsanto and Dow supplying both farmers and the military with similar chemicals. The application of pesticides, herbicides and fungicides is now part of the standard package of technologies upon which industrial agriculture relies. Overall, for over a century now, natural cycles have been replaced by chemical processes. Similarly, animal agriculture has gradually been transformed into an industrial enterprise, with animals subjected to the unforgiving rigours of the input-output logic of manufacturing.

From Solar Energy to Fossil Fuel Energy

The cycle of life is dependent upon the sun as its primary source of energy. Whilst of course, the sun is still indispensable for photosynthesis, industrial agriculture allows for a lot of shortcuts and external inputs through the use of fossil fuels. Both the feedstock and power generation needed to manufacture nitrogen fertiliser and agrochemicals are entirely reliant on fossil fuels. Farm power and machinery, of course, need vast amounts of energy to run, not to mention the energy required for the mining and manufacturing processes required to build and maintain tractors, machinery etc...

Overall, both energy and fertility cycles have become linear, as opposed to cyclical. The three diagrams below show the basic energy and fertility agricultural cycles for:

Figure 1. Traditional Pre-industrial Mixed Agriculture

Figure 2. Contemporary Best Practice Organic Agriculture

Figure 3. Contemporary Conventional Industrial Agriculture

Some preliminary notes on the diagrams below:

- Diagrams, for simplicity, only show the main energy, nutrient, and fertility elements. These are very basic models, sufficient for our purposes.
- There will be other inputs and outputs in each system and other nuances that are intentionally omitted: this is big-picture stuff for the uninitiated reader.
- I have included the basic oxygen-carbon dioxide-water cycle of crops and livestock and omitted human respiration, which we can take as a given.
- I have not quantified any of the inputs and outputs. There is less photosynthesis in Diagram 3 than there is in Diagram 2, and far more fossil fuel energy is used in Diagram 3 than is used in Diagram 2, but the diagrams do not draw a quantitative distinction. The goal here is to show the main flows of inputs and outputs and the basic differences between the agricultural cycles.

- Plants include crops, grassland, and fodder, especially in Figures 1 and 2. Livestock includes the most common farm animals: cattle, sheep, pigs, poultry etc...
- I have omitted the full phosphorus and potassium cycles and focussed on nitrogen. In the first two scenarios, phosphorus and potassium are recycled through the system via the process of decay and through the input of mostly organic fertilisers. In the third diagram, these are inputs originating from mining and manufacturing and come under the "NPK fertilisers" heading.
- I have omitted water inputs other than rain, such as irrigation. This is because in Britain most arable land and pasture are rainfed, whatever the farming system. The use of aquifer/well water could, in principle, apply to all three systems.
- Red shows all those elements that are external <u>inputs</u> (e.g., NPK fertiliser or fossil fuel) and those that are <u>outputs</u> (e.g., pollutants or unrecycled waste) that are not cycled back into the system.

Traditional Pre-industrial Mixed Agriculture

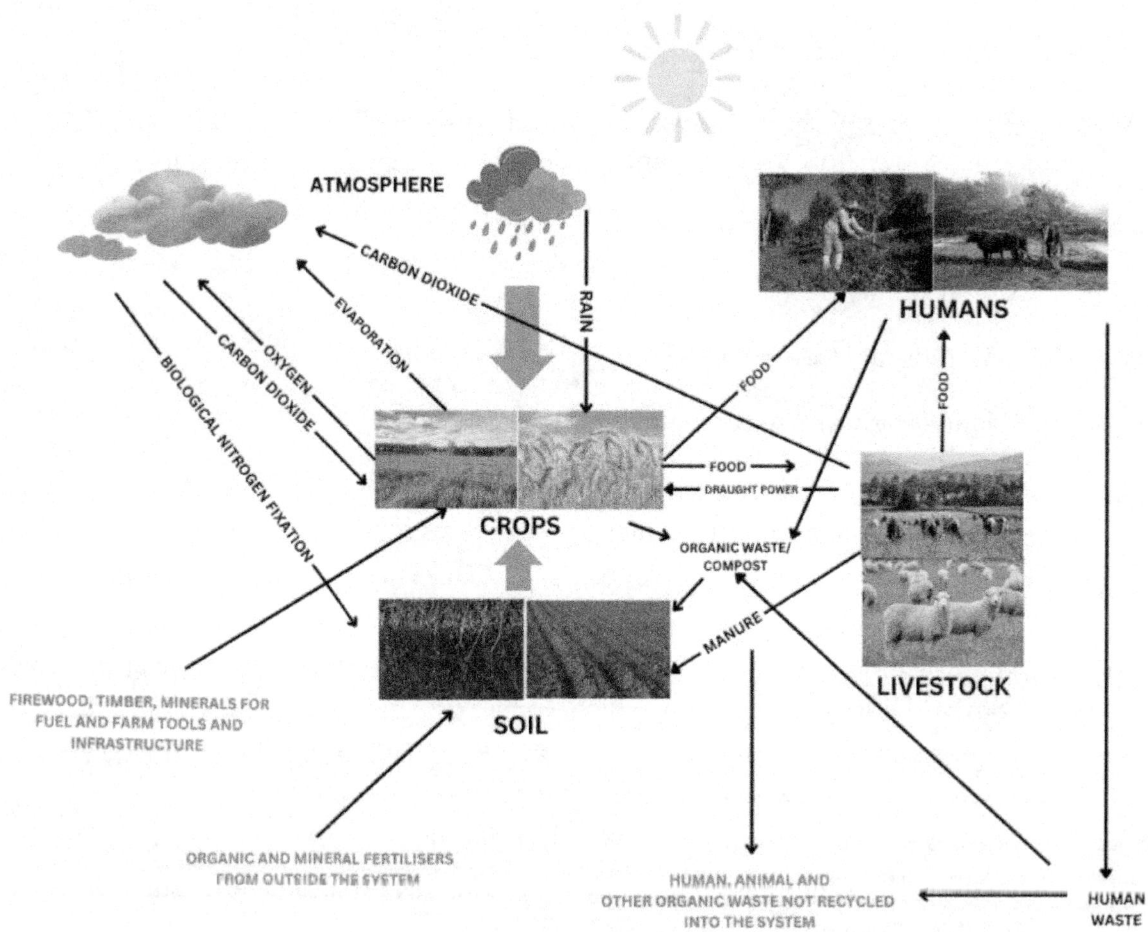

Figure 1

The traditional agricultural cycle is almost a closed system, where energy and nutrients are renewable by definition. There will always be some external inputs (e.g., fertilising inputs, such as wood ashes, seaweed, a few minerals, and other sources of organic waste) and all sorts of other resources that are required as part of the farm's infrastructure. Equally, there will be leaks, with some nutrients running off into waterways. Human waste does not necessarily all come back to fertilise arable land, but much of it does, directly or indirectly. Farmers in China and Korea, historically, were particularly adept at managing "night soil", which was carefully collected and found its way back onto productive land.

Contemporary Best Practice Organic Agriculture

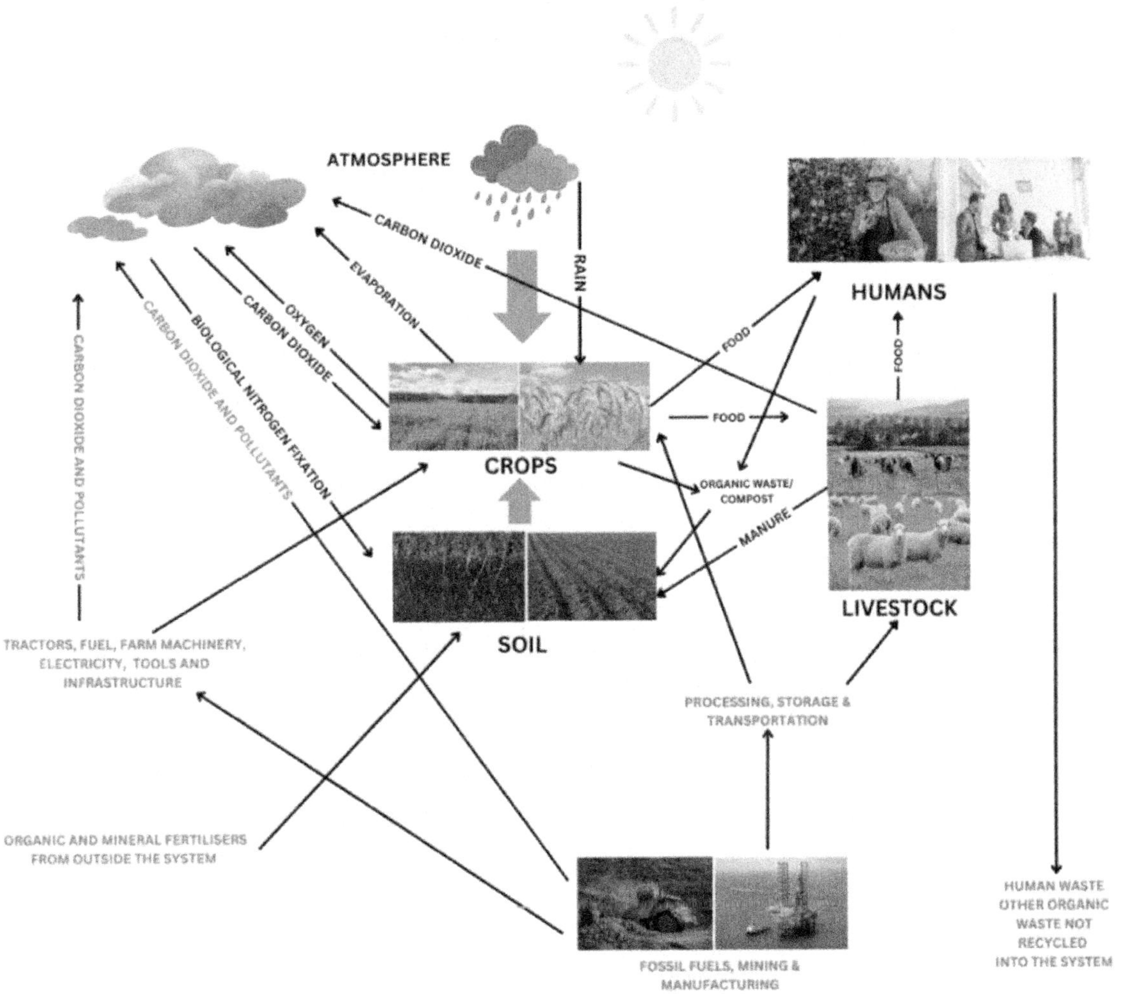

Figure 2

The fundamentals of a well-managed mixed organic farm are the same as those of any preindustrial farming system. It is a system where fertility is by and large maintained within the farm, through the careful cycling of nutrients and the balancing of growth and decay. This is a system where crops, pasture and livestock are intertwined and interdependent. The abundant solar energy captured by grass forms the backbone of the system and indirectly feeds the crops too. In an organic system, the continued process of biological nitrogen fixation and the build-up of fertility in temporary or perennial grassland, as well as additional organic inputs from outside the system, guarantee the maintenance of fertility. Livestock manure is a most precious and irreplaceable resource for the farmer, never to be wasted, requiring careful management.[148] The point here is that this is not an industrial "*inputs → process → outputs*" system. It is a self-sustaining, cyclical system, by and large, that runs on living organisms as opposed to chemistry.

There are inevitable leaks in the system, especially through all the actual food produced, which once eaten never returns as human manure. This is a problem, as sewage presents a double whammy: wasted fertility and a major source of pollution. There are successful examples of small-scale toilet composting projects, sewage treatment reed bed systems and other attempts to turn poop into clean compost, which should certainly be encouraged in rural areas and wherever else it may be possible. Unfortunately, none of this is viable for urban centres and for sewage works. Once human waste is mixed with water and other waste, things generally wrong: water-based sewage is inherently problematic and is probably a mistake to begin with, as convenient as it is.[149] Sewage sludge, which is the residue left over from wastewater treatment, is at times used in conventional agriculture but this is a dangerous practice since sewage sludge is full of toxins, heavy metals, and pollutants, which is why it is not allowed by the Soil Association.

There have been some small-scale attempts to extract clean, pure NPK from sewage sludge and wastewater treatment:[150] this is something we should arguably try to do on a large scale in the future. The technology is potentially there or thereabouts, but sadly there is no serious appetite for this kind of project. I would suggest that instead of wasting time and resources with "precision agriculture", so-called "sustainable intensification" and the latest GM crops, the scientific and industrial communities should be more worried about what to do about sewage. Does that mean that I am advocating the use of NPK, so contrary to organic doctrine? Not quite. Fertility should depend on biomass, organic matter and living soils. However, it is also worth noting that, realistically, even if we decided to go organic as a matter of national or global policy, we could not simply stop using NPK from one day to the next.

[148] Which means no slurry and no waste, for a start. Manure piles and manure spreading needs careful management, as manure can overheat and produce polluting gases, such as hydrogen sulfide and nitrous oxide. They have been omitted from the above as I am presuming "best practice", where emissions will be very limited.

[149] As lamented by Albert Howard, many decades ago.

[150] E.g., a company called Ostara manufactures fertiliser made from wastewater. I cannot comment on the details of their technology, nor can I vouch for its effectiveness, but it certainly looks interesting.

See: https://www.ostara.com/nutrient-recovery/nutrient-recovery-solutions/

We need to wean agriculture off the "free fertility model" over time, and a gradual withdrawal would be more realistic than sudden cold turkey. We should only use NPK from recycled waste and limited mining,[151] as opposed to fertiliser from the conventional Haber-Bosch process. And we should only use it as an additional, supplementary source of fertility to be blended with organic sources of fertility and added to arable land on a rotational basis, if at all, preferably on hungry crops that are not directly used for human consumption, such as fodder crops or fibre and oilseed crops.

There are also other important sources of fertility that provide essential minerals: bone meal and other animal waste, marine sources including seaweed and seafood waste, wood ash, woodchip and leaf litter, tea, coffee and cacao waste, and the biomass from all sorts of food and fibre processing. These are all valuable sources of fertility, which should all end up in fields and gardens as nutrients. As societies, we need to start using all available biomass and sources of organic waste systematically and turning it into compost and fertiliser, that can go back onto the fields.

Cattle at Abbey Home Farm, finding shade by the woodland. Cattle, pasture and woodland should be at the core of the agriculture of the future.

[151] Phosphate is yet another finite natural resource we are using up at alarming speed.

There is another major difference, in the energy cycle, between preindustrial and contemporary organic agriculture. Draught and manpower have been largely replaced by machinery and tractors, which are mostly powered by fossil fuels, which means that there are significant industrial inputs and outputs in the system, leading all the way to the oil well or iron ore mine. The storage, processing and transportation of food are also energy intensive. The ideal farm of the future might produce some of its power from high-tech watermills and windmills, from alcohol/biofuel made on site, and may reintroduce some horsepower for light work like harrowing and will generate its own heat through its own firewood or other clean, renewable sources of energy. Tractors should definitely be smaller and less energy intensive than the extravagant behemoths generally used on farms which, apart from being unnecessary, contribute to soil compaction. But for now, we must rely on fossil fuels to a significant degree, which are irreplaceable and extremely useful as sources of energy. Energy is the key word: we must still rely on fossil fuels for transportation fuel and electricity, but we should not be using oil and gas to manufacture agrochemicals and to manage soil fertility. It is wasteful, unnecessary and hugely damaging.

Contemporary Conventional Industrial Agriculture

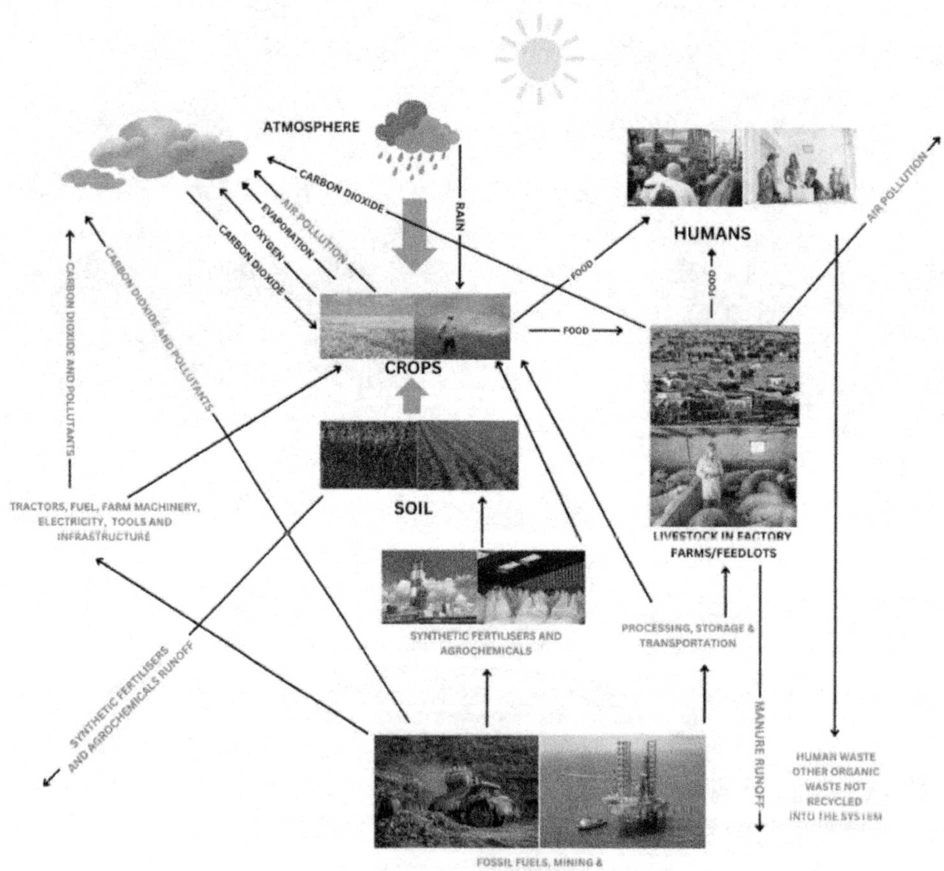

Figure 3

Conventional agriculture is entirely dependent on industrial inputs and consequently also produces a lot of industrial outputs and pollutants. Fertility is centred around synthetic fertilisers applied year on year, which inevitably leak into the waterways and the atmosphere. Livestock are generally almost completely segregated from crop production. The average wheat, barley and oilseed rape farmer in Britain is stockless and relies on synthetic fertilisers. He may sell his byproduct of straw to a livestock farmer, but that's about as far as integration goes. On the other hand, livestock farmers managing indoor dairies and beef fattening units or indoor pig and poultry factory farms are entirely reliant on purchased feed, made with the crops grown by the stockless farmers, and with crops from overseas like soya and maize, and have no use for manure, turning it into a hazardous waste product as opposed to the crucial requirement for fertility. There are also mixed industrial farms of course, and a stockless arable farmer may cooperate with his dairy farming neighbour and manure can find its way onto fields, but, overall, the practice of turning manure into huge amounts of slurry (liquidised fermenting poop, basically)[152] means that a lot of this spoilt, low-quality manure also ends up in waterways and polluting the atmosphere.

Overall, this is a very energy intensive system, starting from the oil and gas required to produce the feedstock for the chemical factory producing the fertiliser and agrochemicals, to the heat, electricity and water needed to maintain factory farms. The environmental costs are huge and include: the gradual death of our streams, rivers and lakes over the last few decades, marine dead zones, the loss of natural fertility in the soil, soil erosion, the decline of wildlife and biodiversity, air pollution, damaged landscapes and impoverished rural communities. Most importantly, the conventional farm is no longer an ecosystem as such, and fails to maintain the nutrient, water, and carbon cycles that a natural ecosystem should support.

Mechanisation and Automation

The combustion engine and industrial processing (for threshing, milling etc...) have revolutionised agriculture by replacing men and draught animals with machinery. This has been one of the primary drivers that has permitted mass urbanisation and a very low farming population. Whilst living and working conditions in the early days of the Industrial Revolution were arguably worse than those preceding it, especially in England, it would be wrong not to see the long-term benefits that mechanisation has brought our societies and it would be naïve to hanker for a return to an entirely pre-industrial society, where poverty and peasantry were often synonymous. One man and a combine harvester can do the work that would have taken several men and horses. With industrial machinery, harvested crops can also be processed *en masse,* cheaply and efficiently.

[152] As we just saw, mixing poop, of any kind, with water is a recipe for trouble. It may be unavoidable for sewage by now, but it is perfectly avoidable for livestock manure.

Harvest, António de Carvalho da Silva Porto, 1893. The traditional harvest has always involved very hard manual labour.

A break in Maremma with a farmer and a team of oxen, Giovanni Fattori, 1875. Draught power was the norm until the early-mid 20th century.

Having said that, we now have an agricultural labour force (spouses included!) of a mere 471,000[153] in Britain, out of a population over 67 million. We therefore have 0.7% of the population entrusted with looking after 69% of the UK landmass: we have gone from one extreme to the other. Whilst of course mechanisation and automation have eliminated a lot of drudgery and increased productivity per unit of labour, we have now gone too far. The demise of traditional mixed farming, the loss of crop and livestock diversity, and the near disappearance of the craftsmanship of artisanal manufacturers have led to the elimination of highly skilled jobs and are undermining our ability to produce healthy food. In their place, we have a relatively shrouded workforce doing precarious and dehumanising work, in factory farms and industrial slaughterhouses, and farmers struggling to make a living growing industrial monocultures on thousands of acres.

The land cannot be looked after properly by so few, often unskilled men. There must be a middle ground somewhere.

Monoculture

The industrialisation of agriculture has led to a simplification of the farming process and to a gradual dismantlement of its complexity and diversity. The artificial fertility of chemical fertilisers, and the crop "protection" provided by agrochemicals, have permitted a focus on fewer staple crops grown as monocultures. Crop rotations, green manures, cover crops, localised crop varieties, folding of livestock on arable fields: all these practices are no longer the norm. Across the UK, 75.1% of land planted with arable crops is dedicated to just three crops: wheat (41.1%), barley (25.1%) and oilseed rape (8.9%).[154] Irrespective of county or soil type, arable production is largely focused on these three crops and dependent on agrochemical inputs for its fertility, pest, weed and disease management. Crops are grown almost continuously or in limited strict rotations based around two or three of these crops.

Moreover, individual crops such as wheat are grown as isolated single hybrid varieties, unrecognisable from the wheats of a century ago. The hybrids created during the so-called Green Revolution, from the 1960s onwards, unlike the early hybrids of Nazareno Strampelli, are specifically designed to be grown as chemically dependent monocultures. An indicative feature of this design is plant height: modern wheat hybrids are very short dwarf varieties, often barely reaching knee height when fully grown. Breeders have focused all their efforts on seed allocation, at the cost of stalk height and development. Armed with herbicides and no longer really needing straw as livestock feed, the average wheat grower does not need a tall, sturdy wheat plant. An early hybrid like the aforementioned Senatore Cappelli, on the

[153] Agriculture in the United Kingdom 2022, pages 25-26.

[154] Ibidem

other hand, created in 1915 and still organically grown in parts of Italy,[155] will grow up to 6 feet tall and will actually overgrow and lodge[156] if fed with artificial nitrogen fertiliser. Given its height, it can co-exist with weeds, grow without herbicide applications and provide a vast yield of very palatable straw fodder.[157]

A consequence of the monocultural approach is that the outputs of agriculture are very limited: cheap grains and unpalatable commodities that are destined to be used as industrial feedstock, for ultra-processed foods and animal feeds. The diversity of choice in the supermarkets is somewhat illusory, given the fact that most food can be traced back to a few monocultures.

More Quantity, Less Quality

The efficiency of industrial agriculture allows for the mass production of a narrow set of traded and often subsidised[158] commodities and the elimination of almost all other crops. Historically, a basic staple like wheat was a precious, expensive resource. Annual grains are labour-intensive, both on the field and off the field, given what it takes to transform an ear of corn into flour and bread. Less than a century ago, a kilo of wheat flour could be swapped for ten kilos of chestnut flour in Tuscany.[159] In Puglia, it was common for the poorest of landless farmers to collect the partially burnt wheat grains left on fields after the stubbles had been burnt.[160] Peasant diets around the world generally revolved around some staple grain or other, but scarcity was always a threat. Bread was revered (not coincidentally bread was in our daily prayers: "Give us this day our daily bread"), as was rice in the Far East. The Korean word for rice, *bap,* is also used to refer to food in general. Maize was equally valued in the Americas and continues to be a major global staple, albeit most of it is now grown for livestock.

There can be no doubt, as discussed in the previous chapter, that the productivity per acre of single crops, from wheat to maize and potatoes, have significantly increased over the last century, as the apologists for industrial agriculture keep reminding us. Meat production has also exponentially increased, thanks to the feeding of these industrial crops to animals. However, as we saw, the historical poverty of peasantry should not be confused with the

[155] Some of the very best pasta manufactured in Italy is made with this wheat.

[156] Lodging: fall over.

[157] Farmers from Puglia who sold me this wonderful wheat have told me that horses generally prefer the Senatore Cappelli straw to most food, including hay.

[158] In the United States, the major industrial monoculture crops (corn, soya, cotton, wheat) are subsidised, with no real benefit to farmers, who barely make ends meet even with the subsidies.

[159] As recalled by the great and erudite food writer Beppe Bigazzi (1933-2019).

[160] Known as "grano arso".

ability of the very best modern mixed organic farms to potentially produce impressive amounts of total food per acre, which can compare relatively well with monocultural production. Furthermore, the productive gains in staple crop production have been accompanied by a marked decrease in both quality, nutritional value and taste, whether we are talking about wheat, tomatoes or chickens. It is for this reason that it is now possible to be both overeating and be malnourished. Nature does not really tolerate short cuts, it seems. Impoverished soils can only give rise to malnourished plants, that need pesticides and fungicides to avoid succumbing to pests and disease. In turn, these crops become the food of unhealthy animals living in unnatural conditions. As concluded in the last chapter, the best of industrial technology needs to be integrated within "organic and beyond organic" principles, so that we can balance quantity and quality.

From Whole Foods to Processed Foods

A corollary of the quantity vs quality conundrum is the fact that industrial technology has allowed ever more intricate processing of the raw products of agriculture. The steps between grain harvest and bread are complex and labour intensive and, from the 19th century onwards, they were revolutionised by the invention of the steam powered roller to grind grain. This allowed the replacement of wind, water or animal drawn stone mills and the ability to produce longer lasting, very refined white flour. White flour was a rarity until then, which only the wealthy could consume on a regular basis. The new technology permitted the cheap manufacture of refined flours, sugars, oils and led to fast and profound dietary changes, especially for the working classes. In and of itself, the wider availability of refined flour and sugar, as maligned as they are now, should not be seen as a negative. The daily inclusion of more palatable and flexible ingredients like white flour and sugar, crucial to the manufacture of many breads, crackers, biscuits, cakes, pastries and all sorts of desserts, can, in the right circumstances, be an enrichment to a diet and to a culinary culture. However, as the rice and beriberi experiment demonstrated, the refining of grains leads to a loss of essential nutrients. The adoption of a diet heavily reliant on highly refined grains and sugar, with the exclusion of many whole foods, is clearly detrimental to nutrition and health, as recent history has amply demonstrated. To compound the problem, since farm animals are also fed with unnatural and impoverished high calorie diets, the increased consumption of meat, dairy and eggs, which in itself was a very good thing for populations that, more often than not, only ever saw meat on a Sunday, has been accompanied by a host of additional health problems.

From the post-war period onwards, food processing and food engineering technology has progressed from industrial refining and gone all the way down to the molecular level, allowing for the manufacture of artificial foods and substances unrecognisable from their source, as well as an array of artificial additives, supplements and flavours. From margarine, high fructose corn syrup and fortified breakfast cereals to chicken McNuggets and flavoured crisps, we are surrounded by food items that could never possibly be reproduced at home from raw ingredients, involve processes that could only be carried out in a factory and include ingredients that are unrecognisable and unpronounceable to the layman. In a nutshell: *ultra-processed* food. This is the main reason why those in the alternative food and agriculture movement generally oppose "processed foods" and opt for "whole foods". This is an important distinction that needs clarification, as we do not want to confuse processing with ultra-processing, as the difference between processed food and ultra-processed food is one of *kind*, not of *degree*.

In the wake of the increasing obscurity and hazards of many contemporary processed food, it makes perfect sense to yearn for simple, recognisable whole foods (tomatoes, apples, rice, potatoes, milk, eggs etc...) that we can source with care and then cook, process and eat as we wish. Indeed, our domestic diets should revolve around the cookery of whole foods: more on this later. This does not mean that all processed foods are bad per se, in fact quite the opposite. We need to draw a very clear distinction between processed foods and ultra-processed foods. The best cheeses and pastas in the world, the best vegetable oils, jams and wines are all *processed* foods, by definition, that can be produced in a factory. The food historian Rachel Laudan, in her attack on the "culinary Luddite" brigade, especially the Slow Food movement, declares that *"for our ancestors, natural was something quite nasty. Natural often tasted bad", "was indigestible"* and *"unreliable"*.[161] She also reminds us of a number of truisms that very few of us have ever questioned, such as the fact that *"to make food tasty, safe, digestible and healthy, our forebears bred, ground, soaked, leached, curdled, fermented, and cooked naturally occurring plants and animals"*.[162] We can't argue with that. Indeed, even hunter gatherers, who do not cultivate grains and other crops that necessitate extensive processing and generally do not ferment, preserve and store food like agricultural people, generally cook the various plants and animals obtained from the wild, which are often inedible when eaten raw. The only fringe movement that has ever questioned the wisdom of all these simple facts about human diet and culture is the so called "raw foodism" movement, including its "raw vegan" wing and fruitarian sub-sect.

So where does the confusion come from? It mostly comes, as we saw in Chapter 2, from a misuse of the word "natural" and from an inability to make qualitative distinctions between different types of processing, which is not surprising given Laudan's praise of McDonald's. "Raw" and "natural" are not at all synonymous, as we saw earlier. A raw chicken, freshly

[161] https://www.jacobinmag.com/2015/05/slow-food-artisanal-natural-preservatives/

[162] Ibidem

butchered, is only as natural as its life story. A raw tomato is only as natural as the methods used to cultivate it. Whether it is eaten raw, cooked or made into tomato paste at a factory is neither here nor there. Domesticated and preserved is not unnatural, either. Once fresh milk from a domestic cow is turned into cheese, it does not suddenly become an "unnatural" product. Ironically, in her attack on the culinary Luddites *extraordinaire* of the Slow Food movement, Laudan laments their excessive emphasis on cheese, cold cuts and wine.[163] And yet, these are all processed, preserved products which, supposedly, according to Laudan, the culinary Luddites of the Slow Food movement should oppose as an act of faith. What both the detractors of industrial food and culinary Luddism should focus on, in my view, is the fact that the only issue we should concern ourselves with, when it comes to processing, are the qualitative differences between processing methods and their resulting products.

Of course, what constitutes "high" or "low" quality cannot be legislated upon and anybody can claim their product is of high quality: these are self-validated, self-certified subjective statements. However, if there is anything you can take away from this book, it is the idea that quality is not a subjective, relative value, but an objective reality, one which whilst impossible to identify quantitively, like a nutrient, is no less real and identifiable through reasoning, understanding, observation, and enquiry. The kind of naïve relativism so popular in all aspects of contemporary culture[164] leads supposedly intelligent people, including decorated professors, to make the following silly statements:

> *Vincent Marks, Emeritus Professor of Clinical Biochemistry at the University of Surrey and co-editor of a new book titled Panic Nation: Unpicking the Myths We're Told About Food and Health, goes so far as to claim that there is no such thing as junk food.*
>
> *"Junk food is an oxymoron," he says. "Food is either good - that is, it is enjoyable to eat and will sustain life - or it is good food that has gone bad, meaning that it has deteriorated and gone off.*
>
> *"To label a food as 'junk' is just another way of saying, 'I disapprove of it.' There are bad diets - that is, bad mixtures and quantities of food - but there are no 'bad foods' except those that have become bad through contamination or deterioration."*

[163] http://www.rachellaudan.com/wp-content/uploads/2011/12/Slow-Food.pdf

[164] Think of how this idea is now enshrined in mainstream art criticism and aesthetics: *"Something is art if I say it's art!"* say the followers of Marcel Duchamp who, one installation and unmade bed at the time, have managed to turn contemporary art into a pathetic and tawdry caricature of serious art... More on this in Chapter 8.

> *Professor Marks says that all foods - whether the dreaded twizzler or a freshly picked apple - are just combinations of protein, fat and carbohydrates, and our bodies will take from them what we need and get rid of the rest."*[165]

In other words: the Professor endorses a relentless commitment to full on reductionist ideology and cultural relativism. Protein is protein, food is food, a chicken is just a chicken and so on… provided it has not gone off!

In a similar vein, Laudan also tells us that two global Italian favourites, namely pasta and tomato sauce, are relatively new industrial products. She reminds us of the fact that in *"the first half of the twentieth century, Italians embraced factory-made pasta and canned tomatoes."*[166] Ergo, she implies, industrial agriculture and processed food are good things that no Slow Food Luddite can deny. Again, I must ask: which pasta and tomato products are we talking about? There are some truly awful pasta and canned tomato producers and some exceptional ones. Is it a good thing that pasta does not always need to be home made any more and that it can be shipped to countries around the world? Of course. Does that mean that all manufacturing processes are the same? Not at all. In Italy, before industrial canning, and up until the post-War period, when many people still tended vegetable gardens, it was common to cook the final tomato harvest at the end of the season in big pots and to carefully put the sauce in jars, to be used in winter. The fact that this is very rare now is not a good thing, but the fact that high quality preserved tomatoes can be produced and purchased cheaply and *en masse* is definitely a good thing.

To conclude: the power of technology in food processing is neither inherently good nor inherently bad. The devil is in the detail.

Urbanisation and Alienation

The mass migration from the countryside to the cities across Europe, that we are now seeing in other parts of the world, is a relatively recent phenomenon. It is estimated that for the first time in human history, there are now more people living in cities than outside of them.[167] For our purposes, the most relevant consequence of this dramatic change has been an increasing severance from food production and from any kind of meaningful interaction with animals and with the wild. Up until the 1950s, it was quite common for city people in Europe to grow some vegetables in the garden or tend to an allotment, or to have some fruit trees. In the past, council homes in England often had fruit trees planted in the gardens. My mother recalls how it was common for city dwelling, office working Romans to go on trips to the

[165] http://news.bbc.co.uk/1/hi/magazine/4304118.stm

[166] https://www.jacobinmag.com/2015/05/slow-food-artisanal-natural-preservatives/

[167] https://ourworldindata.org/urbanization#all-charts

country to pick wild asparagus and mint when in season or to go and forage for mushrooms in Autumn. Hunting and fishing were also more common and the average age of hunters and fishermen in Europe and North America is generally rising.[168] Fruit and vegetables bought at the market were in season and mostly domestic. It was common to prepare and preserve food for the winter. In other words, even in an industrial, mostly urban society, the natural ties to the seasons and to food production had not been completely lost. By and large, this is no longer the case.

There is no question that a lack of knowledge about the seasonal rhythms of the natural world, about the very basic foundations of where our food comes from, how it is made and whether it is any good or not is a very serious problem. The fact that the average child is more likely to play Fortnight than go fishing or climb trees, more likely to eat Hula Hoops and Monster Munch than carrots and pears and unlikely to have ever seen a cow or a pig from up close is fundamentally unhealthy: physically, mentally, emotionally, spiritually. In this respect, mass urbanisation has been a disaster, as there is no remedy or substitute for this kind of alienation in contemporary culture. The only solution, which is available to us all, is to engage with our food in a meaningful way: learn about the seasons, visit some good farms, frequent farmers' markets, plant fruit trees or a small vegetable patch, volunteer to pick fruit at an orchard, try foraging, fishing, stalking and shooting. A few of these things, especially for a young family, would have benefits that are far more important than dietary considerations alone.

The alienation from nature, its rhythms and life cycles are not confined to the cities. The tragedy of contemporary agriculture is that farmers themselves are detached from the essence of what they should be doing: working with soil, plants and animals to produce food, as opposed to commodities. A farmer, one would think, should not need to go to the supermarket very often and should be living off the land, at least in part. And yet, that is not necessarily the case for the average farmer anymore. I will briefly illustrate this point with an anecdote which I will never forget. The BBC used to run a show celebrating the British harvest and one episode featured the cereal harvest across the country.[169] On the show, arable farmers were followed throughout the season and got the opportunity to demonstrate what they did and how. The main protagonist on a particular episode was a farmer called Tom Bradshaw, who runs his family farm, Fletchers Farm, and a contract farming business, spread

[168] My Sardinian great-grandfather Filippi was a great hunter who travelled from Rome for epic seasonal hunting trips in the rough and wild interior of Sardinia, where mouflon and a diversity of game was hunted. My Tuscan great-grandfather, on my mother's side, used to hunt on horseback. It then skipped two generations, and I took up hunting in my mid-30s in spite of no recent family tradition. Mine is an uncommon example, however, as hunting and fishing are in decline.

[169] BBC: Harvest 2013, Cereals "The Seeds of Life".

across around 1,000 hectares in Essex. As it happens, he has recently been appointed as President of the National Farmers Union (NFU).[170]

Fletchers Farm was originally a mixed livestock and cereal farm. It was converted to just growing arable crops,[171]with no livestock, as have so many British farms. It mostly grows the aforementioned unholy trinity of agrochemical agriculture: wheat, barley and oilseed rape. Towards the end of the programme, following the harvest, presenter Gregg Wallace decided to have some bread baked with the wheat just harvested from the fields. Bradshaw's mother duly obliged and produced two loaves of bread. Bradshaw went on to taste the bread in front of the camera and commented that it was the first time he had ever had the chance to eat bread made from wheat produced on the farm.[172] In other words, this fourth-generation farmer was brought up on a farm, manages hundreds of hectares of land and somehow, up until Gregg Wallace suggested making some bread, had never eaten anything made from the crops he grows and fields he manages. Could there be a greater example of the alienation the industrial system creates? To what extent is a stockless farmer who drives tractors, sprays chemicals and produces commodities even a farmer in the real sense of the term? Is there much difference between this model of farming and industrial manufacturing?

There are still farmers who farm and farms where food is available. It was most refreshing, during my last visit to Abbey Home Farm, to eat bread baked with their organic wheat, sold at the farm shop and at the café, where the produce from the farm rules supreme. The fact that Abbey Home Farm is the exception, as opposed to the norm, should worry us all.

From Market to Marketing

The alienation between the average farmer and his craft is accompanied by a further alienation between the producer and the consumer. In a healthy food culture, the supply chain between grower and consumer should generally be relatively short and transparent, and most food should not need to be systematically branded and advertised, nor extravagantly packaged. The best farmers markets, butchers, fishmongers, bakeries, and cheesemongers tend to follow this simple, historically normal model. This was the kind of model I was fortunate enough to grow up with, and I am not exactly Methuselah. I barely have any recollection of supermarket aisles, nor was I continuously bombarded with cereal adverts and visions of Ronald McDonald. I still remember the greengrocer's powerful hands crushing walnuts in season, so that I could try one, and nose to tail bits of carcass at our excellent local butcher, which grabbed my curiosity. I remember the raw tortellini at the

[170] https://www.nfuonline.com/profiles/tom-bradshaw/

[171] https://www.bbc.co.uk/programmes/profiles/2xYcm4hjDGPKx7FL3F4bd7F/tom-bradshaw

[172] https://www.youtube.com/watch?v=S1s6yAEJqu8

gourmet grocery store before Christmas, and the smell of the fishmonger in the summer. That world is now mostly disappearing, as the food industry has industrialised, centralised and consolidated.

At a good farmers market, seasonal vegetables and fruits will still be laid out, with simple labels stating price and variety. The grower, or a person in their employment, will personally sell the product, will be able to answer questions about the product and as a customer, you are able to build a personal relationship with the producer. The producer is accountable to the customer, and the customer can make informed decisions. You will be able to pre-order certain products, you might ask when a certain product will be in season again, you may get tastings, small gifts and discounts, and you will be able to give feedback, positive or negative, directly to the provider of your food. Ultimately, the quality of products shines through, without the shroud of marketing and long, obscure supply chains. There is also a real cultural and social enrichment that comes with frequenting traditional retailers and growers: the opportunity for long-term acquaintances and relationships, a shared awareness of what nature provides and when, and the opportunity to eat lovely food whilst shopping, in a leisurely manner. Most importantly, the traditional market model is one dominated by whole foods and simple processed foods, which are primarily valued for their inherent qualities. These are genuine free markets, where *bona fide* goods are bought and sold between consenting adults, with relatively minimal government interference, apart from the burdensome and often absurd "health and safety" legislation imposed upon them.

None of this normal and wholesome economic activity requires enormous marketing budgets, multi-channel advertising campaigns and targeting children with substandard junk. Sadly, for a lot of consumers, the very idea of a relationship with one's grower and farmer will be obsolete and inconceivable, and food choices are generally mediated through marketers and advertisers. The major ultra-processed food brands sold in supermarkets and the various fast-food multinationals all spend billions of pounds in marketing and advertising per annum to ensure domination and control of the market. My dear reader: the whole point of mainstream marketing and advertising is not to inform consumers, but to induce the repeated purchase of low-quality products, which is why their material is intentionally devoid of any actual facts and reliable information. In principle, according to classical free market theory, buyers in a market should make informed, rational choices. It should be clear that this is the very opposite of what is involved in most consumer choices. It is with bitter irony that one notes that those who invoke free market forces the most, and continuously wax lyrical about Adam Smith, the "invisible hand" and so forth, tend to be corporate leaders, bankers and financiers, with their attendant hordes of lobbyists, politicians, and economists, all of whom are also the most likely to propagate and enforce the very system of irrational choice and market control that "cradle to grave" marketing and advertising inevitably fuels.

Agribusiness and fast-food giants, with their subsidies, tailor made legislation, stock listings, commodity trading desks and marketing budgets, are as far removed from the "free market", if the words are to mean anything, as any economic system can be.

Globalisation

"Globalisation" has become a nebulous and controversial concept, with either positive or negative connotations attached to it depending on who is using the term and for what purpose. One fact that is certain is that, whilst most diets around the world have historically always been "local" by default, some degree of global trade in foods and spices has been a constant since antiquity, especially for seafaring civilisations and, in a way, is nothing new. All sorts of products were transported around the Roman Empire and the people of Rome were likely to be eating bread made from grains shipped in from far flung corners of the Empire, such as Egypt, and the patricians would have enjoyed exotic spices from even further East. The movement of foodstuffs continued to be a constant feature of world history, with new trade routes developing and overlapping periods of domination changing hands as the centuries went by. From the maritime republics of Genoa and Venice to the Arab traders and the Silk Routes from China, through to the trade routes opened by the Age of Discovery and by the British Empire, food, is some form or other, was always a crucial factor in economic history and geopolitics.

Domesticated crops have also travelled far and wide. The most important recent exchange of foodstuffs and domesticates followed the discovery and colonisation of the Americas, which accelerated the expansion of global trade. Many of our European staples, such as potatoes, have only been grown here for a few centuries. There were no horses nor cattle,[173] nor indeed honeybees, in the Americas prior to the European settlement of the continent. Some Italian classics, from tomato sauce to maize polenta and potato gnocchi, were created after these crops were successfully introduced and cultivated on the Italian peninsula. The global trade in spices, sugar, tea, and coffee grew exponentially following the initial Columbian exchange, as did the cultural interchange of agricultural practices, ingredients and foodstuffs around the world. From the 19th century onwards, two major developments took place that sped up these processes: the advent of fossil-fuelled transport and machinery and the rapid cultivation of swathes of land across the British Empire and other white colonies, from the United States to Australia and South Africa. All sorts of staples, such as wheat and beef, were grown and raised extensively on these new lands and imported into Europe, and a whole range of "exotics", like cane sugar and tea, became commonplace,

[173] Both animals were first brought to the Americas by the Spanish. They also brought the first "cowboy culture", which is why rodeo, adopted by the Anglos, retains its Spanish name. It literally means "round-up", as in the rounding up or corralling of cattle.

relatively cheap goods for the masses. Novel and unique cuisines developed in many places across the world in a relatively short time[174] as a result of waves of migration and mixing of cultures and ingredients.

Over the course of the last century, this globalising process has accelerated even further, with modern transportation, including aviation, allowing faster than ever movement of foodstuffs, including fresh goods. There have been some undoubted advantages brought on by industrial transportation technology and its application to global trade. The relative ease of transport, storage and communications technology has made the risk of starvation following crop failure, natural disasters and food shortages far more manageable and unlikely. Most importantly, it has also permitted the cheap delivery of all sorts of goods, all the types of things we now take for granted, across the world. The truth is that we would not want to eat almost completely local, and the fact that we do not need to anymore is a good thing. But have we taken the "globalised diet" too far?

In Britain, where the process of delocalisation started earlier than in the rest of Europe given the imperial and capitalist-industrial model of the 19th century, we have a particularly long legacy of relying on our dominions for food and fertility. As a nation, we are not self-sufficient in food and no longer have any real seasonal variety: strawberries at Christmas and asparagus from Peru are now the norm. I would argue that it makes perfect sense, to anyone but mainstream establishment economists, for any given country to import what it cannot grow (e.g., mangoes or basmati in our case) and avoid importing whatever can be grown domestically. Some degree of self-sufficiency, or at least an effort to make the most of what the land can produce, should be the duty and pride of every country. Some of the outcomes of contemporary globalised food production really make no sense. For example, Britain is a country with over 33 million sheep,[175] more than any other European country, which imports tonnes of cheap lamb from New Zealand every year. Apart from the folly of shipping in lamb from the other side of the planet when we have a domestic excess, this import policy undermines, undercuts and sells out our sheep farmers and their communities. We have also ripped up so many of our orchards all across our country, destroying beautiful landscapes and losing native apple varieties, so that we can import apples from overseas, including from places as far as South Africa and New Zealand, not to mention Argentinian pears. In this age of self-serving and inconsistent free market dogmas, it is imperative to unequivocally state that, for products like lamb, apples and pears, protectionism may be the best and only option available.

[174] In places like New Orleans or Mauritius.

[175] Agriculture in the United Kingdom 2022, page 28.

The other aspect of globalisation that I will briefly touch upon is the damage wrought by the spread of inferior and unhealthy food cultures. I will refer back to my earlier comments: from that first McDonald's that opened in Piazza Di Spagna in Rome in 1986, the spread of junk food has continued unabated. Italy now has over 500 McDonald's restaurants, and this is a symbol of Italy's political and economic servitude and cultural surrender. Laudan argues that *"the McDonald's in Rome was, in fact, just one more in a long tradition of fast food joints reaching back to the days of the Caesars"*.[176] The only way in which this statement is true is in the fact that "fast food" broadly understood, has always existed. Rome has all sorts of wonderful fast food, from rice supplì, panini and gelato, to battered salt cod, sweet pastries and pizza al taglio. Whilst not as easy to find as they used to be, there are still good craftsmen who produce these fast foods with the right ingredients, methods and spirit. Laudan's statement is absurd in its extreme relativism and inability to make any qualitative distinctions between different types of fast food. Fast food *per se*, is perfectly legitimate. The fast food produced by the giants of industrial junk food is not.

Some degree of globalisation is both inevitable and welcome: as with almost everything discussed so far, it is the intent and practical application that makes all the difference.

IN A NUTSHELL

- Industrial agriculture and nutrition science are relatively recent: a lot of what seems normal now is historically abnormal.
- The gains and positives of these rapid developments come with serious drawbacks and negative consequences.
- The Enlightenment and the Industrial Revolution have been accompanied by profound ideological and cultural changes; many of which should be challenged and addressed.
- Science, industry and technology are only as good as their application.
- It should be possible to reform agriculture and food production and, at the same time, retain the progress and benefits of the last century.
- Urbanisation and globalisation are not bad *per se*.
- You do not have to be alienated from nature, its cycles and from food production.
- Not all fast food is the same: quality, or lack thereof, is an objective property of all food.

[176] https://www.jacobinmag.com/2015/05/slow-food-artisanal-natural-preservatives/

Sheep grazing at Bagnell Farm, Somerset. Why should we import lamb from New Zealand?

Chapter 5

THE PROBLEM WITH NUTRITIONISM

One of the main problems that afflicted my dear friend Alex, my original muse, was that he presumed that his poor eating habits, resulting corpulence and health issues were the result of some nutritional deficiency or nutritional excess of some kind or other and that the solution must lie in the latest advice of scientific authorities. He undertook fashionable dietary regimes: one day "carbs" were the problem and the "Ketogenic diet" the solution. Another day, he felt that it was crucial for him to undergo a thorough testing regime to search for "food intolerances and allergies", whatever that even means any more. Some foods were delicious but guilt-inducing, others were puritanically virtuous but punishing and undesirable. At the heart of this all too common, anxious confusion is a widespread faith in the inherent power and certainties of science and, more specifically, in nutrition science and its dietary offshoots. I will strongly suggest that, in the same way that faith in industrial agriculture is not a given, faith in what has been referred to as "nutritionism"[177] is neither obligatory nor wise.

Nutritionism

The contemporary incarnation of nutrition science, nutritionism, can be traced back to van Liebig's work on plants. As we saw, the discovery of the role and importance of NPK in plant nutrition gradually led to the conclusion that these basic nutrients were almost all that mattered in plant nutrition. It is important to note that this is quite a leap from one established fact (the importance of NPK) to an unfounded and speculative inference. It is certainly true that nitrogen, phosphorus, and potassium play a crucial role in plant nutrition, and it is also

[177] The term has been coined by Gyorgy Scrinis (See: G. Scrinis, 2013, Nutritionism: The Science and Politics of Dietary Advice) and popularised by Michael Pollan (see: M. Pollan, 2008, In Defence of Food).

true that we have been enriched by such a discovery. It does not follow that the absorption of NPK is all that really matters in plant nutrition.[178] It also does not follow, most crucially, that the source and method of absorption of these plant nutrients are not as important as the nutrients themselves.

Soil is a living thing and therefore not supposed to be a sterile medium through which artificial applications of nitrogen, phosphorus, magnesium, and a handful of other micronutrients are applied. No such thing exists in nature and plants are, as one would expect, perfectly adapted to living soils rather than to sterile soils. The main reason why plants grown in lifeless soils require default applications of pesticides and fungicides is that lifeless soils are not suitable for raising healthy plants that can look after themselves. The reductive "NPK mentality" applied to plants was gradually applied to animal and human nutrition, with the same results: poorly fed animals and humans are susceptible to weakness and disease. Sadly, almost all research focus in nutrition has focused on the animal and human versions of NPK: proteins, fats, vitamins etc... with no attention devoted to either the source of these nutrients nor to the context in which these nutrients are consumed. Again, whilst it is important and informative to know the difference between protein and Vitamin C, and the fact that we need both of these nutrients to grow and be healthy, it does not follow that all we need to do is to make sure that we absorb protein, Vitamin C and all the other basic macro and micronutrients. Just as with plant nutrients, both the source and method of absorption of these macro and micronutrients are as important as the nutrients themselves. Nutritionism, on the other hand, is an ideology based on the assumption that the scientifically identified nutrients in a food item determine its value and that the nutritional value of a food item is determined by the sum of all its individual nutrients, vitamins, and other components.

The tenets of nutritionism can be summarised as follows:

- A food item is best understood as the combination of its fundamental nutrients.
- A whole food (e.g., a tomato) is identical to the sum total of the nutrients that it contains, per 100g: *18 calories, 2.6g sugar, 1.2g fibre, 0.9g protein, 3.89g carbohydrates, 0.2g fat, 273mg potassium, 5mg sodium, 10mg calcium, 24mg phosphorus, 0.27mg iron, 0.114mg manganese, 11mg magnesium, 0.17mg zinc, 0.059mg copper, <14.6mg lycopene, <21mg Vitamin C, <1.1mg beta-carotene, <4.9mg phenolic acids, <0.3mg lutein, <1.3mg phytoene, <8.2mg flavonoids, <1.8mg Vitamin E, <1.2mg phytofluene.* [179]

[178] Agricultural scientists do of course recognise that a few other elements, like calcium and magnesium, are required by plants, but NPK are the three most important nutrients and are virtually considered to be synonymous with fertility by mainstream agronomists.

[179] https://www.britishtomatoes.co.uk/tomatoes-food-for-health

My very own tomatoes: just bundles of nutrients or something more complex, beautiful and irreducible?

- A given nutrient from one source (e.g., Vitamin C in a tablet) is identical to the very same nutrient from another source (e.g., Vitamin C in an orange), since the Vitamin C molecule ($C_6H_8O_6$) is always identical everywhere by definition.
- The source of a nutrient is not as important as the nutrient itself.
- Some nutrients are healthy, others are not, depending on the latest research.
- The exact quantity of each nutrient required per day for optimum health can be known, depending on the latest research.
- When deciding what to eat, nutrient content and its presumed effects on health and body weight should be the most important criteria.

The wide acceptance of these tenets explains:

- Why people come to believe that there is no difference between our Red Tractor and Abbey Home Farm chickens.
- Why we have now got to a point where people often refer to food as "carbs" or "protein", as opposed to their proper names.
- Why supplements, tablets, protein powders and food substitutes may seem like a great idea.
- Why people are more likely to read the calorific and nutritional content in food packaging rather than the list of ingredients, production method or country of origin.

- Why nutritional advice has changed so rapidly and drastically over time and continues to do so.
- Why certain nutrients are exalted, and others demonised.
- Why people may buy "low fat" and "gluten-free" products and prefer "white meat", believing that these choices will benefit their health.
- Why, incredibly, organic bacon, organic butter and organic jam from a company called Farm Drop were banned by Transport for London as "junk food" advertising in 2019,[180] and Kentucky Fried Chicken (presumably because chicken is low in fat?) is still, at the time of writing, currently advertised on the London Underground.[181]

Nutritionism and Reductionism: The Limits of Science

The key problem with nutritionism is its inherent reductionism. A reductionist approach is characterised by the belief that a complex phenomenon can be fully explained by identifying and analysing its basic components and mechanisms and that ultimately the phenomenon is identical to the sum total of such components and mechanisms. This approach has become all too prevalent in both science and philosophy over the last few decades. A reductionist approach to the human being, for example, would attempt to explain our existence in terms of the genome, of DNA and of other physical processes. It would attempt to explain our experience of the world in neurological terms: in terms of specific cerebral functions, of synapse activity or with reference to the agency of specific chemicals (e.g., dopamine, oxytocin, cortisol etc…), as well as so-called evolutionary psychology. The reductionist relies on a key presumption: that the whole is identical with the sum of its parts and that experience is determined by the different processes that gave rise to it. I would argue that, just as a person and his or her experience cannot be reduced to DNA structures and to neurones firing in the brain,[182] something as complex as soil or a plant or an animal cannot be reduced to a collection of nitrogen compounds, glucose, vitamins etc. Whilst our ability to observe the molecular structure of living things is extremely helpful in understanding their composition and function, it does not follow that the molecular analysis of a living thing fully reveals the living thing as it is in and of itself.

[180] https://www.standard.co.uk/news/health/bacon-butter-eggs-and-jam-banned-from-tube-ad-over-sadiq-khans-new-junk-food-rules-a4083016.html

[181] https://www.mylondon.news/news/transport/sadiq-khan-accused-making-ad-27496962

[182] Fashionable reductionists like Sam Harris, Steven Pinker, Patricia Churchland, Robert Sapolski and Yuval Noah Harari will argue that neurology and brain chemistry supposedly explain and demystify the human experience of free will, conscience and self-consciousness.

As a coherent whole, the living thing is more than the sum of its parts and of its functions. Wholeness is, by definition, irreducible. To see a tomato as a bundle of sugars, vitamins and antioxidants or a cow as a lump of animal protein and fats is to see tomatoes and cows in a very limited way. To see your uncle or daughter as an evolved biochemical automaton made up of DNA belonging to a mammalian primate species is to see people in a very limited way, as objects in the world as opposed to subjects, devoid of personhood. Most importantly, to define plants, animals and people in this way is not only limiting but also fundamentally *untrue*. Whilst a tomato, a cow and a person are physical beings characterised by biochemical processes, that is clearly not all there is to say about them. In fact, such a reductive analysis says very little about them and leaves many other avenues of knowledge and enquiry wide open. I am indebted to Roger Scruton for his powerful and apt analogy when discussing scientism and the humanities.[183] Imagine a scientific, reductionist analysis of a great painting, say a Caravaggio.

The Supper at Emmaus, 1601, Caravaggio.

[183] See: https://www.thenewatlantis.com/publications/scientism-in-the-arts-and-humanities

No doubt a scientific account of the painting would identify its date, through carbon dating, and would identify all the elements present in the paint, giving exact formulas for yellow, blue and so on. It could deduce the type of brush used and describe the material of the canvas. The analysis could also explain how light is refracted from the canvas, how it interacts with our eyes, and how our optical nerves are connected to our brains to create an image in our consciousness etc. Our scientist could also tell us, through the latest MRI imaging, which parts of our brains are activated when we observe the painting, and which chemicals are released in the process, depending on the emotions that arise in our consciousness.

All of this would be both true and interesting. However, such an analysis would at best be incomplete. Is that *all* that is knowable and true about the painting? Surely not. In fact, a scientific analysis of our painting would actually exclude its most important features and cannot tell us what the painting is about. It could say nothing about its meaning and purpose. It could not tell us anything about the intention and message of the artist. Most crucially, a scientific account would have nothing to say about the painting's artistic and *aesthetic value* and about our *aesthetic experience* when we look at it. To refer to optical nerves and neurones firing off in the brain whilst we look at the painting is simply to miss the point.

TO SUM UP: reductive science is very useful at throwing light upon certain aspects of reality, but not others. If we overlook those other aspects, we run the risk of obscuring our overall understanding rather than illuminating it. If we use it to identify the differences between tomatoes, cows, people and works of art, the process of reduction, taken to its logical conclusion, leads to basic misunderstandings and to dangerous conclusions, in all fields of knowledge, from anthropology and farming to art and nutrition.

Reductive tendencies have been exacerbated by the fact that, over time, science has also undergone a process of increasing compartmentalization. The nutrition scientist or dietician of today is highly likely not to know much of anything about agriculture, livestock husbandry, ecology or cookery *and it shows.* He or she is not only not expected to know anything about these crucial subjects but does not even need to study them to qualify in their discipline. A similar problem occurs with the other scientific disciplines connected to food. Chemical engineering, genetics, soil science, pharmacology, entomology and several other disciplines and sub-disciplines that are involved in agriculture and food science do not come together as a coherent whole. Scientists who spend their career studying fungal diseases in potatoes or manufacturing novel pesticides will have very limited exposure to agriculture and food production as a whole, and a very narrow understanding of the complexity of living systems. Reality, of course, is not subdivided into such neat categories and rigid subdivisions. Whilst we (humans) need to categorise and compartmentalize the observable world in order to make sense of it and to help us focus on specific problems, we must not forget that the world in and of itself is not identical to what we conceive through our interpretative tools of reduction.

Revisiting our Chickens

If a scientist decides to analyse and assess the value of a food item from a purely molecular point of view, he or she will gain an incomplete picture and therefore give wrong, or at the very least flawed, advice. Going back to our chickens: both our whole chickens will contain more or less 18.75% protein[184] and similar amounts of fats, minerals etc. From a reductionist, nutritionist point of view there is no substantial difference between our chickens and, since protein is considered to be a necessary nutrient, and since chicken meat is not red, both of our chickens are equally recommended by scientific and medical authorities. It is for this reason that, incredibly, the NHS nutritional guidelines draw no distinction whatsoever between different sources of chicken or of any other meat, for that matter. For our scientific and medical authorities, who most probably have never set foot on a farm or have any idea how to raise an animal, chicken is chicken, no matter where it comes from, how it is raised, in what conditions, how it is fed, how it is slaughtered, its breed, age and so on.

The only advice the NHS nutritional guidelines give is to ask the butcher to take the chicken's skin off,[185] which apparently is bad for us: a remarkably wasteful and stupid idea. Interestingly, the kind of advice given by reductionist nutritionists is flawed even by reductionist standards of enquiry. Further research into our chickens would actually reveal other significant differences in the accumulation of pesticides and other agrochemical toxins, as well as traces of pharmaceuticals and whichever other additives are blended in the feed of our chickens. There would also be differences in micronutrients, given that a chicken with access to the sun, herbs, grasses and insects will have benefited from their nutritional value. The same holds true of tomatoes, cows and any other source of food: whilst the percentage of the main macronutrients will be similar (18.75% protein etc...), their profile will be different (the fats in grass-fed beef are entirely different from those in grain-fed beef, for example) and quantities of micronutrients and toxins will differ in significant ways.

However, the key objection to reductionist analysis should not be framed in reductionist terms: it is not simply a case of analysing pesticide residues and missing micronutrients. I would like to suggest that a holistic approach to food is far more revealing and important than any reductionist account. Holism, which is the opposite of reductionism, is based on the idea that not all the properties of a phenomenon can be determined or explained by its

[184] https://fdc.nal.usda.gov/fdc-app.html#/food-details/768602/nutrients

[185] https://www.nhs.uk/live-well/eat-well/meat-nutrition/

component parts alone: the whole is greater than the sum of its parts and there are aspects of the whole that escape reductionist analysis. If we go back to our analogies, the fact that we cannot detect the aesthetic value of a painting or free will and conscience in a human being through a reductive lens does not indicate the absence of these phenomena, but merely that we are using the wrong lens. Therefore, when it comes to our chicken, our cow or our tomato plant, I would like to suggest that, taken as holistic entities, these entities have properties that cannot be identified with the same method and approach used to identify vitamins and antioxidants. These are living things which are connected to the complexities of soil, vegetation, climate and ecology that they inhabit, or not as the case may be, and cannot be fully understood through reductive analysis. In the case of animals, these are sentient beings, which can experience both contentment and misery. How can we measure such things in a microscope?

I would contend that our Abbey Home Farm chickens, or indeed any livestock that live as their nature intended, have a vitality that their abused counterparts do not have, irrespective of any nutritional analysis. There is a real difference between a flourishing, contented, inherently healthy animal and one that is neither flourishing, nor contented, nor healthy. The reductionist will no doubt dismiss notions of "vitality" and "flourishing" and "contentment" as non-existent and unidentifiable: irrational, sentimental hocus pocus with no scientific foundation. But there is nothing irrational in seeing the limits of reductionist analysis, in fact quite the opposite. If we search for these properties in DNA samples, we are simply looking in the wrong place. And yet we know, through reason and day-to-day experience, that these are real, observable phenomena.

Why You Don't Need Nutrition Scientists and Dieticians to Tell You What to Do

We can go as far as stating that, in order to *know*, with certainty, that our Abbey Home farm chicken is inherently superior to its unfortunate counterpart, we do need *any* nutritional data of any kind. Similarly, we do not need any lab work to understand that a tomato grown in healthy soil is inherently superior to one grown in sterile soil and sprayed with toxic chemicals. Even if we were unaware of the existence of proteins and vitamins, or completely unaware of the specific activity of glyphosate and organophosphates, we would still be obliged to make these sorts of qualitative distinctions. Nutritional data are nonetheless important and will *inform* our decisions, rather than *determine them*. The bottom line is that no scientific sanction, no NHS guideline, no visit to a dietician is required to draw sound qualitative distinctions between food items. This may seem a radical or dangerous position to take, but is it so extreme to believe that a cow eating grass all day, as its nature intended, will produce milk that is superior to that of its confined, mistreated, poorly fed counterpart? Do we really need an agronomist to confirm what should already be obvious?

What Alex and the rest of us need is a radical move away from the scientific and nutritionist orthodoxy of the day. The word *radical* comes from the Latin *radicalis*, which in turn comes from *radix*: root. The modern usage of *radical* is somewhat divorced from its original meaning, as it is often simply used to refer to extremism and excess. As should be clear by now, the only way to get to grips with the problems in our food culture is to identify their roots, which as we saw are best understood in the context of the agricultural and cultural revolution of the last two centuries. A lot of what I propose is radical only in so far as it gets to the root of the problem, refusing to accept contemporary assumptions. None of what is being proposed throughout this book is radical in the sense of being extremist or intentionally contrarian: in fact, quite the opposite. By and large, it is simply a call to normality, to common sense, to a sense of historical perspective[186] and to the independent use of reason. The key message here is that nobody needs any scientific qualifications, medical degrees, agricultural credentials, or dietary accreditations to make reasonable and sound nutritional and dietary decisions by themselves.

No Bad Nutrients

What does a rejection of nutritionism actually imply? The first radical tenet of "anti-nutritionism" is very simple: there is no inherently bad nutrient. All the basic macronutrients (proteins, carbohydrates, fats) and micronutrients (vitamins, minerals, antioxidants) that we have identified since the Chemical Revolution are fundamentally good for us. We would not have the physical ability to digest, absorb and gain benefits from all the various nutrients from plants and animals if we were not supposed to eat them. We now know a lot more about why a specific nutrient is required and what its activity in the body is, which is most helpful, but the fact that it is useful to the body is not in question. Interestingly, many of the traditional dietary practices around the world reflect what we now know about the activity of nutrients. For example, the classic combination of grains with pulses[187] happens to provide the full set of plant proteins, which neither grains nor legumes alone can provide in balanced quantities. Science has provided detailed information on how the nutritional benefit of combining

[186] To what Will Harris (2023) of White Oak Pastures refers to as *"radical traditional"*.

[187] This is a universal phenomenon amongst agricultural people: think of red bean rice in China (*hóngdòu fàn*), Japan (*sekihan*), and Korea (*patbap*), or tofu dishes served with rice or noodles, Mexican maize tortillas and tacos with beans, rice and lentil dal in India, Caribbean rice and peas, hummus and flat breads or mujaddara (lentils with rice or bulgur) in the Middle East, beans on toast in England. In Italy alone, a vast quantity of dishes is based on this grain/pulse combination, such as *orzo e fagioli* (barley and bean soup), *risi e bisi* (Venetian rice and peas), *pasta e ceci* (pasta and chickpea soup) and *pasta e lenticchie* (pasta and lentil soup).

grains and pulses actually works, but the benefit itself was already known and well established. It reminds me of the practice of planting and rotating pulse crops around the farm. Agricultural people have always known that pulses increase soil fertility but, as we saw earlier, it was not until the 19th century that the nitrogen-fixing property of pulses was understood. An even more interesting example is provided by maize. As we saw earlier, pellagra is a disease associated with the low niacin content in maize, which afflicted poor peasants subsisting on maize as their main food source.

Our Daily Bread (Panem nostrum quotidianum), 1894–95, Giuseppe Mentessi. A depiction of pellagra and suffering in a corn field, somewhere in Northern Italy.

However, in Central America, where maize cultivation originated, a practice called nixtamalization, which corrects the niacin deficiency, was traditionally practised. The process involves soaking and cooking the corn in an alkaline solution, usually limewater, washing it, and then hulling it. Therefore, whilst having no knowledge of such a thing as niacin, the ancestral cultivators of maize had worked out a way of rendering this wonderful crop more nutritious. The reason why pellagra was such a problem for the new maize eaters, whether in Alabama or Veneto, was that, having just adopted the crop, they were not aware of nixtamalization and its benefits. Therefore, yet again, science has provided a new model and language to understand what pre-scientific people already knew: maize is nutritionally deficient if untreated before eating. In the field of nutrition, science often seems to confirm and provide an explanation for what traditional knowledge already held to be true.

"Las Tortilleras": women making tortillas, 1836, Carl Nebel. The women are using nixtamalization to improve the nutritional value of the maize.

The same is true of cookery methods and of the traditional combination of specific ingredients. Food ingredients in isolation will have a different effect on the body and provide a different nutritional benefit than when combined with other specific ingredients. The common practice of combining meat with herbs and/or vegetables, for example, has the benefit of providing the dietary fibre and some of the micronutrients missing in meat and aiding the latter's digestion. For instance, rosemary has been proven to offset the potentially negative effects that charring and grilling red meat can have on health, by removing free radicals with their antioxidants.[188] Combining beef and lamb with rosemary is of course a very well-established culinary practice and tasty combination that precedes any research

[188] See, for example: University of Arkansas, Food Safety Consortium. "Spicing the meat also cuts the cancer risk, research suggests." ScienceDaily. www.sciencedaily.com/releases/2010/05/100518105801.htm

about its benefits. The research just confirms what we already knew. Similarly, the reason why cooking pasta *al dente* is a good idea is not just palatability, taste, and texture, but the fact that overcooking pasta breaks down its starches and raises its glycemic index, meaning that pasta will deliver less long-term energy to the body and more simple sugars instead.

Even the medicinal properties of many plants were anticipated by prescientific people.[189] For example, the humble beetroot was renowned for its energising and aphrodisiac properties by the Romans. We now know that beetroots contain nitric oxide, which stimulates bodily functions by improving oxygen utilisation. Nitric oxide opens up blood vessels, increasing blood flow and feeding more oxygen to working muscles.[190] The problem with the nutritionist approach is that, once the key molecule or nutrient is discovered, the assumption is made that if that nutrient is isolated and reproduced in artificial forms, it will have the same or similar benefit as it does when it is consumed through the food that contains it. Nitric oxide supplements, which are available on the market, will not have the same benefits of a fresh organic beetroot, in the same way that Vitamin C tablets are not comparable to oranges and kiwis. Furthermore, even when nutritionists recommend the food source itself rather than any supplement and tablets, they will generally not make any reference to the quality of the food source. Not all oranges and beetroots are the same.

The main benefit of reductionist nutrition is in addressing severe malnutrition. First of all, as we saw, it permitted a whole new diagnostic capability and rendered diseases like scurvy easy to treat and virtually disappear. There is no doubt that if someone has no Vitamin C in their diet, Vitamin C supplements from any artificial form will make a crucial difference. But day-to-day health and diet should not be based on worst-case scenarios or emergency intervention for the severely malnourished. All things being equal, it is nutritious food, rather than nutrients per se, that we should focus on when choosing what to eat and how. Overall, since all nutrients per se are, by definition, inherently good for us, the general rule of thumb is to eat a broad mixture of them, from the best possible natural sources, as I have been arguing thus far. The emphasis should be on the quality of the source of the nutrient (whether beetroot, beef or garlic) and on eating several different sources of such nutrients. We are clearly omnivores and, given the potential abundance of herbs, vegetables, fruits, grains, legumes, nuts and animal products at our disposal, we can be sure to obtain all our basic nutrients by eating balanced amounts of what nature can provide.

[189] That is not to say, of course, that pre-scientific also did not hold false beliefs about the properties of plants. But it is quite clear that a lot of more established cookery practices and beliefs about common ingredients have turned out to be well founded.

[190] Or other body parts… hence the beetroot's reputation as an aphrodisiac. Technically, it is NOT an aphrodisiac, as it does not stimulate sexual desire as such, but will ensure a better functioning of male genitalia given increased blood and oxygen flow.

More on what a "balanced" diet could look like in Section Three. Going back to our beetroots and oranges, the safest and most sensible way to benefit from the antioxidants, vitamins and minerals contained in fruits and vegetables, is to eat a wide array of them, in season. It is not a bad idea to be guided by colour: eating fruits and vegetables that come in a wide array of different colours (green spinach, orange carrot, purple beetroot, red tomato...) is a default guarantee of a wide range of nutrients, as different colours generally correspond to different nutrients. We now know that the orange in a carrot corresponds to beta carotene, but even without such technical expertise, it is a good idea to eat orange-coloured vegetables, as part of a "rainbow" approach to diet.

My carrots and Radicchio di Castelfranco at the allotment.

The only bad nutrients, to be avoided in all circumstances, are the artificial ones that do not exist in plants and animals. A particularly relevant example is the artificial "trans fats", otherwise known as hydrogenated fats, that occur when vegetable oils are chemically altered through hydrogenation in order to render them solid at room temperature, with a longer shelf life. The first most common product containing artificial trans fats was margarine, and trans fats can now be found in a broad range of processed junk food. A more hidden source of trans fats is found in the vegetable oils used in fast food chains to fry potatoes, chicken nuggets and other fried foods, as these oils are cheap and can be used to fry several times. Following decades in which natural animal fats were demonised and margarine promoted as a health product, it is now very well established, and undisputed, that trans fats are inherently unhealthy and have been linked with several diseases, especially cardiovascular, to the point that they are legally restricted in some countries.[191]

Fat is Beautiful?

Unlike artificial trans fats, the fats naturally contained in plants and animals are both essential and good for us. Fat provides storable energy and bodily warmth, is a structural component of the human body, is crucial for a wide range of biological functions and allows fat-soluble vitamins to be absorbed. The Fat Phobia that continues to afflict our culture and compels people to buy 0% Fat Yogurt can be traced back to two real problems. The first problem is that, in the post-war years, there was a marked increase in the production and consumption of cheap, low-quality industrial dairy and red meat products from the nascent industrial livestock farming system. Dairy and red meat were presumed to be very healthy by the medical establishment and were heavily promoted in the 1940s, 1950s and 1960s.

As waistlines expanded and the diseases of abundance, especially heart disease, increased, nutritionists, in one of the many volte-faces that we have witnessed since then, turned against saturated animal fats. By the time I was growing up in the 1980s and 1990s, "lean", "low fat" and "fat-free" products had flooded the market, and the general presumption was that saturated animal fats were fundamentally unhealthy. Chicken consumption, especially chicken breast, skyrocketed,[192] and "diet" food gradually became mainstream. The problem, as should be clear by now, was not animal fats, which have actually always been revered as the most precious outputs of a traditional farming system. Lard, butter, tallow, cream, bacon, and cheese are stores of energy and sustenance that, especially in the temperate and cold parts of the world, have always enriched diets and increased health. The problem of the last few decades has been the very low quality of the animal products that have been eaten in vast quantities since the industrialisation of livestock farming, together with all the other negative elements of the so-called "Western diet".

The second problem is the obvious increase in the average body size of the population. The simplest, but false, assumption made by the average person is that fatness is the end result of eating fat. This is a psychologically understandable presumption. However, it does not

[191] Denmark has banned all but trace amounts of trans-fats in food since 2003.

[192] Not coincidentally Chicken McNuggets were launched in 1983.

stand up to any observation and rational analysis. Globally and historically, there is no correlation whatsoever between obesity and high levels of animal fat in the diet. As we saw earlier, rates of animal fat vs vegetable fat consumption are generally determined by climate, ecology and geography. The same is true of lactose tolerance and dairy consumption, which is fundamental to cultures where herbivores like cows, sheep and camels have been domesticated and used for milk. There is however no correlation whatsoever between a history of livestock husbandry and dairy consumption and obesity or heart disease. The only correlation that is clear is that the arrival of the relatively new industrial food diet in any country and culture centred around refined flour, white sugar, low-grade vegetable oils and masses of low-quality animal products, including red meat and dairy, leads to obesity and related diseases.

The reason why nutritionists keep getting it wrong and will continue to get it wrong until they abandon nutritionist dogmas is simply because they do not make any qualitative distinctions between sources of fat, or any other nutrient. As waistlines keep expanding and as diet-related diseases continue to afflict an increasing percentage of the population, the rational thing to do would be to simply condemn the whole industrial food diet, irrespective of its fat, carbohydrate or sugar content. As it happens, having noticed how the low-fat hysteria of the 1980s, 1990s and early 2000s has not led to any public health improvements and benefits, nutritionists are now gradually backtracking on the animal fat issue: butter is back, apparently.[193] But they were wrong then, and they are wrong now since their sole focus is still on nutrients, not *sources of food.* They will continue to be wrong in the future, for as long as they continue to operate under the ideological constraints of nutritionism.

The steady and relentless increase in obesity in the West since the post-war period, now visible in countries where the industrial food diet arrived relatively recently,[194] has been accompanied by odd cultural trends around the issue of body size and weight. These trends have tended to change over time with the same sort of frequency and superficiality as nutritional fads and diets. The two phenomena are related, to an extent. Historically, and one only needs to look at Renaissance paintings, corpulence and some degree of body fat have consistently been considered both desirable and attractive, especially in women, who need to potentially bear and breastfeed children.

[193] Dear Reader, look up the TIME Magazine cover on the 26th of March 1984 issue, demonising cholesterol and animal fats, and the TIME Magazine cover on the 23rd of June 2014 issue, advising readers to "eat butter", and stating that scientists had been "wrong" to label "fat the enemy".

[194] This is a global and consistent phenomenon. Mexico, since the North American Free Trade Agreement (NAFTA) of 1994, has gradually succumbed to alarming levels of obesity and diabetes, as its market has been flooded by fast food chains, cheap meats and fizzy drinks. Obesity is already a serious problem in the Gulf states and is gradually becoming a problem in China. On many Polynesian islands, the adoption of the "Western diet" has led to a particularly rapid and massive increase in obesity and related illnesses.

The obvious reason for the desirability of physical abundance is that food scarcity and intense physical labour rendered most of the population emaciated or at the very least far from corpulent. Corporeal abundance and some body fat were generally the preserve of the wealthy and land-owning classes. Until not long ago, skinniness was not considered a physical virtue.[195] This held true until the 1950s and 1960s which, as we saw, was a time in which saturated animal fats were still deemed acceptable. The model Twiggy, in the swinging 60s, was the first thin supermodel and was the exception rather than the norm. A quick glance at the sex symbols and great beauties of this period will generally reveal a celebration of Venus-like feminine flourishing and shapely forms. As waistlines began to expand at unprecedented rates, fashion gradually started to demand a thin, super-skinny look, exemplified by runway models and magazine covers. This was especially the case from the early 1980s onwards when rates of obesity accelerated further. By the 1990s, the sensual abundance a' la Marilyn Monroe and Sophia Loren had unfortunately given way to the skinny look.

Venus of Urbino by Tiziano (1538).

[195] My Tuscan Great-Grandmother Clotilde used to refer to any baby she found beautiful as "bello e grasso": literally "beautiful and fat".

Kate Moss' 1990s skinny look coexisted alongside the skeletal look, with extreme emaciation and anorexia becoming very serious problems in the fashion and modelling businesses. Partly as a reaction to the horror of anorexia and its links to the fashion industry, the "body positivity" and "fat acceptance" movement has recently surfaced to prominence, affirming the legitimacy of all sorts of corpulence, especially in the female figure. Whilst partly well-intentioned,[196] this is, yet again, a movement born out of confusion that arrives at the wrong conclusions. Whilst all reasonable people will agree that the body images portrayed in fashion and visual media have contributed to a rise in insecurity, obsessive dieting and eating disorders, this does not mean we should embrace a naïve aesthetic and medical relativism. Body positivity is based on the nonsensical idea that "all bodies are good bodies" that no standards of normality are conceivable and that, somehow, fat is beautiful.[197]

It is certainly true that there is a (limited) spectrum of acceptable, healthy body weight and size and no single, ideal form. One's position along this spectrum may vary according to genetics, ethnicity, climate and choice. But it is not cruel, but in fact kind, to point out that being overweight[198] or obese is not a lifestyle option, nor compatible with health. Not all bodies are "good bodies", if by "good" we mean healthy, well proportioned, and fit. Health and fitness are not relative values. There are very few fat people who make it to old age and obesity, at any age, is associated with all sorts of health problems and chronic diseases. Obesity also leads to debilitating social, emotional and personal difficulties: sexual dysfunction, difficulties in movement and travel and the inability to play sports and be physically active. This does not mean that, as a society, we should not treat obesity with care and compassion, in the same way that we should treat any other serious health and social problem with care and compassion. But outright denial and absurd relativist claims about health do not help, in fact, quite the opposite. Both the importance of personal responsibility and the dangers of being overweight must be emphasised and made clear. Being overweight is not an unavoidable destiny, nor a desirable option, under any circumstance.

[196] The intention of marketing agencies and fashion brands that have embraced this movement is no doubt the same as those of previous campaigns: profit. At the individual level, undoubtedly many people are drawn to the movement out of a legitimate concern for body image issues, eating disorders etc.

[197] See a recent BBC report on "fat pride" (https://www.bbc.co.uk/news/resources/idt-sh/why_we_are_proud_of_our_fat_bodies) and Glamour's report on supposedly beautiful, severely overweight bodies:

https://www.glamour.com/gallery/adipositivity-project-photos

[198] The "fat activist" will reply: what weight is overweight? This is a disingenuous line of questioning used to justify an absurd relativism. Whilst there is no absolute cut off "overweight" point for a man or woman of a given height, there are basic medical guidelines and tests that can measure body fat and diagnose excess fat and/or obesity. In any case, without the need for medical tests, the use of our eyes and common sense will generally indicate whether someone is indeed overweight. I am confident any reader can spot someone who is overweight, even if they pretend not to. As for obesity, that is as obvious as the extreme emaciation of the anorexic.

TO SUM UP: confusion about dietary fat and about body fat are linked. The reality is relatively simple. Dietary fats, including saturated fats from animal products, are both desirable and healthy, provided they are from the right sources and not eaten in gluttonous quantities. On the other hand, excess body fat, just like the absence of body fat, is to be strictly avoided: your health depends on it.

All the Colours of Meat: The White Meat Distraction

My schoolmate Ruben, who was a year above me, went on to study medicine upon leaving school. He became a GP, working in the NHS, before setting up his own private practice. One evening, in our mid-late 20s, at our friend William's house,[199] the subject of chicken came up. Whilst I cannot recall the context of the discussion, Ruben came up with the theory, which he presumed to be mere fact, that the "dark meat" in chicken legs was less healthy than the "white meat" in the chicken breast. He predictably dismissed any discussion about the difference between factory-farmed chickens and "happy" chickens. Chicken is chicken, after all. Given that NHS guidelines are consistent with this worldview, I should not have been surprised by Ruben's concerns about so-called dark meat: it is textbook advice. Nonetheless, the fact that medical professionals are dishing out this kind of advice explains the obtuse obsession with "red" meat, "white" meat and so on.

When it comes to meat, we ought to accept a simple principle: colour is not the issue, quality is the issue. In fact, just as with other foods, a diversity of colours, even within the same carcass, is highly likely to produce a far better diet. The reason why a chicken leg has a different colour from a chicken breast reflects the obvious fact that it is a different part of the carcass with a different function, different muscle type etc. Quality does not come into it. In cultures that are reliant on meat as the main food source, the consumption of every body part is the reason why health can be maintained, even in the absence of plant foods. The Inuit of Alaska, Greenland and other parts of the Arctic did not suffer from scurvy or other vitamin and mineral deficiencies for the simple reason that they ate every part of the animal, from deep purple raw livers to the liquid inside the eyeballs. The explorer Vilhjalmur Stefansson, who lived with the Inuits for months on end,[200] found that, in spite of being born and raised in a plant-eating farming culture like the rest of us, he could adapt and thrive on the Inuit diet precisely because he learnt to consume the whole carcass of land animals and whole fish.

[199] Will was the most committed Coca-Cola addict I ever met. He famously stated that Coca-Cola and toilet paper were the two most important shopping items. Sadly, to my disappointment, he now drinks Coke Zero.

[200] I recommend his "Hunters of the Great North", published in 1923.

This extreme example should not be understood as a prescription for a pure carnivore diet, but merely as an example to highlight the fact that diversity of meats, textures and carcass parts is the best possible deal for us. The obsession with red versus white meat, much like the obsession with singular nutrients, distracts us from what really matters: the health and provenance of the animals we consume, irrespective of species and meat colour. Colour is only an indication of quality when the same cuts of meat from the same species of animal are compared. If you compare pork chops from different pigs, raised in different ways, there will be a colour difference. Factory-farmed pork tends to be of a lighter, pinker, greyer, pallid colour and the fat tends to be thinner and less dense. Outdoor-raised pigs, especially heritage breeds, produce darker, redder, shinier meat, and thicker, denser fats.

These carnivorous considerations should neatly prepare us for the next chapter, where a growing phenomenon is critically examined: veganism.

Sugar Phobia

The nutritionist backtracking on saturated animal fats has been accompanied by the search for a new culprit to explain all the problems associated with the industrial food diet. Sugar is the new fat: the latest nutrient to be demonised as the source of our ills. Gary Taubes, one of the high priests of the new campaign against sugar introduces his book by declaring that his goal is to *"present the case against sugar - both sucrose and high-fructose corn syrup - as the principal cause of the chronic diseases that are most likely to kill us, or at least accelerate our demise, in the twenty-first century"*.[201] Taubes' investigations also claim to reveal the sugar industry's record in funding scientific research to promote sugary products and the anti-fat agenda.[202] A lot of what Taubes and anti-sugar campaigners claim is absolutely correct: the huge amounts of cheap sugar and high-fructose corn syrup (which is a junk product derived from the processing of industrial maize) in a lot of our food is highly damaging and is a major contributor to obesity, diabetes and other diseases. The problem with the anti-sugar campaign is that it ignores two fundamental caveats.

The first problem is that, whilst refined white sugar and high-fructose corn syrup are two of the main negative components of the modern diet, they are merely two of several negative components. The enormous amounts of cheap animal products do as much if not more

[201] G. Taubes, 2016, The Case Against Sugar, Author's Note

[202] Taubes however seems to ignore that the meat and dairy industries have equally done their best to fund research to promote their products and demonise carbohydrates and sugar. The bottom line is that most industry funded research concludes whatever its backers need it conclude. This is yet another reason to be sceptical about a lot of nutrition science, with its competing agendas and sources of funding.

damage to our health and are directly implicated with many of the diseases of modernity. If we give up Coca-Cola, Ben and Jerry's ice cream, Haribo sweets, Mars bars, Kit Kats, Oreo biscuits and whichever other comparable sugary horror we are consuming daily, we will be better off without a doubt. However, if we are still piling in cheeseburgers,[203] chicken nuggets, eggs, bacon, sausages and steaks made from factory-farmed animals and processed with the usual host of vegetable oils, soya, fillers and additives typically found in the industrial food chain, we are still eating very badly and will still suffer from many of the typical afflictions of the so-called Western diet. We would likely not suffer from diabetes and obesity to the same degree, but we would still be eating a diet likely to lead to heart disease, cancer and several other preventable illnesses. It will also be disastrous for farm animals and the environment, an issue that Taubes does not seem to consider.

The second problem, at the risk of repeating the same concept *ad nauseam*, is the presumption that all "sugar" is the same. Just like the presumption that "chicken is chicken" is wrong, "sugar" is not some uniform demonic substance that can be universally condemned, as virtually all food writers, nutritionists, and celebrity doctors seem to do. Professor Tim Spector, author of a recent guide to "The New Science of Eating Well",[204] in spite of his clear opposition to artificial sweeteners, nonetheless condemns "sugar" in virtually all its forms, on account of the fact that, ultimately, all sugar causes blood sugar spikes. Spector warns:

"At least 250 names have been invented for food labels to dupe consumers into thinking they are buying healthier products free from added sugar - from dextrose and maltose to corn syrup, grape sugar, trehalose, fruit concentrate, malt sugar, invert sugar, granular sucrose, corn sweetener, fructose, fruit juice concentrates, glucose, raw sugar, sucrose, sugar syrup, cane crystals, cane sugar, crystalline fructose, evaporated cane juice, coconut blossom extract, and corn syrup solids, to the mysterious silan syrup.... But don't be fooled – they are all sugar, and any differences are trivial. Maple syrup and honey are often promoted as healthy options without any evidence other than our willingness to believe."[205]

The difference is of course very far from trivial, as we cannot lump basic processed sugars (e.g., evaporated cane juice or raw sugar), syrups (e.g., maple or agave syrup) and excellent whole foods (e.g., top-end raw honey) in the same category as out-and-out ultra-processed foods such as high-fructose corn syrup, glucose and common white table sugar (sucrose). They are completely different products and the fact that they all cause blood sugar spikes

[203] With fries or crisps on the side, which are after all sugar free...

[204] T. Spector, 2022, Food for Life: Your Guide to the New Science of Eating Well.

[205] Ibidem, page 336.

(which, incidentally, is not necessarily a problem) is no reason to dismiss them as "all sugar". In fairness, whilst retaining a fundamentally reductionist approach towards all "sugar", Spector, later in the same chapter, is slightly more sympathetic towards honey, at least. He recommends choosing *"good honey from your local beekeeper and enjoy it in small doses as one of nature's finest treats"*[206] and concludes by informing his readers that *"honey produces a similar effect on the body as table sugar, but it may help tickly coughs and hay fever thanks to its active ingredients"*.[207]

In any case, apart from the need to draw qualitative distinctions between sugar-based products, we must also not forget that the quality of the raw materials used to make these products, as should be clear by now, really matters. Presuming they are grown free from the usual agrochemical cocktail, the sugar cane and sugar beet plants, in and of themselves, are botanic and agricultural marvels and should be appreciated for their powers and bounties: we should be glad that they exist. Many plants contain high levels of sucrose,[208] but none more so than these plants. They are also the most productive crops on Earth, or thereabouts, producing a staggering amount of food per acre. Part of the negative perception of sugar comes from the fact that, historically, sugars are hard to come by in nature, leading many to conclude that the human body is not designed for high amounts of extracted, concentrated sugar. This theory has some credibility. In the wild, there are few sweet fruits and, apart from a few tree saps[209] and wild honey, there are no sources of concentrated sugar. Furthermore, natural sugars from these sources are generally made up of a mixture of sugars (fructose, glucose and sucrose) rather than sucrose alone. Since the advent of agriculture, honey intake increased, and sweet fruits and sugary vegetables were domesticated but nonetheless, there was nothing comparable to sugar from sugar cane and sugar beet available in the diet.

Sweetness was not readily available and was not an abundant part of the diet until relatively recently. It is believed that the sugar cane was first domesticated in Papa New Guinea and gradually spread throughout Asia, being cultivated and used in India, where sugar was probably first crystallised, and gradually spreading Westward into Persia. Throughout the Islamic Golden Age, both the cultivation and use of sugar[210] spread further West, including Sicily and Andalusia. But the first large-scale sugar cane plantations in the world and the first industrial sugar mills were only established in the Americas after European discovery and colonisation. It was only then that sugar cane became an important crop, gradually

[206] T. Spector, 2022, Food for Life: Your Guide to the New Science of Eating Well., page 345.

[207] Ibidem, page 362.

[208] Sucrose: fructose plus glucose.

[209] The natives of North America had maple syrup but no honey.

[210] The word sugar (*zucchero* in Italian, *azukar* in Spanish) can be traced back to the Arabic *sukkar* and Sanskrit *śárkarā*.

spreading across the Americas, as well as other European colonies around the world, such as Mauritius. Sugar beet cultivars and plantations were also developed in Europe and North America during the 18th and 19th centuries, with sugar mills being built to process the beet pulp.

Sugar as a food product became popular in Europe during the 18th century and became a mass-produced staple from the 19th century onwards, hugely accelerated by the tools and technologies of the Industrial Revolution. The sort of technology that permitted the mass manufacture of refined white flour was used for the mass manufacture of sugar. Therefore, there is no doubt that, given its relatively recent arrival, sugar as a staple food is a new input into our diets, that only goes back five or six generations for most of us. Does this mean that it is a negative addition to our diet? Not necessarily. After all, sugar cane and sugar beet are simply providing more of something that our bodies have painstakingly obtained from other sources before, but have always desired and readily recognise as food. We are perfectly designed to digest and gain energy from sugars, including sucrose, whether they come from sweet fruits, honey, maple syrup or sugar cane. As we saw earlier, a lot of foods increased in quantity and availability from the 19th century onwards. Tea, coffee and cocoa are also relatively recent introductions into our diets[211] and, unlike cane sugar, are completely different from anything we consumed before. And yet these have arguably enriched our diets rather than made them worse.

As ever, the problem with the sugar extracted from sugar cane and sugar beet can only be understood in terms of its provenance, quality and the amount in which it is consumed rather than with *sugar per se*. The cultivation methods of the sugar cane and the processing and manufacturing methods used to make sugar vary enormously, in the same way that the cultivation of cocoa, its processing and manufacture into its end products varies enormously. There is good sugar and bad sugar. There are good, sweet products and bad sweet products. The fact that the vast majority of products containing sugar on supermarket aisles are poor, unhealthy products does not imply that sugar per se is a problem. Provided that we avoid, as we should, the whole range of ultra-processed junk commonly found on our shelves, the amounts of refined white sugar in our diets will automatically plummet.

It makes no sense to equate the sugar found in a can of Pepsi with the sugar found in a really well homemade iced tea.[212] These are inherently different products: the first junk, the second a wholesome drink. It makes no sense to equate, say, Haribo sweets with confetti from Sulmona. Confetti, the traditional Italian confectionery used for special occasions should

[211] Which are usually paired with sugar in their preparation, especially cocoa.

[212] A personal favourite, made of four ingredients: strong organic Assam tea, rose petals, fresh organic lemon juice and the home-made syrup of organic raw cane sugar. Add slices of fresh peach in season for a touch of wonder.

contain only main two ingredients: Sicilian almonds and a thin layer of high-quality sugar. Some rice starch and arabica gum are also used in the process. They have been made with sugar in Sulmona since at least the 16th century. Most of the sweets in your average corner shop are made with a concoction of glucose syrup, white sugar, gelatine, dextrose, "flavourings", colours and other obscure ingredients. The cheap sugar, gelatine (made from the animal remains from factory farms) and mysterious flavourings are particularly worrisome.

Whilst it is certainly wise to avoid daily consumption of candy, mostly to salvage teeth, there is nothing inherently wrong with candy per se. It is absolutely legitimate and desirable, in spite of what Gary Taubes might think, for candy and sweets to be given as appropriate treats to children. A Happy Meal is not an appropriate treat, but a bag of confetti, a proper ice cream, a pastry filled with cream, cake with marzipan frosting and chocolates are all appropriate treats. The only thing that matters is quality and frequency.[213]

As I mention chocolate, it should be clear that it makes no sense to equate a Mars bar with high quality chocolate.[214] The fact that these are all sweet products containing sugar does not mean that they will have the same impact on our health and diets. From a nutritionist point of view, our two chocolate bars are largely comparable.

Mars Bar, per 100g: 448 calories, 17g fat (8.1g saturates) 69g carbohydrates (60g sugar), 4.5g protein, 0.4g salt.

Ingredients: Sugar, Glucose Syrup, Skimmed Milk Powder, Cocoa Butter, Cocoa Mass, Sunflower Oil, Whey Permeate (Milk), Palm Fat, Milk Fat, Fat-Reduced Cocoa Powder, Barley Malt Extract, Salt, Emulsifier (Soya Lecithin), Egg White Powder. Milk Chocolate contains Milk Solids 14% minimum.[215]

Alter Eco Milk Chocolate per 100g: 569 calories, 37g fat (23g saturates), 51g carbohydrates (50g sugar), 7.2% protein, 0.2g salt.

[213] Having said that, even frequency can be flexible. As a kid in Italy, we had ice cream every single day during the summer months, as well as pastry from the traditional *pasticceria* at times. But it was great ice cream, first of all, and the rest of my summer diet would have been dominated by loads of seasonal vegetables, herbs, fruits, bread, pasta (all dressed or cooked in olive oil) and, as we were right by the sea, fish and other seafood. We had a local farmer, whose bucolic farm we once visited, deliver eggs and the most astonishing fruit and vegetables every week. Today I would happily pay an exorbitant price for a basket of his figs or a bag of his gages. My sister and I were thin and healthy of course, in spite of the ice cream cures. Context is everything: sweet treats need to be understood in the context of an overall diet.

[214] I will use Alter Eco's excellent organic milk chocolate as an example: https://uk.altereco.com/milk-chocolate/

[215] https://www.marsbar.co.uk/products/chocolate-bar/mars-chocolate-snack-bars-multipack-4x394g

Ingredients: Organic cane sugar, organic cocoa butter, organic whole milk powder (20%), organic cocoa mass, organic skimmed milk powder. Cocoa: minimum 36%. 22% milk solids.[216]

Some nutritionists, from the anti-fat and calorie counting camp, would recommend the Mars bar as a better option given its lower calories and percentage of fat. Others, in the anti-sugar camp, would recommend the Alter Eco bar given its relatively lower sugar content. This is clearly completely misguided, as there are irreconcilable qualitative differences between the two products and only a fool would look at the nutritional label, as opposed to the ingredients label, to make sense of these products. In any case, by and large, both sets of nutritionists would not recommend chocolate bars at all, given the demonic presence of high calories, fats and sugar. It is this odd and unnecessary condemnation that has turned chocolate into a "guilty" pleasure. It should only be a guilty pleasure, if "guilty" is the right word, when overindulged perhaps. But a moderate consumption should be a positive and welcome addition to one's diet and one's life with no negative connotations. I say life, rather than just diet, because one of the assumptions of nutritionism that needs to be challenged, apart from the supposed reliability of its dietary advice, is the idea that when deciding what to eat, nutrient content and its presumed effects on health and body weight should be the single most important criteria. When it comes to food like chocolate, the pleasure and clear psychological benefits derived from its consumption are just as important. There is no need to introduce a state of nutritional anxiety and parental guilt to something as innocent and joyful as a kid eating a piece of chocolate, provided it is good chocolate.

The now prevalent sugar-phobic *reductio ad absurdum* leads to a further problem: if sugar content is presumed to be the main problem, sugarless alternatives and diet products containing artificial sweeteners are presumed to be superior. Once all sugar is lumped into the "unwanted" category, Diet Coke starts looking like a really smart idea. Indeed, as previously mentioned, if we were to follow NHS guidelines to the letter, we would feel justified in giving our children Coke Zero instead of organic apple juice. The NHS guidelines, after all, include an arbitrary concept known as "free sugars". This refers to additional sugars in the diet that are not derived from whole foods such as fruits, vegetables and milk. The problem is that everything else is considered "free sugar" and therefore bad:

[216] https://uk.altereco.com/milk-chocolate/

- *"Any sugars added to food or drinks. These include sugars in biscuits, chocolate, flavoured yoghurts, breakfast cereals and fizzy drinks".*
- *"Sugars in honey, syrups (such as maple, agave and golden), nectars (such as blossom), and unsweetened fruit juices, vegetable juices and smoothies. The sugars in these foods occur naturally but still count as free sugars."*[217]

Only a nutritionist could equate raw honey, white refined sugar, Pepsi and beetroot juice and place them in the same category. The only way to sustain such a belief is by insisting that "sugar is sugar"! Personally, I am occasionally fond of a banana milkshake in the morning. Sometimes I may just eat the bananas whole. It is hard to see how my bananas go from legitimate whole food to illegitimate free sugars, all in the one-minute blitz of a food processor. Similarly, I may squeeze oranges by hand and drink the juice, pulp and all: how do oranges become an unwanted "free sugar" product? The logic behind this belief is elucidated by the British Heart Foundation: the sugar in a fruit becomes "free" through juicing because the juicing action releases the sugars from the fruit's cells and break up the fibre.[218] It is for this reason that it is much easier to drink the juice of four oranges than to eat four oranges whole. The latter point is evidently true and simply suggests that, on the whole, we are better off eating fruits whole, rather than in the form of juices and smoothies, especially for the fibre content: this was quite obvious to begin with. It does not follow that freshly made fruit juices and smoothies are in any way inherently unhealthy or that their sugar is more harmful than it was before juicing and processing. At the very least, it is not comparable to the sugar in the vast array of fizzy drinks consumed daily across the country: freshly squeezed orange juice is not remotely comparable to Pepsi Cola. And yet, both the NHS and BHF insist, one should never drink more than a measly 150ml of unsweetened fruit juice and opt for sugar free soft drinks instead. If we were to follow their recommendations, we would feel obliged to drink organic apple juice in great moderation and feel free to drink Coke Zero at leisure.

Ultimately, the sugarless approach is just another form of nutritionism and, as such, is bound to lead into a whole range of other problems and contradictions. Taubes, in an interview, describes his diet, which is effectively a de facto Atkins or Ketogenic diet:[219]

"I eat eggs and bacon or sausage for breakfast every day. At lunch, I might have three quarters of a pound of hamburger with cheese, no bun. Dinner is a pound of steak or half a roast

[217] https://www.nhs.uk/live-well/eat-well/how-does-sugar-in-our-diet-affect-our-health/

[218] https://www.bhf.org.uk/informationsupport/heart-matters-magazine/nutrition/sugar-salt-and-fat/free-sugars

[219] The Atkins Diet was a popular low-carb and sugar diet proposed by Robert Atkins. See: https://uk.atkins.com

chicken or the largest piece of fish I can buy, and vegetables. You eat what you want until you're satiated–you just don't eat the things that will make you fat."

"The weight just dropped off. If I walked down the street, it was like you could see the pounds lying behind me on the sidewalk." [220]

I have no doubt that Taubes did lose weight and that if the average obese person ate Taubes' diet he or she would most likely lose weight. But weight loss cannot be the goal of a diet: the end does not justify the means. After all, there are many unhealthy ways to promote weight loss. Weight loss and stabilisation should be one of the effects, rather than the goal, of a healthy diet. And a diet of daily bacon (no doubt made with factory farmed pork smothered in nitrates and fried in low quality vegetable or animal fats) and tonnes of other animal products from factory farms cannot be a good idea.[221]

Carb Phobia

A corollary of sugar phobia is an irrational fear of foods containing carbohydrates. As previously mentioned, it has become common in our culture to refer to "carbs"[222] as a dietary item (as opposed to, say, pasta or rice or potatoes) and their avoidance is the theme of many diets and weight loss regimes. Carbs are generally presumed to be a major driver of weight gain and obesity and, consequently, demonised. I will simply repeat what applies to all nutrients: all whole foods containing carbohydrates, including complex carbohydrates, are perfectly healthy, suitable sources of nutrition for humans. Yet again, the only thing that matters are quality and quantity. As regards the former, not all bread is the same, not all pasta is created equal: you know the drill by now.[223] As regards quantity, however, and its relationship to body weight, there are some interesting nuances that are worth examining. Historically, for agricultural people across the world, grains and, to a lesser extent, tubers have been fundamental staples in their diets. Wheat, rice, maize, barley and other grains have been the most widely grown food staples since the advent of agriculture. As previously discussed, the issue of weight gain is historically novel: the average citizen, in any agricultural

[220] http://garytaubes.com/wp-content/uploads/2012/02/WWGF-Readers-Digest-feature-Feb-2011.pdf

[221] Taubes, nowhere in his missive against sugar ever discussed the origin and quality of the gargantuan quantities of animal foods he recommends ingesting

[222] Or indeed "carbs on carbs", as my delightful colleague Camilla described my Pasta e Fagioli (pasta and bean soup).

[223] Please see Chapters 10 and 11 for how to select "carb" rich foods like bread, rice and pasta. Preview: organic oats and potatoes are in; Monster Munch and Coco Pops are out.

civilisation, from the Far East all the way to Europe and the Americas, has generally had the opposite problem.

Food scarcity and a lack of body fat have been the historical norm for the masses, in spite of the fact that grains constituted the vast majority of their diets. The simple reason why the historical "high carb diet" of old produced thin people was that, very often, people didn't eat that much else. An over-reliance on grains or other starchy staples, which were at times scarce, and frequent shortages and absences of other nutritious foods, not to mention the frequency of hard physical labour, resulted in a thin population, with corpulence, as discussed, the preserve of the wealthy and owning classes. Therefore, we cannot conclude, from the historical record, whether there is a clear correlation between high carbohydrate consumption and weight gain and obesity, as other factors come into play: the percentage of grains/starches in the overall diet, what the rest of the diet consists of and the average rate of physical activity and calorific consumption. Since the 19th century, following the industrialisation of agriculture, three major changes have occurred:

- We consume more grains per capita, which are now less nutritious (in terms of micronutrients, not in terms of carbohydrates and calories) and are mostly very refined.
- We also, as we saw, consume a lot more other previously scarce foods, especially sugars and animal products.
- Mechanisation and urbanisation have led to less active, more sedentary lifestyles. We also do not need, since the widespread use of central heating, to expend that much energy keeping our bodies warm.

The above is a recipe for a population with increasing waistlines, as a quick glance around any town in Britain will quickly reveal. However, once historical factors are removed, it is still important to consider whether carbohydrates, as opposed to fats and proteins, do correlate to weight gain in a significant manner. The short answer to this question is that there does indeed seem to be a correlation between body weight and excessive consumption of carbohydrates. This has been known before carbohydrates or indeed any other nutrient had been identified or understood. In Leo Tolstoy's *Anna Karenina*, published in 1877, we are told of how Count Vronsky, a keen competitive equestrian, opted for steak and abstained from floury foods and desserts, in order to keep his weight down to acceptable levels for a racing jockey.[224] I am confident that Tolstoy, great man as he was, would have had no

[224] To her credit my dear sister Ilaria, who is far less interested in the intricacies of the human diet than myself, has successfully followed three basic common-sense rules to lose weight post pregnancy: no bread, no desserts, no snacks. Remarkably like Count Vronsky's regime.

understanding of carbohydrates, the biology of fat formation and human physiology in general.

He was merely passing down common knowledge. I sincerely doubt he had read William Banting's *Letter on Corpulence*, published in 1863.[225] Banting, an obese undertaker, published his personal account of successfully losing weight by following a diet in which he generally abstained from sugar, beer, potatoes, and starchy vegetables, as well as milk and butter. He mainly subsisted on meat, fish, non-starchy vegetables, cooked fruit, and very moderate amounts of bread. There were many odd things in his diet, such as excluding salmon, herrings and eel as permissible fish, or cooking fruit before eating it. He also drank wine, whilst abstaining from beer, and indulged in a "nightcap" before bed. Irrespective, the main gist of his diet was the exclusion of what are now referred to as "carbs". As we saw earlier, Justus von Liebig had also observed how pigs could be fattened on potatoes that were rich in starch and could be converted into fat. Farmers have indeed always demonstrated this awareness in raising livestock: animals have been "finished" before slaughter and fattened with starchy foods and grains since times immemorial, should crop productivity afford such a luxury. If you want to fatten a pig, maize, barley and potatoes will do the trick very well. You do not feed an animal or a human fat in order to make them fat.

Are we therefore justified in our carb phobia? The short answer is a resounding no. All we need to be aware of is that, at least in modern industrial societies, we are flooded with cheap grains, and of very low quality. We therefore get fat, with no health benefits. As previously discussed, if we didn't produce crops with agrochemicals, grains would be more hard-earned and expensive, and we would eat less of them: our diets should reflect our soils' natural capacities. Therefore, my very simple suggestion is to eat less "carbs", and make sure they are of high quality.

Gluten Phobia and Other Disorders

Bad ideas seem to be related. This is certainly the case with the recent craze around gluten. Gluten-free products have flooded the market, and an increasing percentage of the population identifies as "gluten intolerant" and swears off any foods, such as wheat, that contain gluten. Such radical dietary enterprises are yet again the result of basic misunderstandings, facilitated by opportunistic marketing. For the uninitiated, gluten is the protein contained in cereal grains like wheat, barley and rye. Gluten intolerance, usually associated with coeliac disease, manifests itself through various symptoms, mostly digestive,

[225] W. Banting, 1863, Letter on Corpulence, Addressed to the Public.

such as bloating, diarrhoea and stomach aches.[226] We should not doubt for a moment that coeliac disease is a condition some people suffer from, but we should also be very sceptical about the relatively sudden explosion of such a condition and the spread of gluten-free products. Some of these products are virtually fraudulent; gluten free oat products being a prime example. Oats do not contain gluten to begin with: selling oats as gluten free is almost the equivalent of selling fat-free water or sugar-free chicken. The industry's justification for such marketing ploys is that oats are often processed in facilities where gluten rich products are also processed or that hulled oats can at times contain the odd grain, given that farmers may grow them alongside wheat and barley and use the same combines etc... and that therefore there might be accidental traces of gluten in oat products. Given that gluten intolerance is not an allergy, it is impossible to see how the tiniest of traces of gluten could possibly make any difference to the gluten intolerant. The more likely explanation is that food marketers are riding the gluten free wave and profiting from the rampant gluten phobia that has recently possessed our culture.

Could it be that the rather common symptoms often associated with gluten intolerance are, in most cases, more likely explained by poor diets which, after all, cause all sorts of digestive difficulties? Whilst a very small minority of people might indeed develop an intolerance to gluten, it is worth noting that most people are diagnosed with gluten intolerance without actual physical tests to confirm coeliac disease. Homespun diagnoses, mail order testing kits, online assessments or verbal descriptions of symptoms to a GP often suffice for a formal diagnosis. I would encourage the reader, next time he or she meets someone who declares themselves as "gluten intolerant", to enquire how they arrived at such a diagnosis. Very often, neither blood tests nor gut biopsies were involved in these largely homespun or verbal diagnoses. Without such quantitative methods, we can dismiss or at the very least doubt the reliability of these diagnoses and explain the digestive difficulties experienced by the many "gluten intolerant" by reference to the fact that poor diets produce poor digestive functions and unpleasant symptoms. A very similar phenomenon explains another increasingly diagnosed condition, irritable bowel syndrome (IBS), for which there is no formal nor quantitative diagnostic method. Its symptoms, which are remarkably similar to those attributed to coeliac disease,[227] can again, in most cases, be far more easily explained by reference to the unpleasant symptoms associated with a poor diet. As opposed to having a

[226] https://www.nhs.uk/conditions/coeliac-disease/;
https://www.coeliac.org.uk/information-and-support/coeliac-disease/about-coeliac-disease/what-are-coeliac-disease-symptoms/

[227] https://www.nhs.uk/conditions/irritable-bowel-syndrome-ibs/symptoms/

chronic "syndrome", most patients are usually suffering from the effects of a poor diet on their gut health, which are reversible through a wholesome diet.

Having said that, there is no doubt that modern diets contain excessive amounts of gluten. This is not, as is generally believed, because wheat per se is the problem. The real problem is that wheat has changed more in the last 100 years than it did in the previous 10,000 and we eat far too much of it. Modern wheat hybrid varieties used for the average loaf of bread or packet of pasta are radically different from traditional wheats. One of the key differences is gluten content, which is much higher in modern strains: more gluten, less micronutrients and less flavour. Pasta made with an old-fashioned tall wheat variety like Senatore Cappelli or Saragolla is not comparable with pasta made with Manitoba or Arizona wheat. Ancient wheats like emmer and einkorn, still grown in pockets of Italy and other parts of the world, are even less comparable with the modern hybrid wheats. Therefore, the first step to avoid gluten intolerance is cut down on the overall consumption of wheat products and try to avoid modern hybrid wheats as much as possible. This is a difficult thing to do, as even most organic wheat products are made from modern wheat hybrids. Nonetheless, once quantity is reduced and quality improved, the whole issue of "gluten intolerance" should dissipate. An even more efficient way to eliminate the symptoms associated with gluten intolerance would be to improve the rest of the diet. The supposedly gluten intolerant among us seem to have poor diets, irrespective of wheat content. Instead of eliminating all gluten from their diets, I would wager that, for the average "gluten intolerant", the adoption of a better overall diet free of ultra-processed foods would generally result in better digestive function and in the decrease or disappearance of those concerning symptoms.

A corollary of the rise of gluten phobia is an unhealthy interest in food intolerance and "sensitivity" as a whole. A quick Google search of "food intolerance" reveals a worrying abundance of available tests and assessments, which supposedly reveal which foods we are individually intolerant to. Apart from the absurd presumption that food intolerance is in any way normal or common, and the intentionally blurred distinction between an intolerance and an allergy, this approach results in the unnecessary elimination of perfectly good foods from individual diets, based on shoddy science and the exploitation of nutritional anxiety. Even the NHS condemns food intolerance tests: *"a number of companies produce food intolerance tests, but these tests are not based on scientific evidence and are not recommended by the British Dietary Association (BDA)."*[228]

The simple truth is that if you have the misfortune of actually being allergic to something, like nuts or kiwis, you will have learnt about that from an early age, given the obvious and

[228] https://www.nhs.uk/conditions/food-intolerance/

dangerous symptoms of an allergic reaction. Similarly, if you are truly intolerant to lactose,[229] you will also likely know that this is the case through the severity of your symptoms but must nonetheless get appropriately tested via quantitative methods, such as a blood test. But the notion that we all have long lists of food sensitivities and degrees of intolerance to several foods and should therefore pick our foods *à la carte* on that basis is false and dangerous. I am reminded of a nameless and attractive colleague who, apart from exhibiting a worrying degree of concern over her already low weight,[230] was supposedly intolerant to all sorts of foods, including garlic and other basic kitchen staples. This miserable diagnosis was based on a very expensive food sensitivity and intolerance test she had purchased, which only led to more anxiety around food, more restrictions, more guilt and more obsession about dieting and losing weight. None of this is necessary: presume that you are neither allergic nor intolerant to *anything*. Unless you have very persuasive reasons not to do so, seek simpler explanations for your common symptoms and focus your attention on the quality of your overall diet.

What About Your Gut Microbiome?

A more recent related trend has been the focus on gut health and the "gut microbiome", as exemplified by the aforementioned Professor Tim Spector, the enthusiastic promoter of "scientifically proven" personalised diets, and the health app ZOE.[231] The gut microbiome or gut flora loosely refers to the microorganisms that live in the digestive tracts of animals. In our guts, invisible to the naked eye, inhabit innumerable bacteria, with which we co-exist in a state of beneficial symbiosis. As with virtually everything else in our bodies, there are varying degrees of microbiome health, and the healthy gut of a healthy human will contain within it the right kind and balance of microbial life. The unhealthy gut of an unhealthy human, on the other hand, will not have a healthy microbiome. As Spector has correctly pointed out, the consumption of ultra-processed foods (most of which, I would argue, can hardly be classified as "food" proper) is laying waste on our gut health, sterilising, damaging and unbalancing our microbial life, with dire consequences. As we saw, unhealthy guts lead to all sorts of symptoms and problems, which are often misdiagnosed and misunderstood.

All of this is perfectly reasonable and indisputable and Spector's broad recommendation, to stay away from ultra-processed foods, is of course commendable. The problem is that

[229] This is extremely unlikely if you are Caucasian but more likely if you are of Chinese or Japanese ancestry.

[230] I personally dreamt of fattening her quite up a bit, with some wholesome Italian pasta and meat dishes like Neapolitan Ragu' and abundant, full sugar desserts.

[231] https://zoe.com/

Spector and his fellows could not resist going two steps further. The first step was the counterproductive leap into reductionism that so many scientists simply find irresistible: an overwhelming focus on "the microbiome" as the Holy Grail of human health, as the *conditio sine qua non* of the new science of eating. Dr Chris van Tulleken, who also recommends staying away from ultra-processed foods, actively invites us to identify with our gut microbiome:

"The gut microbiome is so crucial to its survival that you could invert your idea of a cow and think of it as simply a vehicle for its own microbiome, a four-legged vessel transporting the microorganisms to the plants of their choice. Once you've done that, you can imagine yourself in the same way"[232].

Needless to say, neither a cow, nor your friends and colleagues, should be reimagined as vessels transporting microorganisms. The microbiome is one of many vital bodily features, and in the same way I do not feel any need to identify with my red blood cells or sperm, I do not feel the need to get carried away about the invisible creepy crawlies living in my gut.

The second step is towards the idea that, since every individual's microbiome is not identical to that of any other individual's, which no doubt is true, we therefore all have unique, individual dietary needs which, in principle, are both discoverable and prescriptive. We are told that we all respond to different foods very differently, that we need to feed and cultivate our unique microbiomes accordingly, and that we need a "scientifically proven", "personalised nutrition" which, apparently, will be the norm in the future. By sending in poop samples, wearing a real-time blood sugar sensor for up to two weeks (imagine the tedium), having blood fat tests and so on, we can find out which foods we (or rather our microbiomes, as we are encouraged to think in terms of "feeding our microbiomes" as opposed to feeding ourselves) personally respond to, from a score to 1 to 100, and track our progress accordingly. Some foods, as a consequence, are recommended, others are not. Spector, for example, found out that grapes were his personal "nemesis", but mercifully does rather well with strawberries.[233] He also found out that cous-cous is no-no, and pearl barley is just fine.[234]

The first and obvious problem with this approach is that it leads to yet another Manichean approach to diet: perfectly normal foods to feel good about and perfectly normal foods to strictly avoid, which is eerily reminiscent of the food intolerance craze, or of any restrictive diet that eliminates entire food groups. And, even more problematically, the foods that score low may well be perfectly good healthy whole foods like grapes, or perfectly good staple

[232] C. van Tulleken, 2023, Ultra-Processed People, page 87.

[233] T. Spector, 2022, Food for Life: Your Guide to the New Science of Eating Well, page 119.

[234] Ibidem, page 118.

processed foods like cous-cous. In an age of nutritional anxiety, the last thing we need is personalised lists of perfectly good foods that we must avoid based on some score we have been given. It would be far wiser to worry about the quality of grapes (most grapes in the UK are appalling, super sweet, seedless, heavily sprayed grapes from South Africa) and of the cous-cous (it should always be organic) and simply ensure that we eat a variety of foods: grapes, strawberries, cous-cous, pearl barley etc... Even if we choose to take the ZOE scores seriously, what do they actually tell us? They tell us that, for example, Spector happens to get a particularly high sugar spike when eating grapes. Does that mean he will always get high sugar spikes when eating grapes? Is a high sugar spike necessarily always a bad thing? Will he need to monitor his grape score in perpetuity? Should we not expect his grape score to change as his microbiome health improves? Whatever the answer to these questions, a personalised list of compatible and incompatible foods is, in my opinion, a step in the wrong direction. Eat a sensible whole foods diet[235] and the microbiome, blood sugars, and blood fats will take care of themselves.

In Spector's ideal future, *"everyone will know how their body responds to certain foods and will have access to a list of foods ranked in order of health benefit for their metabolism and microbes. Digital menus in restaurants might sync with your smartphone or watch to give personal recommendations, or automated supermarket labels might change for every customer"*[236]. Furthermore, *"everyone will have access to wearable AI devices to monitor themselves and their metabolic responses to food."*[237] There is something very unappealing about this high tech, screentime future of personalised eating, and sincerely hope it never materialises. If you want 24/7 high tech surveillance, a sort of internal metabolic CCTV, go for it, but it will likely increase anxiety, decrease pleasure and have no tangible positive health outcome.

For now, whilst we wait for the digital, AI assisted of the future, we can nonetheless subscribe to ZOE's services. In an age of mindless individual consumerism and superficial *a la' carte* identities, personalised nutrition via a smart phone makes perfect sense. But in the real world of blood, guts, soil, and breath, it makes very little sense. This is obvious when we observe the correlation between nutrition and health on a population basis, as opposed to an individual basis. In simple terms: natural whole food diets are always good for any human population, and ultra-processed diets are always bad for any human population. And populations are made of individual people, whose microbiomic and genetic differences are secondary and largely irrelevant. As it happens, and to be fair, Spector's general advice is

[235] More on this in Section 3.

[236] T. Spector, 2022, Food for Life: Your Guide to the New Science of Eating Well, page 110.

[237] Ibidem, page 112.

fairly sound. His five basic suggestions are to eat 30 different plants a week, try colourful plants, increase fibre intake, explore fermented foods and limit ultra-processed foods.[238] To his credit, he also encourages people to eat organic fruits and vegetables.[239] No doubt any overweight and unhealthy individual who replaced their microwave meals and Coke Zero diet with 30 different plants a week etc... would improve their health or, to stay true to Spector's emphasis, the health of their microbiome. That does not mean they need to nurture and mollycoddle their unique microbes with tailored menus and high scoring foods.

A quick word on the 30 plants a week: there is no sense, in spite of ZOE's continuous emphasis on "the science", that the magic number 30 is any more or less arbitrary than, say, the NHS 5-a-day recommendation. It could have been 25 or 35, and I would therefore urge the reader to desist from spending much time and effort counting their weekly plants. If you lose count, considering that according to ZOE's classification even spice, coffee or popcorn can be classified as plants for your weekly tally, you are probably on the right track. Furthermore, whilst Spector rightly condemns food supplements as unnecessary or worse,[240] ZOE now retails a food supplement made of 30 plants, to be taken daily. It weighs 15 grams, and contains tiny amounts of: red beetroot, baobab, buckthorn, chicory root, carrot, onion, garlic, chaga, lion's mane, shitake, maitake, tremella, reishi, cordyceps, white mushroom, thyme, parsley, turmeric, cumin, rosemary, chia seed, flaxseed, grape seed, hemp seed, pumpkin seed, sunflower seed, almonds, hazelnuts, walnuts, red lentil, quinoa.[241] This "scoop of ZOE science" comes at £1.11 a portion when bought in bulk directly from the ZOE website at the time of writing, and at a whooping £2.45 at my local Waitrose. The one merit of this supplement is that, unlike most supplements, it is not made from synthetic vitamins and minerals. Nonetheless, none of the ingredients are organic, there is zero information about their origin and, in any case, if one eats a good whole foods diet, there is absolutely no need to ingest little sachets of dried-up seeds, herbs etc... on a daily basis. A far more sensible option, I would suggest, is to make sure we have lots of dry organic spices in the pantry, fresh herbs, organic raw nuts etc... and use them liberally in the kitchen. It will be a lot cheaper too.

Lastly, whilst not advocating for veganism, Spector exhibits a distinct anti-meat and dairy bias throughout his books, mostly due to misguided concerns about the environment. He does not oppose meat and dairy from a nutritional standpoint, and in fact advocates for full fat dairy and organic beef, but in very modest quantities due to their presumed carbon

[238] https://www.youtube.com/watch?v=BloRpfNCjQ8

[239] T. Spector, 2022, Food for Life: Your Guide to the New Science of Eating Well, page 91.

[240] T. Spector, 2020, Spoon-Fed, pages 53-62.

[241] https://zoe.com/daily30

emissions. As such, he flirts with the idea of eating insects, in the form of maggot powder,[242] has no apparent problem with genetically modified salmon and livestock,[243] and is favourable towards "future burgers", in spite of the fact that they are the epitome of ultra-processed junk.[244] Commenting on the Impossible Foods burger, he notes that *"they emit 80-90 per cent less greenhouse gases compared to normal meat burger, and human trials have shown that even with the extra chemicals used to make the patty stick together and taste good, they are still potentially better for your heart (based on blood markers) than the original. The genetically modified plant meat burger looks like it is here to stay"*.[245] Like George Monbiot, Spector views the space age edible protein made by Solar Foods favourably on account of its supposedly low carbon emissions,[246] and is also keen on the growing trend of cultured meats and predicts that *"we will soon be eating meat, fish and fungi protein grown ethically in labs"*.[247] Like so many in contemporary culture, he seems to fall for what I like to call "technological determinism": the belief that just because something is becoming or will become technologically feasible, it will necessarily need to be adopted. I will repeat, yet again: just because we *can* do something, it does not follow that we *should*.

I would also dare to suggest that these futuristic foods, apart from their bogus environmental credentials and gastronomic worthlessness, may very well wreak havoc on our precious microbiomes. I suspect that the potential effect such strange synthetic foods might have, in the case of fake meat and synthetic proteins, will not be dissimilar to that of contemporary ultra-processed foods. As for cultured meat and fish, I would expect it to resemble the flesh of factory farmed animals, in the best-case scenario. In any case, and most importantly, these are all unnecessary distractions from actual solutions and, as such, best forgotten.

TO SUM UP:

- You do not need to know anything at all about the microorganisms living in your gut.
- You are not a two-legged vessel transporting microorganisms to the plants of their choice.
- Unless you are testing for specific disease, or have worrying symptoms, you do not need to have your poo tested in order to decide what to eat.
- You are not special, nor unique. The basic rules of diet and health are universal.
- Fake meat and maggot flour are not necessary to save the planet, and they suck.

[242] T. Spector, 2022, Food for Life: Your Guide to the New Science of Eating Well, page 108.

[243] Ibidem, 103-104.

[244] See Chapter 10.

[245] T. Spector, 2022, Food for Life: Your Guide to the New Science of Eating Well, page 105.

[246] Ibidem, page 104.

[247] Ibidem, page 112.

- GM crops are part of the problem, not the solution. Genetically modified animals are an abomination.
- We will hopefully never eat cultured meat, fish and fungi protein grown "ethically" in labs.

Intermittent Fasting, Juice Detoxes and Other Fads

It has now become quite common to meet people who, when asked why they are skipping lunch, declare, with an air of hard-earned satisfaction, that they are practicing "intermittent fasting". There are various forms of intermittent fasting but, as the name suggests, in essence it refers to the practice of refraining from eating for set periods of time (e.g., 16 hours), which, supposedly, benefits the body in all sorts of ways. Specifically, since it is mostly used for weight loss, intermittent fasting is supposed to stimulate the burning of fat, by simulating short term cycles of quasi-starvation. The evidence for whether intermittent fasting can lead to any weight loss is scant, as is the evidence for whether it has any other health benefits. But let us presume that it can lead to weight loss, without significant health damage. Does that mean that it is a good idea?

As you can probably guess, I do not believe it is a good idea. This is for two simple reasons: it does not come close to tackling the root causes of excess body fat and it is completely unsustainable. Dear reader: if you are overweight it is because of what you have been eating over a very long period of time. There are clearly errors and misconceptions and bad habits that have led you to the point where you need to lose weight. Fasting intermittently simply alters *when* you eat as opposed to *what* and *how* you eat. Therefore, by not addressing the root of the problem, you are destined to regain whatever weight you lose through the painstaking intermittent fasting regime. This takes me to the second point: nobody, with the best will in the world, can sustain the intermittent regime long term. Therefore, even if you manage to lose weight, you will eventually stop intermittent fasting and, when you do, you will gradually regain whatever weight you painstakingly lost.

A related folly that I have had the dubious privilege of observing first hand is the trend of "juice detoxes" or "cleansers", which people order from companies that ship out boxes full of colourful liquids. The principle behind these fads is that by ingesting liquid only diets, often featuring so called superfoods, for several days in a row, both weight loss and "detoxing" will be achieved. These are often marketed as "recharging", "supercharging", offering a "renewal" to those who subject themselves to the rigorous liquid regime. Apart from the lack of any evidence for any of the claims made by the purveyors of these strange dietary plans, it should be quite clear that there cannot possibly be any benefit in liquidising fruits and vegetables as opposed to eating them whole. In fact, quite the opposite. It is always better to eat a whole apple than a pressed apple, and to eat a carrot than drink carrot juice. Furthermore, as a quick scan of the market for these dietary plans and home deliveries will reveal, it is absolutely clear that, most of the time, these juices in plastic bottles are made with cheap, conventional (as in sprayed), out of season produce. Some versions of these liquid diets allow for "protein" juices as well, containing the usual dodgy powders and collagens. Other "juice plans" include sweeteners, "probiotics", superfood "shots" and other questionable ingredients.

In any case, a far smarter approach to a "detox" or a "cleansing diet", might simply be to only eat seasonal, organic, whole fresh fruits and vegetables for 1-2 days a week. Whilst not necessary, it could well have some benefits.

The Skinny Jab Scam and Other Techno-Fixes

Far more alarming than any of the faddish, mostly ridiculous diets swirling around our culture has been the rise of the so called "skinny jabs", now a global business and cultural phenomenon. I dare not mention specific products and their mendacious manufacturers, or I will be sued to bankruptcy or worse by teams of vampiric lawyers. I have to confess that I foresaw the sinister trend before it really took off. I know someone who, well before the jabs were mentioned in any European mainstream media, had them prescribed in the United States, where it was starting to enter the market. This individual was Type-2 Diabetic, a reversable condition, and slightly overweight. It was obvious to me how a pharmaceutical solution to both diabetes and obesity could potentially be a "blockbuster" as Big Pharma's marketing successes are often called. Apart from the enormous potential market, this kind of drug and approach to weight loss conforms very well to a broad range of cultural, economic and ideological trends. In the age of scientism, a magical slimming drug will always find blind faith and acceptance. It also fits in very well with the increasing tendency to look for quick fixes that do not involve taking personal responsibility. Instead of making changes, and taking tough decisions, and taking inventory of one's behaviour and actions, why not "trust the science" and run to the saviour in a white coat and to the pharmacy? In any case, the producers of the various skinny jabs followed the usual playbook and had the usual allies: mainstream media, newspapers and highly regarded magazines gave the miraculous jabs enormous coverage and continue to do so. Then, as is again usually the case, a growing stream of celebrities came out to endorse the products. Once celebrity sponsors, paid or otherwise, came to the fore, it was obvious that the skinny jabs were going to be huge. The most recent trend I have had the displeasure of observing is that the miracle jabs are now being promoted as potential cure-alls that transcend mere weight loss: they may treat anything from cardiovascular disease to Alzheimer's and "addiction".

The chief effect of these jabs on my acquaintance, and on so many others, is very clear: a loss of appetite, often accompanied by nausea, diarrhoea, abdominal pain and/or other unpleasant symptoms. As he and others have found, the "skinny jabs" can lead to weight loss, at least in the short term which is no surprise given the suppression of appetite and common symptoms they cause. Does that mean they are a good idea? The short answer is absolutely not. To begin with, the fact that a substance can promote appetite suppression and lead to weight loss is an insufficient reason to ingest it. Afterall, and I am not being facetious, there are plenty of dangerous substances that promote appetite suppression and lead to weight loss: cocaine hydrochloride, amphetamines and nicotine, for example. One does not need to be a genius to realise that a drug, such as those used for the skinny jabs, which suppresses appetite and alters the body's basic hormonal balance and digestive functions, with unpleasant side effects, cannot possibly come without potentially serious consequences. A quick read of the potential side effects published by the manufacturers of these drugs make for scary reading, with increased incidence of a specific type of cancer recorded by the two main manufacturers.[248] At the very least, we can say with certainty that these drugs will have drawbacks and carry unknown long term health risks.

The promoters of skinny jabs, however, argue that they are not necessarily designed for long-term and indefinite use. But this is a disingenuous argument for the simple reason that, once the patient has followed a 6 or 12-month course, for example, they will almost invariably start gaining weight again. Why? Because, yet again, appetite suppression does not in any way address the root cause of the problem, which is to be found in the dietary habits and types of food eaten by the overweight patient. The drug targets the symptom, not the cause of the condition. Therefore, when our poor patient ends their course of skinny jabs, he or she, having gradually regained their natural appetite, will simply start piling on the pounds again, as they will inevitably go back to the very same habits and foods that made them fat in the first place. From the pharmaceutical industry's point of view, that is not a problem, but a positive development and opportunity for further sales: the patient can simply go back to their doctor and renew their prescription and go on a never-ending rollercoaster of weight loss and gain.

Lastly, I must mention another problematic technological fix: bariatric surgeries. These come in different forms, the most common of which is sleeve gastrectomy, in which the majority of

[248] I have intentionally avoided details and sources and will let you do your own research: this is uncontroversial, publicly available information. Again, I will refrain from names and brands for my own self-preservation.

the patient's stomach is surgically removed, leaving a smaller, mutilated, stitched up digestive organ. The tragedy of such a procedure, apart from its inherent risks and long-term consequences, which the removal of an essential healthy organ must inevitably involve, is that, yet again, it does absolutely nothing to address the root cause of the problem. Is obesity caused by an enlarged stomach or is an enlarged stomach the end result of obesity? Does one eat too much and of the wrong things because of an enlarged stomach or does one have an enlarged stomach as a consequence of eating too much and of the wrong things? It should be quite clear that an enlarged stomach is yet again a symptom, a consequence of obesity and not its cause. The theory behind sleeve gastrectomy is that it will reduce both appetite and stomach space, meaning that the obese patient will literally not be able to eat as much and will therefore lose weight. No doubt some do, albeit not without risks and potential long-term consequences. Just as I have had first-hand experience of observing the impact of skinny jabs, I have also had the unpleasant experience of witnessing how patients do not necessarily lose weight in the long term. Whilst they may not be able to eat anywhere near as much as they used to in one sitting, they can simply end up eating smaller quantities on a more regular basis, in an endless series of snacking. They may even end up favouring some of the worse foods that caused their obesity in the first place: sugary snacks and drinks that can be immediately absorbed into the blood stream and do not occupy stomach space for long. In other words: no surgery can alter the dietary habits and food choices that cause obesity in the first place.

IN A NUTSHELL

- Contemporary nutrition science is based on an ideology, nutritionism.
- Reductive science has its limits, and it shows.
- You are better off without nutritionists and dieticians in your life. You do not need an "expert" to eat well.
- Remember that almost every malpractice in agriculture, food production and dieting has had mainstream scientific sanction at some time or other.
- NHS nutritional guidelines are fundamentally flawed.
- Abandon the false belief that certain nutrients are either "good" or "bad" - all nutrients are good if they derive from the right sources.
- Adopt the belief that nutrients are only as good as the form they come in and the context they come from (e.g., carbohydrates from an organic roast potato good; carbohydrates from Monster Munch, bad. Sugar from honey or organic chocolate, good; sugar from Coca-Cola and Percy Pigs, bad)

- There are no bad food types (e.g., grains, dairy, meat, sugars) only bad food (bad grain, dairy, meat, sugars etc...) and good food (good grain, dairy, meat, sugars etc...).
- You most likely do not have any food allergies or intolerances.
- You do not need to fast for non-religious reasons.
- You do not need to "detox": eat whole foods from healthy soils as much as possible instead.
- Personalised gut health assessments and diets are yet another step towards reductionism.
- Skinny jabs are a disgraceful scam.
- Bariatric surgery is not a solution for obesity.
- Do not fear red meat, animal fats, sugar, "carbs" and gluten.

SECTION TWO

Critical Essays on Alternative Approaches to Food

Chapter 6

VEGAN?

It is hard to gauge just how fast veganism is growing worldwide. If levels of celebrity endorsement and social media presence were our only barometer, we would have to conclude that it is growing very fast. However, both day-to-day experience and anecdotal evidence, and indeed any statistics on the consumption of animal products in Britain reveal that veganism, whilst growing, is still a fringe persuasion. Be that as it may, no discussion about food, cookery and agriculture should be undertaken without a clear position on the legitimacy or illegitimacy of rearing, using and eating animals.

Right Questions, Wrong Answers?

For someone who takes great pleasure in hunting, fishing, butchery and the slow cooking of meats, I have a relatively sympathetic view of the vegan movement. In a sense, the vegan position is superior to the unquestioning, careless position of many, if not most, people in this country. The average vegan, as he or she often testifies, is someone who has reached their radical conclusion through exposure to, and a rejection of, the horrors of the factory farms and feedlots. Having asked the right sorts of questions (Where does my food come from? How are eggs and milk produced?) they have concluded that the best option, and the only morally legitimate option, is to opt out altogether. The reason why this may be a relatively superior position is that at least it lives up to the simple Socratic suggestion that a worthwhile life requires examination. To go from meal to meal, from purchase to purchase without ever wondering or wanting to know anything about the long chain of events that leads to the chicken nugget or pint of milk is the least desirable of all positions: ignorance is not bliss!

I would immediately grant that, if the only way to consume animal products were the enclosed pig factory farm, the 30,000 chicken houses and the indoor Holstein mega-dairy systems, I would embrace and promote veganism. It would be the only ethical option available. It would also, as its proponents often claim, have less negative impact on the environment, in terms of pollution, land use and energy waste. The good news, however, is that this is not the only possible route to redemption. The vegan epiphany only impresses those unfamiliar with the nuances of good animal husbandry and those who are clearly unaware of the workings of the laws of nature and of biological systems. It is no coincidence that veganism is by and large an urban, cosmopolitan, and elite pursuit. The rural, the remote and the poor do not seem to have taken to the vegan gospel and not because they are ignorant simpletons, as vegans often seem to imply. There are many reasons for the urban and cosmopolitan uptake, but clearly it is easier to buy into a seductively simplistic and all-encompassing ideology such as veganism when one's only relationship with the natural world is through television, a passive infertile pet or the back garden. It is also an ideology fit for the 21st century secular liberal mind, which finds the inversion of common sense and the uprooting of historical normalcy too tempting to be resistible.

Basic Anatomy Goes Awry

Let us begin with the simpler arguments: the arguments "from nature". These are retrospective claims about human and animal biology and anatomy used to justify the vegan position. This dated line of argument, as portrayed in the popular, persuasive, successful, and well-made documentary, *The Game Changers*[249] runs along the following lines:

1) A close look at human anatomy reveals that humans are herbivorous or frugivorous,[250] rather than omnivorous or carnivorous.
2) This revelation is clear when the human digestive system and teeth are compared to those of other animals.
3) It follows, therefore, that a herbivorous or frugivorous diet is the optimal human diet, the most natural of diets.

[249] See: https://gamechangersmovie.com/

This chapter on veganism will often refer to this documentary, given its success, popularity and persuasiveness, and given that it encapsulates most of the arguments in favour of veganism. Very similar arguments were prominent in another successful documentary, *Cowspiracy* (https://www.cowspiracy.com/). Prominent and media savvy vegan activists like Ed Winters (AKA Earthling Ed) and Joseph Armstrong (AKA Joey Carbstrong) also tend to present the arguments disputed throughout this chapter.

[250] Primarily subsisting on fruit.

There are a number of basic problems with this line of argument. The first problem is a misrepresentation of human anatomy. In *The Game Changers* and other vegan propaganda, we are reminded about the extraordinary length of our digestive system, which is far longer than that of the Earth's big carnivores, such as tigers and lions, and much closer to that of herbivores. This is certainly true and indicative of the fact that humans do not exhibit the anatomical features of carnivores: a claim which no one on the other side of the debate is making. What is conveniently missed out is the required analysis of the *kind* of digestive system that different animals have, which is quite different from the issue of *length*. Without the need for a GCSE in Biology, some reflection on this distinction will reveal some basic truths, about what we are certainly *not* and about what we probably *are*.

Firstly, humans are certainly not herbivores, in any meaningful sense of the word. Yes, the length of our digestive system relative to height is closer to that of a sheep or a cow than it is to that of a cat or a crocodile, but the *kind* of digestive system we possess is remarkably different from that of herbivores. Herbivores, which generally possess four stomachs as opposed to one, have the unique capacity to digest and nourish themselves from cellulose, which is the fundamental component of grasses. This is of course one of the main reasons why the major species of domesticated animals (cattle, sheep, goats, horses, donkeys and camels) are all herbivores: they have the capacity to feed themselves on the very abundant resources which we are entirely incapable of digesting. We have domesticated herbivores, whose flesh we are perfectly adapted to eat and digest, primarily because we are not herbivores.

As it turns out, our digestive system is closely matched by the pig's. A visit to a local slaughterhouse or butcher would reveal the striking similarities. It is for this reason that pigs are thought to be the best candidates for organ transplants to humans. It is unclear whether xenotransplantation will ever work and, whether we agree with the ethical implications of such practices or not, the choice of the pig as the best potential candidate, as opposed to a sheep, is not insignificant. The pig is of course an omnivorous creature that can digest almost anything, rather than a herbivore. Our closest genetic relatives, the chimpanzees, are not "vegan". Apart from the occasional consumption of insects, honey and bird eggs, male chimpanzees at times hunt monkeys in groups. When they hunt, the male chimps coordinate their efforts and share the meat amongst each other. The reinforcement of social status and the exchange of sexual favours with female chimps also come into play. To sum up, the chimpanzee hunts in ways that are somewhat reminiscent of what we know of early humans and of the most primitive hunter-gatherer societies. Our closest genetic relatives do not eat plants only.

Similar nonsensical arguments are made about vision and its supposed correlation to our ideal, natural plant-based diet. We are told that our ability to identify different colours is due to the fact that, like other primates and fruit-eating animals, the ability to spot ripe fruit is advantageous to us. Humans have trichromatic vision, ideally suited to identifying different sources of food. Carnivores like tigers and lions, apparently, have dichromatic vision and do not have the ability to see a wide spectrum of colours in their vision, which is unnecessary in identifying prey. That's all very well and good, until one considers another key aspect of vision which is conveniently not discussed in *The Game Changers*: the *range* of vision, as opposed to the visible colour spectrum, and the distinction between panoramic and binocular vision. In brief: panoramic vision allows a very broad range of vision, capturing as much of the landscape around oneself, both in front and behind. This is typical of prey animals that have eyes on the sides of their heads: sheep, goats, rabbits, squirrels, buffalo, horses etc... This is what you need if you want to be able to spot movement and potential danger both behind and in front of you: in other words, to look out for predators. Binocular vision, on the other hand, is typical of predators: cats, tigers, wolves, bears and... humans. An animal with binocular vision can focus on a spot, track and follow prey and, in our case, aim and throw/shoot something to kill it with. So, what are we to conclude? That, again, we have the characteristics of an animal that is neither an out-and-out carnivore nor a herbivore. We are ideally suited to both spot ripe fruit and mushrooms as we are to track and hunt our quarry. A quick consideration of our dental faculties, again misleadingly dealt with in *The Game Changers*, reveals the very same truth: our teeth are neither suited to ripping and chewing grasses nor look nothing like those of a cow, who in fact chews her meals more than once[251] and look nothing like those of a panther, whose teeth are designed to rip and barely chew raw flesh. We are, yet again, somewhere in between: the ultimate all-rounders of the natural world, who can rip, chew and bite into most things, whether animal or plant.

None of this necessarily means that we are therefore obliged to follow an omnivorous diet as opposed to a vegan diet. It is quite clear that humans, unlike animals, are capable of transcending their biological inheritances. We are literally the only creature on Earth that can make dietary choices, for ideological and cultural reasons: we have many taboos, we have hunger strikes, eating challenges, eating disorders, cooked food, fine dining and sacred foods. Our choices are not and should not be based solely on biology. But it is not us non-vegans that appeal to biology and digestive systems to justify our choices: we have many other reasons. However, when faced with absurd vegan claims about human anatomy and the natural human diet we must repeat an obvious and indisputable fact: if we were to be guided by biological and anatomical considerations alone, we would have to conclude that nature clearly and unequivocally indicates that we are omnivorous, not vegan, creatures.

[251] Chewing the cud: the regurgitation and secondary chewing of grasses. This, at least. is not recommended by any vegans.

Historical Record 101

A corollary of the "anatomical argument" is an argument that looks back at human history and prehistory. The claim being made is that if we attempt to look back at our prehistory, we discover that, as it turns out, the image of "Man the Hunter" is a misleading one. We were, apparently, fruit-eating, plant-eating primates and meat-eating is a relatively rare and recent extravagance. Our ancestors were "vegetarian", as one of the papers highlighted in *The Game Changers* claims to demonstrate, and humans are simply not built to eat meat. The only evidence that may give this odd theory any kind of plausibility is that mainstream archaeological evidence from prehistory tends to indicate that early hominids progressed from omnivorous primates that supplemented their diets of gathering plants, seeds and fruits with small game and carrion to increasingly skilled hunters that subsisted on increasingly bigger game. In other words, the diet of our earliest ancestors throughout much of the Stone Age was unlikely to contain that much meat, given their smaller size, height and cranial capacity compared to *Homo Sapiens*. These early ancestors, therefore, also lacked sophisticated hunting skills and complex tool-making ability and were also living in the presence of several formidable competing predator species. It apparently took a long time to climb up the evolutionary ladder and become the dominant species.

Whilst we should be cautious with all assertive and simplistic claims about human origins and evolution and not pretend to have certainties about the very distant past, the uncontroversial consensus, backed up by archaeological sites all over the world, is that modern man, who now calls himself *Homo Sapiens,* has always hunted. What is fairly certain is that over time, there was a gradual evolution in weapon manufacture from basic stone and bone tools to ever more complex and well-crafted weapons, as well as the discovery of fire, which was used as a tool to clear land for hunting and corralling animals, as well as a cookery method for the flesh of such animals. Indeed, archaeological evidence has strongly suggested a correlation between the extinction of animals like the Mammoth and the increase and spread of human populations and hunting sites. It has in fact been argued, with some credibility, that it was the ability to manipulate fire, cook and hunt bigger game that led to the accelerated development of human culture in the last 50,000 years.

The last 50,000 years, also known as the Upper Palaeolithic/Late Stone Age is certainly characterised by the omnipresence of artefacts and remains that indicate human hunting, meat consumption, meat cookery with fire and the use of animal parts, such as skins, furs and bones. The most well-preserved ancient human artefacts discovered worldwide from this period, still visible and preserved today, reveal a culture in which hunting was the norm rather than the exception. A well-known example is the cave paintings of animals dated 20,000-40,000 BCE across modern-day Western Europe. A less well-known example is the intricate and skilfully made bone artefacts discovered in the Palaeolithic site in Sungir, modern-day Russia, dated 30,000-35,000 BCE, that demonstrate a very ancient culture of hunting, weapon manufacture and use of animal bones. In the Americas, evidence of Man the Hunter, albeit more recent, still dots the landscape with no exception. The Folsom site in New Mexico, dated at around 8,000-10,000 BCE, demonstrates both the abundance of buffalo and of human hunting and slaughter. There is some debate about whether the extinction of major mammal species from wherever humans spread to (the Americas are a particularly strong example) was a direct consequence of human presence and hunting. There may have been other factors, but human presence was most probably one of them.

The Game Changers makes the claim that the predominance of hunting artefacts is misleading because the leftovers of plant-based meals inevitably deteriorate fast, unlike bones, and leave no visible trace. The remains of fruits and leaves eaten 20,000 years ago are indeed unlikely to show up. Whilst plenty of archaeological evidence of seed and grain consumption has been found across the world, which has in fact allowed us to trace the development of agriculture, it is certainly true that spearheads and bones will outlast plant materials. All this truism tells us is that humans have generally not been *exclusively* hunters and that we should not presume that the absence of evidence for the consumption of plant foods indicates that meat was our main source of food. This, again, is a straw man argument: no claim has been made, by non-vegans, that humans did not feed themselves on plant foods. In fact, as even a cursory look at remaining hunter-gatherer cultures generally reveals, meat is always a precious, highly prized but hard-won resource, with plants usually providing the bulk of the diet. This is especially true in warm, tropical climates where vegetation is particularly rich and abundant all year round.

Most importantly, the historical case for Man the Hunter can be made *in absentia*. There is no record or evidence that a human culture subsisting on a diet free of all animal products has ever existed anywhere on Earth. Every single hunter-gatherer or agricultural society that we know of from past and present has consumed and consumes animal products. The fact that many hunter-gatherer societies and most agricultural societies have traditionally subsisted on diets in which the *majority* of calories derive from plants is irrelevant to the vegan argument: it demonstrates our omnivorous nature and the fact that most ecosystems produce an abundance of edible vegetation and that meat is a particularly rare and precious resource.

There are, in fact, examples of cultures subsisting entirely on animal products: the Inuits of the Arctic regions and the reindeer herders of Siberia. There are also several examples of pastoral societies, such as the sheep, goat, and camel herders of Mongolia, who subsist on a meat and dairy-based diet. This does not demonstrate that humans are carnivores, of course, but merely that an all-meat diet, unlike an all-plant diet, is more suitable to humans and is a diet on which humans have historically been able to subsist on for countless generations. I challenge our vegan friends to produce evidence for a single example of a human culture that has survived on plants alone for a few generations. Modern-day vegans are a subculture, rather than an independent culture, existing within an omnivorous culture. Furthermore, almost all vegans "converted" in adulthood and benefited from omnivorous diets as children and adolescents. It remains to be seen whether strict veganism can survive even a couple of generations within a single family.

The mention of family and "conversion" brings me to a last point: humans are mammals that need milk in childhood in order to survive and be healthy. The human ability to supplement or substitute mother's milk with the milk of other animals is an obvious advantage to our health, growth rate and survival. The fact that human mothers do not need to breastfeed their children until they go to primary school should be seen as a good thing, for both mothers and children, for both physical and psychological reasons. There is a clear correlation between breastfeeding until a late age and extreme poverty. Ownership of a cow in many parts of the world (in many parts of Africa, for example) can make a huge difference to rates of infant mortality, malnutrition and women's health. The "vegan child" is a weird ahistorical experiment that is being played out in a few odd families in the rich urbanised Western world. We will discover its consequences in the future but what we know already is that it is a distinct disadvantage for a child to be fed plant-based milk substitutes and have an impoverished diet free of all animal products. I can already hear the typical counterargument: what about obese children fed on diets of Coca-Cola, Turkey Twizzlers and McDonald's? Well, two wrongs do not make a right. And at least the parents of obese children, whilst being both ignorant and irresponsible, do not claim to be making a *superior* choice based on an ideology and ethic that sets them apart from others.

Misconceptions about Health and Performance

One of the problems with veganism is the seemingly impressive but ultimately vacuous health claims made to promote its virtues. The strategy is usually as follows: a person or select group of people on an average Western diet, high in ultra-processed food and low-quality animal products, is put on a vegan diet. Lo and behold, the health of the participants is measurably and significantly improved over a short period of time: cholesterol readings, blood pressure, weight loss etc... all point in the right direction. Conclusion: the vegan diet is the healthiest of all diets. In our chosen documentary of the age, *The Game Changers*, we have some prime examples of this approach throughout. An experiment with the firemen in New York was particularly relevant. Here we had a group of firemen undertaking to switch from their normal "American diet" to a vegan diet rich in vegetables for a week. Apart from the evident corpulence and lack of mobility of its participants, they admittedly had very poor health indicators and were cases of heart attack waiting to happen, we were told. After a week, there was a general statistically relevant average weight loss and improvement in blood pressure, cholesterol levels etc... This is impressive, at first glance.

However, it should at once be clear that any movement away from a diet of ultra-processed foods and low-quality animal products is a definite improvement, whatever the regime adopted. Of all the issues in the world of food and dieting, the only one on which there is some degree of consensus is the following: that a junk food diet, heavy in cheap animal products and almost devoid of any fruit and vegetables and other whole foods, is fundamentally unhealthy. A diet made up of microwaveable ready meals, cheap eggs, bacon and meat, fizzy drinks, fast food (the various burger and fried chicken chains, kebab shops etc...), pizza deliveries and Chinese take-aways will generally lead to the classic diseases of the West: heart disease, diabetes, cancer, obesity etc... None of this is controversial. Therefore, if our firemen in New York switch from Big Macs, hot dogs and KFC buckets to garden salads, lentil soups and stir-fried tofu the only thing we could possibly expect is improvement. In the United States, celebrity vegan doctors Dr Michael Greger[252] and Dr Michael Klaper[253] continuously testify that their patients, suffering from the comorbidities associated with being overweight, record all round health improvements upon switching to a whole foods plant-based diet. We have no reason to doubt that like our firemen, the average patient on an ultra-processed "Western diet" will benefit from switching to a plant-based whole foods diet. None of this implies that a vegan diet is the best of all diets, but simply that it is better than the All-American diet, which is not difficult to achieve.

A more interesting challenge was presented by experiments aiming to demonstrate that plant-based meals led to higher performances both on the field and in the bedroom when compared with meals containing even high-quality meat.[254] This was supposedly demonstrated by one-off experiments, where the fat content in the blood of three football players was measured after each meal and, equally, the erectile function of another three players was measured (by a less than appealing contraption, rather than by a live volunteer!) during a night's sleep, again after the consumption of different meals. The results demonstrated that the plant-based meals led to both lower fat content in the blood and increased erectile function overnight than the high-quality meat meals. Again, this is impressive at first glance. However, even presuming that proper large-scale trials confirmed this pattern, there is a fundamental and crucial difference between the short-term effect of a meal and the long-term effects of a dietary regime. It may be

[252] https://drgreger.org/

[253] https://www.doctorklaper.com/

[254] Organic/grass fed meats were used in the experiment, to their credit.

the case that a plant-based meal is a better option than a meat-based one just *before* taking to the field or the bedroom. Personally, if I were going for a run or a game of tennis, I would rather have a light plant-based meal[255] and save the meat for afters.

It was amazing to learn that the professional American football players interviewed throughout the programme declared they were in the habit of eating things like steaks, fried chicken and burgers before games. This, even to the uneducated, seems like a remarkably bad idea. Similarly, should I be so fortunate as to have female company one evening, I don't think a large plate of lamb chops, or pork ribs, or fried chicken would be an ideal meal for a night of passion. Their consumption, I must add, has the added disadvantage of encouraging rather unattractive and savage aspects of my table manners, which could well preclude sexual relations to begin with... Be that as it may, our ribs, chops and fried chicken, even if made from the best possible ingredients, might simply be, forgive the unscientific language, *too heavy*. No blood tests are required, day-to-day experience should confirm these simple rules of thumb. A bit of fish and a nice mixed salad, plus a light dessert would be a far better option, for both sports and lovemaking. A nice substantial meat dish would be perfect for recovery and replenishment after both sporting and amorous feats. None of this implies that plant-based meals are to be recommended *all* the time or that long-term abstinence from animal products would not bring other disadvantages. Performance and long-term health are not dependent on abstinence from all animal products, period.

As Michael Pollan recalls in his *In Defence of Food,* a similar experiment to the firemen trial was undertaken in Australia. A group of ten Aboriginal men, who lived in settlements and ate standard junk food Western diets, suffered from the typical conditions that accompany such diet: diabetes, high risk of heart disease and so on. The researchers asked the men to literally take to the bush for seven weeks and go back to their traditional hunter-gatherer diet. This consisted of a mixed diet that included seafood, grubs, reptiles, kangaroos, birds and wild fruits and tubers.[256] As with our firemen, the Aborigines showed marked improvement all around: their traditional diet, rich in all sorts of fish and game and certainly not vegan, turned out to be infinitely better than the super-sized double cheeseburger, fries and beer diet. Again, this is neither a surprise nor a suggestion that the Australian Aboriginal diet is the best of all diets: it is a healthy diet, one amongst many others.

The main problems with our diets, as previously discussed, is the great abundance of very low-quality ingredients and products produced by a chemically dependent industrial agricultural system and food manufacturing industry. There is an important issue here, which superficially seems to favour a vegan approach: the problems are amplified when it comes

[255] For example, lovely bread with olive oil and chopped tomatoes and cucumbers or bananas, fruits and nuts.

[256] M. Pollan, 2008, In Defence of Food, pages 85-89.

to animal products. Animals are at the top of the food chain, so whatever nutrients and toxicities there are further down the food chain, these are accumulated and concentrated in animals. Much of the best *and* worst food usually comes from animals. As bad as a heavily sprayed crop of wheat or potatoes may be, its products (white bread, French fries, crisps etc..) are still relatively less harmful to humans than poor animal products. Animals raised on the factory farm not only eat low quality feed made from the same type of low-quality crops used to make our bread. They are also fed with the waste products of the very same agricultural and food manufacturing system and their diets are often supplemented with a steady stream of pharmaceuticals to keep them alive long enough for slaughter. They are overbred, overcrowded, live in miserable, unsanitary conditions and are fundamentally unhealthy, weak animals. Their products, from bacon and burgers to chicken breasts, are the worst that the industrial food system has to offer, and certainly the most morally objectionable. As per the beginning of this discussion, if these were the only animal products available, veganism would be the better alternative.

This clear verdict on conventional animal products has led many to believe that it is animal products *per se* that are the problem, rather than the methods used to produce such products. Unfortunately, scientific research and public health policy and advice has been unable or unwilling to make this clear distinction. In 2015, the World Health Organisation declared that red meat and processed meats are carcinogenic.[257] This advice has since been repeated *ad nauseam* in the media and across the environmental and vegan movement. The problem with all this is very straightforward: none of the studies used by the WHO make any qualitative distinctions between different sources of red and processed meats. As previously discussed, the difference between the life, welfare, environmental impact, and products of a well raised "happy" pig and that of a factory farmed pig is not just one of degree, but of kind. Similarly, there is a world of difference between beef cuts from animals fattened up in feedlots, on a diet of maize based feeds and additives, and those from rustic cattle that are pastured outdoors for much of the year. A herd of healthy Dexter cattle grazing and raising their calves on a clean, untreated pasture in the West Country, supplemented by hay and fresh fodder in the winter, produce a dramatically different product from that produced by a herd of Angus[258] cattle being fattened on very low-quality dry feed and bovine growth hormones, living in their own filth in an overcrowded feedlot in Nebraska or California. Interestingly, even the colour, texture and flavour of these meats is remarkably different. Unfortunately, none of these fundamental nuances are factored into any of the major studies into the correlation between meat and cancer rates. Red meat is not a uniform product and any study that treats it as all the same cannot be taken seriously.

[257] https://www.who.int/features/qa/cancer-red-meat/en/

[258] Which is not the original Native Aberdeen Angus!

The same principle holds true for processed meats. On rare occasions, I eat *prosciutto* (raw ham) and *salame* made from *Cinta Senese* pigs. This is a very small, rustic, undemanding black and pink breed native of the Siena province. It can be found depicted in Medieval and Renaissance paintings and is a very hardy little pig that will forage a lot of its own food, that includes fallen fruit, chestnuts and acorns. The Cinta Sense ham itself is as good as any of the best hams in the world[259] and is remarkably different from the more commercial and highly valued Parma ham. Whilst undoubtedly very tasty, and free from all nitrates and preservatives, most Parma ham is nowadays usually a very industrial product made from factory farmed pigs and, as such, should not be presumed to be a healthy product. Sliding further down the quality ladder, one will find that the "average" packet of supermarket sausage, bacon and ham is a health hazard that should simply not be consumed on any occasion.

An affresco by Ambrogio Lorenzetti (1290-1348), found in the Palazzo civico del Comune di Siena, dated 1340. Spot the Cinta Senese pig.

TO SUM UP: there is no such thing as a single ideal diet, vegan or otherwise, nor a silver bullet to guarantee maximum sporting and amorous performance. Given the diversity of human populations, crops, animals and climates it would be very strange for a particular diet to be the best of all diets, under any circumstances. What we do know is that there are several healthy diets around the world and, whilst all good diets are based on the same principles, none of them are vegan. At the very least, we can say that a vegan diet is not necessarily the healthiest of diets, has not been proven to be the healthiest of diets, and is as yet an untested

[259] It is certainly as good as the wonderful but relatively overrated *jamon de bellota Iberico*.

and relatively new experiment. The burden of proof must rest with the vegan and, so far, the burden has not been met.

Green Misconceptions and Why We Need Livestock

The idea that veganism is better for human health is generally accompanied by the view that it is also better for planetary health. As should be clear from our previous overview of industrial vis-à-vis organic agriculture, this veganic misconception is based on a failure to distinguish between different agricultural models. As we saw, one of the key distinctions between the biological, organic model of agriculture and the chemical, industrial model is that the former is based on a cyclical soil-plant-animal web of symbiotic relationships, whereas the former is based on a segregation between these three crucial elements, which are managed under the linear input-output logic of the factory system. As such, the role of animals, and their impact on the environment and planetary health, is entirely dependent on the agricultural model we choose to adopt and assess. The strength of each of the now popularised arguments against meat eating and animal husbandry rests on these choices, rather than on meat eating per se.

One of the textbook arguments for veganism, and indeed for eating less meat, is based on the assertion that dairy, egg and meat production is inherently inefficient. Efficiency in this context is measured in terms of the ratio between edible crop used for feed and food outputs from livestock husbandry, also referred to as feed conversion ratio. A quick review of global agricultural trends reveals that, as it stands, animal agriculture is indeed highly inefficient. It is an indisputable fact that a high percentage of crops worldwide are grown for animal feed and crops like soya and maize are almost entirely dedicated to animal feed. Here in England, a high percentage of our cereal crops do indeed end up feeding animals, as does a high percentage of the calories in oilseed rape. As our vegan friends remind us, the crop input to animal product output ratio is very inefficient with X (always a high number) kilos of grain or soya needed to make 1 kg of meat.[260] Therefore, the argument goes, this is a very wasteful use of land and resources, as far less land would be required to feed the same number of people if they switched to a low meat or vegan diet: we could eat crops like wheat and soy directly, instead of eating the animals we feed on these sorts of crops. Wouldn't, say, 10kg of grains and legumes be better than 1kg of beef? Edible crops will always provide more calories overall than meat, once the conversion ratios are considered.

[260] Estimates vary enormously, but the general idea is that it takes several kilos of feed to produce 1 kg of meat. Beef is perceived to be particularly wasteful, with estimates of 5 to 10kg of feed needed for kilo of meat.

At face value, this is a seductive argument and hard to refute. One initial problem, however, is the implied equating of plant and animal foods: the idea that 1,000 calories of plant food are equivalent to 1,000 calories of animal food or that 100g of plant proteins are equivalent to 100g of animal proteins.[261] This is an oversimplification, based on textbook nutritionist assumptions: a calorie is a calorie, protein is protein and so on. In any case, even if we accepted the plant and animal calorie comparisons, we could also argue that, in a context of average or high crop productivity, it makes sense to sacrifice a percentage of the edible crops to produce more high value animal products and therefore enjoy an overall more diverse and rich diet. It may be better to sacrifice some of our weekly bread, oats and potato consumption if it means eating an egg and a glass of milk in the morning, some cheese or yogurt, and beef or pork a couple of times a week. However, we have to concede that in a context of food scarcity and diminishing productive potential, there is no question that, if survival and calorific intake were the be-all and end-all, eating edible crops directly is more efficient and will feed more people per acre. Does this mean that, ultimately, with a growing world population, the inefficiencies of meat production will need to give way to a vegan or mostly vegan diet? The short answer is "no", because the very simple problem with the whole inefficiency argument is that, just like World Health Organisation statements on the carcinogenic properties of meat, this argument is entirely based on statistics derived from the industrial meat production model.

Indeed, if animals are fed on purposefully grown monoculture crops, such as maize and soya, there will always be an inevitable degree of inefficiency. But this is neither inevitable nor irreversible, provided that animals are allowed to fulfil their biological functions. All we need to do is stop feeding farm animals with edible crops and feed them with what they are actually designed to eat: grasses, straw from edible crops, cover crops and crop waste. In one of the very best books on the subject, Simon Fairlie coins a term for the sort of meat produced this way: default meat.[262] The defining feature of "default meat" is the fact that it is a by-product of an agricultural system, rather than its primary goal. It is meat from animals raised for other purposes, such as traction, dairy and eggs, or from animals raised for meat that are fed from plants inedible for humans, such as grass, and from the waste products of agriculture, food manufacturing and human consumption. Meat produced in this way requires no extra land, feed or resources. It is a free byproduct of agriculture. Incorporating this meat into the human diet is inherently sustainable and is a prudent way of maximising available resources. It makes no sense, from an environmental and sustainability point of view, for a potato and vegetable grower not to keep a few pigs on the farm. The vegan or

[261] Plant and animal proteins are not directly comparable. Bioavailability varies, for example, with plant proteins generally less bioavailable than animal proteins.

[262] S. Fairlie, 2010, Meat: A Benign Extravagance.

vegetarian may justify eschewing the addition of animal products from "default livestock" on personal ethical grounds. They may not, however, do so on environmental or sustainability grounds. It is in fact inefficient and wasteful *not to* raise and eat default animals.

Despite these obvious truths, mainstream science, policy makers and the media, unable to see past the dogmas of industrial agriculture, simply focus on *industrial efficiency* rather than *ecological or biological efficiency* and will therefore inevitably argue that we need to improve feed to meat ratios and eat more chicken and less beef, given the former's more efficient grain to meat conversion. How about not feeding grain to beef cattle at all? This option, unfortunately, is rarely considered. In fact, many scientific studies, that do consider this option, have had the audacity to conclude that grass fed beef, and extensive farming, is the *worst* of all options and that factory farms, nasty as they be for animals, are better for the environment.[263] This is because they occupy less space, raise animals to slaughter faster, and therefore, they believe, end up emitting less methane per animal, as if that were the key measure of sustainability. This is sadly the result of a firm faith in the tenets of industrial efficiency and in the belief that, after all, a cow is a cow, a demonic emitter of methane, no matter how it is raised and where. The best we can hope for, in this mindset, is damage limitation, by farming very intensely on some land and sparing the rest. But, as we saw, another option is available: to allow animals to perform their ecological functions and to turn farmland into an environmental asset rather than a liability.

Needless to say, environmentalists like George Monbiot[264] and vegan activists like Ed Winters have latched onto scientific attempts to demonise pasture raised cattle from regenerative systems and have argued that, should we abandon feedlot beef and embrace regenerative grass-based systems, we would need to convert most of the land, forests included, to pasture, just to meet demand, and cause even more environmental damage in the process. This argument is misguided and irrelevant, for three main reasons: 1) Both the actual and potential productivity of grass-fed beef are underestimated; 2) No one on our side of the argument is suggesting that we should meet current demand for cheap beef: we should only supply as much beef as the land can produce through the most efficient regenerative methods;[265] 3) No one on our side of the argument is suggesting that we should

[263] See, for example: Capper, Judith L. 2012. "Is the Grass Always Greener? Comparing the Environmental Impact of Conventional, Natural and Grass-Fed Beef Production Systems" *Animals* 2, no. 2: 127-143. https://doi.org/10.3390/ani2020127

[264] George Monbiot argues that organic, pasture-fed beef and lamb are the most damaging of all farm products, worse than feedlot beef and factory farms. See G. Monbiot, 2023, Regenesis: Feeding the World Without Devouring the Planet.

[265] If this ultimately results in higher average costs, especially for prime cuts, that would be a price worth paying, as we are eating too much cheap, low-quality beef in many parts of the world. We need to focus on quality over quantity. Regenerative grass-based systems, in any case, could potentially still produce vast amounts of meat, especially in countries like ours.

chop down forests or protected wilderness to graze cattle. In fact, quite the contrary: we need to end deforestation and reforest as many recently deforested parts of the world as possible. Most importantly, we should change the way we use all *existing farmland* worldwide, for both crops and livestock, and increase arboreal cover across farmland. The only *additional* productive land should come from the regeneration of degraded marginal land (and there is plenty of it around the world) and use livestock as part of that process.

But what about animals which, unlike sheep, goats and beef cattle, actually need to consume edible crops, especially grains, as part of their diet? The simple answer here is that we must eat less of these animals globally. Daily chicken consumption will never be a sustainable option, under any agricultural system. Just how much poultry could the world raise and consume sustainably? The measure of sustainability here depends on overall grain productivity minus human grain consumption. This will determine how much maize can be fed to poultry or how much barley can be spared for dairy cows and pigs. The more successful and productive a farming system is in raising crops, the more crops can be spared for raising animals. The goal of the sustainable farmer is to keep the soil healthy and fertile, so that it will produce high crop yields, which allows for a greater percentage of crops that can be spared for animals, as well as more crop waste. It must also be remembered that the raising of crops, if it is going be productive and free from chemical fertilisers and agrochemicals, requires animals for their role in maintaining fertility. The simple, inconvenient truth is that the vegan utopia is particularly compatible with industrial chemical monoculture, which requires no animals whatsoever to raise crops. It is no coincidence that vegan activists are comfortable with promoting the use of synthetic fertilisers.[266] It is impossible to see how this is more sustainable and environmentally friendly, in any shape or form.

The vegan rebuttal to this may be that an "organic vegan" system, such as the one promoted by Iain Tolhurst,[267] which featured in Monbiot's *Apocalypse Cow* documentary, is workable. It can sustain itself by composting all plant waste and by growing green manures[268] on rotated fields, in order to allow the soil to regenerate in between vegetable crops. This is certainly a workable system, but it is still ecologically inefficient: even if we allow for rotated green manure fields, it would be far better to have these regularly grazed by animals. It would also make sense for all the crop waste and crop residue to be eaten by animals. Then

[266] E. Winters, 2023, How to Argue With a Meat Eater (And Win Every Time), Chapter 16, Audiobook. Winters argues that we do not need animal manure, *"what we need is the nutrients in manure that help with fertilisation, primarily nitrogen, phosphorus and potassium"* and that these should come from synthetic fertilisers. In other words, Winters is a textbook NPK reductionist.

[267] http://www.tolhurstorganic.co.uk/. Winters also mentions this as a possibility in the Chapter above, referring to it as *"veganic farming"*.

[268] Green manures are crops such as clover and ryegrass that are grown to help regenerate fertility and rest soil in between demanding food crops such as potatoes.

we would kill two birds with one stone: we would maintain fertility *and* produce additional animal products all on the same land, with the same resources. Iain Tolhurst could grow just as many crops, if not more, as he currently does and raise a small flock of sheep and a couple of pigs a year, all on the same land and without additional resources. Vegan organic systems, whilst clearly workable on individual small farms such as Iain Tolhurst's, make little overall sense were organic farming to be the global norm. The inefficiencies of managing organic waste and fertility without animals, and the forced abandonment of farmland unsuited to arable farming,[269] not to mention the complete abandonment of seas, rivers and lakes, render global veganism an undesirable and ineffective solution to our problems.

Another claim that is repeatedly made alongside the feed to meat ratio inefficiency argument, is the claim that, apparently, an enormous amount of water[270] is needed to make 1kg of meat. Again, the answer to this apparent problem lies in the radical distinction between husbandry methods and between geographical regions. Beef raised in a feedlot in the Californian Central Valley will have a completely different water footprint to a steer raised on rain swept lush meadows in the West Country of England. There is no question that a standard industrial beef feedlot in California is an environmental disaster on every level. The enormous amounts of grain-based feed required to fatten these miserable animals, the mind-boggling amounts of bore well water used in what is an arid, hot and dry part of the world and the lagoons of manure produced as a waste product alone render this operation a perfect example of the damage that industrial agriculture can do. If this was the only way to raise cattle, we should side with the vegans, on environmental, ethical and health grounds. But, mercifully, not only we do not need to feed cattle with tonnes of maize feed and growth hormones, we also do not need to waste enormous amounts of water in the process of raising them.

That not every beef cattle can possibly be said to waste Olympic sized pools of water to produce some mince seems very obvious when we leave the feedlot operations of the arid Central Valley and move our attention to responsible, sustainable, holistic grazing operations that do not require drawing water from finite acquirers. As Fairlie observed, looking at his steer Bramley contentedly grazing in a wet Dorset pasture, it is impossible to see how such a steer could possibly consume, or indeed waste, such prodigious quantities of water.[271] Bramley, apparently, eventually produced at least 125kg of beef: even if we took the relatively low 15,000 litre estimate quoted earlier, we would need to conclude that Bramley

[269] Whole swathes of land would become unproductive: what would we do with the millions of acres in Scotland, Wales, the West Country and Cumbria that are unsuitable for crop production? Rewilding, as we saw, is not the answer.

[270] Always in the several thousands and as Simon Fairlie points out, figures as high as 100,000 litres have been bandied about for many years now.

[271] S. Fairlie, 2010, Meat: A Benign Extravagance, pages 63-64.

consumed an astonishing 1,875 tonnes of water throughout its lifetime. This is clearly absurd. As we saw earlier, sound agricultural practice is based on cycles, rather than linear processes, and this naturally includes water. Whilst a steer like Bramley may drink up to 50 litres of water per day, in many parts of the world like Dorset this modest amount would be from rain fed bore well water, which is by definition replenishable. Also, as Fairlie points out, it is impossible to understand why this water is supposedly wasted or somehow disappears.

Bramley's daily drink simply ends up in the pastures, in the form of pee and manure, which is absorbed by the soil, and in respiration, in the form of water vapour which will eventually return in the form of rain. Bramley, much like any other herbivore, simply plays his role in nature's water cycles. His unfortunate Californian counterparts, on the other hand, are denied the ability to partake in such a process. Their water is drawn from diminishing acquirers that are being used faster than they are being replenished, in a parched part of the world, and their pee and manure hits cement and lifeless dirt, rather than grass, and is washed away into lagoons by yet more bore well water. It is probably from these cattle that the sorts of figures quoted in vegan sources like *The Game Changers*, which goes for "2,400 litres of water for 1 hamburger", are drawn from. This should not fool us into falling in a state of aquatic guilt next time we tuck into our roast beef. In fact, unlike intensively managed arable land, grassland has the ability to retain moisture in the ground and is far more resilient to both draught and flood. Well managed pasture and regenerative grazing can prevent or reverse desertification: livestock are crucial to maintaining and regenerating freshwater cycles. The devil is in the detail.

Beef cattle happily grazing on the pastures at Daylesford Organic Farm, Gloucestershire.

The devil is also in the detail when it comes to the supposedly devastating effect of methane emissions from cattle.[272] The first thing to clarify is that, contrary to popular perception, it is burps, rather than farts, that are responsible for bovine methane emissions. But, even if it happened to be posterior flatulence that were primarily responsible for said emissions, we would be wrong to see this as inherently problematic. Methane from herbivores, whether domestic or wild, is part of the natural nutrient and atmospheric cycles of our planet: it is inevitable, necessary and continuously recycled. In a nutshell: plants and soil absorb carbon dioxide → solid carbon is absorbed by herbivores through the consumption of plants → carbon dioxide and methane are emitted by herbivores → methane breaks down to carbon dioxide over time → carbon dioxide is absorbed by plants and the soil. Therefore, in terms of *net carbon dioxide*, herbivores are more or less neutral, *provided they are permitted to live as herbivores should.*

This is true for all herbivores, whether caribou, deer, antelope, sheep or cows, not to mention the millions and millions of bison that once roamed upon the Prairies. I use the words "more or less neutral" quite intentionally, as the very concept of carbon neutrality is somewhat dubious. Apart from the impossibility of tracking the carbon cycle of any system with accuracy, and apart from the natural variability in atmospheric carbon which predates any reasonable concerns about anthropogenic emissions, it is also a mistake to assess the sustainability of an agroecosystem by focusing on carbon dioxide. As Will Harris of White Oak Pastures aptly put it *"the myopic focus that's currently happening with soil carbon measurements and carbon credits is too reductionist. It's not all about the damn carbon."*[273] Agroecosystems are complex living systems, by definition, and carbon dioxide is just one of many elements and factors to be considered. What matters when raising herbivorous livestock is the overall context in which they are raised. Is it a system that mimics wild herbivore behaviour? Do the animals live as their nature intended? Is it a system built upon living soil? Is its fertility mostly self-sustaining? Does it allow for complex biodiversity? Can it cope with climatic variability and extremes? And so on. If the answer to these questions is a resounding "yes", there is basically no need to fret about bovine emissions as the be-all and end-all of sustainability.

[272] The supposedly devastating effects of grazing cattle have been documented in a series of high-profile papers and studies. See, for example. Garnett, T., Godde, C., Muller, A., Röös, E., Smith, P., de Boer, I. J. M., zu Ermgassen, E., Herrero, M., van Middelaar, C. E., Schader, C., & van Zanten, H. H. E. (2017). Grazed and confused? Ruminating on cattle, grazing systems, methane, nitrous oxide, the soil carbon sequestration question - and what it all means for greenhouse gas emissions. FCRN. https://edepot.wur.nl/427016

[273] W. Harris, 2023, A Bold Return to Giving a Damn, page 236.

It is no coincidence that it is proponents of industrial livestock systems, which fail to comply with any of the above criteria, who are now looking at ways to "lower methane emissions" with the usual misguided techno-fixes, exercises in damage limitation and attempts to basically retain the status quo whilst being able to claim lower emissions. There are now mainstream scientists, academic institutions and companies that are developing "methane inhibitors" to feed cattle with, that are developing vaccines that could reduce the activity of methane-producing microbes in a cow's stomach, and that are looking at ways to use gene editing to select animals that produce less methane. Instead of building systems that allow cattle to live as cattle should, the conventional approach is to tinker with narrow elements of the factory farm system in order to achieve very reductive, marginal gains and be able to claim greater "efficiency".

Lastly, it is also important to point out that there is also a clear difference between methane emitted from biological sources and methane emitted from industrial sources. Methane emissions from oil and gas wells is methane that was previously locked underground and, the minute that it is emitted, is a net *addition* to the carbon cycle. Livestock such as those on industrial feedlot operations are substantial net emitters of methane, and therefore carbon dioxide, precisely because they are unable to contribute to the natural carbon cycle and because their whole existence is dependent upon an ocean of petroleum and on a long supply chain of industrial activity. More could be said on this subject but, for our purposes, I would simply urge the reader not to succumb to the fashionable demonisation of the cow. Cows are not the problem. How we currently treat and raise them is the problem. Next time you see cattle quietly grazing on lush pastures or some brisket from a good farmer on your plate on a Sunday, remember that you are not witnessing the destruction of our planet. There is a long list of things you do that are far more likely to contribute to planetary destruction... in your garage, in your home, in your office, in your waste bin, in your shopping basket.

It's Not Easy Being Green: Moving Away from the Plant vs Animal Mindset

The depiction of animal products as environmental liabilities usually implies that plant alternatives are better for the environment. As already conceded, this is indeed often the case when we consider animal products such as feedlot beef as our benchmark. Kilo per kilo, calorie for calorie, nutrient for nutrient, there is no doubt that the most damaging food products on the planet, and indeed in history, are those from livestock factory farms, in all their forms, including intensive fish farms. The same mantra that has been valid so far, however, applies here too: animal products compare badly with plant alternatives only when we compare industrial animal products with plant-based alternatives. The comparison fails however, when we compare high quality animal products with their plant alternatives, especially when those plant alternatives are from conventional, agrochemical dependent agriculture.

It was again Simon Fairlie who explicitly exposed the limits of the veganic environmental thinking, when he lived within an alternative community:

"It (the commune) aspired towards self-sufficiency but spent about £200 a fortnight importing olive oil, sunflower oil, margarine, peanut butter, tahini, soya milk and yoghurt, nuts, chick peas, beans, lentils, molasses, dried fruit, rice, quinoa and more.

Meanwhile the grass and dairy operation on site – for which Fairlie was responsible – produced perhaps 350 kilos of meat, dripping and lard a year. "We were producing, from grass, a substantial proportion of the protein and fat that we required for our nutrition, but this was shunned. Instead we imported it from countries where people go hungry."[274]

There are two primary considerations at play here: locality and production method. Does it make environmental sense to import plant products from the other side of the planet and ignore local, animal product alternatives? Does it make environmental sense to opt for industrial crops when organic animal products are available? These sorts of questions render environmental considerations more complex than simple plant vs animal calculations. Plant foods are, at times, worst for the environment: milk is a perfect example. As Fairlie rightly noted, it makes little environmental sense to consume soya or almond milk from overseas whilst living in England, when our domestic grass-fed cows can produce nutritionally dense whole milk. Plant milk, if indeed we can call it "milk", can often have very dubious green credentials. Where do the almonds or soya come from and what is involved in their production? An estimated 80% of the world's almonds are produced in California. The methods used to grow these almonds are those of conventional agriculture. The California almonds[275] are grown as monocultures on bare, overcultivated soil and are entirely dependent on heavy application of agrochemicals.

Their pollination is harmful to bees and the trees are thirsty for finite acquirer water in a state exponentially prone to drought and wildfires. It is probably a bad idea to grow almonds on such a scale in a place like California to begin with, but it is certainly a bad idea to grow them with these methods. It is impossible to see how someone living in England could argue that drinking imported milk made with such almonds is not worse for the environment than

[274] https://www.flintoff.org/eat-meat-to-save-planet

[275] The almond varieties themselves are part of the problem, as they have been selected for size and for the softness of their shell, rather than flavour and nutrition.

drinking whole cow's milk from the very best of our pasture based organic farms. What holds true for milk, often holds true for butter and animal fats. As Fairlie points out, vegetable oils, apart from being mostly imported in a Northern country like Britain, are rather expensive in terms of land use. The yields of most vegetable oil crops are rather low, especially when compared to the fats of our domestic livestock. Furthermore, some of these vegetable fats, such as palm oil, are particularly destructive: when the deforestation involved in the establishment of palm oil plantations is accounted for, it must be one of the worst foods on Earth, plant or otherwise.

Of course, as the more thoughtful vegan will point out, plant milk and vegetable oil does not need to derive from Californian almonds or Indonesian palm oil plantations. Here in Britain, milk could come from organic oats, for example, which, whilst less nutritionally dense, are perfectly sustainable. All this illustrates is that the division between plants and animals, in environmental terms, is inconsistent and unclear: there is no direct correlation between the plant or animal origin of a product and its environmental footprint, once locality and productive method are taken into account, as the simple table below illustrates. Overall, the two factors most likely to contribute to a heavy environmental footprint are the use of industrial methods and food miles. The worst food items are those right at the top of the table, whether plant or animal: an imported industrial product is generally worse than any of the alternatives.

Whilst this hard and fast rule generally holds, there are a lot of nuances and grey areas, which render shopping and food selection an exercise in judgement and compromise, if environmental sustainability is our main concern. Sometimes, there may be a clash between a concern for farming methods and a concern for seasonality and food miles. Is imported organic quinoa better or worse than conventional Scottish oats? Is it better to import organic apples out of season from Chile or opt for conventional seasonal British apples? Is it better to purchase grass-fed New Zealand lamb or English beef from a feedlot? Whilst, as previously argued, we should certainly not be importing lamb and apples from the other side of the planet, the answer is not always clear when imported high-quality products are compared with mediocre local alternatives.

Having said that, more often than not, productive method does trump food miles: organic olive oil from Italy or Greece is better than our conventional home-grown rapeseed oil, which we could really do without. Similarly, I would generally choose imported organic bananas over our domestic conventional strawberries, which are sprayed with all sorts of nasty products. I would undoubtedly choose Alaskan wild salmon or Icelandic cod over farmed Scottish salmon. The good news is that we don't always need to make these choices, if we take the time and care to select what we eat and if we respect seasonality and prioritise it.

When productive methods are comparable, we should always prioritise local products: domestic organic apples always trump organic apples from Chile. If industrial and imported/out of season is generally the worst option, organic and local/seasonal is generally the best option. As previously argued, it makes perfect sense to enrich our diets with high quality imports, especially of non-perishable foods we cannot possibly produce, but the foundations of our diets ought to be homegrown, and not just for environmental reasons.

Whatever the answer to all these questions and shopping conundrums, one thing that is clear is that there is no direct correlation between plant origin and environmental sustainability, and indeed vice versa. In several instances, the animal product is better than the plant product, as in the case of organic British cow's milk vs Californian almond's milk. In other instances, the plant product is better than the animal product, as in the case of British organic oat's milk vs industrial British cow's milk. The environmental footprint of several plant products can be quite startling. Apart from the obvious problems associated with soya and palm oil, there are many plant-based products that are problematic, from unseasonal conventionally produced vegetables flown across the planet such as Peruvian asparagus, to most wines.

The inclusion of champagne and prosecco in the table below may surprise some of my readers. However, we must bear in mind that grape vines are subjected to an especially potent dousing of chemicals,[276] are grown in monocultures and, given that wine's nutritional value is limited and its consumption optional, represents a rather extravagant use of land. The global demand for Prosecco has led to a massive expansion of its acreage in the North-East of Italy, displacing other crops and pasture, which has led to the poisoning of several tracts of land, soil erosion and well-documented health issues for the local communities.

[276] Pesticide residues in wine are particularly high. In 2014, a French organic farmer in Burgundy was fined for refusing to spray pesticides. This anecdote gives an indication of the entrenched and systematic application of agrochemicals on grape vines. See: https://www.theguardian.com/world/2014/feb/23/french-organic-winemaker-prison-pesticide

Industrial / Local*

Plant Product	Animal Product
Rapeseed Oil	British Feedlot Beef
Conventional Milling Wheat	British Factory Farmed Pork
Sugar Beet	British Factory Farmed Chicken
Conventional Potatoes	Scottish Farmed Salmon
Conventional Broccoli/Cauliflower	Bernard Matthews Turkey
Conventional Apples	Conventional Milk
Conventional Strawberries	Conventional Cheddar Cheese
Conventional Lager/Ales	Red Tractor Eggs

* I use "industrial" in the broadest sense of the word as explained in previous chapters. This can include healthy but unsustainable fish, such as bluefin tuna, which are subjected to industrial fishing methods that seem perfectly designed to decimate them and destroy sea life as a whole.

Industrial/ Imported

Plant Product	Animal Product
Indonesian Palm Oil	USDA Feedlot Beef
Californian Almond Milk	Danish/Dutch Factory Farmed Pork
Soya Products	Vietnamese/Honduran Farmed Prawns
Central American Pineapples	Brazilian Factory Farmed Chicken
Peruvian Asparagus	Foie Gras
Sugar Cane	Bluefin Tuna
Canadian Wheat Flour	Conventional French Cheese
Champagne & Prosecco	Conventional Parma Ham

Organic / Local

Plant Product	Animal Product
Organic Broad Beans and Peas	Organic/Grass Fed Beef
Organic Oats and Oat's Milk	Organic/Grass Fed Lamb
Organic Potatoes	British Wood Pigeon
Organic Root Vegetables	Organic Cheddar
Organic Apples & Pears	Organic Eggs
Organic Lettuce	Rare Breed/Heritage Organic Pork
Organic Milling Wheat	Organic Milk
Wild Mushrooms	Pole and Line Caught Mackerel

* I use "organic" in the broadest sense of the word as explained in previous chapters: it is not a matter of certification. The organic category here includes wild foods, provided they are sustainably sourced.

Organic / Imported

Plant Product	Animal Product
Organic Animal Feed (maize, soya etc...)	Italian/Spanish Sheep Cheese
Organic Italian/Indian Rice	Wild Boar Sausage (EU)
Organic Italian/Greek Olive Oil	Alpine Cow's Cheese
Organic Lentils and Chickpeas (EU/Turkey/China)	Icelandic Cod
Organic Peruvian/Bolivian Quinoa	Cinta Senese Prosciutto
Organic Sugar Cane	Jamon de Bellota
Organic Bananas	Alaskan Wild Salmon
Organic Cocoa, Tea and Coffee	New Zealand Organic Lamb

What should be clear from all the above is that, instead of a plant vs animal mindset, we should mostly be concerned with how plants are grown and how animals are raised. There is no doubt that if the environment is our main concern,[277] we should stick to the sorts of products listed in tables 3 and 4 and stay away from those in tables 1 and 2.

Overall, TO SUM UP: the vegan diet is better for the environment than a conventional Western diet, which is the worst of all diets, and that's all. It is not necessarily better than a conscientious omnivorous diet, in fact quite the opposite.

Pigs Are Not Our Siblings

In the final analysis, once biological, nutritional and environmental arguments are exhausted, the case for veganism must rest on ideological grounds. It is for this reason that, when it comes down to it, most contemporary vegans defend their worldview in terms of "animal rights" which, they argue, are comparable to human rights. Seen in this light, animals have a "right to life"[278] and a right to liberty comparable to that bestowed upon people. They consider themselves "abolitionists"[279] and oppose the concept of animal welfare, on the grounds that animal welfare presumes the amelioration of animal husbandry, the continued use of animals for our purposes and reaffirms the status of domestic animals as property. In the same way that we would not argue in favour of a humane form of slavery, they claim, we should not argue in favour of animal welfare, humane slaughter and so on. This worldview, in fairness, is internally consistent: if humans and animals are broadly comparable, we must apply the same moral standards to both.

Therefore, the key assumption in the philosophy of the animal rights movement is a rejection of human exceptionalism[280] which, as I will argue, leads to the inevitable moral confusion between humans and animals. The first problem with the notion of animal rights lies in a misuse and misunderstanding of what we mean by "right", if we are to use the term with any consistency. When it comes to "rights", what applies to the human cannot apply to the animal, given our intrinsic differences. In the human realm, a right implies a duty. If I claim to have such a thing as a right to life, that is under the understanding that I have a duty to respect your equal right to such a life. We live in a world of reciprocal rights and duties under

[277] Not that it necessarily should be. It ought to be one of our main concerns, not the main concern.

[278] Interestingly, I have not come across any vegan thinkers or activists who believe in the "right to life" of the human foetus or who oppose abortion. This is consistent with the fact that veganism is an ideological offshoot of liberalism and secularism.

[279] A term intentionally borrowed from the 19th Century abolitionist movement. The equating of human slavery with animal husbandry is a strategy deployed by many in the vegan movement, from the thinkers and philosophers of the movement like Gary Francione and Tom Regan, to activists like Joseph Armstrong and Ed Winters.

[280] Understood as the idea that the difference between humans and animals is one of *kind* rather than *degree*.

the presumption that we are members of a moral community, made up of free agents. With freedom, comes the burden of responsibility and with responsibility come consequences. Even our right to life, enshrined in law, can be surrendered when we fail to fulfil our half of the bargain, which is why I can be killed in self-defence, without my killer being convicted of murder or infringing upon my rights.

The animal rights theorists will invariably ask: what about the rights of babies or of other humans who, through circumstance or disability, are unable to fulfil any duties or make any moral decisions? If we respect their rights, why not those of animals? The simple answer here is that youth, misfortune or disability cannot disqualify fellow members of our moral community from equal consideration. A baby is a future member of the moral community and, by default, needs to be educated as such. Someone in an irreversible coma cannot be excluded from the moral community any more than someone with a severe neurological disability can be excluded, as basic human virtues of empathy, integrity and dignity will compel us to include those less fortunate than ourselves into our sphere of protection. However, even if we ignore the demands of virtue and we just take a rights-based approach to understand this problem, it should be clear that accident or misfortune are insufficient reasons for someone to lose their rights, whatever those may be. Mrs Smith's property cannot be stolen just because she is now in a vegetative state; nor can John's trust fund be appropriated because he is born with severe neurological disabilities. The fact that little Jack has Down's Syndrome does not mean that his organs can be extracted and used to save the life of other children. In fact, a person does not even need to be alive for their interests and reasons to matter, which is why we tend to respect wills, trusts and bequests and why we will feel bound to keep death bed promises, to be honoured long beyond the death of the supplicant, unless we have really good reasons not to do so.

In other words, exceptions to the norm cannot be grounds to withdraw our moral concern and neglect our duties towards those can no longer, have never been or will never ever be responsible for themselves. The same can never be said of a crab, of a mouse or of a cat. They are just not the kind of beings that could possibly, ever, be members of the moral community. They are morally innocent and unbounded by our constraints and responsibilities. There is nothing criminal in the cat playing with the mouse or killing songbirds for fun, nor do we judge the lion as a moral monster for killing a rival's cubs or indeed condemn a tiger or crocodile for killing a human.[281] The cuckoo's penchant for nest

[281] This clear distinction between us and predator animals should be morally uncontroversial. The wilful ignoring of this obvious fact is one of the many philosophical failings in Sam Harris' dreadful book on "the delusion" of free will (S. Harris, 2012, Free Will). In his lecture on Free Will at the Festival of Dangerous Ideas 2012 (available on YouTube), Harris argued that if only we had a better understanding of neurology, we would not morally condemn a human murderer any more severely than we would condemn a homicidal crocodile: both are ultimately biochemical automatons with no ability to make free choices. It should be clear that no rational person would pass moral judgement on a homicidal crocodile but would do so for a murderer.

stealing is not an infringement of property rights, as no such right exists outside our rational, moral order. The world of animals, with or without human agency and intervention, is one where the idea of a right to life or property simply does not have any correspondence with reality. Furthermore, it *cannot and must not* have any correspondence with reality, as the natural order relies on the endless interaction between predator and prey, those who are eaten and those who eat them. To wish for a world where animals are protected from their designated end, which is to both eat and be eaten, is to simply wish the world away and demonstrates an inability to accept and face the mysterious but very real fact that life and death are mutually interdependent. Creatures must die so that other creatures may live, in a cycle with no beginning nor end. To opt out of this cycle, apart from being practically impossible, given that all food production, including grains and vegetables, involves suffering, displacement and death,[282] is to opt out of life altogether.

Of course, this does not mean that we must necessarily directly participate in the dance of prey and predator: hunting and animal husbandry is not for everyone[283] and there is much to be said for acts of personal sacrifice and spiritual renunciation. The Buddha and his monks, for example, abstained from the intentional killing of other creatures or indeed from any form of food production and relied on food alms from the lay community for their sustenance. Interestingly, this did not preclude meat eating, as the Buddha and his monks ate whatever was offered. The Buddha did make it clear that he did not want lay people to sacrifice and slaughter any animal specifically for his sake. If, however, he arrived at a village or a home unannounced, which was often the case, he gratefully accepted whatever food was offered, animal or otherwise. In Buddhist ethics, intention is what matters, rather than taboos, ritualistic fasts or indeed any idea of intrinsic rights. The goal is to reduce suffering and transcend selfish desire, in all its forms. The Jains, on the other hand, were careful to avoid all killing and harmful action, even unintentional.[284] The spiritual utopia of the Jains was deemed to be unrealistic and counterproductive by the Buddha. In any case, the Jains did not avoid killing due to any conception of animal rights, but due to their belief that all forms of harm had negative karmic consequences. Be that as it may, no spiritual and religious

[282] Consider the simple fact that cultivation alone, whether ploughing, harrowing or planting, will alter soil and its biology most dramatically. After ploughing, scavenging birds like crows tend to descend upon the field, to feast on the myriads of insects and rodents killed in the process. Consider also the inevitable removal and containment of trees, shrubs, weeds and pests involved in all forms of agriculture and land management, even at its best: this has real life and death consequences for wildlife and for all the animals that coexist with us on the farm.

[283] As my sister often reminds me, she could never bring herself to kill and butcher one of my hares or muntjacs but approves of my doing so and will happily eat them once transformed into classic dishes. This should not be confused with the hypocrisy of those who condemn hunting and eat meat: one can approve of an activity without wanting to engage in it. Afterall, almost everyone will approve of growing and eating vegetables, but only a minority wish to do it themselves.

[284] Jain monks went to great pains to avoid stepping on insects or breathing them in, as even unintentional killing was perceived to be karmically significant.

tradition has ever equated animals to humans or sought to grant animals anything like an inviolable right to life.

To attempt to equate our fellow humans with animals is a relatively novel idea, arguably directly correlated with the abandonment of traditional religion and its replacement with liberal, secular alternatives, fuelled by dogmatic pseudo-Darwinian reasoning. Whatever the ideological roots of this worldview might be, it should be clear to any thinking person that a pig is not comparable to my sister, nor can a cow be compared with my mother. I have killed and butchered many animals, but I can never be said to have committed murder[285] or cannibalism. The anthropomorphic, juvenile attempts to equate persons with animals, no matter how charming or lovable they may be, can only lead to a devaluation of ourselves and to a misunderstanding of animals. It is perhaps no coincidence that animal rights activists, as indeed many environmentalists, often exhibit strong misanthropic tendencies, depicting humans as a scourge on the planet and depicting animals as superior to humans, in their innocence. There is both truth and falsity in this idea. The burden of humanity is indeed that we are capable of both good and evil, unlike animals. We are the authors of both the best and worst acts on Earth. Our cruelty towards other animals can be boundless, but so can our mercy. We may force feed geese in a factory farm, torture dogs or harvest bile from caged bears, but we may also go out of our way, and at times dedicate our whole lives, to rescuing orangutangs, tending to stray cats or replanting forests. We should condemn and praise ourselves accordingly. Animals, in their innocence, are free from both our condemnation and praise.

Most importantly, the anthropomorphic idealisation of animals does not necessarily do animals any good. To ascribe a "right to life" to a deer does not necessarily benefit deer in any significant way. Deer are prey animals which, left to their only devices, usually end their life by being eaten in one way or other: either by a predator or, when they die of starvation or disease,[286] by the various scavengers and creepy crawlies who pounce upon dying animals and act as nature's recyclers. In Britain, there are no predators that can feed on deer and an estimated 350,000 deer are culled annually to keep the estimated population of up to 2 million stable.[287] Vegans and animal rights activists have advocated contraceptive control, rather than culling, to manage UK deer populations and the introduction of wolves to control wild boar populations in Spain and Italy. These examples show that their key concern cannot logically be the "right to life" of animals but a taboo against humans

[285] Animal rights activists often refer to hunters, fishermen, and butchers as "murderers".

[286] All of these alternative ends are likely to be far more prolonged and painful than the average death at the hands of a human hunter with a rifle.

[287] The Mammal Society, DEFRA. There is controversy about the total deer population, which can only ever be estimated. What is certain is that Britain is full of deer.

engaging in hunting. Animal welfare cannot be the main concern either, as it is hard to imagine a deer benefiting from infertility, or a wild boar's life being ameliorated from being killed by a pack of wolves rather than by a human hunter. In fact, surely, a good human hunter is generally the best of all hunters, given his unique concern for bringing about a swift death. A conscientious hunter will avoid shooting a deer if a kill is unlikely and will avoid the risk of wounding an animal or risk a prolonged death. No such scruples will ever trouble a pack of wolves, of course, and rightly so.

The Author after a successful hunt in Hertfordshire, 2019.
This is neither murder, nor the breach of any rights.

If we were to follow the abolitionist principles of animal rights theorists, we would need to abandon all animal domestication,[288] which would inevitably lead to the eventual extinction of domesticated animals, apart from those who manage to survive as feral creatures or a few specimens kept in "sanctuaries". Why a world with no chickens, pigs, sheep, cows, donkeys, dogs, cats and so on is a better world than one with these animals in it can only be understood as yet another expression of misanthropy, rather than real love for animals. Of course, if domesticated animals were only ever abused in factory farms, then the end of domestication would be welcome. But, as I have argued throughout this book, that is clearly not the case: the factory farm is a relatively recent, horrific phenomenon, which is neither necessary nor unavoidable. The life of a contented sheep or pig that has been looked after with care and sacrifice by a good farmer compares very well with that of any wild animal. To "liberate" these animals makes no practical or logical sense, as their very existence and well-being are defined by dependency on and companionship with conscientious humans.

My Great-grandfather Giampietro Filippi in his Sardinian homeland after a day's shooting.

[288] Gary Francione, as many other animal rights activists, has rescued pet dogs but advocates for the end of all domestication. In his ideal world, we would stop breeding dogs, which would eventually go extinct. It seems convenient and somewhat hypocritical for Francione to enjoy the pleasures of dog ownership in his lifetime whilst advocating for its future abolition.

Animal Liberation?

> *"Animals are individuals–their own people–and have the right to live free from human exploitation."*[289]

The argument for "animal liberation" rests upon another erroneous idea: animal "freedom" and hope for the future liberation of animals. It should be clear that one of the great divides between us and animals is that the latter do not have, by definition, anything that could be considered comparable to freedom. Freedom must involve the agency of self-conscious beings that can choose to act in ways which, in principle, could be otherwise. As discussed, it involves self-determination, reciprocal rights and duties, responsibility, the possibility of success and failure, the ability to judge and be judged. A human being may claim to be "liberated" when his or her most basic ability to self-determine is restored, when his or her dignity is finally recognised as sacrosanct. No such freedom exists in the world of animals. To claim that animals are "their own people" is to either misunderstand people or animals or both. What do we actually mean when we say that an animal is free? All that we can actually mean to say is that an animal is free if it lives as its nature intended. A wolf is free if it lives as part of a roaming wolf pack pursuing its prey, a rabbit is free if it lives as a herbivorous rodent living as part of a colony, dwelling in burrows. And that is all, as no other options, other than those that humans might impose upon them, are available. There are no other possibilities, choices and lifestyles available to animals other than those strictly dictated by their nature. A majestic eagle flying in the sky, often a symbol of freedom, is only free in so far that, unlike an eagle in confinement, it is able to live as an eagle should. No other lifestyle is available. In the grand scheme of things, the eagle is no more or less free than a soldier ant or a little sparrow.

The only really useful but misleading use of the term "freedom" when applied to animals occurs when an animal is freed from an unnatural situation which prevents it from living as its nature intended. A bird in a cage is freed when released in so far as flying is a fundamental feature of what being a bird is all about. This is true for both wild and domesticated animals, albeit with important differences. Freedom for a domesticated animal, by definition, is freedom to engage in its natural behaviours *as a domesticated animal*: as in an animal dependent on human care and husbandry. Whereas an eagle's freedom consists in command of the sky and in life as an aerial predator, without human aid or control, a chicken's freedom consists in the ability to express, as Joel Salatin would say, its inherent "chickenness": the ability to roam, fly, scratch, nest, establish a pecking order, nest, lay eggs

[289] https://www.peta.org/about-peta/faq/what-is-speciesism/

and so on. Freedom for a chicken does not consist in being released in a forest or a beach and left to fend for itself. The expression "free-range" when referred to a chicken, provided it is used by a conscientious farmer, refers to the provision of adequate space and resources for a chicken to express its chickenness. It cannot, and should not, mean a release into the wild which would almost certainly spell death at the hands of a fox or of another opportunistic predator.

One freedom that no animal has, both wild and domesticated, is freedom from the inevitable: death. This is true whether death comes at the hand of a human or of another animal. When a mouse is caught by an owl or a chicken slaughtered by a good farmer, no freedom is being infringed, as predation and death is exactly what nature intends for prey animals. Attempts to "liberate" animals does not seem to benefit them in any meaningful way, nor prevent a painful death. The end of hunting wild animals or livestock husbandry would not prevent animals from living, being killed and being eaten: "liberation" from human intervention does not equal an end to the immutable law of nature. It is also worth noting that, even in a world without hunting and livestock husbandry, our vital interests inevitably clash with those of animals. In the vegan utopia, there still remains the problem to how to control pests,[290] whether it is slugs eating our crops, mice entering our homes or those eating our grains and, most importantly, there remains the simple reality that all sorts of human activities, from building homes and roads to taking down trees for timber and fuel, involve displacement of animals and clashes between our interests and their needs and habitats. Therefore, I would suggest, instead of hankering after what cannot possibly be, our efforts should be spent towards the preservation of the natural world, the maximisation of biodiversity and towards developing a healthy symbiotic relationship with our domesticated companions.

[290] My fellow Director and partner-in-crime extraordinaire at Local Organic Growers CIC, Nabs Lilley, is, believe it or not, a committed vegan. Unlike many of her fellow vegans, she is open minded and accepting of our stark differences. The more horticultural experience she gained, the more the complexities of our inevitable clashes with pests became clear to her. During the 2024 season, given unprecedented slug numbers, she assisted in my regular collection of slugs, which I fed to our neighbour's chickens.

Hertfordshire, 2023. The Author with some hares for the pot after a great evening out. The man next to me, Jim Shaw, was a much beloved teacher at my school, who used to bring me the odd brace of pheasants during the shooting season. He took me and a few other boys to shoot clay pigeons on more than one occasion, giving us a taste for his favourite past times. For this and many other reasons, I will always be grateful to Jim.

The Virtues of Speciesism and Aristotle: Swat Flies, Pet Dogs, Eat Rabbits

"Speciesism, in applied ethics and the philosophy of animal rights, the practice of treating members of one species as morally more important than members of other species; also, the belief that this practice is justified."[291]

"Speciesism... is a prejudice or attitude of bias in favor of the interests of members of one's own species and against those of members of other species."[292]

"Speciesism is the human-held belief that all other animal species are inferior. Speciesist thinking involves considering animals–who have their own desires, needs, and complex lives–as means to human ends. This supremacist line of "reasoning" is used to defend treating other living, feeling beings as property, objects, or even ingredients."[293]

[291] https://www.britannica.com/topic/speciesism

[292] P. Singer, 1976, Animal Liberation, page 6.

[293] https://www.peta.org/about-peta/faq/what-is-speciesism/

In the midst of all the "isms" and "phobias" that are casually thrown around as accusatory terms in our culture, "speciesism" is gradually gaining popularity alongside racism, sexism and other labels, real or imagined. As the colourful definitions above illustrate, speciesism is based on the idea that it is wrong for humans to discriminate against animals, when comparable interests, such as the interest to avoid pain or violent death, are in play. In the same way that it is wrong to discriminate against other humans on the basis of race or gender alone, animal rights theorists will argue, it is wrong to discriminate against animals on the basis of species membership alone. As I argued thus far, it should be clear that, given that the differences between humans and all other animals are of kind, rather than degree, the analogy between inter-human differences such as race and gender and the differences between humans and animals does not hold. The difference between men and women, as significant as they may be, are not morally significant because both men and women share the fundamental features of humankind: self-consciousness, rationality, moral responsibility, free will and so on. The same cannot be said of animals. The differences between us and them are morally significant. The inherent differences between my next-door neighbours and a flock of sheep are morally significant and must determine how I relate and behave towards both my neighbours and the flock of sheep. My decision to castrate a ram or slaughter a lamb, instead of castrating my next-door neighbour and murdering his son is not based on an unjustified bias against sheep but on a well-founded and rational understanding of the inherent and morally significant differences between men and sheep.

I plead guilty as charged: I am a "speciesist". I make no apologies for it. That we are superior to animals is not in question: the only question is how we ought to exercise our supremacy. Furthermore, I would argue that speciesism is a prerequisite for any healthy and ethical relationship between humans and animals. Our conduct towards and consideration for animals must not only be different to that which we reserve for people; it must also be adapted to the species of animal in question. We cannot apply the same standards to gorillas that we apply to malarial mosquitoes, slugs, crows or horses. We should relate to each of these creatures differently and what applies to one, may not apply to the other and vice versa. Some rules of conduct do apply to all animals, irrespective of species. It would, for example, always be wrong to torture or beat an animal for the sake of it, whether it is a spider, a lizard, a mouse, a fish or a kitten. It would always be wrong to engage in bestiality.[294] We can all agree that sadism, perversion and cruelty are never justifiable, are indicative of a vicious character, and we rightly condemn these traits in our fellow humans. But whether or not we choose to domesticate an animal, hunt it for food, eliminate it as a pest, keep it as a

[294] Not according to animal rights activist Peter Singer, who controversially, but perhaps unsurprisingly, holds a favourable view of zoophilia. See: https://www.prospectmagazine.co.uk/opinions/56258/heavy-petting

pet or protect it as an endangered species should depend on the nature of each species and on its circumstances. As I have tried to argue throughout this book, we ought to treat animals *as their nature intended*, whether or not this conforms with our desires and interests. As it happens, thankfully, as we saw in previous chapters, there is no necessary contradiction between our desires and interests and those of domesticated animals, provided the latter are treated as their natures clearly indicate. If we are willing to observe and understand what it is that nature reveals about animals, we will have fairly comprehensive guidance on how we ought to behave towards them.

Aristotle argued that animals, like humans, have purpose, and that *telos*[295] is natural and unchanging. In the *Nicomachean Ethics*, he identifies virtue as the chief good for humankind. The ability to reason, and to be virtuous, is what distinguishes us from other life forms:

> *"Life seems to be common even to plants, but we are seeking what is peculiar to man. Let us exclude, therefore, the life of nutrition and growth. Next, there would be a life of perception, but it also seems to be common even to the horse, the ox, and every animal."*[296]

> *"...we state the function of man to be a certain kind of life, and this to be an activity or actions of the soul implying a rational principle... human good turns out to be activity of soul in accordance with virtue..."*[297]

As such, it would be wrong of us to live purely in order to satisfy our appetites, to perform our bodily functions, and to fulfil our carnal desires. Our ideal life is one where our animal urges, those facts of our nature that we share with animals, are moderated through the lens of reason and virtue. It follows, therefore, that the ideal life of an animal, whether wild or domesticated, lies in the fulfilment of all its natural propensities and qualities. If the ideal life of a person consists of virtue, reason, responsible action, aesthetic pursuits and so on, the ideal life of a cow will consist in the full expression of its "cowness": grazing on pastures, being out in the sun and rain, living in the comfort of the herd and so on. "Cowness" does not, and cannot, include a negation of another aspect of "cowness" that animal rights activists wish to deny; that of being a prey animal, whose natural purpose is to eventually feed predator animals. If we wish to use the language of "rights", especially if it helps to cement animal welfare legislation, by all means, we can do so, but the rights of a cow, such as the

[295] Teleology, (from Greek telos, "end," and logos, "reason"): explanation by reference to some purpose, end, goal, or function. (https://www.britannica.com/topic/teleology)

[296] Ibidem

[297] Nicomachean Ethics (Chap. 1.7).

right to graze, are simply not comparable to whatever rights we wish to bestow upon ourselves.

This kind of reasoning also implies that there are species-specific qualities and limitations, which should guide us in our thinking about different species. The reason why we swat flies, pet dogs, eat rabbits and protect snow leopards has as much to do with our own interests as it does with the nature and circumstances of animals per se. It is neither an accident nor an anomaly, nor the result of an arbitrary social and cultural construct that we tend to eat chickens rather than beagles and that we have no compunction about killing a rat or a scorpion but will have grave qualms about killing chimps or elephants, even if these happen to threaten our interests. Some animals, due to their natures and circumstances, should neither be killed nor domesticated, and it would be wrong to do so. The fact that the gorilla and the orangutan are great primates, who undoubtedly share far more characteristics with us than any other animals, is reason enough to protect them and their habitats and to severely punish any abuse or exploitation of these animals. The fact that many species are either in danger or going extinct is also reason enough to refrain from killing them, even if we don't share many characteristics with them.

At this point, the animal rights activist will point to an interesting and obvious fact: that different cultures behave rather differently towards the same species of animals. Typically, they will point out that in parts of China and Korea, for example, dogs are eaten, which is something we would never do. Jonathan Safran Foer, in his emotive but rather shallow call for vegetarianism,[298] goes to great lengths to make this point, suggesting there is no rational basis for our canine bias. Safran Foer and many others will also point out that the intelligence of pigs is comparable to that of a dog and that we therefore have no reason, other than habit and relative cultural norms, to eat the first and pet the second.

Tom Regan, in *Empty Cages*, puts together a captivating illustration of this problem:

> *"A few years ago, the Home Box Office network aired a program entitled "To Love or Kill: Man vs. Animals." It told a fascinating and, at the same time, a disturbing story about how different cultures treat the same animals differently. One especially chilling segment took viewers out to dinner in a small Chinese village. You know how, in some American restaurants, patrons get to choose from among live lobster or live fish? And how, after they make their selection, the animal is killed, and the chef cooks a meal of their choice? At this Chinese*

[298] J. Safran Foer, 2009, Eating Animals.

restaurant, things are the same except the menu is different. At this restaurant, patrons get to select from among live cats and dogs.

The video takes its time. First, we see the hungry patrons inspect the cats and dogs, jammed cheek by jowl into wooden cages; next we see them talk it over; then we see them make their selection; finally, we see a man (the cook, I assume), using long metal tongs, yank a fluffy white cat from her cage and hurry into the kitchen. What follows does not make for pleasant reading, so feel free to skip the next paragraph.

While the cat claws and screeches, the cook hits her several times with an iron bar. Clawing and screeching more now, she is abruptly submerged in a tub of scalding water for about ten seconds. Once removed, and while still alive, the cook skins her, from head to tail, in one swift pull. He then throws the traumatised animal into a large stone vat where (as the camera zooms in) we watch her gulp slowly, with increased difficulty, her eyes glazed, until – her last breath taken – she drowns. The whole episode, from selection to final breath, takes several minutes. When the meal is served, the diners eat heartily, offering thanks and praise to the cook."[299]

At face value, there does seem to be a strong case for arguing that, if we object to the eating of cats and dogs in China, we ought to object to the eating of chickens and pigs in England. If we object to the Yulin Dog Meat Festival, we ought to object to, say, the Game Fair at Ragley Hall or to a swordfish festival in Italy. The only difference between the two practices is cultural, rather than moral.

However, unless we are committed to the doctrines of cultural relativism, we should be willing to judge cultural practices, both our own and those of others, and draw appropriate comparisons. The first point to make is that the horrific treatment and slaughter of cats in Tom Regan's story, and indeed of dogs in the infamous Yulin Dog Festival, is horrific because of what is done to these animals, rather than simply because of the species of animal. If we caged, beat, scalded and skinned a lamb or a pig alive, we would be committing a very comparable cruelty and we ought to be strongly condemned and severely punished by law for doing so.

Regan anticipates this objection and argues that, if cats were killed painlessly, he would have to concede that *"gentle treatment is better than violent treatment"* but *"would still object to what happened"*[300] to the cat. Fair enough, but it is no minor distinction. There could never

[299] T. Regan, 2004, Empty Cages, pages 1-2.

[300] Ibidem, page 2.

be any justification for treating an animal in such a way, whatever the species. But there are other reasons for dismissing the equating of dogs and pigs. The dog is, in essence, a predator pack animal, closely related to the wolf and other canines. We struck a primordial partnership with the dog, who was our first domesticated animal, for the purpose of hunting[301] and living together. Unpalatable parts of hunted animals, such as deer entrails, have traditionally been fed to hunting dogs and humans have generally nurtured and looked after their hunting companions.

After the advent of agriculture, the dog also took on the role of protecting human settlements and their livestock from other predators, including wolves. We generally do not, as a species, eat many other predators, and certainly do not tend to eat domesticated predators that cooperate with us.[302] In essence, dogs are fellow predators, dependent upon us for their sustenance and, if we are to treat them as their nature intended, we will not eat them. The dog is truly "man's best friend", especially given the services they provide.[303] The same cannot be said of the pig and its wild relative, the wild boar. Pigs, much like wild boars, are prey animals. It is noteworthy that in the wild a major predator of wild boar is the wolf: the wild relative of the pig is hunted by the wild relative of the dog. This fact alone should prevent us from simplistic comparisons between dogs and pigs: being killed and eaten is part and parcel of "pigness", it is not part and parcel of "dogness". Domestic pigs are useful scavenging prey animals that mop our waste and provide nutritious meat and fat. This, in brief, is why we eat pigs but do not eat dogs: we tend to treat both of these species as their natures intended. It would only be in the most extreme circumstances imaginable, and maybe not even then, that we would consider eating our animal companions.[304]

In China and Korea, there has never been a tradition of milking livestock[305] and of extensive grazing of livestock that is even remotely comparable to that of the Caucasian peoples to the West. Hunting has also never been as important to their cultures as it is to our own. Consequently, the dog has historically not been used and bred for livestock husbandry and hunting in the way that it has been across Europe. The dog in the Far East is more of a backyard scavenging animal, not too different from a pig, in this respect, or seen as a

[301] It is no coincidence that both myself and my Great-grandfather are pictured with dogs in the images above.

[302] We also do not eat falcons and other birds of prey used for hunting.

[303] Not that the provision of services is an absolute requirement, of course. Cats have never been of much practical use, but are charming predators, whose beauty and subtle friendship we value. Again, it would be inappropriate to farm and eat cats, being solitary predators rather than natural prey like sheep.

[304] In parts of Italy, cats were once eaten, but only in times of war or during late winter hunger and famine.

[305] Which is why lactose intolerance is quite common there.

nuisance.[306] It is therefore no coincidence that the dog is not particularly revered and has been, at times, eaten like other backyard animals. I would still argue that this is nonetheless a mistreatment of the dog, which, as a predator, should not be farmed and eaten like a prey animal. It is also worth noting that dog eating is a relatively rare practice in China and Korea, not comparable to pig eating in Europe, and one that is controversial and not universally approved of within these cultures. Be that as it may, we should not squirm from criticising the practices of other cultures, which may well be worse than our own at times. We should of course apply the same critical standards to ourselves that we apply to others, lest we be accused of hypocrisy: we should just as keenly criticise the industrial force-feeding of geese in France or Hungary as we criticise dog eating in China or Korea.

[306] The culling of stray dogs is common across cities in Asia. My horticultural companion Lam, from Malaysia and of Chinese descent, once recalled how dogs were culled in his city and people, including his aunt, collected them for the kitchen. I am told the dog stew was most palatable.

IN A NUTSHELL

- A concern for animals is an inherently good thing.
- Vegans ask the right questions: the answers are open to debate.
- Anatomy, biology and history strongly indicate that veganism is unnatural and abnormal.
- A vegan diet is better than some diets, but it is not the best of all diets.
- Any diet is better than the stereotypical Western junk food diet.
- Avoid greasy pork ribs before sex or sports, save them for afters.
- It is better for your mother not to breastfeed you until you are four years old.
- Red and processed meats are not necessarily bad for your health.
- Do not blame cows for climate change and pollution: blame human mismanagement of land and livestock.
- We need livestock to restore ecosystems and to secure our future.
- We would be worse off without livestock.
- Turning vegan will not "save the planet".
- Plant foods are not necessarily more sustainable than animal foods.
- Animals are not people and vice versa.
- Speciesism is a good thing.
- Animals cannot be "liberated".
- The dog is man's best friend, after all.

Chapter 7

LIMITS AND MERITS OF VEGETARIANISM

Vegetarianism, unlike veganism, does not exclude all animal products. Vegetarians generally include dairy products and/or eggs and, at times, even fish.[307] One thing all vegetarians have in common is that they do not eat meat, often on similar grounds to those offered by vegans. The latter, for all their flaws, cannot be accused of being inconsistent in their internal logic and usually accuse vegetarians of hypocrisy on the grounds that dairy and egg production are intimately connected to meat production. As any enquiry into even the very best organic dairy farms and egg producers will reveal, there is no question that the vegan charge is grounded on a lot of hard truths. A good dairy farmer controls his herd size and demographics through slaughter, will ensure male calves end up being raised for beef and will, inevitably, send all spent dairy cows and bulls to slaughter. The same holds true for sheep and goat dairy operations. Egg production works under similar constraints.

The bottom line is that dairy and egg production depend on slaughter to be viable and productive in any meaningful way, even under the very best organic farming conditions. But couldn't we produce dairy and eggs without slaughter? The short answer is yes, but with huge and mostly insurmountable limitations, rendering the whole enterprise impractical and unproductive. It is perfectly true that hens do not need a cock to produce eggs[308] and that, if you keep a few hens in your back garden or allotment, you can get eggs without needing to slaughter the hens, which can be "retired" and die of old age or disease. However, what applies on an individual back garden or allotment scale cannot apply at the farm scale, and to the poultry sector as a whole. Any population of poultry will include males and females and, whilst it is perfectly possible for me to adopt a few hens and keep them in my garden, their very existence relies on the continued existence of the overall population of hens, cocks,

[307] Pescovegetarianism.

[308] The eggs collected from hens are unfertilised and cannot possibly turn into chicks.

chicks and so on. What should a poultry breeder or large-scale farmer do with male chicks or spent hens? One option that is not feasible nor sustainable is to keep all male and spent birds as de facto pets. Spent laying hens, in the old days, made fabulous birds for boiling and broth making[309] and old cocks made wonderful slow-cooked stews. Male chicks were traditionally raised as cockerels for meat or castrated and raised as capons, to be fattened up for the festive season. We should bring these thrifty and humane traditions back to every poultry farm in the country. Sadly, with the segregation of egg and chicken production that is inevitable in industrial farming systems, these wholesome practices have almost entirely gone out of fashion. Male chicks are routinely killed at birth[310] and spent hens are no longer part of the human food chain.

If we try to convert to a slaughter-free system on dairy farms, we have many of the same constraints and limitations, as I can personally testify. For eight wonderful seasons, I spent a lot of my spare time working at a vegetarian farm.[311]

Oxen ready for work by my old field. Credit: @escapetheofficejob

[309] I have so far failed to find a single farm or butcher who is willing to sell me an old hen, so that I can resurrect the traditional *Bollito* in its full glory. It is also impossible to find an organic capon for Christmas. If any reader can assist on this front, please do not hesitate to contact me!

[310] The segregation of egg and chicken production has led to the common practice of male chick culling which, if we were conscientious about farming, should be abolished. Similarly, the common practice of killing male calves at birth on dairy farms is neither necessary, nor acceptable and is the result of the segregation of dairy and beef production in industrial systems.

[311] Given the carnivorous feelings expressed throughout this book, and out of respect for my former hosts, to which I will always be grateful, the farm shall remain nameless.

This was a dairy farm, with some arable land, where the cows and oxen[312] were never slaughtered and, quite literally, retired once no longer productive. They undoubtedly enjoyed very high levels of welfare and were happy animals. This policy, however, led to several unavoidable consequences:

- The percentage of producing cows in the herd was necessarily very low: roughly 1 out of 6 animals at any given time. Being unable to slaughter calves for veal and being unable to favour a relatively higher percentage of cows in the herd through selection and slaughter, much of the herd could not produce any milk but still needed land, feed and housing.
- Low birth rates. When the herd cannot be managed through slaughter and meat production, the bull must be kept on a leash and birth rates kept low, or herd numbers will increase out of control and beyond the land's capacity. The consequence of this is that each cow cannot have a calf every year or two, as they normally would, meaning less lactation and lower milk yields per cow.[313]
- No default meat. By eschewing meat eating, this system of farming wastes the opportunity for a lot of free food from a fixed amount of land and resources. On a dairy farm, where milk is the primary product, meat is a secondary by-product, that comes from calves raised for veal, steers raised for beef and all spent animals that are retired to the pot once no longer productive.

Consequently, if every organic dairy farm in the country were to abolish slaughter, milk production would inevitably plummet and there would be no default meat produced. As pleasant as my host farm was, it was not necessarily a model farm. The farm's very low milk productivity and extravagant land use could hardly be replicated or promoted as a viable option for dairy production countrywide.

Is India a Bovine Paradise?

A critic of this simple analysis could point to India as a counterexample where, seemingly, the prohibition of cow slaughter in many of its farming and religious traditions has not led to an unsustainable farming system and to a shortage of dairy products. There are individual farms and communities in India where cow protection, with animals used for milk, traction and manure, clearly works and has worked for millennia. The Indian anomaly, however, can be explained once we look into the details and consider the country as a whole. The first

[312] The oxen were used for traction and cultivation, as they still are in many parts of the world.

[313] Cows have high milk yields after each birth/lactation, which naturally and gradually decreases over time. A cow that has a calf every year or two will have higher average milk yields than a cow that has a calf every three or four years.

consideration to make is that India's system of cow protection exists alongside cow slaughter and meat eating: cow protection and vegetarianism are not universal practices in India, and never have been. Unproductive animals are often abandoned in India, which explains the renowned phenomenon of cows wandering the streets and scavenging amongst waste heaps. This alone is a serious side effect of the cow protection system, as not all farmers have the ability or willingness to protect and keep unproductive animals until their deaths. But, most importantly, cow protection in India takes place within a culture with the strictest and most inflexible of class systems.

In every other agricultural civilisation apart from India, there has usually been a clear correlation between meat eating and class: the dominant, wealthier classes tend to eat more meat and vice versa. This was certainly the case in Europe, where meat consumption tended to be lower amongst the poor, who were also more likely to eat offal and the "fifth quarter" as opposed to prime cuts.[314] In India, it has historically been the other way round: the dominant Brahmanical classes have generally practised vegetarianism and "impure" meat eating has been confined to the lower classes. Abandoned animals, or the carcasses of protected animals that died of old age or disease, have historically ended up in the food chain by being collected and eaten by the *dalits* (untouchables). Pigs[315] and poultry, kept as free-ranging scavengers, have also traditionally been eaten by the poor and untouched by the Brahmanical elite.[316] Let us also not forget that, amongst India's many castes, we have the rat-eating caste,[317] who are usually extremely poor landless labourers who supplement their meagre diets with rats. In fact, the grisliest occupations associated with animals in India, such as leatherwork, carcass disposal and pig keeping, are all designated as the work of the *dalits*. What this means is that whatever the uniquely Indian cultural and religious conditions may be, India is not a vegetarian nation. It is also remarkable that India is generally, year on year,

[314] Working class cookery in Italy, for example, was typical in its use of all the off cuts, from tripes and tails to heads and intestines. Roman and Florentine trattorias still showcase many offal dishes. Fattened poultry and prime cuts such as fillet and loins, on the other hand, were historically more likely to find their place on the tables of the learned and wealthier classes, the nobles and the clergy. This has been a universal phenomenon across cultures and eras. In China, whilst the Imperial courts dined on the now famous Peking duck, the peasantry and the workers ate very little meat and much of it in the form of offal and off cuts, such as chicken feet and pig's trotters. In the Southern States, slaves were most likely to eat pork chitterlings whilst the slave owners ate chops and hams.

[315] Pigs have often served as ultimate waste disposal experts, as they feed on human faeces. This is still very common in India, where feral or semi-feral pigs feed on human waste. This unattractive and unhygienic practice was once also common in China and Korea. In fact, there used to be such as a thing as "toilet pigs" who were destined to feed on the waste of latrines, which were attached to the pigsty. The Adi tribal people of India still have "toilet pigs" whose meat, for some reason, is particularly prized (see: https://www.bbc.co.uk/tribe/tribes/adi/index.shtml)

[316] In recent times, as Indian elites have "Westernised" meat eating has become increasingly popular and religious vegetarianism has declined. The meat consumed by the growing Indian Westernised classes, however, is not from scavenging animals and carcasses, of course, but from farms, supermarkets and fast-food chains.

[317] The Musahar rat eating caste of *dalits* in Northern India and Nepal were traditionally tasked with ridding fields of pests such as snails, insects and rats. They were famed for not only catching rats but eating them as well.

amongst the top 3 beef exporting countries in the world.[318] This fact alone should illuminate us about the interdependence between dairy production, vegetarianism and slaughter, even when the latter is outsourced to other people and to foreign lands.

Spiritual Vegetarianism and Sacrifice

None of this should be construed as implying that there is no value nor virtue in limiting meat consumption or even abstaining from it altogether. The Buddha's nuanced approach towards meat eating, when compared to the contemporary vegan or environmentalist approach, is both rational and compelling, as it is grounded on the reality of suffering and on the need to transcend and curtail our desires. If we also consider the fact that great men like Lev Tolstoy and George Bernard Shaw adopted vegetarianism, for spiritual and ethical reasons, we should not be dismissive of its potential and justifications. To renounce and sacrifice our natural desire for animal flesh can have its place in spiritual practice, much in the same way that chastity and other austerities can have theirs. I may consider it myself in my old age. At the very least, the spiritual practice of renouncing meat should remind us of an obvious truth that, in our urban, sanitised and vacuum-packed experiences of meat, is often forgotten: the taking of a life is a big deal and should not be undertaken lightly and without consideration. The fact that from death springs new life and that the two are mutually interdependent is one of the great, sacred and tragic mysteries of our existence and of the natural world, whether we choose to acknowledge it or not. Killing an animal is not something that should be done lightly and without a full understanding that a life is being taken. Sacrificial slaughter, common to many traditions, originates from this very idea.

This sort of understanding is also implicit in many hunting cultures, where the taking of an animal's life is seen as both a sacrifice and as a gift. Indeed, hunting differentiates between the species and the individual animal, and the hunter ensures that individual sacrifices are matched by gratitude towards the species. The species needs to be respected and protected, the individual animal, on the other hand, can be sacrificed and eaten. Hunters like the Inuit, who traditionally depended entirely on their Arctic prey, used to ritually put a little fresh water in the mouth of killed seal or whale, so that *"it, and all other seals and whales, would know that the hunter respected the willingness of the hunted to be killed and eaten"*[319] and similar rituals are common amongst hunter gatherers worldwide. The Bushmen of the Kalahari Desert, for example, engage in a particularly touching hunting ritual as they finish

[318] Most of the meat is technically from water buffalo, which is classified as beef, but that makes no difference to the point being made. See: https://www.statista.com/statistics/617458/beef-and-veal-export-volume-worldwide-by-country/

[319] Hugh Brody, The Other Side of Eden, 2000: page 256.

off their prey. The hunters, engaging in persistence hunting,[320] honour their stricken prey with ceremonial gestures, by gently stroking it with sand, representing the soil from which it came, and to which its spirit will return.[321]

Whatever the relevance of ancient hunting rituals to us today, to kill an animal for food is, literally, a sacrifice and, as such, needs to be performed with the respect and humility that all rituals, properly understood, ought to involve. It is for this reason that we should unequivocally oppose industrial slaughterhouses, which treat animals as objects and regard their staff as soulless, exploitable, replaceable killing automatons.[322] We should push for on farm slaughter, for the return of the travelling slaughterman and for small, local slaughterhouses and for the re-integration of slaughter and butchery. No animal should travel for hours and hundreds of miles for slaughter[323] and no slaughterhouse should process individual animals as if they were components in a manufacturing plant: it should be illegal. A sense of sacrifice should be accompanied by an attitude of gratitude for both the animal and the food it provides. Perhaps the greatest value of the vegetarian challenge to those of us who persist in our carnivorous habits is to force us to reflect upon such habits and enshrine them is the right attitudes and behaviours. As I have already conceded, the thoughtless purchase of vacuum-packed pieces of questionable, flaccid meat from the supermarket is highly problematic. If this is how we choose to operate, we would be better without meat altogether.

Celebration and Redemption

To help us redeem and justify the eating of animals, following their rearing and slaughter, there are other basic attitudes that we can adopt which, arguably, will also increase our enjoyment of meat. The first is to recall that meat, across cultures, has generally been at the centre of celebration, rites of passage and communal experience. It is not an accident nor a coincidence that Thanksgiving, Christmas, Easter,[324] Eid al-Adha, Chinese New Year and

[320] The ancient practice of chasing and stalking an animal to the point of exhaustion, with the animal eventually collapsing from fatigue and the hunter finishing it off with a basic weapon.

[321] I recommend watching Sir David Attenborough's depiction of the hunt and its final ritual: The Intense 8 Hour Hunt, Attenborough Life of Mammals, BBC Earth (https://www.youtube.com/watch?v=826HMLoiE_o)

[322] For more information on the horrors of industrial abattoirs, see Erik Schlosser's classic *Fast Food Nation* (2002). Whilst his work is based on the American meat packing industry, a lot of what he describes applies to the United Kingdom and the EU as well.

[323] One of the many problems with industrial slaughter is the consolidation of the sector, with small, humane slaughterhouses gradually disappearing. I was horrified to discover that on the Isle of Wight, one of my favourite places, there is longer a single slaughterhouse, and cattle are ferried off to the mainland for slaughter, with some of the meat returning packaged and ready for retail as Isle of Wight beef. This is madness.

[324] In Rome, as a child, I fondly recall my mother roasting half a lamb on Christmas Day and half a lamb on Easter Sunday, to feed a family group of nine. These were the only times of the year when such a large amount of meat would be cooked for one meal.

countless other festivities across the world are based on the communal eating of meat. Meat has always been considered the most highly prized of foods, which is why it has historically been reserved for special days and special company. That is the reason why, in our culture, we still have the Sunday roast[325] and, when we invite people to our homes or host a party, we tend to offer barbeques, roasts and other meat-based meals instead of vegetable soup.

Whilst, at least in the West, access to meat has become so easy and financially accessible that we no longer need to save meat for special occasions, it would be worthwhile considering the timing of our meals and the overall amount of meat we choose to consume. After all, if we are conscientious in our choices, we will find that good quality meat is still relatively expensive. We are certainly better off eating one happy chicken on a Sunday than lots of factory farmed chicken on a day-to-day basis. Apart from thinking about the quality of life and slaughter of the animals we eat, the other way to honour the animals we sacrifice is to ensure we eat most of them. To waste and throw away any food is bad, to throw away meat is worse, given the life sacrificed in order to put it on the table. Learning how to use leftovers and learning how to cook cheaper but delicious parts of the carcass that are no longer in fashion should be at the centre of a healthy attitude towards meat eating.[326]

Giovan Battista Recco (1615-1660). A ligated lamb by a basket of eggs.

[325] Communal meat eating on a Sunday following a largely vegetarian week was ubiquitous across Christian civilization.

[326] I admit I am not overly keen on all offal. I will however happily eat the liver and the heart (if not shot through) of the muntjac I shoot, as it would be a shame to waste such a healthy and perfectly palatable part of the animal. If liver is the sacrificial portion of the animal that must be consumed, the loin is the celebratory part!

Personally, I have found a compromise between the complete renunciation of the spiritual vegetarian and the thoughtless consumption of the meat eater: Lent. Over the past few years, I do not hunt animals or eat meat throughout Lent and celebrate Easter in style, with lamb. It is important to note that Easter, like most of our Christian celebrations, has some pagan, Greco-Roman roots and is intimately tied with agricultural cycles.[327] Lent coincides with what in Europe used to be known as the Hungry Gap. This was the time of the year where there used to be the greatest degree of scarcity: the fall harvest was running out, livestock had long been slaughtered, the hunting season was over, there were very few vegetables in the garden,[328] no fruits would be growing. It made perfect sense for our culture to have a period of religious austerity during this time of the year. In some respects, Easter is a spring festival celebrating the return of life following the decay and darkness of winter, a festival of rebirth and regeneration. Lambs are ready for slaughter and birds are making eggs again[329] and the cycle of life is renewed for another year. Each to their own, of course, but I find this self-imposed austerity to be a great opportunity to reconnect with the seasonal constraints of agriculture and to develop a greater appreciation and gratitude for the pleasures of the flesh. Here endeth the lesson!

IN A NUTSHELL

- Dairy and egg production are intimately connected to meat production.
- Slaughter-free vegetarianism would not be a viable option if everyone adopted it.
- India is not a bovine paradise.
- Spiritual vegetarianism should nonetheless be taken seriously and may be a wise option, depending on circumstances and on stage in life.
- Be grateful for any meat that you eat and never waste it.
- As always: quality over quantity.
- Appreciate and enjoy meat as the best of foods, especially in company, on days of rest, on special days, on religious festivities.
- If you can get hold of an old happy hen or tough old cock, please get in touch with me.

[327] Awareness of this should enhance, rather than diminish, the celebration of Easter throughout Christendom.

[328] As any competent vegetable grower knows, late February, March and early April is the time of the year when most winter vegetables have run their course and very few vegetables can be harvested.

[329] Hence the Easter egg!

Chapter 8

THE DELUSIONS OF POSTMODERN GASTRONOMY

An ideological offshoot of the reductionist and relativist approach that we have examined thus far is what can aptly be referred to as postmodern gastronomy, which now dominates the world of restaurants and cuisine. After all, it is not surprising for a dominant set of ideas to permeate every aspect of a culture, and gastronomy is no exception.

Have you ever thought that many celebrity chefs are overrated? Have you ever suspected that liquid nitrogen and foams do not bring anything of value to fine dining? Have you ever wondered why plates of food increasingly look like something out of the Tate Modern and do not live up the hype? Do the tiny plates of mediocre food feel like a total rip off sometimes? Have you started questioning the wisdom of the celebrated Michelin Guide?

If the answer to any of these sorts of questions is yes, you have started to doubt and challenge the values and practices of mainstream contemporary gastronomy. It is important to realise that it is now almost impossible to gain three Michelin stars or get on the industry "best restaurant" lists without conforming to some or all of its principles. Even the classical chefs and masters of fine dining who do not partake in the practice of postmodern gastronomy have to pay lip service to its tenets and authority, or else!

Why I am not Proud of Massimo Bottura

A critique of postmodern gastronomy could fill volumes, and one is spoiled for choice when looking for examples of both its exponents and their works. I must, however, start close to my roots. Italy is a gastronomic treasure trove, that is hard to match in most respects. But for the gastronomic iconoclasts, Italian or otherwise, nothing is sacred nor worth preserving. In my opinion, no man encapsulates the spirit of the age better than the celebrated chef patron of Osteria Francescana, Massimo Bottura, and will therefore start this polemical piece with a critique of his particular brand of gastronomy.

Osteria Francescana is a three-Michelin-star restaurant based in Modena, Italy. The restaurant has been ranked No.1 on The World's 50 Best Restaurants list twice (2016, 2018) and is currently part of the so-called Best of the Best list.[330] Even if we choose not to give any serious credit to these industry lists and awards, we cannot dismiss their cultural influence, marketing clout and financial muscle. As such, we have to pay close attention to the gastronomic landscape and feel free, as virtually no mainstream food critics do, to be scathing about the sacred temples of contemporary gastronomy and expose them for what they are.

Bottura comes from one of Italy's richest and most impressive culinary towns and provinces of Italy, that showcases a cornucopia of diverse, overlapping, and astonishing ingredients and dishes, including Parmigiano Reggiano cheese, Cotechino and Zampone sausages, balsamic vinegar, Tortellini, Tagliatelle al Ragu', and plenty more. Having spent some time at El Bulli, a bastion of postmodern gastronomy, he came back to Modena to modernise, reinvent, deconstruct, "provoke" and recreate the classic dishes of his region. In typical postmodern fashion, he effectively proceeded, in my opinion, to lay waste to a broad range of traditional ingredients and dishes, justified by shallow, highfalutin and cliched rationales in the process. As ever, the postmodern chef is not content with just adding his dubious and exorbitantly expensive concoctions on his menu, but he feels compelled to provide an explanation, which, he quips or implies, may be too profound for his critics to comprehend, and certainly beyond the average man on the street, who should just be overawed into submission.

A few Italian treasures, amongst the many that he attempted to corrupt, stand out: Tortellini, Mortadella and Bollito.

Let us start with Tortellini. Bottura recalls how he decided to stop serving classic *Tortellini in Brodo*[331] because apparently his customers were eating them by the mouthful, somewhat thoughtlessly, casually, losing themselves *"in the process of eating"*, which apparently is a *faux pas* when... eating. So, quote, he decided to *"serve something very provocative"*[332] instead, as if provocation is what we look for when we go to a fine dining restaurant. The

[330] Restaurants can no longer be voted world no.1 more than once. A "Best of the Best" hall of fame was introduced in 2019 and is made up of those restaurants that have been named No.1 in The World's 50 Best Restaurants since the list's inception.

[331] Tortellini in Brodo are the traditional stuffed fresh egg pasta parcels cooked in a rich meat broth. A fabulous dish that is often served on Christmas Day in many Italian households.

[332] Series 1, Episode 1: https://www.netflix.com/gb/title/80007945

provocative dish consisted of just six tortellini, in one line on a plate, which were, apparently *"walking into the broth"*, which turned out not to be a broth at all, but a very questionable broth gelatine. Why having six tortellini instead of a decent portion and having broth replaced by some ghastly gelatine is an improvement on the original remains an inscrutable mystery. We are comforted, however, by the moral teachings enclosed in this impoverished dish: *"tradition, most of the time, doesn't respect the ingredients"*[333] and through the chastising consumption of the six walking tortellini we are taught not to lose ourselves in the process of eating, humbly respecting each tortellino, presumably because we only have six tortellini to ration and savour to begin with. I would like to suggest that this pretentious charade can only be defined as a mockery of paying customers. Nonetheless, this reckless pillaging of great traditions to grab the headlines proved to be very successful. To Bottura's credit, the reinvented tortellini were certainly provocative, and lots of people at the time were very critical and scandalised. Eventually, the mainstream food critics came round to his "vision". Mission accomplished!

Bottura also plays on the concept of memory and nostalgia in food which, as Marcel Proust famously testified with his madeleines, is undoubtedly a powerful force in our experience of food. As it happens, Bottura has strong memories of Mortadella. Mortadella is a globally well know, unique pork product from the Emilia-Romagna region, which every Italian, including Bottura, remembers from childhood. On a televised presentation of his take on Mortadella, the celebrated Chef recalled how his mother would give him Mortadella sandwiches to take to school. So far, so good. He therefore decided to create a memory of Mortadella[334] by distilling Mortadella water by inserting the hapless cold cut into some machine, with water, to distil some porky liquid from it, which he then proceeded to whip with actual Mortadella[335] into some less than attractive mousse, to be served with some kind of bread. I guess in a way, this does what it says on the tin: it provides a faint memory of the real thing, namely Mortadella and bread.[336]

Where Bottura really hits rock bottom, and ticks every box in the postmodern gastronome playbook, is with the classic *Bollito*, literally "boiled".[337] This is a glorious traditional Sunday dish that we find in many regions of Italy,[338] with different versions, but which generally

[333] What nonsense! Surely, if anything, the opposite is the case. Until two generations ago, the kind of food waste that is now the norm would have been considered unconscionable and traditional cookery revolved around using off cuts of meat, stale bread and other items that would now ordinarily be considered inedible.

[334] See: https://www.youtube.com/watch?v=icks5C1sSqI

[335] Here is the recipe: https://streetfooditalia.it/pdf/bottura.pdf. Warning: you need a lab tool called a Rotavapor, and nitrogen, amongst other things.

[336] When in Rome, I recommend Mortadella inside *Pizza Romana*: hard to beat.

[337] I confess I take this affront personally, as it is one of my absolute favourite dishes.

[338] Similar traditions are found in France (*pot-au-feu*), Iberia (*cocido*), and Austria (*tafelspitz*).

consists of: 1) A broad range of boiled meats that require slow cooking; 2) The production of a very rich broth through the process of boiling the meats; 3) Side vegetables; 4) Various sauces to accompany the boiled meats, ranging from the great *Salsa Verde*, to fruity mustards and horseradish sauce, depending on the region and local tradition. The meal is made up of two hefty courses, as the strained broth is served first as a starter, on its own or with pasta, or rice or other grain in it, and the warm sliced meats are served as a main, with vegetables and sauces on the side. There is clearly plenty of room for a Chef to apply his own personal touch and creativity, with the cuts of meat he uses, the vegetables and the sauces, and he can of course always try to perfect his broth, which can be sublime in its depth of flavour.

Bottura's *Bollito*, however, is cunningly called *Bollito non bollito*[339] (Literally: Boiled not boiled). True to his word, Bottura desists from boiling anything. The dish begins with cuts of meat vacuumed packed in plastic and cooked in the fashionable water bath, usually referred to as *sous vide* in the industry, as it was invented by a Frenchman and, as we know, everything in cookery sounds far more credible in French, even when it is wildly overrated.[340] He explains that unbeknownst to us, boiling meat turns out to be disrespectful to the farmers who produce such meat, because boiling apparently ruins meat by robbing it of its essential qualities. Boiling meat apparently strips it of its flavour, nutrients, and vitamins, and is therefore a thing of the past, that we need to evolve away from. As I am fairly confident Bottura knows, but would not dare confirm with certainty, the whole point of a *Bollito*, apart from rendering several humble cuts of meat tender and gentle on the palate and stomach, is to create a rich broth, where the juices, goodness and flavours that seep out from the meat coalesce to provide something wonderful, both in terms of flavour and health benefits. It is the sort of food your mother or grandmother would make for you when you are ill.

Having been extracted from their plastic enclosures, the meat is then cut into the shapes of "buildings". Why buildings, we might wonder? The inspiration for the dish, we are told, came when Bottura was in New York and, from Central Park, seeing the skyline of buildings and skyscrapers on 59th Street, reaching above the tree cover, he had a moment of gastronomic enlightenment. In the *Bollito non bollito*, therefore, blocks of meat are served in a vertical position. Next to it, are two lines of red and yellow bell pepper sauce, adorned with a few

[339] The recipe and absurd rationale for it are explained in a paper Bottura co-authored (https://www.sciencedirect.com/science/article/pii/S1878450X1400002X) and can be watched here in Italian: https://www.youtube.com/watch?v=icks5C1sSql.

[340] I am sure I must have eaten meat cooked (at least in part, before searing) in water baths at some fine dining restaurant or other, and that it tasted good. What I am disputing is the fallacious idea that *sous vide* is an improvement, or a necessity in the fine dining kitchen. I would also add that the very aesthetics of cooking in plastic in a world that is already drowning in plastic is less than appealing. It may also be worth reconsidering the wisdom of heating food in plastic, even if it is "food grade" plastic.

capers and bits of anchovy. Finally, in lieu of a *Salsa Verde*, Bottura lines the meat "buildings" with a green parsley-based foam containing *"broth from the sous vide bags, soy lecithin, salt and sugar"*[341] that is supposed to represent Central Park's vegetation. In some versions he adds a caper and anchovy jelly underneath the foam. Be that as it may, this dish is not a reinterpretation or legitimate version of *Bollito*, but a sad, tawdry postmodern caricature of a great dish.

There are several problems with this dish. There is the dubious enterprise of cooking food in plastic bags. We have the elimination of the second half of the dish, and possibly the most delicious: the broth. We have no vegetables. We have no great sauces,[342] just a few whiffs and jellies reminding us of the wholesome sauces that normally accompany this dish. We have the horrid, dreadful foam. One must be unequivocal about the dreaded foams: the recently invented and fashionable foams have no place in any great cuisine, as they bring no culinary, textural or flavour improvement to any dish. I cannot emphasise this enough. But most frustratingly, we have the completely vacuous moral and nutritional justification that we somehow owe it to our livestock farmers to stop boiling their meats and should feel obliged to vacuum pack them in plastic instead. Finally, we have the pretention of art and inspiration, through Bottura's Road to New York moment in Central Park. There are many gullible commentators who will buy into this sort of retrospective narratives, and Bottura has been favourably compared to Manet,[343] who I presume must be spinning in his grave.

None of the above should be construed as suggesting that there is only one absolute way to make tortellini or *Bollito*, or to incorporate Mortadella in a meal. There is always room for interesting twists and innovations. No *Bollito* or broth is necessarily the same as the next, and the skill of the Chef consists in perfecting and providing the best possible version of these dishes, first and foremost, and if changes are going to be made, they should not alter and demolish the very essence and value of the dishes.

When he wasn't too busy desecrating great traditions, Bottura also put together dishes that cannot but be understood for what they are: an insult to the intelligence of the customer. One such dish, considered one of Bottura's iconic desserts, is his *Oops! I dropped the lemon tart*.[344] In Chef's Table[345] and on other media, Bottura proudly recalls how his Japanese Sous-

[341] https://www.sciencedirect.com/science/article/pii/S1878450X1400002X

[342] In explaining the dish, Bottura claims that the sous-vide meat is so good that it does not need great sauces. Apparently, the sauces in the traditional Bollito are only there to compensate for the flavourless meat.

[343] For a particularly gushing review, see: https://www.greatbritishchefs.com/features/massimo-bottura-interview

[344] https://osteriafrancescana.it/menu/

[345] Series 1, Episode 1: https://www.netflix.com/gb/title/80007945

Chef Takahido Kondo[346] once dropped a lemon tart on the floor, just before serving it. Frozen in fear, and ready for a scalding, the Sous-Chef was instead taken aback by one of Bottura's customary Road to Culinary Damascus moments: the great Modenese declared that the splattered, broken tart was *"beautiful"*, apparently, if only we looked at it from a different perspective. From that point onwards, lemon tarts are intentionally broken and splattered onto the plate at Osteria Francescana. His Sous-Chef claims that from this episode he learnt that in life we must learn from mistakes. What lesson was learnt, other than Bottura's impressive ability to charge his customers €60 for a broken lemon tart,[347] remains a mystery.

It is hard to know the extent to which Bottura believes in his purported philosophy. Has he cleverly and cynically tapped into a cultural trend that made him successful? Does he truly believe in everything he says? Or is he both a believer and cynical marketer? People are complex and full of internal contradiction, and we will never know the answer to these questions. In many ways, it does not matter. I have no doubt the man can cook very well and could reproduce his pasta mentor Lidia Cristoni's dishes to perfection, if he wanted to. But, in contemporary culture, that would not get him anywhere.

TO SUM UP: I would much rather have eaten with Massimo's mother[348] than at Osteria Francescana.

Why Heston Blumenthal Should Have Been a Chemist

Closer to home, the greatest exponent of postmodern gastronomy (not that he would define it as such) is undoubtedly the celebrated chef Heston Blumenthal. Blumenthal prides himself on his scientific approach to cuisine, and even a cursory glance at his books and television programmes will reveal a keen interest in lab work, chemical formulas, all sorts of machinery and contraptions, as well as psychology, neurology, and other fields of science.

[346] I will risk pathetic and predictable accusations of "racism" and state that whilst I have no particular reason to question Mr. Kondo's talents and abilities, I would immediately question the choice of a Japanese chef for a great Italian restaurant that purports to reinvent the Italian tradition. With the best will in the world, how can a non-native who only moved to Italy as an adult be charged with reinventing a tradition that he has no personal experience of? Even if we presumed that there was a need to reinvent the food of Modena, surely one should know it inside out, on both a personal and professional level before even attempting such a task. It would be equally absurd for an 18-year-old Italian Chef to move to Japan and be tasked with reinventing Japanese cuisine at Japan's top ranked restaurant. The Japanese, I imagine, are far too smart and conservative to do anything as misguided as that.

[347] https://osteriafrancescana.it/menu/

[348] Who let it slip, during an interview, that she felt she was a better cook than her son: https://www.newyorker.com/magazine/2013/11/04/post-modena

Blumenthal was the first chef to be awarded an Honorary Fellowship by the Royal Society of Chemistry.[349] Why would a cook[350] win, or even want to win, a chemistry award? For the simple reason that, in my opinion, Blumenthal is a textbook, committed reductionist, who has embraced the idea that food, ultimately, is just the sum of its chemical components. A molecule is a molecule, and the more we know about molecules, the more we can manipulate food products. This worldview has led to an approach that prioritises the use of techniques, machinery, tools, and chemicals not normally found in the kitchen, and for really good reasons. The use of liquid nitrogen, for example, whose popularity in gastronome circles is broadly attributed to Blumenthal,[351] is certainly relatively novel and high tech but does not actually bring anything of great value to the kitchen.

Blumenthal has long relied on scientific research and methods to justify and inform his school of gastronomy and believes that resistance to new technology is misguided.[352] On bestowing their Honorary Fellowship, the Royal Society of Chemistry informs us that Blumenthal *"researches the molecular components of different dishes to enable a greater understanding of the chemistry behind various tastes and flavours. His original and scientific approach to the molecular art of cuisine has teamed him with fellow chefs, scientists and psychologists through the world."*[353] In The Fat Duck Cookbook, Blumenthal has extensively recalled his collaboration with Firmenich, the flavourings and perfumes company based in Geneva, to make sense of some of his odd flavour combinations, such as caviar and white chocolate,[354] which I cannot claim to have tried. We are told that the purported success of this chocolatey-fishy combination was due the fact that both ingredients *"contain high levels of amines. These are a group of proteins that have broken down from their amino acid state but not so far as to become ammonia. Amines contribute to the desirable flavours that we find in cooked meats and cheeses, among other things."*[355] Not surprisingly, as a review of its website will reveal,[356] Firmenich manufactures all the sorts of products used by the food manufacturing industry to create ultra-processed food and drink items, by providing flavourings, ingredients, sweeteners, and textures. Recently, the company created its first flavour made by using Artificial Intelligence (AI), a lightly grilled beef taste for use in plant-based meat

[349] https://www.rsc.org/news-events/articles/2006/07-july/honors-chef/

[350] Let us remind ourselves that "Chef" is just a fancy French word for a cook who runs a particular kitchen.

[351] https://www.theworlds50best.com/stories/News/seven-ways-heston-blumenthal-changed-the-food-and-restaurant-world.html

[352] H. Blumenthal, 2008, The Fat Duck Cookbook, page 44.

[353] https://www.rsc.org/news-events/articles/2006/07-july/honors-chef/

[354] H. Blumenthal, 2008, The Fat Duck Cookbook, pages 171-172.

[355] https://www.theguardian.com/lifeandstyle/2002/may/04/foodanddrink.shopping

[356] See: https://www.firmenich.com/

alternatives.[357] In other words, no one interested in haute cuisine, or indeed great home cooking, should possibly have any interests in this company's products. Industrial reductionism and lab-based molecule fiddling is, surely, the enemy of flavour, complexity, and quality in the kitchen.

The hypothesis that different foods go well together when they share major compounds that contribute to flavour, also referred to as "foodpairing", is at best a dubious hypothesis and should not, in any case, be a necessary tool for any decent chef. Foodpairing is a now a trademark[358] and, on their website, which features Blumenthal,[359] services are offered to professional chefs looking for flavour combinations and recipes. Call me old fashioned and reactionary if you will, but, surely, if a taste combination is pleasant, it is pleasant, and no scientific sanction is required. Similarly, if it is unpleasant, no number of matching amines or other compounds prove that it is actually a good combination. The idea behind foodpairing, however, is that the method is not only able to confirm why a food combination is successful or unsuccessful, but to predict which combinations will most likely work, based on their matching compounds. The website is free to register and use, with a subscription option for the "Pro" level. I registered for the free service and consulted this gastronomic oracle, just to see what sort of results it might throw up. Due to copyright and trademark legal protection, I cannot reproduce some of the results that are suggested by the foodpairing database. It will suffice to say that, in my opinion, the food pairings varied from the obvious to the absurd. I will leave you to register and draw your own conclusions.

There is something problematic about looking at food ingredients on a molecular, compound by compound basis. Apart from the fact that it does not tell us anything about the quality of the actual ingredients, this sort of approach leads to the isolation of specific molecules and compounds, which, as the flavour industry routinely does, proceed to be synthesised and isolated, in an ever-increasing simplification masquerading as sophistication. Even if through chemical analysis we learn that X compound in Y food is the distinctive compound that we recognise when we eat Y, it does not practically nor logically follow that it would be a good idea to use X as a separate ingredient in food. As ever, reductionism clashes with a holistic view: what makes food X pleasant to eat is the fact that it is indeed a complex, flavoursome whole food, not the mere sum of chemicals responsible for specific flavours. It is the complexity and depth of flavour that enhances our experience

[357] https://www.perfumerflavorist.com/flavor/ingredients/news/21874372/firmenich-sa-firmenich-announces-ai-created-flavor

[358] https://www.foodpairing.com/

[359] https://www.foodpairing.com/chefs/

of food. Extract, reduce, simplify and you end up with an impoverished, contrived version of the same experience.

This simple fact does not deter Blumenthal, who in fact uses individual flavourings as part of his culinary arsenal. In an interview with the admiring food critic Jay Rayner, we are told:

> *"He has jars of flavour essences and refined acids, the chemical versions of tastes we know so well. He has one that smells of cut grass, another of oak, a third of leather."*
>
> *'There are 3,500 of these essences,' he says. 'They are the building blocks. I want to learn them all.'*
>
> *"He gets me to sniff some Benzaldehyde. 'I was shocked by how pure an almond kick it is,' he says, and he's right. Benzaldehyde is almonds."*[360]

In reality, almonds are not benzaldehyde: they are almonds, a complex whole food not reducible to a compound. Using synthesised flavourings, which are normally the ingredients of crisps and pot noodle manufacturers, impoverishes and simplifies cuisine, rather than enrich it. Not content with using food flavourings, Blumenthal even uses non-food flavourings, such as leather.[361]

The same confrontation with reductionism occurs when we consider the human experience of food. As we saw in Chapter 5, attempts to reduce human experience (aesthetic, moral, gastronomic, or otherwise) to neurological and chemical process inevitably leads to a reduced or irremediably flawed understanding of these experiences. They simply miss the point. Just because we can now identify the neural and sensory pathways that are involved in eating, smelling, and tasting food, or we can identify the specific chemicals that are responsible for the distinctive aromas of specific foods, it simply does not follow that gastronomic experiences or the specific foods involved in these experiences are reducible to such an analysis. More importantly, this knowledge can only ever have a very limited influence on actual cookery and eating.

Consequently, given his fashionable interest in the pseudo subject of "neurogastronomy",[362] Blumenthal has also devoted himself to what is pretentiously referred to as "multi-sensory cooking", which roughly refers to the idea that the eating experience involves all the senses,

[360] https://www.theguardian.com/lifeandstyle/2004/feb/15/foodanddrink.restaurants

[361] H. Blumenthal, 2008, The Fat Duck Cookbook, pages 253-254.

[362] Beware of the recent mushrooming of several pseudo subjects starting with the prefix "neuro". See Raymond Tallis' lucid take on the issue: R. Tallis, 2011, Aping Mankind.

other than just taste and smell, and that the context in which we eat affects our experience of eating.

Blumenthal recalls that his first venture into the world of multi-sensory cooking, which resulted in his first research paper in 1997, co-written with Martin Yeomans for the University of Sussex, was made whilst making his signature crab ice cream:

> *"I first made crab ice cream in the late 1990s," he says. "On reflection, this was one of my landmark dishes. It changed the way I thought about food because I realised people's perception changed based on whether I called it a frozen crab bisque or crab ice cream."*
>
> *"In an experiment, people who were told a dish was smoked salmon ice cream thought it was 10-15% saltier than the people who were told it was a frozen smoked salmon mousse, because from memory people expect ice cream to be sweet. This is when I started to use the term multi-sensory."*[363]

If crustaceans are to be made into a cold sweet treat, frozen crab bisque does sound a lot more appealing than crab ice cream, but is this really a surprise or discovery of any kind? One is left wondering about how much time and resources are wasted at British universities. According to an article on the Top 50 Restaurants' website, Blumenthal's *"discovery that what we hear, smell, see, and touch when we eat can have a profound effect on how little or how much we enjoy our dinner is simultaneously obvious and groundbreaking."*[364]

There is of course nothing remotely groundbreaking about these non-insights, as anyone who has ever spent a minute or two thinking about the experience of eating would have arrived at the same obvious conclusion. The ambiance of a restaurant, the lighting, the background noise, the tablecloth and tableware, the narrative of the menu and the very location of a restaurant all clearly influence our dining experience. If taste and smell were all that mattered, our meals could simply be served to us in cheap, dark, silent individual metal cubicles, eating from plastic plates with plastic cutlery, with no views beyond our four walls. Whilst no amount of ambiance and sweet surroundings will rescue a really poor or mediocre meal, clearly context and factors outside of the plate really matter to us.

So where is the supposed innovation and great insight? It lies in the fact that the exponents of multi-sensory cooking, armed with the feeble, reductionist findings of questionable psychological research, believe that sensory experiences can be manipulated and controlled

[363]https://tempusmagazine.co.uk/news/interview-heston-blumenthal-talks-25-years-of-groundbreaking-gastronomy/

[364]https://www.theworlds50best.com/stories/News/seven-ways-heston-blumenthal-changed-the-food-and-restaurant-world.html

in a restaurant setting. On the basis of this sort of research and thinking, Blumenthal and others have therefore been busy artificially stimulating and playing with their customers' senses at their restaurants, under the presumption of promoting a more profound, meaningful gastronomic experience.

Blumenthal has often recalled, as one of his formative experiences, a trip to Provence as a teenager, where he ate at a beautiful countryside restaurant and was overwhelmed by the smell of lavender, sound of cicadas and stunning views and observed how *"the visual splendour of the setting almost seemed to eclipse the food"*.[365] We can all relate to Blumenthal, I imagine. In fact, not only will the eating experience be enhanced by its surroundings, but even the type of food eaten, when matched by its surroundings, will be more pleasant to eat. Eating seafood by the sea, with smells and sounds of the ocean, certainly enhances the pleasure of eating seafood. It is not just the freshness of the seafood itself: if you ate the very same seafood, caught at exactly the same time by the same boat and cooked in the same way by the same chef and ate it in a grotty pub in London, you would most likely not enjoy it or taste it with the same intensity as you do when eating it at a lovely seaside restaurant. The same basic, obvious truth will hold for other foods and landscapes.

Unfortunately, Blumenthal does not seem to have grasped the lesson he could have learnt from this formative experience, as demonstrated by one of his signature dishes, called the *Sound of the Sea*. This is a dish in which seafood, seaweed and edible "sand" are used to create a dish that is supposed to look like the edge of the seashore. The dish itself, like so many dishes in postmodern gastronomy, seems to favour novelty for the sake of novelty, elaborate and pretentious presentation, unnecessary processes, and suspect ingredients (e.g., soya lecithin, sodium caseinate, N-Zorbit M tapioca maltodextrin, blue shimmer powder (a colourant) and brown carbonized vegetable powder amongst others)[366] over substance, flavour, and technique. The full recipe and its rationale can be found on Blumenthal's book[367] and I will leave you to decide whether it is worth making in your own kitchen. I would personally describe it as follows: a weird edible "sand" containing crushed ice cream cones and panko breadcrumbs, amongst other things, is covered with a few bits of shellfish and seaweed. A large amount of white foam (the dreaded foam again!) dominates the plate, supposedly evoking the foam produced by crashing waves and so on. I can think of hundreds of seafood dishes more interesting, skilful, and appetising than this but, be that at it may, it is the sound accompanying the dish that is really troubling. What completes the multi-sensory experience, is that the diner finds a pair of earpieces to wear

[365] As recalled here, for example: https://www.bps.org.uk/psychologist/down-culinary-rabbit-hole and in more detail in H. Blumenthal, 2008, The Fat Duck Cookbook, pages 17, 22, 23.

[366] H. Blumenthal, 2008, The Fat Duck Cookbook, pages 214-215.

[367] Ibidem, pages 206-15.

inside a conch shell, served next to the dish. The diner is invited to wear the earpieces whilst eating, from which he or she will hear the "sounds of the sea": waves crashing, seagulls mewing and so on.

Hearing the sounds of the sea, according to Blumenthal's theory, will significantly enhance the experience of eating the seafood. To justify this questionable belief, the celebrated Chef yet again draws on scientific research. He collaborated with Professor Charles Spence[368] at Crossmodal Research Laboratory in Oxford to investigate the idea that *"sound could radically affect our perception and enjoyment of food."*[369]

In his own words, Blumenthal recalls one of their experiments:

> *"For one of them we fed test-participants (actually members of the audience at the Art and the Senses conference held in Oxford in 2006) a scoop of bacon and egg ice cream. One group of participants ate the ice cream while listening to the sounds of bacon sizzling in the pan. The others tasted the ice cream while listening to the sounds of chickens clucking in the farmyard. In each case the sound appeared to intensify the relevant flavour. In another experiment, we fed participants oysters while listening either to the sound of the sea (think waves crashing gently on the beach), or to the sounds of farmyard animals, after which we asked them to rate how pleasant the oysters tasted. (Listening to the sound of the sea resulted in people rating the oyster as tasting significantly more enjoyable, but no more salty when compared to the farmyard soundtrack. Such results giving further support to the notion that sound can indeed influence our emotional response to food.) It was this last experiment that inspired what is now a classic on the menu at The Fat Duck, "Sound of the Sea"…"*[370]

It should be clear to any reasonable person that no groundbreaking insight can be gained from any of the above. If we are to be afflicted by bacon and egg ice cream, it may well be better to do so with bacon and egg related sounds in the background than to do so in silence or with the sounds of the sea. Similarly, if we are going to be eating oysters during one of Blumenthal's experiments, we would undoubtedly feel more comfortable with the sound of the sea than with the farmyard soundtrack. In other words, these pseudo experiments yielded the results one would expect without any need to actually perform the experiments. Do the results of any of these sorts of experiments remotely imply that it would be a good idea to accompany restaurant meals with soundtracks that match the animals presented on

[368] As has Ferran Adrià: https://www.wired.com/story/staying-creative-ferran-adria/

[369] https://www.bps.org.uk/psychologist/down-culinary-rabbit-hole

[370] Ibidem

the plate? Or that these sounds can significantly elevate a mediocre plate of food? Certainly not.

The *Sound of the Sea*, in a nutshell, is an example of reductionist thinking at its worst, of attempting to reduce complex and unique experiences to transportable, plug-and-play *faux* experiences. The reason why eating by the seaside is inherently pleasant is because of the complexity and uniqueness of the actual, real seaside experience: the smells of the sea and of local vegetation, the sight of birds and boats on the horizon, the sea breeze and indeed the sounds of the sea and the seagulls. And so much more. When eating the *Sound of the Sea* at The Fat Duck in Bray, Berkshire, we are still just eating in a restaurant in the middle of England, with nothing remotely resembling the sea anywhere near us. We are still in Bray, with a pair of earpieces in our ears. We are not magically transported to a marine parallel universe. Blumenthal can play with our senses all he likes but no amount of smoke and mirrors can manufacture or even come close to invoking the experience the smoke and mirrors are supposed to recreate. I would also add, as a sidenote, that this pathetic imitation of a genuine experience breaks all rules of conviviality and tableside manners in its quest to transport the diner on a solipsistic virtual journey to the sea: how are we to converse with our table companions, with seagull noises going off in our ears? We are consoled, however, by the sobering fact that some of Blumenthal's customers are so overwhelmed by the experience, that they are reduced to tears: *"A few people cry over the dish."*[371]

The only lesson the young Blumenthal should have learnt from his Provençal epiphany is one we have already conceded as being true by definition: that the experiential conditions in which we eat are very important in determining the quality of our gastronomic experience. Complexity is the key word: it is the irreducible holistic experience, the coming together of sights, sounds, smells, human interactions etc… that give us a valuable experience. At the Fat Duck, a more earthy, countryside, farmhouse menu would make a lot more sense than any attempt to conjure the seaside. If Blumenthal wants to provide the ultimate seafood "multi-sensory" experience, I am afraid the only option he has is to open a seaside restaurant, in some scenic village in Cornwall. I imagine, but cannot possibly confirm, that this is a project he could afford to undertake.

Blumenthal has been a very successful businessman, therefore if money and fame were his objectives, he has chosen the right career. But his gastronomic achievements are largely illusory: I would suggest he would have made far better contributions to the field of chemistry, in which he undoubtedly excels.

[371] https://www.wired.com/story/heston-blumenthal-chef/

The Alchemy: Why Uncomfortable Lessons Should Not Be Part of the Menu

Like many of my readers, I imagine, I am partial to MasterChef: The Professionals, the popular show on the BBC. Part of the fun consists in spotting culinary trends and fads in haute cuisine, which are often on show when the final contestants get the opportunity to work at top rated restaurants worldwide. In the 2023 Series, in the penultimate episode, the contestants visit The Alchemy, the 5th ranked restaurant in the world at the time,[372] based in Copenhagen.[373] Even a weathered, seasoned observer of human folly like my good self was caught unprepared by some of the misguided absurdities on display at this "restaurant". I use the word restaurant in inverted commas because this establishment sells "tickets" as opposed to tables, and an "experience" as opposed to lunch or dinner.

The enormous restaurant was built inside an abandoned portside industrial warehouse. Inside the building, apart from contemporary art instillations and what I would describe as dancers slash entertainers, we have a planetarium, showcasing video imagery that change over the course of the meal, which is designed to deliver an "experiential" dining experience. In the MasterChef episode, Chef Rasmus Munk takes his charges through some of the dishes, or "impressions", as he calls them, that are served as part of the up to 50 courses tasting menu. There is a definite futuristic, techno-geek feel about the kitchen, which looks more like a lab than a kitchen, which produces, amongst other things, the "Perfect Omelette", made by using a less than appealing eggy membrane, manufactured with a 3D printed mould. The test kitchen is indeed *"filled with state-of-the-art scientific equipment from 3D printers to sound wave machines"*.[374] Apparently, it can take one to two years for some of the impressions to make the grade: quite an R&D process!

Incredibly, Rasmus Munk defines his method as *"holistic cuisine"*, as it apparently combines art, science, and food, guided by the belief that the world can be changed through gastronomy. How does this holistic cuisine change the world? By ensuring that each *"impression"* has a *"story to tell"*, and conveys a message to society, with each experience carefully *"designed to get the diner thinking about everything from blood donation to animal welfare and the environment"*.[375] The contestants are charged with making several dishes, including two particularly poignant and educational dishes: a cod dish, called Plastic

[372] It now ranked 8th: https://www.theworlds50best.com/list/1-50

[373] My critique of The Alchemist is based on watching MasterChef: The Professionals Series 16. See episode 20 on https://www.bbc.co.uk/programmes/m001t4sr

[374] MasterChef: The Professionals Series 16, Episode 20.

[375] Ibidem

Fantastic and a chicken dish called Burnout Chicken. The former consists of the flesh from a cod's jaw, which is usually a low value or discarded part of the fish. So far so good. However, apart from what looked to me like a remarkably mediocre and unappetising recipe, the cod's jaw was topped with various bits of two types of see-through plastic. Edible plastic, but plastic, nonetheless. The plastic elements are used to remind the diner that the oceans are full of plastic, because, apparently, 29% of Danish cod contains microplastics.[376] I cannot claim to have had the dubious pleasure of eating plastic myself, but I have felt plastic in my mouth from a sweet wrapper, or something like that, and it is not something that any normal person would willingly want to put in their mouth and eat. The planetarium also swings into action, as the cod dish is served and consumed, with images of sea creatures surrounded by plastic bags, to ensure that the environmental lesson cannot possibly fail to be taken in by the diner.

Chef Munk concedes that the plastic does indeed have a *"plastic texture"* and that there will be *"a couple of seconds where you will feel like this is not pleasant"* and *"then it will turn into hopefully some good flavours and textures"*.[377] Not surprisingly, the contestants and judges, in spite of the obvious implied and unspoken requirement to praise their host Chef and restaurant, do not seem overly impressed by the actual flavour of the dish. Gregg Wallace does point out that when he first put the plastic in his mouth, *"it feels like you're chewing on a plastic bag. It tastes great at the end, but that is uncomfortable to eat at the start. And it's supposed to be, isn't it?"*[378] Why any food should intentionally be made to feel uncomfortable, at any stage, is a questionable notion to say the least. Marcus Waring, who is a most competent chef himself, and vastly superior to Rasmus Munk, disappointingly praises the dish as "genius", presumably for its ideological virtues as opposed to the taste, which he fails to comment on.

Things arguably get worse with the chicken dish. The dish consists of a chicken drumstick, with its foot on, that is stuffed, coated, and fried and placed inside a metal cage filled with some sort of straw or hay. The diner, who doesn't get the benefit of a plate or any other retrograde crockery, is supposed to literally "free" the chicken from the cage, in order to be taught the sort of lesson I also tried to impart throughout this book: that most chickens in agriculture are abused, unhealthy, miserable creatures that live in cramped, filthy conditions, including cages. Whilst we should all take stock of this fact and amend our actions accordingly (by boycotting all factory farmed chicken, for a start), it is the delivery method of the message that is entirely misplaced.

[376] MasterChef: The Professionals Series 16, Episode 20.

[377] Ibidem

[378] Ibidem

Once the dish is served, the planetarium fills up with images of caged birds, clucking away in their metal prisons, in what Waring describes as a *"hellish vision"*, *"a reality check of what we've been eating for so many years"*.[379] Wallace, again, reports that whilst *"this is quite uncomfortable"*, *"that's the whole point"*. Monica Galletti is also *"quite uncomfortable eating it"* but is comforted by the value of the moral lesson: *"people need to be more aware of their food sources."*[380] At least the three emotional presenters do not get hysterical, and no tears are shed. Nonetheless, lest he should fail to equal Blumenthal's knack for tear-jerking dishes, Chef Munk proudly informs us that a lot of the diners actually cry when confronted by this provocative chicken dish. Call me boring and insensitive, but I would argue that discomfort, hellish visions, tears, and guilt should not play any role in what should surely be pleasant, convivial, and relaxing.

In fairness, Munk does reassure us that the chicken in question does come from a chicken that *"had an amazing life from a little farm in Denmark"*.[381] Of course, all our messianic Chef could do to promote animal welfare would be to keep sourcing the very same fortunate chicken, add some information about it on the menu and website, and, instead of delivering tear filled techno-sermons, he could focus on a serious and fantastic recipe, preferably served without a side of straw, and on a plate, without disturbing images. Similarly, if Munk is truly concerned about the plight of the poor cod and sea creatures in general, he could simply not have seafood on the menu. That would save a few cod, given that according to one of his assistants they consume up to a tonne of cod heads a week.[382]

Overall, it seems to me that in order to deliver this strange multi-sensory sermon, pleasure, aesthetics, and actual food quality are sacrificed on a very expensive altar of virtue signalling. Surely there are better ways to deliver the message, if messages must be delivered, whilst providing great food. But, as we saw, the point here is not to provide pleasure and great food, but to generate shock, surprise, and uncomfortable feelings. Apparently, according to a separate BBC report, *"dishes include "hunger", where thin silver ribs are draped with sustainable rabbit meat, making its well-heeled diners squirm in their seats as they think about starvation."*[383] We can therefore add "squirming" to the long list of emotive reactions we can expect at this vanguard of contemporary gastronomy. One is also left wondering whether there is any room for irony, as one is being reprimanded about world hunger via the

[379] Not I, Marcus!

[380] MasterChef: The Professionals Series 16, Episode 20.

[381] Ibidem

[382] Ibidem

[383] https://www.bbc.com/travel/article/20230110-alchemist-is-this-the-worlds-most-creative-restaurant

expensive consumption of thin morsels of meat, washed down by copious amounts of champagne.

It would also be interesting to know how Chef Munk feels that the supposed green credentials and pretentions of the restaurant can be squared up to the fact that this enormous establishment, with its screens and digital entertainments, must consume a relatively large amount of electricity, and with the fact that it probably uses more machines, computers, and technological gadgetry than a dozen normal restaurants put together. It is hard to imagine a more energy and resource intensive restaurant. Not so green, I suspect, but I may be wrong...

To make matters worse, all the intellectually vacuous, uncomfortable moralising, and impressions of weird techno-food last for an estimated 4-6 hours, at a cost of over £606 per head at the time of writing,[384] excluding drinks. I imagine that a state of constant inebriation must almost be necessary, if not mandatory, to get through this ordeal, raising the cost to not far off £1,000 a head, if not more, depending on the wine pairing selected.

Deconstructing Deconstruction: El Bulli and Ferran Adrià

All of the Chefs criticised thus far have paid homage to the man who has probably done more than anyone to spread the ideology and practices of postmodern gastronomy, which he defines as "avant-garde" or "deconstructivism." In fairness, his influence has been unparalleled, and it is with the Catalonian that this brief critical essay must end.

Ferran Adrià revels in his legacy: *"I see chefs - chefs on the [World's] 50 Best list - still doing things we did 20 years ago. That was the power of El Bulli. After us, everybody started questioning everything."*[385]

Heston Blumenthal has no doubt about his debt to the great Catalonian: *"Ferran's a genius. Without a doubt, he's had the biggest influence on modern gastronomy of any chef alive."*[386]

Massimo Bottura sees him as a *"revolutionary - he taught me how to use the power of emotion and express myself in a million different ways."*[387]

[384] DKK 5,400 per head on 11.10.24, see: https://alchemist.dk/the-alchemist-experience/

[385] https://www.gq-magazine.co.uk/lifestyle/article/ferran-adria-interview

[386] https://www.theguardian.com/lifeandstyle/2006/apr/12/foodanddrink.shopping

[387] https://www.gq-magazine.co.uk/lifestyle/article/ferran-adria-interview

Rasmus Munk has recently run an event with Ferran Adrià and his brother Albert,[388] who are *"the closest you can get to 'culinary royalty' in this business"* and got to *"finally fulfil his dream of bringing some iconic elBulli dishes to his own restaurant."*[389]

Daniel Humm, "plant-based" chef and owner of Eleven Madison Park, number 1 on the World's 50 Best Restaurants list in 2017, informs us that *"what Ferran has done is unbelievable. He changed how we all think about food. Not just for us chefs at the highest level, but he changed the way people think about food on any level. That is beyond, beyond, beyond inspiring."*[390]

Even the way he eats has been described as radically different from the rest of us mere mortals: according to Grant Achatz, Chef and Restaurateur of Three Michelin-starred Alinea in Chicago, *"he computes it, then inhales it – I've never seen anything like it."*[391]

His philosophy is often described as being so profound, so advanced, that it is beyond human comprehension. According to the Financial Times' restaurant critic, Nicholas Lander, Adrià is *"impossible to understand in any language."*[392]

The very experience of eating at El Bulli, now no longer a possibility, was potentially the greatest experience of one's life, and not just at the dining table: *"what El Bulli used to offer was quite straightforward: the best meal on the planet, the best meal of your life and very often one of the best experiences a human being could have."*[393]

I could go on for several pages, as the gushing and mesmerised praise Adrià has received to date goes far and deep, having somehow gained the status of great artist, revolutionary and genius all rolled into one. This should immediately make us suspicious, for the simple reason that no cook nor chef can possibly fit any of these categories. A great chef is neither an artist, nor a revolutionary nor a genius, if any of these appellations are to mean anything at all. Caravaggio, Raffaello, and Rembrandt were great artists. There can be no doubting the genius of Leonardo da Vinci, Wolfgang Amadeus Mozart, and Fyodor Dostoevsky. A revolution, political or otherwise, involves something far more serious than the Michelin Guide. Even if we came to believe that Adrià or indeed Blumenthal were truly great chefs,

[388] Younger brother Albert Adrià worked at El Bulli with Ferran Adrià, specialising in deconstructing pastry. He is credited with many of El Bulli's innovations, including spherification. Their approach and philosophy are by all accounts indistinguishable. I will mostly refer to Ferran Adrià throughout this brief essay given his leadership role and fame, but the critique applies to both chefs.

[389] https://www.four-magazine.com/tasting-notes/ferran-albert-adria-team-up-with-rasmus-munk-in-copenhagen/

[390] https://www.theworlds50best.com/stories/News/ferran-adria-el-bulli-never-wanted-to-cook.html

[391] https://www.gq-magazine.co.uk/lifestyle/article/ferran-adria-interview

[392] Ibidem

[393] https://www.gq-magazine.co.uk/lifestyle/article/ferran-adria-interview

even the greatest of all chefs, it would still be a mistake to categorise them with such labels. It's a simple category error.

This has not stopped Adrià from placing his craft within the history of art: *"there have always been creative movements in Spain" he said, "most recently in art – Picasso, Miró, Dalí – today, that movement is in the kitchen, in cooking. Spanish cooking is the most modern in the world."*[394] Not only is this cuisine an art form, according to Adrià, it is high art: *"these are really two different ways to cook. For the one, the name says it all: it is food for traditional purposes. The other is a high art."*[395] The contemporary art world seems to agree with him: Ferran Adrià's work has been featured at international museums and art galleries[396] and The Centre for Contemporary Culture of Barcelona (CCCB) presented Adrià alongside artists like Salvador Dalí and Antoni Gaudí in their *"Illuminations. Visionary Catalonia"* exhibition.[397]

Let us set the art debate aside for now and look at what Adrià has actually contributed to the culinary field. What does "avant-garde" or "deconstruction" look like in the kitchen? Fundamentally, in his own words, it involves taking a dish or recipe that is well known and *"transforming all its ingredients, or part of them; then modifying the dish's texture, form and/or its temperature. Deconstructed, such a dish will preserve its essence... but its appearance will be radically different from the originals."*[398] For example, early in his career, Adrià deconstructed the classic Spanish Tortilla, which most of us will be familiar with. The deconstructed tortilla *is "a layered construction of potato foam, onion purée and egg-white sabayon, scattered with deep fried potato crumbs."*[399] I have not had the honour of tasting it, but the description does not exactly leave one salivating. In any case, in what sense is this even a tortilla? How is it an improvement on an actual tortilla? Worryingly, Adrià also has a home version of the Spanish Tortilla: Tortilla made using potato crisps from a packet as opposed to actual potatoes.[400] Again, this is definitely not an improvement on the classic tortilla, and one is left baffled by the fact that the world's most celebrated chef would recommend using ultra-processed junk food (potato chips) as opposed to a whole food (actual potatoes). Perhaps it was an attempt to reach out to "the people", to "democratise" his food and pre-empt accusations of elitism and snobbery, which are often levelled towards the high priests of haute cuisine. Having said that, Adrià did use to partner with PepsiCo and

[394] https://eatourwords.wordpress.com/2014/04/01/my-interview-with-ferran-adria/

[395] https://the-talks.com/interview/ferran-adria/

[396] See, for example: https://drawingcenter.org/exhibitions/ferran-adri%C3%A0-notes-on-creativity and https://www.somersethouse.org.uk/whats-on/elbulli-ferran-adri%C3%A0-and-art-food

[397] https://clotmag.com/key-artists/ferran-adria

[398] https://www.theguardian.com/observer/foodmonthly/futureoffood/story/0,,1969713,00.html

[399] C. Andrews, 2010, Reinventing Food: Ferran Adrià: the man who changed the way we eat, page 40.

[400] https://www.phaidon.com/agenda/food/articles/2014/april/15/the-things-people-ask-ferran-adria/

helped them develop a potato crisps brand,[401] so the motive might have been purely commercial. We should not condemn a man for chasing a paycheque, but should a chef stoop so low for a consulting fee? Did he have to include the crisps in the iconic tortilla?

His biographer Colman Andrews describes how Adrià also deconstructed another Spanish classic, the Paella, *by "inventing a 'Kellogg's paella', made out of puffer rice (think Rice Krispies) fried with saffron and mixed with tomato powder, prawn powder and raw prawns, and served with an ampoule of intense brown extract to be squeezed directly into the mouth"*.[402] Reminiscent of Bottura's deconstructed Bollito, the deconstructed Paella is clearly a travesty and desecration of a great dish. Paella, at its best, is one of the greatest dishes one can have the pleasure of eating: certainly, one of the greatest rice dishes in the world. In Valencia, where it originates, it is traditionally cooked in a flat paella pan, on top of an open fire, often fuelled by wood from the pruning of the orange groves. The rice variety, the saffron, the vegetables used, the meats, the seasonings: the care and attention taken in selecting these ingredients at their very best all contribute to the great complexity and depth of the dish. There are of course seafood versions, which are wonderful, and there is plenty of scope for a Chef to create their own twist and version of this great dish.

The deconstructed version is simply not a version or rendition of anything at all, but a disjointed, senseless farce of a fantastic dish. This should not surprise us, however. The postmodern, deconstructive approach in the fine arts and philosophy has also led to a similar process of desecration. It is an ideology based on a wholesale rejection of the past, on a rejection of the very possibility of truth and of objective standards and values, whether in morality or aesthetics. It is a worldview permeated by an extreme form of relativism, that gives its proponents a false sense of freedom and emancipation. Liberated from all tradition, accumulated knowledge, established standards and norms, and any objective frame of reference, the deconstructivist feels unbounded in his ability to break with the past and manufacture his "own truth". Anything goes. Novelty is sought for the sake of novelty: the new and original is celebrated, whatever its form. This is a grave conceptual error and moral failing, as novelty and originality are not inherent virtues, not in cuisine, nor in any other field. Novelty without skill, quality and value is totally worthless.

Going back to gastronomy, in order to deconstruct and create new dishes, Adrià developed a whole host of techniques and methods used to create textures, temperatures and appearances that could not be created via the traditional techniques of boiling, grilling,

[401] https://www.eater.com/2011/6/16/6674725/pepsico-announces-new-partnership-with-ferran-adria
https://www.independent.co.uk/life-style/food-and-drink/renowned-chef-ferran-adria-to-create-products-for-pepsico-2298870.html

[402] C. Andrews, 2010, Reinventing Food: Ferran Adrià: the man who changed the way we eat, page 40.

braising, frying, baking and so on. It is thanks to Adrià that we have been afflicted by foams: *"Without doubt, the most imitated children from the el Bulli kitchen have been the foams, a revolutionary and certainly controversial idea in the field of gastronomy."*[403] However, foams are only one of Adrià's contributions, as he has also been responsible for creating and/or publicising the use of several other products and techniques such as: frozen powders, warm gelatines, liquid nitrogen, spherification, gelification, the use of agars, candy-floss machines, chemical baths and plenty more. Needless to say, he cooks some of his dishes in microwaves and sous vide.

The Chef has also felt free to play with untested flavour and food combinations, resulting in weird and less-than-appealing concoctions, which divide his customers. Of course, there is no such thing as weird for Adrià: *"The concept of weird does not exist for me. And if you have to talk about something "weird" there is no such thing as weird food. There are only weird people."*[404] This way of thinking is a logical consequence of breaking with the past: if we start cooking with a tabula rasa, with no preconceived notion, any combination goes and cannot be criticised. It should be quite obvious that the reason why there are tried and tested combinations and combinations which are just not done is because some combinations work, while other combinations do not and cannot. Don't tastes change and vary over time and place? Is there room to attempt new combinations, is there room for trial and error? Of course. But the collected wisdom, culinary techniques and recipes of the past are nonetheless the foundation of any great cook. Throwing ingredients together just for the sake of creating something new has no inherent value: anyone can do that, in any case. Some combinations do not exist for really good reasons, and vice versa. The reason why there is no traditional recipe combining, say, mussels, coffee and English mustard is not because of a lack of imagination but because some ingredients and flavours simply do not go together and cannot be made to work together. The reason why most cultures and cuisines combine legumes with pork, for example, is because they go very well together.

In fairness to Adrià, he freely admits that not everyone will like his food, and in fact does not believe this is a necessary goal, for the avant-garde Chef:

"With elBulli, the aspect of creativity was always most important for us. Worrying about whether or not people were able to experience good food and a nice time just wasn't the point"[405]

[403] https://eatourwords.wordpress.com/2014/04/01/my-interview-with-ferran-adria/

[404] https://www.phaidon.com/agenda/food/articles/2014/april/15/the-things-people-ask-ferran-adria/

[405] https://the-talks.com/interview/ferran-adria/

"First of all, El Bulli was probably the first restaurant in history that had people who hated it. Why? Because we took that experience to the limit. We cooked to open new paths and to make you reflect on things."[406]

"I am happy when people enjoy my food. But it's not my first priority."[407]

"For the first time, people [who ate there] hated a restaurant. And why? Because we required them to do something that wasn't in the normal framework. We did provocation, irony, things that weren't normal [at a restaurant], and all of this made you think about life. At El Bulli, there was no middle ground - either you hated it or you loved it."[408]

The aforementioned Chef Grant Achatz also sees this as a positive, rather than a negative: *"I fell in love with his thought processes and his risk-taking, how he would openly admit to creating a dish that did not taste good, on purpose. To me, that was so courageous."*[409]

Incredibly, even his adoring biographer, who hails Adrià as a genius, recalls not enjoying or being indifferent to quite a few of his dishes. One example stands out:

"Sea Anemone 2008. Just your everyday mix of sea anemone, raw rabbit brains, oysters and calamondin (a sour-sweet Southeast Asian citrus) in lukewarm dill broth. I wouldn't go so far as one blog entry I later happened to come across, which described this creation as 'Vile. Vomitous. Nightmare!' but I found it so utterly unpleasant and cacophonous that I wondered for a moment whether Ferran had gone off the rails. It made my teeth ache."[410]

I would put it to my dear readers that no great chef can possibly produce ill-conceived food that a significant percentage of people find inedible and disgusting. It shows a lack of palate and judgement, which is the very basis of cookery. No great chef can consistently create flavour and texture combinations that produce "love it or hate it" food. Graver still is the fact that Adrià does not seem concerned by this and that his chief goal is not creating flavours that people will love, but flavours that are new, that provoke, challenge, surprise, and divide. We need to be clear about this: the idea that dividing the crowd is synonymous with virtue and refinement is complete nonsense. Whilst we will all have our preferences and what is amazing for me might not be amazing for you, surely a great dish cannot elicit such strong negative feelings in a significant percentage of those who eat it.

[406] https://www.splendidtable.org/story/2015/12/18/chef-ferran-adria-how-do-you-define-cooking

[407] https://www.independent.co.uk/life-style/food-and-drink/features/bulli-for-him-ferran-adria-on-why-he-s-the-world-s-greatest-chef-395311.html

[408] https://www.scmp.com/magazines/post-magazine/article/1540814/ferran-adria-man-very-big-plan

[409] https://www.gq-magazine.co.uk/lifestyle/article/ferran-adria-interview

[410] C. Andrews, 2010, Reinventing Food: Ferran Adrià: the man who changed the way we eat, page 40.

In response to my critique, one might try to argue that there are particular foods that tend to divide people, such as coriander and blue cheese, or very culturally restricted ingredients, such as *nattō* (fermented soybeans) in Japan, that people who did not grow up eating them do not tend to like: the so-called acquired tastes. But the subjective preference or dislike for individual ingredients or the fact that there are inevitable acquired tastes in every culture is not relevant to the argument. These are both different cases from that of a chef intentionally creating specific combinations, recipes, dishes, and menus that, surely, should be designed to please the palates of all his customers, from the least to the most refined. No great restaurant, especially one that is ranked number 1 in the world (!), could possibly produce dishes that people hate or just find weird and not particularly pleasant.

Whilst the Catalonian does not seem to mind if some people hate his food, he demands respect for it nonetheless:

"What does he think now if people find one of his dishes unappetising or even disgusting? "Well, I think that lacks respect," ... Adria, who is sometimes painted by the Spanish press as a mad professor, a figure of fun, doesn't like any implication that his food is in any way "strange". "If there was a sculpture that I didn't like, I wouldn't say it was disgusting, I'd just say I didn't like it. So long as there is freedom for people not to go to a place, then there is freedom for the cook to do whatever he wants."[411]

This kind of self-serving relativism should not be allowed to go unchallenged. Apart from the ridiculous idea that there can be no badly made sculptures, or indeed paintings or dishes and that it is all just a matter of personal taste, we must also confirm that we have the freedom to criticise a cook's work, even deeming it repulsive, should we feel the need to, in the same way that the cook demands the freedom to do whatever he wants. Adrià and his followers can keep producing foams: I will keep pointing out that they are at best totally unnecessary and at worst disgusting.

Of course, Adrià is hostile to hostile opinions, which he considers illegitimate and unprofessional: "*One of the [conclusions] I've come to is that since everyone eats, everyone feels bold enough to give their opinion. If I were to talk to you about nanotechnology, would you be bold enough to [argue with] me about it? But [everyone] would feel comfortable to talk to me about cooking. It's fascinating."*[412] If anything, I would argue that the only reason why Adrià gets away with his avant-garde cuisine and is taken seriously at the highest levels of gastronomy is precisely because we have an impoverished food culture, with an

[411] https://www.independent.co.uk/life-style/food-and-drink/features/bulli-for-him-ferran-adria-on-why-he-s-the-world-s-greatest-chef-395311.html

[412] https://www.scmp.com/magazines/post-magazine/article/1540814/ferran-adria-man-very-big-plan

increasing percentage of people, including critics, who do not cook at all and are raised on mediocre food. It is easier to impress those with no standards and frame of reference. Had Adrià turned up amongst great chefs in Italy and France a generation or two ago, with his foams and spheres, he would never have been taken seriously.

In any case, the comparison between cooking and nanotechnology clearly does not hold. Nanotechnology is a niche, specialised, recently invented subject that over 99.9% of the human population knows absolutely nothing about. Eating and cooking are fundamental activities of mankind, in which we all have a stake and that we all engage in, albeit to differing degrees. We may not all have benefited from the same culinary education, we may not all have benefited from good home cooking as children, we may not cook very much, and we may not all have the same discerning palate or budget, but we all eat! Surely, if we pay for the benefit of a meal at a restaurant, we can form an opinion on it, even if we are not professional cooks like Adrià. A more appropriate comparison than nanotechnology might have been clothing. We all wear clothes and, even if we are not fashion designers or seamstresses, we can and will have opinions on the quality, design, and appeal of different items of clothing. I do not need to work in fashion to hold the belief that a particular shirt is tacky and ugly, or a particular suit is elegant and well-made.

If food critique is to amount to anything, we must be able to make qualitative distinctions. There are clearly foods, like the aforementioned coriander and blue cheese, or indeed anchovies and oysters, that we might subjectively find disgusting but recognise are not actually disgusting: it is just a matter of taste or upbringing, and we just do not order them on the menu. But the same reasoning does not apply to dishes, menus, and restaurants, where qualitative distinctions really matter. In fact, El Bulli customers were asked before the meal if they had any strong dislikes ("You have no problem with shellfish?" and so on) so that they were not served dishes that contained ingredients they simply did not like.[413] Therefore, presumably, it was the actual recipes and weird combinations which elicited disgust and "hatred" in some of the former El Bulli customers. This is not surprising, as ill-conceived, poorly combined, senseless food can be disgusting and generally unpleasant, and we should not be afraid to say so. Adrià wants to have his cake and eat it: he doesn't mind if you hate *Sea Anemone 2008* but wants you to respect his artistry and innovation and leave opinions to the professionals.

In any case, the tendency to sacrifice flavour and pleasure for technical showcasing, provocation and effect is after all part and parcel of the postmodern approach. One of the reasons for this is a general disinterest in the quality and integrity of whole food ingredients,

[413] C. Andrews, 2010, Reinventing Food: Ferran Adrià: the man who changed the way we eat, page 59.

which are the foundation of all cuisine, from the simplest to the most refined. Without great ingredients, there is no great cuisine. The avant-garde gastronome, on the other hand, fits the ingredients around the techniques, ideas, concepts, and innovations that are being pursued:

"You don't only start the creative process just with products [ingredients]. You can start it from a technique, or a concept."[414]

Even a cursory look at Adrià's menus and famous dishes confirms this, as there is no clear celebration and respect for individual ingredients, no evidence of any interest and appreciation for the best products of agriculture, as well as a penchant for using additives, colourants and chemical products not normally found in a kitchen.

This did not go unnoticed and, whilst postmodern gastronomy now rules supreme, Adrià was not without his critics. Chief amongst them was the late Santi Santamaría, chef of the 3-starred Can Fabes. Much has been made about the rivalry between the two men and about their personal relationship and motives.[415] These do not matter for our purposes: what matters is what they said and did, not their personal issues. Santamaría, unlike us mere eaters and non-professionals, could form an opinion that Adrià presumably considered to be legitimate and well-informed: *"I have an enormous conceptual and ethical divorce with Ferran; he and his team are going in a direction contrary to my principles."*[416] Santamaría denounced *"molecular or techno-emotional cooking, promoted by Ferran Adrià ... that fills our plates with gelling agents, stabilisers and laboratory emulgents."*[417]

The Chef lamented the rise of fast food and bought directly from local producers[418] and insisted on the produce of *"organic farming, traditional fishing. Fish from Blanes, mushrooms and lamb from the Montseny, truffles from Osona, peas and strawberries from the Maresme, rice from the Ebro delta, game out of the hunter's pouch." You can get an idea of his culinary style from the "amuse bouches" on his set menu: "Iberian cured ham from Extremadura, wild mushroom flan, razor clams with herbs and goat-milk curd with kumquat honey" - the only concession to today's foodie globalisation being the kumquat honey."*[419] I probably do not need to tell you whose approach I champion. Whatever you, dear reader, might think about Adrià and Santamaría, one thing cannot be denied: it has now become virtually impossible

[414] https://www.wired.com/story/staying-creative-ferran-adria/

[415] C. Andrews, 2010, Reinventing Food: Ferran Adrià: the man who changed the way we eat, pages 277-294.

[416] http://www.gourmet.com.s3-website-us-east-1.amazonaws.com/restaurants/2008/11/ferran-adria-santi-santamaria-dueling-spanish-chefs.html

[417] https://www.theguardian.com/lifeandstyle/2011/apr/10/santi-santamaria-obituary

[418] Ibidem

[419] https://www.independent.co.uk/news/obituaries/santi-santamaria-michelinstarred-chef-who-provoked-outrage-when-he-attacked-the-school-of-molecular-gastronomy-2218299.html

to make the top 50 restaurants in the world by taking the Santamaría approach, no matter how good the food and cookery might be. In the battle of ideas, and we must be clear that this is a battle of ideas as opposed to a mere culinary disagreement, the postmodern approach is winning hands down.

There were others who were alarmed by Adrià's open use of chemical agents to create his novel textures and preparations. German food journalist Jörg Zipprick denounced Adrià's use of additives and chemicals as a potential health hazard, a claim which Adrià has strongly denied.[420] I sincerely doubt whether eating at El Bulli constituted any sort of health risk, especially given the unlikelihood of anyone eating there on a regular basis. Far more important is the simple fact that the Catalonian's cuisine does include and celebrate a vast range of ultra-processed, low-quality ingredients, the very kind of ingredients we want to avoid in all food. What is also clear is that Adrià's cuisine clearly does not focus on quality whole food ingredients, on great artisanal products or on heritage livestock breeds. Adrià and his brother Albert do indeed retail a broad range of what are, in my opinion, very questionable products, which can be purchased online from specialised retailers at great cost.[421] These are products that can be used for the processes they have been using and promoting: spherification, gelification, emulsification, thickeners and "surprise" products, such as maltodextrin, dehydrated tomato flakes, powdered yoghurt (yum!), crystalline polyol and so on.[422] Neither the techniques nor the ingredients have any tangible culinary value and the fact that they are the distinctive contributions of the world's greatest chef is indicative of how worthless the top restaurants lists and guides actually are.

Heston Blumenthal is also devoted to the ingredients of labs and ultra-processed food manufacturers. Apart from an inordinate use of gelatin and glucose, his recipes include: acids, salts, chelating agents, emulsifiers, enzymes (transglutaminase, anyone?), milk powders and milk derivatives, sweeteners, starches, gums, gels, synthetic flavourings etc...[423] This is coupled with far less interest in the importance of quality whole food ingredients, seasonality and the agricultural practices involved in the production of cooking ingredients. There is very little mention of these crucial topics throughout *The Fat Duck Cookbook* and, should one be so enterprising as to attempt to reproduce the sci-fi dishes on display, one would have little guidance to go by when it comes to sourcing quality whole-food ingredients. To his credit, Blumenthal does acknowledge the importance of animal

[420] C. Andrews, 2010, Reinventing Food: Ferran Adrià: the man who changed the way we eat, pages 272-274. https://www.thetimes.co.uk/article/top-chef-ferran-adria-poisons-el-bulli-diners-with-additives-bcvzh6mcxpt

[421] For example, see: https://www.bienmanger.com/2R551_Sole_Graells_Products.html

[422] https://www.albertyferranadria.com/

[423] H. Blumenthal, 2008, The Fat Duck Cookbook, pages 454-461 specifically and as evident from the recipes throughout the book.

welfare and some of his animal products are clearly well sourced,[424] albeit one has to question his confidence in the lack of cruelty involved in the production of the foie gras produced on the farms he visited.[425]

A longstanding and popular Italian political satirical television programme, *Striscia la Notizia*, paid Adrià a short visit back in 2009.[426] Whilst it was a brief and light-hearted encounter, it was very revealing. The presenter asked Adrià, who was busy signing books, if he used *"chemical additives"* and Adrià replied *"no"* and confirmed that it is *"all natural"*.[427] Following the book signing, the reporter got Adrià's reluctant attention and again pressed him on the same question. The Chef replied with the kind of circular, obtuse reasoning that we have seen from other dogmatic reductionists. He tells the reporter that *"he is chemistry"*, *"all food is chemistry"*, *"sugar is chemistry"*, *"salt is chemistry"*, *"gelato is chemistry"*, *"everything is chemistry"* and confirms that his Texturas products are *"natural"*, in spite of the fact that, by definition, they are largely the products of labs and ultra-processed food manufacturers. It is interesting to note how this dogma is unanimously supported by our reductionist chefs and their muses: Harold McGee, the food scientist who Blumenthal refers to as a major inspiration, and who wrote the Foreword to the Chef's tome,[428] stated, as if it were a serious insight, that *"like everything on earth, foods are mixtures of different chemicals"*.[429] Similarly, Dr Simon Campbell, in awarding Blumenthal with his Honorary Fellowship at The Royal Society of Chemistry, reminds us that *"food and drink are composed of chemicals, as are our bodies, and all the materials that make up our world. However, "chemicals" are frequently projected in derogatory terms in the marketing of foods in the UK"*[430] Ergo, our obstinate reductionists imply, there is no real difference between a piece of celery and aspartame or between a lamb chop and Monosodium glutamate. Everything is chemistry: your mother, your dinner, this book...

As we saw in Chapter 2, to confuse the rational distinction between natural and unnatural is a textbook strategy used by all reductionists to justify their vacuous ideology. According to our Catalonian chef, anything that is touched by a human is unnatural:

[424] H. Blumenthal, 2008, The Fat Duck Cookbook, page 224 (pigeons), page 365 (venison), page 377 (pigs).

[425] H. Blumenthal, 2008, The Fat Duck Cookbook, page 177.

[426] See: https://www.striscialanotizia.mediaset.it/video/cucina-molecolare-ii_33509/

[427] Ibidem - the rest of this interview is translated by the author into English.

[428] H. Blumenthal, 2008, The Fat Duck Cookbook, pages 8-11.

[429] H. McGee, 2004, McGee on Food and Cooking, page 3.

[430] Dr Simon Campbell, Royal Society of Chemistry: https://www.rsc.org/news-events/articles/2006/07-july/honors-chef/

"First of all, the most important part about El Bulli is that we have made people think in relation to cuisine and gastronomy. It's pretty clear that we're supposed to eat organic, natural food, right? So it's clear that an organic tomato is a super natural product, right?

That's a lie. This is objective. Something natural is something that's in nature, but that the human being has not touched. The natural tomato is up in the Andes. That one you cannot eat. It's super bad. Ninety-nine percent of the natural vegetables are not edible. The organic tomato is the least natural thing in the entire world because it has been made -- man has participated to make it a better product. That's what El Bulli did."[431]

Again, this absurd and disingenuous argument is a feeble attempt to counteract those who rightly object to laboratory methods and chemical processes and champion quality whole foods: if an organic tomato is just as unnatural as sucralose and any of his "Texturas", then anything goes, there is nothing to object to.

It should be quite clear by now that these sorts of evasive non-arguments do not hold. To say that everything is chemistry is to say nothing at all. It is like saying everything is physics, everything is molecules, atoms or waves or whichever reductive category we wish to use or is currently in vogue. If words are to mean anything, and language is respected as our chief method of communication, we must see this strategy for what it is: either misguided ideological commitment or, most likely, cheap trickery to evade debate. We all know, including our reductive Chefs, I imagine, what we mean when we say that a product is "chemical" or artificial or synthetic. When we say that glyphosate, acesulfame K, sodium benzoate, dioxin etc... are chemical products and when we say that Heston Blumenthal, your cat, and an apple are not "chemical products" we are making a clear and logical distinction. The fact that there are chemical reactions going on inside the bodies of Blumenthal, of the cat and inside the apple is simply irrelevant. It also does not tell us anything about whether it is a good idea or not to use a chemical product. Imagine, for a moment, that a Chef's dish included generous additions of pure mercury or lead. Would the Chef be able to justify such additions simply by reminding us that, after all, "everything is chemistry", so who are we to criticise?

The video ends with the late Beppe Bigazzi, one the greatest culinary experts and minds I can think of, dismissing molecular gastronomy as "*la cucina fatta da furbacchioni per dei coglioni con i soldi*" (roughly translates to: "cuisine made by cunning people for the benefit of morons with money"). Santi Santamaría also called the molecular cooks *"a gang of impostors whose work is to distract snobs."*[432] These departed men may have been onto something.

[431] https://www.splendidtable.org/story/2015/12/18/chef-ferran-adria-how-do-you-define-cooking

[432] https://www.independent.co.uk/news/obituaries/santi-santamaria-michelinstarred-chef-who-provoked-outrage-when-he-attacked-the-school-of-molecular-gastronomy-2218299.html

El Bulli closed in 2011, and Adrià launched El Bulli Foundation, a centre for culinary creativity, which includes a museum, an R&D centre, and the putting together of *Bullipedia*, a mammoth encyclopaedia that supposedly can answer all questions related to food, and apparently far more: *"In order to understand Bullipedia, we need to study how the world began..."*[433]

Another ambitious project is "Sapiens", which will hopefully not be inspired by Harari's namesake tome. It is, apparently, *"a research methodology with a holistic and systemic vision, since it considers that everything is connected and is based on systems theory and systems thinking, and also with a historical vision."*[434] Sapiens, whatever it actually is or purports to be is, I daresay, a tad overambitious: *"There's a world of information out there and no general system that can link it together," "Sapiens is that system. Use it correctly and you'll be able to understand anything"* including questions about the nature of the universe.[435] Given that Adrià has taught a culinary physics course at Harvard University's School of Engineering and Applied Sciences,[436] and is known to be proud of his Honorary Degree in Chemistry,[437] in spite of never completing secondary school,[438] one cannot blame him for his forays into astrophysics. Blumenthal is also threatening to publish a book on what he calls *"Quantum Gastronomy"*.[439]

Reminiscent of a theologian reminding us that we cannot get inside the mind of God, Noma's René Redzepi humbly admits he cannot quite get to grips with what Adrià's profound Sapiens concept actually means: *"Ferran talks about his projects a lot," said Redzepi, "but sometimes when you speak to him it's beyond you. At some point, it's all going to click into place and make sense, I'm sure. But I'm not going to grasp it until I see the whole thing come together."*[440] A key to all knowledge would be a wonderful thing, as well as historically unprecedented, so unlike René I will personally remain highly sceptical. We live in hope.

It might not be tactful to inform the Catalonian deconstructionist that he may be suffering from severe, chronic delusions of grandeur. After all, the world is enabling and encouraging this delusion on a daily basis: call someone mediocre a genius long enough, they will come to believe it. We are reassured, however, that whilst *"he has the ego befitting of any world-*

[433] https://www.scmp.com/magazines/post-magazine/article/1540814/ferran-adria-man-very-big-plan

[434] In the great man's own words: https://metodologiasapiens.com/en/que-es-sapiens/

[435] https://www.gq-magazine.co.uk/lifestyle/article/ferran-adria-interview

[436] https://lareviewofbooks.org/article/finer-dining-through-chemistry/

[437] Colman Andrews recalled an incident in which, to defend his views on "natural" vs "unnatural" foods, Adrià claimed that he knew what he was talking about because he had a degree in chemistry! See C. Andrews, 2010, Reinventing Food: Ferran Adrià: the man who changed the way we eat, pages 255-57.

[438] C. Andrews, 2010, Reinventing Food: Ferran Adrià: the man who changed the way we eat, page 256.

[439] https://www.theworlds50best.com/stories/News/heston-blumenthal-food-meets-talent.html

[440] https://www.gq-magazine.co.uk/lifestyle/article/ferran-adria-interview

leading talent, he balances it with modesty well. To him, the real best chef in the world is his pastry chef brother Albert."[441] Indeed Ferran has declared *"that Albert has had the great misfortune of being"* his brother and that he sincerely believes that Albert *"is the best cook"* he has *"ever known."*[442] So modest! Be that as it may, the fact that we have elevated Chefs like the Adrià brothers, Blumenthal, and many others to the status of great artists and geniuses, and the fact that contemporary art awards and galleries are almost entirely dominated by creative and intellectual nullities, says a lot about the decline, degradation, and lack of integrity of Western culture. A whole other book would be needed on the subject.

"What would have happened to cuisine if El Bulli had not existed?"

"It's a very interesting question, it's a science-fiction question. When I think about what we did in 1995, even [by today's standards] El Bulli is avant garde. That's when you realise what El Bulli meant."[443]

It does not seem like a science fiction question, I must say. I would be tempted to suggest that we would be far better off, and would have had less Botturas around, with their foams, pretentions, and deconstructed dishes. However, Adrià is very much a man of his age and, in an alternative universe where he didn't end up working at El Bulli, chances are someone else would probably have come up with similar strategies and techniques somewhere else. Postmodern gastronomy, molecular gastronomy, deconstructivist gastronomy or whatever else you want to call it is very much in tune with the times, part of a much broader ideological, cultural, and social movement that has been several decades in the making.

If we look back, we can see that, to an extent, the predecessor to postmodern gastronomy was "nouvelle cuisine", a French attempt to modernise classic haute cuisine, which unsurprisingly took hold from the 1960s onwards, with an emphasis on novelty (hence "nouvelle") and presentation, and our chefs all openly drew from it and took it to new, extreme levels, which the early proponents of nouvelle cuisine probably would not recognise.[444] This is a shame, given that the French, to their credit, have done more than any other culture to systematise their great cuisine, to document technique and gastronomic ideas, to create the very concept of the "culinary school" and of the "great restaurant", as well

[441] https://www.theworlds50best.com/stories/News/ferran-adria-el-bulli-never-wanted-to-cook.html

[442] https://www.foodandwine.com/chefs/albert-adria-the-legend-continues

[443] https://www.scmp.com/magazines/post-magazine/article/1540814/ferran-adria-man-very-big-plan

[444] The postmodern cuisine of today arguably resembles Filippo Marinetti's "Futuristic Cuisine" from earlier in the 20th Century. Marinetti's outlandish vision for cookery, laid out in his 1930 Manifesto of Futurist Cooking and in his *La Cucina Futurista* (1932), includes food as a performance art, an interest in controlling all the diner's senses, a fascination with high tech, a yearning for synthetic foods, and an emphasis on complete originality and on shocking food combinations, on progress and on being *avant-garde*. Marinetti's vision had very limited impact at the time, but one feels our postmodern chefs might have a copy of his book tucked away somewhere, given the similarity of vision and approach.

as developing formalised, ritualised, ceremonial table service. They also have a great tradition of manufacturing kitchen equipment, as their excellent brands of pots, pans and the like clearly demonstrate. This does not mean, as all our postmodern chefs tend to believe, that the French, whilst objectively having a grand culinary tradition, have the best of all cuisines.[445] They tend to believe this because, as evident from Blumenthal's cookbook, they often came from a very limited culinary culture (as Blumenthal himself concedes when recalling his upbringing) and do not know any better.[446] Even when they do come from a high food culture, like Bottura and Adrià, they all train in classical French cuisine anyway, whether formally[447] or informally.[448]

The French, after all, have also done an incredible job in promoting their cuisine overseas, in institutionalising haute cuisine as the global benchmark, in setting up the Michelin system, and in marketing their goods and reputation.[449] They also export excellent chefs: think Raymond Blanc and Michel Roux,[450] here in the UK.[451]

Anyhow, going back to our Catalonian chef, and to sum up: Adrià, in my opinion, is a contemporary artist, as opposed to a great chef. If you value contemporary art, in all its mediocrity and superficiality, you will probably value Adrià. If you value great cuisine, I encourage you to look elsewhere.

[445] I am no relativist, as should be clear by now: it is quite clear that not all cuisines are equally sophisticated, varied and accomplished. There are real and profound qualitative differences between culinary traditions. There are no more than a handful of cuisines that can claim to have reached the pinnacles of gastronomy. Both French and Italian cuisine are certainly amongst this elite group.

[446] Rasmus Munk openly admits growing up in a house with little or no cooking and recalls McDonald's visits every Friday (see: https://www.esquire.com/uk/food-drink/a28936203/rasmus-munk-creates-food-that-asks-questions-and-blows-minds/

https://www.3daysofdesign.dk/post/the-playful-life-of-an-alchemist)

[447] Bottura spent time with Alain Ducasse.

[448] Both Blumenthal and Adrià immersed themselves in French cuisine and techniques before they came up with their postmodern style.

[449] That classical French cuisine at its best is excellent is without question but it is also relatively overrated as a consequence of its unparalleled promotion, driven by the commendable patriotic fervour of the French. My favourite example, and there are many, to highlight this phenomenon are the famous snails (escargot) and frog legs: all around the world people tend to presume that these are French specialities and delicacies. They certainly are, but did you know there are literally hundreds of snails and frog leg recipes all over the Italian and Iberian peninsulas, in Crete, and elsewhere? The French have *croissant*, Italians have *cornetto*, which most people presume is an Italian take on croissant. It is not, and the two excellent desserts are distinct in both form and origin. Steak Tartare is a world-renowned French dish: is anyone familiar with the Italian equivalent, *Battuta al Coltello* from Piemonte?

[450] One of the many reasons to dismiss the Top Restaurants list and the Michelin Star system is that classical exponents of haute cuisine and fine dining like Roux and Blanc could never make the top 10 list nowadays. I am not saying they should be on the list, or that we even need a list to begin with, but there is no doubt that, in spite of being vastly superior to the Adriàs of this world, they could not compete with the postmodernists who dominate at the top.

[451] Italians on the other hand generally do a very poor job of promoting their food and products overseas. In spite of that, Italian food is still one of the most popular around the globe, if not the most popular by some measures. Given the culinary and artisanal treasures that we have, many of which are unparalleled, it is a real national shame. We have so much to learn from the French on that front.

The Principles of Postmodern Gastronomy

To recap on what we learnt from our chefs, the philosophical and cultural basis of contemporary gastronomy can be summed up as follows:

Novelty for the Sake of Novelty

Irrespective of claims to the contrary,[452] novelty is sought for the sake of novelty in contemporary gastronomy. There is no question that one of the main reasons why the chefs we have looked at so far, and many others, make the top restaurant rankings is due to their innovations and originality, as opposed to their ability to cook great food. An overemphasis on "creativity" and an over-inflated sense of his own creative powers is apparent in many of Adrià's musings:

"I'm being generous when I say that in the entire world there are maybe five chefs who are really, really doing what I consider creative."[453]

Adrià is aware of his critics and defends innovation: *"when it comes to creativity in cooking, it's the only field where that is under debate, which is incredible. I know of no other field in the world where they debate whether they should have innovation."*[454]

Apart from the fact that innovation is debated in many other fields, it is not innovation *per se* that we oppose, but *the kind* of innovation. If creating foams, gels and weird faux caviar is the only way to be amongst such an elite group of creatives, we have every reason to dismiss creativity as an inherent value. What we create, why we create it and how we create it is what qualifies the value of any creation in any field, after all.

Just like contemporary artists, who mistakenly repeat the false cliché that geniuses are never appreciated in their own time, Adrià prophesises a future where spherification and emulsification will be the norm: *"don't forget that the cutting edge of today will be tomorrow's classicism."*[455] Maybe so. But we must not forget that cultures and societies do not always progress or improve, and in fact often decline. Perhaps a future where classical haute cuisine is the avant-garde cuisine of today's postmodernists is not a future we should look forward to.

[452] See the Statement on the 'new cookery' penned by Heston Blumenthal, Ferran Adrià and Thomas Keller: https://www.theguardian.com/uk/2006/dec/10/foodanddrink.obsfoodmonthly and reproduced by Blumenthal on H. Blumenthal, 2008, The Big Fat Duck Cookbook, page 126-127.

[453] https://time.com/108688/10-questions-with-ferran--adria/

[454] https://www.scmp.com/magazines/post-magazine/article/1540814/ferran-adria-man-very-big-plan

[455] https://www.wired.com/story/staying-creative-ferran-adria/

Breaking with the Past

A misguided desire to do away with tradition, a contempt for established techniques and norms and an overwhelming desire to be "progressive" are part and parcel of postmodern gastronomy.

Adrià sees a questioning of the culinary establishment as crucial to his endeavour: *"that was our philosophy, in two words: question everything."*[456] Heston Blumenthal also question everything,[457] apparently. The motto is emblazoned on a coat of arms he was asked to create: *"question everything," it states. "The opposite is to question nothing, and that wouldn't be human. If we did that, then computers would take over."*[458] Why the only available options are to question everything or to question nothing is another one of those inscrutable mysteries that are left unexplained, as is the looming threat of computers taking over.

In a telling introduction to his very own episode of Chef's Table, the younger Albert Adrià summarized the philosophy of the avant-garde with the following nonsense:

"We play to discover the avant-garde. There aren't limits. There is total freedom. Let's say that we skip the rules. One plus one is three. If you always think that one plus one is two, you will never do anything different. Those who think that one plus one is three are the ones who dare. They are the brave ones. They are the avant-garde."[459]

The idea that everything must be questioned, and even basic facts disputed, charmingly adolescent and decadent as it may be, makes no sense at all in any craft or artisanal activity, or indeed any serious field of human knowledge and inquiry. A chef cannot even call himself a chef until he has learnt a broad range of established, successful, intelligible methods and techniques. Before he can even consider becoming creative or innovative, there are a lot of facts that he will need to accept as true, as established, as tried, and tested. He will need training, practice, learning and discipline. If you do not take certain steps, mayonnaise will split. Water has to get to 100 °C in order to boil. Panna cotta either wobbles or it is overset. Overcooked pasta is overcooked pasta, period. None of these facts are open to question. Established methods and techniques are generally what they are precisely because they are the result of historical enquiry, collective experience, recorded knowledge, and skills that are passed on from one generation to the next. Ferran Adrià, nonetheless, in another customary moment of culinary rapture, declares that *"I have discovered that I know nothing; that what I*

[456] https://www.gq-magazine.co.uk/lifestyle/article/ferran-adria-interview

[457] https://ten-membership.com/in-conversation-with-heston-blumenthal/

[458] https://www.wired.com/story/heston-blumenthal-chef/

[459] Series 5, Episode 4: https://www.netflix.com/gb/title/80007945

thought I knew wasn't right. I am unlearning everything to start learning again."[460] It would be very interesting to learn how he eventually figured out how to boil an egg from behind this culinary veil of ignorance and gastronomic amnesia.

Adrià not only questions everything but he takes the fight to the culinary dinosaurs: *"it is a war with those that seek comfort from the past and believe that tradition is more important that evolution."*[461] Massimo Bottura takes matters a step further and relishes the process of defecating on tradition, which in fairness he does achieve with his deconstructions. In a telling passage of *Chef's Table*, the Modenese chef recalls a visit to the Venice Biennale (where else?) in 1997. In the rafters, we are told, there was an installation: stuffed pigeons, the products of taxidermy, that an "artist" (my inverted commas) had placed right at the top of the structure. The work was completed by painting their "poop" on the walls and on some of the other artists' artwork.

Bottura found this to be *"genius"*,[462] of course. The pigeons were like him, apparently: he was trying to change the Italian kitchen and the only way he was going to get noticed was if looked down from above and, in Bottura's wife's retelling of the incident: *"deface the generation that came before"* and *"felt part pigeon in his own defiance"*.[463] The defacing, the desecration, the loathing for tradition is not my unkind interpretation of the postmodernists' work: it is literally what they are proudly telling us they are doing.

Finally, given his fixation with untrammelled progress, Adrià even has contempt for food nostalgia. When asked if he missed the way fruit and tomatoes used to taste, he replies: *"This is all part of people's nostalgia, that tomatoes were different. I hear 20-year-olds saying it. Sixty years ago, people were dying of hunger and there were 1,000 kilos of tomatoes. Now there's 1,000 million kilos, and so of course proportionally you're going to have bad ones."*[464] Here again our great chef demonstrates an astounding ignorance about how the changes in the methods of food production have resulted in serious changes in quality, taste, and variety. Or perhaps, dare I suggest, does he demonstrate a lack of discerning palate? If he travelled down to the south of Spain, he could witness the endless polytunnels mass producing tasteless tomatoes, that are now the supermarket norm. A trip to Holland would be even more revealing. A lot has changed in the last sixty years. That quality has dropped as quantity has increased is without question, not because of "proportionality" or misplaced nostalgia, but because it turns out that intensive

[460] https://www.theworlds50best.com/stories/News/ferran-adria-el-bulli-never-wanted-to-cook.html

[461] https://www.greatbritishchefs.com/features/massimo-bottura-interview#google_vignette

[462] The word "genius" is really played around with fast and loose by our chefs and culinary commentators. I am reminded of Isaac Davis' line in Woody Allen's classic film Manhattan (1979): *"Oh really, he was a genius, Helen's a genius and Dennis is a genius. You know a lot of geniuses, y'know. You should meet some stupid people once in a while, y'know, you could learn something."*

[463] Series 1, Episode 1: https://www.netflix.com/gb/title/80007945

[464] https://time.com/108688/10-questions-with-ferran-adria/

growing conditions dependant on agrochemicals and sterile soils result in lower overall quality of produce. Quality has also dropped due to the widespread cultivation of hybrid varieties of tomatoes and the gradual loss or marginalisation of more flavoursome heritage varieties. The disappearance of seasonality, which all year-round availability seemingly overcomes, has also led to a loss of quality and flavour, which any chef worth his salt should be most concerned about.

Adrià even polices his own nostalgia: when writer Michael Paterniti asked Adrià to describe the best meal he'd ever eaten, the chef *"said he erases his memories so he doesn't live for a moment he can never bring back"*.[465]

Worship of Technology

A prominent and consistent feature of postmodern gastronomy is the sort of faith in technology we have already observed in industrial agriculture, nutrition science and the fast-food industry. Our postmodern chefs not only embrace new technologies, or enthusiastically bring lab techniques and tools into the kitchen, but also work under the presumption that there is a direct and consistent correlation between technological and culinary advancement. Technology can undoubtedly enable culinary advancement, but it can also lead to culinary abasement. This is true in both the domestic kitchen and in haute cuisine. There is no question that the wide availability of high quality and relatively cheap pots, pans and basic kitchen tools has made cookery safer and easier. Gas hobs, electric ovens, food blenders, refrigerators, and plenty of other tools that a lot of us now take for granted have been positive additions, overall. On the other hand, the now ubiquitous microwave[466] has not brought any culinary advancement, but in fact enabled the culture of fast food, junk food, ready-made ultra-processed meals and convenience at all costs.[467] Similarly, our postmodern gastronomists have so far failed to prove the benefits of their dehydrators, 3D printers, water baths and sound machines. If anything, they have brought some of the techniques, ingredients, and approaches of ultra-processed food manufacturing into haute cuisine, which is a step in the wrong direction.

New technologies should always be questioned. What purpose do they serve? Do we need them? What are the benefits? What are the negatives? Are they wasteful and too energy intensive? Most importantly, I ask, yet again: just because *we can* do something, does that mean *we should*?

[465] https://www.esquire.com/food-drink/restaurants/a25809/esq0701-july-ferran/

[466] See Chapter 10.

[467] The more recent and rapidly spreading cult of the air fryer (which is not a fryer if the word fryer is to mean anything) is also based on a similar principle: prioritising speed and convenience over skill, quality, and flavour.

Commitment to Scientism and Reductionism

The worship of technology is based on the very same commitment to scientism and reductionism that we have seen in other fields: it is the ideology of the age. We have covered this extensively and I will not dwell on this any further, but will highlight, yet again, both the confusion and intellectual dishonesty it leads to:

"In the end, everything is science, everything", Adrià tells us. *"People see molecular gastronomy as something almost like magic. But frying an egg is a chemical process that is probably much more complex than trying to do spherification."*[468] In the same vein, Blumenthal recalls how when journalists asked him for examples of molecular gastronomy, they would be *"disappointed"* when he replied, *"a boiled egg or a roast chicken"*.[469]

This is yet again indicative of a mixture of ideology (Everything is molecules! Everything is chemistry!) and a disingenuous strategy to deflect criticism, as our chefs are well aware of the fact that a lot of people are (rightly) suspicious of their additives, powders, and chemical baths. By implying that there is no difference between roasting a chicken and, say, using liquid nitrogen, PH meters or transglutaminase, they are negating language, common sense, and the possibility of having any grounds for rational debate. In any case, our chefs cannot have it both ways: they cannot claim to be doing groundbreaking, innovative work and also claim that there is no actual difference between normal cookery and their laboratory techniques. They seem to want to have their deconstructed cake and eat it.

Globalised and Homogenous

A lot of the restaurants at the highest echelons of haute cuisine tend to be detached from their respective locations. There is no sense in which El Bulli used to represent Catalonian cuisine, agriculture and produce. There is no sense in which The Fat Duck represents British cuisine, agriculture and produce. You could transplant either of these restaurants from one part of the world to the other with little effect on the menu.[470] Osteria Francescana is slightly different: in its misguided and unnecessary quest to reinvent Italian cuisine, it draws on a lot of local produce and local recipes. However, as we saw, it does so by using the kind of fashionable techniques exhibited by El Bulli and other postmodern establishments and its cuisine resembles other three-star establishments around the world far more than it resembles genuine Modenese cuisine. Noma in Copenhagen, which prides itself in its stringent use of Nordic ingredients, also uses postmodern techniques and approaches, resulting in a cuisine that arguably resembles its peers

[468] https://www.wired.com/story/staying-creative-ferran-adria/

[469] H. Blumenthal, 2008, The Fat Duck Cookbook, page 124.

[470] When The Fat Duck opened its pop-up restaurant in Australia, its menu was virtually indistinguishable from the menu at The Fat Duck in Bray. See: https://www.theguardian.com/lifeandstyle/australia-food-blog/2015/mar/20/heston-blumenthals-fat-duck-in-melbourne-wonderful-but-no-wizard-in-oz

across the world far more than it resembles traditional Nordic cuisine. Everywhere you look in contemporary haute gastronomy, the foams, powders, and deconstructed dishes keep popping up. Like fast food culture, it is homogenous, globalised, and soulless.

Trendy Ingredients and Senseless Fusion

A feature of postmodern gastronomy, being inherently faddish, is that ingredients go in and out of fashion and end up being used by our postmodern chefs for no particular reason other than the very fact that they happen to be fashionable. The reader must have noticed how yuzu and miso, for example, seem to show up everywhere nowadays, often for no culinary reason or benefit. There is nothing inherently wrong with these Oriental ingredients, of course, and there is room for introducing them into our cuisines but there is no doubt that the great ascent of these ingredients has more to do with fashion than their inherent virtues. Do contemporary master chefs regularly use yuzu on their menus due to this citrus fruit's incomparable virtues and as a result of careful gastronomic consideration or because it has become *de rigeur* in haute cuisine? I imagine one day it will simply go out of fashion and some other exotic ingredient will replace it. Some ingredients, on the other hand, never go out of fashion. Chief amongst them is the overrated foie gras, the fatty liver of an overfed, sick goose, which still features supreme on the top tables. What has changed is the form in which it is used and presented, and not necessarily in a positive direction. According to French celebrity Chef Eric Ripert, for example, Adrià's freeze-dried foie gras powder is a fascinating presentation, but a slab of seared foie gras is more satisfying.[471] Again, I cannot claim to have tried foie gras powder, but I challenge any reader to salivate at the thought of it.

A related trend that appeals to our globalist gastronomes is so called "fusion". This involves the careless blending of unrelated traditions and ingredients. Fusion is often based on the same mentality that led to the universal adoption of ingredients such as yuzu: an *a priori* belief that the fusion of cuisines and cultures is inherently more progressive and desirable. This is not to say that cultural interchanges and the wide availability of a diverse range of ingredients are undesirable. There is no doubt that cuisines change over time and that both ingredients and recipes travel around the world. Not only is this inevitable, but it can be wholesome and enriching. There are also genuine fusion cuisines in many parts of the world, where unrelated culinary cultures have coalesced over time.[472] The difference is that these fusions have happened organically, as the natural consequence of immigration, conquest, and trade, as opposed to the usual obsession with "novelty for the sake of novelty".

[471] https://lareviewofbooks.org/article/finer-dining-through-chemistry/

[472] As mentioned in Chapter 4, Mauritius and New Orleans stand out as wonderful examples of successful "fusion" cuisines. There are many other examples around the world.

Historically, when ingredients and recipes were adopted by a culture, this generally happened with a certain logic and rationale.

A good example would be the tomato, which plays such a crucial role in the cuisines of Italy, Spain, and other countries across the Mediterranean. This native of the Americas, brought over by the Spanish, was gradually adopted and cultivated in the Old World, with new localised varieties developing over time. The fruits were gradually introduced into the existing cuisines and recipes, with genuine innovation taking place over time. Similarly, the various spices that arrived in Europe from the Orient via the travels of the Venetians, Portuguese, and others over the course of the centuries were gradually incorporated into local cuisines, with iconic local dishes often including non-native spices. The traditional *Tortellini in Brodo* we discussed earlier contain nutmeg, for example, that would only have reached the Italian peninsula from the 15th century onwards.[473]

A similar process has occurred with many, now classic, recipes and dishes, where distant traditions "fused" over time: kedgeree is a good example of British and Indian tradition coming together, with smoked haddock joining Indian rice and spices to make a breakfast dish. None of this is the same as the common contemporary practice of adopting random "cool" ingredients or mixing completely unrelated recipes and traditions for the sake of being original. When Massimo Bottura produced the broth for his walking tortellini, he put all *"the traditions together in one pot–duck, pigeon, guinea fowl, chicken, veal, beef, pork, eel, and frog's legs, with some kombu seaweed from Japan, for a wise cultural contamination"*.[474] Contamination is the right word, I believe, and is indicative of an unwise attitude that respects neither Italian nor Japanese tradition.

Sensationalism and Provocation: The "Shock Factor"

As we saw throughout our discussion, a sense of rebelliousness and provocation abounds amongst our postmodern chefs. The parallels with contemporary art are uncanny, in both theory and practice. Apart from the pretentious presentation of a lot of contemporary dishes, which does intentionally resemble the works of contemporary art, the attitude is almost indistinguishable. The desire to shock, disturb, provoke, "challenge" and lift a virtual middle finger to an imaginary establishment is palpable amongst our postmodern artists and chefs. Up until the early part of the 20th century, the traditional aim of art, as perfectly outlined by

[473] In *The Opera di Bartolomeo Scappi 1570*, a Renaissance cookbook by Bartolomeo Scappi, Chef to Popes and Cardinals, the recipe for tortellini also contains cloves, cinnamon and most surprising of all, sugar! Throughout this era, spices and sugar, which were luxury products, were found in all sorts of main courses on the tables of the very wealthy and powerful, especially for formal banquets and events. There was undoubtedly status attached to sugar consumption, which would have been absent from the cuisine of ordinary people. The obsession with sugar gradually faded away, and sugar ended up being confined to desserts in Italian cuisine.

[474] https://www.newyorker.com/magazine/2013/11/04/post-modena

the late Roger Scruton,[475] was beauty. Eventually the pursuit of the beautiful was replaced by the pursuit of originality, of provocation and of "breaking boundaries", no matter how valuable or important these may be. Technique, skill, virtuosity, and knowledge gradually gave way to incompetence, tawdriness, vulgarity, and ugliness.

Similarly, the aim of great cuisine and the goal of the gastronome has always been good taste and pleasure. The very notion of producing food that many will likely hate, as openly declared by Adrià, would have been anathema to any chef before the contemporary period. The idea that diners might be induced to cry or feel uncomfortable during dinner is also a recent absurdity. To put it simply: the idea that food should do anything other than produce great flavour and give pleasure to the diner is both novel and highly questionable.

Massimo Bottura was very clear about his intent: *"only with that kind of sort of sensationalism and that kind of provocative attitude am I going to be able to break through and open up the doors for another generation of Italian Kitchen."* [476]

In the kitchen, our postmodern chefs often create specific dishes for the very purpose of shocking and provoking. Most of the public is familiar with Blumenthal's notorious bacon and egg ice cream, for example, which caused some raised eyebrows at the time of its creation and earned him significant media coverage. He is also known for his sardine on toast sorbet and snail porridge. We must ask ourselves whether the creation of these dishes was the result of the groundbreaking discovery of superior taste, or whether it was created to achieve what it did: novelty, debate, controversy, and popularity. There is no such thing as bad publicity, we are told, and there are enough impressionable people who will be overawed by celebrity chefs. Whether, when it comes down to it, a perfectly made pistachio ice cream is simply more palatable and pleasant than the weird "Nitro-Scrambled Egg and Bacon Ice Cream"[477] is a question I will leave the reader to ponder.

It is not just weird combinations that are used to achieve the shock factor. It can also be achieved via less than conventional ingredients, the sort of ingredient that invokes both surprise and suspicion. Noma, for example, is known for its use of live or cooked ants in its dishes.[478] Apart from the shock factor and publicity, ants are ideologically sound: given the current agitation for insects as sources of more "sustainable protein", their use is very much in keeping with the times. I confess to having had a tendency of tasting odd things from the wild as a child and I have certainly tasted ants on a few occasions. I can confirm, but please

[475] See Scruton's BBC documentary "Why Beauty Matters", 2009, for a concise presentation of the argument.

[476] Series 1, Episode 1: https://www.netflix.com/gb/title/80007945

[477] H. Blumenthal, 2008, The Fat Duck Cookbook, pages 256-263.

[478]See: https://www.telegraph.co.uk/foodanddrink/foodanddrinknews/11379809/Worlds-best-restaurant-Noma-serves-live-ants.html; https://www.zdnet.com/article/in-copenhagen-daring-to-innovate-on-the-plate/

do your own research, that their taste is bearable but rather unpleasant. They have a sharpish, acidic taste, which I would not describe as citrussy, nor like *"lemongrass and kaffir lime"*.[479] At best, they would not add much to a plate, other than the shock element. Ants are one of the most abundant, widespread insects on the planet. In Europe, in spite of their abundance, they have never been eaten. Was this an oversight? Or could it be that there were always better, more palatable options available?

The Chef as "Artist"

Bottura openly draws inspiration from contemporary art, which has *"real value for him"* and *"really had a great influence on the way he thought through the recipes"*.[480] As we saw, Adrià also sees himself as part of the new creative wave, following on from the Spanish painters. Blumenthal also wonders: *"if an artist or a musician can generate emotions from painting and music, why can't a chef do the same with food?"*[481] In their joint Statement on the "New Cookery", our chefs have the gall to declare that *"preparing and serving food could therefore be the most complex and comprehensive of the performing arts."*[482] According to our chefs, therefore, a dessert or a starter can be more complex and comprehensive than the opera, a symphony or a great film. Cookery is not just art, but the greatest of all the arts!

Once and for all, we need to be absolutely clear: a great chef is not the equivalent of Beethoven or Michelangelo, for cuisine is not strictly speaking an art form and no dish can be compared to the Sistine Chapel. Cookery, even at the very highest level, is a craft and a trade, not an art. A great Chef can be a great artisan, but not a great artist. Cuisine is limited in scope; it is easier to imitate and learn. In the kitchen, perfection is attainable, both for the home cook and the great chef: a perfect cake, sauce or stew is potentially doable for most people, if they try hard enough. The fine arts are far more elitist and selective, by definition, and very few people could ever achieve any degree of greatness. Artistic boundaries and limits are far higher and less definable and belong to a different realm.

Classical arts, such as music, painting, and sculpture, are purely aesthetic: the very definition of art is that it does not and cannot have any utilitarian purpose. Its goal is beauty, and it is imbued with meaning and value. Cooking, no matter how sophisticated, remains what it is: the production of food for the table. Food can be produced with artistic flair, especially patisserie and chocolatery, but it is not, nor could it ever be, defined as art. Of course, in this age of "anything goes" and extreme relativism, *anything* could be art, including gastronomy. It may seem as I have contradicted myself as I have claimed that cuisine is not art, and postmodern

[479] https://www.zdnet.com/article/in-copenhagen-daring-to-innovate-on-the-plate/

[480] Series 1, Episode 1: https://www.netflix.com/gb/title/80007945

[481] H. Blumenthal, 2008, The Fat Duck Cookbook, page 424.

[482] Ibidem, page 127.

chefs are basically contemporary artists. But I do not consider the latter to be serious artists, nor the former to be serious cooks. Serious cooks are not artists, and "gastronomic artists" are not serious cooks. Overall, dear reader, be vigilant and wary of all chefs with artistic pretentions.

An Alternative Vision for Gastronomy: Radical Conservation and Genuine Innovation

I would like to end this critique of contemporary gastronomy on a positive note and offer a vision of what the future of gastronomy, freed from its postmodern shackles, could look like. I will suggest that it can and should rest on two mutually compatible goals, namely radical conservation and genuine innovation. I will use two wonderful restaurants that I had the pleasure of visiting in the summer of 2024 during a trip to Sicily, which perfectly exemplify this vision. I will pre-empt the accusation of Italian bias: had I travelled to Spain or France, for example, I could have found equally valid examples and case studies to make the very same argument. I happen to be Italian, happened to be travelling in Sicily, and, after all, it is only natural for me to use Italian examples of much needed alternatives to Massimo Bottura.

Radical Conservation: l'Osteria 4 Archi, Milo, Sicily

The first duty of any great culinary tradition is the conservation of all its agricultural, artisanal and gastronomic wealth. The crops, livestock, products, techniques, recipes that have been painstakingly developed and perpetuated over generations must be preserved and passed on. One of the tragedies of our food system is that we have already lost unique crop varieties and livestock breeds, with biodiversity steadily decreasing, as industrial monoculture and factory farms have expanded their range. Artisanal products and skills, culinary traditions and recipes have also gradually made way for junk food and a uniformly inferior food culture. Before even thinking of creating anything at all, the first concern of a cook, professional or otherwise, should be to play some part in the preservation and continuation of the natural and cultural capital embedded in their food culture. This involves being truly rooted to the landscapes and traditions that have got us so far, and a conscious effort to both preserve and save them from literal extinction.

On the foothills of Etna, I purposely made an unannounced visit to one of Italy's most prominent exponents of the Slow Food movement, the charismatic Saro Rosario Grasso, who opened the restaurant in 1995 to showcase and preserve the mountain food of the region. It is important to understand that the Etna region, which is in an incredibly beautiful, green, lush, largely unspoiled corner of Italy, has an absolute wealth of products and traditions that it can both offer and lose. Apart from producing some of the best wines in the world, and the renowned olive oil and citrus fruits, this mountainous region is full of unexpected and unique surprises. It would take an entire chapter to paint a comprehensive picture of what is on offer, so I will only touch upon a few examples. It is home to the unique pistachios of Bronte, the Etna hazelnuts, chestnuts and walnuts, and almost every fruit one can imagine, from the now rare black mulberry to the yellow skinned Etna apple. Vegetables abound, including unique local varieties, as do wild herbs such as wild fennel, that find their way into the local recipes and products.

The Etna region does not seem to have suffered from the historical deforestation that has afflicted so many parts of the Mediterranean, which explains its relative moisture, coolness and greenery, even in the heat of summer. From a gastronomic point of view, this has resulted in a great tradition of wild mushroom foraging, including the Etna Porcini mushrooms. Honey production is very widespread and reflects the biodiversity and richness of the vegetation. As one travels around the region, it is common to find cattle[483] grazing on the side of the road, sheep and long horned goats crossing the road and climbing up steep slopes, and you might see the odd donkey *Ragusano* grazing in a paddock. The cheeses, virtually unchanged for centuries if not millennia, are examples of dairy at its best. A jewel in the crown, originating from the forested mountain range to the North West of Etna, is the heritage black pig of Nebrodi (*Suino nero dei Nebrodi*),[484] which like all the ancient heritage breeds, are raised in the old-fashioned way, producing meats of unique quality and flavour. Living semi-wild, and foraging in the woods, these pigs produce cold cuts that are at the very top end, including a *Prosciutto* (ham) that cannot be improved upon.[485]

What Saro has done is take the best ingredients of the region, with an almost obstinate passion, and his Chef Lina uses all her mastery and knowledge to showcase the great recipes and traditions and recipes of the region, with menus that change over the course of the seasons. I was fortunate enough to be there as the first Porcini mushrooms had been gathered. This is a cuisine that does not aim or purport to be creative, as its goal is to preserve and present what has already been created, at its very best, supporting the wholesome web of agricultural and productive activities, many of which at risk of disappearing, that make it possible to make this food. Their work, and that of others like them, is the most important work in the field of gastronomy, as everything and anything else of value depends upon it.

[483] Sicily has three main local breeds: Modicana, Cinisara, Siciliana.

[484] https://www.fondazioneslowfood.com/en/slow-food-presidia/nebrodi-black-pig/

[485] It is the most expensive product of these pigs, and I paid a hefty €18.00 per 100g. This is still far cheaper than the top end *jamon de bellota* which, whilst excellent, is no better that the *Prosciutto di Suino Nero dei Nebrodi*.

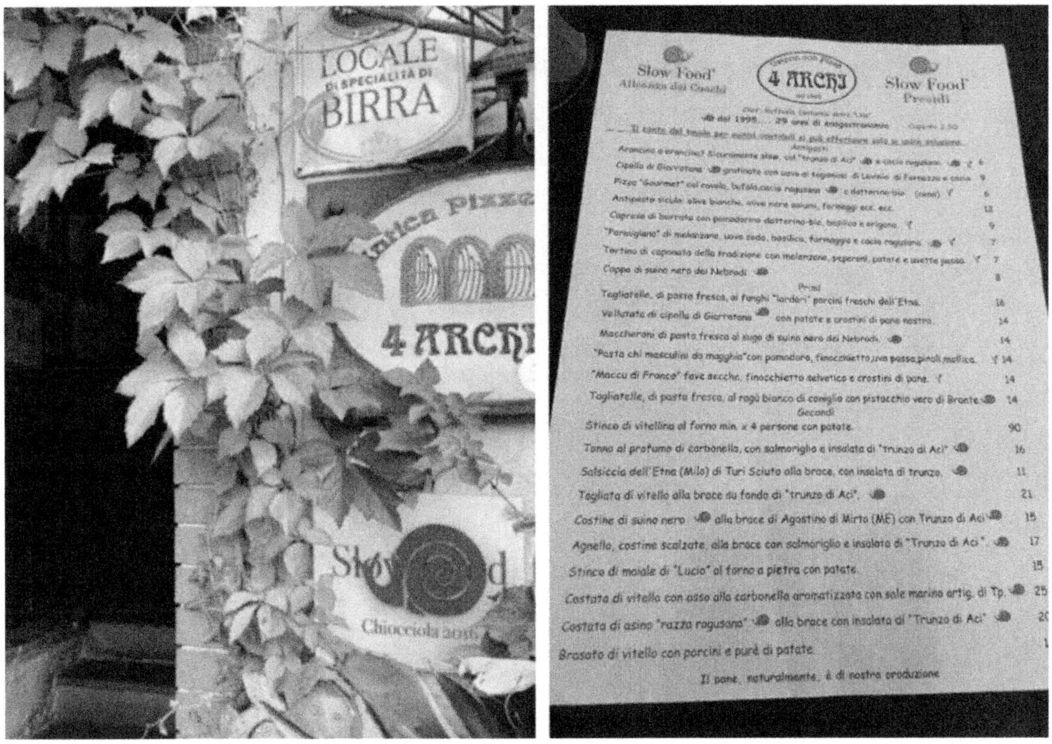

Credit: https://www.instagram.com/4_archi_milo/

Left: Caponata, made with aubergines, peppers, potatoes and raisins. Exceptional. **Right**: Arancino, the classic fried rice ball of Sicily. This one featured the pecorino cheese of the mountains and was the best arancino I have ever had by some distance.

The menu features the great meats and cheeses of the Etna region, the homemade pastas and pizzas, the unique vegetables of the region, especially the *Trunzo di Aci*, a cabbage/turnip or kohl rabi type vegetable, the Giarratana onion and so much more, as the seasons change. I would happily have tried the whole menu, but here is a selection of what I had:

Tagliatelle with the fresh Porcini mushrooms of Etna, perfectly made.

Left: Tagliatelle with rabbit ragu' and Bronte pistachio. So good! **Right**: Another Sicilian Slow Food Presidium on display inside the restaurant: the unique garlic of Nubia, from the far West of Sicily. See https://www.fondazioneslowfood.com/en/slow-food-presidia/nubia-red-garlic/

Left: Baba' al Rum, with pistachios of Bronte. **Right**: Panna Cotta with Black Mulberry Compote.

What follows will horrify some of my readers: donkey steak, grilled on their wood fired *brace*, served with yet more *Trunzo di Aci* salad. The Ragusano donkey,[486] once primarily used for labour, is now still bred by a few passionate farmers who want to preserve this unique animal, producing excellent meat and dairy products in the process.

One might argue that donkeys should just be kept in sanctuaries, but the best way to preserve these animals, and indeed any livestock breeds, is to farm and eat them. Incidentally, they are raised the old-fashioned way, are as happy as livestock can be, and are an inherently sustainable source of food. I could accept the objections from those who object to all meat consumption, but not from the average meat eater.[487]

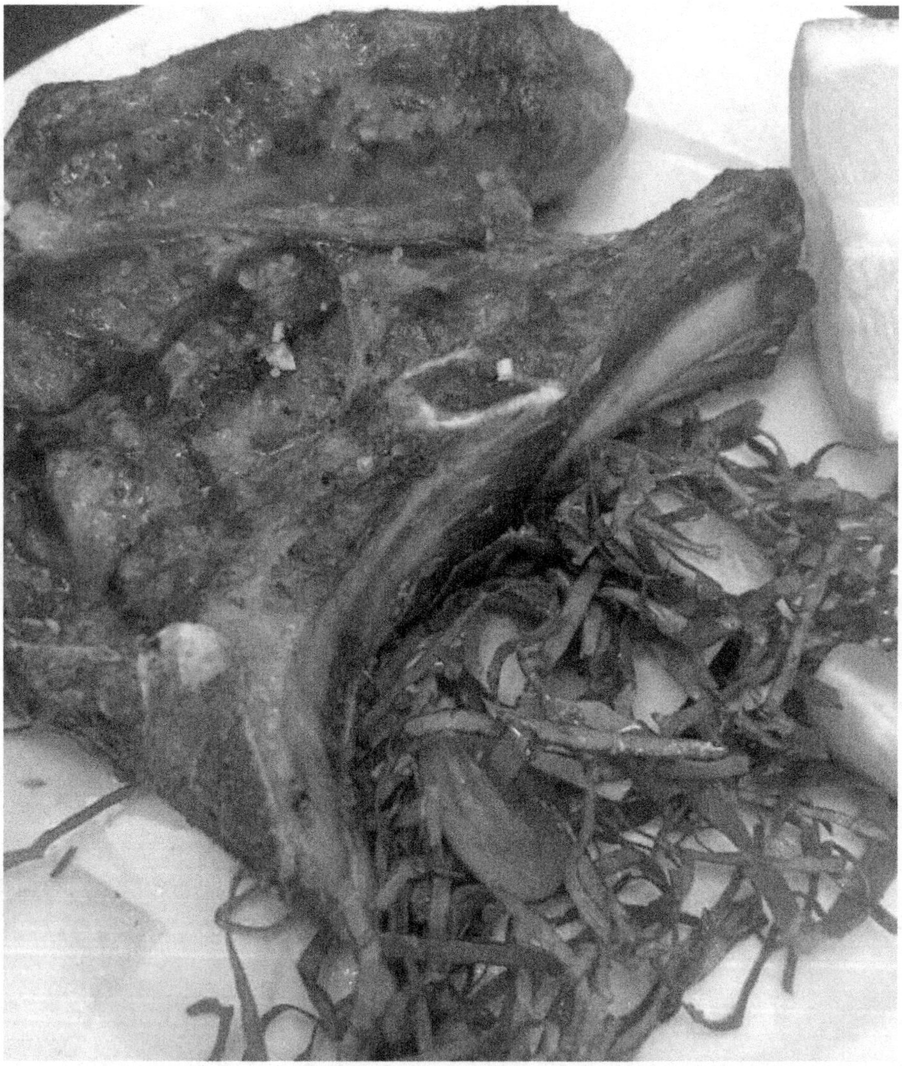

[486] See: https://www.fondazioneslowfood.com/en/slow-food-presidia/ragusano-donkey/

[487] As my witty schoolfriend William jokingly said, having seen the image of my donkey steak: *"That's just immoral, you shouldn't eat animals that have been successfully anthropomorphised by Disney and the like."*

Overall, whilst some of the food was relatively simple, everything was exceptional because of the purity and quality of the ingredients, the perfect execution of the recipes, and their seasonality. The rustic ambiance, which is hard to describe, was comforting and warm, and took me back to younger days. Saro ended up having coffee with us, whilst smoking his Toscano cigar, and the whole experience was an immersion in his world of Etna country life. It was the traditional Sunday lunch at its best, with families eating together.

Left: Saro Rosario Grasso with the Author. **Right**: Saro comparing himself to a mushroom.
Credit: https://www.instagram.com/4_archi_milo/

Genuine Innovation: Ristorante Da Antonio, Tenute di Villa Giulia, Randazzo, Sicily

Close to the beautiful town of Randazzo, the nearest town to the summit of Etna, I had the pleasure of visiting Chef Antonio Fucile's countryside restaurant.[488] Antonio trained with some of the best chefs in Italy, including the modernist Gualtiero Marchesi, before returning home to apply his craft and skills to showcase an elegant, refined and innovative take on the local cuisine, with a cornucopia of ingredients at his disposal. He bought and restored Villa Giulia and took over its organic vineyards and winery, producing his own wine. His seventeen-year-old son Vincenzo works in his kitchen with him, and the restaurant combines a family feel with the utmost professionalism.

[488] Three times in a week!

Credit: https://www.ristorantedantonio.com/ristorante-etna-da-antonio

Ibidem

Just like Saro, for whom he has the deepest respect, the basis of the Antonio's cuisine rests upon an uncompromising commitment to the livestock, produce and artisanal products of the area, and broader Sicily. His selection includes the aforementioned black pig *dei Nebrodi*, which formed the backbone of my first antipasto at the restaurant, served with Sicilian cheeses, black mulberry jam and orange blossom honey. He bakes his own range of breads, some of which were yellow in colour, due to the addition of turmeric, an exotic ingredient which, I imagine, his grandmother would not have recognised. This immediately gave me an indication of where he differs from Saro: Antonio's aim is to respect tradition whilst also innovating and experimenting, whilst providing his customers with a refined, elegant dining experience as they enjoy the beautiful views and winery experience.

Credit: https://www.ristorantedantonio.com/ristorante-etna-da-antonio

Over our few visits, we had a range of excellent dishes, many of which had clear elements of innovation, and which blended techniques and ingredients in ways that, whilst creative, did not detract from the primacy of the ingredients.

An immediate comparison I would draw is between Saro's very traditional tagliatelle with Porcini mushrooms and Antonio's take on the dish. In essence, the dishes are the same, but Antonio added, instead of the optional chopped parsley, a "parsley chlorophyll gel", which worked very well. The dish had a freshness and a depth which, whilst mostly due to the exceptionally well-cooked fresh Porcini and perfect handmade pasta, was augmented by Antonio's little twist. Is it inconsistent for me to promote a dish made with a gel, after lambasting Heston Blumenthal and others for their endless gelifications? The answer is no, because Antonio prepared a perfect *Tagliatelle ai Funghi Porcini*, did not deconstruct, adulterate, and make a mockery of this great traditional dish, but simply added a modernist (as opposed to postmodernist) twist.

To the left of the tagliatelle, we have Antonio's off the menu, improvised raw Porcini mushroom salad, with Grana Padano (a milder counterpart to Parmigiano Reggiano), flowers, and fresh vegetables and herbs that I cannot accurately recall. There were no ingredients or techniques here that Saro could not have used in his rustic establishment, apart from the green sauce perhaps. What is different about this dish is its elegance, design and modern look: it could grace any fine dining restaurant table. The creative use of herbs and flowers, the attention to textural balance, and the ultra-thin cutting of the mushrooms all made for a perfect salad.

Next, here are two dishes showcasing one of the great bounties of the Etna region: the pistachios of Bronte. The *Montanina* veal fillet[489] to the left came with a rich but delicate pistachio cream, which is not a traditional combination, but worked extremely well. To the right, traditional Cappellacci pasta filled with ricotta and spinach was served with a pistachio cream and crunchy Speck, the smoked ham of the Dolomites.[490]

[489] The red Modicana cattle of Sicily is referred to as Montanina when raised in the mountain areas.

[490] Antonio uses ingredients from all over the country, but the basis is always Sicilian.

Being mountain food, meat dominated the main courses. To the left we had the unique sausages *al ceppo di Linguaglossa*, a Slow Food Presidium produced within miles from the restaurant.[491] They were served with a soft mash potato and black truffle. This was simply a more luxurious version of a classic. To the right of our sausages was probably my favourite dish, which blew me away. These were perfect *Montanina* veal meatballs, aromatised with the grated rind of lemon *verdello* (green lemon, before it is fully ripe), wrapped in lemon leaves, and cooked *alla Brace*,[492] served with the unique purple onions of Tropea, the classic onion from Calabria, and a saffron infused potato purée. This is a Sicilian dish, which Antonio elevated, with perfect sides and dressing.

[491] https://www.fondazioneslowfood.com/en/slow-food-presidia/al-ceppo-sausage-of-linguaglossa/

[492] The closest translation is barbecued, on wood embers.

The most elaborately designed dish that we had, almost painted onto the plate, was his pork fillet, with black mulberry sauce, caramelised peach, and a smooth, perfect reduction on top. This was a creative pork dish, which combined the distinctive products and flavours of Etna. To the right we have the classic Sicilian Cannolo. Antonio used the same basic recipe his grandmother would have used but made it as light and as refined as possible and presented it beautifully.

I was struck by Antonio's generosity and humility, his recollections of his farming background, and his composed, understated love of the land and its gifts. As we walked through his vineyards, and as I ate my way through his grape varieties,[493] in spite of having demolished yet another four course meal, he pointed out the specific weeds which his grandmother taught him to use in the kitchen. Indeed, this was the norm in many rural parts of Italy, with seasonal weeds providing nutritious and tasty additions to the local cuisine.[494] One particular weed, belonging to the cabbage family, *cauliceddi* (*Brassica fruticulose*), had

[493] Including grapes from enormous pre-phylloxera grape vines, which had survived the pest onslaught. Phylloxera is an insect from North America that devastated most grape vines in Europe in the 19th Century, especially in France. The solution was to import resistant grape vine root stock from North America, on which the European varieties were grafted.

[494] It is also a common feature of traditional Greek cuisine, and wild foraged herbs are still used on some of the Greek islands.

featured in one of best dishes I had at the restaurant. Traditionally, Antonio explained, these weeds were harvested in the vineyard and added to sausage and/or pork off cuts (ears, snouts, tail etc.), to make a sauce that could go with pasta or some other staple. This was humble peasant food, which inspired Antonio to create a richer, refined version of it, resulting in a modern, luxurious, unique dish.

Cauliceddi (Brassica fruticulose) in Antonio's vineyard.

In his dish, Antonio served excellent Sicilian spaghetti with a pesto made from the vineyard weed, which he combined with crumbled sausage *al ceppo di Linguaglossa*, dried Pachino cherry tomato, crunchy Avola almonds, served with grated pecorino cheese from the mountain and coarse black pepper on the side. This was genuine innovation, inspired by a peasant dish. Not all of Antonio's innovations are or will be equally successful, but the thinking around this particular dish was exemplary. Apart from the unique gastronomic experience, the dish also made me think about what we lose when we use herbicides. Apart from poisoning the land and waterways and decreasing biodiversity, we lose culinary and nutritional opportunities.

Final Words on the Best Restaurants Lists, and on Fine Dining

The reader might be wondering whether I am suggesting that Antonio's delightful establishment should be on some Best Restaurant list or other and displace the postmodernists. Whilst the postmodernists do not belong in any conceivable roll of honour, and do not deserve any of the accolades and respect that is routinely bestowed upon them, the short answer is no. The very idea of having a top 50 restaurants list does not make much gastronomic sense, it is merely useful for marketing and commercial purposes. Intelligent regional or city guides to the best restaurants, without rankings, are the way to go, and Antonio's establishment would unquestionably feature as one of the best restaurants in the Province of Catania.[495] Furthermore, whilst Antonio's restaurant is wonderful, there will be others across Italy which are eminently comparable and, as he would be the first to concede, there will also be others that are, for now, more sophisticated and accomplished. Antonio has great talent, work ethic and humility, and his son is still learning his trade. As such, Antonio still has room to improve, develop and grow as a Chef and wine producer. Watch this space!

I must also clarify that Antonio's restaurant, whilst elegant and refined, is not strictly speaking a "fine dining" establishment, nor does it purport to be, and a fantastic meal will not cost more than €50-60 a head. Not that fine dining establishments necessarily make *better food* than the conservative food of 4 Archi or the creative food of Antonio, far from it. What a fine dining restaurant can and should do is provide ever more refinement, sophistication, complexity, elegance, and luxury. Its formal service should be perfect, it will have deeper cellars, a dedicated pastry Chef, perhaps, and particularly rare, expensive ingredients not normally found on the menus of excellent but humbler establishments. Fine dining can be either radically conservative or genuinely innovative, and there is certainly a place in gastronomy for fine dining at the highest level, provided it does not fall in the pitfalls of postmodernism. Nonetheless, fine dining ultimately lives and dies by the same rules that apply to all restaurants, irrespective of whether dinner costs €60 or €300. Are their kitchens built upon the very best products and ingredients that the land and seas have to offer? Are the best artisanal products being sourced by the Chef? Is the kitchen free from the culinary and ideological adulterations of postmodernism? Does the restaurant showcase classical technique at its very best? Is any innovation, not that it is a requirement, genuine? What improvement does innovation add to the dining experience and to gastronomy as a whole? Will it leave a positive legacy?

[495] As would Saro's, of course.

Antonio's vineyard seen from the terrace where we ate our second and third lunches.

The Author with Antonio in the vineyard.

IN A NUTSHELL

- Contemporary high-end gastronomy is mostly a worthless fad.
- Postmodernist approaches are ruining gastronomy.
- There is a direct ideological correlation between postmodernism in the kitchen and the art gallery.
- Most of the trappings of postmodernist gastronomy (the foams, synthetic flavourings, specification and so on) add little or nothing of value to the kitchen.
- Beware of all chefs who have the airs and pretensions of activists, artists, revolutionaries and scientists.
- Michelin stars do not necessarily shine bright, and the Michelin guide is no longer a guarantor of quality.
- Gastronomy, cuisine, and cookery, even at their best, are not classifiable as fine arts.
- Creativity cannot take place without very firm foundations of knowledge, technique, tradition, and discipline.
- Without the very best whole food ingredients, there is no great cuisine.
- The best chefs understand the primary importance of agriculture, viticulture, artisanal production and seasonality.
- Genuine innovation is both possible and desirable.
- Spend your time and money on more valuable things and experiences than postmodern gastronomy.
- Conservation is the first duty of every high food culture.
- Fine dining is not necessarily better than simpler alternatives and is not exempt from the same principles that apply to all cuisine.

Saro's beloved *Trunzo de Aci* (Brassica oleracea var. gongylodes) at a local market.

Antonio's dreamy organic grapes. Notice the weeds!

SECTION THREE

Navigating Food and Dietary Choices

Chapter 9

HOW TO EAT: A BRIEF GUIDE

(General Principles, In No Particular Order)

No Calorie Counting

A good start to any healthy approach to food is to avoid doing many of the things that are both popular and widely recommended. Being a contrarian, when it comes to food, is generally a good idea, in this day and age. One of the most established practices in our culture, encouraged by dietary guidelines and food packaging, is to count calories and to use such dubious accounting as a basis for daily food choices. Apart from adding unnecessary anxiety to such choices, it serves to shift our focus from the *qualitative* to the *quantitative*. Calories, to be clear, are not indicative of the quality, value, and desirability of a food item. An item of food which contains a lot of calories could be excellent and a low-calorie item could be dreadful. Organic double cream from a happy cow is full of calories but is inherently good; diet soda may have almost no calories at all, but it is always junk.

Furthermore, putting health aside, calorie counting makes little sense even if we are purely concerned with weight gain and weight loss. 2,500 calories of meat, fish, fruit, and vegetables do not have the same effect as 2,500 calories of bread, potatoes, and white sugar. If you don't believe me, run the experiment. Calories are not created equal and are not interchangeable. Calories, depending on where they come from, are not equally metabolised and absorbed, have differing effects on the body and are simply not a predictable indicator of weight gain and weight loss. This is even true for the same categories of food. A given amount of average white supermarket bread containing the same number of calories as an equal amount of traditional sourdough bread will have a very different impact on the digestive system and on body weight, if that is the main concern of the calorie counters. Two people consuming the same number of calories could be getting completely different results.

It is also worth noting that there is no precise method of measuring calories from any single food, and that the numbers you will read from labels are rough estimates at best. Food is not fuel, and the body is not a machine, and there is no simple "calories in, calories burnt" formula that actually maps onto reality. Furthermore, the rate and speed of calorie absorption varies from food item to food item, will differ depending on the combination of foods eaten together, the time of day in which they are eaten and will vary from person to person depending on their gut and overall health. The other problem with calorie counting for those who are overweight or obese is that it does not generally lead to a change in diet and food quality. It is often based on a reduction of the same types of foods, and the consumption of yet more sugar free sodas and low-fat dairy products. The overweight or obese person will inevitably have an unhealthy, compromised gut, will suffer from a hormonal imbalance and will therefore be primed for keeping or adding excess weight, even if the foods that he or she consumes are reduced in quantity. A key concept in all biological systems, human or otherwise, is homeostasis, a concept that can be traced back to Hippocrates, which refers to the process that living things use to actively maintain fairly stable conditions and maintain equilibrium. Therefore, what is needed in order to shift from one state of equilibrium to another is a radical change in the type and quality of food eaten, as opposed to a change in quantity.

Finally, having said that, the only obvious thing that anybody can appreciate, without the need for calorie counting and other dietary accounting, is that eating huge amounts of food, even healthy foods, coupled with a lack of physical activity, can lead to weight gain. Exercise, walking, sports, manual labour etc... have an impact on general health and, indirectly, to body composition (muscle vs fat) and weight. Nonetheless, diet has far more impact on body weight and health than exercise: exercising without radical dietary change does not lead to weight loss. Calorie counting at both ends[496] is redundant, impractical and misleading: it is not necessary and does not work.

TO SUM UP: do not count calories. Do not look at calories on packaging, on the internet etc. Ignore the very idea of food as calories.

No Nutrient Bans & No Food Type Bans

As should be clear by now, you should not ban any nutrient from your diet. Better still, do not think of foods as bundles of nutrients. Think of them as foods. If you ever catch yourself thinking about "what protein to have for dinner" or about whether you are "eating too much fat", force yourself to think about what meat or rice or whatever *food* you are actually having

[496] As in counting calories consumed through food and calories burnt running, for example.

for dinner. As we saw earlier, all the macro and micronutrients contained in the plant and animal products we eat are perfectly appropriate for us. The only thing that really matters is the quality and diversity of the foods that we eat. You can be extremely well nourished without having a clue about amino acids, polyphenols, and fat-soluble vitamins. If you focus on sourcing quality *whole foods*, which are very complex products made from living things, you will do well. The corollary of not banning nutrients is that we must not ban food types: dairy, meat, grains, tubers, nuts or whatever else. This, by now, should be crystal clear.

TO SUM UP: *do not ban any nutrient or food type from your diet.*[497] *Do not buy into any diet that has any X-free recommendations (fat-free, sugar-free, meat-free, gluten-free etc...) and which promotes products that have added nutrients (added vitamins, minerals, fortified with X, Y and Z).*

Prioritise Whole Foods

The obvious consequence of the latter recommendation is that as a general rule, you should always prioritise recognisable, basic whole foods. Whole foods should constitute the vast majority of any human diet, anywhere in the world.

We can consider the following as clear examples of whole foods:

- **Herbs**: e.g., parsley, coriander, sage, rosemary, thyme.
- **Vegetables**: e.g., onions, carrots, cabbages, celery, lettuce.
- **Fruits**: e.g., apples, pears, plums, grapes, bananas.
- **Nuts**: e.g., walnuts, almonds, hazelnuts.
- **Fungi**: mushrooms and truffles.
- **Pulses and grains**: e.g., lentils, beans, chickpeas, peas, rice, barley, quinoa.
- **Animal products**: e.g., whole milk, eggs, fresh meats, fresh seafood.

It is important to note that some relatively processed foods (e.g., tomato paste, cheese, or coconut milk) are from a single source and share many of the characteristics and benefits of their plant of origin (tomatoes, milk and coconuts in this case) and are, in any case, one ingredient processed foods. Other whole foods need some processing by definition in order to be turned into edible foods or to maximise their use and viability in the kitchen (e.g., most spices, grains, and oily seeds).

[497] Not for health or dietary reasons anyway. There may be religious and cultural taboos that preclude from eating certain foods, of course, but that's another matter.

These should be considered "secondary whole foods" and are not in any way comparable to the multi-ingredient ultra-processed foods that now dominate the supermarket aisles. For example:

- **Spices**: e.g., turmeric, cinnamon, saffron, aniseed.
- **Vegetable oils**: e.g., olive oil, sunflower oil, hemp oil.
- **Grain flours**: e.g., wheat flour, maize flour/cornmeal, buckwheat flour.
- **Pulse and nut flours**: e.g., chickpea flour, almond flour, chestnut flour.
- **Plant "milks"**: e.g., oat milk, almond milk, rice milk.
- **Preserved fruits and vegetables**: e.g., fruit jam, canned tomatoes, pickled cucumbers.
- **Fruit juices and smoothies**: e.g., freshly squeezed orange juice, apple juice, mixed fruit smoothie.
- **Syrups, honey and unrefined sugar**: e.g., maple syrup, rapadura sugar, wildflower honey.
- **Dairy products**: e.g., butter, Greek-style yoghurt, cheddar cheese.
- **Preserved fish**: e.g., salted anchovies, smoked Alaskan salmon, canned tuna.
- **Preserved meat**: e.g., streaky bacon, prosciutto, venison jerky.

As ever, the quality of the raw ingredients used to make these foods makes all the difference. Flours and oils are wonderful ingredients, but only if made from quality grains and oilseeds/olives, using the appropriate processing methods. The gulf in quality between one bottle of oil and another is similar to the gulf in quality between a bottle of milk and another. The gulf between low-quality bacon made from factory-farmed pigs and high-quality bacon from happy pigs is equally stark, if not more so.

TO SUM UP: ensure that quality whole foods constitute the vast majority of what you purchase and have in your fridge and larder. See Chapter 10 for more information on how to select the right products.

Superfoods?

A consequence of prioritising whole foods and rejecting nutritionist tenets is the dismissal of increasingly popular beliefs in the existence of "superfoods". Whilst I do not wish to doubt the potential benefits of any whole food designated as a "superfood", it is worth noting that the very belief in the existence of superfoods stems from two forces, one ideological, one commercial. The first belongs to the same reductive mentality that seeks to find THE nutrient or food item that is either good or bad, part of the ongoing hopeless quest for a dietary silver bullet. The second is the obvious work of the food industry and its marketing efforts, through which an item of food can be promoted by appealing to its quasi-magical qualities. There is no doubt that the various popular, fashionable superfoods, from goji berries to acai seeds, are, in and of themselves, wholesome and nutritious whole foods. But they are almost certainly no more valuable than less exotic, domestic alternatives like blackberries and raspberries. Relatively common and underrated fruits and vegetables, from beetroots and onions to apples and blackcurrants, are all, in principle, classifiable as "superfoods".

The simple truth is that, mercifully, all edible herbs, vegetables, fruits and nuts are, in and of themselves, wonderful gifts of the land which are inherently good for us. Some may be particularly nutritious or hold specific properties. Tomatoes and carrots may be more nutritious than radishes or iceberg lettuce, overall, and some plants, such as lemons and garlic, are particularly valuable for our health, but the whole notion of "superfood" is somewhat misleading. By all means eat kale, now considered a superfood, but do not consider the humble cabbage or head of broccoli to be in any way inferior. Also, as ever, the fashionable attraction towards somewhat exotic and mysterious foods like the now ubiquitous goji berries detracts attention from what should be of far greater importance: the soil health and cultivation method which gave rise to such a mysterious food. The vast majority of goji berries are grown in China, where for the most part they will be grown under intensive and pesticide-laden conditions. It would surely make more sense to opt for, say, home grown organic blackberries than dubious berries from the Orient.

TO SUM UP: do not get caught up in superfood fads. Nature has mercifully provided a cornucopia of superfoods.

Seasonality & Locality

> *Nothing important comes into being overnight; even grapes or figs need time to ripen. If you say that you want a fig now, I will tell you to be patient. First, you must allow the tree to flower, then put forth fruit; then you have to wait until the fruit is ripe. So if the fruit of a fig tree is not brought to maturity instantly or in an hour, how do you expect the human mind to come to fruition, so quickly and easily? – Epictetus, Discourses I, 15.7-8*

> *You must remind yourself that you love a mortal, and that nothing that you love is your very own; it is given you for the moment, not for ever nor inseparably, but like a fig or a bunch of grapes at the appointed season of the year, and if you long for it in winter you are a fool. So too if you long for your son or your friend, when it is not given you to have him, know that you are longing for a fig in wintertime. – Epictetus, Discourses III, 24.86*

As we saw in previous chapters, both locality and seasonality are complicated variables that add an extra layer of complexity to our food choices. It may at times be better to source an exotic product than a local product and it may at times be better to ignore the rhythms of the seasons. Having said that, as a general rule, we must absolutely prioritise seasonal[498] and local produce as a starting point. We are actually blessed with a lot of variety here on the British Isles. As I write this chapter, in late February, I can refer to my Saturday morning trip to the Farmers' Market on Pimlico Road. I came home today with a wealth of vegetables, herbs, and apples that no reasonable person could possibly be dissatisfied with. A particular highlight this morning was the organic purple sprouting broccoli, which puts the conventional imported "tender stem broccoli" in most supermarkets to shame. And this is late February, one of the scarcest times of the year in the Northern Hemisphere. All of my purchases were UK-grown, organic (some certified, some not), and wonderfully fresh. It generally makes no sense whatsoever to go and purchase fresh tomatoes, strawberries, and aubergines in late February on a regular basis.

If the sustainability and environmental angle is of no interest to you and if you do not care about supporting British agriculture, at least consider your health and, importantly, your palate. I still recall, as a child, the pleasure of the seasonality and ephemerality of many of the foods that we ate. Each season was delineated by specific smells, flavours, and colours: ripe persimmons, clementine and oranges in the autumn and early winter, figs and melons during summer, peas, and broad beans to be hand shelled in spring, and so much more! I was fortunate enough to be educated accordingly and I used to look forward to seasonal produce and happily accept its transience. I remember the arrival of *agretti*[499] and spring asparagus, which only lasted a few weeks, peaches, and apricots in summer and roast chestnuts in autumn. Rare and fabulous chicories, endives and escaroles were available in the colder times of the year. None of this led to a shortage of ingredients or lack of variety: quite the opposite. By understanding the seasons and their culinary implications, there is more pleasure to be had and less repetition. Seasonal and fresh produce tastes better, is more nourishing and can only lead to more pleasure and better health.

TO SUM UP: prioritise local and seasonal food.

[498] Relative to where you live of course!

[499] A unique Italian vegetable, adapted to salty terrains. Known as Monk's Beard in English. It is similar to the fashionable samphire but better.

"Organic"

I will insist on placing inverted commas when using the word "organic" as I am keen for you to appreciate the spirit, rather than the letter, of organic principles. Whilst I certainly recommend organic certification overall, there are plenty of organic products that are not certified, as well as plenty of certified products that are not necessarily particularly good or worth buying when other options are available. Be that as it may, if there is one take away from this book is that the single most important thing in food, dieting, cookery etc... is the quality of ingredients and raw materials that you eat and or cook with. Whether we are talking about apples, bread or complex dishes, the most important requirement is that quality of the ingredients is prioritised above all other considerations. And, as we saw in previous chapters, quality is not a relative, arbitrary property, but an objective, discernible one. Our happy chicken is objectively better than our factory-farmed chicken. Cows that eat grass for most of the year produce far better milk than those stuck inside a barn eating dry feed. Organic potatoes grown in living soil are objectively better than potatoes grown with a host of agrochemicals in sterile soil. This principle holds true across the board and must be at the forefront of any sensible approach to food, cookery and eating.

TO SUM UP: source, cook and eat "organic", as much as possible.

Learn how to Cook

One of the main goals of this book is to provide the criteria and tools needed to make better food choices. One crucial option at your disposal is to learn how to cook: this alone will change your whole attitude towards food and generally improve your life. It will benefit your health, and you will make the most of your food budget. Prioritising high-quality *ingredients* (e.g., eggs, raw vegetables, flour, grains, dried pulses, whole joints of meat etc.) that require assemblage and/or cookery as opposed to manufactured, processed, readymade foods, not to mention deliveries and take-away, will generally guarantee far better food quality and the maximisation of your budget. The most often quoted reason as to why this recommendation is supposedly impractical and unrealistic is that in the hustle and bustle of day-to-day life, we simply *do not have time*.

There are two main objections to this supposition. Firstly, by historical standards, in Britain, and indeed Europe, we generally have more spare time available than at any given time in history. It would be helpful to remember that the average person has fewer working hours, more days off, and more holidays than ever before. Even accounting for the fact that the traditional division of labour between working husband and housewife has largely disappeared, there are still enough hours left in the day for the average adult to prepare food. In Britain, we currently spend over 4 hours a day watching television and other video content.[500] Add to that all the time spent on social media, and it is quite easy to see that time availability is not the problem nor a sufficient reason to explain the gradual disappearance of cookery. Kitchen work, furthermore, has never been faster or easier, given the myriad tools, electric devices and other technologies we now have at our disposal. None of us need to grind our own grains, thanks to cheaply available ground flour, whip our own cream, thanks to the electric whip, or shop every day, given the advent of refrigeration.

None of this implies that everyone can or should spend several hours a week making egg pasta with a rolling pin, plucking pheasants or baking their own biscuits, far from it. Between engaging in these niche occupations and no cooking at all there is an achievable happy medium.

TO SUM UP*:* ensure you find the time to cook and prepare your own food.[501]

Conviviality and Hospitality

Prioritising and finding time for food is clearly non-negotiable if we are to have a healthy food culture. The decline of home cooking and the emphasis on dieting and nutrition have had a deleterious effect on our culture. The scarcity of kitchen time and the increasingly popular pseudoscientific understanding of food have both chipped away at the cultural and social functions of food. The context in which we eat food, and the way in which we eat it, should be as important as any dietary and nutritional concerns. Communal eating of the same meal, as opposed to solitary eating or individualised dietary choices within the same family unit, is at the heart of every healthy food culture. The ritualistic and formal elements of the meal are more important than misguided considerations about gluten and cholesterol. Conviviality[502] is about a way of living together, communally, and of celebrating life. The meal should be a source of consolation and connection, rather than a source of anxiety and opportunity for "refuelling".

[500] https://www.ofcom.org.uk/media use-and-attitudes/media-habits-adults/gen-z-swerves-traditional-broadcast-tv-as-less-than-half-tune-in-weekly/

[501] Of course, as long as someone is cooking in the household, not everyone necessarily needs to cook. The key point here is that home cooked food is irreplaceable, and someone needs to do it. It would still be advisable for anyone, however, whatever their circumstances, to learn some very basic cooking, because it is a simple life skill that everyone should have.

[502] The word has Latin roots, from *convivere*, to live together, and *convivium*, a party or a feast.

TO SUM UP: try to eat with other people. Look at meals as opportunities for companionship, as opposed to opportunities for refuelling. Cook for other people, be a good host and gracious guest.

The Pleasure Principle

Conviviality is intimately connected with pleasure and thankfully there is no contradiction between pleasure and health. Healthy food can be extremely pleasurable, rather than some sort of punishment. The association between guilt and pleasure in food is, by and large, misguided. Unfortunately, thanks to false nutritionist assumptions, the idea that delicious food is usually "bad for you" and healthy food plain and austere often passes unchallenged.

The first problem with this way of thinking is that foods that are widely perceived as delicious but unhealthy are not necessarily unhealthy. A perfect example are "fatty foods" and "sugar". As we saw earlier, the fear of animal fats and sugars is often unfounded and there is no need to feel guilty about eating a very fatty meal or a dessert: the devil is in the detail. A chocolate cake or bacon sandwich can be healthy or unhealthy. It all depends on the quality of the ingredients and the methods used to produce them. What is also important, of course, is the context in which these items are eaten: in other words, the overall variety and balance of one's diet. Last night I had a wonderful dish, which would have made many nutritionists, not to mention vegans, shudder in disapproval: a large, very fatty, rib eye steak bathing in a generous amount of peppercorn sauce. The steak was butter basted, and the subsequent sauce was mostly made up of a blend of the cooking butter and double cream. However, and this is the key issue, as ever, these delightful fatty ingredients were carefully sourced and originated from the finest of British pastures. Grass fed, organic beef and dairy is simply not comparable to its factory farmed equivalents.

It is important to note that I also had a nice portion of "peperonata" alongside it, a sweet bell pepper dish, cooked with white onion and tomato sauce. For lunch, I had an enormous fresh salad of seasonal raw vegetables and soft-boiled eggs, and a slice of sourdough bread. Breakfast was a banana, and a couple of apples were eaten as snacks during the day. A bowl of top-quality ice cream completed the day after dinner. In other words: one thing is eating a rib eye steak with a heavy sauce in the context of crisps, microwave pizzas and other junk, quite another is to eat it in a context of healthy whole foods.

The other problem with the seeming paradox between health and pleasure has more to do with education and upbringing. Many of my readers could argue that they can only enjoy and gain pleasure from Big Macs, Doritos and KFC and no pleasure at all from vegetables. It is certainly true that the palate needs to be educated and that, if one were unfortunate enough to have been raised on junk food and had no exposure to a broad range of whole foods and great home cooking, the palate will be stunted in adulthood.[503] The whole point of a gastronomic education, which most people do not receive, is to encourage and instil the natural and virtuous association between gustatory pleasure and quality food. It is never too late for further education.

Furthermore, it is also true that the healthy, wholesome counterparts of many junk foods can be successfully reproduced. I am yet to meet any fan of the Big Mac or KFC bucket who would not enjoy a well-made grass-fed beef hamburger or a homemade organic fried chicken or indeed my special Southern Fried partridge! Furthermore, the palate is malleable and changeable and open to new experiences: someone who hates vegetables as a child can come to love them as an adult, given the right inputs and stimuli. I have met many people in England from an older generation who recall dreadful childhood experiences of poorly cooked vegetables at home and at school. These were often "boiled to death", with no finesse, seasoning nor spice. Many of the same people come to love the very same vegetables they dreaded, such as cabbage. Ultimately, the best cuisine and the finest of foods can be both pleasurable and healthy. It is a win-win situation.

TO SUM UP: source and create healthy versions of the foods you already like. Try to experiment with all kinds of vegetables, pulses, and herbs. As a general rule, do not eat anything you simply cannot enjoy. You can have both pleasure and health if you seek it.

Celebratory Foods and Occasional Overeating

The connection between food and celebration is an ancient and precious one, which thankfully we haven't completely lost. Most people still make some sort of effort to put together a Christmas meal, or special birthday dish, for their loved ones. The roots of this connection are deep and complex but, at the simplest level, apart from the fact that we are social animals, it has to do with the fact that, since food scarcity has been the historical norm, any celebration, religious festival and rite of passage has traditionally been accompanied by special, precious and abundant foods. Often, celebrations had to do with *food itself*: think of the countless harvest festivals, often dedicated to a single ingredient,[504] that were the norm across Europe. In Italy, there were, and to an extend there still are, hundreds of seasonal food festivals, celebrating anything from snails to chestnuts, artichokes and radicchio. The

[503] The idea that ultra-processed food, including the food of fast-food chains, is popular because it is "hyperpalatable" should not be confused with the idea that it is actually delicious, or the height of gustatory pleasure. In fact, it takes childhood habituation and continuous exposure to find these inferior foods palatable.

[504] Or indeed slaughter: pig slaughter has always been at the centre of celebrations and partying.

Catholic calendar, with its saints and festivities, also revolved around certain foods. I recall how, on the 19th of March, St Joseph's day, we always had what could be loosely translated as cream puffs. During Carnival, we still have, just once a year, fried pastries called *Frappe*, *Struffoli* and *Castagnole*. We also always have lentils on New Year's Day for good fortune, apparently.

Frappe and Struffoli from my home kitchen. The latter are covered in honey.

In our part of the world, scarcity, seasonality, religious observance and agrarian lifestyles have all largely declined or disappeared. The idea of inviting people round to an asparagus festival or to a hog killing party would be odd for most. It is not always possible, practical nor necessary to resurrect certain traditions, but celebratory food or indeed the celebration *of* food is a commendable and crucial part of any healthy family and culture. I would also add that it is not a bad idea to overeat at times, and to struggle getting up from the table after a very long lunch. This is again an ancestral experience that we can share with family and friends on great Sunday dinners or special days, on holiday or when we need to celebrate something.

TO SUM UP: take the time to prepare or source special foods for special occasions, starting from the Sunday lunch or dinner. Stay close to the seasons and be willing to prepare certain foods no more than once or twice a year. It is commendable to overeat at times and to enjoy festivities.

Respect Your Elders

One of the most pleasant sources of inspiration I found in recent times is a book and YouTube channel called "Pasta Grannies".[505] It contains hundreds of videos featuring grandmas across Italy, often in their 90s, who present and prepare a traditional dish: not all pasta in spite of the name! These documents are in some way more valuable than cookbooks, for there is no substitute for an erudite demonstration from those who will not be with us for much longer. It's historical record, cultural treasure and technical showcase rolled into one. An obvious fact that is often lost in contemporary cuisine is that an established recipe and technique is what it is for good reasons: it's the result of tried and tested methods that have stood the test of time. Cuisine, like agriculture, is inherently conservative.

The first task of any budding cook should be to acquire basic technique and to learn a broad range of established recipes and preparations, before even trying to be inventive. There is, as previously discussed, a place for innovation, but it has to be rooted on firm ground. One of the reasons why the Pasta Grannies' granddaughters are, on average, less likely to know how to cook is because vital cultural transmission has largely skipped the last two generations. The extinction of crop varieties and livestock breeds, which rely on continuous sowing, breeding and preservation, has been mirrored by a similar process of extinction in the kitchen.

Some traditions came to an end for good reasons. For example, in Liguria, meat from dolphins caught as bycatch was traditionally eaten by fishermen and their families. The meat was dried and preserved: *mosciame di delfino*. Given the dramatic depletion of the seas, the need to end bycatch of all major marine species, and given our increased concern for sea mammals, and given the fact that unlike poor fishermen we certainly do not need to eat dolphins anymore, this is a tradition that we do not need to revive. But in the vast majority of cases, the loss of valuable traditions is quite literally *a loss*. Mercifully, some traditions can be revived. Nothing is stopping the granddaughters, or indeed grandsons, from keeping the Grannies' legacies going.

[505] See V. Bennison, 2019, Pasta Grannies. See also www.pastagrannies.com and the YouTube channel: https://www.youtube.com/user/pastagrannies

TO SUM UP: learn everything you can from those who preceded you and know what they are doing. Before attempting to invent anything, learn the basics.

Produce it Yourself?

One way to transform and improve our eating habits is to engage in some form of food production. Before I get accused of expecting everyone to pick up a hoe and sickle and forcibly march out to the countryside, I can only reiterate what I have already made clear: that between the largely agrarian societies of our relatively very recent past and the newly urbanised, alienated industrial societies of today, there are some happy mediums and plenty of nuances and grey areas. There are ample opportunities to spend some spare time engaging in some form of food production. It could be growing a few herbs at home, a few vegetables in the garden, tending to a couple of fruit trees and grape vines or keeping bees and a few hens.

There is an astonishing amount of spare land dotted around the country that is misused, abandoned or undervalued: gardens, lawns, parks, wasteland, all sorts of nooks and corners, both private and public. It doesn't even have to be all on soil: how many raised beds and pots can be placed on brick and mortar and on roofs? In parts on North London, old council homes with gardens still have fruit trees, which were planted at a time when it was presumed that back gardens could and should be put to some purpose. Council land and gardens are no longer maintained with any food production in mind, unfortunately. Equally, every school, university, prison, hospital and army barrack ought to have a growing area, but we currently do not have the political will and regulation in place to implement a national policy with domestic and community food production at its heart. Having said that, we cannot and should not wait for government policy to be enlightened and it is not an exaggeration to say that virtually anyone could grow some herbs and vegetables or plant some fruit trees if they really want to.

Apart from the inherent wholesomeness and prudence of localising food production and making the most of our domestic spaces and unproductive land, engaging in food growing transfers a lot of skill, knowledge and enthusiasm into the kitchen and into our diets, as well as being a healthy, intelligent pastime. Knowing when and how to grow potatoes or processing one's apples into cider does more than just provide some food and drink. It provides a natural understanding of what food and drink are really about and reconnects us to those living processes upon which we ultimately all depend on.

TO SUM UP: consider growing something, anything, even just lots of herbs in pots. Or at least engage with someone who does. Turn up for fruit picking or harvest days, volunteer somewhere. Visit and buy direct from a good farm.

Be Willing to Kill

If you become willing to grow food, you may wish to become willing to kill for it. Putting vegan extremes aside, the reality is that the vast majority of the population still consumes meat, fish and other animal products but has never witnessed or participated in the inevitable act that precedes such consumption. The distance, both physical and psychological, from animals and their fate has rendered their consumption a very thoughtless, superficial act. As we pick up cellophane wrapped or vacuum packed[506] pieces of meat[507] and filleted fish,[508] we are comfortably separated from the last breath and slaughter that must have occurred at the hands of someone, somewhere. This alienation has led to a number of negative consequences. The first is that the worst practices of industrial farming, fishing and slaughter are protected and shrouded by the detachment and ignorance that is involved in thoughtlessly picking up bits of meat from the supermarket. The less people know about what is involved in these activities, the more malpractice can become institutionalised. It is only with knowledge and a questioning attitude that one can become a conscientious and selective consumer in this day and age.

Another negative consequence is a naïve sentimentalism and hypocrisy about killing animals, which manifests itself most clearly in the increasing opposition to shooting, fishing, hunting and domestic slaughter. Such opposition is both legitimate and consistent when it comes from vegans and animal rights activists but cannot be taken too seriously when it comes from the average omnivorous urbanite, who may thoughtlessly gobble a fish finger and buy a £3-4 whole chicken from the supermarket and, at the same time, consider the average hunter to be a cruel, unreconstructed caveman in need of re-education. I have met many such people: those who, unlike myself, will buy cheap meat from abused factory

[506] A terrible way to package and store meat, now virtually compulsory under so called health and safety regulations. Meat, for the record, should not be vacuum packed in plastic. Meat should "breathe" and only wrapped in butcher paper. If plastic packaging is going to be used, there is no need for it to involve vacuuming, which only encourages the formation of the horrid liquid that you get every time you open a vacuum pack of meat. Vacuum packing is only useful for freezing.

[507] Which are also not very reminiscent of the animals from which they came from. The heads, tails, organs and other bits are almost entirely absent from the supermarket shelves, as steaks and chicken breasts dominate. Again, this makes it even easier not to see the life behind the piece of meat.

[508] Which usually originate from intensive fish farms or from the destructive methods of most fishing fleets.

farmed animals and, at the same time, object to my deer stalking activities or would look down on someone fortunate enough to wring the necks of their own chickens.

Perhaps the main objection to the activities of those who procure some of their own meat and fish themselves is based on the fact that hunters and fishermen clearly *enjoy the process*. This is considered to be sadistic: we should not enjoy killing. But, in truth, we do not enjoy killing *per se*. Whilst there will always be a small minority of sadists involved with hunting and fishing, just as there will always be a small minority of sadists in the medical, teaching and law enforcement professions, hunting and fishing are plainly not about inflicting pain for the sake of it. Some degree of suffering is part and parcel of it, of course, but is not the goal of pursuing prey. Hunting and fishing are about many things, including reconnecting with our most ancestral and instinctive communal or solitary occupation, enjoying communion with our canine (and equine) friends, love of the land and the great outdoors, actively engaging with land management and pest control and, most importantly, the procurement of excellent food. If suffering and indiscriminate killing were the goal of the hunter and fisherman, he would have devised the most prolonged and unnecessarily painful methods of slaughter possible and would also use explosives and machine guns to kills as many animals as possible. As anyone vaguely familiar with so called "blood sports"[509] will know, the opposite is true: the goal is to dispatch prey as swiftly and as painlessly as possible. A hunter that takes a pot shot at an animal, with high chance of wounding it without killing it, is generally frowned upon. A fisherman who enjoys torturing a fish or a slaughterman that abuses the animal at his mercy are universally considered to be cruel at best and criminal, bordering on psychopathic, at worse.

Therefore, once the distinction between the right way and the wrong way to do things is made clear, there should be no objection to those who take matters into their own hands. The only objection can be one of taste and aesthetics. I dare say, at the risk of being martyred by the guardians of political correctness, that many women would never want to engage in any kind of animal killing but do not disapprove of it, which is a perfectly coherent position. They may be extremely keen on having pheasant or venison on their plate but would never wish to shoot animal and find the very idea of gutting and butchering a carcass repulsive. Hunting, fishing, slaughter, butchery etc... are undoubtedly more attractive to the males of our species and less agreeable to the more delicate tastes of the ladies of the world. There are of course men who would never wish to hunt and women who do hunt, especially in

[509] Hunting and fishing, are not sports, strictly speaking, but traditional activities with a sporting element. The reference to "blood" is derogatory and misleading, as the shedding of blood is not the goal of such activities, but just an inevitable part of them, if successful. To call deer stalking a "blood sport" makes as much sense as calling football and rugby "mud sports". You will often play on turf and get muddy when you play these sports, but that's not their end goal.

cultures where it is encouraged, but there can be no serious doubt about the broad gender divide. Be that as it may, if you do consume meat and fish, you may want to try and procure it yourself once or twice. It may serve as an interesting experience and spiritual exercise or even as the beginning of a new activity. If you cannot stomach the prospect of ever taking a life, that is perfectly legitimate, but remember, every time you take a morsel of steak or fish, that it was once living and breathing and someone, somewhere, did the dirty work for your sake and, usually, for your money.

TO SUM UP: have a go at catching a fish or shooting a woodpigeon, or something like that. Visit an ethical, small slaughterhouse or take a butchery course. If none of this is for you, be supportive, or at least tolerant, of others who are happy to get blood on their hands.

No Waste

It is not worth repeating what was already make clear and discussed in Chapter 3[510] but it suffices to say that food most food waste is unnecessary, unconscionable and avoidable. Making a "no food waste" policy a cornerstone of your attitude towards food is non-negotiable. With better planning, purchasing and cookery, decreased food waste is very attainable.

TO SUM UP: do not waste food.

[510] See "The unbearable problem of waste".

Chapter 10

WHAT NOT TO EAT - A TO Z

Let us begin with the negatives: what not to eat. We start with the negatives because the beginning of a healthy and wholesome diet, in contemporary Britain, really begins with a rejection and boycott of what is most commonly eaten. By avoiding or completely abstaining from a lot of conventional foods, it will be far harder to go wrong. You will note that it's not food *types* (e.g., dairy, red meat, legumes etc.) or *nutrients* (e.g., saturated fats, proteins, vitamin C etc.) that feature on the list of what not to eat, but *specific foods and their production methods*. Needless to say, as in every other aspect of life, progress is far more realistic than perfection. We will inevitably stray from our best laid plans and life is full of compromises: actively avoid, rather than swear off, all the below!

A brief disclaimer: my original intention was to present specific examples of brands and products to avoid, in great detail, listing their ingredients and challenging their specific claims. Unfortunately, given the less than complementary comments that would have been made, and a copyright and libel legal system that seems to be largely designed to defend corporate interests over and above anything else, I have had to desist from going into great detail. All I can safely say, for example, is that my readers ought to abstain from drinking Pepsi or Fanta and eating Monster Much or Percy Pigs, which are, in my opinion, very poor products but I cannot extensively reproduce the claims their manufacturers make on their websites and call them out for being false. I can recommend that you do not buy the basic, barn raised chicken from Tesco, Sainsbury's, or Waitrose but I cannot necessarily quote, even if I give full references, what these retailers say about these chickens on their websites. I can also say that I personally find Nutella's sustainability claims ludicrous and McDonald's targeting of children reprehensible but will not get involved in anything more quantitative.[511] Lastly, any references to products and ingredients provided in this chapter are presented as they are at the time of writing; there may be some changes by the time you read this chapter.

So, here they are, in alphabetical order:[512]

Added Nutrients

A simple start: do not eat food with added nutrients. There is no positive reason why a food item would need to have nutrients added to it. The only food items that advertise the addition of nutrients on their packaging, or the prevalence of specific nutrients, tend to be ultra-processed foods of low quality that, in reality, are not redeemed by the addition of artificial nutrients. A particularly relevant example are cereal based foods that have been denuded of any nutritive quality through processing and are "fortified" with added nutrients and marketed as health foods.

As a rule, do not eat foods that are labelled with:

- Added "protein".
- Added vitamins.
- Added minerals.
- Added fibre.

You should similarly stay away from products that advertise nutrient *reduction*, not just addition. If a product is "fat reduced" or "less sugar" and so on, that is again a sign of low quality. What we need, as should be clear by now, are whole foods that naturally contain nutrients in their proper context.

TO SUM UP: do not eat food with added or reduced nutrients.

All You Can Eat

As a rule of thumb, any place that allows you to eat unlimited amounts of food for a fixed price cannot be offering you anything good. This is for the simple reason that the only way unlimited buffets and all-you-can-eat deals can be commercially viable is by focusing on sourcing great quantities of low-quality ingredients. In fact, I would go further: be suspicious

[511] In the famous McLibel trial, the reason why the defendants were sued by McDonald's for libel was because they made substantive and specific claims about McDonald's operations, which had to be proven in court in order not to be found guilty of libel. I will not tread in those waters.

[512] The themes and genres are so varied and interconnected, that I opted for a neutral alphabetical.

of any restaurant that offers enormous portions. Between the greasy all-you-can-eat venues on one end of the spectrum and the minimalistic portions of some of the more highfalutin establishments, there is a reasonable, wholesome alternative: normal quantities of high quality, unpretentious food.

TO SUM UP: do not frequent buffets and all-you-can-eat joints. Do not enter eating competitions. Be suspicious of massive portions.

BBQ*[513]

Barbecue is, by and large, a crowd pleaser. I will not dwell into the specific national, regional, and cultural differences and similarities worldwide. In Italy, we refer to what Anglophones call barbecue as *brace*, which literally means *embers*, given that it is not flames that cook meat but the white embers of a fire. In my ancestral land of Sardinia, it is traditional to bury whole lambs or piglets in soil, covered with hot embers, dressed with herbs like myrtle, to cook for hours. Or they are slowly cooked on a spit in all sorts of ways, lubricated with hot melted fat. Be that as it may, the cookery of meat with fire worldwide is as old as cookery itself and there are not many more universally enjoyable forms of communal eating. There is also nothing inherently wrong or unhealthy about it. But there are three potential perils that come with the pleasures of barbecue: the low quality of the meat, the low quality of the combustible fuel and the high degree of carbonisation.

Therefore, first and foremost, strictly avoid BBQ made with conventional, factory farmed meats: that's a golden rule for all meat consumption irrespective of cookery method. Secondly, avoid barbecues unless made by a real pit master or by someone who uses good wood and knows what he is doing. It should be no surprise that good wood is important. In Puglia, the traditional wood ovens used to roast all sorts of meat, *fornelli*, are fuelled with olive wood from the vast olive groves that dominate the region. Almond tree wood is also traditionally used. Similar practices abound around the world. In Texas, old BBQ hands have assured me that mesquite wood is arguably the best fuel for the pit.[514]

When it comes to charcoal, it should be untreated, the source of wood stated clearly and not come in the form of briquettes, which is always a sign of low quality. This is not to say that a domestic barbecue fuelled by little more than B&Q charcoal is unacceptable, but it is

[513] For many of the headings here, those marked with an asterisk (*), I will not be referring to ALL food items in the given category - not ALL BBQ or breakfast cereals or chocolate are bad of course, but most of them are. I will clarify which good options are available within each category when we get to the What to Eat section. The headings with no asterisk, on the other hand, are always to be avoided: there are no good crisps or all-you-can-eat deals.

[514] I can testify that mesquite, a wood that grows well in arid regions, produces excellent wood for barbecue and occasionally use it myself, mixed with hickory, when cooking beef on my small but efficient barbecue.

certainly inferior. At the very least, invest in the best possible fuel. Do not use fire starters, unless you want your meat to taste like it has been dipped in a barrel of gasoline. Lastly, we have all heard that blackened meat is inherently unhealthy. There is some debate around the extent to which it is harmful[515] but common sense suggests that eating carbonised meat cannot be a great idea. Furthermore, it is simply bad cookery. If your ribs and sausages are coming out looking like lumps of coal, you are not cooking them properly.

TO SUM UP: do not eat low quality barbecue. Three things matter: meat quality, fuel quality and not carbonising everything.

Biscuits, Cakes & Desserts*

I must again point your attention to the asterisk next to the heading again. It's not ALL biscuits, cakes and desserts that are the problem, just the majority of what it marketed and sold across our food retailers, unfortunately. I will make myself wildly unpopular and "attack" some of the most popular treats across the land: Oreos, Chocolate Hob Nobs, Chocolate Digestives, Jaffa Cakes, Custard Creams, Ginger Nuts, Bourbons, Cadbury cakes, Mr Kipling cakes, all the various Nestle, Bonne Maman and Muller desserts etc... not to mention supermarket/own-brand custards, puddings, sundaes, chocolate pots, logs, mousses, biscuits, cakes etc...

The average biscuit, cake and dessert is largely made up of one combination or other of the typical building blocks of industrial ultra-processed foods: white flour, glucose-fructose syrup, white sugar, palm oil, soya derivatives, rapeseed oil, cocoa derivatives, gelatine, vegetable fats, emulsifiers, starches, sweeteners, flavourings, fillers, and stabilisers. The ingredient lists will be very long. Many will contain ingredients of animal origin: highly processed derivatives of eggs, milk, and dairy,[516] which are undoubtedly from factory farm operations. Doughnuts, another popular dessert, share the same basic characteristics and typology of ingredient as all the other sweet foods, but have the added disadvantage of being deep fried, rather than baked, and are often full of colourings. There is no doubt that food that is fried at high temperature in industrial vegetable oil, often containing trans fats, is fundamentally unhealthy and some of the least desirable food, right at the bottom of the list.

TO SUM UP: do not buy any popular biscuits, cakes, desserts, and doughnuts.

[515] See T. Spector, 2020, Spoon-Fed, pages 101-102.

[516] None of which you would find in a normal kitchen: would you use "egg powder" or "dried whey" to bake at home?

Bread*

In many parts of the world, and certainly across Europe, bread has always been a mainstay of the diet. It is part of our culture and rituals: we have been asking Our Father for our daily bread for countless generations and, much like rice in the Far East, bread is a symbolic representation of food per se. The bread of the masses tended to be dark in colour and made from a variety of relatively unrefined grains, not necessarily all wheat, and its quality was variable. However, at its best, traditional wood oven baked bread has always been and remains some of the most valuable foods one can eat. Finely ground white flour, as we saw earlier, became widespread with industrial milling and white bread became the norm rather than the exception. White flour is made through the removal of the germ and bran, which are the most nutritious parts of the wheat grain, and then fortified with artificial vitamins and minerals. Most importantly, changes to bread production methods, such as the use of artificial yeast and electric ovens, and the gradual disappearance of bakeries and trained bakers, led to a complete transformation of bread. Industrial white bread is now both cheap and ubiquitous. Sadly, the long-term consequence has been that most bread is now a nutritionally deficient, tasteless imitation of actual bread.

The main problem with most supermarket breads (think Hovis, Warburtons, Kingsmill, for example) is a combination or other of the following features:

- Being made with conventional wheat from chemically dependent agriculture. Conventional wheat bread production is heavily reliant upon the use of glyphosate, pesticides etc… It is important to note that whenever you read on any ingredients label, "wheat flour" this always refer to conventional, industrial wheat: hybrid varieties grown with agrochemicals. If it were organic wheat, a local heritage variety or anything like that, *it would say so on the label*.
- Made with hybrid wheat varieties, which are less nutritious and have higher gluten content.
- Usually made with highly refined white flour.
- Fortified with artificial nutrients.
- Made with artificial yeast.
- Contains several fillers and added ingredients, such as soya flour, vegetable oils and sugar. Contains emulsifiers and preservatives.
- Baked in factory ovens, instead of wood ovens.
- Not made by skilled bakers, but by machines and machine operators.

The news that eating copious amounts of conventional white flour is not a great idea has gradually seeped into common knowledge, to a degree. The response of the food industry has been to promote "brown bread" or "wholemeal bread" as the healthier option. The problem with this approach is that, following textbook nutritionist tenets, it does not address the main problem: the low quality of the ingredients and the poor production methods. White bread and "medium" brown bread or wholemeal bread are all made with the same conventional, glyphosate dependant wheat. Furthermore, these breads still contain all the same fillers (soya flour, rapeseed oil etc...) and are baked using the same methods and techniques. Overall: are these products better than white bread? Yes, but only very marginally: the differences are insignificant. They have some natural wheat fibre but, apart from that, have all the same problems as white bread. A similar problem is found in "wheatgerm" products: the nutritious part of the grain is incorporated back into the bread, without any improvements to the quality of the ingredients nor of the production method. We still have the same fillers, such as soya flour, and false improvements, like the addition of barley fibre. The bog-standard supermarket loaf of bread is an ultra-processed low-quality product, irrespective of whether it is white, brown, wholemeal, wheatgerm or whichever other variation.

TO SUM UP: do not buy and eat the average supermarket loaf of bread. It's not bread.

Breakfast Cereals*

Breakfast cereals are a well-entrenched component of our food culture, certainly for my generation. The idea that having a bowl of cereals for breakfast is normal is, nonetheless, relatively recent. It was men like John Harvey Kellogg (1852 - 1943) and his brother William Keith Kellogg (1860 - 1951) who pioneered the production and promotion of cereal flakes. Much like the popularisation of white bread, the production and marketing of cereal flakes was rendered possible by the new conditions created by the industrial revolution: the increased availability of cheap, refined grain, mechanisation, and large-scale industrial manufacturing. It is worth pointing out that the Kellogg brothers, especially John Harvey, held a number of beliefs about nutrition and lifestyle that most current consumers of breakfast cereals are unlikely to endorse, such as: vegetarianism, low protein diets, no masturbation, the use of enemas and electrotherapy. Be that as it may, the breakfast cereal gradually became a supermarket staple and has been heavily marketed to children and, indeed, to their mothers.[517]

[517] A lot of ready-made food, fast food and microwaveable food in the post War period was specifically marketed to women. The message was that these foods would liberate the modern woman from the domestic drudgery of previous generations.

Overall, breakfast cereals are bad news. Again, not because there is anything wrong with cereals per se, but because of their ingredients and the processing methods used at the manufacturing plant. The classic, original corn flakes, it must be said, taste pretty good. If corn flakes, with no added "reinforcements", were made with organic maize and a little organic cane sugar and salt, and nothing else, it would be a pretty decent food item to add to the larder for occasional use. The problem is that this is not the case for the bog-standard corn flakes and breakfast cereals. This is because they are, by and large, highly processed, low-quality cereals, grown with agrochemicals. Highly refined and nutritionally depleted, they are then reinforced with artificial vitamins and minerals, with the addition of white sugar and whatever other flavourings are required to distinguish one product from another.

Kellogg's Frosties, popular with children, are, in my opinion, very similar to plain cornflakes, with the addition of copious amounts of white sugar. According to their nutrition information label, they contain 37% sugar.[518] Overall, they are certainly worse than the plain cornflakes and not something to feed your children. They are not "Grrrreaat", in spite of what the tiger tells our children. Other brands, again marketed to children, are pretty awful and camouflage their awfulness in the usual insidious nutritionist jargon,[519] such as promoting their Vitamin D content or the fact that they contain "fat-reduced cocoa", as if cocoa fat were the problem or something to avoid. It is also remarkably unclear what % of the overall product is made up of cocoa in most industrial chocolate products: it is probably embarrassingly low, hence the lack of clarity.

The breakfast cereal industry in many ways mirrors the bread industry, in so far as they attempted to create seemingly healthier options. Again, the strategy is to re-engineer the product by inserting the missing fibrous parts of the cereals. This is still a product made with low quality cereals, irrespective of the bran content, sugar and the usual range of artificial vitamins and minerals. The various brands of whole wheat breakfast cereals and bran flakes products have all the same basic characteristics of the other low fibre products. Are these, in my opinion, better than Frosties and Coco Pops? Yes, they are, marginally, in the same way that wholemeal bread is generally better than white bread. But are these healthy, wholesome, high-quality products? No. Do not be fooled by the high fibre narrative and allusions to regular bowel movements.

TO SUM UP: do not buy conventional breakfast cereals of any kind. It's not the breakfast of champions.

[518] https://www.kelloggs.co.uk/en_GB/products/frosties.html

[519] Unlike the fuzzy animal characters and colourful boxes, which are aimed at children, the nutrition claims are marketing devices aimed at their clueless parents.

Candy*

I know of parents who deny their children candy, or turn them into guilt-laden occasional treats, presumed to be inherently bad. This is based on a sad and unnecessary misconception, for reasons that should by now be clear. Nonetheless, it is certainly true that most candy, sweets, and "treats" are woefully under par. They are also, if we add gustatory and aesthetic considerations to the equation, not very nice sweets to eat to begin with. There are far nicer, and far healthier, candy options available.

Be that as it may, the problem with conventional candy is generally a combination of:

- Cheap refined conventional white sugar, sugar derivatives and other sweeteners.
- Colours, additives, artificial flavours.
- Nasty ingredients that are added to create certain textures, like gelatine or palm oil.

Sadly, yet again, the nation's favourites (Skittles, Fruit-tella, Fruit/Wine Gums, Tic Tac, Haribo Sweets, Chupa Chups, Percy Pigs, Jello Babies etc...) should not, in my opinion, be given to your children, nor indeed to anyone else you know.

TO SUM UP: do not buy conventional candy. Do not deny your children sweets or sugar and attach no guilt to it. But make sure you always focus on quality and context.

Chocolate*

The fundamental problem with chocolate is that, for the most part, it is not strictly speaking chocolate if, by chocolate, we are referring to a product primarily composed of cocoa beans, the wonderful gifts of the cacao plant. It may sound like a facetious and patronising thing to say. But, then again, the facts speak for themselves. That's not to say that only dark chocolate, which is indeed mostly made from cocoa, is the only genuine chocolate. Even milk chocolate and white chocolate can lay claim to being chocolate products, of course, provided that the cocoa component is the single most important ingredient, accompanied by no more than two or three basic ingredients, usually sugar and milk. As chocolate production embraced the philosophy of ultra-processing and industrial mass production, it gradually became a complex concoction of low-grade ingredients, often the same as those found in other ultra-processed junk food. The sugar and milk components, furthermore, tend to conform to the same ruling principles: cheap, of obscure origin, produced with no regard for the fields and animals from which they derive.

Most supermarket and high street chocolate products are therefore best avoided. Not because chocolate is "fattening" or is "high in calories", of course. Even plain milk chocolate fits the basic description of a cheap contemporary chocolate, high in low grade sugar and milk derivatives. Most notably, it usually contains vegetable oils, including palm oil, to supplement the more valuable cocoa butter. As products get more complex and undergo more processing, with, say, soft or biscuit fillings, there is ever more room for things to go wrong.

When you read the ingredients labels of chocolate products, you need to look out for:

- Low cocoa contents
- Sugar and sugar derivatives
- Palm oil and other vegetable fats
- Milk and egg derivatives
- Emulsifiers
- Flavourings
- E numbers

It is worth repeating that, as a rule, long lists of ingredients, most of which cannot possibly be found in your kitchen, is an indication of very low quality. This rules out, in my opinion, all the chocolate that are prominent in both supermarkets and corner shops: Cadbury,[520] Twix, Mars Bars, Smarties, Toblerone, Snickers, Kit Kat, Maltesers, Galaxy, Bounty, Aero etc...

Close scrutiny of these products and their ingredients paints a grim picture, and no amount of marketing should derail us from their homogeneous low quality. Mars, for example, truly excels itself in its saccharine attempts to pass itself off as a producer of "sustainable" (whatever that even means anymore), healthy and quality foods, whilst of course pursuing the now mandatory commitment to the vacuous and unscientific utopia of Net Zero. Did you know that the Mars Bar is now "carbon neutral"?[521]

A commitment to "the science"[522] permeates the food industry and nutritionist circles, after all. Some of Mars' common taglines, which are littered across their marketing material, have what I would call a "techno-optimistic" feel about them:

Better Food Today. A Better World Tomorrow.[523]

[520] I appreciate that is an almost blasphemous thing to say in England, but the reality is that the broad range of Cadbury chocolates is neither good nor desirable.

[521] https://gbr.mars.com/marslovesearth

[522] Look out for sentences and statements that start with "the science": they are usually appeals to authority used by those under the spell of scientism.

[523] https://www.mars.com/en-gb/our-brands

Better Lives Through Nutrition.[524]

The last slogan is an eery and appropriate reminder of DuPont's "Better Living Through Chemistry" slogan, first adopted in 1935.[525] DuPont was a major chemical manufacturer, which merged with Dow Chemical in 2017 and has been responsible, amongst other things, for the manufacture of all sorts of plastics,[526] of chlorofluorocarbons (now mostly banned given the fact that they are responsible for the depletion of the ozone layer) and, during the time of its optimistic slogan, the company was a major contributor to the Manhattan Project, which led to the atomic bombing of Japan and ushered in the age of nuclear war. Dow Chemical, on the other hand, as we already saw, has a truly toxic and bellicose track record and has been a major producer of the full destructive arsenal of industrial agriculture: pesticides, herbicides, GM seeds and so on. These are hardly the sort of institutions you would want to entrust with your food.

I do not wish to pick on Mars and in order to demonstrate that, at least on this occasion, I am not an Italian chauvinist, I would also not recommend some of the most popular chocolate products that a notable Italian company, Ferrero, has been spreading and marketing around the world: Kinder Surprise, Ferrero Rocher and Nutella. The Ferrero company is from the Piemonte region in the Northwest of Italy, home to some of the best chocolate makers in the world, comfortably as good as the very best Swiss, French, or Belgian counterparts. *Gianduja*, a unique chocolate preparation containing hazelnuts, has been produced in Piemonte for over two centuries and chocolate makers still make *gianduiotti*, wonderful and unique chocolates Italians of the past four generations will be familiar with. They are hard to match.

The Ferrero company, founded by Pietro Ferrero in 1946, left its artisanal roots behind many decades ago and gradually grew into an enormous global company. As with many post-War industries, its initial goal was to turn a luxury product into something that could be more affordable and accessible. This is not dissimilar to the fast-food industry's desire, at its very beginnings, to produce cheap restaurant food that the average working Joe could afford. In and of itself, this cannot be reproached, in fact, quite the opposite. The problem is that the strategy and *modus operandi* of Ferrero, as it expanded operations worldwide, is based on the same principle that, as we have already seen, characterises most food manufacturing:

[524] https://esp.mars.com/en/made-by-mars

[525] https://en.wikipedia.org/wiki/Better_Living_Through_Chemistry

[526] Not that we can superficially condemn plastics. Plastic is a very useful material, and we are all dependent on it. My point is that these are chemical companies, first and foremost, which have specialised in producing a broad range of toxic and environmentally problematic products: consequently, their contributions to food and agriculture have been negative.

quantity over quality. Nutella is mostly made up of sugar, palm oil and, of course, "fat reduced cocoa"[527] and is, in my opinion, a low-quality product which I would not recommend. Ferrero is now the second biggest chocolate producer and confectionery company in the world and the world's largest consumer of hazelnuts[528] and will operate under the same principles of any major industrial food manufacturer. Needless to say, its website dedicates many pages and words to "sustainability", with well-crafted and glossy content about the supposed quality of the ingredients and Earth friendly policies of the company.[529] No amount of marketing babble about sustainability, "climate action" and animal welfare, which all the major companies feel obliged to incorporate in their messaging, can obfuscate the true nature of their operations and the low quality of their products, if only we are willing to look beyond the headlines.

TO SUM UP: avoid conventional chocolate, avoid all the popular brands.

Crisps

Britain is a nation of crisp eaters. Superseded only by the United States, the British lead the way in per capita crisp consumption, with billions of crisp packets consumed each year, with an average of 2-3 packets per person each week.[530] It is not a coincidence that the nations which industrialised their food production earlier and more radically than any others should also hold such an unwelcome record. After all, the potato crisp is the epitome of ultra-processed food: cheap, uniform, unhealthy, full of additives and impossible to reproduce in the kitchen. It is also ideally suited to palates used to artificial flavours and inferior foods.

After all, the flavours contained in crisps are gustatory delusions of the lowest order: there is no real cheese nor onions in "cheese and onions" crisps, but only poor derivatives and imitations of such ingredients with the addition of "flavourings". It is highly unlikely that any adult exposed to flavoured crisps for the first time would find them palatable, apart from the classic "ready salted". I still recall almost retching the first time I had the misfortune of putting flavoured crisps in my mouth as a teenager. It takes childhood habituation to find the harsh, synthetic pseudo-flavours of most crisps attractive: crisps are symptomatic of a base gastronomic culture. Be that as it may, what is certainly true is that crisps should be in the list of foods to completely avoid and never have in the larder. They certainly have no place in your children's lunch at school.

[527] See ingredients list: https://www.nutella.com/uk/en/products/nutella

[528] https://www.bbc.co.uk/news/magazine-27438001

[529] See: https://www.ferrero.com/int/en/

[530] https://onepoundcrisps.com/30-facts-about-crisps-that-will-blow-your-mind/

Let us start with the best-case scenario: the plain old ready salted crisp. Of all the crisp products, this is the least undesirable, for the simple reason that it does not involve the host of ingredients and processes which the flavoured counterparts require. It is also the only crisp that does not have a horrid synthetic taste, and which is highly palatable. So, what's wrong with it? Its fundamental components (conventional potatoes and vegetable oils) are not good. As is always the case with industrial processed foods, which ultimately rely on the processing of a few monoculture crops, these are never going to be high quality raw ingredients to begin with. Furthermore, frying is a cooking method that lends itself to unhealthy preparations. It involves high temperatures and volatile fats. The quality of the oil is crucial in determining the healthiness of the final product, as well as the number of times in which the same oil is used. Needless to say, on both counts, as the crisps fry in gigantic vats of oil, the crisps on the supermarket aisles and corner shops leave much to be desired.

As we move from ready salted crisps to flavoured crisps, things get worse, as more and more additives get added to the mix to create the ghastly snacks, featuring things like flavour enhancers (monosodium glutamate, disodium 5'Ribonucleotide), obscure flavourings, E numbers, industrial salt, colours, sugars, soya derivatives, milk derivatives and so on. The artificiality and nastiness of flavoured crisps is highlighted by considering the fact that products that are marketed as having meat or seafood flavours are suitable for vegetarians. Thanks to our nemesis monosodium glutamate and other laboratory concoctions, these crisps supposedly conjure a hint of "steak" or "chicken". Similarly, the popular but repulsive "prawn cocktail" crisps are also suitable for vegetarians.

TO SUM UP: do not eat any crisps. Place them in the top 5 foods to avoid list.

Dressings & Sauces*

Sauces and dressings can make food more interesting and complete. As with all asterisked items here, there is nothing wrong with enriching food with all sorts of additional condiments that add flavour, modify texture, and increase nutritional value. Sadly, most people don't bother making their own salad dressing or mayonnaise, which are easy to make and taste infinitely better, and this is where the problem lies. The supermarket aisles provide less than healthy alternatives to the homespun originals. There are factory made dressings and sauces available on the market which are perfectly healthy and well made, of course, but as ever, we should be concerned about the mainstream market rather than the niche products.

Store bought mayonnaise, for example, is an all-round poor product that contains very little egg and what egg it contains is mostly barn raised or free range, which is not that much different or better. But this is not the only problem with the popular mayonnaise brands and supermarket ranges. The main problem is that it is mostly made with one of our "to be avoided products": rapeseed oil.[531] That alone disqualifies it from being an ingredient you would want in your fridge. Vegan mayonnaise is even worse, potentially, because whilst lacking the egg element it tends to have more additives, such as starches, sugar, and synthetic preservatives. Similar issues to those we find in the various regular and vegan mayos are found in salad creams and salad dressings and vinaigrettes, which are usually full of sugar as well.[532]

The popular sweet sauces, such Ketchup, HP Brown Sauce, and Worcester Sauce, are marginally better than mayos and salad creams, given the lack of eggs, vegetable oils and many of the additives added to mayos and salad creams, but they are nonetheless very sugary sauces that are also best avoided.

TO SUM UP: avoid ready-made dressings and sauces and try to make your own.

Drink*

Alcoholic drinks have been part and parcel of many cultures for millennia. The natives of Europe, in particular, have been committed to regular, daily, and communal drinking to such a degree that it is hard to imagine our world without it. It is worth noting that the root of the human love affair with alcohol is fundamentally agricultural: with few exceptions, hunter gatherers do not traditionally produce and consume alcoholic beverages. Alcohol is the natural result of fermentation, which can occur without any prompting to sweet fruit that is overripe. The main reason why farming people across Eurasia took to alcohol, in a nutshell, is that it was a way to preserve the abundant seasonal harvests of domesticated plants, including fruit. There are only so many grapes and apples we can eat fresh and alcoholic beverage is, by definition, a preserved, extremely long-lasting product.

Turning crops into alcoholic beverages is a traditional way to make use of crop surpluses: grains and potatoes can be stored or fed to animals but can also be turned into drink. The fermentation of grains and fruits was also a way to produce a sanitised, clean drink: alcohol, as we know, is a natural germicide. Needless to say, alcohol's effect on the mind has generally been considered most desirable too. This is not the place to discuss the respective benefits and disadvantages of inebriation, nor the ravages of alcoholism, but there is no

[531] Interestingly, in the USA, the ultra-processed food sector tends to use soyabean oil instead of rapeseed oil: these two oils generally play the same role of unhealthy building block on the two sides of the Atlantic.

[532] Would you use white sugar as an ingredient for a homemade salad dressing?

question that alcohol, in its proper context, can add to life, rather than detract from it.[533] Alcohol is, in any case, here to stay.

Most importantly, alcohol is also food. Alcoholic drinks are very high in energy. In the colder regions, the immediate energy and soothing effect of drink has always been a welcome consolation.[534] Furthermore, especially in the warmer regions, wine and other beverages have always been crucial components of meals, both simple and refined, and natural accompaniments to specific dishes, as well as being important cooking ingredients.[535] What this means is that the general principles that apply to non-alcoholic drinks and to all other foods, apply to wine, beer, spirits and so on. In other words, a drink is only as good as the ingredients and processes employed to manufacture it.

The most problematic aspect of alcoholic beverages is not alcohol itself which, in moderate amounts, is not necessarily unhealthy. The trouble is that the main crops used to manufacture bog standard beer, wine and all other alcoholic drinks are subjected to the standard regime of agrochemical treatment that most food crops are subjected to and manufactured with several dubious additives which are not listed on the label. As we saw earlier, even expensive bottles of Champagne and Prosecco are relatively toxic and unhealthy.

TO SUM UP: cut back on conventional alcoholic drinks. Try to drink less, but higher quality drinks.

*Eggs**

The egg[536] is a basic and wonderful whole food that plays a crucial role in both nutrition and cuisine, given its versatility and transformative powers. It's a great example of how the same food item can swing from desirable to undesirable and from healthy to unhealthy depending on its origin. We must take the usual precaution: if no information is provided by the packaging and retailer of your eggs, presume that the eggs are factory farmed and do not buy them. They will be very cheap, which is a sad reflection of the horrible conditions in which they are laid. Some of these eggs will be sold with some labels and certifications. As we have

[533] Alcohol can be used OR abused; it is not an inherently abusive substance.

[534] Scientists will tell you that alcohol makes the body lose heat rather than gain it. This may be physiologically true but is amply compensated by the experience of the drinker, who undoubtedly feels warmer. It is no accident, nor the result of ignorance, that strong alcohol is the drink of choice in so many mountainous and cold regions.

[535] Even a teetotal like myself is stocked with wine and liquors: I would not wish to cook without it.

[536] As wonderful as duck, quail and goose eggs are, I will presume we are dealing with the eggs produced by hens here, which make up most of the egg market.

already seen, the Red Tractor label is not indicative of quality, and neither is the British Lion Quality logo.[537]

However, eggs do have an advantage over many other products, in terms of transparency, because they are all stamped.[538] There are 4 basic grades for eggs, corresponding to the first number stamped on them: 0 for organic, 1 for free range, 2 for barn raised, 3 for caged.

The last two are strictly to be avoided. Number 3 eggs are normally referred to as "Class A eggs from caged hens" and number 2 eggs as "Class A barn eggs". The above eggs are easy to avoid. However, most eggs in the UK now are actually category 1: free range. There is a real problem with free range, which is that whilst it allows consumers to feel as if they are purchasing a high welfare product, free range is actually based on a very intensive method of egg production which is often not far off barn raised egg production standards.[539] It has lower stocking densities[540] than barn or caged systems, and some (rather) limited access to the outdoors.[541] But it has the same feed and medication standards, as well as the routine practice of debeaking.[542]

As ever, there are exceptions, and there will be small free-range producers that exceed the minimum standards and give their birds a very good life. But none of this applies to standard free-range eggs from supermarkets.

There is an interesting twist to the tale. During several months over 2022/23 the UK government imposed what could be correctly referred to as another "lockdown", only not for humans this time but for poultry, as a measure against the spread of avian flu.[543] As a consequence, free range and organic eggs had to be temporarily relabelled, as the birds had no access to the outdoors. This was a typically misguided policy, reminiscent of the absurd policies used to deal with mad cow disease, bovine TB and foot and mouth disease. The fundamental cause for the outbreak and spread of avian flu, or indeed any other

[537] All the British Lion logo indicates is that the hens producing the eggs have been vaccinated against salmonella. Over 90% of British eggs are produced under this scheme: https://www.egginfo.co.uk/british-lion-eggs

[538] Check the shells of the eggs in your kitchen!

[539] Please refer to Chapter 2 to our discussion of Red Tractor approved barn raised broiler chicken. Similar standards apply to barn raised laying hens.

[540] Set to a maximum of 16,000, still a huge number:

https://www.egginfo.co.uk/egg-facts-and-figures/production/free-range-egg

[541] A mere pop-hole for every 600 birds.

[542] The horrible practice of beak trimming involves the partial removal of the beak of young hens, in order to prevent the hens from pecking, attacking, and injuring one another. Of course, as ever, industrial systems treat the symptom rather than the cause of the problematic behaviour (overcrowding, boredom, and stress).

[543] It was a draconian and absurd lockdown: it was even impossible for private citizens with a few backyard hens to purchase new hens, which were not allowed to be moved from place to place. My friend Ian, in deepest darkest Devon, had a single hen left and could not legally purchase a hen or two to add to his garden "flock".

infectious epidemic, is overcrowding, unsanitary conditions, compromised immune systems, poor nutrition and the routine use of antibiotics and other pharmaceuticals: in other words, the standard conditions of poultry farming. Epidemic diseases in livestock are an inevitable reality, as indeed they are for humans, but we have created the ideal conditions for diseases to develop and spread.

The same discourse applies for swine flu and other domestic animal epidemics. Rather than eliminate the causes of disease, the industry reinforces them: more confinement, more crowding, more unsanitary conditions and, most importantly, very weak immune systems and unhealthy birds. In fact, DEFRA, the World Health Organisation, and the various industry bodies involved in intensive agriculture tend to shift the blame on free ranging birds and on wild birds for the spread of avian flu. Hence the absurd avian lockdowns. A more sensible long-term approach would be to finally "free" laying hens from industrial systems and allowing them to live a natural, healthy lifestyle away from the cages and crowded Red Tractor approved barns. No doubt avian flu would inevitably take down some birds in the short term, but healthier flocks would gradually build immunity and resilience, and the disease would eventually become manageable or die down.

Will Harris of White Oak Pastures, in his excellent book, recalls how, when one of his birds tested positive for avian flu, the vet found that, whilst the bird did test positive for avian influenza, it was not for the high pathogenic strain and, most interestingly, the *"bloodwork showed antigens that seem to be antibodies against the high pathogenic strain of avian influenza, which is highly unusual"*.[544] Harris, quite rightly, speculated that the bird might have picked up the virus from a wild bird, like a duck, but, *"because she had been exposed to millions of microbes her all life and had a strong immune system, she got the illness, got over it, and developed the antibodies to protect her for the rest of her life"*.[545] In other words the best way to manage avian influenza, and indeed any other livestock disease is *"to put livestock in the environment they were supposed to be in"*.[546] It would also be a good idea to breed hardier, heritage hen breeds that are far more resilient than the standard industrial layers, and to recover biodiversity in domestic poultry.

TO SUM UP: do not eat factory farmed eggs or products containing factory farmed eggs. Factory farming should be abolished, period. Free range eggs are not as "free" as they seem and it's always worth investing in organic eggs and in farms that you know a lot about.

[544] W. Harris, 2023, A Bold Return to Giving a Damn, page 133.

[545] Ibidem

[546] Ibidem

"Fast Food"

As previously discussed, there is nothing wrong, in principle, with street food, or fast food, or food that is cheap and simple. Give me a really well-made Cornish pasty, sausage roll, gelato, or *pizza al taglio* and I will be grateful for these pleasant foods. This is not what I mean by "fast food". I am mostly referring to "fast food" understood as the mass produced ultra-processed food originating from the major restaurant chains that sprang up in post-War America[547] and spread around the world since. I mean fast food as described by Eric Schlosser in his classic book, *Fast Food Nation* (2001). The food produced by the mainstream fast-food sector is fundamentally unhealthy and bad for you, of inferior quality and inherently linked to systems of food production that are damaging to farm workers, to the environment, to animals and to the oceans.

There are many people who, whilst aware of these problems, still feed this food to their brainwashed children[548] "as a treat". This is a shame and, had they given their children a strict but joyful food education and exposed them to a high quality and diverse range of whole foods from birth, and given them genuine gastronomic experiences, they might not find themselves in a situation where their children consider a Happy Meal to be the apotheosis of eating. Be that as it may, this way of eating is bad at any age and avoiding it completely would be a great achievement.

I will not go into details about which fast food chain and which particular products to avoid, because fundamentally they are homogenously bad. Therefore, in my own opinion, you should not frequent:

- McDonald's
- Burger King
- Pizza Hut
- Dominos
- KFC
- Starbucks
- Subway
- Nando's
- Five Guys
- Wendy's

[547] Needless to say, not all fast food is American in origin, ownership, or manufacture, but the philosophy and methodology largely originate from the United States.

[548] This is no exaggeration nor facetiousness: billions of dollars are invested worldwide in marketing and advertising fast food to children, to ensure cradle to grave consumption.

- Taco Bell
- Papa John's Pizza
- Greggs
- Chicken Cottage
- Krispy Kreme
- Dunkin' Donuts
- Please add all the other fast-food giants to the list.

An important clarification to make here is that one should not presume that non-branded fast-food joints, such as the myriad kebab shops and Chinese take-aways around the UK are any better than the big names. In fact, quite the contrary. A big corporation like McDonald's will have a degree of traceability and consistency that no dodgy kebab shop can guarantee, not to mention relatively high standards of hygiene. Give me Chicken McNuggets over a sketchy Chinese or kebab any day.

TO SUM UP: do not eat "fast food" and, most importantly, do not feed it to your children.

Fish, Crustaceans & Shellfish*

Fish and other aquatic creatures, all things being equal, provide a very valuable source of whole foods, which we are ideally suited to eat and benefit from. No amount of vegan ideology can dispel the fact that these foods have always benefited the populations that relied upon their consumption and that they remain one of the cornerstones of the human diet. However, there are plenty of examples of foods to avoid in this category, for a mixture of health, conservation, and environmental reasons. There is no question that there are plenty of complex problems with both freshwater and sea fisheries, which lead to difficult and partially uninformed consumer choices. The below is a brief guideline on what to avoid.

Farmed Fish & Prawns

Not all fish farming is bad and there are examples of sustainable and desirable aquaculture, especially in small-scale freshwater operations. However, the mainstream aquaculture sector is a mirror image of livestock factory farming: inherently unsustainable, unnatural and in breach of basic ecological principles. Furthermore, unlike livestock, aquatic creatures are not domestic animals: these are wild animals that have been bred to be held in manageable containments. That is an immediate non-starter and insuperable problem for most fish farming. The best example must be that noble and wonderful fish: the salmon. The salmon is an extraordinary creature renowned for its mysterious and long migrations and need to live in both fresh and salt water. Furthermore, it is a predatory fish that feeds on other sea creatures. It should be rather obvious that it is impossible to truly domesticate a predatory and migrating fish: the very nature of the salmon is a non-starter for farming it and all attempts to do so are effectively forced. Consequently, even organically certified salmon is, effectively, a rather dubious enterprise. It is somewhat better than conventional salmon farms simply because organic salmon farms have to comply with standards requiring lower stocking densities, lower chemical use, and more sustainable sources of fish meal.[549] I would still not recommend it as a great fish choice.

Overall, salmon farming is a very wasteful system, as farmed salmon are generally fed with fishmeal, which is made with "forage fish", namely edible fish of little commercial value. Millions and millions of tonnes of wild fish, including perfectly desirable species like sardines, herrings, mackerel, and anchovies,[550] are caught each year to feed farmed salmon, with inefficient conversion rates. The other issue is that tightly confined salmon develop problems, such as sea lice infestations, that require chemical treatment. Salmon are routinely fed with drugs and even dyes to colour their flesh to the appealing colour you see on the supermarket and fishmonger shelves. Add to that the enormous amounts of concentrated salmon poo produced by each farm, and the spread of disease from farmed salmon to wild salmon, and we have an industry that has a devastating effect on the oceans. Most importantly, farmed salmon is an inherently unhealthy, stunted fish that is a pale imitation of its wild counterpart and is best avoided altogether. I will not go into the details, but similar problems apply to all other forms of mass aquaculture, whether it's farmed sea bass in Greece or farmed prawns from Vietnam.

As a rule: avoid all farmed salmon, sea bream, sea bass and prawns. See them as the aquatic equivalent of factory-farmed poultry and pigs.

When it comes to purchasing a lot of the seafood on the market, it is now safe to presume that, for certain popular species, unless the package or fishmonger's label specifically states "wild" or "caught in X", it will be a farmed product. In other words, farmed is the default position, especially for the following: salmon, sea bass, sea bream and prawns. At the fishmonger, when selecting whole fish, rather than a filleted packaged fish, or loose prawns, you can make a similar presumption. When a sea bass or sea bream is wild, it is usually clearly stated and promoted as such and will be more expensive. The good news is that there are plenty of wild fish species that are far cheaper than seabass and sea bream, which are always

[549] Some of the fish meal on the market is made with fish trimming and waste, which is obviously much better than using fish meal made with forage fish.

[550] A lot of the species caught for fish meal, like sand eel, currently have no commercial value as a table fish, albeit there is no reason why they couldn't be eaten as whitebait. In any case, their depletion has a damaging effect on all the predatory sea fish, including on many that we have an interest in, that feed on these small creatures.

going to be more expensive and should be eaten as very rare, extravagant treats. More on this in the "What to Eat" Section.

Precooked and Processed Seafood

The usual principle applies here: once you outsource basic cookery to an industrial manufacturer, a lot more can go wrong. Most fish fingers, fish cakes and the like involve processes and ingredients that are similar to those we find in other unhealthy processed foods: rapeseed or other industrial vegetable oils, flours, flavourings and, indeed, deep frying. Furthermore, the origin of the fish or crustaceans used in these products, which is usually farmed, tends to be even more obscure than in unprocessed fish products. Usually, it is simply unstated. Of the various options on the market, if health concerns were the main criteria behind our choice, cod fish fingers are arguably the better option, as at least the cod is wild-caught somewhere in the Atlantic. But why not get fresh cod and make something yourself?

Endangered/Vulnerable Fish

Wild seafood is a fundamentally valuable whole food and, if diet and health were the only considerations, we should not hesitate to include it in our diet on a very regular basis. However, as I have argued extensively throughout this book, we should not make diet and health the only criteria upon which we choose what to eat. The state of many fisheries is very concerning, and the stocks of most species have been severely depleted. Probably the most notable example is tuna,[551] a fish that is highly prized, very expensive and increasingly rare. Similar problems afflict marlin, grouper, swordfish, and sturgeon. Here in the UK, our great fishing ports of Grimsby and Lowestoft have shrunk to insignificance, with cod stocks collapsing decades ago and never truly recovering. Cod from British waters is now a relatively rare species. On the other hand, Icelandic cod is relatively abundant, and Iceland has been far more successful in managing its fisheries than we have.[552] Nonetheless, overall, Atlantic cod, from the American and Canadian east coast to the Barents Sea, has been severely depleted all round and is best avoided or eaten on special occasions.

The other problem with wild fish is that, due to the now ubiquitous pollution of seawater, even healthy fish can carry high levels of pollutants. Tuna is, again, a good example, and is known to contain relatively high levels of mercury. As a rule of thumb, the big, slow-growing

[551] There are several species of tuna: they are almost all depleted, especially blue fin tuna. Albacore and skipjack tuna are relatively less depleted.

[552] Iceland also had to defend its fisheries during its Cod Wars against Britain from the late 50s to the 70s. Britain had already depleted her cod fishery by then and wanted to gain access to Iceland's. By threatening to pull out from NATO, during the Cold War, Iceland managed to protect its fisheries and win the Cod Wars.

predatory game fish that feed on smaller fish tend to accumulate more pollutants. Smaller, fast-growing fish such as mackerel tend to accumulate less pollutants. This does not mean that we should think that the benefits of eating big fish like tuna are completely outweighed by the negatives, but that we should eat these fish in moderation and with caution.

My top ten list, in no particular order, of wild fish to avoid:

1. Cod (apart from Icelandic).
2. European hake.
3. Bluefin and bigeye tuna under all circumstances.[553] Any other tuna species (albacore, yellowfin, skipjack) that is not pole and line caught.
4. Halibut, turbot, and Dover sole.
5. Swordfish and marlin.
6. Sturgeon and caviar.
7. Skate and rays.
8. Grouper and snapper.
9. Trawled prawns and langoustines.
10. Dredged scallops.

You will find other writers coming up with similar or slightly different suggestions; by all means, expand your research. The more you research this complex subject, the better.

The Products of Destructive Fishing

It is not only certain species that we should avoid, but also certain fishing methods. This only makes things more complicated as the two do not always neatly overlap. There are species that are not particularly scarce or endangered, such as scallops, which are often dredged, which damages the seabed. There are also species which are not as common as they used to be, such as wild sea bass, which can be pole and line caught, which tends to be the least damaging fishing method. In many cases, unfortunately, the species are severely depleted AND caught with destructive methods, as the latter is the primary cause for the former.

[553] The bluefin is making a comeback in British waters over the last few years. The South West Handline Fishermen's Association (https://www.linecaught.org.uk/) have been given a permission in 2023 to establish a small-scale sustainable hook and line fishery. This is positive news, but it is early days and there is no real market or access to blue fin tuna that we can be comfortable about just yet. One thing we can say for sure is the following: if the bluefin makes a great comeback, it should only ever be caught with pole and line/hook and line methods, under tight seasons and controls. Similarly, if the bluefin makes a major comeback in the Mediterranean, the traditional *mattanza* of Sicily and Sardinia (and indeed the traditional *almadraba* of Spain) could flourish. This was a very bloody but selective and sustainable ancient fishing method that has almost disappeared due to the collapse in bluefin tuna fishing stocks, caused by the destructive methods of industrial fishing.

Examples abound, such as: flatfish and cod caught by bottom/beam trawlers and tuna caught by massive fleets of purse-seiners, pair trawlers and drift nets.

The fundamental problem with the fishing industry is remarkably similar to the fundamental problem with industrial agriculture: the application of large-scale industrial technology and ideology to ecosystems is inherently destructive. From the post-war period onwards, the expansion of fishing fleets and the development of new technologies have had the same sort of dramatic and accelerating negative impact on the seas that monster tractors, factory farms and agrochemicals have had on land. Fishing boats often resemble those of the military, and indeed use similar technologies.

Mainstream industrial fishing is also incredibly wasteful and unselective: a staggering amount of sea life is destroyed and killed in the pursuit of a limited range of targeted species. Most shark species around the world have decreased in numbers and are routinely caught and killed as bycatch by fishing boats. A similar problem afflicts dolphins, sea turtles and a myriad of other species. For every fish that ends on your plate, several others may have been needlessly killed and tracts of seabed destroyed.

The worst kinds of fishing generally involve one of these methods:

- The very use of large, "super-trawlers". Some methods of fishing that could be used without causing too much damage, such as pelagic or midwater trawls, can become extremely damaging due to the sheer scale and size of the nets and their indiscriminate catches. Therefore, the monstrous size of fleets, boats and nets is the initial problem.
- Bottom/beam trawling. This can be compared to a relentless ploughing of the seabed and is generally very destructive. It is also highly unselective, as all manner of species are scooped up in the nets. Some stretches of seabed, especially those naturally exposed to intense disturbance and hosting limited numbers of species, may be less vulnerable to bottom trawling with small nets. Nonetheless, overall, it is a very damaging method of fishing.
- The use of FADs (Fish aggregating devices). These are often placed on top of the seawater to attract fish prior to closing them into purse seine nets. The problem is that these devices attract all sorts of fish and marine life, rather than just the species targeted by fishermen.
- Longlines. Longlining would not be so problematic if it weren't for the sheer scale of these fishing lines and hooks. Longlining for tuna can involve, literally, miles of lines and hooks, which inevitably end up catching a lot more than just tuna.
- Dredging. Very similar to bottom trawling and used for scallops in the UK.

Unfortunately, there is often very little information about fishing methods and, as a purchaser and consumer of wild seafood, you generally need to presume, unless there is specific information about the fishery and region from where the product originates, that when the fishing method is not stated it generally belongs to the more destructive, mainstream industrial norm. Again, just as with most food items: the best ways of producing and harvesting food are generally always openly promoted by those that sell it, and often carries a premium cost. If you are selling hook-and-line caught wild sea bass or dived scallops, you will definitely state it on the label and would be a fool not to, as you could also charge a lot more money for it.

You can often get better information and more options from good, trustworthy fishmongers, which are generally, but not necessarily, better than supermarkets. Nonetheless, you will still find a lot of products that present us with similar dilemmas. How were the fish and crustaceans caught? Where were they caught? Is it a depleted species? And so on. We need to ask questions, investigate and be inquisitive before we buy seafood.

TO SUM UP: be very selective with all fish, crustaceans and shellfish purchasing. Ask questions, read labels, and do some research - even more so than you would for other foods. Avoid all four categories above and limit total seafood consumption.

*Fizzy/Soft Drinks**

It will not be a struggle to persuade you that fizzy drinks are best avoided. Whilst sales of fizzy drinks remain very robust, they have been the subject of widespread criticism, as part of the ongoing anti-sugar campaign. What I aim to persuade you of is that, whilst the amount of white sugar in most drinks is very high and very problematic, the fundamental problem with these drinks is not the fact that they are sugary drinks. Fizzy drinks are the liquid counterpart of the various ultra-processed foods that we have seen thus far. Apart from the low-grade white sugar, they contain all sorts of harmful artificial additives and ingredients. When the sugar is substituted, and this is really the main point I would like to get across, the situation doesn't improve. In fact, it arguably gets worse. Replacing sugar with aspartame and acesulfame K (see the published list of ingredients in Diet Coke[554] and Coke Zero[555]) doesn't make these "diet" drinks better options.

Diet Coke and Coke Zero, great marketing successes designed for the sugar-phobic, calorie-obsessed and diet-conscious amongst us, are arguably as low we can go drinks wise. They

[554] https://www.coca-cola.co.uk/brands/diet-coke

[555] https://www.coca-cola.co.uk/brands/coca-cola-zero-sugar

have all the same building blocks and defects of regular Coke and substitute the sugar element for something even worse: industrial sweeteners. Aspartame is a laboratory accident,[556] as is saccharin,[557] that happens to taste very sweet. Unlike sugar, it is totally artificial, it is quasi-toxic[558] and its long-term use is most likely to be harmful. There is also ample evidence accumulating to indicate the fact that drinking or eating something that tastes sweet but is not actually made of sugar, confounds and destabilises the body's control of insulin, and triggers more hunger and uncontrolled eating. Whatever the research might or might not indicate, one thing is clear: sweeteners have zero positive impact on weight loss, dieting and health. Do not be reassured by the fact that regulatory agencies permit their use, as these are the same agencies that permit the most harmful practices in agriculture, food production and manufacture. These are also the same agencies that systematically abolish or curtail wholesome practices under the ruse of "health and safety", such as raw organic milk, which is considered to be more dangerous than Coke, vodka, and glyphosate.

Disclaimer: I think Coca-Cola, especially in a glass bottle, and served icy cold, is extremely pleasant and I would happily down bottles of it on a regular basis if it happened to be as harmless as fresh water. It is literally the only junk food that actually tastes good for me. Not eating Big Macs or flavoured crisps is a relief, rather than a sacrifice, as I would not enjoy eating them at all. But Coca-Cola… Unfortunately, it is definitely part of the package of foods to completely avoid. It is no coincidence that Coca-Cola, Pepsi, and other similar drinks are sold in fast food outlets as part of the meals and occupy massive aisles in the supermarkets. The classic Coke has a reputation as being loaded with sugar. That reputation is justified, as it contains 10.6g of sugar per 100ml: a whopping 35g per can.[559] The sugar quality is always low, but variable. In the US, much of the sugar is in its lowest form: high fructose corn syrup. In the UK, it's slightly better, as it is made with actual white sugar, almost certainly from sugar beets.

The best Coke I have ever had the pleasure to drink was in Texas, where, for more money, one can buy Coca-Cola manufactured in Mexico, where they use sugar from sugar cane, which makes a big difference. If you are going to drink an unhealthy drink, do it right, I guess. Coca-Cola also contains phosphoric acid, which rots teeth, synthetic caffeine, and a wide range of so-called "natural" flavourings: the exact formula is a trade secret. Do not get caught up in the "Coca-Cola contains cocaine" bandwagon. The original formula certainly contained

[556] It was first produced in 1965 as part of pharmacological drug development.

[557] First produced in the 19th Century by Constantin Fahlberg, a chemist working on coal tar derivatives.

[558] The International Agency for Research on Cancer lists aspartame as possibly carcinogenic to humans. Whilst not comparable to out and out carcinogens, long term, daily use of many substances like aspartame is certainly unwise.

[559] https://www.coca-cola.com/gb/en/brands/coca-cola-original-taste

extracts from the coca plant (and indeed the stimulant kola nut), but the stimulant agent has been replaced with synthetic caffeine over a century ago. Coca leaf flavourings may still be part of the flavourings, but there is no coca active agent involved.

In essence, the major soft drinks, in their original versions, diet or otherwise, both fizzy and flat, have the same basic flaws. In my opinion, you should avoid all the drinks made by the major soft drink brands (Coca-Cola, Fanta, Pepsi, Red Bull, Ribena, Dr Pepper, Tango, Sprite, 7Up, Oasis, Schweppes, Irn Bru, Old Jamaica Ginger Beer, Lipton Iced Tea, Monster Energy, Lucozade etc...) and the own-brand supermarket equivalents.

TO SUM UP: avoid all soft/fizzy drinks.

Flour*

As discussed in previous chapters and as clear from the (above) discussion of bread, conventional white wheat flour is one of the building blocks of a lot of the foods we should try to avoid. It is usually made from hybrid wheat varieties that are dependent on agrochemicals, and then processed through the removal of the germ and bran, which are the most nutritious parts of the wheat grain. The flour is then fortified with artificial vitamins and minerals, in order to try and compensate for the nutritional loss. I will not dwell on this further. Suffice to say, unless a bag of flour clearly indicates cultivation method, wheat variety and country of origin you can be certain that it matches the above description.

TO SUM UP: minimise the use of white flour in your kitchen, especially conventional non-organic white flour.

Foie Gras

There is no doubting the greatness of the French culinary tradition. However, one of its trademark ingredients, foie gras, is arguably not a product to be particularly proud of, at least not since the advent of industrial agriculture. The culinary roots of fattened duck or goose liver are ancient and deep, from the Egyptians to the Romans, as well as being part of the Jewish tradition, which makes sense given the absence of pork fat in the traditional Jewish diet. The French have been producing some kind or other of fattened liver for centuries, and South-West France is the undoubted home of what we generally refer to as *foie gras* (literally "fatty liver"). I confess I have only had dishes containing *foie gras* less than a handful of times, notably at Michel Roux's *Le Gavroche*, which sadly closed in early 2024.

Geese and ducks, it must be understood, have a natural ability to increase their food consumption and accumulate fat with the onset of winter, which is something which a migratory bird needs to be able to do as part of its life cycle. As such, domesticated geese and ducks are birds that can quite easily be overfed and fattened, producing very fatty meats and indeed livers, which is where fat tends to accumulate. *Foie gras* started as a domestic tradition, in which a goose would be singled out for excessive feeding and fattening in the build-up to Christmas. Traditionally, in the pre-Industrial era, producers of this delicacy would literally pick up their free ranging birds one by one throughout the day and shove lots of feed down their hatch, speeding up the fattening process in the final stage of their lives. It always involved excessive feeding, but it was not a particularly cruel practice, and not one which we would condemn if it were still the norm. Given the extravagant use of feed, fatty liver has generally been an expensive, delicious luxury product and there is no questioning its potential in the kitchen, albeit the devotion of contemporary chefs to *foie gras* is grossly exaggerated.

As seems to be case for all forms of animal husbandry, the industrialisation of agriculture has turned a niche, traditional method of poultry farming into something that has become controversial and is now illegal in many countries. Industrial chicken farming is horrific enough: industrial *foie gras* production ups the ante. This is because apart from all the usual welfare problems of indoor industrial poultry farming, it involves an industrial approach to *gavage* (force feeding), using metal or plastic tubes that remind one of petrol pumps. The degree of overfeeding and the size of the livers has also massively increased, resulting in what can only be described as the sick, oversized liver of an abused bird. We can be certain, beyond reasonable doubt, that the vast majority of *foie gras* made in France and Hungary, the second leading producer, is of the intensive, industrial variety. Apart from the cruelty involved in forcefully feeding a bird to produce a massive liver, it is also a very wasteful, unsustainable method of food production.

Needless to say, not all producers in France or Hungary use the cruellest, industrial methods: there are and there will be a very tiny minority of small producers who raise birds destined for *foie gras* as their forefathers would have done. But none of these products are available and identifiable from afar: you would need to personally search for them somewhere in the *campagne* or follow a very educated and specific recommendation. If you purchase *foie gras* on line, or from luxury retailers, or at 3 Michelin Star restaurant, there is no telling how the *foie gras* was produced and you can be confident that, if it made the export and retail market, it was almost certainly produced at scale, with industrial methods, with all the horrors that these methods entail.

There is a producer in Extremadura, Spain, who produces an organic *foie gras* made from fully free ranging geese who are not force fed at all.[560] The birds follow their natural seasonal pattern of fattening up before winter, as part of their migratory cycle, and seem to have as good a life as can be expected for any poultry. At Eduardo Sousa's traditional mixed farm, the geese eat the acorns, olives, grass, lupins and other vegetation growing on the land. Their diets are sometimes supplemented with organic corn, to ensure the liver's colour is as yellow as possible, which is the colour consumers and chefs expect from *foie gras*. The resulting *foie gras*, apart from only being produced seasonally once a year, is far smaller than the conventional supersized fatty livers. To many of the purists, and no doubt many producers in France, this unconventional *foie gras* is not *foie gras* at all, given that without *gavage* and with a much smaller liver size and lower fat content, it is a very different product. It is certainly different, and, I would add, certainly a far better product. In fact, on the face of it, it cannot be faulted. Don't get too excited though: when in stock, a jar of this delicacy will set you back €199.[561]

TO SUM UP*:* do not buy or order foie gras. If you can afford a can of Eduardo Sousa's special gavage free foie gras and can get hold of one, go for it!

Health and Nutritional Claims

When a food item is marketed with some health or nutritional claims, you should immediately get suspicious. There is no good reason why the packaging of a food item should promote its nutritional virtues and supposed health benefits. The best food items never do, with very few exceptions.[562] Those items that do make health claims are almost always ultra-processed foods of low quality that use health claims as part of their marketing strategy, based on very tenuous grounds. Some claims are outright false. Sometimes the claims are true by definition but irrelevant and misleading. For example, there will be products that should never have added sugar to begin with, such as yoghurt, that are advertised as having "no added sugar" or products that are low in saturated fats, which may be true for that particular product but is not an actual health benefit. Similarly, there will be products advertising the fact that they contain only X number of calories: it may well be true, but so what?

The fact that the advertising regulatory bodies allow these marketing practices should neither surprise nor impress us. There are many products on the supermarket shelves that

[560] As narrated by Dan Barber throughout his book (D. Barber, 2014, The Third Plate).

[561] https://lapateria.eu/products/foie-gras-de-ganso-extremeno-entero-mi-cuit-min-180grs

[562] There is a brand of organic Kefir (fermented yoghurt) that I can think of that carries a number of health claims on its bottles. But this is an exception that confirms the rule.

make these claims, just look out for them. They are designed to address and monetise on contemporary anxieties and confusions about dieting and specific nutrients.

Here are examples of the sort of claims you might find:

"Proven to lower cholesterol."
"No added sugar."
"High in Fibre"
"Nutrient X contributes to the normal function of the heart."
"Low in saturated fats."
"Only X Calories"
"X Calories per Bar"
"X Grams of Protein"
"High in Vitamin X"
"Packed with Protein"
"High in Protein"
"High in Fibre"
"X% less sugar"
"0% added sugar"
"0% Fat"
"Natural Flavours"
"Cholesterol Lowering"
"High in Omega 3"
"Heart Healthy"

TO SUM UP: do not buy any products that advertise any sort of nutritional, health, and calorie content claims on their packaging.

Ice Cream*

There is some debate around the origins of ice cream, as one would expect, and various attempts to manufacture some sort of cold sweet dessert were clearly made in more than one culture. Having said that, I must claim ice cream and frozen dessert supremacy for my native homeland, as any reasonable assessment of the world of ice cream will reveal. *Gelato*, and indeed sorbets, are wonderful desserts created in what eventually became Italy.[563] The

[563] To be clear: there were of course other similar cold desserts in other cultures, such as *kulfi* in the Indian subcontinent, but the true ancestor of ice cream, and certainly its best representation, is *gelato*.

De Medici in Florence enjoyed sorbets[564] and possibly the first gelato[565] during the 16th century and Francesco Procopio dei Coltelli (1651 - 1727), the Sicilian creator of gelato, opened the first ice cream parlour that we know of in Paris in 1686. Needless to say, before refrigeration, electricity and modern transport, cold desserts were the preserve of the very wealthy. By the late 19th century and early 20th century, ice cream underwent the sort of revolution that, as we have seen thus far, swept over other foods, such as white flour, sugar, and pasta, enabled by industrial technology and accelerating urbanisation. By the early 20th century, ice cream parlours were gradually spreading, with the ability to manufacture on scale and at lower costs increasing exponentially.

Italo Marchioni (1868 - 1954), an Italian immigrant in the United States, invented the ice cream cone in 1903, which turned ice cream into a dessert that could be eaten on foot. The popularisation of ice cream, like the popularisation of chocolate, was an inherently good thing. However, as we saw with chocolate, the ramp up of industrial production and industrial agriculture eventually led to a progressive decrease in quality. This is true of both packaged ice-cream (think Cornetto) and gelato from the ice cream parlour. Even in my lifetime, the drop in quality across all ice cream categories has been clear: the average ice cream parlour in Italy is worse than it would have been decades ago. Egg powders, low quality industrial milk, artificial colours and other lowly ingredients gradually replaced wholesome fresh ingredients, and artisanal skills are increasingly harder to come by, as they are in all comparable trades.

Moving to the present day, most ice cream is yet another ultra-processed product produced with the same philosophy and ingredients that you will find in all the kinds of foods we saw in this chapter. The basics of ice cream are by and large the dairy and egg products[566] of factory farms mixed with the addition of refined white sugar. A broad range of additives,

[564] The word *sorbetto* has Arabic (*shariba)* and Iranian (*sharbat*) roots and the basic principle of mixing ice or snow with fruit and sugar (more of a sherbet than a sorbet) was most likely brought to Sicily by the Moors. From these *sorbetto* was gradually developed, in both Sicily and Naples. The Sicilians also invented *granita*, a frozen dessert related to sorbet, and the Neapolitans invented *spumone*, a layered ice cream confectionery, and plenty of other frozen or semi-frozen desserts were developed across the Peninsula. In any case, whatever the origin of *sorbetto*, no equivalents, in terms of technique and quality, are found anywhere else. Antonio Latini (1642-1692) wrote down the first recipe for *sorbetto* in his cookbook *Lo scalco alla moderna*.

[565] Bernardo Buontalenti (1531 - 1608) has been credited with inventing modern gelato in Florence.

[566] Vegan ice cream is no better. If anything demonstrates the limits of veganism, it is vegan equivalents of normal foods, such as dairy. Ice cream, by definition, ought to include cream which, mercifully, we can get from happy cows. In any case, even if we want to eat inferior imitation foods, we must rid ourselves of the presumption that somehow, animal free is necessarily better. To manufacture plant based imitation foods, a lot more ingredients are needed in order to create the textures that give an impression of the food being imitated. The go-to ingredients of vegan ultra-processed foods are the building blocks of industrial monoculture: sugar, all sorts of low-grade vegetables oils, soya and its derivatives, isolated vegetable proteins etc... As we saw, these are far from healthy and, despite belief to the contrary, these are not "planet friendly": agrochemical dependent monoculture is never planet friendly.

emulsifiers, vegetable fats and flavourings complete the ice cream mix. Overall, it is an unhealthy, ultra-processed food product and, just as importantly, the average ice cream does not taste nearly as good as it should.

In my opinion, one should steer clear of all the major ice cream brands, from Haagen-Dazs to Ben & Jerry's. It is not only the major brands of ice cream tub that one should avoid, but also the various ice cream sticks, bars, and cones. The iconic Cornetto, for example, and similar products, should also be avoided. I am sure I will be accused of sentimentalism and false memory, but I can guarantee you that Cornetto, and other packaged ice creams, were far better 30-40 years ago than they are now. Production methods, and indeed the location, of many manufactured goods has altered familiar brands, which are often owned by some massive global corporation. In Cornetto's case, it is now owned by Unilever, hardly a purveyor of quality food.

TO SUM UP: avoid conventional ice cream.

Margarine/Butter Substitutes

Margarine and other butter substitutes sit high on the rankings of top 10 ultra-processed foods to shun at all opportunities, for both health and gastronomic reasons. They are largely made up of a lowly concoction or other of rapeseed, palm, sunflower and olive oil,[567] emulsifiers, industrial salt, and flavourings. Furthermore, as we saw earlier, artificial "trans fats", proven to be harmful, are found in many of these products.

TO SUM UP: Never use margarine or any kind of butter substitute. Get the real thing (butter), get the best quality you can afford, and don't eat silly amounts of it.

Meat*

A lot can go wrong with meat production and, if there is one whole food where extra caution is needed, that is meat. Factory farmed livestock operations are an ethical failure and environmental disaster which produce low quality, unhealthy products. I will repeat, yet again, what I have written countless times: when no information is provided on your meat products and packaging, this indicates that the product will most likely originate from intensive industrial systems. At a traditional butcher, where quality is generally higher, there is no packaging, so one has to ask clear questions and build a relationship with a competent

[567] The olive oil spreads, sold as health foods designed to "lower cholesterol", are fundamentally no better than any other vegetable oil spread.

and conscientious butcher. What breed of pork is this? Is it certified organic? Is it outdoor reared? Do you know which farm it is from? And so on.

Here is a brief overview of what to look out for and avoid:

Chicken

Unfortunately, the first and unequivocal indication that you should desist from purchasing a chicken is its low price. Chicken cannot be a cheap everyday food. Anything less £10k per kilo tends to be of poor quality, sadly. For intensely raised factory chicken, costing £3-4 per kilo, you will generally find, as already stated, no real details of the farming method described on the packaging. This chicken is usually described as "Fresh Class A British Chicken". They may also refer to the fact that they are "free to roam" in barns, on a wholegrain diet, and so on. These reassuring statements should be ignored, as they simply refer to the fact that these are indoor raised birds living in the horrid conditions described in Chapter 2.

The bog-standard free-range chicken, normally costing £6-7 per kilo, is somewhat better but still not recommended, for the same reason we don't recommend free-range eggs.

Other Poultry

Farmed duck presents similar problems to chicken and the vast majority of the market is made up of factory farmed duck, Red Tractor or otherwise. Guinea Fowl, which is a wonderful bird, is also normally a French import from intensive farms, and therefore also best avoided. Sadly, I cannot recommend any supermarket duck nor guinea fowl. Even more goes wrong with turkey. This poor bird from the New World, mostly reared for the Thanksgiving and Christmas period, is another domestic animal made to live in unnatural, unsanitary, and miserable conditions in massive factory farm operations. A bog-standard turkey from the supermarket costs around £5 per kilo and, again, will simply be described as a "Fresh Class A whole turkey" from "trusted farms". A good representative, in my opinion, of the type of turkey to strictly avoid, whether whole or broken down into various products, is Norfolk's Bernard Matthews, the largest turkey producer in the UK. Free range turkey is an improvement on the cheapest turkey and costs around £8 per kilo, but, again, we can do better, especially once a year.

Pork

Of all the meats, pork is probably the one where we must be the most careful. This precious and engaging animal, the mainstay of small-scale agriculture and domesticity across Europe for millennia, has been grossly abused by the adoption of industrial methods. The average pig farm is a horrible, hellish, unhealthy operation that we do not want to finance and feed ourselves from. A lack of labelling information indicates that the pork you are purchasing does indeed come from factory farm operations, by default. The only information available on the average piece of fresh pork is that it comes from "trusted farms" and that it is British.[568] It is also remarkably cheap.

Free-range will be better, albeit there is no clear legal definition nor enforcement of definitive standards for free range pork in the UK. You need go online and look up the farm, if possible, and find out as much information as you can on a case-by-case basis. Some free-range farms and labels will be good, but generally not the ones that supply supermarkets. There are also pork cuts sold at supermarkets with "outdoor bred" or "outdoor reared" labelling. Outdoor bred refers to system where pigs are born in outdoor facilities, albeit not necessarily with any access to pasture nor woodland. The piglets are then brought inside shortly after weaning and spend the rest of their lives indoors to fatten up for slaughter. Outdoor reared refers to a system where pigs are born and raised outdoors for roughly the first half of their lives and are brought indoors for the second half of their lives for intensive fattening. In both systems, the sows do remain outdoors their entire lives, which is a relative good. What you need to keep in mind, however, is that, apart from serious welfare considerations, the feeding regimens and quality of the feed used in free range and outdoor systems will not necessarily be much better than those used in intensive indoor systems.

Similar principles apply to cured pork products, where even more can go wrong. This is because as well as the unhealthy meat from intensive pork operations, which is a non-starter, the bog-standard cured pork products such as bacon, ham and sausages also contain plenty of nitrates, industrial salt and, sometimes, other additives. Meat content will also differ; industrial bacon will have a relatively lower meat content than traditionally dry-cured bacon and is pumped with triphosphates to increase water content.[569] Overall, there is no doubt that these are amongst the most harmful food products available and must strictly be avoided.

Beef

Beef quality, on average, is better than both pork and poultry in the UK and indeed Ireland. This is because our rain swept islands are blessed with abundant rain fed grassland, unlike the rest of Europe, where beef cattle are more likely to be stuck in feedlots for much of their life. Therefore, even the lowest quality beef "from trusted farms", tends to be relatively decent, as beef cattle more than likely spent some time eating grass, before being finished

[568] Most fresh pork tends to be British. A lot of cheap factory pork is imported from Denmark and Holland and is used to manufacture bacon and sausages. Because it is manufactured in the UK, it is labelled as a British product.

[569] H. Browning, 2018, Pig. Tales from an Organic Farm, page 259.

indoors on dry, grain-based feed and silage. Nonetheless, there are all sorts of unpleasant and undesirable practices that inevitably take place whenever cattle are confined to feedlots and finishing units and therefore, beef from our "trusted farmers" should still be avoided. Having said that, our finishing units are not yet comparable[570] to the horrors of the USDA[571] approved feedlots in America. As we will see in the next chapter, there are things you can look out for when buying beef, so that you can secure the best products. British beef, at its best, is some of the best in the world and is a genuine health product.

A quick word on Wagyu: it is mostly a fashionable trend, and its exorbitant cost is generally not justified by the quality of the product. Wagyu simply refers to cattle that has the genetics of Japanese crossbreeds developed in several prefectures in Japan during the early part of the 20th century. It makes sense in Japan, and it will taste good, albeit there is better and healthier beef out there. But a lot of the Wagyu beef on the market is from the UK, Australia, and the USA, where all you really have is cattle with Wagyu genetics. Wagyu beef is famous for its marbling, which, apart from genetic predisposition, is achieved by a long, sedentary lifestyle and a high calorie, grain-based diet. Apart from being extraordinarily wasteful, this sort of regimen does not produce healthy meat. I may be wrong, but I don't believe there is any major Wagyu producer that produces 100% grass fed beef, as the whole point of Wagyu beef is the marbling, which means that the animals have to spend a significant part of their lives fattening up. Overall, you can do better.

Lamb

Sheep are the domestic animals that have been the least affected by the industrialisation of agriculture[572] and there is no ovine equivalent to the factory farm that afflicts poultry, pigs, and dairy cattle. Sheep generally still spend much of their lives outdoors, on their natural grass diet. Non-organic sheep are still dipped[573] and their grassland might be managed with synthetic fertilisers and some agrochemicals[574] but welfare and health standards are generally high in the UK. I do not recommend any New Zealand lamb, not because of welfare or health concerns but because it is a lunacy for us to import lamb from overseas.

[570] Not yet anyway. The beef and dairy sectors are undergoing a process of intensification in the UK, which is very bad news.

[571] There are steak restaurants and retailers in London that sell "USDA Prime" beef, sometimes even labelled as "grain fed" (as if that were a good thing!), for a premium. USDA Prime beef, full of marbling, is amongst the least healthy products available and, as we saw earlier, pretty disastrous from a welfare and environmental perspective.

[572] Apart from slaughter, which sadly generally involves long journeys, enormous slaughterhouses, fast conveyor belts and exploited, brutalised workers.

[573] See Chapter 3.

[574] Not comparable to conventional arable land, however, which is entirely dependent on the heavy use of agrochemicals.

Overall, when in doubt, the safest and healthiest meat from all farmed animals is lamb. Far less can go wrong and even cheaper, less traceable lamb from the supermarket is a relatively safe bet, certainly when compared to other meats. The same discourse applies to goat meat which you should definitely consider eating if you can get hold of it.

Game

Game meat generally refers to meat coming from wild animals that are not farmed as livestock and do not belong to domesticated species: the products of hunting, shooting, stalking and pest control. In terms of gastronomic value and health benefits, there is no doubt that wild meats are an excellent addition to our diets. If you get the opportunity to buy venison, woodpigeon, rabbit, grouse, hare and any other legal quarry, you should do so. I particularly recommend venison: it is a very abundant resource in the UK, and, unlike woodpigeon, that will feed on oilseed rape seeds and wheat grains on arable land, deer will almost entirely feed themselves with wild plants and grasses.

A slight grey area is game birds like pheasant, partridge, and mallard, which are reared by the gamekeeper and grain fed throughout their lives and medicated if needs be. They are quite unique examples of animals that live on the frontiers of domesticity and wildness, which in my view accounts for the fantastic flavour. As critics of shooting often remind us, with much exaggeration, there is no question that chicks on game farms often start their lives in intensive farming conditions[575] and that the grain feed gamekeepers leave across the land will not be dissimilar to conventional poultry feed, and non-organic. Nonetheless, what we have with pheasant, partridge, and mallard are birds that are as "free range" as it gets, fending for themselves, supplementing their diets with what nature provides and, at times, surviving their first shooting season and still be flying high the following season.

Another potential issue is the fact that these birds are usually shot with lead shot, which slightly taints the meat and pollutes the environment. Major supermarkets and retailers, who are content to sell £3-4 chickens from factory farms living in their own poo, have recently banned meat from lead shot birds, which is an absurdity. In any case, lead is gradually being phased out and being replaced by steel.[576] Just watch your teeth!

Whatever one thinks of the complexities and ethics of game shooting, there is no question that pheasant, partridge, and mallard are still very healthy options when compared to most

[575] Gamekeepers used to raise their own pheasants from eggs, using broody hens to lay them. Nowadays, they tend to buy in chicks from game farms.

[576] A major estate where I shoot has a steel only policy and, in any case, I only buy steel cartridges these days. It is definitely a positive move for the countryside, going forward, and I have barely noticed any difference: I am an equally poor shot, whatever the cartridge.

of the poultry on the market and you should eat them throughout the shooting season and put some in the freezer whilst you are at it.

Exotic Meats

By exotic meats, I am referring to domesticated (e.g., ostrich, camel, or reindeer) or wild (e.g., wild boar, mouflon, zebra) meats from overseas, from animals that we do not have here in Britain. Overall, tread with caution. Common meats from Continental Europe, especially wild boar, are desirable, but the further out we go, the more obscure the supply chain is, and the more pointless it is to import fresh meat from afar. With wild meats, there should be even further caution given potential conservation issues.

Halal/Kosher

Halal and kosher are ritual slaughter methods that involve the severing of an animal's throat, with the goal of bleeding an animal to death and rendering it unconscious as blood stops flowing to the brain. It is similar to how animals were generally slaughtered in Christendom and in many other societies around the world[577] before the invention of stunning and other techniques that render the slaughtered animal unconscious, prior to the use of a knife. Historically, using a sharp knife to sever the throat of an animal has certainly been a sensible way of dispatching an animal with limited tools available. This does not mean that it's the best possible slaughter method or that we cannot do better.

Be that as it may, we need to remind our observant Jewish and Muslim friends that slaughter is only the final stage before an animal ends up on their plate. How an animal is slaughtered is not indicative of its health, quality, and life on the farm and a visit to the average London halal and kosher butcher shop does not fill one with confidence, to be honest. There is generally a distinct lack of information about the origin of the meat. There is no doubt that the best meat on the market is unlikely to be from animals that have undergone ritual slaughter. Having said that, there are a small minority of retailers that sell halal and kosher meat from animals that are certified organic or from similar high welfare, wholesome farming operations. If ritual slaughter is important to you, make it your job to find these niche retailers and butchers. When in doubt, lamb and mutton are the safest bets.

Lastly, the pious must ask themselves: what is more ethical, to purchase the meat from a factory farmed animal that has been ritually slaughtered or to purchase meat from a happy animal that has been slaughtered without any religious ritual and method? There is no doubt

[577] Mongolian sheep herders practice an impressive, fast, and efficient traditional method of slaughter in which a small incision is made in the belly and the aorta is severed by hand, leaving all the blood inside the animal. Look it up.

in my mind that reason and virtue demand that we choose the latter. If both high welfare and ritual slaughter can be achieved, so much the better.

Fake Meat/Meat Substitutes

The attempt to create the sensation and texture of meat, like any attempt to create a plant-based substitute for an animal product, involves the manufacture of ultra-processed foods that can be liberally dismissed as vegan junk. Apart from any gastronomic considerations,[578] no-turkey turkey, vegan bacon, meat free sausages, meat free burgers and so on are made up of reconstituted plant proteins (yum!), low quality vegetable oils and all sorts of additives and flavourings needed to create something remotely resembling the real thing.[579] Therefore, what they lack in taste is not redeemed by any health benefit of any kind. If you don't want to eat meat, just eat organic legumes and whole grains.

TO SUM UP: take great caution when buying meat and try to be as informed and conscientious as you can. Do not trust the anonymous "trusted farmers" on the conventional meat aisles. Never buy anything that comes from a factory farm.

Microwave Meals

I often shock and amuse my friends by my refusal to use a microwave, which is now the norm. The microwave came to prominence in post war America and swept through the industrial world as the new kitchen item to go alongside ready-made meals. It is part and parcel of the philosophy of convenience at all costs and a domestic representation of fast-food culture. As any good cook should know, this odd implement is not a genuine cookery tool, but merely a heating device, a task which, in any case, is better accomplished via a conventional thermal oven. The meals that supermarkets retail for the very purpose of sticking them in the microwave are generally of very low quality and fit the description of ultra-processed foods. As a rule, if you outsource your cooking to an industrial manufacturer, you will end up with a low-quality product made with ingredients and processes that you would never find in your kitchen.

[578] Plant based meats, despite the enthusiastic media coverage, have been remarkably unsuccessful thus far. The main reason is that no amount of food engineering and lab work can ever, and will never, produce something that tastes anything like the real thing. Vegan sausages, burgers, bacon etc... are simply not good to eat for the average human and certainly have no role whatsoever to play in great cuisine, especially when compared with high quality meat, sausages, burgers, bacon etc... There may come the day when human palates have been dumbed down and habituated to such an extent that vegan bacon will be popular, in the same way a lot of other awful cultural artefacts are popular; but that will not be a day to rejoice.

[579] Beyond Burger, for example, contains: Water, pea protein (15%), rapeseed oil, flavouring, rice protein, coconut oil, dried yeast, preservative (potassium lactate), vinegar, stabilisers (methyl cellulose, calcium chloride), potato starch, salt, apple extract, colour (beetroot red), concentrated pomegranate juice, potassium salt.

See: https://www.beyondmeat.com/en-GB/products/the-beyond-burger/beyond-burger

Putting microwave meals aside, the same discourse applies to any of the sort of ready meal products that need re-hydration in order to be ready to eat, such as the various brands of pot noodles. Similarly, most of the ready-made soups, the various "cream of chicken" or "cream of mushroom" tins, are also to be strictly avoided. They contain very little of the supposed main ingredient and are bulked up with rapeseed oil, sugars, white flour, milk powder and other fillers.

TO SUM UP: do not own/use a microwave. Even if you do, do not buy any microwaveable ready-made meals. Stay well away from any rehydrated junk like pot noodles and from the average soup tin.

*Milk and Dairy**

Milk and dairy do not get very good press these days, given the animal fat phobia and vegan propaganda swirling around our culture. It is nonetheless still a staple, widely consumed food, especially across Europe. Dairy consumption has been gaining ground in other parts of the world where it was previously not the norm, such as China, which has become a big export market for the EU. China has unfortunately also been building mega-dairies, modelled on American and European models of production. Milk powder, whey and other milk derivatives are also found in so many ultra-processed foods and women across the world are bombarded with advertising suggesting that milk formula is better than mother's milk.[580] Milk is a big and growing sector.

Nonetheless, as already argued, cheese and other milk derivatives are excellent foods, in principle, provided they originate from high quality milk and are made with appropriate methods. Sadly, a lot of the cheese consumed globally does not meet this requirement. Most dairy products, especially those made with cow's milk, are made from the inferior milk of unhappy, enclosed animals. The time trusted methods upon which great cheese production depends on have also increasingly been replaced by industrial processing. Germany and the USA, for example, are the world's major cheese producers, but their cheese, let's be honest, is pretty awful.

But first things first: let us look at milk. Milk is an ultimate healthy whole food which provides dense nutrition that is hard to match. There are some basic things to look out for and think

[580] As discussed in Chapter 6, it is a good thing that cow's milk can supplement and eventually replace mother's milk, and we should strictly avoid the vegan approach on this matter. However, at the other extreme, milk formula has been relentlessly and shamelessly pushed as a *better* option than mother's milk and women are being actively discouraged from milking their children at all, practically from birth, which puts babies at a distinct disadvantage, as well as denying the unique mother-child bond that is created via breastfeeding.

about when purchasing milk. Apart from the farming method, which should always be "organic"[581] in the broadest sense of the word, there are other aspects to consider:

- **Fat content**: never presume that skimmed or semi-skimmed milk is in any way better for you. It is also less tasty and nutritious. There are no real health reasons to shun whole milk.
- **Homogenisation**: homogenisation is the process by which milk fats are broken down into smaller fat molecules, evenly dispersed throughout the liquid, in order to create a homogenous white product. This process was introduced in the early 20th century and was certainly the norm by the 1980s, coinciding neatly with the fat phobic movement. Most people born in the 1950s can still recall milk bottles than came with their "golden top" of cream, that formed at the top end of the milk bottle: this was the naturally solidifying fat that accumulated at the top of the milk. There is literally no benefit, other than a superficial aesthetic one, to homogenising milk. In fact, quite the opposite: it disrupts this wonderful whole food.[582] These days, milk producers that do not homogenise their milk also tend to be the same producers who have organic dairy herds, pasture-based system etc…
- **Pasteurisation**: pasteurisation is the process by which, through heat, milk is sanitised, and its bacteria killed off. The method started being used in the early days of urbanisation and industrialisation. The longer transport, the lengthening of supply chains and the often unhygienic conditions of early urban development meant that milk could often go bad and potentially pose a threat to health. Pasteurisation allowed milk to be relatively safer and last longer. It has been the norm for over a century. Overall, in a largely urbanised society, it makes sense. However, we have now gone to the other extreme: there is an ongoing campaign to demonise and eliminate the retailing of raw milk,[583] no doubt encouraged by mainstream dairy producers and by major supermarket retailers. Raw milk comes with a health warning now. Each bottle has to state: "This milk has not been heat treated and may contain organisms harmful to health". No health warnings can be found in all the junk food we have looked at so far, including drinks such as Coca-Cola and Red Bull. According to contemporary scientific advisers to government, fresh milk from a cow is more dangerous than any other drink on the market. I cannot think of a single drink retailed

[581] There are some milk producers without organic certification that produce excellent milk. These are pasture based, grass fed dairy systems, often from breeds like Jerseys, for example. Read labelling closely and see Chapter 10.

[582] It may alter the way the body absorbs milk's fat, by accelerating it. There is conflicting research on this. One thing is certain: there is no benefit at all to homogenising milk.

[583] It is currently legal in England and Wales, but in limited retail settings and with health warnings. It is illegal in Scotland! See https://www.food.gov.uk/safety-hygiene/raw-drinking-milk

in the UK that carries a health warning, including liquor with over 40% alcohol. This is insane, and we must set the record straight: there is absolutely nothing wrong with raw milk per se. In fact, quite the opposite. With heating, all sorts of positive benefits are eliminated: heat destroys beneficial bacteria and enzymes and reduces or eliminates the bioavailability of certain nutrients. Provided hygiene is very carefully monitored, there is no serious risk with raw milk and only benefits. Therefore, whilst realistically even in the best-case scenario most of us urbanites will continue to consume pasteurised milk, do not shun the possibility of a raw milk bottle, should it be on sale at your local farmers' market.

- **UTC**: Ultra High-Temperature Pasteurisation or UTC is a very fast, high temperature version of conventional pasteurisation, that zaps the milk to such a point of sterility that it can sold as "long-life milk". In the United States, this is the norm. I can recall buying the most expensive organic milk on the market at Whole Foods in Austin, Texas, and being both surprised by its tastelessness and long expiry date. Again, there is no benefit to UTC milk other than the lengthening of its shelf life. This may be an advantage for catering and food supply in remote or very hot environments but makes no sense here in Britain or indeed anywhere else in Europe.

Average British milk tends to be better than average milk from the Continent, and certainly better than average milk in the United States. This is mostly because British dairy cows are more likely to see some blades of grass throughout their lifetimes. Having said that, the cheapest supermarket milk, which makes no reference to neither cow breed nor farming method on its labels, is most likely to come from overmilked, oversized, overfed Holsteins living indoors for much of the year, who do not see or eat much or any green grass. The Red Tractor label, as we saw, is no guarantor of quality and animal welfare. Therefore, you must strictly avoid the nondescript milk from supermarkets or corner shops which is usually devoid of any information, simply labelled as fresh milk "from British farms".

The same discourse applies to butter, yogurt, and cheese. When there is no information on the farming method, breed of animal, precise location of manufacture or any other relevant certification that indicates quality, you must presume that these products will most likely originate from the same obscure supply chains that produce cheap industrial milk.

Lastly, I suggest staying away from all so-called vegan dairy products, such as vegan cheese and yoghurt. These are generally ultra-processed junk food products[584] with no redeeming qualities. A notable exception is tofu, which is a genuine "vegan cheese" and a traditional food of East Asia, where dairy is virtually non-existent. Most Europeans seem to find it tasteless and not particularly pleasant, but if you enjoy organic tofu, go for it.

TO SUM UP: avoid conventional nondescript milk and dairy products. Avoid any low or zero fat products. Stay away from "plant-based dairy" products.

Pasta*

Pasta is one of the most versatile and popular staples on the planet and, thanks to the mountain of wheat produced since the so-called Green Revolution and thanks to the economies of scale and efficiencies of industrial production, it is a very cheap, easily accessible product. Unfortunately, it has become too cheap for high quality to be sustained. A 500g packet of dried pasta cannot cost less than £2-3 if it going to be a quality product. You should not eat, or at least let us say that you do not need to eat, more than 120-160g of pasta per meal: it does not need to cost more than £0.80-1.00 per portion.

As ever, a lack of information is a sure sign of low quality. To begin with, the average pasta packet does not specify which wheat variety was used to manufacture it and often states that it is made with "EU & non-EU durum wheat", meaning a mixture of hybrid wheat from the big wheat growing regions of Eurasia and North America. It will also not state what cultivation method was involved, meaning that it is made from wheat produced through conventional agrochemical arable operations, nor how the pasta was dried. The latter is important, as most pasta is dried at very high temperatures which in a sense pre-cooks it and explains its yellow colour. As a general rule, the more yellow the pasta, the lower the quality.

The other pastas to avoid are the "gluten free" or "low gluten" varieties. As previously explained, the misguided gluten phobia that has taken root over the last decade has led to all kinds of campaigns to market gluten free or low gluten products, which are entirely unnecessary. As it turns out, the best pasta, made from the older wheat varieties, is naturally low in gluten. Conventional pasta, made with modern hybrid wheat varieties, has a higher

[584] The only brand of "vegan dairy" I could find that, to its credit, uses 100% organic ingredients, no trans fats, and none of the additives, emulsifiers and stabilisers used by other manufacturers is Miyoko's Creamery (https://www.miyokos.com/), which featured in the recent Netflix documentary Watch You Are What You Eat: A Twin Experiment (2024). These are probably not unhealthy products and clearly better than the usual vegan alternatives. My main objection to these *faux* dairy products would be gastronomic: it cannot and will not compete with real dairy. Needless to say, I also dismiss the presumption that we need to replace dairy products with plant alternatives for health and environmental reasons.

gluten content. Therefore, if you are worried about gluten, for some reason or other, simply go for the best pasta and don't eat a lot of it.

A brief word on egg pasta: similar principles apply, with the added issue of egg content and complex fillings. Egg pasta, part of the great tradition of Northern Italy, used to be homemade or sold in the traditional *Alimentari* (Grocery) shops, and consumed fresh on special occasions.[585] Giovanni Rana, much like Ferrero, turned an artisanal product into something anyone could afford to buy from the supermarket. Just like Ferrero, the massive scaling up and global spread of the company gradually led to a drop in quality, especially when we consider the industrialisation of egg, dairy and cheese production. In fairness to Rana, the company's egg pasta is not an ultra-processed food product,[586] as it does not contain any of the signature ingredients: emulsifiers, stabilisers, flavourings, colourings, gums etc... The simplest pasta, like tagliatelle, are simply made with flour, eggs, and water. We could do a lot worse. Nonetheless, we must not forget the basic principle underpinning all food: the quality of whole food ingredients is paramount. When this is lacking, we should desist. We must think agriculturally before we think gastronomically.

TO SUM UP: eat less pasta and eat better pasta. Do not be gluten phobic.

*Out of Season**

There are many food writers and chefs who celebrate our freedom "from the tyranny of the seasons". As previously argued, this freedom is undeniable to an extent, especially when we consider the extraordinary and historically unprecedented availability of exotic produce that we cannot grow here at home.

However, there is no wisdom in buying, on a regular basis, produce that we can grow here from overseas. Even if we put aside the obvious inefficiency and dysfunctionality of importing fresh produce that we can comfortably grow here, there is an issue of taste and quality. At the risk of stating the obvious, there is no comparison between a fresh vegetable grown locally, at the right time, and one that is out of season and travels great distances to get to our tables. It will be nutritionally and gastronomically inferior, period. Furthermore, there is real value in diversity when it comes to diet: not eating the same things all year round is good

[585] I only ate Tortellini from the Alimentari on Christmas Day growing up, not out of poverty but out of cultural habit. There are organic tortellini available on the market nowadays, at a decent price, and I will have them a maximum of 2-3 times a year around the Christmas period.

[586] Pasta in general, including all the household brands, is not an ultra-processed food product and is relatively benign. My contention is that there is a still a gulf in quality between the best pastas and the average commercial brands, for the reasons outlined above. In the next chapter I will outline the key criteria to use to identify the best pasta on the market, which is tastier, healthier and derived from the best wheat varieties.

for you and each season has its products and flavours. The simplest way to avoid out of season produce and follow the seasons is to familiarise yourself with what grows in our temperate climate and when,[587] going to your closest farmers' market on a regular basis and reading supermarket labels very closely.

Here are some basic examples of what to avoid:

- Asparagus from Peru and Mexico.
- Tomatoes and cucumbers from Holland.
- Butternut squash from Argentina.
- Aubergines from Kenya and Holland.
- South African grapes.
- Apples and pears from Argentina, Chile, and New Zealand.
- Green beans, sweetcorn, and fresh herbs from Africa.
- Chinese garlic.
- Courgettes from Spain, Morocco, and Holland.
- Strawberries from Spain, Morocco, and Egypt.
- Blueberries from South America.
- Peppers from Holland.

Many more examples could be listed. The bottom line is that there are two basic principles you can follow:

- Avoid out-of-season produce (e.g. strawberries, cucumbers, and courgettes in winter).
- Avoid produce that we can grow perfectly well locally and currently import (e.g. apples from New Zealand, garlic from China, and green beans from Kenya)

TO SUM UP: prioritise seasonal and local fruit, vegetables, and herbs.

Prepped Fruits & Vegetables

Outsourcing kitchen labour to manufacturers is not always a bad thing. As Rachel Laudan reminds us in her misguided attack on "culinary Luddites", it is a good thing that people no longer have to grind their own flour or churn their own butter. But the culture of speed and convenience has many evident downsides, which the high priests of progressivism casually ignore.

[587] Consider buying a book about organic horticulture to learn about what grows in our climate and soils throughout the year. See the next chapter for a very brief guide.

As someone who grows a lot of his own produce, I am familiar with the painstaking work involved in transforming a mixture of muddy radishes, huge endives, and thick stemmed cultivated rocket into a nice, clean, edible salad. Or the time it takes to prepare and flash boil chard and spinach before any dish can be made with it. There is the cleaning, the various bugs you need to dispose of, the trimming, chopping etc... At the other extreme, there are plenty of supermarket aisles with pre-cleaned, pre-cut, pre-mixed fruits and vegetables. The main problem with all the prepped products is that fruits and vegetables lose freshness, flavour, and nutritional value from being cut, packaged, and stored in plastic packaging on the supermarket aisles. There is a world of difference between a freshly cut salad and a pre-cut salad poured out of a plastic bag. The other serious problem with prepped produce is that it is usually made with less traceable, lower quality fruits and vegetables. You are far more likely to find, say, high quality lettuces, cucumbers, and tomatoes as individual, unprocessed products than you are likely to find them in the ready-made mixed bags.

You will definitely need to dedicate more time to sourcing and preparing produce, but you do not need to scrape mud off your radishes! For the vast majority who do not grow their own produce, whatever they purchase from retailers, whether supermarkets or farmers' markets, will be cleaner and easier to process than the allotment or garden grown produce.

TO SUM UP: avoid prepped fruits and vegetables.

Smoothies/Juices/Cleansers*

Liquidised fruits and vegetables seem to be either demonised, mostly by the sugar phobic movement, or exalted by those susceptible to detoxing, "cleansing", and intermittent fasting fads. The truth is somewhere in between. There is nothing inherently wrong with pressing fruits and vegetables for the purpose of making juices and smoothies: the primary concern, as always, should be the quality of the fruits and vegetables. For example, there are obvious problems with run of the mill supermarket orange juice, made with unidentifiable fruits from all over the world[588] and grown on plantations that make ample use of pesticides and glyphosate. The worse juices are made from concentrates, which is juice that has had most of its water content removed through a filtration and extraction process which removes most of the nutrients and fibre from the fruit. The pulp is then reconstituted by adding water back in. Most juices from concentrates also have sweeteners, preservatives, flavourings, and are fortified with synthetic Vitamin C, AKA ascorbic acid. As we have seen over and over again,[589] ultra-processed foods are often designed on the same model: denude a whole food, in this

[588] The average orange juice is likely made from massive orange plantations in Brazil, Mexico, Florida, or Spain.

[589] Cereals and bread are primary examples.

case oranges, of any nutritive quality through processing, following which the product is "fortified" with added nutrients and additives to recreate, without success, something resembling the original whole food.

Even the juices that are not made from concentrates and are made with 100% squeezed fruit are problematic if the quality of the fruit is low, and it usually is. The main brands (e.g. Tropicana, Innocent, Copella and supermarket own brands) are not, in my opinion, purveyors of anything desirable. In any case, even the very best juices and smoothies, made from the best fruits and vegetables, are not better than whole fruits and vegetables. It is better to eat whole oranges and apples than to drink the juice made from these same fruits.

TO SUM UP: avoid the average fruit juice and smoothy. Press your own fruit or source unfiltered organic juice. Prioritise whole fruits and vegetables.

Sports Drinks & Supplements

As an amateur, ageing sportsman I can appreciate the temptation of looking for a quick fix, a performance enhancer, something to give me an edge. Under the guise of state-of-the-art nutritional science, which is fundamentally flawed, a huge range of "sports drinks" and supplements have flooded the market to cater for people like me. These products can be bought everywhere: gyms, pharmacies, supermarkets, corner shops, health shops, and petrol stations.

The problem is that sports drinks are normally made up of refined sugars and/or sweeteners, synthetic vitamins, minerals, colours, and obscure and pointless components, such as "electrolytes",[590] which are currently very fashionable. Whatever the supposed benefits of any of these nutrients, it should be clear that there are far better natural sources of nourishment for sportsmen than these artificial drinks. If the idea is to provide a sweet drink that provides instant energy, as well as vitamins and minerals, one would be better off with good old mineral water, with a whole lemon squeezed into it and perhaps a banana. No amount of buzz words and images of sweating athletes will make bright blue or sickly orange drinks and electrolyte sachets any better than what they are.

In any case, as previously discussed, irrespective of whether you are a marathon runner or a sedentary person allergic to exercise, you do not need artificial vitamins and minerals if you eat real food of high quality and drink plenty of clean water. The only real benefit of vitamins

[590] A word now commonly used to refer to minerals such as sodium and calcium.

and minerals is for those who are generally malnourished and do not eat what they need to in order to function. In other words, they are useful for damage limitation and survival.

The supplements sector operates under the usual nutritionist tenets. One of the main categories of supplements are those marketed as "protein" products, usually in the form of powders, to be blended in bland, medicinal, and artificial liquid meals. Whilst it is clear that greater physical exertion and muscle development implies an increased need for food rich in protein, it simply does not follow that low-quality protein powders are the way to go about it. The usual justification for the consumption of such supplements is that it is difficult to ingest the extra protein required from normal meals and that bodybuilders regularly supplement their diet with such products. There are three basic responses to such justifications:

1) If you find it difficult to eat any more protein packed foods on a daily basis, you should see this as a sign that your body does not really want or need any more of these nutrients. If you are unable to fit any more steak or fish in your daily diet, perhaps you should listen to your body and desist from stuffing protein powders down your gullet.
2) There are plenty of simple liquid whole foods that you could consume straight after the gym, outside of mealtimes, to add protein and minerals to your diet: drink a large bottle of organic milk or homemade beef broth from a hot flask.
3) The fact that professional bodybuilders consume an enormous range of supplements[591] and protein shakes is all the more reason not to do it, since professional bodybuilding is fundamentally unhealthy.[592] Just as there is no health reason to take steroids and HGH, there is no health reason to ingest extraordinary levels of protein and other synthetic nutrients.

TO SUM UP: stay away from all products marketed as "sports" products and stay away from all supplements, even if you are an amateur bodybuilder. Eat real food and drink normal drinks.

Sugar*

I refer you back to Chapter 5 for our discussion of sugar phobia: there is no doubt that refined white sugar and other industrial sugars, such as glucose syrup and glucose-fructose syrup,

[591] Such as creatine, another supplement to stay away from.

[592] For many of us boys who grew up in the 80s, in the era of Arnold Schwarzenegger, there is a certain attraction towards extreme bodybuilding. I love Arnie! However, we need to accept the fact that professional bodybuilders often develop all sorts of health issues, have a lower life expectancy than other athletes and that the extreme diets are a big part of the problem.

in a lot of our food are highly damaging and a major contributor to obesity, diabetes, and other diseases.

There are some notable exceptions: even the best gelato parlours, patisseries and restaurant will usually use conventional white sugar and icing sugar for their desserts and confections. This is not a reason to avoid them, far from it. What really matters is that we do not keep these products in our kitchens and larders and think carefully about what we buy for day-to-day use.

TO SUM UP: do not use white refined sugar, and do not buy products that contains it or which contain glucose syrup and glucose-fructose syrup.

*Sweeteners**

Using artificial sweeteners, prevalent in so much food and drink, is a counterproductive method to replace refined white sugar. Apart from their inadequate taste, these are laboratory-made products whose effect on health is suspect. More importantly, high-quality foods never contain sweeteners, which tend to be the building blocks of a lot of junk food. For that reason alone, when you find sweeteners listed on a label, you know that the product as a whole is of low quality. The NHS lists the following as the sweeteners approved for use in the UK:[593]

- acesulfame K (E950)
- aspartame (E951)
- erythritol (E968)
- saccharin (E954)
- sorbitol (E420)
- steviol glycosides (E960)[594]
- sucralose (E955)
- xylitol (E967)

[593] https://www.nhs.uk/live-well/eat-well/food-types/are-sweeteners-safe/

[594] Steviol glycosides are at least derived from the stevia plant, unlike aspartame and others on the list (acefultame K, saccharin, sucralose) which are entirely synthetic. I grow a stevia plant or two in a cold frame these days and I recommend its use with teas and drinks. The dried leaves, its powder and other basic derivatives are sold by a few producers and can be purchased online and in shops. Ironically, the Food and Drug Administration has opposed stevia leaves and its natural products, in the same way it opposes raw milk, which we should take as an indication of stevia's wholesomeness. The FDA declares that *"the use of stevia leaf and crude stevia extracts is not considered GRAS (generally recognized as safe), and their import into the U.S. is not permitted for use as sweeteners."*

See: https://www.fda.gov/food/food-additives-petitions/aspartame-and-other-sweeteners-food

The NHS nutritional advice, which, as we saw, considers apple juice as more dangerous than Coke Zero, can be safely ignored.

TO SUM UP: do not use artificial sweeteners of any kind.

Tea and Coffee*

Putting aside any debate about the merits and demerits of caffeine, there is nothing inherently problematic with tea and coffee. In fact, there is plenty of evidence to suggest that quality tea and coffee might add to life and health rather than subtract from it and we are probably better off with these interesting plants in our lives than without them.

Irrespective, as ever, the main limit is posed by the fact that these are both crops which in most plantation systems are heavily sprayed with poison. The main agricultural challenges stem from the fact that these crops suffer from being grown as monocultures and from the impoverishment of the soils in which they are grown, which are low in organic matter and reliant on synthetic fertility, as already documented many decades ago by Sir Albert Howard across the British dominions in Asia and Africa. Coffee, for a start, is a shade plant, which should grow in the company of taller trees, in polyculture systems. "Sun coffee", grown in monocultures in major producing countries like Brazil, requires extensive chemical treatments in order to survive the pests that plague it in such an unnatural setting. Tea is also blighted by similar problems, when grown in massive monocultures.

Our best bet is to avoid tea and coffee products which do not specify cultivation method, crop variety and country of origin. It is also better to avoid blends and focus on single-estate teas and coffees.

TO SUM UP: be willing to spend a bit more money on tea and coffee and read labels very closely.

Unrecognisable Chemical Formulas and Flavours

As a general rule, do not eat or at least be very suspicious of any food item which:

1) Lists ingredients which you cannot recognise as remotely connected to food.
2) Lists ingredients which are obscure names of chemicals. Disodium 5'-Ribonucleotides, anyone?

3) That contains ingredients which start with the letter E; the so-called E numbers.[595] These are not all harmful, but the best foods generally do not contain them.
4) Is marketed as being made with an ingredient which is entirely absent from its actual list of ingredients (e.g., chicken pot noodles with no chicken).
5) Has a very long lists of ingredients. Be suspicious of any food item that contains 20+ ingredients, many of which impossible to source and use in a normal kitchen: what was the last time you thought about adding maltodextrin, palm fat or dried whey to your dishes?

There has been pushback on the need to avoid chemical formulas as food ingredients from all quarters, based on the tautological argument that everything, after all, is made from chemicals, so why should we fear chemicals? The reductionist fightback, as we have already seen, includes scientists, chefs, food critics and, believe it or not, vegans. Ed Winters, in one of his many media appearances, tried to defend the fact that vegan burgers contain many unpronounceable ultra-processed ingredients by arguing:

"Well, I sometimes hear this phrase "don't eat anything that you can't pronounce". Oh, so just about all the different vitamins and minerals that we need to be healthy. If you look at the names of these vitamins.... Cyanocobalamin.... Or alpha linolenic acid... these are essential vitamins and minerals that we eat..." [596]

The elementary answer to such gormless bleating is that there is a world of difference between a whole food ingredient (e.g., milk) which contains vitamins or minerals that we can refer to with a chemical formulas (e.g., cyanocobalamin) and the use of synthetic chemicals and lab formulations as actual ingredients. This is yet again another example of how the reductionist mind works: reduce everything to its basic components and voilà! Everything is the same as everything else! I am chemistry, you are chemistry, my dog is chemistry, this book is chemistry... Even van Tulleken, who has been campaigning against ultra-processed foods, and would surely oppose the average vegan burger, reminds us: "*Food is, after all, made of chemicals. We are made of chemicals.*"[597]

[595] See full list: https://www.food.gov.uk/business-guidance/approved-additives-and-e-numbers

[596] How to Argue With a Meat-Eater With Earthling Ed, The Plant Based News Podcast, 31 January 2024.

[597] C. van Tulleken, 2023, Ultra-processed People, page 209.

TO SUM UP: If you need a chemistry degree to make sense of a label, you should immediately dismiss the product therein as unfit for human consumption.

Vegetable Oils*

We should view a staple like vegetable oil with the same lens that we use for flour, pasta, and sugar. These are kitchen essentials that vary greatly in quality and where close attention to labels really pays off. Basically, the quality of vegetable oil is greatly variable, and depends on the quality of the oilseeds or fruits from which they are derived, as well as the processing method.

The low-quality oils tend to exhibit the following features:

1) The oil seeds are stated as being the product of more than one country.[598] In other words, the oil is made up of a blend of oilseeds that have come into a single processing plant. For example, most of the big Spanish and Italian brands are not producing olive oil made with Spanish and Italian olives, but with blends of whatever cheap olives the producers could get on the market.
2) There are no details of cultivation method.
3) There are no details of crop variety (e.g., olive variety).
4) There are no details of processing (e.g., extraction process).
5) Contain additives, like anti-foaming agents in rapeseed oil.
6) Seed oil type: strictly avoid all soya oil, which is made with GM soya from overseas, and avoid rapeseed, groundnut, and maize oil.
7) Very low price. This is a comparative exercise which you can do quite easily when you shop. It's not simply a case of "the more expensive the better", but as a rule you get what you pay for. With olive oil, it is simply impossible to grow olives with care and respect for the environment, harvest them, cold press them, bottle the oil, market it and charge, at today's market rate, less than around £15-18 a litre. The best sunflower oil, and those of other oilseeds, generally cost less.

Lastly, in spite of all my bias for olive oil, which objectively speaking is a real gift of nature, there is no sense in which we should be overly focused on what type of oil we go for. There are cultural, geographic, and economic reasons why we may prefer one type of oil over another. What matters is simply the quality of the oil you use. I would always much prefer, if

[598] This is true of olive oil and sunflower oil. With rapeseed oil, it is normally British, but it should nonetheless be avoided given the agrochemical scourge on the land that rapeseed oil truly is.

I were forced to make the choice, to dress my salad with the best organic sunflower oil on the market than a really poor olive oil.

TO SUM UP: avoid the cheap industrial vegetable oils. Strictly avoid rapeseed oil, unless it's organic, which is very rare, and avoid all soya oil. Get better quality oils and use less.

Chapter 11

WHAT TO EAT: A SHOPPING GUIDE - A TO Z

It has to be presumed that the majority of us will shop for our food, as opposed to growing, gathering, or catching any of it. It is therefore imperative to know how to read labels, test quality, seek out the best suppliers and make wise decisions. I recommend you consult this chapter whilst keeping an eye on the previous chapter, as many of the categories are the same.

Lastly, as we will see in the next chapter, there will be some categories that you will need to avoid completely if you are on a slimming diet but, nonetheless, in principle, there are good ways to eat virtually any food category, including desserts and sugar, in spite of what sugarphobes keep telling us.

So, here we are again, in alphabetical order:

Biscuits & Cakes

This may seem like an odd place to start, but this is the burden of an alphabetical list. As we saw in the previous chapter, there is a lot that can go wrong in this category. It is imperative that you read labels very closely and when in doubt, desist.

Here is what to look out for:

- Relatively short lists of ingredients.
- Sugar (preferably raw cane sugar) or honey or pure organic syrup based.
- Butter based.
- Whole milk or double cream-based.
- Free-range eggs, at a minimum.
- Fruit or nut-based may be an advantage.
- Whole spices (e.g., cardamon, saffron, aniseed) may be an advantage.

- Some or all organic ingredients, ideally.
- No bright colours and additives.
- Artisanal, small-scale manufacture may be an advantage.
- Products that are baked in a wood oven often tend to be better.

TO SUM UP: eat moderate amounts of biscuits and cakes and buy very selectively. This is a food category in which making your own really pays off.

Bread

I am old and fortunate enough to remember the smell of traditional bakeries selling bread made in wood ovens, where the bakers started work on the dough before dawn and produced products of sublime quality and flavour. This sort of artisanal production is mostly a thing of the past, but we can still look out for a few basic features when purchasing bread:

- **Very short list of ingredients, usually just three**: wheat (or other grain) flour, water, and sea salt. Of course, if a bread is seeded, or is a milk loaf or some other very specific type of bread, there will be more ingredients, but bread 101 should only really be made with a list if three ingredients.
- **Sourdough**: made with natural airborne yeast.
- Any information about the **cultivation method** used for the wheat or whatever other grain in question. As ever, organic is better.
- **Process**: there may be positive information about the baking method (e.g., wood-fired oven) or milling method (e.g., stoneground flour).
- **Origin**: the best breads tend to indicate some reference to a locality, bakery, or recipe, as opposed to non-descript factory products with a brand name.

Nutritionists and dieticians would generally ignore all the above and just recommend people choose brown or wholemeal bread over white bread. I will argue that if all the above boxes tick, it doesn't really matter what bread you go for, it is mostly a matter of taste. Darker breads, especially those made from rye, are particularly good, but it is always better to go for a quality, traditional sourdough white bread than for a poor brown bread, such as those described in the previous chapter.

Lastly, do not waste bread, which is one of the most wasted foods around. Bread freezes well, for a start, so there is no reason not to save bread when you know you will not be able to consume what you purchased in the short term. If you do not wish to freeze it, or do not have a freezer, and you do get a large quality loaf, you can use the hard, stale bread for some wonderful dishes, including soup.[599]

TO SUM UP: eat actual bread, rather than the ubiquitous imitation products. Be suspicious of anything that contains more than 3-4 ingredients.

Breakfast Cereals

We have all been brought up in the breakfast cereal era and we would all be better off leaving it behind. For those who are in the habit and need to "crunch" in the morning, there are some niche options, of course: organic corn flakes, organic granola, or organic muesli.

A notable and particularly wholesome exception is oat porridge, traditional to the British Isles. It is a fundamentally good staple, which has been consumed for a very long time for good reasons. Similar preparations, made with other grains, exist in other cultures and climates. Go for wholegrain organic oats and do not add any sugar to it.

TO SUM UP: consider avoiding breakfast cereals altogether, apart from porridge and a few other niche products, and only if you like them.

Chocolate

Chocolate is often associated with guilty pleasure and body fat. This is an easy error to make considering that most of the chocolate on the market is junk, as described in the previous chapter. The main features and ingredients to look for when purchasing chocolate bars from retailers:

- The main ingredient, **cocoa**, will preferably be organic.
- The origin of the cocoa is listed, as a "**single origin**" product from one specific region or country (e.g., São Tomé, Dominican Republic, Peru, Ecuador).
- **Cane sugar**, preferably organic, rather than just "sugar".
- **High percentage of cocoa**, even for milk chocolate, ideally above 50%.
- Organic milk solids.
- No other ingredient, apart from vanilla, normally. An exception is chocolate that has specific additions, such as nuts. As long as the above criteria are followed, then this is not a problem.
- White chocolate is also acceptable, provided it follows the above parameters, with cocoa being substituted by cocoa butter.

[599] Look up Pappa al Pomodoro, Ribollita and Panzanella: Tuscan classics designed to use old bread.

It is worth noting that if you go to the great artisanal chocolate shops in Turin or Paris or other European capitals, they rarely if ever use organic cocoa. Does this contradict the above? Not necessarily, as they will get the very best single-origin non-organic cocoa and other quality ingredients and, unlike the chocolate we looked at in the previous chapter, will not contain any of the usual ingredients of low-quality chocolate, such as palm oil.

TO SUM UP: chocolate is a good thing. Be very selective and read labels. If you are able to enjoy dark chocolate, so much the better.

Cold Cuts

Cold cuts or processed meats in general get a really bad press these days and, as we saw earlier, are even considered a carcinogen by the WHO. This is a fundamental error based on the presumption that processed meats products somehow all fall under the same category and are all made the same way and with the same meat, which is nonsense.

The best cold cuts, which will most likely be eaten as treats, snacks, or small starters rather than daily staples,[600] are excellent foods with much to offer and are a precious addition to the larder. So much can go wrong with cold cuts, however, so here are the features we need to look out for, presuming we are looking at pork products, which make up the majority of cold cuts:

- As ever, the meat has to come from **organic or equivalent systems of husbandry** and this needs to be stated clearly on the label or counter. If a ham is labelled as being made with "pork" and nothing else is stated on the label, you can be certain that the pork will be from a factory farm. If a cold cut fails this first test, we must desist.
- **Rare Breed** is a very good indicator of quality. Some of the very best pork products are not necessarily certified organic but are made with rare breed pigs raised with the same principles. These products are in fact often better than some certified organic pork products. Basically, the old fashioned, rare breeds of pork are simply not designed nor suitable for factory farming systems and the good farmers who raise these animals do so specifically because they want to provide an alternative to the

[600] The exception might be if one buys an entire ham from a great farm. We used to occasionally do this as a family, buying a whole *prosciutto* directly from a traditional farm in Tuscany. The ham would be in the kitchen and get carved almost daily. Spaniards will do similar things with their *jamon*. It really depends on your circumstances, where you live and what you want to spend your money on. But the main point is that hams can be regular/quasi daily foods, albeit in moderate quantities. The extra fat and the skin, as well as the bone, all end up being used in the kitchen as well. A classic Roman countryside dish is *fagioli con le cotiche*, a delicious bean soup made with the skin/rind of *prosciutto*.

factory farmed mainstream products.[601] These pigs tend to grow slowly, are relatively undemanding, hardy, and able to look after themselves, to an extent. For example, they traditionally forage for acorns, chestnuts, and orchard fruit. They enjoy eating fresh grass from pasture and clearing up arable fields. They have a certain "wildness" about them and struggle in confinement.[602] They tend to develop a thick layer of beautiful, dense fat, which is the part of the pig which we should value the most. The meat is outstanding in texture, flavour, and nutritional value.

- There are heritage pig breeds left in many parts of the world. Closer to home, here are some examples:
  - England: Gloucestershire Old Spots,[603] Tamworth, Large Black, Berkshire, Oxford Sandy and Black, British Saddleback.
  - Italy: Cinta Senese, Nero dei Nebrodi, Mora Romagnola, Nero Casertano, Porcu Sardu, Maiale Nero dei Monti Dauni, Nero d'Abruzzo, Nero di Parma, Nero di Calabria. Italy is objectively unparalleled, pork wise, both in terms of breed diversity and breadth and quality of creative end products.
  - France: Noire de Bigorre. I had the pleasure of eating this pig in France, and like all heritage breeds at their best, it was fabulous.
  - Hungary/Austria: Mangalitza. This is a very hairy pig with a coat! Looks most distinct and I had the pleasure of finding its wonderful products (I specifically looked for them), including the lard, during a memorable trip to Vienna.
  - Spain: Iberico. When buying Iberico, which is the classic black-skinned breed of the Iberian Peninsula, always look for the words *de bellota*. This indicates that the pigs were finished on acorns, and it is a legally valid label. You will taste the difference, it is fantastic.
- **Very few ingredients**: normally just pork, sea salt and spices.
- The **nitrates/preservatives** issue: most cold cuts, even the very best ones, contain sodium nitrate (also listed as E251). Historically, a rock called saltpetre was mined to make this salting product, it is now produced synthetically. It preserves the meat and makes it easier to store and avoid rotting. There is no doubt that sodium nitrate is generally not good for us. However, industrial cold cuts tend to contain more

[601] Most pigs in the industry are Large Whites, and even the very best organic pig farms often have Large Whites or cross breeds with Large White genetics. To be clear, there is nothing inherently wrong with the ubiquitous Large White, as these pigs can be raised as happy outdoor pigs and excellent products made from them. Sadly, the fate of most Large Whites is confinement in factory farms. The point is that the heritage rare breeds cannot and are not raised in factory farm conditions and should therefore grab your attention when you come across their products.

[602] ALL pigs struggle and suffer in confinement, but the old-fashioned heritage breeds are particularly hard to control and manage when compared to the unfortunate Large Whites.

[603] Used to be known as the "orchard pig": a perfect example of how crop and livestock farming can and should be integrated.

preservatives than traditional cold cuts: most low-quality bacon, for example, tends to contain both sodium nitrate and potassium nitrate.

- The Porcine Holy Grail, which can be found, is a cold cut that ticks all the above boxes (organic, heritage breed etc…) and does not contain nitrates. Many of the Cinta Senese products I have had the pleasure of eating do not contain any preservatives of any kind. The best *prosciutto* and *jamon* also never do. Helen Browning, the CEO of the Soil Association, has recently launched organic bacon that is entirely nitrate-free.[604]
- Nonetheless, my general advice is that if you do find a great pork product that ticks all the boxes but does contain nitrates, you should still buy it, as you may be missing out on some of the very best products you could find. However, I would recommend you eat it in even greater moderation and in the best possible context.[605]
- Other labels: any products that fall under the **Slow Food** banner will generally be very good. Most of the heritage breed pigs are indeed championed by the Slow Food Presidium system. **Protected designation of origin (PDO)** and **protected geographical Indication (PGI)** are other labels that you will find on a range of cold cuts. These EU and UK labels aim to preserve the designations of origin of food-related products, by linking them to their locality, history, and manufacturing techniques. For example, Parma Ham is a PDO product: only ham that complies with the Parma Ham protocol and produced in a defined area in the hills around Parma can legally be labelled as Parma Ham. The PDO does not guarantee that the products are made with the best quality of meat, unfortunately. Parma Ham can be made with great pork or, more often than not, with factory-farmed pork, as long as it is raised in Italy. Therefore, whilst it is always better than non-descript supermarket cold cut products (e.g., your average supermarket cooked ham is definitely far worse than the lowest quality Parma Ham, which is at least preservative free), PDO and PGI products should not be presumed to always be desirable per se, especially if no other information is available.

There are also cold cuts made from beef, mutton, goose, goat, horse, donkey, water buffalo[606] and other livestock and the exact same principles outlined above will apply. Wild boar can be very good, but you must read the label closely, as often it is made with a blend of wild boar (which is an excellent food) and factory-farmed pork (which is awful). All the

[604] https://helenbrowningsorganic.co.uk/shop/bacon/

[605] As in: are you eating lots of vegetables and other wholesome foods on the same day?

[606] I have had the pleasure of eating water buffalo salame in Sicily: it is excellent.

same principles will apply to other cold cuts from around the world, such as biltong in South Africa and jerky in the United States.

TO SUM UP: enjoy cold cuts as some of the kitchen's great highlights but be very selective and moderate with your consumption.

Desserts & Ice Cream

The key, as ever, is quality of ingredients, followed by a call for moderation. As we saw in the previous chapter, so much can go wrong, given that the four key components of desserts tend to be: flour, sugar, dairy and eggs. The same is true of ice cream, with the absence of flour.

Here is what to look out for:

- Relatively short lists of recognisable, pronounceable ingredients.
- Sugar (preferably cane sugar) or honey or pure organic syrup based.
- Butter-based (for desserts).
- Free-range eggs, at a minimum.
- Fresh dairy ingredients (whole milk, double cream etc..) as opposed to dairy derivatives.
- Fruit or nut-based may be an advantage.
- Some or all organic ingredients, ideally.
- No bright colours and additives.
- Artisanal, small-scale manufacture may be an advantage.

The same point I made about chocolate applies here: the very best traditional pastry and gelato shops may not always follow all the above, but closely enough. There are not many of these shops around, so if you find a really good one, by all means use it on special occasions.

Overall, there is nothing inherently wrong with sugar or desserts, in spite of contemporary beliefs. It is wrong to deny your children these simple pleasures. Nonetheless, quality is the non-negotiable criteria you need to keep referring back to. It is also important to remember that one of the reasons why desserts come at the end of a meal, or are associated with festivity and celebration, is precisely because they are not absolute staples, but optional highlights.

TO SUM UP: same as cakes and biscuits. In a nutshell, be both moderate and very selective. Make your own, as much as possible.

Drink

Grape vines, as we saw earlier, are some of the most sprayed crops in agriculture. Nonetheless, there is no question that a great Barolo or Bordeaux, most of which will not be organic, will be wonderful to drink and that ultimately you get what you pay for.

Here are some basic criteria that are helpful in selecting healthier wines:

- Organic or Biodynamic certification. There are plenty of uncertified small-scale organic growers of course, but you need to know who you are buying from and look at each wine and producer on a case-by-case basis. In Sicily, I had the pleasure of visiting the Barone di Villagrande winery[607] on the foothills of Etna in Milo. Their wine is not certified as organic but is grown with organic methods, and the only source of external fertility used is donkey manure. There are plenty of growers like them: seek and you shall find.
- Grape variety, farm location and region are clearly labelled.
- Preferably low in sulphites.
- Cost: anything less than £10 a bottle tends to be poor.

Barone di Villagrande, Milo, Sicily.

[607] https://www.villagrande.it/en/barone_di_villagrande_en/

One of the many interesting results that arose from the Blue Zones study was that, in both Sardinia and Greece, the local centenarians drank simple wines that were made with organic grapes and zero additives. It makes perfect sense, in spite of what doctors and nutritionists might think.

The same principle applies to other traditional drinks, from lager and ales to stout, cider and perry, as well as spirits. Since the end of the War, we have lost many of our orchards, and private gardens do not feature fruit trees, generally speaking. If we were to increase fruit tree cover across the land, as we should, we would drink more cider, which lends itself particularly well to small-scale and organic production. In the meantime, whilst we wait for the arboreal revolution, let us support the best cider producers in the country.

TO SUM UP: the oenologists and wine club members will dismiss me as a fool, but if you prioritise organic and biodynamic wines, you will be much better off. We should grow more apples and drink more cider.

Eggs

Eggs are one of nature's great gifts and should form part of any sensible diet. In many ways, as we saw in the previous chapter, the labelling is somewhat easier to interpret than other products. If buying from a supermarket or shop, the simplest thing to do is to get the eggs that are stamped with a zero.

Here are the basic rules of thumb:

- Buy eggs with a 0 number stamp on them, which means that they have organic certification.
- If you don't live in town, there will be uncertified, free-range eggs on sale across the countryside from small producers: these are obviously worth going for.
- Farmers markets always have good eggs. Sometimes they sell misshapen ones for less!
- If you find eggs from rare breeds like Bantams, go for them.
- Never waste any part of the egg and plan your meals accordingly. If you are using the yolks for mayonnaise or ice cream, keep the whites for an omelette or meringues, for example.
- Eat more eggs in spring and summer than in autumn and winter.

TO SUM UP: good eggs are worth every penny. Prioritise them as one of the most important items on your shopping list.

False Grains

In case you are wondering, false grains (or "pseudo-grains") are not fraudulent cereals! The major cereal crops (wheat, barley, rice, maize, rye, oats etc...) are members of the grass family, *Poaceae*. False grains are seeds from crops that are neither cereals nor members of the grass family,[608] but which do a decent job at substituting cereals in the human diet. The main three false grains are quinoa (very popular nowadays), amaranth and buckwheat. The latter used to be an important secondary crop in many parts of Europe,[609] especially in altitude and marginal lands.

These seeds have an interesting characteristic absent in the main crop cereal grains: they contain all the essential amino acids and are therefore very nutritious. On the downside, they are not as versatile and palatable as culinary ingredients, especially quinoa. It is hard to see how false grains could ever significantly substitute wheat or rice in the human diet. Realistically, they diversify and enrich the overall diet rather than provide a staple food.

In the midst of the contemporary debate about veganism, there has been criticism of our increasing taste for quinoa, due to the fact the increased production of this crop for export in Peru and Bolivia, according to many reports, has had a negative impact on the population.[610] There may be some truth to this claim, as when crops become commodities designated for export, this does not necessarily benefit farming communities or the poor who rely on cheap staples. However, at times, the ability to produce and export a high-value cash crop can be beneficial to farming communities if done with the right principles and practices: context and detail are everything.[611] In spite of the claims of both "free trade" and anti-neoliberal dogmas, the world is complex and there are no simple answers to the problems afflicting farmers around the world.

Anyhow, even if we accepted the idea that quinoa production has had a negative impact on the populations of Peru and Bolivia, this is not a particularly fair criticism of the vegan enthusiasm for quinoa, given the damage caused by the production and export of other crops eaten by the average omnivore or by the animals that are raised for meat, eggs and dairy. We certainly cannot underplay the damage done by monoculture soya plantations in

[608] The exception being wild rice, which is not actual rice but an edible seed-bearing aquatic grass.

[609] In Italy, whilst a very minor crop, it is still grown in a few regions and made into breads, cakes, and pasta. The world's main producer by a long stretch is Russia.

[610] Arguments tend to focus on issues arising from monoculture replacing diverse cropping systems and from the increase in the price of the crop, which negatively affects the poor.

[611] There are definite examples of coffee or cocoa producing schemes, with Fair Trade, organic and/or other relevant certifications and guarantees, that benefit farmers involved in these projects.

South America that end up feeding livestock around the world, which is far more extensive and consequential than the production of quinoa. Of course, one of the most sensible solutions would be to start growing quinoa domestically here in the UK,[612] on a modest range, as part of organic crop rotations. The plant is almost identical to the common weed Fat Hen (*Chenopodium album L.*) and will grow very well and with few inputs.

As ever, when it comes to purchasing these sorts of whole foods, opt for organic options and read labels closely, but bear in mind that there is a limit to the options you have with imported crops grown in relatively few regions.

TO SUM UP: incorporate the pseudo grains in your diet if you like them. It's wholesome food.

Fish, Crustaceans & Shellfish

As we saw in the previous chapter, this is a difficult area to navigate, as there are many overlapping issues and concerns involved in all our choices. Ask yourself: 1) Farmed or wild? 2) If the latter, is it an endangered species? Is it being caught during its spawning season? 3) From which sea/freshwater/country? Is fresh fish travelling from far?[613] 4) If wild, which fishing method was used? 5) Are there any certifications/schemes that the fishery is monitored by?

In a nutshell, my recommendations are as follows:[614]

- Wild fish, rather than farmed, with few exceptions.
- Always try, within reason, to identify the fishing method used. Sometimes it is stated on the label, even at the supermarket fishmonger or on the packaging for packaged and filleted fish on the shelf. Refer to the previous chapter about what to avoid (e.g., Bottom/beam trawling).
- Fish that is pole and line caught is probably the gold standard. This is not possible for many fish species, like cod and haddock, but it is possible for tuna, sea bream, sea bass and pollack.[615]

[612] There are a few growers/farmers who do grow it, but it's extremely rare.

[613] E.g., Is it worth getting fresh grouper or Patagonian toothfish (AKA Chilean seabass) from the other side of the world, even if they came from sustainable, well managed fisheries?

[614] Bear in mind that I am presuming you are living in the UK. The same principles will apply wherever you live around the world (e.g., wild caught fish instead of farmed) but you will have different options and species depending on where you are.

[615] A good certifying body is the South West Handline Fishermen's Association. See: https://www.linecaught.org.uk/

- Never buy tuna that is not pole and line caught. The label on a can of tuna should specify: 1) Fishing method - pole and line caught; 2) Species - e.g. skipjack, yellowfin, or albacore, do not purchase anything else; 3) Sea/Origin: e.g., Azores.
- Sardines/pilchards, sprat, and anchovies. These humble fish are mostly used for farmed fish feed[616] and should really be in our larders instead.
- Pot/creel caught crab, lobster, and langoustines from British waters.
- Dived or farmed scallops, as opposed to dredged scallops. Dived razor clams.
- Fresh mackerel from British waters.

I can literally catch a bucket full of mackerel on a good day in the English Channel. It is still an abundant fish.

- Rope-grown mussels: possibly the most sustainable seafood option available, as well as cheap[617] and delicious. Top 3 seafood choices in my view.
- Dorset clams and cockles. Whelks and winkles from British waters. All of these may need revisioning in the future. [618]

[616] And even for livestock feed on land.

[617] Tends to go for £4 to £5.50 a bag.

[618] Whilst the "hydraulic pump-scoop dredge" method used to collect clams in Poole Harbours is not comparable to dredging for scallops, and is MSC certified, it is still relatively disruptive and may need more regulation in the future. As for whelks and winkles, these are being caught (in pots) in huge numbers which may not be sustainable long term.

- Jig-caught squid and cuttlefish from British waters.

My own squid, caught in the English Channel, which later made its way into my kitchen. I am not suggesting you need to catch your own squid!

- Farmed oysters from British, Irish, and French waters.
- Spider crab. Huge numbers in British waters and up for grabs.
- Alaskan wild salmon and pollack. Alaska has done a relatively good job of managing its fisheries and the products are excellent.
- Icelandic cod, in great moderation.
- Icelandic or Norwegian haddock, in moderation.
- Icelandic Lemon sole and herring, in moderation.
- Dogfish from British waters.
- Flatfish like flounder, megrim, witch, dab, and brill, from British waters, in moderation. These are good alternatives to plaice and Dover sole, which have been overfished and should be eaten on rare occasions if at all.[619] For all flatfish, check their certification and try to avoid beam-trawled fish.
- Grey mullet, red gurnard, and garfish from British waters.

[619] Personally, I catch 2-4 plaice a year with rod and reel, if any, and eat Dover sole at a posh London restaurant once or twice a year. I would apply the same principle to monkfish, another overfished species that is usually caught by bottom trawlers.

- Two very productive "invaders": blue velvet swimmer crab (sea) and signal crayfish (freshwater).
- Try to get hold of the cheap, delicious fish that amateur fishermen like my good self regularly catch but which have limited commercial value, for no good reason: pouting, whiting, horse mackerel.
- Freshwater wild fish such as carp, zander, grayling, and pike from relatively clean waters.
- Organic brown and rainbow trout and any other fish from small-scale sustainable aquaculture. Read labels carefully, gather information and, when in doubt, desist.

Certifications/Guides:

- Some seafood products have the blue Marine Stewardship Council label (labelled MSC Certified Sustainable Seafood). The MSC has recently been coming under attack from critics, as exemplified by the recent successful documentary Seaspiracy.[620] Whilst the documentary exhibited the same sensationalist vegan agenda as its predecessor Cowspiracy, some of this criticism is justified: it is far too easy to get an MSC label and a lot of depleted fisheries and destructive methods are certified. In and of itself, it is an insufficient guarantor of sustainability. That is not to say that the MSC certification is worthless: it is still, on average, better than no certification at all.
- The Marine Conservation Society has a downloadable App[621] with a guide to sustainable seafood. It is far from perfect and a bit clunky to use, I find, but certainly useful and an added tool at your disposal.
- The Soil Association certifies a few farmed fisheries. As already argued, this is a dubious exercise, both in theory and practice, especially with salmon or indeed prawns. It is nonetheless still better than conventional aquaculture and can work quite well with freshwater aquaculture, with fish such as carp and trout.
- Read a book or two on the subject, to familiarise yourself with the main issues surrounding seafood, and to gain confidence in the kitchen.[622]

620 https://www.seaspiracy.org/

621 The Good Fish Guide (https://www.mcsuk.org/ocean-emergency/sustainable-seafood/the-good-fish-guide/)

622 I recommend: H. Fearnley Whittingstall and N. Fisher, 2007, The River Cottage Fish Book. If you wish to read up on the broader topics surrounding fisheries and the state of the oceans, I recommend Charles Clover's contributions (The End of The Line, 2004, and Rewilding the Sea, 2022).

My first seabass, which I caught off Poole Harbour, Dorset, thanks to my friend Oliver. I never buy seabass: it was a special treat.

A few words on good practices once you have selected what fish you wish to buy:

1) **Freshness**: when buying fresh fish, as opposed to frozen,[623] of whatever kind, make sure you check that it is actually fresh. There are three basic tests:
   - Smell: does it stink?
   - Touch: if you touch the skin and it bounces back up immediately, it is fresh, if you leave a dent, it is not fresh.
   - Look: the eyes must look alive, as opposed to glazed over.
2) **Thrift**: use offcuts, heads, bones, shells etc… to make stocks, soups, bisques.
3) **Consider deliveries and bulk buying**: you can order seafood from fishermen, fishing companies and fishmongers online nowadays, which allows for more room for research before you purchase anything and developing a relationship with a good supplier. You can also buy in bulk at times, for efficiency and economies of scale: whilst we all like fresh fish, there is no harm in freezing very fresh fish.[624]

TO SUM UP: fish, crustaceans & shellfish are excellent food items. Pay very close attention to what you purchase and be particularly conscientious about what you buy and order.

Flours

Wheat flour is relatively cheap and is, at the end of the day, a staple that belongs in the kitchen.[625] The best wheat flour, whether plain white, self-raising, wholemeal or strong bread flour, is relatively cheap and goes a long way. The key indicators to look out for when purchasing flour:

- **Cultivation method**: organic flour is always better than the alternatives, as a rule. Make this your key criteria.
- **Wheat variety**: it is very rare for the variety to be stated on the flour packaging. The vast majority of flour, including organic flour, is made with hybrid wheat varieties. If

[623] There is nothing wrong with frozen fish, but it will not be as good in the kitchen. However, between a quality, relatively sustainable frozen fish and a fresh fish of obscure origin and quality, go for the frozen.

[624] My dear friend Jeff and I have had the pleasure of having lobster and crab delivered from Cornwall from a fisherman I met whilst on a spearfishing trip. Buying in bulk made logistical and financial sense. We ate some of the lobsters (which arrived alive and kicking) fresh and froze the rest.

[625] In the UK, during the 2020 lockdowns, flour was apparently one the main grocery items to be hoarded. Instinctively, flour (and indeed bread) is perceived, even subconsciously, with food. Whether it was ever used by the panicking lockdown bakers or not is another matter.

you happen to find flour made with a single wheat variety or landrace, and this is stated on the packaging, that is a positive sign.[626]

- **Milling method**: most flour is made with a roller mill, including the highest quality organic flour. Stoneground flour tends to be excellent, so if you come across it, give it a go.
- **Any "colour"**: as previously discussed, it is not a simple case of white vs brown flour. The very best white flours will still contain some fibre and most importantly the living wheat germ. Furthermore, in any case, the type of flour you choose will depend on what you are cooking. You will need white flour for certain dishes and baked products, and that does not need to be a problem.
- **Country of origin/location**: the worst flour will be made with wheat from multiple countries and the packaging will not state a single country of origin, as it is made from a blend of cheap commodity wheat. The best flours will be from one country and, ideally, will state region and farm as well.
- **Added ingredients**: the vast majority of flour, including a lot of the organic flour on the market, has added nutrients (Calcium, Iron, Niacin, Thiamin). Flours that do not have any added nutrients are even better and the very top-end flours generally do not.

The same principles will generally apply to the flours made from other grains: rye, corn/polenta, rice, spelt etc… and those made from crops other than grains (e.g., chickpea, potato, buckwheat, chestnut). Make sure at least some of these flours find their way to your kitchen cupboard.

TO SUM UP: avoid eating too many products made with white flour. Use organic white flour when needed. Explore and use other flours as opposed to just wheat flour.

Fruit

Fruit should be one of the fundamental pillars of the human diet. In the UK, and indeed in the rest of Europe and North America, that is no longer the case and high-quality fruit is harder to get hold of, far more so than high-quality vegetables, meat, and dairy. Generally speaking, we have ripped up so many of our orchards, no longer bother with homegrown fruit in the garden and have lost all sense of seasonality. At the farm level, fruits are some of the most heavily sprayed crops on the market, and are mostly eaten raw, which increases the

[626] In England, an old wheat variety like Red Lammas will produce top quality flour. In Italy, it will be with wheat varieties like the aforementioned Senatore Cappelli.

I am a little bit biased, of course, but the best example of a flour mill I can recommend is the Italian Mulino Marino, which ticks every possible box: https://www.mulinomarino.it/images/brochure_eng.pdf

problem.[627] Fruit variety has also plummeted, with many varieties going extinct or becoming increasingly rare. Most apples on the market, for example, tend to come from a few varieties: Gala, Braeburn, Golden Delicious, Granny Smith, Pink Lady, Discovery etc... Like all other sectors in agriculture, the tendency in fruit production has been towards monoculture, simplification, homogenisation, loss of quality and a focus on superficial qualities.[628]

Nonetheless, if you frequent enough farmers markets, supermarkets, greengrocers and other suppliers, there are still decent options available. Here are some guiding principles:

- **Cultivation method**: organic or equivalent.[629]
- **Local unless exotic**: buy British-grown fruit for those types of fruit that actually grow in the UK: apples, strawberries, blackberries, pears, raspberries, plums and so on.
- **Heritage varieties**: look for heritage fruit varieties and for suppliers selling heritage apple varieties and old-fashioned plums like damsons or gages, for example. These will generally be good, irrespective of certification.
- **Seasonality**: eat fruit that is in season, by and large. Leave berries, cherries, and plums for the summer, don't eat them for the rest of the year. Make the most of the British apple and pear harvest. Apples store well pretty much all year round, so if you find good organic apples, they are a staple fruit you should have in your kitchen. Citrus fruits should be abundant in autumn and winter, and it is possible to find quality fruit in this category, albeit it will not come cheap.
- **Preserve and/or cook with good fruit**: if and when you find good fruit, make jams, preserves and desserts. Autumn should be the time to fill the jars. Freeze fresh berries for winter.
- **Dried fruit**: if you find quality dried figs, apricots, mango, pineapple, plums etc... you should absolutely have them in your larder. Look for minimally treated/untreated fruit, and preferably organic.

[627] Peeling or washing is not really a solution, contrary to popular belief. Agrochemicals are systemic and affect and shape the growth and quality of fruit throughout their lifecycle.

[628] There is nothing wrong with the popular apple varieties but bear in mind that they are mostly popular due to their aesthetics and uniformity, as opposed to flavour, nutrition, and potential in the kitchen. Having fewer varieties simplified the supply chain for supermarkets. Furthermore, specific fruit varieties have been favoured due to their ability to sustain packaging and transport without much bruising.

[629] As previously explained: there are uncertified growers who use organic methods. You will find some at farmers markets.

- **Exotic[630] fruit**: by all means go for citrus fruits, dates, kiwi, Japanese Persimmon,[631] tropical fruits like mango and so on. As ever, organic matters. Do you know how many pesticides are used to grow conventional oranges and pineapples?
- **Leave some on the shelf**: some fruit varieties are almost impossible to find. Good quality, that is. Specifically, I am thinking of peaches, apricots, figs, grapes and clementines. Cherries are not much better. These fruits are almost always bland, tasteless,[632] and heavily sprayed. It is a great shame and loss, and I wouldn't bother with them, unfortunately.
- **Bananas**: when in doubt, organically grown bananas are a cheap and valuable all year-round option.
- **Grow some?** I planted an orchard over the last two years. One of the many motivations is to have good fruit and of rare varieties. If you have even a tiny garden, plant both top and soft fruit. Find an allotment, go on the waiting list. Ask a friend or neighbour with a garden to plant trees together. We need a horticultural revolution in this country, be a part of it if at all possible.

TO SUM UP: try your best to get good fruit and incorporate it into your daily diet. Eat fruit at its best, follow the seasons and don't shy away from exotics.

Herbs

Herbs, both fresh and dry, are another important pillar of both diet and culinary pleasure. It is important to incorporate herbs in daily cooking and to add them to salads, sandwiches, and other simple dishes. There is no question that all the various herbs that we have traditionally used in Europe and elsewhere (mint, thyme, bay leaf, rosemary, sage, basil, parsley, coriander, marjoram, oregano, dill, tarragon etc…) are fundamentally good for our health and our palates. The same applies to the native herbs used in other regions and cultures around the world. Some of the properties of individual herbs are well known, others

[630] By exotic, I don't just mean tropical, but also fruit that simply doesn't grow here, like oranges and lemons from the Mediterranean. My own Central London home grown lemons do not count.

[631] AKA Sharon Fruit or Kaki: a wonderful fruit.

[632] I have eaten these at their best, and of several varieties. What we have available at every retailer in the UK is less than mediocre by comparison. You can still eat these fruits at their best from when travelling in the Mediterranean regions, (and even in Italy, Spain etc... the average quality has significantly dropped) but of course we can only do that on holiday, if indeed we can go on holiday… The last time I ate great figs was in Sicily and in Crete. In Crete they were straight off a tree, from an old couple who looked after a monastery shop. The smell and flavour took me back to my childhood.

less so. Herbalism is undoubtedly an interesting subject,[633] however, in essence, the details of the properties of different herbs do not really matter for our day-to-day diet. Just as it is a good idea to eat a broad range of vegetables of different colours, textures, and flavours, it is a good idea to apply the same reasoning to herbs: by using a broad range of quality herbs on a daily basis in one form or other, it will be beneficial.

Here are some guiding principles:

- **Seasonal when fresh**: don't bother with basil and coriander in winter, there are plenty of other fresh herbs in winter. Use dry herbs all year round.
- **Local**: it is dispiriting to see fresh parsley from Kenya or fresh rosemary from Ethiopia on the supermarket shelves. It simply makes no sense to import such simple herbs, that can so easily be grown domestically and which, in any case, have lost flavour and fragrance by the time they end up on the supermarket shelf. Therefore, shun fresh herbs from overseas, unless they are exotic herbs that are not grown in the UK.
- **Farmers markets**: tend to have local, fresh, and cheapest herbs, that come in large bundles. It is definitely the best place to buy herbs.
- **Organic or equivalent**: herbs are not generally grown very intensely and some, like rosemary, are so easy to grow that it is unlikely any producer would feel the need to bombard the plants with agrochemicals. Having said that, look for herbs grown with organic methods, certified or otherwise.[634]
- **Herbal teas**: make use of them. It is better to have loose-leaf single herbs (e.g., mint, lemon verbena) than to buy ready-made blends, but there are some good blends on the market.
- **Try to grow some**: some herbs, especially perennials like thyme, bay, and rosemary, are easy to grow in a pot and will be so fresh and fragrant when you pick them just before cooking. If at all possible, grow some of your own herbs.
- **Plan menus around good herbs**: if you get hold of great parsley, make *salsa verde* or *chimichurri*, if you get hold of great basil, make *pesto*, if you get hold of great coriander, make a curry with a raita on the side.

[633] There is an overlap between culinary and medicinal herbs: mint, for example, is both a traditional remedy for cold and a kitchen herb. Basically, all culinary herbs have some medicinal properties. Some herbs, on the other hand, are purely medicinal, such as feverfew and St John's Wort.

[634] One of my favourite greengrocers at a Farmers Market in West London was not certified but was proud of the fact that she did not use chemicals. You could argue that there is no way of knowing what a farmer sprays on their crops, irrespective of what they say. I will respond by saying that we need to make judgement calls on a case-by-case basis. If you have a good relationship with a grower, if they give you satisfactory answers and their produce is clearly of high quality, you may well choose to trust them.

TO SUM UP: go to the farmers market for quality fresh herbs. Do not buy fresh herbs imported from other countries. Have quality dry herbs in your larder. Try to grow some herbs in pots.

Honey

In most cultures, and in most religions, honey is treated with a special reference, one not bestowed upon the other ordinary foods of mankind. It has often been depicted as a gift, a blessing of the land, as a healing balm and sweet respite from the vicissitudes and trials of life. The average materialist-nihilist-reductionist Westerner will see this historical legacy as all the more reason to dismiss honey as just another "sugar". But as argued in our deconstruction of nutritionist ideology, sugar is not just sugar, and honey is not just a combination of fructose and glucose. Bees, their activities, their collective intelligence, their symbiotic relationship with flowering plants, as well as their end product, are part of a complex and dare I say beautiful, somewhat mysterious, web of life. Again, those who dismiss awe towards Creation will dismiss everything I say as reactionary sentimentalism. I will simply respond by saying that accepting that complexity and beauty cannot be reduced to sugar analyses and entomological studies is far more rational than the alternatives.

The medicinal and healing qualities of honey have, in part, been confirmed by science, but insufficiently so, especially as there are great differences in the quality of honey, which goes from the mediocre to the sublime. Furthermore, each honey is unique to some extent, with its characteristics depending on where bees have travelled and what they foraged. Each honey is a sweet reflection of local soils, vegetation, ecology, climate and so on. Honey also takes up some of the flavours and medicinal properties of the plants it forages on; linden honey will aid sleep and relaxation, for example, and eucalyptus honey will help relieve coughs and colds.

This is what to look for:

- **Flower/s**: the best honeys will state what the bees have been foraging on. An acacia honey is made from bees that have been foraging on acacia, a heather honey is made from been that have been foraging on heather and so on. Wildflower honey refers to honey that is made from bees that have been foraging on meadows and a mixture of wildflowers. When no flowers and forage are stated, it's usually not a great sign, for commercial honey. The same discourse does not apply for domestically produced honey, in the back garden or allotment, as the honey will be multifloral and the bees will simply forage whatever is around.
- **Raw/cold filtered/unpasteurised**: pasteurisation/heat makes honey smoother and more uniform but kills off a lot of its wonderful properties. Raw honey is effectively

honey straight out of the hive, with the most minimal processing. Always go for the raw honeys.

- **Unblended**: do not go for honeys made from different sources, even if they are of the same floral category. Do not go for an acacia blend, for example. Honeys that are "product of multiple countries" are no good. A jar of honey should be from a single hive or from a few local hives managed by the same beekeeper/company.
- **Location/region:** a good honey should specify where it is made. Yorkshire moors heather honey is clearly made from bees foraging up on the moors, for example. A lack of information is a bad sign.
- **Bee species**: some honeys may be marketed as having been made of a particular honey bee species. Much like heritage livestock, this is usually a positive sign, both in terms of bee conservation and the quality of the product.
- **Organic?** What does organic honey mean? In terms of what the bees actually forage, it makes little sense for honey made from bees that forage from wildflowers like heather or ironwort, as these are uncontaminated by agrochemicals by definition. Some of the very best honeys are not organically certified. There are also cultural and practical reasons, as many of these honeys are produced on a small scale by beekeepers who have no practical need to get certified and can still get a premium for their precious product. Certification makes a lot more sense for honeys made from domesticated crops, like fruit trees or arable crops that flower before setting seed. According to the Soil Association regulations, a beehive cannot be situated within 3km of conventional crops (e.g., next to your average oilseed rape field in the UK, which will not be good for bees nor produce great honey).[635] Lastly, organic certification enforces or encourages good practices, such as not mutilating the queen bee, using minimal chemicals to treat disease, leaving as much honey as possible for the bees over winter, using local bee species[636] etc... Therefore, overall, it is an additional tick in the box.

[635] My friend Mervyn, formerly a commercial beekeeper, informed me that commercial large-scale beekeeping in the UK would not be viable without oilseed rape. I am sure this is correct, given that there are so few flowering plants left in British agriculture. If we rebuilt an intensive organic agriculture built around flowering pulses, such as beans and peas, flowering vegetables, wildflowers meadows, orchards, and soft fruit, we would have more than enough forage for extensive beekeeping.

[636] The diversity of honeybees has decreased over time, in the same way that so many domesticated and wild animals have gone extinct or become increasingly rare.

- **Diversify**: treat honeys like fine wines and explore honeys made from different flowers, from different regions and places around the world.[637] Honey has no real expiry date, so it is the ultimate food for import and storage.

TO SUM UP: honey is indeed a somewhat miraculous food. Make the most of it and be grateful. Incorporating at least a teaspoon of great honey a day is a sound idea.

Legumes AKA Pulses

Legumes have been a fundamental part of the diet of agricultural societies around the world since antiquity. Throughout the history of agriculture, legumes have generally served the crucial purpose of compensating for the scarcity of meat and fish in the average diet.[638] As is often the case, we have gone from one extreme to the other: in Europe and North America, we eat enormous amounts of low-quality meat and consumption of legumes is now almost negligible. Is there a middle way available between the default consumption of legumes and their abandonment? The short answer is yes. We could eat less, but far better, meat and eat a lot more legumes than we currently do.

I am fortunate to have grown up in what I would define as a "residual legume culture". It is residual because legume consumption in Italy has steadily declined since the post-war period, just as it did in other industrial nations. The average Italian now no longer eats legumes as a staple food. However, Italy has an extraordinary variety of unique legume varieties across its peninsula and islands[639] and a residual legume culture has managed to survive. Pulses still feature in domestic and trattoria tables across the country and, most importantly, high-quality legumes are still grown, albeit on a relatively small scale, with countless heirloom varieties being preserved.

At the certain risk of perpetuating every Italian stereotype (and let's face it, most stereotypes tend to contain significant elements of truth, including the following), I am most grateful to my mother. She was bucking the trend in the 80s and feeding us with all the classic legume dishes on a very regular basis. It is fair to say we were in a minority. I recall shelling fresh borlotti beans, peas, and broad beans and seeing bowls of dry pulses soaking in water in the kitchen as part of normal domestic routine. All the classic staple dishes featured: pasta and

[637] For exotic experiences, try forest honey from Zambia, strawberry tree honey from Sardinia, carob honey from Crete, savory honey from Abruzzo, lavender honey from Provence and so many other wonders from around the world. It is remarkably easy to get these sorts of products online nowadays. The best honey I have ever had might be a special honey my dear sister Ilaria got for me from a monastery in Japan.

[638] Legumes are still consumed in large quantities in parts of Asia, Africa, and Latin America.

[639] Many of the small islands have their own legumes. For example, the little islands of Ustica and Ventotene have their own unique lentils.

chickpea soup (with rosemary, in Rome), Borlotti or butter beans and pasta soup, fresh peas and pasta soup in the spring, lentil and pasta soup, Cannellini beans in tomato sauce and so on. The pasta shapes varied, and pasta was often substituted for rice or whole barley grains. Potatoes sometimes featured as well. Traditionally pulses are also eaten by themselves, just boiled, and dressed with excellent olive oil and sea salt, and perhaps some good vinegar. Minestrone, a seasonal classic soup featuring all sorts of vegetables, sometimes featured freshly shelled Borlotti beans or fresh peas depending on the time of year. Lentils were also combined with pork, famously at New Year, when lentils are cooked with unique sausages, *cotechino* or *zampone*. Chickpeas in Rome are combined with salt cod, and, especially in Tuscany, cannellini beans are combined with tuna. We kept up many of these good habits when we moved to England in the early 90s, as dried legumes are not difficult to find and last forever in the larder.

In Britain, for geographical and agricultural reasons, legumes have generally not been as prevalent in the diet as they have been on the continent. Having said that, peas, and field beans (both the broad bean, *Vicia faba*, and the so-called horse bean variety, *Vicia faba var. equina*) have been grown here since antiquity and were a very important part of the diet of the poor. Mushy peas, the accompaniment of fish and chips, and pease pudding are modern remnants of British legume culture. By the early 20th century, the most prevalent legumes were, and still are, the pre-cooked and canned baked beans that feature on toast and in the English fried breakfast. These, however, were an import from America, as the Heinz company increasingly exported its products overseas from the late 19th century onwards.

Apart from the Indian community, and a few other minorities, legumes play a very marginal role in the British diet. This is a shame, and we should be growing far more legumes on farmland and gardens and should be importing quality legume products other than the common and extremely mediocre canned baked beans. The good news is that excellent dried legumes can be bought online and in shops, which gives us plenty of scope for incorporating these precious plants into our diets and recipes.

Here are some suggestions:

- **Dried**: it is far better to get dried pulses as opposed to pre-cooked pulses. They taste better once cooked and, not surprisingly, the best quality pulses are never generally sold pre-cooked. Pre-cooked pulses also contain synthetic preservatives, at times. To prepare dry beans, chickpeas and so on: place the pulses in a big bowl of cold water, add a pinch of bicarbonate of soda and let them soak overnight. The following day, wash them and boil them in water and sea salt and they will be ready to eat or use for whatever recipe you wish to make. If, however, you really can't be bothered, there are plenty of cans of organic pre-cooked pulses in water which are not bad and certainly better than the average product sold on supermarket shelves. They are also very cheap and nutritious, and versatile in the kitchen.

- **Origin/location**: the best legumes tend to specify the location where they are from, with the country at the very minimum. Do not buy blends of pulses labelled as being "from EU and non-EU countries". Apart from the country, the best products will also denote the region and farm where the pulses were grown.
- **Organic or equivalent**: there are plenty of organic legumes on the market thankfully and legumes lend themselves particularly well to organic cultivation. Many of the old heritage varieties actually would not perform well with chemical fertilisers (just like old wheat varieties) and are therefore generally grown organically by default. The best organic legumes on the market, in terms of quality and diversity, tend to be from Italy and Greece. Turkey is also a major producer of good organic pulses, as is India.[640] China and Canada are also major producers, but quality tends to be lower. Nonetheless, if you are on a tight budget, a bag of generic organic legumes from any of these countries, which costs around £2.00-2.50 for 500g, is still a very good call.
- **Heirloom/single varieties**: as we have often seen throughout this book, specific, single-crop varieties and livestock breeds should be sought after, as they often correlate with quality. If you come across common single varieties like Borlotti or Cannellini, that's good, provided they are grown in their country of origin. If you find heirloom specialist varieties (such as the aforementioned Saluggia Beans), you have hit the jackpot!
- **Diversify**: the broader the types of pulses you try to use, the better. Legumes are plentiful: beans, peas, chickpeas, lentils, chickling peas, black-eyed peas, broad beans, and a few other minor legumes that do not fall under any of the previous botanical categories. Again, go for different colours (did you know there are black chickpeas?), sizes and textures. Inevitably, you will find your favourites but broaden your horizons.
- **Bulk**: given that there is some time and effort involved in soaking and boiling pulses before eating or using them for recipes, it is better to prep a large batch (say a 500g bag or more depending on family size) and use it during the week for more than one meal.

[640] India is a particularly impressive source of legume biodiversity. It is just harder to source organic legumes from India if you live in the UK or elsewhere in Europe. Turkish organic legumes, on the other hand, are very easy to find and are relatively cheap.

TO SUM UP: legumes should be one of the foundations of diet and culinary culture; bring them into your kitchen on a regular basis.

Meat

Meat has always been a most desirable food, if not the most desirable. As should be clear by now, there is no absolute ethical, medical, or environmental reason not to satisfy that ancestral desire. The key features we should look at when selecting meat products are the following:

- **Farming method**
  The best farming standard is organic or equivalent to organic.[641] With beef, we want animals that are almost entirely grass-fed and outdoors for much of the year. With lamb and goat, mercifully, that is generally always the case in Britain. With poultry and pork, we need to be extremely careful, as these are the meat products most likely to come from factory farms. Do not buy anything unless you have some solid information about the farming method involved in the raising of these animals. Be sceptical of "free range". For poultry, it is a legal definition which, as we saw in our section on eggs, is indicative of better, but often far from optimal, production methods.[642] For pork, lamb, or beef, it doesn't necessarily mean anything and has no legal grounding. For pork, as we saw in the previous chapter, "outdoor reared" is the very minimum standard that we can consider, but we can do a lot better.[643]
- **Feeding regimens**
  There is rarely anything about what livestock are eating on the labelling. The words "grass-fed" alone, unfortunately, are not legally binding and may not necessarily mean that the animals have been grass-fed throughout their whole lives. Having said that, it should still draw your attention, and some "grass-fed" labels specify what they mean by "grass-fed", or the % of grass feeding. With poultry, sometimes, we find "corn-fed" chicken, which is not, on its own, a guarantee of quality, for the simple reason that a corn-fed chicken might very well be a barn-raised bird of the kind we want to avoid. With pork products, if you find a producer that has finished his animals on acorns or chestnuts, you have done very well.

[641] Please refer to Chapter 3 for a discussion of what we mean by "equivalent to" and why some of the best products are not certified organic.

[642] There are some farms producing quality free range chicken with no organic certification (I have had very good chicken from this free range chicken producer in Suffolk: https://www.suttonhoochicken.co.uk/) but unless you actually know about the farm and its operations, you must presume that the bog standard free range chicken in the supermarket is a mass produced bird that too closely resembles the cheapest £3-4 kg chicken.

[643] Refer to the section on Cold Cuts above.

- **Certifications**

  The Soil Association organic certification, or the European organic certification, is a guarantee of a respectable standard of quality. USDA Organic standards are generally much lower, but better than their local alternatives. Therefore, always look out for organic certification, especially in supermarkets. The other very valuable certification to look out for is Pasture for Life.[644] Other labels, such as Red Tractor and RSPCA Assured, do not mean very much and are not indicative of quality.
- **Country/region of origin**

  Always look for where your meat comes from. With few exceptions, it generally makes little sense in Britain to buy fresh meat products from overseas. Products from a specific farm should be welcome, as you can look at the farm's website and get a clear idea of what you are buying. Furthermore, low-quality meat products never specify the farm they originate from.
- **Breed of animal**

  This is really important because when a breed is specified, this is very often indicative of quality. Therefore, a lack of information about this is another negative sign.
- **Supply**

  It's very important to find good suppliers. If you only have access to supermarkets most of the time, organic is the safest and best option and there is certainly value in using them when convenient and do not have time for shopping at more than one venue. However, it is worth investing time in finding professional, traditional butcher shops and going to the Farmers' Market and developing a relationship of trust. It is also worth considering having large deliveries online directly from a farm: you can get meat of the highest quality this way. Make use of your freezer.
- **Diverse cuts**

  One of the reasons to diversify away from the supermarket is that they only sell the same few cuts of meat. They also tend to be the most expensive cuts! It is healthier to eat most of the carcass, it is a more prudent and respectful use of the animal, and it makes for more varied and interesting culinary experiences. At the very least, try different cuts. If you just do not like kidneys (I must admit I am yet to enjoy them), do not eat them but do overcome our contemporary aversion to the grisly cuts and try all sorts of offal and offcuts. Even if you cannot stomach (pun intended) the internal organs, I do not believe anyone who likes sirloin and fillet would not enjoy shin or brisket.

[644] See https://www.pastureforlife.org/. In the USA, some products are sold as "pasture raised", which is a very positive sign, and more valuable than grass-fed, as it means the animal actually grazed as opposed to being fed cut grass or hay in a barn.

- **Thrifty cooking**
  Never waste or throw away meat. Use your freezer and just buy what you need if you have a really small freezer or do not have one. Cooked meat, especially stews, keeps for long in the fridge. In fact, slow-cooked meats and game tend to improve after a day or two of rest. When you buy whole joints and when you are preparing whatever cuts you need for a dish, keep all trimmings, extra fat, and bones for other dishes. When buying chicken, it is always best to buy it whole and use it for more than one dish unless cooking it whole. It is more economical and gives you the opportunity to eat the whole bird, which is tastier and healthier. The best butchers include a little bag with the neck and giblets. Cut the whole chicken up and if not using the carcass, freeze it and keep it for another day. The other option you have in the kitchen is not to make meat the absolute centrepiece of a meal. A small portion of meat with a lot of other items (grains, pulses, potatoes, vegetables etc..) is a good policy for a lot of meals.
- **Bones and carcasses**
  Following on from the last point, use bones and carcasses (the butcher will sell these separately and for a low cost) to make broths and stocks, which are healthy and delicious, and useful for other dishes (soups, risottos etc…).
- **Ageing**
  One of the many failings of supermarkets, apart from the now obligatory vacuum packing of meat, is that they do not hang and age meat, especially beef, which is standard practice for traditional butchers. The best butchers will hang and age meat, which will tenderise it. The length of the ageing can be a matter of taste, however, and ageing itself is not an absolute necessity. Given the choice between beef from 100% pasture-fed, rare breed beef that hasn't been hung very long and USDA feedlot beef that has been dry aged, you should always and unhesitatingly choose the former.

Referring back to the Meat section in the previous chapter, here is what to look out for:

Chicken

Organic or equivalent is the way to go, or top of the range free range.[645] It is expensive to produce and purchase, as it should be, and should not be considered a staple, daily sort of food. As said, buy it whole. The bird's flesh should not be flaccid and should be relatively dark in colour. Always look very carefully at what you buy.

[645] Which is not available at the supermarket. Free range at the supermarket is not recommended.

Other Poultry

With turkey, organic or equivalent is again the way to go. It is a very expensive once-a-year investment, but worth it. We bought the "Rolls Royce" of organic turkey this year, from the Rhug Estate in Wales[646] at a hefty £120. It was fantastic and can feed at least 8 people on the day, in my estimation, with ample leftovers. For a once-a-year special meal (plus leftovers), £15 a head is very reasonable. It is worth bearing in mind, and anecdotal evidence will confirm this, that a high percentage of the Thanksgiving or Christmas turkey is wasted, especially any other part of the carcass that is not breast. Therefore, it is far better to buy a smaller one or share a larger one with more people. Whatever you do, make sure you use all the leftovers for several days.[647] It may be a good idea to buy a whole turkey and just cook the breasts on the crown for the festivity and butcher down the rest of the bird (legs, wings, etc...) and freeze it for the rest of the year. The same principles apply to farmed duck and goose. With these birds, keep the fat in jars and bottles for the rest of the year, for roast potatoes and other dishes.

Pork

Organic or equivalent, including rare breed pork,[648] is the way to go. Alternatively, consider top of the range free range/outdoor reared. Only go for the latter when you have done some research. Earlier this year, I had a roast pork sandwich at Borough Market with my friend Imraan, who had recommended the place. As we queued, I checked the supplier of pork, which had a website and several YouTube videos. What was immediately clear, and later confirmed by retrospective investigation, was that it was pork produced on an extensive, 100% truly free-range basis, on pasture and muddy fields. The flavour lived up to Imraan's enthusiastic review.

Pork is famous for being 100% palatable and edible, so try and eat as much of the carcass as possible. Pork belly and ribs will be cheaper than pork chops and pork loin, so keep that in mind if your budget is tight and you want to eat quality meat from happy pigs. If you are adventurous, I recommend pig's feet, which are very cheap and not difficult to find, and any other offcuts you can find, including ears, cheeks and so on.

[646] See: https://rhug.co.uk/about).

[647] I recommend making turkey croquettes with the leftovers.

[648] Refer back to Cold Cuts for examples of breeds to look out for.

Beef

The usual principles apply; organically certified or equivalent, such as 100% grass-fed or certified by Pasture for Life.[649] The best beef will be sold with clear information about the farm, county and breed it comes from. Here in Britain, always look out for traditional breeds like Dexter, South Devon, Gloucester, and Native Aberdeen Angus.[650]

One of my favourite beef suppliers is a farm in Devon called Eversfield Organic, which ticks virtually every single box, and I will use as an example of best practice.

The farm was developed over conventional farmland and converted to an organic farm, with miles of hedgerows reinstated and over 30,000 trees planted over time, encircling lush pastures: a perfect example of how livestock can improve, rather than destroy, the environment. The cattle are Native Aberdeen Angus and are pastured all year round on a rotational basis.

Boxes ticked:

- Organic certification (Soil Association).
- Pasture for Life certification.
- 100% grass-fed.
- Heritage breed: Native Aberdeen Angus.
- Slaughtered locally on small family-run slaughterhouses.
- Meat is hung and dry-aged.
- Broad range of cuts available.

It is expensive beef and not for daily eating for most of us, but we have no reason to eat beef all the time, nor do we need to choose the most expensive cuts. In any case, I am giving this example to provide a very high benchmark and give readers an example of the various criteria they need to look out for.

[649] 100% grass or pasture fed does not necessarily mean that animals literally graze 12 months of the year, which is not possible in most of the country. It means that animals graze as long as conditions allow, including autumn brassicas, and eat appropriate herbaceous fodder when not grazing, such as hay and arable sileage.

[650] The actual native Aberdeen Angus is relatively rare. "Angus" beef is popular on menus and farms across the world, but most of these are cross bred animals at best (they are allowed to be called Aberdeen Angus when only sired by a bull, therefore 50% Aberdeen Angus) and black cattle at worst (in the USA they only need to be black to qualify for the Certified Angus Beef Scheme).

Another example of best practice and high benchmark is undoubtedly Daylesford Organic Farm,[651] in Gloucestershire, which ticks the same boxes and has the added benefit of having its own slaughterhouse. Its meat is simply excellent, the "Rolls Royce" of beef.

It is important to go beyond sirloin, fillet, and rib-eyes, great as these cuts are, and eat far more of the carcass. Try brisket, shin/ossobuco, oxtail, short ribs, cheek, tongue, and all sorts of other cuts. Get good mince, which is cheap and versatile, and marrow bones for stocks and broths. If you can find British veal that meets the same standards, you should not hesitate to go for it.

Beef cattle at Daylesford Organic Farm living as cattle should.

Lamb

Lamb is the safest choice when information is lacking. Nonetheless, look out for organic or Pasture for Life certification. Again, look for products that indicate the farm, county, and breed of sheep, as these tend to be the better products. We have a wonderful biodiversity

[651] https://www.daylesford.com/discover/sustainability/regenerate

of 63 heritage native sheep breeds in the UK and we should take the opportunity to help preserve them by eating them and patronising the best farmers.

Supermarkets tend to stock a limited range of cuts, as usual, and restaurants tend to focus on the delicious but limiting lamb cutlets and loin chops. These are expensive cuts, and there are several cheaper and delicious cuts. Of the common cuts, that even supermarkets stock, shoulder is the best value for money. Of the less common cuts, which you can find online, or at the farmers market or traditional butcher, try lamb breast (very cheap), scrag end, foreshank, leg shank and offal. Mince is always good value as well.

Apart from lamb, get hold of hogget (a juvenile sheep aged 1-2 years old) and mutton, we should be eating it on a regular basis, and goat if you can get hold of it.

Game

As we saw, game is generally a very good, safe, wholesome and tasty choice, and one you should not hesitate to include in your kitchen. Pheasant and partridge are in low demand and relatively cheap, so make the most of the shooting season. Try to include venison in your culinary repertoire and any other British quarry. To get good game, unless you take up shooting, stalking and frequent gamekeepers, simply head to traditional butchers and farmers markets.

TO SUM UP: eat meat with a clear conscience. Focus on absolute quality over quantity and source more carefully than any other food item.[652]

Milk & Dairy

Referring back to the Dairy & Milk section in the previous chapter, here is what to look out for:

- **Farming method**
  The broken record continues; organic or equivalent is the way to go, as that is the best way to raise livestock. With milk, butter, creams, and yoghurt it is relatively easy to find organic products and you should target them as your port of call. Virtually all supermarkets stock some organic milk and its basic derivatives, relatively cheap. With milk, ideally, it should be unhomogenised and full fat. Cheese is somewhat more difficult to select. When choosing cheese, you want to look at cumulative criteria and

[652] I recommend, as a useful and thorough guide on the subject: H. Fearnley-Whittingstall, 2004, The River Cottage Meat Book.

facts and make a case-by-case assessment. There are excellent organic cheeses on the market, and you should certainly go for them. However, many excellent cheeses are not certified but are produced by traditional dairies that practice good husbandry, graze animals, and produce cheese with exceptional skill. For example, one of the best cheesemongers in London, Neal's Yard Dairy, sells traditional cheeses that are not certified organic but are of very high quality. For these sorts of cheeses, whether from Britain, Italy, or France, you need to look at other criteria, as outlined below.

- **Certifications**
  Apart from the Soil Association, look out for cheeses that are listed on the Slow Food Ark of Taste list,[653] that are listed on Pasture for Life and on the Great Taste Awards. Look at cheeses at cheesemongers as opposed to supermarkets.
- **Country/region of origin**
  All dairy products need to be labelled and sold as from a specific region and country, and ideally from a single farm, unless made with a blend of milks from a group of farms within the same region. Protected designation of origin (PDO) and protected geographical indication (PGI) is again an additional qualification that you can include in your overall assessment.
- **Ingredients**
  The best cheeses are made with (often raw) milk[654] and, if needed, natural rennet. The exception are those cheeses that include sea salt, a particular herb or spice or single ingredient.[655] Some of the low-quality cheeses, especially spreadable and soft cheeses, are made with milk derivatives (Milk Powder, Milk Fat, Whey Powder, Milk Protein etc..) and stabilisers.
- **Breed of animal**
  With milk, here in the UK, milk made from Jersey and Guernsey cows tends to be exceptional,[656] and it is virtually a guarantee of quality, as these lovely cows do not lend themselves to intensive systems of production and tend to be the cows of choice for farmers who want to run traditional, grazing based dairies. Look out for milk from Ayrshire, Shorthorn, and British Friesian breeds as well. The same principle applies

[653] https://www.fondazioneslowfood.com/en/ark-of-taste-slow-food/

[654] Some cheeses, most notably ricotta and cottage cheese, are second cheeses made from the whey leftover from primary cheese production, which is a wonderful piece of thrift and ingenuity.

[655] Red Leicester cheese includes annatto dye, which gives it its distinctive colour, and truffle pecorino cheese includes truffle, by definition.

[656] If I had to select one milk here in the UK that encapsulates all the best features, my unsponsored vote goes to Ivy House Farm in Somerset (https://www.ivyhousefarmdairy.co.uk/) as it ticks key boxes: organic, pasture based, Jersey cows, unhomogenised. They also make butter, buttermilk and creams using traditional methods. Everything is excellent.

overseas. For example, mountain cheeses made by Alpine cows are high quality by definition, and Parmigiano Reggiano (AKA Parmesan)[657] made with the milk of the local Reggiana red cow will be excellent.

- **Cost of cheese**
  With cheese, there are more nuances as some of the best cheeses on the market are not certified organic, in which case you need to look for other indicators of quality. One of them, I am afraid, is cost! You really get what you pay for. At current prices, good cheese cannot cost less than a very minimum of £1.00 per 100g. The best cheeses tend to cost £2.00-5.00 per 100g. Eat less cheese but eat good cheese.
- **Diverse**
  As ever with food, diversity is a positive. Consume a broad range of dairy products and whilst making the most of the dairy bounties of the British Isles, do not hesitate to consume great cheeses from the continent as well.
- **Yogurt/Kefir**
  Yoghurt, fermented or otherwise, is a fantastic whole food. Make sure that, apart from organic or equivalent, it is plain, full fat, with zero added ingredients.
- **Buffalo products**
  Buffalo mozzarella is an exceptional Italian delicacy with few parallels. Some of the herds are intensively reared, however, so make sure you read labels closely and opt for organic when possible.
- **Sheep and goat products**
  Dairy products made from the main herbivores other than the cow are generally a very good option, for the same reasons that lamb and kid meat are generally good options. They tend to be extensive, outdoor, high-welfare husbandry systems producing niche products. Most of the great sheep and goat cheeses of Italy, Spain, France, and Greece are quality products, as are sheep and goat milk and their derivatives. There are far less sheep and goat dairy products here in Britain, but those that are made are generally of high quality and should be sought after.

TO SUM UP: milk and dairy remain a pillar of agriculture and diet, especially in Britain. Do not let fat phobia nor vegan follies get in the way.

[657] Little note of interest for the protein obsessed and bodybuilders out there: Parmesan is one of the very few cheeses that contains more protein (32.4%) than fat (29.7%).

Nuts

Nuts are a basic whole food that we should be eating more of.[658] Nuts are mostly a niche health food or a marginal snack in corner shops, pubs, and a small section of supermarket aisles.[659] There are some clear principles we can use in selecting nuts:

- **Raw**: avoid roasted, salted, and flavoured nuts. Always go for pure raw nuts. If you want salted peanuts, it is easy enough to make your own. They will taste far better and be far healthier than your average KP nuts.
- **Occasionally in their shell**? You will probably curse me, but I do recommend occasionally buying nuts in their shell, especially walnuts and hazelnuts, not because I want you to work for each nut, but because they are fresher and more flavoursome in their shell.
- **Untreated/Unblanched**: get nuts that have their skin on, that have not been blanched or treated in any way. You will gain in flavour and nutrition.
- **Cultivation method**: organic or equivalent for all cultivated nuts. Brazil nuts are wild harvested, rather than cultivated, with other major nuts mostly cultivated, with widely spread degrees of intensity. At the most industrial end of the spectrum, we have Californian almonds and pistachios, for example, and, at the end of the least industrial end of the spectrum, we have traditional chestnut and pine nut forests in Italy, Spain, and Portugal, with everything else in between.
- **Country/region of origin**: leading on from the latter point, completely avoid conventional almonds, pistachios, and walnuts from California, which make up a big slice of the total market. They are not grown for quality or flavour and depend on massive amounts of agrochemicals. The USA does produce some organic pecans, which are very good and recommended. As ever, always read labels: there is always a country of origin somewhere on the packaging. Do not buy anything that is "product of multiple countries". The best temperate climate nuts (walnuts, almonds, hazelnuts, pistachios) tend to be from European countries and Turkey, and organic ones are not difficult to find. Do not hesitate to go for tropical or Southern Hemisphere nuts such as cashews, macadamia, and Brazil nuts. Again, prioritise organic, raw, and untreated nuts.

[658] Not just to diversify and improve our diets, but to diversify agriculture: we need more perennials across all agro-ecosystems. The major nuts all come from perennial plants, with the exception of peanuts, which are an annual legume.

[659] Go to your nearest supermarket and observe how much greater the space devoted to crisps is, when compared to raw nuts.

- **Diversity:** nuts are little treasure troves of flavours and nutrients, try to diversify as much as possible. Some nuts do have some degrees of toxicity;[660] even more reason to diversify. It is recommended to buy them as single nuts and mix them yourself in a jar or Tupperware and have a readymade nut mix for regular use.
- **Little and often:** unless used in cooking or in desserts, they are best eaten little and often, as a snack or addition to a light lunch or breakfast.

TO SUM UP: natural, raw nuts are an excellent source of food. Ideal for snacking and for everyday use.

Pasta

Pasta has become a global food, one of the most popular and recognisable in the world. Contrary to popular storytelling, it has literally nothing to do with Marco Polo, noodles, or China,[661] and is a product of the Italic Peninsula.[662] I have always been interested in the psychological and historical fallacy that leads many to search for the single inventor of any particular thing, which presumes that human ingenuity can never work in parallel and stem from different, separate roots. For the record, no evidence linking Marco Polo to pasta has ever been found, noodles only partly resemble spaghetti and, even if we accepted the Marco Polo spaghetti tale, we would still need to account for the existence of thousands of pasta shapes and preparations found nowhere else in the world but Italy. It should be quite clear that different societies and cultures, in similar conditions, have come up with similar solutions and ideas quite independently. Can anybody claim to have invented bread or wine? The simple answer is no. Agricultural civilisations that started growing annual cereals and tending to grapevines often came up with similar uses for them: there was no Levantine bread inventor or Georgian wine inventor from whose invention everyone else learnt how to make these products.[663] The Chinese, who have been cultivating cereals for over four millennia,

[660] Brazil nuts contain some toxins, bitter almonds (spit them out) contain cyanide, and all nuts can form toxic moulds.

[661] I could not resist mentioning this to my readers, especially to my Chinese friend Lam, who bangs on about Marco Polo.

[662] The only other culture that has a local, albeit relatively limited, pasta culture is Greece. John Dickie, in his *Delizia! The Epic History of Italians and their Food* (2007) argues that spaghetti and dried pasta are likely to be of North African and Islamic origin, due to the fact that the first documented mention of a dry pasta factory in Sicily dates back to 1154, following the Islamic Era (831–1091), through a document written by Muhammad al-Idrisi, the 12th-century cartographer and explorer, who uses an Arabic word, *itriyya*, to refer to pasta (even though Dickie concedes that *itriyya* is likely a transliteration of a Greek word). Even if we take a single document as evidence of "the origin" of pasta production, the fact that nowhere in the Muslim world there exists, or has existed, anything like a pasta culture (one would have thought that the Muslims would have both preserved and spread their invention more widely) is sufficient reason to dismiss such claims. What the Muslim Era certainly did bring to Sicily was cous-cous, a North African staple that has been cooked in Sicily ever since.

[663] The same is true of many agricultural technologies: no single culture invented the wheel or the plough.

came up with noodles, dumplings and so on, the heirs of Greco-Roman culture on the Italic Peninsula came up with their own creative uses for flour, including dried pasta.

Anyhow, historical clarifications aside, there are now few food items so universally loved and known as pasta, of whatever shape and type. As we saw in previous chapters, mass-produced dried wheat pasta for daily consumption really took off exponentially in the post-war period and egg pasta, which was traditionally always freshly homemade, also became widely available. As industrially processed foods go, less can go wrong with dried wheat pasta, given its simplicity and single main ingredient. The cheapest spaghetti on the market will still be less risky than many of the ultra-processed foods of the kind we saw in the previous chapter. However, as we also saw, quality varies hugely, and there are many degrees of pastas quality available on the market.

This is what to look out for, with dried pasta:

- **Country/region of origin**: the origin of the wheat should be mentioned on the packet. The best pastas will mention country (Italy) and region.
- **Wheat variety**: the very best pastas will state the single wheat variety used (e.g., Senatore Cappelli, Saragolla etc..).
- **Cultivation method**: organic or equivalent.
- **Colour**: the lighter the colour, the better.
- **Slow dried at low temperatures**: this accounts for the lighter colour, and the fact that the pasta will not have been effectively pre-cooked.
- **Bronze drawn**: using bronze as opposed to Teflon gives the surface area a more granular and rougher texture, which grabs and holds sauce better.

When it comes to egg pasta, a great tradition of Northern Italy, wheat variety, cultivation method and place of manufacture matter just as much.[664] The main difference will be the addition of eggs. Use the same criteria for eggs in egg pasta that we have seen thus far for all eggs and egg products.

TO SUM UP: eat high-quality pasta, in more modest portions.

Plant Milk

I am an old-fashioned lactophile, and only use milk from a happy cow, or very occasionally, a goat. Plants do not make milk and "plant milk" is a slightly odd turn of phrase. Nonetheless,

[664] With regards to country of origin, there is a difference. Being fresh, there will be some local UK manufacturers as well, they will not all be in Italy.

we all know what we mean by plant milk these days, and it is becoming quite popular, mostly for the wrong reasons. It is a very marginal and inadequate substitute for actual whole cow's milk, it is low in nutrition (it is mostly made of water) and, as we saw in Chapter 6, there is nothing inherently virtuous about them. However, there is nothing inherently wrong with them either, it really depends on the quality of the products and there are a few decent products out there.

Here is what to look out for:

- **Cultivation method**: organic plant milks are definitely the ones to go for. Bear in mind previous comments about intensive almond production, for example, or consider how conventional GM soya is produced. A lot of milks also contain rapeseed or other low-quality vegetable oils which, as we saw, we must always avoid.
- **Country of origin**: the labelling tends to be very obscure. Usually, I have found that it just denotes whether the plant (almond, oat, soya or whatever it is) is from EU Agriculture or non-EU Agriculture. The best products will state country of origin (e.g., UK-grown oats or almonds grown in Spain).
- **No added sugar**: do not go for any plant milks with added sugar in them.
- **No additives/fortifications**: a lot of plant milks have additives added for texture and synthetic vitamins and minerals. Go for milks that only contain the actual plant, plus water and sea salt.

TO SUM UP: use plant milk if you are (actually) lactose intolerant or simply like them. Plant "dairy" is mostly junk, and there is no need for it in your larder.

Preserved Fruits & Vegetables

Fruit and vegetables are perishable goods, and their preservation has always been a chief concern of agricultural people. What used to be a domestic task can now be done cheaply and industrially and, overall, that is a good thing, as discussed in Chapter 4.

This is what to look out for:

- **Cultivation method and country/region of origin**: whatever applies to fresh fruit and vegetables applies to their preserved counterparts. Read labels closely. Are these pickled cucumbers organic? Where are those frozen peas from? And so on.
- **Ingredients**: do not confuse a preserved product with an ultra-processed one. Apart from the basic natural preserving agent and seasoning (e.g., vinegar, salt,

sugar), if any, you should not be getting a long list of ingredients and preservatives.

- **Frozen:** it is worth freezing or buying frozen produce at times, but only really for products with a very short season. Fresh garden peas and sweetcorn do not last long, and it makes sense to eat good frozen peas out of season. It makes sense to freeze summer berries. It makes little sense to buy frozen spinach and carrots, for example. Apart from being locally available throughout the year, much of the flavour and texture is lost by freezing and defrosting.
- **Canned vegetables:** canning has the great advantage of preserving food for a very long time, and very cheaply, without any need for refrigeration. Canning was a revolutionary industrial technology of great use to people living and travelling in remote places or in extreme climates, for long-distance travel by sea and for the military. Most of us do not live in such circumstances and with vegetables, it is not worth it in most cases, as fresh alternatives are easily available. It is definitely worth it for seasonal crops like tomatoes that need to be preserved after the summer harvest. Bear in mind that the only single ingredients of canned tomatoes are… tomatoes. If the tomatoes are good, they will also be good in a can. One issue with canning is that the metal is often lined with BPA (bisphenol-A), a toxic chemical used to avoid metal corrosion, and its traces can, apparently, be found in the food. There is no way of knowing this when you buy canned products. As a rule, it is probably prudent to avoid eating a lot of canned food anyhow, and you will be fine. Products in glass jars tend to be safer and better, so look out for those.
- **Canned fruit:** fruit is also not worth it for the average shopper. Canned fruit tends to be of low quality and best avoided unless absolutely necessary.
- **Pickled:** pickling is a great way to preserve lots of fresh produce, from cucumbers to onions and beetroots. Apart from being a preservative method, pickling actually alters the food being preserved, creating something altogether different in texture, flavour, and nutrition. Provided we make the usual considerations around cultivation method, origin of the produce and limited lists of ingredients (which may include herbs and spices) that we would make for any other product, then pickled vegetables are a great addition to the larder.
- **Oil-based preserves:** vegetables can also be preserved in vegetable oil which, again, provides a new world of texture, flavour, and nutrition. Same principles that we have seen thus far apply, especially around the quality of the vegetable oil.
- **Salted/fermented:** vegetables are also traditionally preserved with salt, the ultimate agent of preservation throughout history, especially for meat and fish, but has a limited use for preserving vegetables, as there are more palatable ways

to preserve vegetables.[665] There are however plenty of products preserved in brine (salted water) and salt is the key ingredient in fermented vegetable presentations such as Sauerkraut and Kimchi. Again, provided they are made with quality ingredients, these are very valuable foods. Capers are also traditionally preserved in sea salt and are definitely worth using in the kitchen.

- **Dried:** sundried tomatoes were very fashionable at some point and are undoubtedly healthy and delicious when done right. In Basilicata, sweet peppers (*Peperone Crusco*) are dried and used all year round. In Spain, *pimentón* consists of both sweet and hot peppers that are dried and pulverised. With few exceptions, most vegetables do not really need drying these days. With fruit, on the other hand, we have less preservation options available than we do with vegetables. In China, Japan and Korea, persimmon fruits are traditionally hung and dried, as are figs all over the Mediterranean. Dried fruit remains both palatable and sweet and develops new layers of flavour. As we saw earlier, dried fruit is worth adding to the larder.
- **Chutneys**: chutneys can be made with either or both vegetables and fruits. Worth making at home as opposed to buying ready-made.
- **Jam/Marmalade:** fruit jam, much maligned in our sugar-phobic age, is a wonderful way to preserve and enjoy fruit. Easy to make, you should consider using the best seasonal fruit you can find and making jam. However, if you cannot, there is some good jam on the market. The best jams are made with organic fruit, organic raw cane sugar (as opposed to standard white sugar) and, sometimes, a little lemon juice or pectin. Look out for the fruit-to-sugar ratio: whilst all jams have a high sugar content (usually 1.5:1 / 2:1 fruit-to-sugar ratio), the cheaper jams have even higher sugar content, with more sugar than fruit at times.
- **Syrup/Alcohol:** fruit is traditionally preserved in liquor or sugar syrup but is increasingly rare. If you can get hold of old-fashioned cherry preparations in liquor or syrup, it can be a great treat and something to use for desserts.

TO SUM UP: preserved produce has an important place in the kitchen, and it is a good idea to selectively stock up on a few things. Consider pickling, freezing, and preserving some produce yourself.

[665] On its own, that is. Salt goes into pickles and other preservation methods.

Salt

Salt is of enormous historical importance, as both a preservative and as a basic whole food ingredient. The English word "salary" comes from the Latin *salarium*, which stems from the word for salt, *sal*. One of the main roads built by the Romans, the *Via Salaria*, still in use, was built to transport salt. Whilst it is unclear what the link between wages and salt was, with some speculating that salt may at times have been used in lieu of salary, there is no doubt that salt has historically been a key resource and commodity.

Salt has also undergone one of the many, variable cycles of demonisation that we find in the world of nutrition science and dieting, and is often linked, with scant evidence, to heart disease and other conditions. Whilst there is no doubt that excess salt is a bad idea, daily use of salt in cookery and seasoning has not been proven to be harmful in any way. In fact, a complete lack of salt may be more harmful than moderate salt use, which the vast majority of cultures have always included in their diet. As ever, the problem is one of quality, as well as quantity.

Salt is an interesting battleground when facing the promoters of nutritionist ideology. Surely, salt is just salt, right? Sodium chloride is just sodium chloride, after all. If you espouse reductionist dogmas, then of course salt is just salt, and the cheapest table salt is just as good (or indeed bad!) as the best sea salt. In 2011, Professor Graham MacGregor, currently still Chairman of Consensus Action on Salt, led a study demonising what he called "gourmet salts" which predictably concluded that there was no real difference between the various salts on the market, which are equally bad: *"gourmet salts contain approximately 100% sodium chloride, just like your average table salt, meaning they will have exactly the same effect on your blood pressure and health."*[666]

In reality, salt, like anything else, is a complex product that comes in different forms and from different sources and it is not "just sodium chloride". Its origins are very diverse. Common table salt comes from salt mines and chemical works, and it is not necessarily produced as a food item, it is used for a wide range of industrial manufacturing processes that require chemically pure sodium chloride, such as cleaning products, paper, and plastics, among other things. It is therefore highly refined, stripped of all trace minerals and contains anticaking agents. Sometimes it is fortified with iodine: this follows the usual trend of fortifying impoverished products. The best sea salt is literally salt from the sea, cleaned of impurities, with all its trace minerals in place. It is a substantially different product.

[666] https://www.actiononsalt.org.uk/news/surveys/2011/gourmet-salts/

It is also unclear what the maximum quantity of salt we should ingest is, presuming there is even such a thing as a maximum or ideal amount of salt we should ingest. The NHS claims we should have no more than 6 grams of "salt (or sodium)" per day,[667] not specifying what kind of salt, or the context in which we ingest it. The prudent option here, without having to engage in dubious and difficult salty arithmetic, is simply to use salt in modest amounts and get used to food that is not heavily salted. It is always good to be sparing with salt whilst cooking, as salt can always be added but not taken away. It is also good to avoid having salt at the table and adding to food as a routine. In any case, one of the easiest ways to avoid both excess salt and poor-quality salt is not to eat ultra-processed food, microwave meals and the sort of junk food we looked at in Chapter 10.

The latter point I wish to make is one of taste: super fine table salt does not taste anywhere near as good as the best sea salt. It is sharp, too strong, devoid of any pleasant notes. Of course, the high priests of relativism will claim there are no qualitative differences between different types of salt, that taste is purely subjective and so on and so forth. No good chef would use the sharp, unpleasant salt found in so many fast-food stores and pubs, of course, and not because he is a snob, but because it is clearly inferior. Very salty food is also something that the palate gets used to, and which undermines other flavours, leading to a loss of palate and diminished culinary experience. In other words, food can be over-salted, objectively so, and it is not a good idea.

What to look out for:

- **Origin**: the best salt will state which sea and region it is from. Think Anglesey, Trapani, Guérande etc… these are dried outdoors, in the sun, or heated at low temperatures.
- **From the sea**: the sea is the best source of edible salt. Himalayan salt has become very fashionable and, whilst it can be a good product, old-fashioned, naturally dried sea salt is the way to go.
- **Both finely ground and coarse salt**: make sure you have coarse salt at home, it is far better for seasoning water when cooking pasta or rice, and for seasoning stocks. Grind coarse salt to make finely ground salt, ideally, or get ground salt for seasoning your cooking and salads.
- **No additives and fortifications**: the best salt does not contain anticaking agents and is not fortified with iodine or other minerals.
- **Reduced Sodium**: do not buy salt with "reduced sodium".

TO SUM UP: get the basics right. Salt is important; invest in quality sea salt and use it parsimoniously. Do not add salt at the table.

[667] https://www.nhs.uk/live-well/eat-well/food-types/salt-in-your-diet/

Spices

Even a cursory overview of the history of global trade, of nations and empires that have come and gone reveals the great importance of spices since antiquity. They combine powers of flavour, medicine, pleasure, and fragrance and the history of many lands and cultures is intertwined with particular spices and the plants they originate from. Spices are normally distinguished from herbs in so far as they do not come from leaves, flowers, or stems of a plant, but from seeds (e.g., black pepper, cardamom), arils (e.g., mace), barks (e.g., cinnamon), fruits (e.g., cayenne pepper), flower buds (e.g., cloves), stigmas (e.g., saffron), roots (e.g., liquorice, horseradish), rhizomes (e.g., turmeric, ginger), and resins (e.g., mastic). Classification is not always straightforward, as some plants produce both herb and spice (e.g., coriander leaves and coriander seeds), and some produce vegetable, herb, and spice (e.g., fennel bulbs, fennel leaves and fennel seeds).

There is no question that like herbs, spices have complex properties and contribute to health and wellbeing. The details are interesting (e.g., turmeric is very beneficial, but not in large quantities and is far more effective when consumed with black pepper) but you do not necessarily need to know much about them in order to benefit from their consumption.

Here are some basic guidelines:

- **Diversity**: use the broadest diversity of spices in cookery and seasoning. Remember that spices are integral ingredients in all sorts of dishes, from starters to desserts. Learn new recipes.
- **Cultivation method**: organic or equivalent.
- **Country/region of origin**: as usual, the better spices are from a single location (e.g., organic vanilla from Madagascar, organic cloves from Sri Lanka), as opposed to non-descript mixes from different countries.
- **Prioritise single spices over blends**: we can find very good quality blends and mixes on the market for products like curry powder, garam masala, harissa, or Cajun spice mix. However, as a rule, make sure you always have single spices (e.g., cumin, aniseed, black mustard seeds, asafoetida, Szechuan pepper etc...) in your kitchen cupboard and, perhaps, try to combine them and make your own curry mixes etc...
- **Crush/grind your own**: it is better to get whole nutmeg and grate it fresh and whole peppercorns and crush them when needed.

TO SUM UP: spices are inherently good. Use them liberally.

Sugar

As discussed in Chapter 5, sugar has a welcome place in our lives, for all sorts of positive reasons. Just like with salt, one of the easiest ways to avoid both excess sugar and poor-quality sugar is not to eat ultra-processed food, microwave meals and the sort of junk food we looked at in Chapter 10.

The language around different types of sugar (refined vs unrefined, white vs brown) can be somewhat misleading and confusing. All sugar, apart from unrefined whole cane sugar (such as *rapadura* sugar) undergoes some degree of refining. Unrefined "non-centrifugal" whole cane sugar is basically made with the unrefined crystals of boiled sugar cane juice, which retain all the molasses and do not undergo any centrifugation and further processing. It is a very distinct product, that differs in colour, texture, and flavour from what we normally associate with sugar.

There is a lot of refined sugar that is sold as "unrefined" sugar. Usually what this means is that it is partially refined, as opposed to completely refined. For example, there is granulated sugar on the market that is sold as "unrefined cane sugar" which is clearly refined but not as refined as pure white sugar and retains a very light brown colour and a more profound flavour than pure white sugar.

Here are the actual grades of sugar, in a nutshell:

1) Non-centrifugal unrefined whole cane sugar - as above. The nutritional data on the packet will generally show sugar content in the 95-96% range.
2) Raw sugar: sugar crystals that have been centrifuged to remove most of the cane molasses but retain some of the molasses and are generally produced in a sugar mill, as opposed to a refinery. All the sugars in this category will fall within some shade of brown, from very pale blond to brown. The colour and sugar content will depend on the % of molasses left on the crystals. The nutritional data on the packet should show less than 100% sugars and will generally be in the 97-99% range. Read labels very carefully: there is brown sugar on the market that is white sugar with some molasses added back in, in which case it is not raw sugar. Look out for the words "raw sugar" on the label.
3) Fully refined sugar: fully refined sugars have the same basic process as raw sugar. The sugar undergoes concentration, crystallization, and centrifuging. The difference is that only a single cycle produces raw sugars whereas fully refined sugars are purified through a series of cycles that take place in a sugar refinery. There is no certified organic pure white sugar available on the market in the UK. White sugar is

rendered fully white through a complex refining process that involves the use of synthetic chemicals to help remove all impurities. The nutritional data on the packet will always show 100% sugar.

Here are some basic guidelines on what to go for:

- **Cultivation method**: organic sugar is best, for the usual reasons.
- **Sugar cane as opposed to sugar beet**: there is no raw or unrefined sugar available on the market from sugar beet, which all ends up in fully refined white sugar products.
- **Colour**: never buy any sugar that is completely white. It has to be at least pale blond in colour. It also tends to have a coarser texture, even when granulated.
- **Raw sugar as the most refined**: with the exception of icing sugar,[668] always use raw sugar as opposed to fully refined sugar. There is no dessert you cannot make with granulated raw sugar, from gelato to custard and cakes.
- **Unrefined whole cane sugar**: consider using this product for coffee, tea, and milkshakes or in some desserts.[669] It is sold as rapadura[670] or muscovado, panela, jaggery, and piloncillo. Still containing its natural minerals and vitamins, this kind of sugar is a valuable whole food, and I would go as far as stating that it is a "health food" that you should have in your kitchen. It is also worth mentioning that organic unrefined coconut sugar also falls under a similar category and can be used as a substitute for unrefined whole cane sugar.
- **Organic sugar molasses**: can be used as a cooking ingredient for desserts and marinades. This is not to be confused with golden sugar syrup, which is made from refined sugar in the first place and, like icing sugar, is best reserved for special desserts on special occasions.

TO SUM UP: use moderate, high-quality sugar and enjoy it.

Syrups

Natural syrups made from sugary plants are wholesome products that, whilst not necessary and relatively marginal, are useful additions to the kitchen cupboard. Syrups are made from sugary plants that either produce a sap or have a naturally high sugar content and are usually

[668] Organic icing sugar is irreplaceable for some preparations but should only be used on special occasions.

[669] It will not work on many desserts that need more refined sugar but will work on certain types of biscuits and cakes.

[670] For example: https://biona.co.uk/products/biona-organic-rapadura-wholecane-sugar-2

produced through relatively simple processes, involving pulping/extraction, heating, and filtering.

In a nutshell:

- **Cultivation method**: organic or equivalent.
- **Diversity**: maple is one of the most renowned and delicious syrups, but syrups are also made from sugar cane, sorghum, agave, dates, carob, yacon, coconut, rice, and other less common plants. It is worth trying different syrups and if you enjoy them and can incorporate them into your cooking and diet.

TO SUM UP: if you like them, use syrups with the same attitude and parsimony with which you use quality sugar.

Tea & Coffee

Tea and coffee are relatively easy to purchase, provided you look out for a few basic features and read labels closely:

Tea

- **Cultivation method**: organic or equivalent, as usual.
- **Country/region**: all good tea will specify where exactly it is from, as opposed to being a blend of untraceable leaves from several unknown plantations and countries. The vast majority of the tea and coffee on the market from the big brands are made with such nondescript leaves from obscure origins.
- **With tea blends, read carefully**: with tea, there are some classic blends that are very desirable and of great quality, provided that their components are clearly identified, and the cultivation methods and country of origin clearly specified (e.g., an organic English Breakfast made from Ceylon tea, and Assam, Kerala, and Darjeeling from India). Please note the vast majority of English Breakfast blends, apart from not being organic, do not specify the list of varieties and countries, or only partially so.
- **Prioritise single tea varieties**: plunge into the extraordinary world of tea varieties, from the common but excellent Assam and Darjeeling to the less common Nilgiri, Rwanda Pekoe or Lapsang Souchong. Apart from enjoying distinct flavours and benefits, this adds greater traceability.

- **Tea Grades**: look out for OP (Orange Pekoe[671]), the highest tea grade (made from whole leaves) and BOP (Broken Orange Pekoe), which includes broken leaves but is still high quality. The other grades, fannings and dust, make lower-quality tea. These grading terms are typically used for teas from Sri Lanka, India, and countries other than China. Virtually all the black tea bags from the main brands in the supermarket are made from tea dust, yet another reason not to buy them.
- **Flush**: you may have read "First Flush" or "Second Flush" on a tea box. This refers to the fact that some tea varieties have flushes (new growths within a season), and the harvests are referred to as flushes, in chronological order. For example, there are four Darjeeling flushes: first (between February and May), second (between May and June), monsoon (July to September), and autumn (October to November). The quality of the tea generally follows that order, with the first flush being the best tea.
- **The best black tea?** Teas that tick all the boxes will specify all the above criteria on their packaging and labels and are the best on the market. I will share a few examples of teas that I am familiar with and/or drink on a very regular basis, which will help you with reading and interpreting labels. Notice how you have cultivation method, tea grade, tea variety, plantation and country all specified on the label:
    - Organic SFTGFOP Nilgiri from Thiashola Estate, India.
    - Organic GBOP Assam from Ethelwold Estate, India.
    - Organic[672] SFTGFOP1, 1st Flush Darjeeling from Puttabong Estate, India.[673]
- **Oolong, green tea, yellow tea, white tea, Pu Erh**: these are teas which, unlike black tea, have not been fully oxidised (with white the least oxidised), but belong to the very same wonder plant, *Camellia sinensis*. They are the most important teas in the Far East, and are excellent products, in principle, provided that the same basic criteria are applied. There is no grading or flush, however, so in a sense it is a little bit less complex to read and interpret the labels.
- **Milk and sugar?** Yes, if you like it, referring to the sections on milk and sugar we saw earlier in this chapter. However, milk and sugar only really go well with very dark, full-bodied blends like English or Irish Breakfast or single varieties like Assam. They simply do not go with Darjeeling and many other black teas, and certainly not on any green or other type of tea.

[671] There are many categories within the Orange Pekoe category, such as Tippy Golden Flowery Orange Pekoe (TGFOP) or Special Finest Tippy Golden Flowery Orange Pekoe (SFTGFOP), which makes it all rather complicated! But in simple terms, Orange Pekoe denotes quality.

[672] There are of course some great teas that tick all the boxes (grade, flush, variety, estate, country) but are not certified organic. But why not tick all the boxes when possible?

[673] I have an absolute personal preference for Indian tea, which at its best is sublime, but there are fantastic and comparable teas from other parts of the world as well, of course.

Coffee

- **Cultivation method**: organic or equivalent, as usual. Look out for "shade grown" coffee: this is always a good sign.
- **Country/region**: all good coffee will specify where exactly it is from, as opposed to being a blend of untraceable beans from several unknown plantations and countries. The vast majority of coffee on the market from the big brands are made with such nondescript beans.
- **Prioritise single origin coffees**: the best coffees will state the estate or cooperative that they originate from.
- **Prioritise single varieties and transparent blends**: the best coffees will tend to be made from single varieties or from blends made from clearly specified varieties.
- **Fairtrade Certification**: fairtrade is not necessarily always indicative of great quality coffee[674] but there is often an overlap, with many organic coffees and other quality coffees being certified by the Fairtrade Foundation. Whilst it is not entirely clear the extent to which Fairtrade Certification benefits farmers, it is probably more positive than negative. Organic certification is certainly better and more reliable, as the benefits for farmers, the environment and consumers are far more tangible.
- **Arabica or Robusta**? There are two main species of the coffee plant, Arabica, and Robusta. The best coffees, especially as single varieties, are made from Arabica varieties. Robusta is mostly used in blends and for instant coffee.
- **Beans or Ground**? My friend Reggie, an old-fashioned and wise Jamaican, grinds his own Blue Mountain coffee. It is a great idea; I am personally too lazy to do it and buy ready ground!
- **Roast/Intensity**? This is really a matter of taste, with a gradation of 1 to 5, with 5 the darkest and most intense roasts.
- **Technique**: there is much cultural variation from the classic Italian Caffettiera, to the French Press and the coffee pot used in Greece, Turkey, and the Levant. Ultimately, use whatever method you prefer, as long as the coffee is good and the water clean. If you go down the manual coffee machine route, opt for the classic barista style Italian manual coffee machine that requires ground coffee and do not go for any of the machines requiring coffee capsules.[675] Away from home, the coffees available on the global retail/coffeeshop market (mostly Italian, I must say: espresso, cappuccino,

[674] Or indeed chocolate, bananas, and other certified products.

[675] Not because the coffee that comes out of them is unpleasant, far from it. Avoid capsules because they never contain the best quality coffee, which is never used for the capsule industry.

Americano, Latte, macchiato, mocha etc...) will be as good as the quality of ingredients and the skills of the barista.

- **Instant?** Instant coffee is profoundly inferior. It has a role to play for a quick and milder coffee fix, however. There are good and cheap organic instant coffee brands available at most supermarkets.
- **Milk and sugar?** Yes, if you like it, refer to the sections on milk and sugar we saw earlier in this chapter.
- **Decaffeinated?** There is something slightly self-defeating about decaffeinated coffee. However, if you cannot handle caffeine, like the taste of coffee and are able to find coffee that ticks the various boxes and is decaffeinated, go for it.

TO SUM UP: tea and coffee are great pleasures, and their popularity is not surprising. It is one of the very few addictions with no real negatives attached to it. Be very selective and inquisitive with what you buy: it is better for farmers overseas, for your health and for your tastebuds.

Vegetables

Vegetables are a pillar around which menus and meals should be built. Apart from a few odd proponents of the carnivore diet, the benefit of vegetables is one of the few facts every nutritionist agrees upon, as well as every traditional diet,[676] albeit there is little discussion, especially in nutrition science and dietician circles, about the fundamental importance of the quality of vegetables.

- **Cultivation method**: organic or equivalent.[677] There is no new way to emphasise that healthy soils produce healthy plants, and toxic agrichemicals are toxic for all forms of life, animal and human alike. The fact that the ideologues at DEFRA, the WHO and the NHS are unable or unwilling to understand this simple reality should not deter us from using our own better judgement.
- **Local unless exotic**: we are blessed with a climate and landscape that is most suitable for growing a very broad range of vegetables. We can and should prioritise British vegetables, which are abundant all year round.

[676] Cato the Elder was already praising the virtues of cabbage in his famous agricultural treatise *De agri cultura* in around 160 BC.

[677] As previously explained: there are uncertified growers who use organic methods. You will find some at farmers markets.

- **Heritage varieties**: keep an eye out for heritage vegetable varieties, which offer fantastic opportunities in the kitchen. They are hard to come by, as most vegetables on the market, even of the best quality, tend to belong to a narrow range of (mostly hybrid) varieties. You will find specialties like Romanesco Cauliflower at farmers markets.
- **Seasonality**: eat vegetables that are in season, by and large. See Chapter 10 about out-of-season vegetables to avoid. Here is a brief, basic list of seasonal vegetables that grow in Britain and are available in season:
    - <u>Spring</u>: garden peas, broad beans, asparagus, spring cabbage/greens, spring onions, purple sprouting broccoli, radish, lettuce, spinach, chard.
    - <u>Summer</u>: new potatoes, tomatoes, cucumbers, courgettes, French green beans, runner beans, beetroot, carrot, fennel, broccoli, sweetcorn, celery, spinach, chard, radish, lettuce, summer cabbage, cauliflower, chillies/peppers, aubergines, onions, garlic.
    - <u>Autumn</u>: pumpkin/winter squash, maincrop potatoes, kale, autumn cabbage, parsnip, celeriac, turnips, swedes, leeks, radish, spinach, chard, lettuce, chicory/endives, beetroot, cauliflower, broccoli, onions, Jerusalem artichoke, carrot, celery.
    - <u>Winter</u>: parsnips, celeriac, brussels sprouts, cauliflower, winter cabbage, kale, swedes, leeks, purple sprouting broccoli.
- **The seasons are now longer**: a lot of vegetables are now available pretty much all year round, due to improved and efficient storage. We can get British potatoes, carrots, garlic, onions, and many brassicas all year round, for example. Thanks to polytunnels, a lot of other vegetables benefit from much longer seasons than in the past, from tomatoes and cucumbers to all sorts of leafy greens.
- **Retail options**: as ever, it is best to diversify. Farmers markets are great, but expensive: try to go if and when possible, and prioritise the cheaper, more "plain" vegetables, like cabbages and potatoes, as opposed to tomatoes and peppers which, even in the height of summer, are very expensive. Unless, of course, cost is not issue. Traditional, quality greengrocers are mostly a thing of the past, and the corner shops or convenience stores with boxes of fruits and vegetables stacked outdoors, common in many parts of London, are not recommended. All supermarkets will have some decent options: we need to read labels and be very selective with our purchases. Some organic vegetable

box schemes delivered to your home can be good: consider them as an option if you can afford them.

- **Preserve good vegetables**: see section above on preserved vegetables.
- **Exotic**[678] **vegetables**: I personally barely even bother with a lot of the vegetables that I would like to eat throughout summer: plum tomatoes, aubergines, peppers. Unless I grow them myself, I might get a few in season at the farmers market on rare occasions and that is it. There is little point going for the imported stuff: rarely any good or fresh, and very expensive, even when in season. There are some truly exotic vegetables that are worth getting however: organic sweet potatoes and avocadoes, for example.
- **Mushrooms:**[679] there are plenty of organic cultivated mushrooms available at supermarkets at decent prices which are worth purchasing. Wild mushrooms are hard to come by[680] and even if you find fresh wild mushrooms, they will rarely be in great conditions and they will also be ruinously expensive. The best bet are dried porcini (cep) mushrooms, or other types of dried mushrooms, which can be rehydrated and used in all sorts of preparations. Read labels carefully, as the provenance of wild mushrooms can be quite obscure.
- **Seaweed**: seaweed, both wild and cultivated, are potentially valuable food sources. Organic certification is a plus, as organic seaweed can only use naturally derived fertilisers to start off and only use natural nutrients that are available in the marine environment to grow. There are also rules around where the seaweed farms can be situated (as in: away from pollutants) and how much seaweed can be gathered if it is wild harvested, and an overall emphasis on protecting the marine environment and promoting biodiversity.
- **Grow some?** Consider taking any opportunity you can to actually grow some vegetables.[681]

TO SUM UP: try your best to get good vegetables and ensure they form a key component of your daily diet. Eat vegetables at their best and follow the seasons. Exceed the famous "5 a day".

[678] By exotic, I do not just mean tropical, but also vegetables that simply doesn't grow outdoors here, like plum tomatoes, large aubergines, and peppers from the Mediterranean.

[679] Mushrooms are not vegetables, of course, but fungi. For convenience, I have included them here.

[680] Even when you forage for them!

[681] Your back garden? Instead of a mowed lawn? Share an allotment? Someone else's garden and share the produce?

One of my beautiful homegrown Marina di Chioggia pumpkins.

Some of my homegrown courgettes Romanesche.

Vegetable Oils

Vegetable oils are staples where people tend to be more likely to opt for really cheap options, preferring to invest more heavily on other sections of the food aisles. This is a mistake, as vegetable oil is one of the key components of the contemporary industrial junk food diet.

What to look out for:

- **Cultivation method**: organic or equivalent. With olive oil, there are a lot of small producers who use organic methods but cannot afford or do not need certification, and are therefore "equivalent", but you then need to know a lot of information about them and their product.
- **Country/region**: most vegetable oils other than olive oil are almost entirely made from blends, so even some of the very best cooking/frying oils only specify EU or outside EU origin.
- **Olive oil origin**: with olive oil, on the other hand, the bottle must state the origin of the olives in order for it to be any good. Certainly, it should state the region and country, ideally the farm or "single estate". The PDO and PGI labels we saw earlier are also a positive with olive oil. Do not be confused by country of manufacture: for example, the popular Filippo Berio olive oil is made and bottled in Italy, but the olives are a blend of olives from several countries, not just Italy. To sum up: "product of" a particular country only means the oil is made and bottled in that particular country.
- **Processing**: the basic process to look out for is "cold extracted" or "cold pressed", for all oils, olive, sunflower or otherwise. Oil pressed without heat retains the nutritional value of the olives/seeds, along with preserving their flavours and aromas. Olive oil bottles should also state on the label that the oil is obtained "solely by mechanical means": this means that the oil has not been obtained by using heat or solvents throughout the whole process.
- **Extra Virgin?** Extra virgin olive oil is one of the most known terms in common "food language" (AKA EVO) and is now an overrated term, as there are plenty of rubbish extra virgin olive oils. To be extra virgin the oil must have been extracted from the olives on its first pressing, without the use of heat or chemicals, and produce an oil of less than 0.8% acidity. This is all good of course, but it tells us nothing about the quality of the olives used in the first place. Therefore, extra virgin olive oil is one of the basic characteristics to look for, but very insufficient on its own. Definitely stay away from oils that contain "refined olive oil".

- **Crop variety**? With the main oilseeds, the oils are marketed without any reference to crop variety. With olive oil, like with grapes, the best oils tend to specify the olive variety used, and single varieties are often best.
- **Plant/type of oil**: I have already sung the virtues of olive oil. There are of course other oils on the market that are worth using. For example, organic sunflower frying oil is a quality product and easy to find. Other seed oils will be a matter of taste, intended usage and cultural background: sesame, hemp, flax, pumpkin seed, coconut etc... The same principles will apply; look out for cultivation method, pressing method, origin etc... read labels closely!
- **Cost**: sadly, decent vegetable oil, made from any plant, cannot be that cheap. Use less and buy in bulk if possible. I always invite my more sceptical followers to remind themselves that very few of them believe that spending £15-20 for a bottle of wine is a huge extravagance. We can consume a bottle of wine in one sitting quite easily, and do not think much of it. If we spend £15-20 on a bottle of great olive oil, which will certainly a lot longer than one sitting, we feel we have overspent. This is clearly a mistake, given that olive oil is a long-term investment in health and pleasure.
- **Use animal fats instead**? It is relatively cheap and tasty to cook with organic butter so consider using it to replace vegetable oils for some dishes. Other high quality animal fats, from pork, goose, or beef, can also be used to replace vegetable oils for many recipes. Do not let cholesterol phobia cloud your judgement.

TO SUM UP: invest in quality vegetable oils. If you are on a tight budget, use quality oil with parsimony. Substitute with organic butter or other high quality animal fats if and when it makes sense to do so.

Water

That plenty[682] of water is a good idea is again one of the very few ideas upon which almost everyone agrees. As discussed in Chapter 2, we find ourselves in a paradox with water, in so far as water has never been more sanitised and cleaner than it is now whilst, at the same time, industrial pollution has permeated all water sources, to varying degrees, even the most pristine. There is no question that water contamination is an issue, and an unescapable one. Tap water, at least here in Britain, is fundamentally clean and will not give us any of the diseases associated with unsanitary conditions. It is, however, relatively low quality and

[682] There is no such thing as an optimum about of water, it will depend on many individual factors and conditions. Estimates tend to be between 1.5-2.0 litres per day.

tainted with the contaminants that are ubiquitous in rivers and aquifers,[683] the chemical residues from water treatment processes and from the piping system through which it travels. Even if we do not drink it, we are likely to use it for cooking and cleaning produce in the kitchen and is therefore almost inescapable.

Bottled mineral water, by comparison, will have far less chemical contamination, and come from relatively cleaner natural sources of water. Some mineral waters really are rich in minerals, depending on the springs and altitude sources they come from. Overall, it is certainly better. There is also no question (and no, I am not suffering from some kind of aquatic delusion) that it tastes better and does not have the occasionally "eggy" tinge that tap water can have.

However, the great downside of mineral water is that it is bottled in plastic, meaning that we certainly end up ingesting microplastics from the water, which are also an invisible threat to our health. Furthermore, there is no question that there is a heavy environmental cost associated with producing and disposing of all these plastic bottles, with recycling being an exercise in damage limitation at best. Glass bottles would be the solution,[684] which could literally be recycled by being used again, but the mineral water market is almost entirely plastic bottle based. There is no easy solution. My advice is to opt for a filter for tap water or bottled mineral water, microplastics included, depending on your taste, budget, and level of desire to do away with plastic bottles.

A quick word on sparkling water, which is always bottled. You should opt for naturally carbonated water, as opposed to water that is artificially carbonated.[685] You are also more likely to find it in glass, which, considering you are unlikely to drink sparkling water with the same frequency as still water, is a more realistic occasional purchase.

Lastly, desist from all "flavoured water" products.

TO SUM UP: drink plenty of water, irrespective of the above comments.

[683] From agrochemicals which leach into water ways, from industrial activity, from water that goes from sewage treatment plants back into waterways and from many other sources.

[684] If you can afford it… consider it.

[685] The ingredients, in this case, will be listed as water and carbon dioxide on the label.

Whole Grains

In spite of our love affair with flour, whole grains still can, and should, form an important part of our diets.

Here is a brief overview:

- **Rice:** rice is the single most important whole grain on the planet, and it is an inherently wholesome food source. There are parts of the world where people are too reliant on rice, as indeed there have always been agricultural people over-reliant on specific grains. Nonetheless, if you like it, and it is a big part of your culture, there is no reason for rice not to be one of your staples. As previously argued, there is always room for import and consumption of quality products we cannot produce, especially non-perishables. This is what to look out for:
    - **Cultivation method**: organic or equivalent.
    - **Origin/location**: as usual, the best rice on the market is labelled with clear information about where it is grown. You will normally never get more than the country of origin. The lower quality rice bags will be blends or in any case, will not specify the origin of the rice.
    - **Varieties**: most of the thousands of varieties in the world are only accessible locally where they are grown. Much of the rice on the market tends to belong to a few varieties. Most of the UK market is dominated by the *indica* long grain rice such as Basmati and Jasmine from Asia and, closer to home, the plump, short *Japonica* rice such as Arborio and Carnaroli from Italy and paella rice from Spain. Nonetheless, it is worth going for the right variety for the right dish: you cannot make a biryani with Arborio, and you cannot make a risotto with Basmati!
    - **White or Brown?** In principle, it would be better to eat less white rice and more brown rice. In practice, just like the average human enjoys white flour and bread, we all tend to enjoy the culinary virtues of white rice. The solution? Get the best quality rice possible, whether white or brown, and try not to eat one or the other exclusively. Brown rice is very good for rice salads, soups and boiled as a side dish, especially with fish.
    - **Raw**: do not buy precooked or microwaveable rice. No really high-quality rice is sold that way.
- **Ancient Wheat**: there is still a niche market for ancient wheats, to be eaten whole. The three main ancient wheat varieties that can still be found on the market are: einkorn (*Triticum Monococcum*), emmer (*Triticum dicoccum*) and spelt (*Farro spelta*).

In Italy, where there is a niche market for these grains, which were never fully abandoned in Tuscany and other regions, they are still grown and used for traditional soups, bread, and other fantastic products. Often simply referred to as *farro*, they can be purchased online. Ancient wheats are extremely nutritious whole grains with a low gluten content and, as we saw earlier, would be very beneficial to those suffering from the symptoms of overconsumption of white flour made from hybrid wheat, often confused with so called "gluten intolerance". These grains have the added advantage of generally being organic by default: they overgrow and lodge with synthetic fertilisers and the few farmers who do grow these grains are catering to consumers who are interested in organic products.

- **Other whole grains:** barley grain, or pearled barley, is another valuable whole grain that should make its way into soups and salads.
- **Oats**: oats are very valuable grains, which provide a slow release of energy and plenty of other benefits. The main use for oats is in porridge, oatcakes, and a few desserts.
- **Diversify**: consider trying alternative grains like millet, teff and sorghum, still widely consumed in parts of Asia and Africa.
- **Popcorn**: keep organic popcorn seeds at home and make your own popcorn.

TO SUM UP: it is important to include whole grains in our diets. As ever, quality over quantity.

Chapter 12

DIETS AND DIETING: A NEW APPROACH

Disclaimer

In this chapter, I will outline my very own dietary advice for readers from all walks of life, based on the ideas and arguments outlined in this book thus far. I will pre-empt the objections and legal challenges that may come my way if I do not state my position clearly: I am not a qualified Dietician,[686] nor do I have any professional qualifications that pertain to medical or nutrition science. What follows does not constitute medical advice and does not involve prognoses and prescriptions. These are personal lifestyle suggestions for your interest and consideration. I am also not a Nutritionist, even though unlike a Dietician, anyone can call themselves a "nutritionist" without any formal qualifications.[687]

I am legally permitted to give my own personal dietary and lifestyle suggestions, and it is up to the reader to make of them what they will. If the very notion of receiving dietary suggestions from anyone other than someone wearing a white coat offends you, this chapter is not for you, and you can go back to counting calories and drinking diet sodas or, as increasingly fashionable, succumb to the so-called skinny jabs. One of the basic premises of this book is that scientific and medical advice on nutrition and dieting is ill-founded and unreliable and partly to blame for widespread obesity, diet related illnesses and the general confusion around diet, as well as the loss of the great pleasure potential that food promises. The logical consequence of this premise is that I have no qualms pitching in with my own unprofessional suggestions.

[686] Only those who are registered with the Health and Care Professionals Council (HCPC) are able to refer to themselves as Dieticians in a professional capacity.

[687] See: https://www.bda.uk.com/about-dietetics/what-is-dietitian/dietitian-or-nutritionist.html

It is also worth noting that the major opponents of ultra-processed foods from the medical profession, such as Professor Tim Spector and Dr Chris van Tulleken, both openly narrate how they ate ultra-processed foods quite unthinkingly until relatively recently, and only came to the conclusions they came to much later in life. Spector's *"curiosity about food and nutrition was first piqued"* after a health scare in 2011,[688] which started his *"food journey"*.[689] He flirted with reducing salt, with veganism, then vegetarianism, before settling on his current low-meat diet[690] and focusing on the microbiome, detailed throughout his latest book. Spector also recalls that, before his conversion to full-fat dairy, he *"insisted for about ten years on buying spreadable (healthy fat) margarines, and then olive oil spreads with pictures of Italian olive groves on the tub"*.[691] As for van Tulleken, as he was about to embark on his commendable ultra-processed food-eating experiment, he noted:

"I was surprised to find from keeping a food diary over a typical week that I was generally getting around 30 per cent of my calories from UPF. After years of writing and broadcasting about food – and slow but steady weight gain – my usual diet looked something like this: black coffee for breakfast, a sandwich and crisps for lunch, and a fairly healthy home-cooked dinner (chicken,[692] rice and broccoli is a staple), followed by a supermarket dessert. Every few nights, rather than cooking the main course, we'd have a UPF microwave lasagne or a UPF oven pizza. I'd have a takeaway about once per week, usually UPF thanks to liberal use of modified starches and flavour enhancers."[693] He also regretted the fact that he could not eat his favourite mayonnaise (Hellmann's) when he came off ultra-processed foods for the first part of his experiment.[694] Also, incredibly, van Tulleken recalls how, before his experimental diet, he had *"never even read an ingredients list"*.[695]

Therefore, and to my point, it is absolutely clear that both Spector and van Tulleken, in spite of their extensive medical and scientific training, clearly had no idea, by their own admission, how to distinguish healthy food from junk food, and only came to realise that ultra-processed foods are highly damaging to human health in the latter part of their career. Despite no scientific nor medical background, I could have informed both gentlemen that margarine, microwave meals and crisps were a bad idea long before they had their late epiphanies and published their books. This is because I have mercifully never fallen for the tenets of textbook

[688] T. Spector, 2022, Food for Life, page ix.

[689] Ibidem, page 114.

[690] Ibidem, pages 114-116.

[691] Ibidem, page 325.

[692] What kind of chicken, I wonder?

[693] C. van Tulleken, 2023, Ultra-processed People, page 36.

[694] Ibidem, page 36.

[695] Ibidem, pages 152-153.

nutritionism, have never taken NHS guidelines seriously, and appreciate that the debate around food and diet is primarily ideological, as opposed to scientific. Once you truly see the vacuous principles and reductionist dogmas of nutrition science and mainstream agriculture, you cannot unsee them.

I can only reiterate what I have tried to express throughout this book: no thinking person needs the sanction of a dietician, nutritionist, or doctor, to eat well, with joy, pleasure, and health, whatever their circumstances. Not only am I stating that what follows is not the work of a licenced Dietitian, registered Nutritionist, doctor or Professor of Epidemiology, I am also stating that this could be a distinct advantage in my favour.

General Principles & Guidelines to Dietary Suggestions

Please refer back to **Chapter 9**. Whatever our circumstances, the following principles always apply, anywhere, anytime:

- **No calorie counting**.
- **No nutrient bans**. We do not need to look at nutritional data on labels (the legally mandatory information about protein, fat, sugar contact etc…) or at the very least do not make any decisions solely based on nutritional data.
- **No food type bans.** We do not need to ban any food type (e.g., legumes, meat, dairy, nuts) from our diet unless we have a real, as opposed to imaginary, intolerance/allergy.
- Always prioritise **whole foods** above all else.
- Prioritise seasonality, freshness, and locality.
- **Organic or equivalent**, as much as possible.
- **Be willing to cook**. The level of time dedicated to cooking will depend on your time and interest, but a total unwillingness to cook is a complete nonstarter.[696]
- Conviviality and hospitality.
- The pleasure principle.
- Respect for culinary tradition.
- Try to **engage** with growers, farmers, fishermen, hunters, foragers. Consider taking part in any of these activities, even on a one-off basis.
- Avoid all food waste!

[696] Unless of course someone can cook for you based on the principles outlined.

As outlined in **Chapter 10**, the following foods are simply not recommended, whatever our weight, age, and station. In no particular order:

- Crisps.
- Salted and roasted peanuts.
- Supermarket biscuits, cakes and desserts.
- Supermarket bread, whether white, brown, or seeded.
- Breakfast cereals.
- Store-bought dressings such as: mayonnaise, salad cream, ketchup, brown sauce.
- Soft drinks of any kind. Diet sodas.
- Synthetic sweeteners.
- Low-fat dairy products.
- Anything marketed with nutritional claims on the labels.
- Any food from all the major fast-food chains and greasy takeaways.
- Farmed seafood.
- Seafood from destructive fishing practices.
- Really cheap corner shop/supermarket booze.
- Really cheap corner shop/supermarket tea and coffee.
- Factory-farmed chicken, other poultry, and pork.
- Factory farmed eggs.
- Preserved meats from factory-farmed pork.
- Beef and lamb that is not truly grass/pasture fed.
- Bad BBQ.
- Conventional[697] milk and dairy products.
- Conventional white flour and white sugar.
- Conventional pasta and bread.
- Conventional vegetable oils.
- Conventional candy, chocolate, and ice cream.
- Any microwavable meal.
- Prepped vegetables, out of season vegetables.
- Margarine and butter substitutes.
- Non-organic plant milks.
- Vegan cheese or meat substitutes.
- "Protein" foods / bars.
- Cleansers and "detoxing" drinks.

[697] I use the word "conventional" to denote bog standard, non-organic, hyper industrial, supermarket average, low value products.

- Fruit juice and smoothies from the supermarket and corner shop.
- Sports drinks and supplements.
- Any foods containing unrecognisable ingredients that sound like chemical formulas.

How to Read the Menus

Keep all the above in mind when reading the menus. Please also bear the following in mind:

- **Quality of ingredient above all other considerations.** When any food type is mentioned (e.g., chicken or apples) presume that I would strongly recommend that it is sourced as outlined in **Chapter 11**. By "chicken" or "apple", I mean organic or equivalent, with all the nuances and shopping tips that go with it. If I refer to "cold cut", I am referring to ham or salame as described in Chapter 11. I will not be specifying "organic" or any other details for any food item in the menus: take them for granted.
- **Localised and culturally appropriate**: there are universal principles that apply to all human diets but no such thing as a universal or ideal diet. If I relocated to Australia or Japan, my diet and meals would have to adapt to my new locality and supply chain: the principles remain unchanged. Apply the principles laid out thus far to your location, geography, taste, and culture. The menu on Chapter 13 reflects my own culture, background, location, and interests: Italian ancestry, England, London, ties to the land etc… When I have risotto, you might have paella or biryani. When I have minestrone, you might have borscht or French onion soup. What matters is the principles adhered to, as per Chapters 9 to 11.
- **Personal taste and open-mindedness**: if fundamentally you prefer beef to lamb, eat more beef than lamb. If you just don't like coriander, do not eat it. However, it is recommended to challenge your palate and try (or try again, under far better circumstances) things we have not tried or think we do not like. Vegetables are the best example: a lot of the antipathy towards certain vegetables is the result of negative past experiences, low-quality produce and bad cooking.
- **Seasonality and flexibility**: for the 8 weeks of menus, **each 2 weeks correspond to one of the four seasons**. The order of lunches and dinners is, again, just an example. Personal circumstances and logistical limitations will also determine some choices: lunches away from home may have to be simpler and easier to prepare and carry. You may prefer lighter breakfasts and heavier dinners or vice versa. Again: I am suggesting principles and ideas, not exact meal plans.

- **Realities of cooking**: sometimes similar dishes follow from one day to the next. This is because there is time and resource efficiency in making, say, a meat stew or a soup and eating it over 2-3 days. There are also meals with no cooking involved, especially salads, again reflecting the fact that whilst we absolutely need to cook again, we cannot and do not need to cook all the time.

Suggestions for an Overweight Friend

What follows is what I would recommend for an overweight friend. If my original muse Alex asked me for my specific suggestions again, what follows is what I would recommend for him.

Dear Alex,

My suggested approach:

- Think about why you want to lose weight and consider the following reasons:
  - Long-term health and a longer life span.
  - Greater quality of life: being more active, energetic, productive, attractive, comfortable, confident, and useful to yourself and others.
  - Better culinary and gastronomic experiences.
  - Supporting the best agricultural and animal husbandry practices.
- Visualise **weight loss as a symptom of a healthy diet as opposed to its primary goal**. There are many bad ways to lose weight and weight loss cannot and must not be a standalone goal.
- Target weight: do not fret about an "ideal weight", as there isn't one. Have a rough range for your height (say 80-90kg for a 6 foot 3 in male) and aim towards it.
- Rational approach: despite the follies of body positivity and the politically correct curb on the word "fat", any thinking person knows whether they are overweight or not. You will know when you are no longer fat, and you will also know that it is a positive achievement.
- Remember that a diet is not a punishment. Aim for an enjoyable, pleasurable long-term diet that can be sustained once health has been restored and you are no longer overweight.
- No time limit: give yourself time. It will take several months to gradually lose weight.
- Just stay away from everything in Chapter 10 and you will be just fine.

A few **basic rules:**

- Drink plenty of still **water** throughout the day, including first thing every morning.
- Feel free to **season** food with sea salt and black pepper and other spices as appropriate.
- **Tea and coffee**: liberal use, albeit with very small quantities of rapadura sugar, if sugar is to be added at all. Try to drink **herbal teas**.
- Drink naturally sparkling water with freshly squeezed lemon juice (and mint leaves if you like) when you feel the need for a soft drink. Organic lemon juice on a daily basis is a very good idea.
- **Dressings**: you can, in fact should, dress and season your salads or steamed/boiled vegetables very nicely, and liberally. One of the many moronic trends in the diet world, backed by many professional dieticians, is to denounce vegetable oil as "fattening", based on the belief that "calories are calories". Vegetable oil is, after all, the most calorie dense food in our larders. Of course, what matters is the quality of vegetable oil, as opposed to the amount. Therefore, make simple high-quality dressings made with vegetable oil, vinegar or lemon juice to dress salads and vegetables and do not waste your time measuring teaspoons of oil.
- Feel free to add things like olives, pickled cucumbers, mustard, chillis and capers to salads as you see fit, these will not be mentioned in the menu.
- Quantities are usually not stated (rice, pasta and bread are notable examples),[698] as you need to **eat to satiety**, we are not calorie counting and a big man like you should be free to fill up. This is especially true for meat, fish, legumes, and vegetables: there is no good reason to portion control. The size of your steak or fish is down to you. You must not be hungry all the time and need to be satisfied. Of course, there must be a rational element here: fill up a very large plate, take seconds, especially of vegetables, but do not binge eat!
- Whilst quantities will not be policed nor calories counted, our diet will be:
    - High in vegetables, fruit, nuts, herbs, legumes, and spices.
    - High in organic meat and wild seafood.
    - Will include full-fat dairy, grains, and eggs.
    - Low in sugars, will include honey.
    - Relatively low in processed grains.

[698] Not because "carbs are bad" but because as we saw earlier grains, especially processed grains, are undoubtedly correlated with weight gain, as every farmer trying to fatten up a pig will know. The key is to eat less processed grains, and only of high quality, and more whole grains.

- Use the below as **guidelines only** - come up with your own menus, provided you follow all the principles, do not eat from the banned list, use the approved ingredients etc...
- **Alcohol**: avoid drinking more than 1-2 nights per week and avoid more than 5-6 drinks per week. The less, the better.
- **Cooking**: find time to cook something every day. It does not need to take long and be complicated. Learn basic recipes.
- **Mealtimes**: flexible, but roughly stick to breakfast, lunch, and dinner. Do not eat after 8-9pm. Try to eat at a table instead of in front of a screen; and take your time.
- **"Seasonal salad"**: when you read seasonal salad, this refers to a salad made with fresh UK grown raw vegetables that are in season. Do not just use salad leaves, but mix with things like shredded cabbage, celery hearts and leaves, fennel, carrot, radish and so on, depending on what is available. Do not buy prepped/pre-cut salad. Make salads a key part of what you eat. Again: the reason why people find salads less than appealing is because they often use pre-cut salads, out of season vegetables, low quality produce and do not dress them properly. A well-made salad should be delicious to the average palate, and surprisingly filling. Salads should be regular staples: this is true for everyone, not just people who need to lose weight.
- **Chewing**: food that requires lots of chewing and exercising your jaw, such as raw fruits and vegetables, is very important as you abandon easy to chew ultra-processed foods. As well as being better for your teeth, food that you need to "work for" takes longer to eat and is more filling, in a way. Eating two large raw apples is far more laborious than a packet of crisps and brings one to satiety.
- **Soups**: soups are another foundation of healthy, seasonal eating. Go big on soup and fill yourself up. You should try and make big batches of seasonal soup at home and use it as a weekly staple. I can already hear you complain and moan that there is far too much cooking involved here. I will grant that there are some organic brands that make decent ready-made soup with good organic ingredients and no nasties and unpronounceable fillers and additives that just need re-heating: this is an option that can complement cooking your own. However, it will usually cost more, and not be as good as what you can make at home.
- **Snacking**: avoid snacking altogether or as much as possible, ideally. When needed, the permitted snacks are:
  - Small quantities (20-30g) of mixed raw nuts.
  - Seasonal raw vegetable sticks (e.g., carrot, celery, fennel, whole radish) dipped in olive oil, lemon juice, and sea salt.

  - Fruit that is not overly sweet (e.g., apples or pears rather than sweet berries or melon).
  - Remember: as a rule of thumb, if you cannot eat a whole apple or a bowl of raw vegetables when you are hungry, you are not truly hungry.
- **Eating out**: I am including one meal outside the home every two weeks. Irrespective of any weight loss and dietary concerns, go to a really good restaurant and make the best possible choices based on the principles outlined in chapters 10 and 11. Avoid bread and desserts when eating out.
- **Desserts**: there is no getting away from the fact that to achieve dramatic weight loss, desserts are the main food category that needs to be cut out. Not because desserts and sugar are evil, but because once the threshold into overweight has been breached, cutting out sugar and excessive starch is one of the most effective ways to lose weight.[699] My recommendation for a sweet treat if you need one: a 100g organic dark chocolate bar (min 70%) a week.
- **Tailored to your preferences/culture**: I made the menu consistent with some of your preferences (carnivorous, British slant, some expensive ingredients, some Italian dishes…).
- **Budget**: following from the last point, this is not a cheap menu, but your income and food expenditure are already well above average,[700] so I am not asking you to necessarily spend more, but to make far better choices.
- Lastly, you should enjoy every dish, and never forget the **pleasure principle**.

[699] As we saw earlier, this was already understood in the 19th Century before the era of nutrition science.

[700] For a guide on how to eat perfectly well on a tight budget, see Chapter 13.

ALEX'S WEEKLY MENUS

WEEK 1 - SPRING

Monday

- ***Breakfast:*** *Yoghurt with teaspoon of honey*
- ***Lunch:*** *2 poached eggs, asparagus steamed/boiled al dente*[701]
- ***Dinner:*** *Lamb chops/steaks - grilled or pan-fried*
  Garden peas cooked with onion and bacon
  Steamed cauliflower with olive oil and lemon juice dressing

Tuesday

- ***Breakfast:*** *Porridge*[702] *with a teaspoon of honey*
- ***Lunch:*** *Fresh garden pea soup with fresh mint*
- ***Dinner:*** *Icelandic cod or haddock fillets Meunière (cooked in butter and lemon)*
  Pan-fried purple sprouting broccoli with garlic and chili

Wednesday

- ***Breakfast:*** *Yoghurt with teaspoon of honey*
- ***Lunch:*** *Massive mixed seasonal salad with tuna*
- ***Dinner:*** *Pan-fried/grilled pork chops*
  Sweet and sour spring onions, seasonal salad

[701] Again, just to reiterate: the asparagus can be dressed and seasoned as you please, provided the guidelines are respected. Maintain the same principle throughout.

[702] A nice bowl, around 70-80g of oats.

Thursday

- ***Breakfast:*** *2 fried eggs; pan-fried cultivated mushrooms*
- ***Lunch:*** *Fresh garden pea soup with fresh mint*
- ***Dinner:*** *Spaghetti (125g) with crab or lobster*

Friday

- ***Breakfast:*** *Porridge with teaspoon of honey*
- ***Lunch:*** *Beetroot, broad bean, and feta salad*
- ***Dinner:*** *OUT FOR DINNER*

Saturday

- ***Breakfast:*** *2 eggs, bacon, baked beans*
- ***Lunch/Snacks:*** *Seasonal mixed vegetable soup*
- ***Dinner:*** *Asparagus Risotto (125g rice)*

Sunday

- ***Breakfast:*** *Yoghurt with teaspoon of honey*
- ***Sunday Lunch:*** *Roast lamb or lamb stew*
  Spring cabbage, broad beans with mint, roast new potatoes
- ***Dinner:*** *Seasonal mixed vegetable soup*

WEEK 2 - SPRING

Monday

- ***Breakfast:*** *Banana, mixed raw nuts*
- ***Lunch:*** *Leftover roast lamb or lamb stew*
  Spring cabbage, broad beans with mint, roast new potatoes
- ***Dinner:*** *Onion and herb frittata*
  Massive mixed seasonal salad

Tuesday

- ***Breakfast:*** *Yoghurt with teaspoon of honey*
- ***Lunch:*** *Mixed wild rice (125g) and raw vegetable salad*
- ***Dinner:*** *Chicken Cacciatora*

Pan-fried asparagus

Wednesday

- ***Breakfast:*** *Banana, mixed raw nuts*
- ***Lunch:*** *Massive mixed seasonal salad, Cottage cheese, Slice of sourdough bread*
- ***Dinner:*** *Leftover chicken Cacciatora,*
  Purple sprouting broccoli boiled/steamed al dente

Thursday

- ***Breakfast:*** *Porridge with teaspoon of honey*
- ***Lunch:*** *Spring cabbage soup*
- ***Dinner:*** *Risotto (125g) with fresh garden peas and parmesan*

Friday

- ***Breakfast:*** *Banana, mixed raw nuts*
- ***Lunch:*** *Spring cabbage soup*
- ***Dinner:*** *Fried British whiting or pollock, homemade mayonnaise*
  Massive mixed seasonal salad

Saturday

- ***Breakfast:*** *Yoghurt with teaspoon of honey*
- ***Lunch:*** *Raw vegetables, hummus, grilled halloumi*
  Slice of sourdough bread
- ***Dinner:*** *Frittata with spinach/chard, massive mixed seasonal salad*

Sunday

- ***Breakfast:*** *Banana, mixed raw nuts*
- ***Lunch:*** *Boiled butter beans with olive oil and vinegar*[703]
- ***Sunday Dinner:*** *Roasted rolled lamb breast stuffed with herbs and garlic*
  Massive mixed seasonal salad

[703] Do NOT underestimate how delicious high-quality legumes are when you boil them yourself and serve them warm and nicely dressed and seasoned. Filling, delicious and wholesome. If you do the same with canned pre-cooked pulses you simply do not get the same results.

WEEK 3 - SUMMER

Monday

- ***Breakfast:*** *Fresh herbs frittata*
- ***Lunch:*** *Massive tomato, cucumber and fresh herbs salad, with British goat cheese*
- ***Dinner:*** *Chickpea and vegetable curry; basmati rice (100g)*

Tuesday

- ***Breakfast***: *Porridge with teaspoon of honey*
- ***Lunch:*** *Chickpea and vegetable curry*
- ***Dinner:*** *Al Fresco - cheeses, cold cuts, pickled/preserved vegetables, fresh melon*
  Slice of sourdough bread

Wednesday

- ***Breakfast:*** *Yoghurt, mixed summer berries*
- ***Lunch:*** *Tuscan bean salad: Cannellini, tuna, fresh white onion.*
- ***Dinner:*** *Roast chicken thighs/drumsticks/wings*
  Sauteed courgettes, roasted sweet peppers

Thursday

- ***Breakfast:*** *2 fried eggs, roast tomatoes*
- ***Lunch:*** *Mixed seasonal salad with shredded leftover chicken*
- ***Dinner:*** *Penne or other short pasta (125g) with tomato sauce, parmesan cheese*

Friday

- ***Breakfast:*** *Mixed summer berries*
- ***Lunch:*** *Minestrone soup with Borlotti beans*
- ***Dinner:*** *Fresh Cornish mackerel*[704] *roasted, grilled or pan-fried*
  Potato and beetroot salad with fresh herbs
  Steamed French green beans

[704]Or other oily fish: sardines or horse mackerel.

Saturday

- ***Breakfast:*** *Banana milkshake with cinnamon and cardamom*
- ***Lunch:*** *Minestrone soup with borlotti beans*
  Fresh plums
- ***Dinner:*** *OUT FOR DINNER*

Sunday

- ***Breakfast:*** *Mixed summer berries*
- ***Sunday Lunch:*** *Homemade BBQ: lamb cutlets, beef steak, sweetcorn, mixed seasonal salad*
- ***Dinner:*** *Minestrone soup with borlotti beans*

WEEK 4 - SUMMER

Monday

- ***Breakfast:*** *Mixed summer berries*
- ***Lunch:*** *Massive seasonal salad with leftover beef strips*
- ***Dinner:*** *Minestrone with Pudding Rice (75g)*

Tuesday

- ***Breakfast:*** *Yoghurt with teaspoon of honey*
- ***Lunch:*** *Minestrone with Pudding Rice (75g)*
- ***Dinner:*** *Grilled/pan-fried Alaskan Wild salmon, with roast potatoes*
  Pan-fried courgettes with herbs

Wednesday

- ***Breakfast:*** *Mixed summer berries*
- ***Lunch:*** *Aubergine Parmigiana*
- ***Dinner:*** *Al Fresco Dinner: fresh mozzarella and tomato salad, cucumbers and mint salad, slice of sourdough bread*

Thursday

- ***Breakfast:*** *Yoghurt with teaspoon of honey*
- ***Lunch:*** *Massive seasonal salad with crab meat*
- ***Dinner:*** *Aubergine Parmigiana*

Friday

- ***Breakfast:*** *Strawberry and blackberry milkshake*
- ***Lunch:*** *Massive seasonal salad; 3 soft-boiled eggs*
- ***Dinner:*** *Baked dived scallops starter*
  Spaghetti (125g) with loads of Dorset clams

Saturday

- ***Breakfast:*** *Seasonal fruits*
- ***Lunch:*** *Beetroot and Feta salad with fresh herbs*
- ***Dinner:*** *Grilled rump steak, rocket salad*

Sunday

- ***Breakfast:*** *2 eggs, bacon, sausages, tomatoes*
- ***Lunch:*** *Seasonal fruits*
- ***Dinner:*** *Homemade BBQ: spatchcock marinated woodpigeons,*[705] *courgettes, peppers, onions*

WEEK 5 - AUTUMN

Monday

- ***Breakfast:*** *Porridge with teaspoon of honey*
- ***Lunch:*** *Pumpkin/Butternut squash soup*
- ***Dinner:*** *Venetian-style liver (pork/lamb/calf/venison) with onions*
  Sauteed Kale and Broccoli

[705] I had these with Alex one memorable evening! Hence their inclusion...

Tuesday

- ***Breakfast:*** *Yoghurt with teaspoon of honey*
- ***Lunch:*** *Pumpkin/Butternut squash soup*
- ***Dinner:*** *Roasted seasonal fresh whole flatfish from British waters*
  Mixed seasonal salad

Wednesday

- ***Breakfast:*** *Porridge with teaspoon of honey*
- ***Lunch:*** *Fresh pears/apples, Stilton/mature cheddar, pickled/preserved Vegetables*
  Slice of sourdough bread
- ***Dinner:*** *Mutton Stew with roast root seasonal vegetables (parsnip, celeriac, swede, turnip)*

Thursday

- ***Breakfast:*** *Yoghurt with pear/apple compote*
- ***Lunch:*** *Massive mixed seasonal salad; 2 poached eggs*
- ***Dinner:*** *Mutton Stew with roasted carrot and Jerusalem artichokes*

Friday

- ***Breakfast:*** *Seasonal fruit: pear, Japanese persimmon, pomegranate*
- ***Lunch:*** *Leek soup*
- ***Dinner:*** *Risotto (125g rice) with mushrooms*

Saturday

- ***Breakfast:*** *Baked Apple (butter, spices, 1 teaspoon of honey), mixed raw nuts*
- ***Lunch:*** *Leek soup*
- ***Dinner:*** *OUT FOR DINNER*

Sunday

- ***Breakfast:*** *Yoghurt with teaspoon of honey*
- ***Lunch:*** *Massive mixed seasonal salad; 2 soft-boiled eggs*
- ***Sunday Dinner:*** *Roast Beef or Beef Stew, Roast Pumpkin, Sauteed Cabbage with bacon*

WEEK 6 - AUTUMN

Monday

- ***Breakfast:*** *Seasonal fruit: pear, Japanese persimmon, pomegranate*
- ***Lunch:*** *Massive mixed seasonal salad; mixed cheese platter*
- ***Dinner:*** *Leftover roast beef or beef stew, roast sweet potatoes, buttered kale*

Tuesday

- ***Breakfast:*** *Seasonal fruit: pear, Japanese persimmon, pomegranate*
- ***Lunch:*** *Boiled lentils with olive oil and vinegar*
- ***Dinner:*** *Mallard with orange*
  Pan-fried cauliflower

Wednesday

- ***Breakfast:*** *2 fried eggs, pan-fried mushrooms*
- ***Lunch:*** *Boiled lentils with olive oil and vinegar*
- ***Dinner:*** *Mallard with orange*
  Roast celeriac and swede

Thursday

- ***Breakfast:*** *Yoghurt with teaspoon of honey*
- ***Lunch:*** *Winter cabbage soup*
- ***Dinner:*** *Tagliatelle (125g) with porcini mushrooms*

Friday

- ***Breakfast:*** *Grapefruit*
- ***Lunch:*** *Winter cabbage soup*
- ***Dinner:*** *Homemade Fish*[706] *and Chips, mixed seasonal salad*

[706] Again, refer to chapters 10-11 for the most sustainable options. It could be British or Icelandic white fish, depending on species and fishery. Read labels!

Saturday

- ***Breakfast:*** *Blood Oranges*
- ***Lunch:*** *Homemade baked beans, pork sausages*
- ***Dinner:*** *Mixed Vegetable Curry, Brown rice (100g)*

Sunday

- ***Breakfast:*** *Yoghurt with teaspoon of honey*
- ***Lunch:*** *Mixed Vegetable Curry*
- ***Sunday Dinner:*** *Shepherd's Pie*

WEEK 7 - WINTER

Monday

- ***Breakfast:*** *Grapefruit*
- ***Lunch:*** *Onion and herb frittata, mixed seasonal salad*
- ***Dinner:*** *Beef brisket, salsa verde*
  Carrots, onion, celery with mustard dressing

Tuesday

- ***Breakfast:*** *Yoghurt with a teaspoon of honey*
- ***Lunch:*** *Massive mixed seasonal salad, shredded leftover beef*
- ***Dinner:*** *Beef broth with pearled barley (100g)*

Wednesday

- ***Breakfast:*** *Apple, a few dates*
- ***Lunch:*** *Beef broth with pudding rice (75g)*
- ***Dinner:*** *Smoked Alaskan salmon, slice of sourdough bread, butter, lemon juice, mixed seasonal salad*

Thursday

- ***Breakfast:*** *Orange and pomegranate*
- ***Lunch:*** *Boiled Cannellini beans with olive oil and vinegar*
- ***Dinner:*** *Mixed cheese platter, cauliflower salad, fresh pear, slice of sourdough bread*

Friday

- ***Breakfast:*** *Apple, a few dates*
- ***Lunch:*** *Boiled Cannellini beans with olive oil and vinegar*
- ***Dinner:*** *Mussel Soup/Mussels Marinara, slice of sourdough bread*

Saturday

- ***Breakfast:*** *Bacon, mushrooms, baked beans*
- ***Lunch:*** *Parsnip soup*
- ***Dinner:*** *Penne or short pasta (125g) with broccoli and pecorino cheese*

Sunday

- ***Breakfast:*** *Apple, blood orange*
- ***Sunday Lunch:*** *Pheasant stew, roast swede & turnips, sauteed cabbage*
- ***Dinner:*** *Parsnip soup*

WEEK 8 - WINTER

Monday

- ***Breakfast:*** *Grapefruit*
- ***Lunch:*** *Spelt and Borlotti bean soup*
- ***Dinner:*** *Leftover pheasant stew, Braised Cauliflower, Sauteed Kale*

Tuesday

- ***Breakfast:*** *Apple, a few dates*
- ***Lunch:*** *Spelt and Borlotti bean soup*
- ***Dinner:*** *Steamed/Boiled/ Icelandic Cod or Haddock with Salsa Verde, Pan Fried Broccoli*

Wednesday

- ***Breakfast:*** *Porridge with teaspoon of honey*
- ***Lunch:*** *Massive mixed seasonal salad; 2 soft-boiled eggs*
- ***Dinner:*** *Lentils (or Beans) and Pork Belly & Ribs Stew*

Thursday

- ***Breakfast:*** *Apple and orange*
- ***Lunch:*** *Lentils (or Beans) and Pork Belly & Ribs Stew*
- ***Dinner:*** *Jerusalem artichoke and celeriac soup*

Friday

- ***Breakfast:*** *Orange and grapefruit*
- ***Lunch:*** *Jerusalem artichoke and celeriac soup, slice of sourdough bread*
- ***Dinner:*** *OUT FOR DINNER*

Saturday

- ***Breakfast:*** *Porridge with teaspoon of honey*
- ***Lunch:*** *Eggs, black pudding, baked beans, mushrooms*
- ***Dinner:*** *Onion Soup*

Sunday

- ***Breakfast:*** *Apple and pear*
- ***Sunday Lunch:*** *Venison stew or medium rare venison loin, mash potatoes, brussels sprouts*
- ***Dinner:*** *Onion Soup*

Maintenance & Long-Term Approach

Let us presume that, after a year on the above diet, Alex is no longer overweight, his health has improved, and he is no longer a prime candidate for Type 2 Diabetes. What if Alex was already suffering from Type 2 Diabetes? As already discussed, Type 2 Diabetes is normally correlated with being overweight[707] and is almost entirely caused by diet. Therefore, both obesity and Type 2 Diabetes can be reversed through diet rather than pharmaceuticals. Alex could follow the very same diet outlined above, minus the honey, minor chocolate doses and the rapadura sugar. He could eat even less refined grains and sweet fruits and increase vegetables and animal products. Not because any of these foods are in inherently bad, but as a radical short and medium-term measure to reverse a chronic condition like Type 2 Diabetes.

In any case, after a year on the diet, Alex (and his diabetic alter ego) would have been cooking for a long time, would have learnt lots of simple recipes, would have acquired sound shopping habits, would be friendly with his butcher, and would eat tasty food every day, without having been restricted and "punished" in the ways that the various fashionable diets normally do. People who lose weight through the very restrictive, unpleasant diets that involve obsessive calorie counting, fat-free foods, protein shakes, hunger, sweeteners, horrid gluten free products, intermittent fasts and so on generally put weight back on as soon as the diet ends.

There are various reasons for that. The primary reason for that is that they have not actually learnt how to eat well nor how to cook, have not learnt the value of whole foods and of wholesome ingredients from healthy soils and happy livestock. They will not have learnt how to engage with food in a way that is pleasurable, healthy, and principled in equal measures. Therefore, as soon as the diet ends, they resume previous bad habits, the very same ones that led to being overweight in the first place. Another important reason is that people who lose weight through bad diets do not necessarily improve their gut health, their hormonal balance, and their metabolic health. Therefore, they are doomed to fail in the long run.

Once normal weight and overall health has been restored, Alex should keep the same basic foundations, principles and gradually intersperse the diet with more of the food types that were restricted. The main restrictions were the low amounts of processed grains and natural sugars, and the only major item missing was the category of desserts. Therefore, the long-term approach simply consists in continuing with *the same sort of diet*, with a more relaxed

[707] There is undoubtedly a correlation between Type 2 diabetes, heart disease and obesity, which tend to occur as comorbidities. The cause and remedy are the same for all three conditions: primarily diet.

approach to processed grains and natural sugars and the occasional addition of some high-quality desserts. Basically, that is all. I would also expect some normal weight fluctuations: putting on some weight in the winter, where food will be heavier and lives more sedentary, and toning up during the warm season.[708] Provided the foundations of a diet are stable and sound, the fluctuations and variabilities in weight will always be slighter and easier to manage.

Feeding Children & Taking Responsibility

There is a disastrous percentage of overweight children in modern Britain and other countries where the ultra-processed junk food diet dominates. This is precisely what you would expect, as there is an obvious and direct correlation between what adults eat and what children eat. As is often the case with complex issues, there is no single cause or answer to this enormous problem. If little Johnny is obese, who is to blame? Certainly not Johnny. If his parents are obese, who is to blame? Does it even make sense to blame anything or anyone? As we generally find with many public debates, there has been a relatively shallow polarisation between two extremes: the claim that obesity is simply a poor lifestyle choice, and the claim that obesity is a disease for which the patient bears no responsibility.

The contemporary approach at the time of writing tends to favour the apportioning of blame on impersonal entities and institutions, from sugar manufacturers and advertisers to the government's policies on school meals, or on genetics and poverty. There is indeed no doubt that there are many impersonal, systemic factors at play here, ranging from the mass production and marketing of ultra-processed industrial food to woeful government policy and counterproductive medical advice. We have created conditions in which it is very easy to make bad decisions, and far harder to make sound ones. The recent and accelerating explosion of obesity cannot simply be explained by a collective loss of personal responsibility, especially when we consider how the adoption of Western junk food leads to increased obesity wherever it goes, irrespective of culture. An interesting exception might be Japan where, apart from the fact that Western junk food has not yet managed to supplant the traditional diet, obesity is stigmatised and self-discipline expected and institutionalised.

In any case, closer to home, the causes and conditions of obesity are now well entrenched, and in North America and Western Europe, this is now an intergenerational problem, with fat, unhealthy parents raising fat, unhealthy children. In countries where the junk food diet

[708] I also recommend an old fashioned fast from all desserts during Lent, to keep things in balance after the festive season.

has arrived more recently, such as Mexico, Brazil[709] and Polynesia, the effects on public health have been immediate and devastating in a relatively short space of time, with the worst yet to come. Here in Britain, Johnny's parents are highly likely to be eating rubbish themselves and to be overweight. A high percentage of adults born in the 70s, 80s and 90s, who now have children, were brought up on Happy Meals, crisps, soft drinks, and microwave meals, and there is no reason to expect well-meaning people who are ignorant about food, cookery, and health to make sensible choices for their own children.

Whilst it is quite clear that children do not have a choice over what they eat, and the consequences of their diet, what about *compos mentis* adults, who might be reading this book? In his condemnation of ultra-processed foods, van Tulleken takes a clear position in claiming that obesity is not a choice, and obese people bear no responsibility at all for their condition.

As a scientist, he could not resist presenting this idea in very reductionist terms, which stand out in his dubious genealogy of eating:

"For a start, to eat is to compete in an arms race[710] that has lasted billions of years. The world around us has a relatively fixed amount of available energy, and all life is engaged in a competition against other forms of life for that energy. Life has, after all, only two projects; reproduction and extracting energy to fuel that reproduction."[711]

"Life captures the energy released by passing electrons from food to breath. So food can be anything that wants an electron less than breath does."[712]

In the midst of such a struggle for life and invisible subatomic activity, it is no wonder that human choice goes out of the window:

"Food intake is under little more conscious control than breathing or drinking, and this is why it is nearly as hard to limit food intake as it is to limit water or oxygen intake."[713]

[709] See C. van Tulleken, 2023, Ultra-processed People, pages 236-243, for an interesting account of the arrival of ultra-processed food and its impact communities in Brazil.

[710] Note the language of competition and struggle, typical of Darwinian reductionism, as discussed in Chapter 4.

[711] C. van Tulleken, 2023, Ultra-processed People, page 4.

[712] Ibidem, page 82. In a footnote to the above sentence, van Tulleken writes: "You can now sagely say to people, 'Life is nothing but an electron looking for a place to rest,' a quote from the Hungarian Nobel prize winner Albert Szent-Györgyi." This is a textbook example of scientific reductionism that sounds sage and profound, but is ultimately meaningless nonsense, much like the fashionable idea that "we are all stardust", often repeated by celebrity physicists like Lawrence Krauss.

[713] Ibidem, page 102.

"Eating is far less of a choice than it appears…We're controlled by ancient neuroendocrine feedback systems, which evolved to ensure we consume everything we need to pass on a few genes."[714]

"The difference in people's weight has nothing to do with willpower. It's simply a collision of genes and the constraints of the food environment."[715]

Van Tulleken also goes on to claim that ultra-processed food is addictive and that people can develop an addiction to it, with many unintended consequences.[716] Whilst van Tulleken makes a fairly credible argument about the addictive potential of many ultra-processed foods, that seem to be designed to encourage uncontrolled consumption, this does not necessarily negate individual agency and choice. Even if we draw the very imperfect analogy between addictive substances and junk food, it is quite clear that, unlike addictive substances, for which there is no substitute and must be given up entirely, junk food can be replaced with real food. We have no choice about eating, but we can choose what to eat.

In any case, the chief problem with such a reductive view of life, of eating, of food and of human agency is that it is false and, ultimately, self-defeating. Whilst there are clearly many environmental, genetic and economic factors that determine our food choices, we do have a degree of autonomy and we are able to make better or worse choices, in whatever circumstances. Even if we recognise, as we should, the many constraints and difficulties people can and do face, we should not absolve ourselves from all individual responsibility. The buck has to stop somewhere. It is wrong to simply blame "society" or the "system" or corporations or the government or genetics or addiction or whichever other higher power we can appeal to and to avoid taking individual responsibility, especially parental responsibility. Ultimately, the average fat child is fat due to poor parenting[717] and upbringing. If little Johnny eats Happy Meals on a regular basis and stuffs himself with crisps, Nutella and soft drinks at home, his parents are primarily responsible for the problem. It is very hard to raise children on the food front, given the broad range of negative influences they will be subjected to outside of home. It is certainly true that junk food companies spend billions of dollars a year in marketing and advertising to persuade both children and adults to eat their products. But that is no reason not to take responsibility for what we can control and lead a fight back on several fronts. Part of the motivation for writing this book is to

[714] C. van Tulleken, 2023, Ultra-processed People, page 108.

[715] Ibidem, page 148

[716] Ibidem, "How UPF hacks our brains", pages 151-168.

[717] As far as food education is concerned, of course, as opposed to anything else. There are plenty of very good parents who fail in this particular aspect of parenting.

provide readers with knowledge and with strategies to make better choices in their day-to-day life, whatever their circumstances.

None of this is easy. It is actually a lot easier to go with the flow and take your child for a Happy Meal, keep junk food at home, park children in front of the television and not bother to cook any decent food. Good parenting usually requires more effort, confrontation, and resilience. I loved Coca-Cola as a child, and yet never saw a can or bottle of it at home, not even on my birthday. I still drank it on occasions outside of the home, and at other children's parties, but at home it was simply not allowed. That was not harsh treatment, but good parenting. Sadly, a lot of parents associate junk food with "treats" and "rewards" and take their child to McDonald's, even when they know that the food is junk, to supposedly treat and reward their child. This is again a mistake, as there are plenty of fantastic food items that can be used to treat and reward a child. It also sends the wrong message to the child, who internalises it: junk food is a treat, healthy food is not. Growing up I thought Tuscan prosciutto and Pecorino, or the best ice cream were treats, not McDonald's.

I was clearly quite fortunate in my upbringing and cannot take credit for it. This brings me to a serious argument that van Tulleken raises, and which I will further deal with in the next chapter, which is that choice is constrained and limited by poverty. There is no doubt that people living in deprived and degraded areas, on relatively low incomes or benefits, with very serious day-to-day challenges, and surrounded by retailers that almost exclusively sell ultra-processed food and takeaway junk, have very limited scope to manoeuvre and will struggle to make better choices. However, calls to end poverty,[718] well-intentioned as they may be, do not really address the problem at hand. Firstly, whilst there is a strong correlation between obesity and poverty in the UK, obesity and its comorbidities are nonetheless a problem across all levels of class and wealth: junk food is eaten by most of the population, in varying degrees. Secondly, it is also worth considering that it is only in the West, where junk food diets were first adopted, that we find a clear correlation between obesity and poverty. In nations that have recently adopted junk food diets, such as China and India, obesity has struck the rich, as opposed to the poor. There are also entirely wealthy populations that are becoming obese: the Gulf States are a prime example, where a very wealthy native population has been piling on weight as their traditional diet is being supplanted by the Western diet.

Paradoxically, van Tulleken, whilst wishing to end poverty, does not *"think that the aim of policy should be for people to eat less UPF"*, does *"not have a moral opinion about eating*

[718] C. van Tulleken, 2023, Ultra-processed People, page 323.

UPF" and does *"not care how you feed yourself and your child".*[719] Most worryingly, in spite of being a qualified doctor, he expresses a range of problematic ideas:

"I don't accept that you should lose weight. I don't have a 'correct' body and I don't have an opinion about what one would look like. I don't have an opinion on the food you should eat; that's up to you."[720]

He also offers *"almost no advice"* ... *"about how to live your life or how to feed your children. Partly it's none of my business, but mainly I think advice is a bit pointless. What we eat is determined by the food around us, its price and how it's marketed - this is what needs to change."*[721]

In my opinion, a doctor who is, even in principle, unwilling or unable to form an opinion about whether someone is fat[722] or not and is unwilling or unable to give someone clear advice on what they and their children should be eating is a doctor that is failing to live up to the Hippocratic oath. It is also a mistake to promote the idea that what we eat is entirely determined by the food around us, as if Big Macs and crisps from the high street next to our homes somehow end up down our gullet, in spite of our best efforts to avoid them.

In any case, why should policy not aim to reduce or eliminate the consumption of ultra-processed foods? What is the point of public policy and of legislation, if not to reduce or eliminate the problem? If, as van Tulleken and others rightly suggest, ultra-processed foods are the source of obesity and its comorbidities, then surely, we should tackle them head-on. It is also strange to deny the moral implications of food choices given that, as van Tulleken clearly believes, ultra-processed food is harmful to people, livestock and the environment. In the same way that I would advocate for the abolition of factory farms and pesticides, I would also advocate for the abolition of many ultra-processed foods, which harm both individuals and society as a whole. As van Tulleken carefully records, many of the substances used to manufacture ultra-processed foods are poorly regulated, if at all, and could often be considered to be hazardous substances. Why not push to eliminate them?

[719] C. van Tulleken, 2023, Ultra-processed People, page 300.

[720] Ibidem, page 9.

[721] Ibidem, pages 9-10.

[722] Many doctors don't think using the word "fat" is appropriate any more. Only "fat activists" seem to be allowed to "own" the word apparently, which is why so-called body positivity is pushed by organisations such as the National Association to Advance Fat Acceptance or NAAFA, the world's longest-running "fat rights" organisation. The NHS now polices the language around body weight very carefully, and is careful not to offend, referring to fat/obese patients as "people living with obesity". Van Tulleken also insists on the third person perspective: he points out that people *have* obesity, as opposed to *being* obese (C. van Tulleken, 2023, Ultra-processed People, page 35).

Instead, van Tulleken only has *"a demand to improve information about UPF, and access to real food"*.[723] The goal, he argues, *"should be that you live in a world where you have real choices and the freedom to make them"*.[724] It seems very odd for van Tulleken to both believe that eating, diet and obesity are not ultimately bound by individual choice, whilst also advocating for freedom and "real choices". Whilst van Tulleken is correct in calling out the conflicts of interest between regulators and the food industry, and whilst he is right to advocate for regulating labelling, marketing and advertising,[725] which undoubtedly reduce people's ability to make informed choices, it is very hard to see how we go from a scenario in which we have no choice at all to a scenario where we can make "real choices", including the "freedom" to eat ultra-processed foods and feed them to our children. This attitude arguably betrays a very liberal, secular bias, which we have seen throughout this book, common to so many of our friends in the scientific community. The negation of free will and a penchant for reductionist explanations for human behaviour are indeed usually accompanied by extreme moral relativism, by a shallow commitment to a vague notion of liberty and by an aversion to any kind of prohibition and authority. It would be far better, I would argue, to reaffirm and emphasise personal responsibility first and foremost, and, if possible, and when appropriate, promote unashamedly interventionist and strict policies that aim to eliminate the worst practices in agriculture and food production, which damage us all in the long run.

Lastly, I must add that you should also really care about "how you feed your child", who are the innocent recipients of adult choices. How should we feed our children, ideally?

In a nutshell: children should simply eat more or less what adults should eat, as outlined in chapters 10 and 11. All the same principles apply, and children should eat a broad diversity of wholesome adult foods as early as possible: from the moment they can chew and eat, there is no such thing as children's food and menus. As a side note, it is worth mentioning that so-called "fussy eaters",[726] which we often hear about, and who virtually did not exist until a generation or two ago, are also the result of questionable parenting. If little Johnny only eats chicken and potatoes and does not like any fruits or vegetables, that is not the result of some innate predisposition. It is due to a lack of exposure to different foods and flavours from a young age and to being allowed to choose meals and snacks on a whim. The palate, like any other aspect of human taste and discernment, has to be educated and cultivated or

[723] C. van Tulleken, 2023, Ultra-processed People, page 9.

[724] Ibidem, page 300.

[725] Ibidem, "What we could ask governments to do", pages 288-302.

[726] I am referring to children as opposed to babies or toddlers, whose propensity and willingness to eat can vary greatly irrespective of parenting.

it will not develop to its full potential. This is true both in terms of the diversity of foods eaten and in terms of their quality. In spite of relativist claims to the contrary, there is such a thing as a good palate and good taste.

A few suggestions:

- Eat meals as a family.
- Have at least some of the week's meals at the table, as opposed to having them all in front of the television.
- Do not have individual, tailored meals: generally speaking, everyone should eat the same food.
- Do not allow children to choose which courses they will eat (e.g., you cannot eat dessert if you want to skip the soup, and you should eat the vegetables next to your meat).
- Cook. I will not dare suggest that mothers should cook for their children, as such a suggestion will be condemned as patriarchal hate speech. I will therefore suggest that it is imperative for one or both parents or some other responsible adult to cook for the family, for everyone's benefit. Encourage your children to join in a few cooking chores.
- On occasions, bring your children with you to buy food, especially at farmers' markets, traditional butchers, fishmongers etc... instil curiosity and interest in them from an early age.
- Teach children that food should be valued and appreciated, and that waste is a sin. Inform them of the fact that plenty of children around the world are malnourished or hungry.
- Do not deny children desserts, good ice cream or jam.
- Associate celebrations and festivities with particular foods and create happy food memories.
- If possible and affordable, give your children great restaurant experiences.
- Take hard decisions and unpopular decisions, at times.
- Take personal responsibility for yourself and your loved ones.
- Do not wait for government and legislation to bring about positive change, as it may well never do so.

Athlete?

There is no particular reason to believe that athletic activity requires a radically different approach to diet and nutrition. The fundamentals are in no way different to those that apply to the non-athletes amongst us. As previously argued, there is no good reason to resort to supplements, protein powders, electrolytes etc... and everything an athlete needs will be found in normal, wholesome food as described in Chapter 11.

Nonetheless, there are three basic variables: energy requirements, endurance and stamina, and muscle development. There is no doubt that athletes who expend great amounts of energy simply need more food than those who do not, meaning that it is not so much a question of what type of food is required, but the amount. A professional swimmer or boxer training intensely on a daily basis will need more food than a sedentary person. If Alex, having recovered his health and reached a healthy weight, became a full-time athlete (highly unlikely, I must say!) he would undoubtedly need to increase his food intake. Nonetheless, yet again, there are no fundamental differences between the kind of food Alex would need, irrespective of whether he remains sofa-bound or becomes a professional rugby player.

Sports that revolve around great endurance and stamina, such as long-distance running and cycling, will likely require greater amounts of foods that provide the release of abundant long-term energy, such as whole grains and other complex carbohydrates. There is also no question that muscle repair and development, especially in the kind of sports that involve explosive movements and muscle growth, require greater protein intake, which means that we need to eat more protein-rich foods, as opposed to "protein".

Lastly, the timing of meals and the kind of meals required before and after exercise will vary greatly, depending on the sport, individual preference, and other factors, which are beyond the scope of this brief sidenote.

Old Age

The logical consequence of all the above is that, again, there is no fundamental difference between the food of adults in their prime and the food of the elderly. There is one crucial difference, however, and that is summarised in one word: quantity. The basic rule of thumb is that the older we get, the less food we need. It makes sense from a basic biological point of view: having fully grown, and past one's physical and reproductive prime, the body is working on a maintenance and damage limitation basis, as opposed to a growth and development basis.

It is also increasingly important to accept a brutal truth: there are very few fat people that get to old age and those that do are likely to struggle with all sorts of ailments. The best chance to get to old age and in decent shape is to gradually decrease food intake from middle age onwards and maintain a healthy weight. Less is more!

Eating Out

The foundation of a healthy relationship with food begins and ends at home, in the kitchen and the domestic milieu, not with delivery apps and restaurant meals. Having said that, eating out is sometimes a necessity, especially when travelling or on the move, or simply a pleasure we choose to engage in. Going to any sort of restaurant is not necessarily about healthy eating and dieting, but about the experience, new foods, the aesthetics, and the company.

When eating out, whilst the pleasure principle should dominate our motivations, we can still make informed choices, which reflect our concerns as outlined in previous chapters. There is no need to choose foie gras or sturgeon caviar just because it is on the menu, even at a great restaurant. Thankfully, there is generally a direct correlation between great restaurant food and quality ingredients, and many of the other features that we look for in food.

Having said that, we clearly do not have the same level of control when we eat out, nor as much information about what we are eating. We can, and should, be more relaxed about the minutiae of the kind of standards outlined in Chapter 11, which whilst relatively easy to follow at home, are not entirely applicable on the road. Whilst Alex is in his first phase of weight loss, he should not eat out too often, as suggested by the menus above, and think carefully about menu choices.

There are some basic features we can look out for when selecting restaurants, based on their website, menus, and reviews. We should do our research and also ask questions, sometimes, when possible and appropriate. Here are some suggestions of what to look out for:

- An emphasis on ingredients.
- Details about the animals that feature on the menu (e.g., Dexter beef as opposed to "beef"; Cornish lobster as opposed to just "lobster", dived scallops as opposed to just "scallops").
- An emphasis on seasonality. The best restaurants have seasonal menus, as opposed to the same menu all year round.
- Relatively short menus. Very long menus do not usually correlate well with quality.

- Absolutely no images of plates of food on menus or outside the restaurant: this normally spells disaster.
- An emphasis on locality. In true cosmopolises like London or New York, it makes sense to enjoy cuisines from around the world, even with their obvious limitations. On the other hand, it makes no sense whatsoever to go for sushi in Madrid or for pizza in Prague when visiting these great cities: enjoy the local cuisine. Outside of cities, a link to the land, seas and region is even more important, and restaurants, no matter how simple, should reflect that.
- A traditional approach, or genuine innovation. As we saw earlier, this simply means a cuisine that has solid foundations, a respect for technique and for ingredients. In other words, the antithesis of postmodern gastronomy.
- A genuine cultural identity, as opposed to a dubious fusion cuisine or postmodern fad. What a restaurant is about should be clear, and credible, and reflected in the food served and the way it is presented.
- Quality above sophistication. What I mean by this is that it is not the level of gastronomy that matters, but its quality. A trattoria, brasserie, barbecue joint or gastropub can offer great, unsophisticated food. A very expensive restaurant aspiring to present fine dining can be very mediocre or poor. Therefore, go for quality and get value for money, irrespective of whether you choose to go very low or very high on the gastronomic spectrum.
- Impeccable hygiene.
- Professional and warm service.
- Aesthetics and atmosphere really matter; avoid eating anywhere that is not pleasant and inviting.

What about the meals of necessity, such as the quick lunch bought near the office, the service station, or at the airport? In such cases, we have to stick as close as possible to the principles laid out in Chapters 10 and 11: even with very few good options, or no good options at all, there are still better and worse choices to be made, in every circumstance. In some cases, desisting altogether can also be an option, as we can skip the odd meal and make up for it later in the day.

All of the considerations above become irrelevant when we are guests, as opposed to paying customers. When we are guests, the only thing that matters are courtesy and gratitude, and short of being served something that is truly inedible, we need to be good guests and just go with the flow. If our hosts make very questionable choices, serving foods that we would ordinarily disapprove of, we should not make a fuss, nor feel morally compromised by eating it. It is our own choices that matter, and being a gracious guest takes precedence.

Chapter 13

THE AVERAGE JOE EXPERIMENT

The Challenge

The greatest obstacle to making the best food choices is a knowledge gap, rather than a financial barrier which, although not unimportant, is not insuperable. No doubt such a statement will leave me open to being accused of being "elitist" and "out of touch". There may be many who will agree with my broad recommendations, but will argue that they are not realistic, not affordable, and simply unattainable for the average person. My critics will argue that it is all very well for me and others like me to eat organic food, order the best tea online, get the best meat and fish and to frequent farmers' markets. The average Joe Bloggs, unfortunately, cannot afford such luxuries. People like me, they will argue, are detached and out of touch, living in our Kensington & Chelsea bubble. There is no doubt that organic food is often associated with elitism, urban wealth, and aristocracy. Afterall, King Charles, to his great credit, has been a champion of organic farming for decades!

Many commentators will rightly point out that we do not all have the same financial means at our disposal, or indeed access to the same suppliers and retailers, as many people live in what have been referred to as "food deserts", places where it is hard to find anything other than junk food. My simple pre-emptive response to this is that it is a truism to say that we cannot all afford the same food, in the same way that we cannot all afford the same clothing, housing and transport. There is no denying that not everyone can afford beef fillet steaks, oysters and organic chicken on a regular basis. The real question is whether we should adopt the "Let Them Eat Junk Food!" position promoted by many of my supposedly democratic opponents or try an alternative. My response is that whatever one's budget, there are better or worse choices available, and my goal is to provide a framework that helps everyone choose the best available options, whatever their means and personal circumstances.

Is it really the case that organic food is inaccessible? More importantly, is it really the case that it is impossible for the average person to eat well, even if they have the willingness to do so? When we look at the sort of dishes and ingredients I suggested for Alex in the previous chapter, there is no question that only people in the affluent middle classes and above could afford to eat the same kind of food on a daily basis. Therefore, I decided to embark on a simple experiment, to answer five key questions:

- Is it possible to eat well[727] on the average[728] UK budget?
- Can this diet be mostly organic?
- What are the realistic conditions and constraints that would need to be met?
- Can all the intersecting considerations that should determine our food choices (health, pleasure, conviviality, animal welfare, environmental protection etc...) still be respected on an average budget?
- How would one go about navigating a below-average budget?

The experiment is relatively simple:

- I set out to eat on the average food budget for an average adult male in the UK, which totals **£51 per week** as of 2024.[729] The average adult female spends £38.90 per week and both the average "young, active adult male" and "young, active adult female" spend more: £63 and £58.40 respectively. I ran the experiment based on my own category: whilst I qualify as active male, I no longer qualify as young!
- The experiment lasted 4 weeks during the spring of 2024. This required me to use a budget to **£204**.
- All food expenditure and consumption were recorded as clearly and as faithfully as possible.
- A final review to assess whether the recommendations in chapters 9-11 can be followed on an average budget was undertaken at the end.

Shopping

The experiment required some preliminary shopping, especially for products bought in bulk, and some regular shopping for fresh food. In that respect, it was not dissimilar to what I would normally do. One difference was that, whilst I shopped at many of the retailers I would

[727] As defined in previous chapters.

[728] Statistical average. See: https://www.nimblefins.co.uk/average-uk-household-cost-food#nogo

[729] The average adult male spends around £38 on groceries, £13 on food out and £51 altogether on food each week.

normally use, I also shopped from places I would not normally use (Sainsbury's and Whole Foods Online), and bought products I would not normally purchase (e.g., Clipper Organic Tea, organic lentils and chickpeas from Turkey), and also went without several products I would normally want to purchase. There were compromises and choices to be made, and interesting discoveries along the way. Some of the products I bought were either not used, nor finished, and this was recorded in the records below. Here follows the full shopping list, marked by category.

Fresh fruits, potatoes, vegetables and herbs

Preserved vegetables

Dairy and eggs

Meat

Seafood

Cereals, Grains, Bread, Pasta etc

Pulses

Sugars

Oils

Coffee, Chocolate, Tea

Nuts

Retailer	Product	Cost	Eaten by Author	Total
Farmers' Market Notting Hill Gate				
	16 apples and pears	£4.00	All	£4.00
	Large Carrot bunch	£2.00	All	£2.00
	Large Celery	£2.00	All	£2.00
	Broccoli X 2	£2.00	All	£2.00
	White Cabbage	£1.50	All	£1.50
	Parsnips and swede	£3.00	All	£3.00
	5 Large White Onions	£1.00	All	£1.00
	Spring Onions Bunch	£0.80	All	£0.80
	Lettuce X 2 (Romaine and Red Batavia)	£3.60	All	£3.60
	Garlic X 1	£1.00	All	£1.00
	12 Apples	£4.00	All	£4.00
	Dill Large Bunch	£2.00	All	£2.00
	Lettuce Oakleaf X 1	£1.80	All	£1.80
	Lettuce Romaine X 1	£1.80	All	£1.80
	Fennel X 2	£1.00	All	£1.00
	Radish bunch	£1.50	All	£1.50
	Spinach bunch X 2	£2.00	All	£2.00
	Parsley Large Bunch	£1.00	All	£1.00
	5 Large White Onions	£1.00	All	£1.00
	Potatoes 1.5kg X 2	£4.00	2kg	£2.67
	Asparagus bunch large X 1	£4.80	Half	£2.40
	Red Cabbage	£1.50	All	£1.50
	Rookery Farm Organic Free Range Eggs X 12 (Misshapes)	£4.40	All	£4.40

Bagnell Farm				
	Pork Trotters & Hock - 990g	£6.44	All	£6.44
	Short Ribs - 1.014kg	£14.70	1/2	£7.35
	Oxtail - 1.128kg	£16.92	In freezer	£0.00
	Lamb Neck Chops - 542g	£6.72	In freezer	£0.00
	Lamb Neck Chops - 590g	£7.38	All	£7.38
	Lamb Ribs Pack X 3	£6.00	1/3	£2.00
	Beef Minute steak - 158g	£4.03	All	£4.03
	Beef Minute steak - 190g	£4.85	All	£4.85
	Pork Tail, Ears, Snout - Free!	£0.00	In freezer	£0.00
	(Discount (£60 instead of £67.04) + free pork off cuts)	-£7.04		-£3.76
Waitrose				
	Duchy Organic Medjool Dates 180g X 1	£2.00	All	£2.00
	Organic Kalamata Olives	£3.25	1/3 Jar	£1.08
	Organic Halkidiki Olives	£3.25	1/3 Jar	£1.08
	Yeo Valley Organic Butter (Unsalted) 200g	£2.00	100g	£1.00
	Duchy Organic Unsalted Butter 250g	£2.60	All	£2.60
	Duchy Organic Mature Cheddar Cheese 350g	£4.50	All	£4.50
	Duchy Organic Unhomogenised Whole Milk 2 Pints X 3	£4.95	All	£4.95
	Waitrose MSC Tuna Steak in Spring Water 4x150g (drained)	£7.00	All	£7.00
	Mussels 1kg	£3.66	Half	£1.83
	Duchy Organic Wholegrain Italian Rice 500g	£2.35	150g	£0.70
	Wainwright's Organic Zambian Forest Honey 380g	£5.00	175g	£2.30
Whole Foods Online				
	Organic Basmati Rice 1kg	£4.12	500g	£2.06
	Organic Arborio Rice 500g	£3.54	150g	£1.06
	Organic Popping Corn 1kg	£3.46	250g	£0.86
	Organic Plain White Flour 1kg	£2.68	500g	£1.34
	Organic Pudding Rice 500g	£3.54	300g	£2.12
	Organic Chickpeas 1kg	£2.44	700g	£1.71
	Organic Brown Lentils 1kg	£3.91	All	£3.91
	Organic Rapadura Sugar 500g	£3.36	165g	£1.11
	Organic Sunflower Oil (Clearspring) 500ml	£3.65	All	£3.65
Amazon Fresh				
	Odysea Organic Extra Virgin Olive Oil, PDO Kalamata, 500ml	£10.00	All	£10.00
Ocado				
	M&S Organic Fairtrade 10 Bananas	£2.50	All	£2.50
	Ocado Organic Beef 400g Mince 15% Fat X 3	£12.00	400g	£4.00
	HLS Cornish 200g Sardines Butterfly Fillets X 2	£3.80	All	£3.80
	Waitrose Icelandic Haddock Fillets MSC 240g X 3	£12.00	1	£4.00
Sainsbury's				
	Organic Celery	£1.00	All	£1.00
	Organic Carrots 700g X 2	£1.80	All	£1.80
	Organic Potatoes (Reduced) 1.5kg X 2	£1.10	All	£1.10
	Sainsbury's Fairtrade Bananas, SO Organic X 6 - X 2	£3.20	All	£3.20
	Organic Plum Canned Tomatoes 400g X 2	£2.20	All	£2.20
	Sainsbury's SO Organic Tomato Puree 312g X 4	£4.60	2 ¼	£2.59
	Yeo Valley Organic Greek Style Natural Yogurt 950g	£3.85	All	£3.85
	Organic Parmigiano Reggiano 200g	£4.10	All	£4.10
	Sainsbury's Woodland Free Range Large Eggs, SO Organic X 2	£5.40	All	£5.40
	Flahavan's Organic Jumbo Oats 1kg	£2.70	600g	£1.62
	Nairn's Organic Oatcakes 6 X 4 (250g)	£1.20	125g	£0.60
	Mayan Gold Organic Ground Coffee 200g pack X 3	£9.75	495g	£8.04
	Clipper Organic Everyday Tea Bags x160 464g	£5.00	x60 174g	£1.88

Marks & Spencer				
	M&S Collection Italian Organic Pasta 1X Pache (500g)	£3.20	300g	£1.92
	M&S Collection Italian Organic Pasta 1X Spaghettoni (500g)	£3.20	All	£3.20
	M&S Collection Italian Organic Pasta 1X Spaghettoni (500g)	£3.20	100g	£0.64
Daylesford Organic				
	Organic Sourdough Loaf 500g	£4.99	All	£4.99
	Organic Non-homogenised Whole Milk 1l	£1.99	All	£1.99
Eversfield Organic				
	Beef Marrow Bone	£2.50	Half	£1.25
	Chicken Carcass	£2.50	Half	£1.25
Whole Foods				
	Equal Exchange - Organic Raw Cane Sugar - 500g	£2.49	350g	£1.74
	Alter Eco Organic Milk Chocolate	£2.89	All	£2.89
	Organic Almonds 500g	£7.39	200g	£2.96
		£303.51		**£207.63**

Disclaimer: the prices above were faithfully recorded from purchases made during late winter/early spring 2024. Some of the prices will no doubt have changed since. Any errors made are my own and made in good faith.

Budget Split

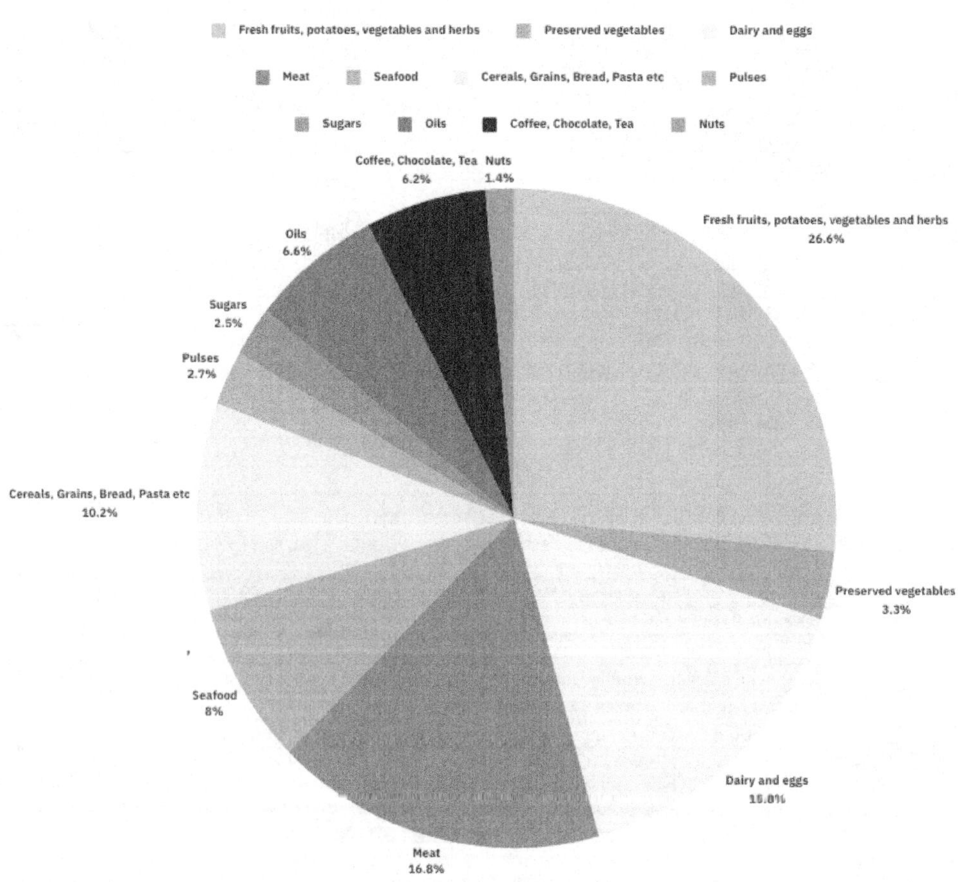

Shopping and Budget Notes

Some interesting statistics:

- **Organic certification**: out of £207.63 spent, £119.14 was on organically certified food: 57.4%.
- **Spending**: £51.90 average per week, 90p over budget per week.
- **Fresh produce** (fruits, potatoes, vegetables, herbs) was the most expensive single category in my shopping. This is symptomatic of a serious problem: quality fresh produce is more expensive than a lot of junk food. This is especially true in Britain and America. In mainland Europe, it is still easier to access quality produce for relatively low prices. On a recent trip to Sicily, I went to a random greengrocer in Bronte, a small town in the foothills of Etna and home of the legendary Sicilian pistachios. I purchased 4 fantastic Etna heritage apples, 4 peaches and a dozen figs. Total cost: €2.36 (£1.97). In the UK, a similar amount of quality fruit would cost at least 3-4 times as much. Anyhow, here in the UK, the average Joe inevitably must devote a significant percentage of his budget to fresh produce.
- **Meat** consumption was approximately 3.4-3.6kg total, with a particularly low carcass availability.[730] This would roughly work out to approximately 44-47kg per annum, well below the UK yearly consumption of 79kg per annum.[731] Considering the low carcass availability, I would estimate my meat consumption to be no more than 55-60% of current average consumption. This makes perfect sense, given my uncompromising quality over quantity approach, and given the fact that, if we give up factory farms and agrochemicals, we will have to eat less meat overall, especially chicken and pork.
- **Seafood** consumption was approximately 1.5kg total, which works out to around 19.5kg per annum, slightly higher than the UK yearly consumption of 18kg per annum.[732] A key differentiator is that none of my seafood consumption was derived from the inefficient and damaging practices involved in the production of farmed fish such as salmon and prawns.
- **Sugars**: organic raw cane sugar, rapadura sugar and honey consumption totalled 690g, which equates to 24.6g per day, plus around 40g of cane sugar from 1 bar of

[730] The meats I have tended to use, from chicken carcass to short rib, have a high percentage of bone and low percentage of meat. The average person is far more likely to eat pure meat in the form of chicken breast or steak.

[731] It is hard to get clear and decisive figures. This is the best I could find and seems to be the most often quoted: https://ourworldindata.org/grapher/daily-meat-consumption-per-person

[732] https://ourworldindata.org/grapher/fish-and-seafood-consumption-per-capita

chocolate, which takes the total to approximately 26g of "free sugar" per day, under the 30g recommended by the NHS, not that I particularly care about the NHS' recommendations. Normally, I am confident that I break the 30g barrier on a regular basis for the simple reason that I eat more mostly homemade desserts than the chocolate and homemade biscuits I had during the experiment.

- **Grains** and starches came from a decent variety of sources: 1,100g rice, 900g pasta, 705g oats, 500g wheat flour, 250g corn, plus a 500g wheat sourdough loaf of bread. I got through 5kg of potatoes, which I listed under produce. Overall, bread and flour consumption was lower than the national average, and fresh potato consumption higher.[733]
- **Milk, dairy and eggs** formed a crucial part of the shopping. Reliable and consistent statistics are hard to come by, but they were roughly consistent with the national average. The weekly average was: 6 eggs, 1.102 litres of milk, 238g of yoghurt, 138g cheese, 88g of butter. It is important to note that, apart from minor amounts of milk in a bar of chocolate, there was no hidden dairy or eggs in any of the food. One of the many problems with ultra-processed foods is the vast quantity of low-quality dairy and egg derivatives they contain.
- **Pulse** consumption was high and totalled 1.7kg, which would work out to 22.16kg per annum, which is more than double the UK average of 10.22kg per annum.[734]
- **Oil** consumption was low for my standards and below the national average.[735] I went for an excellent organic olive oil and rationed it as I have never done before. This was by far the most challenging part of the experiment. I used a cheaper, good quality organic sunflower oil as a substitute for the additional olive oil I would normally have used or cooked in butter whenever possible. There was a very small amount of organic palm oil in my oatcakes, which is not great, but no other oils anywhere in my diet.
- **Coffee** was relatively expensive, as this was an important item for me. Each average Joe will make his own choice on what matters the most and where the budget can be stretched. The tea I drank was decent, but not great, and not what I would normally drink. The chocolate was fantastic, and it is the same one I would normally

[733] Potato consumption statistics are hard to come by, perhaps due to the various forms in which they come. Whilst processed potato consumption is very high in the UK (in crisps, frozen chips etc..), consumption of fresh potatoes has fallen over time. I am fairly confident that the average Joe does not normally consume 1.25kg of fresh potatoes per week.

[734] Lane L, Wells R, Reynolds C. Beans, peas and pulses for improved public and planetary health: Changing UK consumption patterns. Proceedings of the Nutrition Society. 2024;83(OCE2): E203. doi:10.1017/S0029665124004270

[735] We consume almost twice as much per capita (https://ourworldindata.org/grapher/vegetable-oil-vs-gdp). Much of our consumption in the UK, however, is through fried take away foods, crisps and other ultra-processed foods.

purchase. I should really get dark chocolate, but when push comes to shove, I prefer milk chocolate.

- **Nut** consumption was low for my standards, a mere 50g per week. The almonds were of very high quality and relatively expensive, and therefore had to cut down on my usual rations to keep within my budget. Nuts are a very good addition to any diet but, in any case, are not required in large quantities.

Approach and lifestyle:

- With some exceptions, I mostly used suppliers and retailers I would normally use, but just altered and managed my choices with the budget in mind. In other words, I just went for a cheaper version of my existing diet and cuisine, and there was no radical change. Someone who is used to spending their budget on ultra-processed foods from supermarkets would, on the other hand, need to make some radical changes. The main change would be one of choice and lifestyle, as opposed to financial.
- The £51 per week average budget includes both groceries and eating out (£38 groceries, £13 eating out). I chose not to eat out, and simply ate at home. I had guests on some occasions, or cooked for a family member, and the meals for two are clearly marked in the food diary. If I cooked a meal for two that cost me, say, £10, I would mark £5 as part of my personal budget.
- No allotment supplies: I would normally have a steady supply of crops from the allotments, but I desisted from harvesting and, thankfully, the experiment took place during the quietest time of the year, where there is less growing.
- No game nor fish: I did not use any of the "fruits of my gun", as my friend Ian calls them, nor of the fishing rod.

Seasonal limitations:

- Some of the purchasing was repetitive and somewhat limited, because of seasonal constraints in spring, as opposed to pure financials. The only fruits I had were apples, pears, bananas and a few dates. These were the most sensible choices I had available, and they were good. Had the experiment taken place in summer, I would have no doubt had plums and berries, and a greater variety of vegetables.

Notable absentees, obvious restrictions:

- There were no mushrooms, which were the only distinct food group that was missing from my shopping list. This was because unless foraged, the only mushrooms I normally buy are dried porcini mushrooms, which are excellent but expensive. I also tend not to eat them outside of autumn and winter. There are cheap organic cultivated mushrooms easily available at most supermarkets, so that could have been a viable option.

- There were no pork cold cuts, such as bacon and salame. These products, when made as they should, are inherently expensive. I could have picked up a pack of bacon from the supermarket instead of another meat item, of course, but chose not to on this occasion. One thing is certain: the average Joe cannot eat a bacon sandwich every other day, if good bacon is to be used. That is no bad thing, as there is absolutely no need to eat bacon, or indeed salame, with the excessive frequency that is now commonplace.
- Low on desserts, apart from the many delicious homemade aniseed biscuits and some chocolate. I could have baked an apple pie or yoghurt cake at relatively low cost and made some custard and eaten less of other things. However, there is no doubt that regular dessert consumption, if wholesome ingredients are to be used, is not sustainable in the long run. Desserts are best seen as treats or Sunday specials.

Shopping strategies:

- Bulk buying: as clear from the shopping list, I bought some items in bulk, which makes perfect sense, irrespective of whether one in on a tight budget or not. However, do not bulk buy anything that cannot be stored, frozen or otherwise kept. Meat is a particularly good product to buy in bulk. At the farmers' market, I get a handy discount and a few freebies, as outlined on the shopping list above.
- Offers: I bought some items on offer (e.g. Ocado Organic Beef 400g Mince 15% Fat X 3 for £12.00 or Mayan Gold Organic Ground Coffee 200g pack X 3 for £9.75) with a view to using what I needed for the 28 days and keeping whatever was left over for the future.
- It is also important to note that if I were on the average Joe budget long term, I would have purchased certain products in even greater bulk or taken even more advantage of offers and saved more money in the process.
- Maximising deliveries: when ordering online, I ensured I bought enough for free delivery (e.g., Whole Foods Online) or as part of a broader shop (e.g., Ocado, from which I bought plenty of non-food items).
- Expiring products: supermarkets sell products that are about to be past their sell by date at a discount. These are usually perfectly good products, as the date is arbitrary. Use your eyes, touch and smell and make a judgement call. I did not specifically look for expiring products, of course, but came across a few in my shopping (e.g., Organic Potatoes 1.5kg X 2 from Sainsbury's for £1.10).

Thrift and no waste:

- There are so many things that we regularly waste which are perfectly good and useful. For example, carrot tops can be used for soups, radish leaves can go in a mixed salad, potatoes do not always need peeling, cauliflower leaves are delicious.
- The produce at the farmers' market is particularly conducive to thrifty cookery. This is because it is not trimmed, or over trimmed, as the produce at the supermarket always is. For example, the celery I bought at the market may have been £2.00 but was twice the size of a supermarket celery because all the outer stalks and top leaves had not been removed. These can form the basis of soups, stews and stocks. A similar discourse applies to a lot of the vegetables at the market.
- There are simple strategies to stretch the life and freshness of produce. For example, lettuce heads are best used from the outside: use outer leaves first and work your way in. When you have any leafy greens or herbs that have gone a bit limp, just place them in a large bowl submerged in cold water for half an hour and they will come back to life and regain their freshness and crunch.
- Assess what you have in your fridge and storage and make use of things which are more likely to go off soon. If tomatoes are starting to go, make tomato sauce. When bananas are getting black and overripe, it is time for a banana milkshake or banana cake, or indeed if you have extra milk that is about to go off. Apples that are going mouldy or are partly damaged can be cut up and trimmed and still used. During apple harvest time, I end up making more than my fair share of baked apples or apple pies with the trimmings and good halves of damaged apples.
- The freezer is your friend. Even bread never needs to be wasted: what cannot be eaten can be frozen.
- Overall, I managed to avoid almost all food waste, without too much effort.

Personal preferences:

- All the dishes and menus are personalised, but that is to be expected. I could have prepared a different food diary for someone else on the same budget once I knew their preferences.
- Some of the choices and biases (e.g. olive oil, sardines etc...) reflect my personal tastes and preferences. Other choices reflect my habits, such as regular tea and coffee. None of these products are necessary, of course.

Vegetarian and vegan considerations:

- There is no question that meat and seafood are relatively more expensive, and if the average Joe went vegan or vegetarian, it would be far easier to stick to the budget. Whole food staples like rice, pasta, potatoes, pulses, flour are all relatively cheaper and provide more meals than meat, seafood and indeed dairy.
- None of this means that the average Joe has to go vegan or vegetarian: there are plenty of ways of consuming animal products on a tight budget. Furthermore, some animal products, such as whole milk, butter and eggs, are relatively cheap, even if they come, as they always should, from organic agriculture or equivalent.

Food origin and food miles:

- The average Joe relied on both the best from the British Isles and overseas but ensured that what can and is widely grown or raised in the UK took precedence in the kitchen.
- Most importantly, key staple foods and fresh and perishable foods (vegetables, dairy, meat, eggs etc…) were generally from the UK, and what came from overseas tended, with very few exceptions, to be non-perishable food (e.g., lentils, canned tomatoes) or food that could never be grown here (e.g., bananas, cane sugar, basmati rice).
- Foods from the UK:
  - All fresh vegetables and herbs
  - Potatoes
  - Apples and pears
  - Eggs
  - Milk
  - Butter
  - Yoghurt
  - Cheddar cheese
  - Wheat flour
  - Sourdough bread from Daylesford Organic Farm (Gloucestershire)
  - Oatcakes
  - Beef, lamb and pork from farmers' market (Bagnell Farm, Somerset)
  - Marrow bone and chicken carcass from Eversfield Farm (Devon)
  - Mussels (Scotland)
  - Fresh sardines (Cornwall)

- Food from Ireland:
  - Oatmeal
  - Beef mince
- Food from Italy:
  - Pasta
  - Rice: Arborio, Pudding, Wholegrain
  - Plum canned tomatoes and tomato puree
  - Parmesan cheese
- Food from the rest of Europe:
  - Chickpeas and lentils from Turkey
  - Olives and olive oil from Greece
  - Almonds from Spain
  - Sunflower oil from EU agriculture, bottled in Italy[736]
  - Icelandic Haddock
- Food from the rest of the world:
  - Coffee (Mexico)
  - Tea (mixed blend)[737]
  - Rapadura sugar (Ecuador)
  - Organic Raw Cane Sugar (Paraguay)
  - Chocolate (Ecuador)[738]
  - Bananas (Dominican Republic)
  - Dates (Israel)
  - Honey (Zambia)
  - Popping corn (Argentina)
  - Tuna (Maldives)
  - Basmati rice (Pakistan)

Calorific considerations:

- Whilst I have made it clear that calorie counting is a fundamentally bad idea, and leads to poor decisions, I retrospectively counted and estimated the average number of calories consumed by the Average Joe, lest I be accused of starving him.

[736] This is a blend, but cold pressed and organic. It is one of the best sunflower oils available on the market.

[737] This would never be my first choice. Whilst organically certified, this blend is from teas harvested across different regions.

[738] The organic sugar and organic milk used will be from elsewhere, and not identifiable from the packaging.

- The methodology was simple: at the end of the experiment, I went through the Shopping list and noted the calorific content for each product consumed. For most products, it was on the labelling (e.g. pasta, rice, lentils, tuna, beef mince etc...). For others, especially fresh produce, it was an estimate based on basic nutritional guidelines (e.g., the average apple contains around 77 calories, apparently).[739]
- Some estimates were more approximate than others: the meats I bought from the farmers' market were all quite different and, apart from the weight, bore no nutritional data as such.[740] Also, some of the meats were very fatty (therefore high calorie) but contained a high bone mass (with less edible weight, and therefore bringing the average calorific content down), which meant the need to approximate was even greater.
- Total calorie count for the 28 days amounted to an approximate total of 64,000, which averages out to approximately 2,285 calories per day.
- This is not far off the recommended 2,500 calories per day for an adult male which, in any case, and to be clear, is literally a *recommendation and rough guideline* rather than a law of nature. What matters is the quality of what the average Joe eats, its variety and whether he is satiated at the end of meals.
- The other important consideration to reiterate is that other factors beyond calorific content are all important, from nutrient density to micro-nutrient content and medicinal value. For example, whilst vegetables and herbs only account for around just over 6% of the calorie intake, they are hugely impactful on the overall diet and indispensable.
- Similarly, the richness and nutritional density of the best organic dairy products from pasture raised animals cannot be reduced to mere calorific count. One could consume the exact same number of calories from low quality dairy or from dairy substitutes, and one would not be anywhere near as well nourished. A person eating 2,000 calories of excellent whole foods will be far better nourished than a person eating 3,000 calories of ultra-processed foods.
- Lastly, just to clarify, I must emphasise that I am not recommending calorie counting, nor the calorie % below as a guideline.

[739] https://www.weightlossresources.co.uk/calories/calorie_counter/fruit.htm

[740] Not that they should!

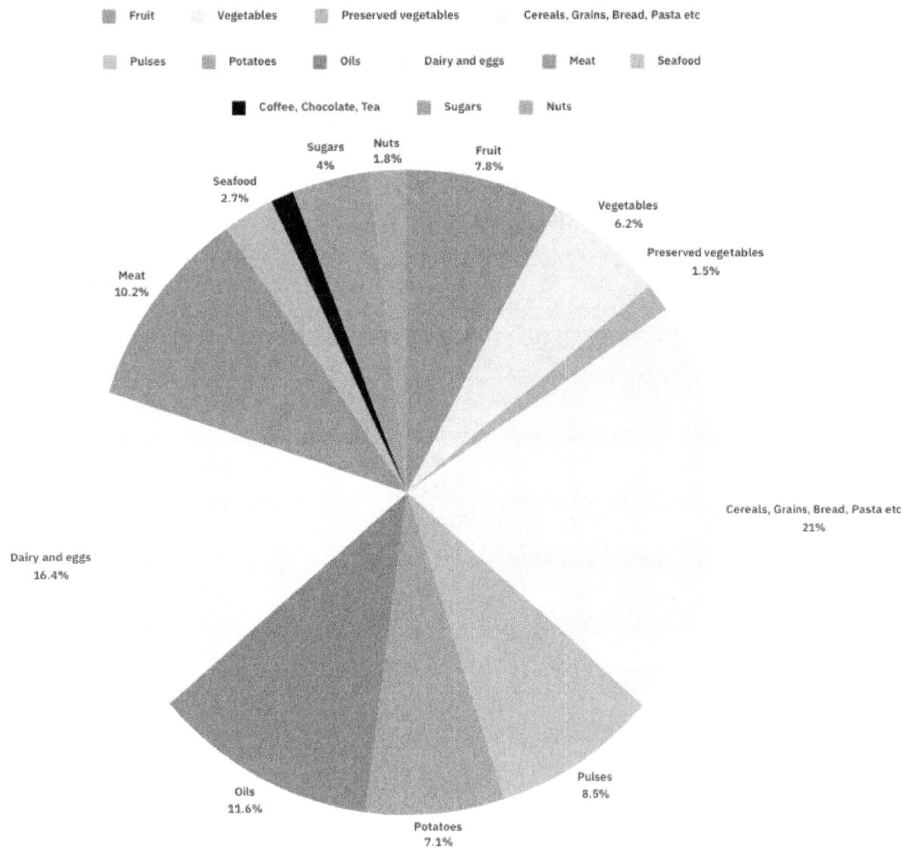

A little cheating:

- There were some herbs from my home potted plants (rosemary, thyme, bay etc..), a couple of lemons from the trees, and a handful or two of lovage added to some soups. Virtually anyone can grow a few herbs, but be that as it may, I do not believe these additions devalue the results of the experiment.
- I also dipped into my spice pantry, to use pinches of sea salt, pepper etc… not to mention more exotic spices for curry and aniseed for biscuits. I also used a tablespoon of capers, some home pickled chillies, splashes of apple vinegar. This may seem like a lot. However, even expensive organic black pepper will cost £2-3 per pot, and I would only have used a fraction of it over 28 days.
- If you wish to add £5-10 to my overall budget, I will accept the addition. What I would point out is that anyone wishing to embark on a different dietary regime, with whatever budget, ought to invest in a small pantry of essentials (good sea salt, some quality spices, vinegar etc..) as an initial start-up cost. The initial cost will be high, but it does not work out to very much in the long term. And grow some herbs, somewhere, somehow!

28-Day Food Diary

Wednesday

- ***Breakfast:*** *2 banana whole milkshake with spices*
- ***Lunch:*** *Mixed vegetable salad with 1 tuna can; 2 X sourdough bread bruschetta*
- ***Snacks****: 1 pear*
- ***Dinner:*** *3 egg onion frittata; large potato salad with fresh herbs*
  1 X Coffee
  2 X Cups of Tea

Thursday

- ***Breakfast****: Porridge (100g oats, whole milk)*
- ***Lunch****: Chickpea (200g) salad*
- ***Snacks****: 1 apple*
- ***Dinner****: Pasta (Pache) Al Pomodoro: (pasta 150g, ½ can organic plum tomatoes, ¼ tomato paste, fresh parsley, chilli, parmesan cheese)*
  1 X Coffee
  2 X Cups of Tea

Friday

- ***Breakfast****: Greek yoghurt (200g), honey (25g)*
- ***Lunch****: 3 egg spinach and herbs frittata*
- ***Snack****: 2 bananas*
- ***Dinner****: Spaghettoni with Tuna (150g pasta, 1 tuna can, ¼ tomato paste, parsley)*
  1 X Coffee
  2 X Cups of Tea

Saturday

- ***Breakfast****: 1 banana*
- ***Lunch****: Lentil (200g) salad*
- ***Snacks****: 3 X pears*
- ***Dinner****: Roast haddock fillet, roast potatoes*
  1 X Coffee
  2 X Cups of Tea

Sunday (Allotment Working Day)

- ***Breakfast***: *Porridge (100g oats, whole milk)*
- ***Snacks***: *Large bottle Caffellatte - (Coffee and whole milk)*
  2 X bananas; 1 apple
- ***Dinner***: *Chickpea (150g) and potato curry with basmati (100g)*
  Half bar chocolate
  2 X Coffee
  1 X Cup of Tea
  (Made mixed vegetable and chickpea (200g) minestrone & made aniseed biscuits - 500g flour, 200g raw organic sugar, butter, olive oil, white wine, aniseed)

Monday

- ***Breakfast***: *3 banana whole milkshake with spices*
- ***Lunch***: *Mixed vegetable and chickpea minestrone with pudding rice (100g)*
- ***Snacks***: *50g organic mature cheddar, 2 X pears*
- ***Dinner***: *Spaghettoni with Mussels (for 2)*
  My portion: 150g pack pasta, ½ bag mussels, ⅛ tomato paste
  2 aniseed biscuits
  2 X Coffees
  2 X Cups of Tea

Tuesday

- ***Breakfast:*** *Porridge (100g oats, whole milk)*
- ***Lunch:*** *3 Eggs in tomato sauce (1 can organic plum tomatoes), fresh herbs*
- ***Snacks:*** *50g organic mature cheddar, 3 oatcakes, 2 aniseed biscuits*
- ***Dinner***: *Mixed vegetable and chickpea minestrone with pudding rice (100g)*
  1 X Coffee
  3 X Cups of Tea

Wednesday

- ***Breakfast***: *2 banana whole milkshake with spices*
- ***Lunch***: *Mixed vegetable and chickpea minestrone with fresh herbs*
- ***Snacks***: *50g organic mature cheddar, 3 oatcakes*
  2 X pears
- ***Dinner***: *Haddock fillet Meunière*
  Broccoli al dente, simply dressed
  1 X Coffee
  2 X Cups of Tea

Thursday

- ***Breakfast***: *2 apples, glass of milk*
  (Made lentils (400g) soup, ½ tomato paste)
- ***Lunch***: *Lentil Soup*
  2 aniseed biscuits
- ***Dinner***: *Minute steak Pizzaiola (½ can plum tomatoes, ½ tomato paste)*
  Mashed potatoes; mixed vegetable salad
  1 X Coffee
  3 X Cups of Tea

Friday

- ***Breakfast***: *2 pears*
- ***Lunch***: *Lentil Soup*
- ***Snack***: *1 apple, glass of milk, 2 aniseed biscuits*
- ***Dinner (for 2)***: *Asparagus Risotto*
  My portion: Asparagus (half bunch) Risotto (Arborio 150g)
  1 X Coffee
  2 X Cups of Tea

Saturday

- ***Breakfast:*** *3 scrambled eggs, pickled chillies, 50g organic mature cheddar*
- ***Lunch:*** *Lentil Soup*
- ***Snacks:*** *2 apples*
- ***Dinner:*** *4 herby/spicy beef meatballs (200g)*
  Broccoli al dente, simply dressed
  Roast potatoes
  1 X Coffee
  3 X Cups of Tea

Sunday (Allotment Working Day)

- ***Breakfast***: *Greek Yoghurt (250g), honey (25g)*
- ***Snacks***: *Large bottle Caffellatte (Coffee and whole milk),*
  2 X bananas, 3 X dates, 6 X oatcakes
- ***Dinner***: *Bowl of mixed vegetable soup*
  2 aniseed biscuits
  (Made mixed vegetable soup for the next couple of days)
  2X Coffee
  1 X Cup of Tea

Monday

- ***Breakfast***: *Greek yoghurt (250g), honey (25g)*
- ***Lunch***: *Large bowl of mixed vegetable soup with fresh dill, olive oil, parmesan*
- ***Snack***: *Homemade Popcorn (125g)*
- ***Dinner (for 2)***: *My portion: Pasta (Pache) 150g, with lamb breast Ragu' (1 X lamb breast, ⅛ tomato paste)*
  1 X Coffee
  3 X Cups of Tea

Tuesday

- ***Breakfast***: *2 banana whole milkshake with spices*
- ***Lunch***: *Minute steak sandwich (sourdough bread, mixed lettuce, mustard)*
- ***Snack***: *Homemade Popcorn (125g)*
- ***Dinner***: *Baked fresh Cornish sardines 200g (with breadcrumbs, olives, capers, fresh herbs)*
  Potato and herb salad
  1 X Coffee
  2 X Cups of Tea

Wednesday

- ***Breakfast***: *Greek yoghurt (250g), honey (25g)*
- ***Lunch***: *2 fried eggs, mixed vegetable salad*
- ***Snacks***: *2 aniseed biscuits, 2 apples, 50g almonds*
  (Made lamb curry - 1 X neck chops. 400g basmati used over three meals, made fresh each day)
- ***Dinner***: *Lamb curry with basmati*
  1 X Coffee
  2 X Cups of Tea

Thursday

- ***Breakfast***: *2 banana whole milkshake with spices*
- ***Lunch***: *Lamb curry with basmati*
- ***Snack***: *1 apple*
- ***Dinner***: *Bowl of Minestrone with pudding rice (100g)*
  1 aniseed biscuit
  1 X Coffee
  2 X Cups of Tea

Friday

- ***Breakfast:*** *2 soft boiled eggs*
- ***Lunch:*** *Mixed vegetable salad with tuna (1 can)*
- ***Dinner:*** *Lamb Curry with basmati, 2 aniseed biscuits*
  1 X Coffee
  2 X Cups of Tea
  (Made simple broth for 2 with a big beef marrow bone and a whole chicken carcass)

Saturday

- ***Breakfast***: *1 aniseed biscuit*
- ***Lunch***: *Wholegrain rice (150g) salad with raw vegetables, spices, and fresh herbs*
- ***Dinner***: *Meat broth with parsnips*
  Homemade potato chips
  1 X Coffee
  2 X Cups of Tea

Sunday

- ***Breakfast:*** *2 aniseed biscuits*
- ***Lunch:*** *Meat broth with swede, carrot, onion, celery*
- ***Dinner***: *Spaghettoni (150g pasta) Burro & Parmigiano*
  Mixed vegetable salad
  2 X Coffee
  1 X Cup of Tea

Monday

- ***Breakfast***: *Porridge (100g oats, whole milk) with honey (25g)*
- ***Lunch***: *2 soft-boiled eggs, potato salad with fresh herbs*
- ***Snacks***: *2 apples*
  (Made lentil (400g) and pork stew, using trotters and hock)
- ***Dinner***: *Lentil and pork stew*
  Quarter bar chocolate, glass of milk
  1 X Coffee
  3 X Cups of Tea

Tuesday

- ***Breakfast***: *2 aniseed biscuits, glass of milk*
- ***Lunch***: *Pan-fried broccoli with garlic and chilli*
  Homemade potato chips
- ***Snacks:*** *50g almonds, 1 apple, 3 dates*
- ***Dinner***: *Lentil and pork stew*
  1 X Coffee
  2 X Cups of Tea

Wednesday

- ***Breakfast:*** *Banana*
- ***Lunch****: Potato salad with fresh herbs*
- ***Snack****: 1 apple; 2 aniseed biscuits*
- ***Dinner****: Lentil and pork stew*
  1 X Coffee
  2 X Cups of Tea

Thursday

- ***Breakfast****: Banana*
- ***Lunch****: 2 fried eggs; homemade potato chips*
- ***Snack****: 1 apple*
- ***Dinner****: Spaghettoni al Ragu' AKA Spag Bol![741] (for 2)*
  My portion: 150g pasta, 200g beef mince, ¼ tomato paste
  1 X Coffee
  2 X Cups of Tea

Friday

- ***Breakfast****: Porridge (100g oats, whole milk) with honey (25g)*
- ***Lunch****: 2 X sourdough bread bruschetta, 100g mature cheddar, mixed vegetable salad*
- ***Snack****: 50g almonds*
- ***Dinner****: Pan-fried fresh Cornish sardines 200g (with butter, lemon, herbs), potato and herb salad*
  1 X Coffee
  3 X Cups of Tea

Saturday

- ***Breakfast****: 3 dates, glass of milk*
  (Made beef stew – 2 whole short ribs, ½ tomato paste)
- ***Lunch:*** *2 soft-boiled eggs*
  Pan-fried broccoli with garlic and chilli
- ***Dinner (for 2):*** *Beef stew and roast potatoes*
  1 X Coffee
  2 X Cups of Tea

[741] Let's clear this one up once and for all. The traditional Bolognese from Bologna is served with Tagliatelle, the classic egg pasta. However, Bolognese sauce can be served with any pasta, fresh or dry, with polenta, or even on crunchy bread, with great results.

Sunday (Allotment Working Day)

- ***Breakfast***: *Banana, glass of milk*
- ***Lunch/Snacks***: *Sourdough bread slice; 50g mature cheddar, pickled chillies; 50g almonds*
- ***Dinner (for 2):*** *Beef stew and mash potatoes*
  2 aniseed biscuits
  2 X Coffee
  2 X Cups of Tea

Monday

- ***Breakfast***: *Porridge (100g oats, whole milk) with honey (25g)*
- ***Lunch***: *Chickpeas (150g) salad*
- ***Snacks***: *2 apples*
  (Made mixed vegetable soup with all leftover vegetables and meat/bone broth)
- ***Dinner:*** *Vegetable soup*
  2 egg spinach frittata
  1 X Coffee
  2 X Cups of Tea

Tuesday

- ***Breakfast***: *Banana*
- ***Lunch***: *Mixed salad with tuna (1 can)*
  Homemade potato chips
- ***Snack:*** *1 apple*
  Quarter bar chocolate
- ***Dinner:*** *Vegetable soup*
  Sourdough bread slice with butter
  1 X Coffee
  3 X Cups of Tea

NOTES ON TEA & COFFEE:

- *Single French Press Coffee: 15g coffee, 5g rapadura, a little milk*
- *Cup of tea: 1 teabag, with approx. 5g sugar, splash of milk or black with no sugar*
- *Total coffee: 33 (at 15g each = approx. 495g)*
- *Total cups of tea: 60 (approx. 50/50 black or white with sugar)*
- *Rapadura sugar: 165g for coffee*
- *Raw Cane Sugar: 150g for tea*

NOTES ON QUANTITIES:

I used scales to measure pasta, rice, pulses and other things that needed to be quantified in order to track total consumption and cost.

I did not measure oil, butter, or sugar on a daily basis. I simply used these ingredients and if there was anything leftover at the end of the experiment, this was quantified for.

The salads, soups, stews, mashes, cooked vegetables, sauces, curries etc... would have contained varying levels of the onions, potatoes, vegetables, herbs that were purchased. Again, all I had to do was measure if there were any leftovers at the end.

Assessment

Is it possible to eat well on the average UK budget?

Can all the intersecting considerations that should determine our food choices (health, pleasure, conviviality, animal welfare, environmental protection etc...) still be respected on an average budget? The short answer is yes. It is just about possible to eat a varied, enjoyable, fresh, seasonal, healthy, nutritious, whole foods diet on the average UK budget. All the basic ideas and principles outlined in chapters 9-11 are compatible with the average Joe's budget.

Can this diet be mostly organic?

The statistics reveal that 56.9% of the food I ate was certified organic. Based on this narrow metric, we could say the food eaten during the experiment was *mostly* organic, by definition. However, what I did with the remaining 43.1% really matters. If that money was devoted to ultra-processed foods or factory-farmed meat, our Average Joe would have failed miserably in his experiment!

The remaining 43.1% of the budget was in fact spent on what I have defined as "equivalent" to organic throughout this book: food that originates from processes that are broadly organic in practice and principle, but not in certification, or from foods that cannot possibly be certified as organic, such as sustainably harvested wild meat or seafood.

The 43.1% of the budget was split as follows:

<u>21.2%: fresh produce from the farmers' market</u>

Most of the fruits, vegetables, potatoes and herbs used during the experiment were bought from two of the regular producers selling their goods at Notting Hill Gate's Farmers' Market.

These are small scale producers (one in Kent, the other in Lincolnshire) growing a broad variety of seasonal produce using methods which they publicly and openly describe as "chemical free". When asked for a definition of chemical free, they defined it free from all the pesticides, herbicides, and fungicides used by mainstream producers supplying supermarkets. On the fertility front, the lines are more blurred, as the Kent producer disclosed that they occasionally boost productivity with NPK based fertiliser. Of course, the reader may well argue that there is no absolute certainty that these producers are not using noxious chemicals, and that their customers are being taken for a ride.

My response to that would be threefold. Firstly, there is no questioning the sheer quality, vitality and flavour of the produce, which is indicative of organic methods of production, in spite of what the naysayers will claim. I cannot claim that I can taste herbicide residues, but I can taste overall quality. Secondly, at the farmers' market we develop personal relationships of trust with hardworking people, which I would be happy to vouch for in terms of their honesty. I must say that, should they be intent on deception, they have chosen a highly unprofitable and strange way to defraud people. Selling chemical free produce that is not chemical free at a farmers' market is not a logical career choice for a fraudster. Thirdly, when asked why they do not have organic certification, the answer I have always received from these producers and others like them across London's markets, is that it is a purely business decision. Organic certification is an annual cost to the business, and many small producers do not wish to add, or cannot afford to add, this extra fee to their annual expenditures. Furthermore, they explained, they have a loyal customer base that will purchase their products, irrespective of certification.

Overall, whilst there are, no doubt, some imperfections, I would be comfortable in classifying this produce as comparable or equivalent to organic produce.

<u>13.8%: meat from the farmers' market</u>

Some of the meat bought during the experiment was organically certified, but most of it was not. I put my faith in a farm in Somerset, Bagnell Farm,[742] which raises beef cattle, sheep and pigs over 174 acres of grassland and woodland. Nick Booth, who runs the farm with his brother-in-law, stated, in writing, that *"for all intents and purposes, we are organic farmers, but without the need for certification. All our cattle and lambs are pasture fed, as nature intended, and our pigs have 62 acres of woodland to forage in"*. Fertility is managed without inputs: *"our manure is spread in the early part of the year, Jan-Feb, for preparation for summer grazing and haylage prep. There is no other form of fertiliser"*. One downside, and the only one that is certainly not consistent with organic principles, is that Nick reported that they *"do spray and pull ragwort"*. Ragwort is a yellow flowering weed that can pop up on pasture, and is hated by most farmers, given its potential toxicity to horses, cattle, and sheep. My own preference, for the record, would definitely be to just pull them out, from the roots, painstaking as that would be. However, it is important to note that ragwort plants are sprayed individually, and only when and where needed: there is no blanket, routine spraying of pasture, or extensive herbicide use that is in any way comparable to the kind of chemical weed control that is the norm on conventional arable land.

[742] https://www.bagnellfarm.co.uk/

Most importantly, and this is what attracted me to Nick and his farm, is that he specialises in heritage rare breeds: the Red Ruby Devon cattle and Jacob sheep. These are exactly the kind of animals that you would select if you were looking to establish a traditional pasture-based system. The former is a traditional Devon breed, which has fallen out of favour due to an increased demand for faster growing continental breeds. These cattle do very well on grass-based systems and are ideally suited to grazing on land that is unsuitable for crops, and in living outdoors for much of the year. The cattle at Bagnell Farm are grazing for most of the year, *"on a rotational 7-day turnaround grazing in two groups"* and only *"housed from the end of December through to the end of February, weather dependent and if the cattle have finished calving"*, and fed *"on haylage from long term herbal leys upon housing"*. The animals are 100% pasture-fed, therefore, with no additional feed entering their diet, apart from a copper supplement, designed for cattle on grass or forage-based diets, in situations where soil and forage copper levels are low or where known copper antagonists are high. Permitted mineral supplements, or indeed salt lick, are sometimes used by organic farmers as well, and are not problematic. To my great satisfaction, the farm does not use artificial insemination, and Nick advised that the *"cows are served by our magnificent Red Ruby Devon bulls"*.

The Jacob sheep is an ancient breed, bearing up to four horns, that is renowned for its "wildness" and rusticity, behaving more like a goat than a sheep! The sheep are also 100% pasture raised, of course, and I was very pleased to learn that *"there is no dipping at all, and sheep are only treated individually if there is a problem"*. Furthermore, *"rather than worming annually, all livestock is dung sampled for worms"*: there is no routine or prophylactic use of pharmaceuticals at the farm which, again, is consistent with organic principles. The pigs, which Nick calls "Iron Age pigs", are wild boar and domestic pig hybrids. These are slow growing animals that produce a think, dense layer of fat, and are ideally suited to foraging and living outdoors all year round. Nick advised that *"the pigs are housed in outdoor arks in a semi-ancient woodland of about 3 hectares, the piglets are castrated and left with mother until around 5 months,"*[743] and are fed on *"vegetable waste (wonky carrots, potatoes, celeriac and beetroot) and bought in pig feed from our local supplier"*.

[743] Which exceeds the minimum weaning time recommended by the Soil Association of 40 days. Conventional systems wean as early as 21 days. This is an excellent and commendable practice, as it significantly increases both welfare and health for the pigs.

Lambs at Bagnell Farm

Lastly, the *"slaughterhouse is small, expensive and selected for our cattle to be housed in their own pens and housed overnight"*. Overnight housing, I would note, is a very sound and humane practice that is sadly no longer the norm. These kinds of practices, as Nick rightly pointed out, *"ensure the least stress possible for the livestock"*.

As discussed in Chapter 11, we should always look out for heritage breeds in livestock, as this is an almost automatic guarantee of quality and integrity. Only a fool would try to raise these animals intensively, and only farmers who are interested in raising animals in the old-fashioned way could possibly take any interest in them. Are there any weaknesses and imperfections in Nick's system? Yes. For example, the happy pigs he raises, which unlike sheep and cattle cannot be pasture-raised, are reliant on non-organic purchased feed, which is an issue. The limited, selective use of herbicide for ragwort is not great. But is this the kind of agriculture that we want to see, promote and financially support? Yes. Is Nick raising happy, healthy animals that produce wholesome food? Yes. Is this the kind of food you would want to be eating and feed to your family? Yes. Is any of this in any way comparable to the horrors of the factory farm and feedlot? No.

Sheep at Bagnell Farm

8.1%: seafood

I will briefly examine the seafood products I bought:

Waitrose MSC Tuna Steak in Spring Water

This tuna has three key positive features going for it:

1) Pole and line caught.
2) Single species: skipjack tuna.
3) From one fishery: Maldives.

Overall, it is a decent seafood option. I would normally prefer tuna in a glass jar, as opposed to a can, and in olive oil.[744] In this case I opted for the spring water option as the oil used for the Waitrose MSC Tuna Steak in Olive Oil is of very low quality and would need to be drained out of the can anyway before using.

The inclusion of tuna may be somewhat controversial. I purchased a 4 pack for £7 for the experiment, and ended up using it all, with an average of a can a week. If I were to extend the Average Joe experiment for another month or more, I would not consume quite as much tuna and would diversify my shopping, which would naturally happen over time. But, in any case, I would argue that, whilst far from perfect, this is a better source of seafood than much of what we currently consume, especially farmed fish or wild fish caught by massive bottom trawlers, or indeed better than any other tuna that has none of the features of this particular brand. Incidentally, this tuna is more expensive than most supermarket tuna, which is almost completely untraceable and unidentifiable.

Waitrose Scottish Mussels

Mussels, as previously discussed, are the ultimate sustainable seafood, and we should be growing and eating far more of them. Whenever you hear nonsense about the future of food (e.g., insects, lab meat etc...) your response should be: how about mussels?

HLS Cornish Sardines Butterfly Fillets

Sardines are traditionally a poor man's fish, and very cheap. They are nonetheless delicious, healthy and underrated. They are often used to make fish meal, to fatten more expensive farmed fish, which is a remarkably bad idea. It is far better to eat sardines directly, as previously discussed. One issue with the rather generic sardines sold on supermarket shelves is that it is hard to trace. Which fishery is it from? And which fishing method has been used? Nonetheless, it is usually a relatively sustainable and safe option. This is due to the sheer abundance of sardines, and to the relatively less harmful fishing methods involved, given that shoals of sardines are caught in midwater, as opposed to the seabed, with purse seine nets and pelagic trawls.

The particular sardines I went for are as good a fish option as one can find on the market. Fresh Cornish sardines, usually referred to as pilchards, are a very valuable domestic option. They are caught with similar methods to those used in the open Atlantic, but on a smaller

[744] My favourite tuna on the market here in the UK is Fish4Ever Azores skipjack tuna in organic olive oil, which is also pole and line caught, but sits in far better oil than all the alternatives available on the market, which can actually be used for your tuna salad. I am not sponsored by Fish4Ever. But would like to be.

scale, and with less impact. They were the MSC Product of the Year 2022 and, overall, if fish is to be eaten, this is a product to feel happy about.

Waitrose Icelandic Haddock Fillets MSC

I decided to include one white fish meal during the 28 days, and there are no easy straightforward options. Given budget constraints, I opted for a relatively cheap and rather delicious MSC certified fresh haddock described as follows: *"produced for Waitrose with haddock caught using hooks and lines in Iceland Grounds"*. The reference to hooks and lines is a sanitised way to describe long lining which, as we saw in chapter 10, is not without its potential problems and is nowhere near as selective as pole and line commercial fishing. However, the haddock stocks are generally considered in far better shape than cod and many other common fish, especially in Iceland, and this specific fishery is considered to be a good choice by the Marine Conservation Society.[745]

Overall, even acknowledging some grey areas and imperfections, the average Joe managed to do pretty well on the seafood front.

What are the realistic conditions and constraints that would need to be met?

There is no doubt that with a limited budget, there are conditions and constraints that are inescapable. I would summarise them as follows:

Strategic shopping: as clear from the above, the average Joe has to shop more broadly and going to one or two supermarkets will not suffice. Some research, some time spent thinking about where and what to buy is a prerequisite for any successful transition to a wholesome diet. The average Joe may live in an area with very few options available, a "food desert", and may need to travel further and wider for good food, as well as rely on more online retailers. Thankfully, in the UK, we are seeing a growth in the online supply of organic and healthy foods. This makes buying in bulk and using storage and freezer space even more important, as he will need to leverage economies of scale and gain greater efficiency. None of this is easy, and is a definite challenge, albeit not insurmountable.

Compromises: when shopping for the experiment, I had to make compromises that I do not normally need to make. For example, I bought relatively cheap organic pulses from Turkey. These lentils and chickpeas were of very decent quality, but ordinarily, outside of the experiment, I would be purchasing organic pulses of higher quality and traceability from Italy and Greece, which cost more than double what I paid for the Turkish ones. I also settled for

[745] https://www.mcsuk.org/goodfishguide/ratings/wild-capture/67/

a generic Clipper organic tea which, whilst far better than the average teabag, is not a patch on my usual loose-leaf magic. On the other hand, I purchased a very fine Greek organic olive oil that I often use outside of the experiment, and the very same sugar and chocolate I would normally purchase.

Cooking is the key: there is no getting away from the fact that some degree of cooking is inescapable for the average Joe, or for whoever lives with him. Someone in any household of more than one person needs to do some cooking. The widespread abandonment of the pots and pans is indeed part of the reason why we are in such a mess with the national diet. Cooking saves money and increases quality, pleasure and health. One example stood out during my experiment. As part of my research, I spent quite some time visiting most of the major supermarkets (Tesco etc..) that I do not normally frequent and from which, even during the experiment, I did not buy any food. There is a large section of ready-made chilled soups in these supermarkets, which are by far not the worst option available. I made note of the weight and prices and can report that they cost more or less the same as my soups, once all ingredients are accounted for. My soups were made with organic pulses, with fresh vegetables and herbs from the farmers' market, dressed with a splash of excellent olive oil, and perhaps some organic parmesan depending on the soup. My soup is definitely far better, on every conceivable level. But the soups cost the same because I contributed my free labour, which brings me to the next point.

Efficient and fast cooking: soups and stews, which are the foundations of good eating and family meals, do not have to take that much time and labour. Learn simple and good recipes and cook in quantity: make a stew that lasts 2-3 meals at the very least. Eggs, meat and fish can also be cooked in all sorts of different ways without too much effort, with extremely tasty results. There are so many YouTube or Instagram Channels with videos of simple recipes, and of course there are tonnes of cookery books on the market. My recommendation for the beginner is to start simple and easy, learn basic technique, and build confidence over time. Many of the dishes I made during the experiment (e.g., the haddock Meuniere, beef Pizzaiola, the egg frittatas) take very little time and effort to cook. Most of the dishes my average Joe had were extremely simple. There are also many whole food options that require zero cooking: fruit, nuts, raw vegetables, salads, sourdough bread, cheese, pork cold cuts, canned or smoked fish, yoghurt, butter, cream, honey, jam etc... It is technically possible to eat well with very minimal cooking, but I do not recommend it, as there is more pleasure and other benefits to be had from some degree of cooking. It is also less financially viable, as many quality whole foods like cheese and cold cuts are inevitably expensive and cooking allows for cheaper ingredients (think rice, potatoes, cheaper cuts of meat) to be turned into something delicious. Having said that, if the average Joe[746] assures me that with his 12-hour working day and other impediments, he simply cannot and would not want to cook anything, I will still argue that he would be better off with simple, quality whole foods than with microwave meals and fast-food takeaways. Personally, I would rather eat the best sourdough bread, cheese and fruit every day for lunch instead of any substandard cooked food.

Limited luxuries: there is no getting away from the fact that the average Joe cannot always afford culinary luxuries. I can guarantee you that I normally spend far more than £51 a week average, and many things that someone on my budget might take for granted are not affordable on an average budget. On an average budget, whole chickens costing £15-20, or special cheeses costing £3.00-4.50 per 100g, can only be occasional treats as opposed to regular food items. This is an unescapable reality. But the other reality is that this is true of any other major living cost: the lower the income, the lower the access to all sorts of expensive goods and services. The only interesting question is what choices are available to someone on an average income, and how to best navigate such choices.

Raising the average: lastly, another issue is that we arguably devote too low a percentage of our incomes on food, and the average Joe could consider spending a little bit more of his income on food. In the UK, we tend to spend a lower percentage of our incomes on food than in other European countries. There are multiple reasons for this, and there is no simple answer. Generally speaking, a relatively low percentage of income being spent on food is a sign of societal affluence: as incomes rise, the proportion of total income spent on food tends to fall. But this does not explain why the UK (and the United States) lag behind other European countries that have similar standards of living and comparable levels of income.[747]

Several reasons have been proposed, such as the UK's relatively higher housing and transport costs,[748] but I would like to suggest that this disparity is not necessarily driven by differences in the cost of food relative to other living costs but might mostly be due to cultural differences in attitudes towards food.[749] The reason why the average Thierry in France and the average Giuseppe in Italy spend a higher percentage of their income on food than the average Joe is arguably because they place a higher value on food and are willing to sacrifice more of their income on it. In the UK, a lot of people on above-average incomes spend

[746] Or his female equivalent. Just to be clear: everything in this chapter applies to any man or woman in the UK.

[747] See, for example: https://ec.europa.eu/eurostat/web/products-eurostat-news/-/ddn-20201228-1

[748] See, for example: https://ahdb.org.uk/news/consumer-insight-why-uk-consumers-spend-8-of-their-money-on-food

[749] And indeed alcohol. The percentage of income spent on alcohol, which varies greatly between European countries, will mostly be determined by cultural factors. Economic factors always matter of course, but I would argue that culture comes first.

relatively low percentages of their income on food, out of choice. There is no doubt that a lot of people prefer to save money on food than on other things. Whilst appreciating that this is purely anecdotal, I have often found that a significant percentage of people on higher-than-average incomes, on six-figure salaries, would rather save on food than on other things, and may think that paying £15-20 for a chicken is an extravagance.

How would one go about navigating a below-average budget?

What about people on a below-average budget, who cannot spend £51 a week? At present, in the UK, people who spend less than the average are most likely to feed themselves from diets devoid of any decent whole foods, dominated by ultra-processed junk and takeaways. The consequences are dire, and generations of children are growing up without eating any decent food, which is both a health hazard and cultural impoverishment.

How could the average Joe adapt to a lower-than-average income? The structure of the diet could be identical in one fundamental respect, namely in the fact that it could still be built around whole foods, and he would have no need to resort to any ultra-processed foods.[750] That would already be an enormous improvement and radical change from what the below-average Joe currently eats.

Here are some suggestions:

Some organic cutbacks: the below-average Joe will not be able, in our current agricultural and food production system, to eat as much organic food as he did when he had an average income. Where would the "organic cutbacks" come from? I would recommend the following:

- More fruits and vegetables would come from the supermarket, and the farmers' market would be an occasional treat. By careful shopping, he could find cheap fresh produce in many supermarkets. Even in supermarkets that barely have any organic produce, the produce section is still one of the few sections where decent food is to be found at low cost. Conventional broccoli, peppers, spinach, beetroots, tomatoes etc... could still be the basis of the diet. For certain cheaper produce, such as potatoes, carrots and bananas, he could potentially still go organic. Had I not bought most of my produce from the farmers' market and had used the cheapest London supermarkets instead, I would have saved a lot of money.
- The average Joe had very expensive pasta, coffee, sugar, flour, rice etc... these are again products where cheaper alternatives could be found. Sainsbury's sells organic

[750] I will happily take on the challenge of taking anybody's budget and demonstrate that ultra-processed junk foods are not the only option.

pasta at £1.35 for 500g, which is far less than I spent for my fancy £3.20 packs, and organic rice and pulses can cost about the same when bought in bulk.[751] Conventional non-organic rice and pulses in bulk are cheaper still, if the below-average Joe needs to cut back on his budget even further. Decent quality nuts (please avoid Californian nuts) and sugar can be found for a lot less than what the average Joe paid. What the below-average Joe does not need to do is to go for the very bottom end of the market (e.g., some supermarkets sell spaghetti at 28p per 500g, and the cheapest vegetable oil, which is dreadful, costs a fraction of what the average Joe paid for his organic sunflower oil).

Do not sacrifice animals: I will be even more controversial and tell the below-average Joe that the one part of his diet where there are far less shortcuts available is animal products. The purchase of products made from factory-farmed animals is never justifiable and, in any case, are harmful to Joe's health, irrespective of his budget. Cheap bacon is terrible for the animals, the environment and for the below-average Joe. It is a lose-lose situation. The cheapest organic milk, eggs and butter from the supermarkets are truly relatively cheap considering their great nutritional value: these will be invaluable foods for the below-average Joe. Organic whole milk can cost as little as £1.00 per litre and eggs 40-45p each, not an enormous difference from their factory-farmed counterparts.[752] As a rule of thumb, in terms of quality, it is always better to cut back from plant products (grains, pulses, vegetables etc...) than from animal products.

Less meat or cheaper cuts: meat is more expensive. The average Joe had a combination of fancy cuts (beef short rib) and cheaper cuts (hock and trotters) and had lots of meat with low carcass availability. The cheapest and most efficient meat he had was supermarket organic beef mince, which generally costs a minimum of £1 per 100g. It has a lot going for it, however, as it has no bones nor waste and is extremely flexible for all kinds of dishes, from meat sauce to meatballs and burgers. The same is true of organic diced beef (usually around £1.20 per 100g), which is widely available, costs about the same and is extremely versatile and nutritious. Had the average Joe spent all his meat budget on organic mince and diced beef, he could have bought up to 3.2kg of beef (2.4kg mince, 800g diced beef), with zero waste, for the same budget. The below-average Joe can focus on these kinds of cheaper, more efficient meats.

[751] The cheapest organic pasta, rice and pulses oscillate between £2.40 and £3.00 per kg. A large meal for an adult would consume 150-200g at the most, costing around 40 60p, which would rise to up to £1.00 once simple sauces and condiments come into play. Bearing in mind that the average Joe had over £7 a day at his disposal, this sort of meal on a regular basis would cut the budget back significantly.

[752] The cheapest milk will still cost 60p per litre and the cheapest eggs around 20p each.

Lastly, the below-average Joe could also venture into the odd butcher shop or farmers' market occasionally, where the very cheapest cuts are truly accessible.[753]

Less seafood: the below-average Joe, in the real world, consumes very little seafood, and what he does consume is highly likely to come in the form of fish fingers or other precooked preparations. Therefore, I suggest that the below-average Joe could go for the same sort of products I went for during my experiment, but no more than once a week (I had some seafood an average of 2/2.5 days per week, albeit in small portions).

More pulses and grains: there is no doubt that many of the traditional staples from many cultures, such as rice, potatoes, pasta, lentils, beans, chickpeas, homemade breads etc... would form the backbone of the diet. This would be a very positive change from the current ultra-processed food diet of the below-average Joe. Some basic dishes are very cheap and very good. One of the go-to breakfasts of the average Joe was porridge: 100g organic oats, 250ml organic whole milk, 25g forest honey. An all-organic, healthy, filling breakfast, over 600 calories. Cost: 52p for oats and milk, plus 32p for the honey. Honey is not necessary, so it could be a 52p breakfast for the below-average Joe.

Greater bulk and zero waste: buying staples in bulk is even more important, as is the avoidance of all waste.

Keep cooking: baking biscuits and cakes from time to time and making hearty soups and stews will be the only conceivable way for our below-average Joe to eat well and with pleasure.

Allotment/growing space? Even in very deprived areas, one is surprised to find that allotments are underutilised, as are other potential growing spaces and gardens, many belonging to the council. We need the Joes of all stripes to consider finding opportunities to grow some food. Seek and you shall find!

Perspective: it may seem harsh to condemn the below-average Joe to a relatively austere diet and lifestyle. My critics will insist on accusing me of elitism and snobbery. But what is the alternative? The ultra-processed foods and factory-farmed animal products which the below-average Joe is currently eating are far worse. All the options recommended by nutritional experts, government, the NHS and retailers are far worse. What we need to focus on is on giving the below-average Joe the tools to make the best possible choices that are at his disposal, limited as they may be.

[753] My lamb breast for £2.00, which is enough for a good meal, is a great example.

In Conclusion

What began as a quest to answer Alex's question, which I hope to have answered to his satisfaction, ended up taking me on a journey back in time, to try and answer why we ended up in a situation where someone like Alex would be utterly confused about what to eat, how, and why. A rejection of reductionist science and its consequences required digging deep into the ideological, cultural, economic and technological changes that took place over the course of the last few generations. Without understanding these changes, we cannot confidently reject the competing, interrelated contemporary dogmas besieging us from all corners. Without regaining some humility in the face of Creation, without rediscovering the truth of both human exceptionalism and the burdens that go with it, we will never heed the call to sanity and normality that I have tried so hard to express.

Something that is as simple and as complex as food requires a holistic, multidisciplinary approach which, nonetheless, once applied and distilled, can be summarised in very basic principles, which anybody can potentially understand and follow. As humans our motivations, desires, ideas and practices around food can seem conflicting and full of inevitable zero-sum games. We also tend to fixate on one concern, at the expense of others. As I have argued, it is a mistake to eat purely for health, or purely for pleasure, or purely out of concern for the environment, or indeed out of any other single concern.

We can and need to address all seemingly competing concerns. As I have attempted to demonstrate, our concerns around health, body weight, pleasure, gastronomy, conviviality, animals, ethics, landscapes, the environment, and more, can actually all be addressed with the same consistent choices and attitudes. It turns out that what is good for our health and body weight is also good for animals, for soils and the oceans, and can bring pleasure, optimism and conviviality back to our tables and homes, without the anxieties and doubts of the contemporary food labyrinth. We can have our cake and eat it, after all.

Afterword

Dear Reader,

I have made it quite clear that, on the basis of this book alone, and plenty of willingness to change, Alex, or anybody like him, can turn their lives around, without any professional assistance or outside help.

Many have nonetheless asked me for my guidance and help. As such, I offer Food Consulting services, as well as Horticultural Consulting services to help people get started on the journey.

Please see: www.ffoodconsulting.com

Email: federico@ffoodconsulting.co.uk

Instagram: @cook.farmer.fred

Lastly, all comments and queries are welcome, as is debate around the subjects discussed throughout this book. I am potentially interested and available for events, workshops, interviews, conferences, and other relevant engagements.

I look forward to hearing from you all.

Federico

Index

B

D

E

F

G

H

J

K

L

M

O

P

Q

R

T

U

V

W

Y

Z

Printed in Dunstable, United Kingdom

66485990R00275